ALSO BY ROGER DANIELS

The Politics of Prejudice (1961)
American Racism (with Harry H. J. Kitano, 1970)
The Bonus March (1971)
Concentration Camps, USA (1971)
The Decision to Relocate the Japanese Americans (1975)
Concentration Camps, North America (1981)
Asian Americans, Emerging Minorities (with Harry H. J. Kitano, 1987)
Asian America: Chinese and Japanese in the United States since 1850 (1988)
History of Indian Immigration to the United States (1989)
Coming to America (1990)
Prisoners without Trial (1993)
Not Like Us (1997)
American Immigration: A Student Companion (2001)
Debating American Immigration (with Otis L. Graham, 2001)
Guarding the Golden Door (2004)
The Japanese American Cases (2013)

For Judith
A partner in everything

Contents

Preface

IT IS MY HOPE IN THIS BOOK TO make it clear how Franklin Roosevelt managed to achieve liberal results in peace and war in a nation whose people were far from liberal and with a Congress that was increasingly conservative. Roosevelt's claims on our attention are indisputable. If a truly great president must deal with and largely master a major national crisis, only Washington, Lincoln, and Franklin Roosevelt can qualify. My original intention, in 2001 with retirement from teaching just around the corner, was to write a one-volume biography of about 120,000 words. Such a book seemed a logical outgrowth of my teaching, which had focused on twentieth-century America, whereas most of my published scholarship concentrated on immigration and ethnicity. I signed a contract to produce such a biography and, once retirement finally came, began to devote most of my time to reading and rereading the most important books and articles about Roosevelt and his times.

As I continued to read, and began to write about Roosevelt's family background and youth, I became increasingly aware that my initial assumptions about the size of the book were inadequate. It took considerable time for me to lay out a new course. I had lived through Roosevelt's presidency—my earliest political memories are of the 1936 election—and was painfully aware of the succession of failed and inadequate presidencies that have followed his death. My own views of Roosevelt had been largely shaped by a small group of historians beginning to publish when I began graduate school at the University of California at Los Angeles (UCLA) in 1957 whom I have described as the founding scholars of the Roosevelt presidency. I already knew the work of Frank Freidel (1916–83), James M. Burns (1918–2014), and Arthur M. Schlesinger Jr. (1916–2007), and in my first graduate seminar I learned that William E. Leuchtenburg (b. 1922) was preparing what remains the finest survey of the New Deal. In time, I met all but Burns, and Freidel became my friend.

I came to graduate school believing that I would write a dissertation on some aspect of the civil rights movement and its interplay with the federal government in the first half of the twentieth century. Theodore Saloutos (1910–80), to whom I was assigned as a teaching assistant and who became my mentor, quickly disabused me of that notion. It was, he thought, a good topic, but not for me, then. He pointed out that I would soon be thirty, that the brightest of my generation were already beginning to get tenure, and that I needed a topic that I could develop while I did my course work, prepared for my doctoral examinations, and performed my duties as his teaching assistant. He eventually suggested that I look into the unwritten history of the discrimination against Chinese and Japanese immigrants in California, a topic well covered by materials contained within the libraries of the University of California.

This practical advice put me on an unexpected career path, which I never would have taken without Saloutos's prodding guidance, but I always intended to write a book about Roosevelt. I had regularly offered courses about the Roosevelt era while teaching in the United States and Europe over five decades, and I now believe that trying to explain Roosevelt and his America to European students, mostly in Germany and Austria during the eighties and nineties, and their responses, subtly modified my own views of the man and his era.

My original design, to which I have largely adhered on a greatly expanded scale, dubbed the book "a political biography." This was to signal that I would all but ignore his personal life apart from his well-documented childhood. I merely note the basic outline of the forty-year marriage of Franklin and Eleanor and its great divide at the end of what they called the Great War. I attempt no judgments about it. Eleanor Roosevelt is a more important historical figure than my treatment of her here might suggest. I pay little attention to his sons; daughter Anna is examined only for her crucial role in the late wartime White House.

Despite a professional lifetime spent reading, writing, and, above all, thinking about Franklin Roosevelt, I have not the slightest notion of what his inner essence was like. None of the attempts to describe that essence, including those of his wife, inspires confidence. The man who seems so outgoing and frank in his public and private discourse was in fact quite secretive. It is not surprising that one of his favorite cartoons featured his face on the Sphinx in the Egyptian desert. What I have tried to do is to present, in as much detail as is feasible, a clear picture of the ways in which Roosevelt presented himself to the various publics that he addressed. This means that I have focused, to a very great degree, on what Roosevelt said and wrote as put forth in public documents, the press, and in the testimony contemporary witnesses recorded about him and try to supply a rational analysis of his intentions and the results of his actions.

As I embarked on the project, my concept of what events a twenty-first-century political biography should stress was largely within the parameters laid down by the founding scholars. In my teaching, I had always stressed matters of race and ethnicity to a greater degree than any of them, and as a former trade unionist and election worker for the Congress of Industrial Organizations (CIO), I would have a greater concern about trade union matters and also about Roosevelt's contributions to what has become our national security state. I had come to believe that all of the founders had undervalued Roosevelt's intellectual accomplishments, particularly the vital postgraduate tutorials that began during his gubernatorial years and were capped by those conducted by Lauchlin Currie and others in the White House that made the president a kind of closet Keynesian. I was also persuaded that the prevailing view, developed by Alan Brinkley (b. 1949) and other historians in the 1980s and 1990s, that meaningful Roosevelt reform had come to an end in 1938 or thereabouts was ill-considered. Nor did I agree that the domestic side of World War II could be characterized by phrases like "the mess in Washington" or likened to what seemed an American Thermidor.

Although I was fairly clear about most of the messages I wished to deliver, it was difficult to decide on the method I would use to craft my version of the Roosevelt story. In the summer of 2004, I read Lawrence and Cornelia Levine's *The People and the President: America's Conversation with FDR* (2002). I had always known that I would pay more attention to Roosevelt's speeches than his other biographers had and that I intended to quote from them extensively, so I paid particular attention to their detailed analysis of each of Roosevelt's Fireside Chats and less so to their analysis of the mail the White House received in response to each. Some days thereafter, I believe within the week, what I call my inner lightbulb flashed on, and I asked myself what kind of book would result if I reversed the Levines' emphasis and made Roosevelt's verbal messages to the American people and the world an organizing principle. These were largely in plain sight and, one way or another, part of the public record and relatively easy to access in printed sources and online. The chief of these were his *Public Papers,* the stenographic texts of his more than one thousand press conferences, the stenographic or recorded texts of a very small number of meetings and conferences, Roosevelt's published personal correspondence, and the testimony, in various forms, of a variety of witnesses who provide what they claim Roosevelt told them and others.

As it turned out, the *New York Times'* coverage of Roosevelt, which begins in 1905 and becomes intensive after his 1928 nomination and election as governor, provided hundreds of examples of otherwise unrecorded and obscure examples of formal, semiformal, and reactive utterances by Roosevelt. The fact that modern technology placed a searchable version of the *Times* on my desktop facilitated my ability to extract even passing references. Throughout his presidency, Roosevelt spent weeks and even months away from the White House. The coverage of the traveling president by reporters and members of his entourage is more intimate and revealing than accounts from Washington and is treated more fully than has usually been the case.

My utilization of all these materials, even in excerpted form, means that a quite large percentage of the book is direct discourse. Roosevelt loved to talk; despite a good deal of persiflage, it is often the case that knowing what Roosevelt actually said—or did not say—is important in understanding what he was about. That during 1938, for example, the word *purge,* so far as the record shows, never crossed his lips calls into question much that has been written about the off-year 1938 election.

After a truncated account of his first forty-six years, relatively detailed coverage begins with his gubernatorial campaign in 1928 and intensifies after 1931. I provide, in roughly chronological order, an annotated narrative of what seem to me to be the more important aspects of the longest presidency in U.S. history. It treats, in some detail, how Roosevelt campaigned for public office and becomes increasingly concerned with how he learned to govern.

The lengthy result will, I hope, enable readers for whom Franklin Roosevelt is not even a memory to understand the accomplishments of a man who, more than any other individual, shaped the world in which we live. Remembering, as Roosevelt's contemporary the Dutch scholar Pieter Geyl (1887–1966) tells us, that history is "a debate without end," I do not in the least imagine that I have written the last word.

Some readers may well question whether I have even written the first one. I make no attempt to explain why this somewhat coddled son of American gentry became a tribune of the people. The inner life of Franklin Roosevelt remains a closed book; the man who insists on telling us all kinds of petty details about his life—some of them quite imaginative, if not fictional—is consistently silent about his motives and inspirations. He was a mystery to his wife, family, and closest associates. These volumes are an attempt to explain what he did and what he hoped would result.

Acknowledgments

ALTHOUGH THE ACTUAL WRITING OF THIS BOOK took place in the past dozen years, my entire formal education, all but two years of it in public institutions, and those who taught me must be acknowledged. My teachers in the Miami public schools pushed me to read beyond textbooks and to question what I read. When I finally got to college in the 1950s, faculty members in the History Department at the University of Houston gave me what I now realize was an inordinate amount of personal attention. I shall always be grateful to them, particularly Louis Kestenberg and Charles Bacarisse. During my graduate work at UCLA, apart from my mentor, Theodore Saloutos, I was most influenced by Eugene N. Anderson.

In a long professional career at five American universities with visiting stints at two Canadian and four European universities and guest lectures at dozens of others as well as professional encounters of various kinds, I came into contact with a considerable number of the historians of my time. I can mention only a few. Al Larson at Wyoming, Ed Saveth at Fredonia, and Bill Aeschbacher at Cincinnati were instrumental in bringing me to those places. I learned much from the men—and eventually women—who became my departmental colleagues, but here I will mention only two: Zane Miller, who was the rock upon whom the modern Cincinnati department was built, and Henry Winkler, who joined us there as a president who actually taught classes regularly while president. Of colleagues in the larger profession, none were more important for me than Rudolph Vecoli, the acknowledged leader of the immigration historians of our generation, and Robert Skotheim, a historiographer who became a college president and then re-created the Huntington Library.

As I note elsewhere, teaching about the Democratic Roosevelt helped me to envisage the kind of narrative I wanted to present. I am particularly grateful to those students who wanted more information and those who didn't quite get it. Questions from both groups helped me to understand some of the inadequacies of what I had originally presented. In the same way that newspapers can claim to be the first drafts of history, my classroom lectures provided the foundation on which I built my narrative. I continue to maintain contact not only with former colleagues and graduate colleagues from all of my permanent appointments, but also with a few former undergraduate students such as James E. Wright from Platteville and Sue Fawn Chung from UCLA.

Among the platoons of historians and others who enabled my efforts in these Roosevelt volumes, Judith M. Daniels, a historian and editor in her own right, must take precedence. Everything I have accomplished since 1960 owes much to her probing intelligence. Beginning with conversations about whether even to attempt a Roosevelt biography, she has participated in every phase of the process, listening to me read daily work product and commenting upon it, editing chapter drafts and redrafts in more versions than I am now able to count. Above all, her faith that I would endure after my original publisher could no longer continue sustained my resolve at times when scrapping the project seemed the better part of valor.

The writing process itself, begun in Cincinnati, was largely completed in Bellevue, Washington, from late 2005, much of it based on materials acquired in visits to the FDR Library, the Truman Library, and various branches of the National Archives. I can no longer retrieve the names of most of the skilled librarians and archivists who helped to continue my education, as I am twenty-three hundred miles away from my stored papers, so I can here mention only the senior reference librarian at UCLA in the 1950s, a Ms. Grey, and Sally Moffitt, the history bibliographer at Cincinnati's Langsam Library who still gently guides students and faculty through bibliographic labyrinths.

Of those persons directly connected with the forging of these volumes, the three most vital, apart from Judith, are two persons in the book trade and one historian. Ivan R. Dee, who had published an earlier book of mine, contracted to publish the biography and provided good advice and a valuable full first editing of the entire text. To our mutual regret, economic considerations made it impossible for him to continue. He facilitated my affiliation with agent Georges Borchardt who negotiated the contract with the University of Illinois Press. Its editor in chief, Laurie Matheson, led me through a complete reediting, whose aim was to prune a hundred thousand words from the text, and did so with intelligence, precision, and grace. Early in the writing, I asked Max Paul Friedman to look over what I had to say about international relations. He generously took on reading the draft chapters as they were written, giving good advice and encouragement on every aspect of the work. Most of this was via e-mail, but I remember particularly a long dinner conversation in Washington, D.C., in which we talked out some of the thrust of the volumes.

To many of my doctoral students, particularly those who wrote on Roosevelt-era subjects, I owe a double debt: not only did I learn much by preparing to help them pursue their specific topics, but their findings invariably expanded my knowledge. In addition, some of them answered my queries and made suggestions as I worked on the text. I thus thank Mike Anderson, Allan Austin, Mark Cowett, Andy Kersten, Kris Lindenmeyer, Bob Miller, Rick Reiman, and Matthais Reiss.

Of my senior colleagues in the larger profession, Frank Freidel, whose five biographical volumes about Franklin Roosevelt remain unrivaled, gave encouragement and advice and commented on a first brief outline for what became these volumes. Most of the assistance I received is acknowledged in the footnotes and in the list of works consulted, but I must mention two government historians, Jan Kenneth Hermann of the Navy and Larry DeWitt of Social Security, for materials gleaned from their own researches.

Of the large squad of specialists who put the materials together, I worked personally with senior project editor Tad Ringo, copy editor Annette Wenda, and indexer June Sawyers, each a skilled professional who imposed their high standards cheerfully while improving the final result. Behind the scenes, art director Dustin Hubbart transformed my vague suggestions into a stunning cover and Lisa Connery composed the pages producing a clean, effective look. Many others, unknown to me, toiled to produce a most attractive volume.

Abbreviations

AAA	Agricultural Adjustment Administration
ALP	American Labor Party
ANB	*American National Biography*
AVG	American Volunteer Group (Flying Tigers)
BEW	Board of Economic Warfare
CCC	Civilian Conservation Corps
CES	Committee on Economic Security
CIO	Committee/Congress of Industrial Organizations
DALLEK	Robert Dallek, *Franklin D. Roosevelt and American Foreign Policy, 1932–1945*
DNC	Democratic National Committee
EDB	Economic Defense Board
EOP	Executive Office of the President
ER	Eleanor Roosevelt
FBI	Federal Bureau of Investigation
FCA	Farm Credit Administration
FCC	Federal Communications Commission
FDR	Franklin Delano Roosevelt
FDRL	Franklin Delano Roosevelt Library, Hyde Park, N.Y.
FDR Letters	Elliott Roosevelt, ed., *F.D.R.: His Personal Letters*, 3 vols.
FERA	Federal Emergency Relief Administration
FLA	Federal Loan Agency
FRB	Federal Reserve Board
FSA	Farm Security Administration (1937–46); Federal Security Administration (1939–53)
FTC	Federal Trade Commission
FWA	Federal Works Agency
GNL	Good Neighbor League
GPA	*Public Papers of Franklin D. Roosevelt, Forty-Eighth Governor of New York*, 4 vols.
HHPP	Herbert C. Hoover, *Public Papers of the Presidents of the United States*, 4 vols.

Hist Stat	U.S. Department of Commerce, *Historical Statistics of the United States: Colonial Times to 1957*
ICC	Interstate Commerce Commission
ILGWU	International Ladies' Garment Workers' Union
LNPL	Labor's Non-Partisan League
NDAC	National Defense Advisory Committee
NDMB	National Defense Mediation Board
NIXON *FDR & FA*	Edgar B. Nixon, ed., *Franklin D. Roosevelt and Foreign Affairs,* 17 vols.
NLB	National Labor Board
NLBR	National Labor Relations Board
NRA	National Recovery Administration
NRB	National Resources Board
NYT	*New York Times*
OCD	Office of Civilian Defense
OEM	Office of Emergency Management
OGR	Office of Government Reports
OPM	Office of Production Management
PPA	Samuel I. Rosenman, ed., *Public Papers and Addresses of Franklin D. Roosevelt,* 13 vols.
PRA	President's Reemployment Agreement
Press Conf	FDR, *The Complete Presidential Press Conferences of Franklin D. Roosevelt,* 25 vols.
RFC	Reconstruction Finance Corporation
SPAB	Supply Priorities and Allocations Board
TERA	Temporary Emergency Relief Administration
TR	Theodore Roosevelt
UMW	United Mine Workers
USDA	United States Department of Agriculture
USHA	United States Housing Authority
VA	Veterans Administration

Franklin D. Roosevelt

1 Beginnings
1649–1905

FROM LATE IN THE NINETEENTH CENTURY until the middle decades of the twentieth, three Roosevelts—Theodore (1858–1919), Franklin Delano (1882–1945), and (Anna) Eleanor (1884–1962)—played major and often dominating roles in American politics.[1] The first Roosevelt in the New World, a shadowy figure named Claes Martenzen van Rosenvelt (d. 1659), was settled in Manhattan by 1649. Obviously Dutch, Claes probably came from a village on Tholen Island in Zeeland's Scheldt Estuary. He seems to have arrived with enough capital to purchase a farm of some forty-eight acres whose southern boundary was about where Twenty-Ninth Street is now.[2] He and his son, Nicholas (1658–1742), were the only male American ancestors that Franklin shared with Theodore and Eleanor. Nicholas, the first to spell the name Roosevelt, was also the first to hold political office: he became a city alderman in 1700. His two sons, Johannes (1689–1750) and Jacobus (1692–1776), are ancestors of Theodore and Franklin, respectively. Each branch of the family got rich largely through the efforts of one outstanding entrepreneur.

For Franklin's branch of the family, the moneymaker was Jacobus's son Isaac (1726–1794), who was also the lone member of either branch who could be called even a minor founding father: he served in the first New York provincial assembly in 1775, the first state constitutional convention in 1777, and the first state senate, and was a member of the New York convention that ratified the federal Constitution in 1788. In family legend, he is referred to as "Isaac the Patriot." More important for the family, he became wealthy as one of the major sugar refiners in New York. His ties to Caribbean plantations meant that, like so many well-to-do New Yorkers, Franklin's Roosevelt wealth had its roots in slavery.

On Theodore's side of the family, significant wealth did not arrive until the nineteenth century. His grandfather Cornelius Van Schaack Roosevelt (1794–1871) made a good deal of money in New York real estate and established a major plate-glass business: at his death, he was described as having "amassed a fortune of many millions."[3]

Although it is common to refer to the two branches of the Roosevelt family as the Hyde Park Democrats and the Oyster Bay Republicans, both families remained in Manhattan into the nineteenth century, and before Theodore's generation there were Democrats in each branch.[4] Franklin's great-grandfather James Roosevelt (1760–1847) broke the residential pattern by moving from the city and building a large house, Mount Hope, on the outskirts of Poughkeepsie in 1818. The family lived in it until it burned down while Franklin's father, James Roosevelt (1828–1900), and his first wife were in Europe in 1855.[5] Rather than rebuild, they purchased and remodeled an existing house and grounds a few miles north on the west bank of the Hudson, called Springwood, on the southern edge of the village of Hyde Park. This is the house in which Franklin was born and raised; the first modern presidential library is on its grounds, and he and Eleanor are buried there. As for the Oyster Bay branch, Theodore and Eleanor's forebears stayed in the city; the first purchase of what became the Sagamore Hill estate near Oyster Bay on Long Island was made by Theodore shortly after his first marriage in 1880.[6]

Many Roosevelts of both branches, as was customary for their class, had performed public roles: two of them served one term each in Congress as Democrats.[7] Theodore, however, the first family member to become a major political figure, entered New York City Republican politics near the lowest level. His meteoric career took off when Franklin was a teenager and was such an influence on and advantage for Franklin's choices and opportunities that some account of "cousin Theodore's" rise should be given here.

Intellectually adventuresome, Theodore ranked 21st in his Harvard class of 171, and, as he put it, "second among the gentlemen." He earned a Phi Beta Kappa key and went on to take a master's degree in history. A year after his 1880 graduation and marriage, he won election to the lower house of the New York Legislature from Manhattan, not a normal habitat for gentlemen, where he served from 1882 to 1884. Energetic, ambitious, egocentric, and a mild reformer, he fought against the nomination of the corrupt spoilsman James G. Blaine for president in 1884. But when "the continental liar from the state of Maine" won the nomination, Theodore supported him. Many of the so-called mugwumps, largely gentlemen reformers of Theodore's own class who bolted to support the Democratic victor, Grover Cleveland, never forgave him for what they thought was his political apostasy, and he never forgave them for questioning his reform convictions.

His unbroken party regularity won him appointment to the U.S. Civil Service Commission by President Benjamin Harrison in 1889. He served for almost six years, became its chair, and helped make the commission at least marginally effective with his activism and genius for publicity and self-promotion.

In 1895 he returned to New York City politics, accepting appointment as head of the city's police department in the reform administration of Republican mayor William L. Strong (1827–1900). His two years there brought energy and real reform to the department, and, mentored in part by the muckraking

Danish American journalist Jacob A. Riis (1849–1914), he gained some insight into the lives of the city's poor.[8]

William McKinley's triumph over William Jennings Bryan in the epochal presidential election of 1896 gave Roosevelt the opportunity to return to the national scene, though it took extensive maneuvering by friends, particularly Henry Cabot Lodge (1850–1924), in his first term as a senator (R-MA) after three terms in the House, to get him appointed assistant secretary of the navy. At that moment, in May 1897, no one could have imagined the circumstances that would conspire to make Roosevelt president in a little more than four years.

The crisis with Spain over its oppressive rule of Cuba made Theodore's position in the Navy Department more significant than it would have been a decade earlier. He applied his habitual energy to the job, to which he brought a number of preconceptions. Two of his mother's brothers had served with distinction in the Confederate navy, and he had published an expanded version of his Harvard master's thesis, *The Naval War of 1812; or, The History of the United States Navy during the Last War with Great Britain* (1882). In addition, along with his friend Lodge, he had been converted to the navalism of Captain Alfred Thayer Mahan (1840–1914), whose *The Influence of Sea Power upon History, 1660–1783* (1890) became a part of the intellectual baggage of a generation or two of American thinkers who wished to end what they regarded as the nation's isolationism, an isolationism exemplified by Grover Cleveland's nullification of the de facto annexation of Hawaii in 1893.

Even before the explosion that sank the battleship *Maine* in Havana Harbor on February 15, 1898, Theodore had been eager for war with Spain. The issue was its colonial rule in Cuba where an insurrection for independence had raged, intermittently, since the 1870s. He quickly announced his conviction, as headlined by William Randolph Hearst's *New York Journal* two days later, that "the Explosion of the War Ship Was Not an Accident." Hearst's editors commissioned a drawing of the *Maine* with an explosive mine shown moored underneath, accompanied by a story headlined "Naval Officers Think the Maine Was Destroyed by a Spanish Mine."

The same day's *New York Times,* conversely, merely mentioned Roosevelt's name in a story headlined "Naval Experts Confer," which reported that the cause of the explosion was unknown.[9] It was the sensational story that was more widely believed, and the slogan "Remember the *Maine*" became the watchword of an all but politically irresistible furor for war. (We now know that the *Maine* blew up from an internal explosion and that its class of battleships had a design flaw—the boilers and ammunition lockers were in too close proximity.) On February 25, Theodore, technically acting secretary of the navy in the temporary absence of his chief, on his own initiative, cabled George Dewey (1837–1917), commander of a small American naval force based in Hong Kong, that if war with Spain came, he should "see that the Spanish squadron does not leave the Asiatic coast, and then [undertake] offensive operations in Philippine Islands."[10]

On April 11, President William McKinley asked Congress to authorize "forcible intervention" by the United States to establish peace in Cuba. Nine days later, on April 20, after considerable debate and over the objections of a number of doves, Congress passed a series of resolutions, often called war resolutions but which did *not* declare war. Instead, Congress recognized the independence of Cuba, demanded the withdrawal of all Spanish armed forces from Cuba, empowered the president to use the army and navy to carry out these demands, and in the so-called Teller Amendment, named for Senator Henry M. Teller (R-CO), disclaimed any intent to annex Cuba and promised to give Cuba independence after the Spanish had gone.

McKinley signed this joint resolution the day it was passed. Madrid was informed that if its terms were not met, Washington would take steps to see that they were carried out. The next day, April 21, Spain broke relations with the United States; on April 22, the United States announced a naval blockade of Cuban ports. Two days later, on April 24, Spain declared war, a blockade being one of the traditional ways of beginning a war. On April 25, Congress also declared war and made it retroactive to April 21.

Unlike most politicians who instigate wars, Theodore was himself ready to take risks. Although thirty-nine years of age and father of six children under the age of fifteen, he helped Leonard Wood (1860–1927) organize the First United States Volunteer Cavalry Regiment, popularly known as the Rough Riders, and on May 6 resigned his desk job to become its second in command. Wood's promotion shortly after their regiment's arrival in Cuba in June left Roosevelt, who had just three years of part-time military experience in the New York National Guard, which involved little training beyond close-order drill, in command. On July 1, he led his unmounted troopers into the brief victorious battle for Kettle Hill, outside of Santiago.[11] Sixteen days later, the Spanish army in Cuba surrendered.

Meanwhile, Dewey's squadron steamed to Manila Bay as instructed, and there on May 1 it destroyed the outgunned Spanish flotilla in a battle that was essentially target practice. When troops dispatched from California after the naval battle arrived in the islands, they and Filipino insurgents led by Emilio Aguinaldo (1869–1964) quickly overcame light resistance. The Spanish authorities in Manila surrendered on August 17. Early the next month, the Rough Riders were mustered out on Long Island, and soon thereafter Theodore, an authentic war hero, obtained the Republican nomination for governor, despite the initial reluctance of the state party boss, Thomas Collier Platt (1833–1910). Franklin's father, forsaking his traditional Democratic affiliation, voted for Theodore. Such family loyalty was not shown by Theodore's descendants when Franklin later ran for national office.

Theodore, running as a reformer/war hero with former Rough Riders as part of his campaign entourage, won a victory by 17,794 votes out of more than 1.3 million cast.[12] He ran ahead of the Republican ticket, and Platt himself later observed that "no man beside Roosevelt" could have won in 1898. On the other hand, Theodore knew that he could not have won without the party machine. Although sincerely dedicated to good government, he was a self-styled practical reformer, who, in the eyes of some, compromised himself by association with corrupt machine politicians. Although Platt, then a U.S. senator, had no constitutional role in New York state government, Theodore, during his term as governor, openly breakfasted with him at his Manhattan hotel on many Saturday mornings and devoted much of the chapter on his governorship in his autobiography trying to justify his ongoing relationship with Platt and the machine.[13]

Despite his accommodations, Roosevelt was a stronger governor than the machine wanted. When the death of McKinley's vice president Garret A. Hobart (1844–1899), at a time when there was no way to appoint a replacement, created a vacancy on the McKinley ticket in 1900, Platt decided to push Theodore for the job. Theodore issued a statement saying that he would stay in New York and run for another term as governor. But when he made a conspicuous late entrance to the Republican National Convention in Philadelphia wearing a broad-brimmed civilian version of his Cuban campaign hat, one veteran politician whispered correctly that it was "an Acceptance Hat."[14] He was nominated unanimously two days later. There had been serious opposition from Marcus Alonzo Hanna (1837–1904), McKinley's manager, who famously muttered about the recklessness of putting "that damned cowboy"[15] a heartbeat away from the presidency, but, outmaneuvered by Platt, he bowed to the inevitable. Theodore campaigned vigorously against Bryan, probably without significantly affecting the result, which was a second McKinley victory by a slightly larger percentage of both the popular and the electoral vote than in 1896.[16]

Once the excitement of the campaign and the inauguration was over, Theodore began to realize what he should have known from the outset: his position as vice president was ornamental and the vice presidency was then largely a blind alley. As one of his successors, John Nance Garner, Franklin Roosevelt's first vice president, remarked, "The vice presidency is not worth a bucket of warm spit."[17] This belated realization caused a kind of depression unusual for the normally ebullient Theodore. He contemplated resuming the study of law and speculated that his public career was probably over. Some three weeks after his inauguration as vice president, he wrote a friend, "I have always thought that I might end as a professor of history, but if possible I should prefer a more active life."[18]

Less than six months later, everything changed. On September 6, 1901, the American-born anarchist Leon Czolgosz (1873–1901) managed to get into a public receiving line to shake hands with President McKinley at an exposition in Buffalo, New York, while carrying a pistol concealed by a handkerchief wrapped around his gun hand as if it were a bandage. When the president clasped the other hand, the assassin fired into McKinley's stomach. The wound was not immediately fatal, and doctors issued reports of the president's expected recovery. But infection set in, and he died on September 14.[19] Theodore took the presidential oath in Buffalo that day. Mark Hanna's worst nightmare had become reality.

Roosevelt, while outwardly correct, rejoiced privately. As he put it in a letter to "Dear Cabot" nine days after McKinley's death, "It is a dreadful thing to come into the Presidency this way; but it would be a far worse thing to be morbid about it."[20]

He had found his niche. For the next seven and a half years, Theodore would contribute importantly to the creation of the modern presidency, a creation significantly augmented by Woodrow Wilson between 1913 and 1921 and transformed by Franklin between 1933 and 1945. For decades historians wrote off William McKinley, blinded by Theodore's brilliance and savoring his disloyal, cruel, and inaccurate put-down of McKinley as having "no more backbone than a chocolate éclair." In recent decades, however, many historians, led by H. Wayne Morgan, have suggested that McKinley was the first of the new presidents rather that the last of the old ones.[21] But what cannot be doubted is that many elite contemporaries, including young Franklin, saw in Theodore not only a leader but a role model, whose example suggested to them that a career in politics was possible and not a dream, even though a cynic like Henry Adams might scoff. Eleanor remembered Adams saying to Franklin when they visited him in his house on Lafayette Square sometime in the early Wilson administration, "Young man, I have lived in this house many years and seen the occupants of that White House across the square come and go, and nothing that you minor officials or the occupants of that house can do will affect the history of the world for long!"[22]

*   *   *

On January 30, 1882, James Roosevelt recorded the birth of his son in his wife's diary: "At a quarter to nine my Sallie had a splendid large baby boy. He weighs 10 lbs., without clothes."[23] He was christened Franklin Delano, after his mother's brother, in Hyde Park's St. James Episcopal Church on March 20. His father, then fifty-four years of age, had married Sara Ann Delano (1855–1941) in 1880, two years after the death of his first wife, Rebecca Howland (1831–78).[24] Sara, called Sallie by her intimates, was almost twenty-seven years younger than her husband.

The Delanos were part of the same Hudson River gentry as the Hyde Park Roosevelts, a tightly knit group well described by Edith Wharton.[25] When Sara married, she moved from her father's home near Newburgh on the west bank of the Hudson across to her husband's home on its east bank, a journey of some twenty miles. After the couple's wedding, they went about halfway in her father's carriage and then got into her husband's waiting carriage to complete the journey.[26] One indication of how interconnected the families were and became is that among the three persons Sallie chose as godparents for Franklin was her friend Elliott Roosevelt, Theodore's brother, whom she had known since he was a small boy. The following year, Elliott's engagement to Anna Rebecca Hall was announced at a party at the Delano home because Anna was a close friend of Sallie's younger sister Laura. A year later, their daughter Eleanor was born; she would marry Franklin twenty-one years later.[27]

The Delanos had arrived in America even before the Roosevelts. The first, Phillipe de la Noye, a Huguenot, landed in Plymouth in 1621, hoping to marry Priscilla Mullins—yes, *that* Priscilla Mullins—who turned him down for John Alden. Thirteen years later, he married Hester Dewsbury; one of the their sons, Jonathan Delano (1647–1720), was rewarded with an eight-hundred-acre tract of land at New Bedford, Massachusetts, for his service in King Philip's War (1675–76), which became the base for three generations of seafaring Delanos. Sallie Delano, part of the sixth generation of American Delanos, was much interested in genealogy and passed that interest on to her son, insisting that the Delanos had a more distinguished lineage than the Roosevelts. There is some evidence to support that claim. Before Theodore's generation, three Delanos as opposed to a pair of Roosevelts are listed in the *American National Biography*. On the political side, each family sent two members to Congress: each Roosevelt served only one term, whereas the Delanos served five terms between them. The more prominent, Columbus Delano (1809–96), seconded Abraham Lincoln's presidential nomination in 1860, was his chief election manager in Ohio, served three terms in Congress, and was an undistinguished secretary of the interior in Ulysses S. Grant's cabinet. The most interesting member of the extended family is Amasa Delano (1763–1823), a ship captain who had what we would call today "multicultural attitudes" and whose memoir provided the inspiration for Herman Melville's short masterpiece "Benito Cereno" (1856), an exploration of slavery that the novelist called "America's national sin."[28]

Sallie's father, Warren Delano (1809–98), like his father and grandfather before him, was involved in the China trade. He first sailed for Canton (Guangzhou) as a supercargo in 1833 after an apprenticeship in Boston and New York mercantile houses. In China he became a partner in two trading companies, came back home and got married in 1843 to Catherine Robbins Lyman (1825–96), and took her back to China. Each trip from or to the American East Coast took about four months. She could not accompany Delano to Canton, as China would not allow Western women to live there, so she lived in the Portuguese enclave of Macao (Heungshan), some eighty miles downriver. In 1846 they returned home with one China-born child, presumably to stay. Delano had earned a medium-size fortune, much of it in the opium trade.[29] Although he maintained his mercantile interests, Delano invested in a variety of enterprises.

He and his growing family lived in a fashionable Manhattan town house and summered in a rented house on the Hudson, north of Poughkeepsie. In 1851 he purchased a sixty-acre farm with a river view a few miles below the house he had been renting and hired the celebrated Andrew Jackson Downing (1815–52) and his firm to expand the existing farmhouse into an elaborate villa, which, with its grounds, required ten full-time servants. Delano called it Algonac.

Six years later, the panic of 1857 wiped out most of Delano's investments. He sold his Manhattan residence and even tried to sell Algonac. Finally, in 1860, he returned to China and the opium trade, this time basing himself in British-leased Hong Kong, and had more than recouped his fortune by the end of the American Civil War when he left China. Because he had summoned his family to Hong Kong in 1862 and leased Algonac to an associate until 1867, the better part of the next two years was spent in residence in Europe.

Warren Delano was obviously not proud of the source of most of his fortune. In a memoir he wrote for an unpublished history of one of the firms he led in China, the word *opium* was never mentioned. And even though he brought his family, including Sallie, to Hong Kong, he so insulated all of them from China that they were forbidden to learn even one word of its language.

Although his grandson Franklin heard much about China from his grandfather—and used the Delano connection while he was president to claim a spurious special knowledge of and relationship with China[30]—he certainly never heard the word *opium* from his grandfather's lips.

In any event, after 1867 Warren Delano's household at Algonac was calm, ordered, and patriarchal. Sallie Delano had been born there in 1854, the sixth of eleven children.[31] When she moved across the river to James Roosevelt's Springdale in 1880, it was to a similar but distinctly smaller establishment. Warren Delano was much wealthier than his son-in-law, who was twenty years his junior. After they both died, two years apart, the estate Sallie inherited from her husband was worth three hundred thousand dollars; she got a one-million-dollar legacy from her father's estate. And Sallie controlled that money into the third term of her son's presidency.

Franklin was his father's second son; his half brother, James Roosevelt Roosevelt (1854–1927), all but universally called "Rosy," was twenty-eight years his senior—just a year older than his stepmother—and was married and no longer lived in his father's house by the time his half brother was born. So Franklin was, for all intents and purposes, an only child. Rosy was graduated from Columbia University with honors and practiced law for less than a year. He gave that up when he married Helen Schermerhorn Astor (1855–93) of the very rich and socially prominent New York City family: his mother-in-law was the doyenne of the "400," those who mattered to New York society, of which he became a part.

His father's friend Grover Cleveland appointed him to diplomatic posts: he was secretary to the legation in Vienna during Cleveland's first administration and held the same position in London in the second. Naturally, he also made appropriate campaign contributions: ten thousand dollars for the 1892 election. While serving in London, his wife died, leaving him with two motherless children. Theodore Roosevelt's older sister, Anna "Bamie" Roosevelt (1855–1931), who was an intimate of the Algonac household, went over to supervise their care and to be hostess for the legation. After McKinley's election ended Rosy's diplomatic career, he never held another job, though he did function as a trustee of the enormous Astor estate, served as a railroad director, and supported several philanthropic activities, most notably the New York City Episcopal cathedral St. John the Divine.

Frank Freidel opens the final volume of his biography of Franklin with the following chilling thought:

> If, as Franklin D. Roosevelt's parents had wished, he had grown up to become another Hudson Valley aristocrat, managing the vestrymen of his church, there would have seemed nothing memorable about his rearing. It would have been of no wider interest than that of his half-brother, James Roosevelt Roosevelt, an estimable socialite. Indeed, Franklin Roosevelt did mature to fill all of the expected functions, to become, as one of his most acerbic critics called him, a country squire, but a country squire with a difference.[32]

It is one thing to note the difference, another to explain it. The things that make one life different from another are often inexplicable, and explaining Franklin, whose inner life is an enigma, is all but impossible, though even his earliest years are exceptionally well documented.

I think that I had a glimmer of insight into Franklin's casual assumption of authority in the late 1990s when I hosted Ahmed Kathadra, one of Nelson Mandela's "classmates" in the prison on Robben Island and the senior Indian in the African National Congress, for a day at the University of Cincinnati. I asked him how he thought it had been possible for Mandela, after years of confinement, to emerge from prison and immediately take his place on the world stage as if it were the natural thing to do. Kathadra smiled and said, "You know, he was the son a king, and he always expected to rule." Like most such explanations, it really does not explain: there are dozens of kings' and chiefs' sons in African politics, and not one can hold a candle to Mandela. But, since then, whenever I have pondered how Franklin became what he became, the South African's words come back to me.

Franklin was, for the first fourteen years of his life, a kind of little king, the center of his parents' world. Like other women of her class and time, Sallie had a lot of domestic help, but unlike many of them she nursed the baby for almost a year and remained intimately involved with every detail of her son's care and development. James Roosevelt delegated the disciplining of Franklin to her. As his mother remembered, after he had become president, "We never subjected the boy to a lot of unnecessary don'ts, and while certain rules established for his well being had to be rigidly observed, we were never strict merely for the sake of being strict. In fact, we took a secret pride in the fact that Franklin instinctively never seemed to require that kind of handling."[33]

Sallie's diary, after Franklin's birth, is dominated by the word *baby,* which she continued to use in place of his name long after he had been christened.[34] Even as a baby, Franklin often, but not always, traveled with his parents. The longest separation occurred when he was four and they both went to Mexico for three months. He was not left at home with servants but stayed with the Delanos at Algonac. From the time Franklin was a small boy, his father, who like his son Rosy was not much involved in either his private or his public duties, spent most clement afternoons outside with Franklin on his thousand-acre estate or on the adjoining river. These were not just for recreation; Franklin was being schooled in an understanding of the land that would someday be his to manage. On one of the three occasions Franklin voted for himself at Hyde Park while president, he listed his occupation as "tree farmer." He sometimes went on long railroad trips with his father, comfortably ensconced in the family's private railcar, a mode of transportation he would again utilize and enjoy as president.

Until he was fourteen, with one brief exception, he was homeschooled, which meant that he spent much more time with his parents, his live-in teachers, and the servants than with other children. On nine separate occasions, beginning when he was three, he accompanied his parents to Europe for extended stays, traveling on liners that were essentially huge floating luxury hotels for those in first class, with, as he put it in a letter to a boyhood friend written at sea, "a library, a barber shop, lots of baths, and lots of other things where you get quite lost."[35] Already a voracious reader, it is not just happenstance that Franklin put the library first.

At home he had, in succession, a German and a French governess. His one public school experience was six weeks in a *Volksschule* in Germany when he was nine while the family was at a spa in Bad Nauheim, where his father went regularly to take the waters. Even as an adult, he retained a working knowledge of both German and French and was able to give running translations of Adolf Hitler's broadcast speeches to aides during the Munich crisis of 1938, and during World War II he could converse with Charles de Gaulle, who refused to speak English.

In addition to his reading, philately became a lifelong pursuit after his mother passed on her childhood stamp collection to him. Franklin eventually became the most famous stamp collector in the world.[36] He also began lifelong collections of books and marine prints, and he enjoyed another hobby of briefer duration, bird-watching. When he was eleven, he was given a gun to shoot birds; he soon became a proficient amateur ornithologist.

In addition, he became a most accomplished sailor while still in his teens. He sailed first in small boats on the Hudson and later in the more challenging waters around Campobello, an island just off the coast of Maine but a part of the Canadian province of New Brunswick, where the James Roosevelts built what was called a "summer cottage"—a house of thirty-four rooms, eighteen bedrooms, and without electricity. Franklin summered there almost every year, boy and man, through 1921. His knowledge of those waters, navigational skills, and supreme self-confidence were such that as assistant secretary of the navy in 1916, he actually took the conn of the destroyer USS *Flusser* to take it through the Lubec Narrows, the strait between the mainland and Campobello. Its nervous commanding officer, Lieutenant (later Admiral) William F. "Bull" Halsey, wrote in his memoirs thirty years later:

> The fact that a white-flannelled yachtsman can sail a catboat out to a buoy and back is no guarantee that he can handle a high-speed destroyer in narrow waters. A destroyer's bow may point directly down the channel, yet she is not necessarily on a safe course. She pivots around a point near her bridge structure, which means that two-thirds of her length is aft of the pivot, and that her stern will swing in twice the arc of her bow. As Mr. Roosevelt made his first turn, I saw him look aft and check the swing of our stern. My worries were over. He knew his business.[37]

When he was fourteen, his parents sent him away to Groton, a fashionable prep school in Massachusetts northwest of Boston, founded by Endicott Peabody (1857–1944) only twelve years earlier. Peabody, from a prominent Boston banking family, became an Episcopal clergyman and modeled Groton largely on the English "public" school—that is, *private* in American usage—in which he had been educated. With an elite group of trustees that included Phillips Brooks (1835–93), the Episcopal bishop of Massachusetts, and J. P. Morgan (1837–1913), it quickly became a prestigious place for the sons of the northeastern gentry. Peabody espoused a nonintellectual brand of muscular Christianity in which character and, above all, success in football, which all boys had to play, were the most important yardsticks of judgment.[38]

Franklin was neither a great success nor a great failure during his four years at Groton. Socially, he was doubly handicapped: he and one other boy entered only in the third form; the other seventeen boys in their class had been at Groton for two years, and thus Franklin began as an outsider. In addition, his half brother's son, known as Taddy in the family but called Rosy at school, was a year ahead of Franklin and well established as a misfit. As he described it to his parents, "The boys call me Uncle Frank, but I would sooner be Uncle Frank than Nephew Rosy as they have been calling Taddy."[39]

If Taddy was a drawback, it must have boosted Franklin's prestige when newly appointed assistant secretary of the navy Theodore Roosevelt came to speak at Groton in June 1897. As he wrote his parents, "After supper tonight Cousin Theodore gave us a splendid talk on his adventures when he was on the Police Board. He kept the whole room in an uproar for over an hour, by telling us killing stories about policemen and their doings in New York." Franklin also told rather than asked his parents that he would be spending part of the Fourth of July with Theodore at Oyster Bay.[40]

Academically, he did reasonably well. The detailed but incomplete grade reports available show him to be a B student at a time when grading was much more severe than it is today. His B average in his first year, based on four separate reports, ranked him second once, third once, and fourth twice in a class that numbered between sixteen and nineteen students. The eleven brief written assessments by Peabody between October 1897 and April 1900, after an initial "very fair," consisted of six "good," two "very good," and two "excellent" appraisals. His marks were boosted by strong grades in German and French, languages in which he had been tutored at home. And though he failed Latin in his first year, when he was graduated in 1900 he took the school's prize for Latin. Peabody's final report to his parents reads: "He has been a thoroughly faithful scholar & a most satisfactory member of this school throughout his course. I part with Franklin with reluctance."[41]

Most Roosevelt biographers assume that Peabody and Groton were a very important shaping influence upon him.[42] But perhaps his four years there merely heightened certain tendencies that already existed. If his religion resembled, in some respects, that of Peabody, it was not much different from that of his father. The adult Franklin went to church—but not every Sunday—sang hymns, and, even while president, followed in his father's footsteps as senior warden of the church in which he had been christened.

When times of crisis came, he could write a prayer, as he did for D-Day, the invasion of France on June 6, 1944, and read it on the air. If you look at the famous newsreel of Roosevelt, Churchill, and their aides at church services on the deck of the ill-fated *Prince of Wales* in Argentia Harbour during the signing of the Atlantic Charter in 1940, you see that Churchill and the others have their noses in their hymnbooks, while FDR is singing lustily with no book needed. To his dying day, Franklin seemed to believe that good people, like himself, would go to heaven. Irving Brandt reports an incident in 1937 when the president, shown an area on Washington's Olympic Peninsula where lumbermen had clear-cut a vast area of forest, leaving utter devastation, exclaimed, "I hope the lumberman who is responsible for this is roasting in hell." Brandt adds, "One has the feeling that FDR believed in a real hell."[43]

Eleanor's later comments on Franklin's religion are germane. In her 1937 memoir, she speaks of asking him about what kind of religious instruction their children should have.

He looked at me with his amused and quizzical smile, and said that they ought to go to church and learn what he had learned. It could do them no harm. Heatedly, I replied: "But are you sure that you believe in everything you learned?" He answered: "I never really thought about it. I think that it is just as well not to think about things like that too much." That effectively shut me up, but in the years to come, whenever he played golf on Sundays and I took the children to church, I used to feel a kind of virtuous grievance.[44]

Franklin had Peabody officiate at his wedding, sent his four sons to Groton, and had him conduct the first three preinaugural services. Once he became president, he and the rector made use of each other. One of Peabody's goals was to inspire the sons of the upper class to seek careers in enlightened public service, and though he had voted for Herbert Hoover in 1932, he did vote for the Democratic Roosevelt in 1936 and 1940. The president had become what we would now call the poster child for Peabody's claim that Groton was preparing many of its sons for public careers. While any such list, headed by a president, from a small school that had perhaps a thousand graduates during Peabody's lifetime seems impressive, a calculation shows that there were perhaps ten such persons, which means that 99 percent of Groton's sons turned a deaf ear to the rector's exhortations. The overwhelming majority of the Old Grotonians in the 1930s regarded Roosevelt as a traitor to his class.[45]

For Franklin the Groton-Peabody association was valuable as evidence of his orthodoxy in religion, if not in economics. In June 1934, for example, the president and much of his family came to Groton. It was not only Groton's fiftieth graduation but also the occasion of the graduation of John Aspinwall Roosevelt (1916–81), the president's youngest son. According to the *New York Times,* which ran two stories on the event, the president, in a speech not open to the press, hailed Peabody and claimed that "as long as I live, the influence of Dr. and Mrs. Peabody means and will mean more to me than that of any other people next to my father and mother."[46]

This is surely the politician's hyperbole. The slight correspondence from him cited in Peabody's biography is friendly and largely perfunctory. In the only published letter from Peabody to Franklin commenting on the New Deal, he praises the "Social Securities Act" and the Civilian Conservation Corps (CCC) but posits to the president that "your going to church means more to the people . . . than anything else that you can do."[47]

After Groton came Harvard. It was not a family tradition—his father was a graduate of Union College but did take a law degree at Harvard—but it was *the* place to go from Groton. And, of course, cousin Theodore had gone there. While Franklin was still at Groton, plans had been made to send him to Harvard, and he took enough advanced courses at the prep school that he was able to graduate in three years, taking a bachelor's degree in history in June 1903.[48]

Unlike Theodore, who made Phi Beta Kappa and had taken his master's by the time he was twenty, Franklin did not excel in his studies, though he did take and pass a thoroughly respectable array of courses in the liberal arts, primarily in history and economics.[49] But Franklin was not at Harvard to get high marks. As Freidel has written, putting the best face on it, "At Groton, Roosevelt learned to get along with his contemporaries; at Harvard he learned to lead them."[50] He was much more concerned with the social and political aspects of college life than with his course work. One of Franklin's nonacademic biographers sneers that there is "no evidence that he ever developed, at Harvard or later, anything that could properly be called a philosophy of history."[51] An undergraduate with a "proper" philosophy of history is an exceedingly rare commodity; the only ones I have encountered in nearly five decades of teaching were so-called red-diaper babies who had picked up Marxism at home. Franklin, as we shall see, like most presidents, would use "history" for his purposes, time and again, and he certainly knew more about it than most.

Harvard students in those days were divided into two parts, unequal in both size and influence. There was the relatively small social elite, what Theodore called "gentlemen," and everyone else. Almost any Roosevelt would have been in the select group, but Franklin's nephew Taddy, who preceded him by a year at Harvard, quickly put himself beyond the pale. Possessed of an annual income of forty thousand dollars from his mother's estate, he spent much time in New York City when he should have been in Cambridge, and, unbeknownst to any member of his family, he was married in June 1900 at New York's City Hall to a young immigrant woman of dubious reputation whom he had met in a dance hall.[52] Shortly after his family learned of it in the fall and his father had a stormy confrontation with the couple in the New York apartment, the story broke in the newspapers. Some reports mentioned the family connection to the state's governor and Republican nominee for vice president and the closer connection to the Astors. The Hyde Park Roosevelts were horrified. Taddy's father disowned him but could not affect the legacy from his mother. James Roosevelt was mortified and deeply disgraced by the stain on the family name: he had a heart attack two days after he learned of the marriage, and both Sara and Franklin may have blamed it on Taddy. Franklin wrote home:

> The disgusting business about Taddy did not come as a very great surprise to me or anyone in Cambridge. I have heard the rumor ever since I have been here, but in the absence of facts the best course has been silence. I do not wonder that it has upset Papa, but although the disgrace to the name has been the worst part of the affair, one can never again consider him a true Roosevelt. It will be well for him not only to go to parts unknown, but to stay there and *begin* life anew.[53]

The letter makes Franklin sound more priggish perhaps than he was. He had just learned of his father's heart attack, and the letter's subtext was an assurance that *he* was not like Taddy.

Taddy and Sadie went to Florida for a while and then returned to New York; they remained married until her death in 1940 but did not always live together. Taddy worked at repairing cars, became a teetotaler, and apparently never touched the principal of his legacy. At his death in 1958, he left five million dollars to the Salvation Army. There is no evidence that he ever saw or communicated with any of the Hyde Park Roosevelts again, though in 1927 Theodore's compassionate sister Bamie tracked him down and invited him to lunch at her Connecticut home. He told her, among other things, that he bicycled up to Hyde Park every summer to put flowers on his mother's grave.[54]

Taddy's disgrace *may* have been the cause of the one serious setback that Franklin's extracurricular career at Harvard suffered. He failed to be accepted by the most exclusive elite club, Porcellian, something Theodore had achieved. The secret selection process was by the "black ball" system: one negative vote eliminated a prospective member. Eleanor Roosevelt wrote that it gave Franklin an inferiority complex but made him more democratic than he would have been. Freidel calls it a "serious blow," which may have "developed in him a trace of humility." But he balances this by quoting an anonymous Harvard friend who denied the significance of the snub and argued that "Franklin had an inherited social position which nothing except his own actions could change. Any feeling of inferiority was that of a young man standing uncertainly before the awakening body politic of the United States." I have never seen a direct reference to the matter attributable to Franklin.[55]

Franklin was elected to three other elite clubs and became the librarian of two of them. He took the positions seriously and, with his collector's proclivity, haunted the used bookstores of Boston to acquire appropriate volumes for them as well as adding to his own collection. He also joined the Harvard Republican Club and cast his first presidential vote in 1904 for cousin Theodore. As he explained in a speech to the 1938 Jackson Day Dinner: "My father and grandfather were Democrats and I was born and brought up as a Democrat, but in 1904, when I cast my first vote for a President, I voted for the Republican candidate, Theodore Roosevelt, because I thought he was a better Democrat than the Democratic candidate. I have told that story many times, and if I had to do it over again I would not alter that vote."[56]

But his chief extracurricular activity—really his primary activity during his later years at Harvard, although he did not often cut classes—was writing for and then editing the student daily, the *Harvard Crimson*. He won election as the paper's president and also as permanent chairman of the class committee of the class of 1904. The latter was the first popular election victory of the future champion campaigner. He became active in alumni activities and served as a Harvard overseer during the period 1918–24.

While at Harvard, two important changes in Franklin's family life occurred: his father died in his first year, and he got engaged in his third. James Roosevelt, who had become increasingly frail over several years and had been gradually forced to abandon all of the outside activities that had been a center of his life, died in the early hours of December 8, 1900, in the apartment the elder Roosevelts maintained in a New York City hotel. He was seventy-two. Forewarned, both his sons had been with him the evening before. Sallie, who would be a widow for four decades, after a period of mourning refocused her attention on "my boy Franklin." She spent the next two winters in Boston, not Cambridge, explaining later that her quarters were "close enough to the University to be on hand should he want me and far enough removed not to interfere with his college life."[57]

In later life, Franklin often spoke of his "Dutch stubbornness," but if that trait is a heritable characteristic, it surely came from his mother rather than his father. Both Sallie and Franklin were stubborn, determined individuals: while Franklin tried to please his mother whenever possible, he was determined to be his own man. At two key turning points of his life, his engagement and marriage to Eleanor in 1903–5 and the resumption of his political career after his paralysis in 1921, Franklin's will prevailed and Sallie accepted it. There is no evidence that they ever shouted or raised their voices to each other, as occurs in most American family disagreements, but there can be no doubt that there were battles and that he won them when they concerned matters that he thought were important. Both he and his mother were extremely self-centered and self-assured.

We do not know at which family function Franklin and Eleanor first became aware of one another: there is a well-documented visit of her family to Springwood when he was four and she two during which she rode happily on his back as he crawled across the floor, but neither of them remembered it as adults. Eleanor, who depicted herself as a wallflower, did remember one social occasion at which Franklin danced with her. Their romantic attachment seems to have grown from a chance meeting on a train in 1902, when Franklin and Sallie were going back to Hyde Park and Eleanor was returning to her grandmother's home at Tivoli, a few miles farther north.[58]

Although both Franklin and Eleanor were born into the American patriciate,[59] their childhoods, in emotional terms, were at opposite poles. Whereas Franklin's family life was stable and revolved around him, Eleanor's was dysfunctional, and she must have felt herself a distant minor satellite. Her father, Elliott Roosevelt (1860–94), whom she adored, was an alcoholic who used morphine and perhaps other drugs;[60] her mother, Anna Rebecca Hall (1863–92), was a celebrated beauty obviously disappointed in her daughter, whom she often called

"Granny." Orphaned before she was ten, Eleanor clearly felt herself abandoned: her parents had separated, and she was, even before their deaths not two years apart, largely raised by her grandmother.

Her most accomplished biographer, Blanche Wiesen Cook, reminds us that the first words of Eleanor's initial memoir are "My mother was one of the most beautiful women I have ever seen" and argues persuasively that it "represented an unending reproach and longing" about her relationship with her mother—and, I would suggest, a feeling of guilt about not being made in her image.[61] Her early education was haphazard. Her maternal grandmother, Mary Livingston Ludlow Hall (1843–1919), was shocked to discover, when Eleanor came to live with her, that at age seven she could not read. She hired a tutor to remedy that situation. For the next seven years, Eleanor's schooling was either at home or in small groups of other girls from elite families.

Then in the autumn of 1899, she was sent to England to study at Allenswood, a girls school just outside London run by a remarkable Frenchwoman, Marie Souvestre (1830–1905). There were family precedents: her father's sister Bamie[62] had gone there, her parents had met and admired Souvestre in Europe, and her mother had intended to send her to Allenswood.

At Allenswood, where she spent three years, Eleanor for the first time began to have a real sense of who she was and what she might become. If one can doubt the impact of Peabody on Franklin, there can be no doubt, given Eleanor's repeated testimony and their correspondence between 1902 and her teacher's death, of the lasting impact of Souvestre on Eleanor.[63]

Her encounter with Franklin on the train took place shortly after her final return from Allenswood in the summer of 1902. There followed a series of meetings that became a courtship, culminating in his accepted proposal while both were at Groton on Sunday, November 22, 1903. Eleanor, well chaperoned, had come up to Cambridge for the Harvard-Yale game and accompanying social events and then went to Groton to see her younger brother Hall (1891–1941), for whom she felt responsible.[64] Franklin noted the event in his diary in a simple code: "After lunch I have a never to be forgotten walk to the river with my darling."[65]

Since the first public disclosure of Franklin's affair with Lucy Mercer during World War I in two books by Jonathan Daniels, some of the accounts of Franklin and Eleanor's courtship and the first dozen years of their marriage seem written through the prism of that searing event.[66] But there can be no doubt that, at the beginning, it was a love match.

The first shadow on that relationship was caused by Franklin's mother and by his almost congenital reluctance to tackle difficult personal situations head-on. He told Sallie of his feelings face-to-face over Thanksgiving: her diary entry speaks of Franklin's "startling announcement."[67] Back at Harvard a week later, he wrote:

Dearest Mama—I know what pain I must have caused you and you know I wouldn't do it if I really could have helped it—mais tu sais, me voilà! That's all that could be said—I know my mind, have known it for a long time, and know that I could never think otherwise: result: I am now the happiest man just now in the world; likewise the luckiest—And for you, dear Mummy, you know that nothing can ever change what we have always been & always be to each other—only now you have two children to love & to love you—and Eleanor as you know will always be a daughter to you in every true way—.[68]

Two days before, Eleanor had written from New York City:

Dearest Cousin Sally:
    I must write you & thank you for being so good to me yesterday. I know just how you feel & how hard it must be, but I do so want you to learn to love me a little. You must know that I will always try to do what you wish for I have grown to love you dearly during the past summer. . . .
Always devotedly,

                                          Eleanor

Eleanor had been summoned to a meeting in the New York City apartment Sallie still maintained: her future mother-in-law laid down conditions that the nineteen-year-old Eleanor could only accept, though Franklin overrode some of them. The older woman insisted on delay and secrecy, arguing that they were too young and probably hoping that her son's ardor would cool. She arranged an extended Caribbean cruise for herself, Franklin, and his college roommate but without Eleanor in February and March 1904. Eventually, she agreed to the announcement of the engagement in November 1904, a full year after Franklin's proposal. The wedding did not take place until the afternoon of March 17, 1905.

It was a spectacle, described by the *New York Times* as "one of the most memorable weddings of the year."[69] Because Eleanor was an orphan, it was natural that her father's brother should give the bride away. Whatever reservations Eleanor's future mother-in-law might have had, her uncle was typically enthusiastic: he had congratulated Franklin on the engagement, in a letter signed "Your aff. cousin," and later offered to give the bride away from under his own roof. But the marriage took place in the Manhattan home of the cousins with whom she lived before and during most of the engagement.

But Theodore was president of the United States, so, as would be the case for the rest of the couple's lives, the personal was subordinated to the political. The date was set to mesh with his political schedule. He was to make two speeches at banquets that evening, one to the Friendly Sons of St. Patrick, the other to the Sons of the American Revolution.[70] After the ceremony, he congratulated Franklin loudly on "keeping the name in the family."[71]

But, of course, a presidential presence is always disrupting. Theodore's carriage, held up by the parade crowds, was late, and the ceremony had to be delayed. In addition, such crowds assembled to see him in front of the house on East Seventy-Sixth Street that some guests could not get in until after the ceremony. As soon as Theodore arrived, the ceremony proceeded. Immediately afterward, the inner doors between the two houses were opened, and the guests who were not family members poured in. Theodore, who may or may not have kissed the bride first, headed straight for the refreshments, and most of the guests followed him, leaving Franklin and Eleanor all but alone.

2 Roosevelt Enters Politics

1905–20

BECAUSE FRANKLIN HAD ENROLLED IN COLUMBIA University's Law School in the fall of 1904 after graduating from Harvard, the newlyweds lived in a Manhattan hotel apartment for the remainder of the school year. The couple then sailed for Europe and a proper honeymoon for Americans of their class. Their identification with a sitting president gave them added prestige. On the trip across, Eleanor was seated on the captain's right; a London hotel ushered them into the "Royal Suite," which Franklin described to his mother, facetiously, as costing "$1,000 a day."[1] The couple then toured for three months through much of western Europe. Everywhere they went, they met relatives and friends. Both were experienced travelers. Eleanor noted that in France, Franklin did the talking, while her superior Italian was used in Italy.[2]

During the trip, Franklin got his law school grades. He had failed two subjects. Sara sent him the necessary texts, and he studied enough to be able to pass remedial examinations and continue his studies. He failed no more courses and was able to pass the New York bar exam in early 1907. He then stopped going to classes and never received a law degree.[3] He and Eleanor socialized with their extended family and others of their stratum of society, including two memorable trips to Washington for Theodore's inauguration and for the marriage of the president's daughter, Alice, to Nicholas Longworth in February 1906.

After their return from Europe, the couple had moved into a house in Manhattan that Sara had rented for them and supplied with servants. This was their home for two years until the two connected houses at 47–49 East Sixty-Fifth Street that Sara paid for were completed. Franklin participated in the planning and furnishing of these houses, and Eleanor did not. Within a few pages of her 1937 memoir, published while Sara was still alive, Eleanor put two different spins on the situation. Initially, she explained: "My early dislike of any kind of scolding had developed now into a dislike of any kind of discussion, so, instead of taking an interest in these houses, one of which I was to live in, I left everything to my mother-in-law and my husband." But a few pages later, she related: "A few weeks after we had moved into the new house . . . I sat in front of my dressing table and wept, and when my bewildered young husband asked me what on earth was the matter with me, I said I did not like to live in a house which was not in any way mine, one that I had done nothing about and which did not represent the way I wanted to live."[4]

About the same time, she wrote, but never published, a third version, a bitter paragraph of failure that expressed her feelings about her mother-in-law—and her own children—perhaps as well as they could be expressed: "She determined to bend the marriage to the way she wanted it to be. What she wanted was to hold on to Franklin and his children; she wanted them to grow as she wished. As it turned out, Franklin's children were more my mother-in-law's children than they were mine."[5]

Franklin's views are not on record. Clearly, he had imposed his will upon his mother in the matter of the marriage and seems to have been incredibly insensitive to Eleanor's ongoing unhappiness with the way that Sara dominated so much of their lives. Perhaps he did not understand Eleanor's unhappiness. But throughout his life, he tried, often with great success, to avoid certain kinds of personal and political confrontations. His refusal to intervene between his wife and his mother was not one of those successes.

Both Franklin and Eleanor were independently well off, with trust funds and other assets. Early in their marriage, each agreed to contribute half of an estimated $1,200 monthly to meet normal household expenses at a time when the average annual earnings of federal employees were calculated at $1,072.[6] This covered their expenses, including servants' wages, in both New York City and Campobello, where they summered. Account books had to be kept, and Eleanor reports that Franklin taught her how to maintain them.[7]

Their first child, Anna Eleanor, named for her mother and herself, was born on May 3, 1906. Five other children, all boys, were born between 1907 and 1916: thus, Eleanor, who tells us that she was "perfectly miserable" for three months before each birth, was pregnant for four and a half years between mid-1905 and March 1916.[8] From the first, Franklin left the discipline of their children largely to Eleanor, to her despair and with unfortunate results.

After passing the bar and spending the summer of 1907 at Campobello, Franklin took his first job, at age twenty-five, with the prominent Wall Street law firm of Carter, Ledyard, and Milburn, in September. The terms were typical for elite firms. Law clerks, as beginners were called, got no salary for the first year and a salary, small at the beginning, after that. His assignments, while not as menial as Franklin had predicted—"full-fledged office boy"—were clearly bottom-of-the-ladder tasks. He wrote "logs" of cases handled by partners and other senior lawyers and defended the firm's corporate clients, such as the American Express Company, against suits in small claims court. He clearly enjoyed the give-and-take of the latter and quickly became managing clerk for such cases.[9]

Sometime during his three years at the Carter firm, Franklin decided that a political career was what he wanted. One early evidence of his ultimate goal is the oft-quoted obituary remark of fellow clerk Grenville Clark: "I remember him saying with engaging frankness that he wasn't going to practice law forever, that he intended to run for office at the first opportunity, and that he wanted to be and thought he had a very good chance of being president." Clark went on to say that Franklin had laid out a hypothetical course parallel to the one Theodore had taken: New York State Assembly, assistant secretary of the navy, and then governor of New York. Once that was achieved, he remembered Roosevelt remarking that "anyone who is Governor of New York has a good chance to be President with any luck." Perhaps even more striking is Clark's memory of his fellow clerks' reactions to it: "I do not recall that even then, in 1907, any of us deprecated his ambition or even smiled at it as we might perhaps have done. It seemed proper and sincere, and moreover, as he put it, eminently reasonable."[10]

The opportunity that Franklin sought came in 1910, and he seized it. Nationally, it was a tumultuous election, even though the presidency was not at stake. What historians have called a progressive revolt was building up steam, as the presidential performance of William Howard Taft (1857–1930), TR's handpicked successor, was a distinct disappointment to the Rough Rider and his followers. And though the progressive movement had begun largely in the Republican Party, by 1910 the conservative-progressive struggle had broken out among the Democrats as well. Some contemporaries and many later historians have minimized the differences between conservatives and progressives, but to most of those involved in the struggle and the first couple of generations of historians who wrote about them, the differences seemed real and polar.[11] As it turned out, it was a most fortuitous time for the twenty-eight-year-old Roosevelt to enter politics: entry even two years later would have almost certainly denied him the promotions he received in 1913 and 1920 as assistant secretary of the navy and vice presidential nominee.

He apparently never considered joining the Republican Party and simply adopted the party of his father, in the same way that he adopted his father's religion. To be sure, he had cast his first presidential vote for Theodore in 1904, but that was a family matter. Theodore, to a degree, felt the same way. In response to a query from Franklin about entering politics, routed through Theodore's accommodating sister Bamie, the Rough Rider president gave his encouragement: "Franklin ought to go into politics . . . is a fine fellow," but wished that he were a Republican.[12]

His political debut was easily accomplished. The Dutchess County Democrats had tried without success to get his father and his half brother to run for office. Not only would a young "squire" add strength to the ticket, but he, his family, and friends could be called upon for financial support. Roosevelt decided to run for an open state senate seat, even after he learned that it covered rural Columbia and Putnam Counties as well as Dutchess and had gone to a Democrat only once since 1856. He showed up to be looked over by a gathering of Democrats in Poughkeepsie, made a speech or two, and was duly nominated on October 6, 1910, a month and two days before election day.

Roosevelt and a more experienced Democratic candidate for Congress, Richard E. Connell (1867–1912), conducted a joint campaign. Connell, a Catholic and longtime reporter and editor for a Poughkeepsie paper, had run unsuccessfully for Congress once and for the state assembly twice and had held local public offices.[13] The religious issue would be very important in Roosevelt's New York political career, and this early willingness to work in tandem with a Catholic candidate is worth noting.

Roosevelt's penchant for the dramatic gesture and his assets gave the pair a decided advantage: he purchased a red Maxwell touring car—which he called "the machine"[14]—festooned it appropriately, and with Connell canvassed the whole three-county area. To avoid accidents, they would stop the car when meeting oncoming horse-drawn vehicles, using those opportunities to talk to individual farmers. Roosevelt's campaign speeches stressed that he was an independent who favored the reforms advocated by the former progressive Republican governor Charles Evans Hughes (1862–1948).

These efforts might have been of no avail in most years, but 1910 was not a normal year. Nationally, Democrats gained fifty-six seats in the House of Representatives, winning control of that body for the first time since the election of 1892. In New York State, the Democratic triumph was even more pronounced. Theodore, now usually referred to as "Col. Roosevelt" in the press, took on the Republican establishment, won control of its state convention, and forced through the nomination of Henry L. Stimson (1867–1950) for governor. As a result, many of the Republican bosses did little or nothing for the statewide ticket. Even the weather—snow and rain in much of the state on election day—kept many Republican farmers home. The result was a Democratic sweep. *New York Times* headlines described the result:

DIX IS ELECTED GOVERNOR;
SWEEPS STATE BY 64,074

Well down in the story, but still on the front page, were adjacent paragraphs about the Roosevelt and Connell campaign. It was the initial appearance of Franklin's name in a political context in the paper.[15]

Roosevelt did not just float in on a Democratic tide, but ran ahead of the ticket, garnering just over 52.2 percent of the vote, more than any other candidate on the three-county Democratic slates.

The name Franklin D. Roosevelt quickly became familiar to *Times* readers. A New Year's Day story about Governor John A. Dix's (1860–1928) inauguration mentioned Roosevelt as a possible candidate for leadership of the senate. Three weeks later, a full-page spread—with a portrait—was devoted to him in the paper's magazine section, and by the end of the month a story headlined

"Murphy Confers with Roosevelt . . . Tammany Chieftain and Insurgent Leader Meet" showed that he had achieved an amazing prominence for a political newcomer who had just turned twenty-nine the day before.[16]

This unexpected attention was but another example of what a latter-day Horatio Alger might have styled "pluck and luck." Franklin Roosevelt was lucky, but he was prepared to succeed. Politics become his day job. He was what his son called a "more or less inactive partner" in the firm of Marvin, Hooker, and Roosevelt.[17] Franklin had had the assets, the leisure, and the foresight to move his family plus assorted servants to Albany for the legislative session, even though the capital was less than seventy miles from Hyde Park—his voting address—and not even a hundred miles from Manhattan, where he actually lived. He rented a large three-story house in Albany for four months at four hundred dollars. Most other legislators lived alone in hotels or small apartments. Most of the New York City delegation, men such as Senator Robert F. Wagner and Assemblyman Alfred E. Smith, went home for weekends.[18] Thus, when a group of Democratic legislators rebelled against the Tammany leadership, it was "natural" that they found the Roosevelt "home" a convenient place to meet and for their host to become what the *Times* called "chief insurgent." Roosevelt, from his earliest press interviews, showed that instinct for effective self-promotion so important in a political career. Speaking of the endless insurgent meetings at his home, he told a *Times* reporter, "I will betray one secret. There is little very little business done at our councils of war. We just sit around and swap stories at the bivouac fire."[19]

The issue that provoked the insurgency was which Democrat should become U.S. senator. The Constitution of the United States originally provided in Article I, Section 3, that the "Senate of the United States shall be composed of two Senators from each state, chosen by the legislature thereof." Thus, since 1788 New York had chosen its senators by votes of each legislative chamber in which each legislator had one vote, and a majority of all legislators was required for victory. Because the term of one of New York's two Republican senators expired in 1910, the Democratic sweep meant that the first order of business for the new Democratic majority in the legislature would be to choose that senator. The 200-member legislature was divided between 110 Democrats and 90 Republicans. The rules under which the Democrats in the legislature operated provided that a caucus of Democrats would meet separately and choose a candidate by majority vote and that all Democrats who attended the caucus were bound to support that choice. But any Democrats who did not attend the caucus were not bound by its results. If all Democrats attended the caucus, a mere 56 votes could choose a senator. Because party leaders, concentrated in the New York City organization called Tammany, could control that many votes, Tammany's leader could normally choose the senator on those infrequent occasions when Democrats controlled the legislature.

Tammany leader Charles F. Murphy (1858–1924) had let it be known that he would support William F. (Blue-Eyed Billy) Sheehan (1859–1917), a wealthy lawyer-politician of dubious reputation. Many Democrats, including New York's mayor, protested. When Roosevelt learned that 18 assemblymen had informed Murphy that they would neither attend the caucus nor support Sheehan, he joined them. By the time of the first vote on January 17, there were 22 insurgents.[20] At the caucus, 62 of the 68 attendees voted for Sheehan, who became the caucus choice. When the legislature voted, Sheehan got the 68 caucus votes, 13 shy of the needed majority. The deadlock went on for sixty-one days before a deal was made. Sheehan withdrew, and James A. O'Gorman (1860–1943), a Tammany stalwart but a man of good reputation, was chosen and became the last New York senator elected by the legislature.[21] The Seventeenth Amendment to the Constitution, mandating the direct election of senators, was ratified in 1913.

Murphy's biographer points out that although the insurgents claimed a "symbolic victory," in the final analysis Murphy could be pleased with the result. He was relieved of an embarrassment and was able to send a respectable Tammanyite to Washington.[22] But to say, as many writers do, that Roosevelt's revolt failed is to miss the point. The senatorial election controversy served Roosevelt well. It is difficult to imagine another scenario that would have advanced his career so effectively so fast. He came to Albany a relative unknown despite his famous name, so green that Al Smith had to explain how things worked. Within weeks his name had become familiar to readers of the state's newspapers; he had negotiated, publicly, with the state's most powerful politicians; and he had managed to please many of his constituents who were not regular Democrats while not completely alienating the party regulars. Like his role model, Theodore, he had established reform credentials while staying within the limits of party loyalty.[23] This was but the first dance in what would become a long ballet between Roosevelt and Tammany, the Protestant patrician reformer and the plebeian, largely Catholic political machine. Initially, Tammany made the rules, but eventually Roosevelt, as president, became its master. In the final analysis, each needed the other for success.

Roosevelt's legislative service, though brief, had real significance for his career in two distinct ways. First, it gave him some basic lessons in practical politics. He learned, some critics would say too well, that while it was good to fight for principles, it was necessary to know when to compromise. He soon came to understand that he needed to embrace urban issues as well as those that chiefly concerned his largely rural constituency. The second significant consequence of Franklin's brief legislative career is that Louis McHenry Howe (1871–1936) became the first member of his political entourage and his most important mentor. Born in Indianapolis, Louis was the only child of an "old-stock" middle-class family of steadily deteriorating fortunes.

Louis, self-described as a "mediaeval gnome" and "one of the four ugliest men in the State of New York," was a sickly child who became a sickly adult. Barely five feet tall and weighing less than a hundred pounds, his face was severely pockmarked by a childhood tumble from a bicycle onto a graveled surface. He dressed like an unmade bed. Despite a chronic cough so severe that he had to wear a truss, he smoked cigarettes incessantly and was usually bedecked in ashes.

By the time Louis was five, his father had gone bankrupt in Indiana during the panic of 1873, resettled in Saratoga Springs in upstate New York with the help of his wife's relatives, and had taken charge of a struggling weekly newspaper and print shop. Educated in two local academies prepping for a college career that never materialized, Louis read widely. Beginning with minor tasks for his father's paper as a teen, he developed a popular, purplish-prose style despite an often uncertain syntax and eccentric spelling. When he was twenty-one, he was made coeditor and took over his father's role as stringer for two New York papers, the *New York Herald* and its companion, the *Evening Telegraph*. While most such assignments were trivial and involved Saratoga Springs affairs, he scored one notable scoop: the first account of Theodore Roosevelt's breakneck trip from an Adirondack cabin to Buffalo to be sworn in after McKinley's death.

In 1898 he married Grace Hartley, the daughter of a well-to-do Fall River, Massachusetts, family, over the objections of her widowed mother, who nevertheless bought the new couple a substantial house in Saratoga Springs. They had three children, one of whom died in infancy. After the failure of the family paper in 1900, Louis had no full-time job, but beginning in 1906 he was added to the *Herald*'s Albany staff but only during the annual legislative session, which could be as brief as two months. Thus, Louis had to constantly hustle for additional employment. He was regularly hired by metropolitan newspapers during election campaigns and took on political chores for politicians, including a wealthy Democratic reformer, Thomas Mott Osborne (1859–1926).[24]

By 1911, when Franklin came to Albany, Louis was a seasoned political reporter with unsatisfied political ambitions and a continuing need for any kind of employment. We do not know exactly when they first met, but since Franklin was central to the big story of the 1911 session—the fight over Sheehan—it must have been in January, and Louis would have covered some of the press conferences in Roosevelt's home. The first association between them that can be documented came during the 1912 presidential campaign, when Franklin and Osborne organized a short-lived organization to muster support for Wilson's candidacy and hired Howe to run it.

Franklin had gone to see Wilson (1856–1924), the newly elected governor of New Jersey, sometime late in 1911 and supported his presidential bid. Boss Murphy and Tammany wanted no part of Wilson and kept Democrats like Franklin and Osborne off the New York convention delegation.

The 1912 Democratic National Convention was one of the most dramatic and crucial in American political history. By the time the convention met in Baltimore on June 25, Theodore Roosevelt, after losing his bid to replace Taft, had announced plans to organize a new party and regain the presidency. Wise politicians assumed that whoever was nominated in Baltimore would become the first Democratic president elected in twenty years and only the second since before the Civil War.

The pro-Wilson Democrats in New York were either kept off the delegation— Franklin was supposed to be an alternate but was frozen out at the last minute—or neutered by the unit rule, which, like the caucus in the legislature, bound all delegates to vote for whomever the majority of the delegation supported. As was the case in the legislature, that usually meant Tammany control. The entire convention scenario was governed by the traditional Democratic stipulation that a successful candidate must have a two-thirds majority. Only after forty-five bitter ballots was Wilson selected on the forty-sixth; it was the eleventh day of the convention.

Despite being kept off the New York delegation, Franklin went to Baltimore to lobby for Wilson. There is no evidence that his lobbying changed a single vote: he was, at best, a spear-carrier. But his energetic support of Wilson during the convention—including an unauthorized incursion onto the floor to lead a vigorous pro-Wilson demonstration—caught the attention of many national leaders. Even without such activity, Franklin enjoyed greater prominence after the Wilson nomination as one of only three prominent New York Democrats who were preconvention Wilson supporters. He and Eleanor shared a rented house with two other Democratic couples. Eleanor attended the convention for a while, disliked its noise and general vulgarity, and left early to return to New York and take the children to Campobello.[25]

Before the convention, Franklin and Osborne had organized the short-lived New York State Wilson Conference, financed largely if not exclusively by Osborne, and hired Louis Howe to do publicity work out of an office in lower Manhattan. After the nomination, Franklin paid his respects to the candidate in New Jersey. He and Osborne quickly morphed the Wilson Conference into the fleeting Empire State Democracy, which threatened to field an independent Democratic slate.

Meanwhile, Louis Howe was desperate for a job. In expectation of more or less steady employment, he had turned down offers of election-campaign work from the *Herald,* but Osborne let him go. In September a telegram from Eleanor informed Howe that Franklin had come down with a serious case of typhoid fever and needed someone to manage his campaign, as he would not be able to stump the district in person. Howe jumped at the chance and was hired at fifty dollars a week.

From that point on, Howe became almost a member of the Roosevelt household. Eleanor, the Roosevelt children, and particularly Sara resented and protested the presence of the "dirty little man," but Franklin was adamant. Louis remained. Eleanor, but not Sara, learned first to accept and then to appreciate Louis, as did at least some of the children.[26]

Howe's tactics to manage a campaign without a visible candidate included an unusual amount of newspaper advertising and direct mail. One letter went to more than ten thousand recipients. Although Franklin received fewer votes than in 1910 from a larger electorate, he faced two opponents in 1912. His percentage of the vote dropped from 52 percent in the two-candidate election in 1910 to 48.5 percent in the three-candidate race in 1912. He still beat his closest rival by some seventeen hundred votes in a canvass of just over thirty-two thousand and ran ahead of the Democratic ticket.[27] Nationally, Wilson's triumph was achieved with only 41.9 percent of the popular vote.[28]

Thus began a close relationship that endured until Howe's death. But even before this formal arrangement, Howe, according to Eleanor, had urged Franklin to think about running for governor. In June, while he was still working for the New York State Wilson Conference, Howe wrote to Franklin with the salutation "Beloved and revered Future President."[29] We do not know if Franklin had shared his dreams of political glory with him.

The nomination and election of Woodrow Wilson opened up exciting vistas for Franklin. As had been the case from the beginning of the Republic, the new administration would not begin until March 4, 1913, so Franklin again took his seat in Albany and Louis went back on the *Herald*'s payroll there. One indication of Franklin's confidence that he would get a post in Washington was that, unlike 1911, he merely took hotel rooms in Albany. He and Eleanor commuted, while the children stayed with the servants in their Manhattan house.[30]

Franklin trolled for a position in the administration all during the interregnum. Several days before the inauguration, he declined two separate job offers from the treasury secretary designate, William Gibbs McAdoo (1863–1941): the number-two slot at the Treasury and the collectorship of the Port of New York.[31] The job he most wanted, of course, was assistant secretary of the navy. In another piece of Roosevelt luck, the new navy secretary was the veteran North Carolina editor-politician Josephus Daniels (1862–1948). Franklin had met and impressed him at the Baltimore convention, and they saw each other again during the campaign when Daniels was based in New York City as Wilson's national director of publicity.[32] Franklin went to Washington some days before the inauguration and, knowing that Daniels's appointment had been announced, managed to meet him in the lobby of the Willard Hotel shortly before the inauguration. As the North Carolinian told the story in his memoirs, after Roosevelt congratulated him on his appointment Daniels asked: "'How would you like to come to Washington as Assistant Secretary of the Navy?' His face beamed with pleasure. . . . 'How would I like it? I'd like it bully well. It would please me better than anything else in the world. . . . All my life I have loved ships and have been a student of the Navy, and the assistant secretaryship is the one place, above all others, I would love to hold.'" Wilson sent Franklin's nomination to the Senate on March 11, and four days later Daniels recorded, "On the very day that I received the letter from Mr. Wilson I immediately determined upon having Mr. R. as assistant if it was agreeable to the President. It is singular that I never thought of any other man in that connection. . . . His distinguished cousin TR went from that place to the presidency. May history repeat itself?"[33]

Not surprisingly, the career replication was noted by many, including the distinguished cousin. Theodore wrote Franklin on March 13 that he was "much pleased" with his appointment, adding, "It is interesting to see that you are in another place that I once held. I am sure you will enjoy yourself to the full. . . . and that you will do capital work."[34] He was thirty-one years old; Theodore had been thirty-seven when he achieved the same office.

Franklin began his job on March 17. Charles H. McCarthy, a carryover old Navy Department hand, served as Franklin's secretary during most of his tenure. Louis Howe came to Washington almost immediately as Roosevelt's other secretary—at two thousand dollars a year—and would later become his special assistant at three thousand dollars. Even the smaller sum was a larger assured income than he had ever earned.[35]

When Eleanor and the children came down from Campobello in the fall of 1913, they lived initially in the home of Eleanor's aunt Anna (Bamie) Roosevelt Cowles, at 1733 N Street, but in the autumn of 1916 they moved to a larger home at 2131 R Street. The Roosevelts' pattern of life in Washington was both similar to and different from what it had been in New York City. They continued to have servants and summered at Hyde Park and Campobello, with Franklin visiting when he could. But the national capital was a far cry from metropolitan Manhattan. Washington was, in 1913 and for decades to come, a medium-size southern city with few cultural attractions. It ranked sixteenth among the nation's cities with some 330,000 persons, more than a quarter of whom were black, who do not seem to have impinged significantly on the consciousness of either Franklin or Eleanor except as servants.

Franklin's official position imposed complex social obligations on Eleanor. She complained in her first autobiography of the endless social calls she had to make "repeating the formula which I can remember to this day: 'I am Mrs. Franklin D. Roosevelt. My husband has just come as Assistant Secretary of the Navy.'"[36]

She tried to do without the social secretary who was de rigueur for most wives of senior Washington officials "but finally engaged one for three mornings a week."[37] Shortly after her move to Washington, she became pregnant for the fifth time: Franklin D. Jr. was born on August 17, 1914, at Campobello, followed by their last child, John Aspinwall, born on March 13, 1916, in Washington.

Franklin would remain in the Navy Department for seven years and five months, from his thirty-first into his thirty-eighth year. Both his immediate boss, Daniels, whom he continued to call "Chief" even while president, and his ultimate superior, Woodrow Wilson, were major influences on his life and outlook. The influence from Daniels was personal, subtle, and democratizing; that from Wilson was relatively distant, obvious, and programmatic—it would be fully observable only in the latter years of Franklin's presidency.

Josephus and Franklin were seemingly a mismatched pair, and the new assistant secretary seriously underestimated his boss. Impatient with what he took to be Daniels's "hillbilly" ways, a notion that was neither culturally nor geographically correct, Franklin often chafed at Daniels's slowness and unwillingness to accept all his suggestions, and sometimes he gave comic imitations of his chief at his club and private gatherings. Daniels was quite aware of his subordinate's minor disloyalties. In his diary—but not in his memoir—he wrote at the time of Franklin's resignation in 1920, "He left in afternoon, but before leaving wrote me a letter most friendly & almost loving wh. made me glad I had never acted on my impulse when he seemed to take sides with my critics."[38]

Josephus was born and lived in small towns in coastal North Carolina. His shipbuilder father died when the boy was three. His mother, who kept a millinery shop and was postmistress, raised him and two brothers. When he dropped out of an academy at eighteen, his mother mortgaged the family home so he could buy and run a small newspaper. He remained an editor-owner for the rest of his long life. In addition, he studied law and was admitted to the bar, though he never practiced. In 1894, with outside financial backing, he bought the *Raleigh News and Observer* and made it North Carolina's leading daily and one of the most important in the South.

Active in Democratic politics without running for office, Daniels supported the progressive, agrarian wing of the party, embodying what C. Vann Woodward called "progressivism—for whites only."[39] Daniels was important enough to receive a patronage appointment in each of the three Democratic assumptions of national power in his lifetime. He was the second ranking official of the Interior Department under Grover Cleveland, navy secretary under Wilson, and Franklin Roosevelt's ambassador to Mexico. Although many felt at the time that he was a poor choice for the latter two posts, he filled both well.[40]

Apart from their temperamental differences and backgrounds, Daniels and Roosevelt had very different agendas for the navy. Daniels, who had two naval officers as brothers-in-law, wanted an expanded and efficient navy, but one that was somewhat democratized: he insisted that one hundred places at Annapolis be held for qualified enlisted men and that civilian faculty be appointed there. As a lifelong prohibitionist, he initiated the regulations that forbade the serving of alcohol in the officers' messes. Although not a pacifist, he was very much on what we would call today the dovish side of most foreign policy questions. He also was largely unconcerned with pomp, circumstance, and protocol. Socially, he tended to mix with members of Congress, more often than not his fellow southerners, who dominated the Wilson administration.

Franklin's views on these matters were quite different. He was, like Theodore, very much a big navy man and much more hawkish than either Daniels or, for that matter, Woodrow Wilson. Franklin was not in sympathy with the ban on shipboard liquor. He got along well with most naval officers, many of whom were openly scornful of his chief, and he and Eleanor tended to socialize with members of their own class, regardless of party affiliation.

One reform that both Daniels and Franklin pursued was what Ronald Spector has called the "reinvention of the enlisted man." Both men understood—as did the contemporary British Admiralty—that a modern navy needed men with modern skills.[41] However, this impulse did not extend to racial policies: segregationist Daniels continued the diminution of the black presence in the navy that had begun in the early Progressive Era. As he explained to a senator: "There is no legal discrimination shown against colored men in the Navy. As a matter of policy, however, and to avoid friction between the races, it has been customary to enlist colored men in the various ratings of the messman branch . . . and in the lower ratings of the fireroom, thus permitting colored men to eat and sleep by themselves."[42] There is no evidence that the assistant secretary ever lifted a finger to ameliorate this policy; he did, however, write a "strong letter" to the surgeon general on behalf of an African American doctor who wished to enter the Army Medical Reserve Corps.[43]

Franklin absolutely reveled in the trappings and perquisites that came with his position. An assistant secretary was entitled, on boarding a naval vessel, to a seventeen-gun salute with four ruffles and a guard of sixteen men and to be met by the ship's officers in dress uniform. Roosevelt even designed a special pennant to be flown when he was aboard, adding to the existing arrangements that called for such emblems only for the president and the secretary of the navy. He made much use of two small naval vessels, which he could commandeer much of the time. The secretary's yacht, the *Sylph*, and the dispatch boat *Dolphin* were often seen at Campobello and Hyde Park. And to celebrate the Fourth of July in 1914, Franklin arranged for the battleship *North Dakota* to put in at Eastport, Maine, adjacent to his vacation home at Campobello.[44]

Despite such wonderful "toys," Franklin, who had not previously administered anything more complicated than his household budget, quickly demonstrated an ability to execute the major functions of his new job. Franklin's chief responsibilities were navy yard personnel and, after the basic political decisions had been made, budgetary matters. As he liked to say, "I get my fingers into everything and there's no law against it."[45] No twelve words better express

Franklin's activist approach to running anything—the Navy Department, his therapeutic spa for "polios" at Warm Springs, and, eventually, the government of the United States during the Great Depression and World War II.

In the Navy Department, Franklin made his job, in present-day terms, roughly that of a chief executive officer, while Josephus was an alert chairman of the board. For its time, the naval enterprise was huge: in 1913 there were more than fifty-two thousand officers and men in the U.S. Navy and almost ten thousand more in the Marines. The department's budget was $143 million. Franklin, despite his inexperience, soon mastered both personnel management and detailed budget making to a degree surprising to most of those with whom he dealt. With the help of Howe, he soon also became adept at dealing with the American Federation of Labor (AFL) trade union leaders who represented the dockyard workers and learned how to talk to the rank and file as well. He stressed accommodation, and during his tenure the navy had an exemplary labor record. Thus, Franklin would enter the White House more experienced in labor relations than any president before or since, unless, of course, one counts the experience of George Washington and several of his successors in slave management as labor relations. He worked very hard at his job from the beginning, but still found time for frequent weekday golf games.

In mid-August 1914, Franklin made a serious political misstep. Apparently egged on by treasury secretary William G. McAdoo, the transplanted Georgian who had made New York his political base, he agreed, precipitously, to be an anti-Tammany candidate in the Democratic primary for New York's other U.S. Senate seat. The adoption of the Seventeenth Amendment to the Constitution meant that the senators elected or reelected in 1914 were the first to be directly chosen by the voters.[46] Because Elihu Root chose not to seek reelection, his seat was open.

Daniels had urged Franklin not to run, predicting that he would lose to Tammany and that, with a divided Democratic Party, the GOP would hold the seat in the general election. Tammany's Murphy waited to name a candidate until just before the filing deadline of September 8. Then, in a striking coup, he named a respectable candidate, James W. Gerard (1867–1951), a former associate justice of the New York Supreme Court, who was currently in the headlines as Wilson's ambassador in Berlin, helping Americans caught there by the outbreak of World War I. The ambassador remained at his post, did not campaign, and left Franklin looking foolish.[47] The result was as Josephus had predicted: Gerard won the primary easily—Franklin got only about a third of the votes—but lost the general election in a Republican sweep of the state.[48] Franklin and boss Murphy each apparently came to realize that the Democrats could win consistently in New York only if, whatever their differences, they presented a united front.

When what we now call World War I began in Europe in August 1914, Franklin, unlike most of his American contemporaries, realized immediately that this was a major event that would impact American life. On Saturday, August 1, 1914, after learning that Germany had declared war on Russia, he wrote to Eleanor, "A complete smash up is inevitable, and there are a great number of problems for us to consider. Mr. D. totally fails to grasp the situation and I am to see the President Monday a.m. to go over our own situation. . . . These are history-making days. It will be the greatest war in the world's history."[49]

Before examining Franklin's role in the American preparation for and participation in World War I, his involvement in the "gunboat diplomacy" aspects of American imperialism in the Caribbean should be noted. He did not get his fingers into the muddled naval intervention in Mexico in April 1914. He was in the midst of an inspection of Pacific naval facilities from San Diego to Seattle, his first visit to the Far West, and had no part in the decisions that led to a fatal encounter that the leading authority describes, ironically, as "an affair of honor." The short-term cost of "honor" was an American occupation of the Mexican port of Vera Cruz and fighting that cost at least two hundred Mexican and nineteen American lives, the first of the more than fifty thousand battle deaths accrued during the Wilson administration.[50]

Franklin was, however, deeply involved in another aspect of American imperialism, the ongoing occupation of Haiti (1915–34), an occupation executed by the navy's Marine Corps. Like so many of his fellow progressives, he naively believed that a benign American imperialism would lead Caribbean and other Western Hemisphere nations into a prosperous if second-rate modernity, which would improve the lives of its peoples. Freidel puts it nicely, speaking of Franklin's "enthusiasm for [the] dramatic employment of violence to achieve presumably democratic aims."[51] Roosevelt supported and executed policy toward Haiti, but had no decisive policy-making role in 1915–16.[52]

He did, however, go to Haiti in early 1917—the senior American official to make such an inspection—and the records and accounts of that trip provide an interesting preview of his later complex and contradictory attitudes toward less developed nations and peoples when he was making policies for the planet. On the one hand, he was an apologist for the often brutal and humiliating treatment the Marines inflicted on both the peasantry and the local elite; on the other, he genuinely believed that foreign capital would be useful in raising the standard of living of its people. He could repeat and relish racist remarks, like the comment by one of his entourage in Haiti about a muscular Haitian cabinet member: "I couldn't help saying to myself that that man would have brought $1,500 at auction in New Orleans in 1860 for stud purposes."[53] Yet Franklin could, unlike most white Americans there, ignore the color line, treat black officials with courtesy, and charm them by making speeches in French. He wrote, "I cannot agree . . . that just because the Haytian native population does not use knives, forks, cups, etc. that they never will use them. As a matter of fact I feel convinced that during the next generation the Haytian population will adopt the living standards more generally in vogue."[54] Some friendly scholars have seen the roots of Roosevelt's Good Neighbor policy in such sentiments, but it seems quite a stretch: in 1917 he was clearly an out-and-out imperialist, if one of the more benevolent kind.[55] The following year, he tried to promote the purchase of Curaçao from the Netherlands.[56]

Franklin thoroughly enjoyed his inspection tour of Haiti, which included an overland trip to the neighboring Dominican Republic and was in essence a winter vacation. Some twenty-six years later, while flying back from the Casablanca Conference on his sixty-first birthday, he had the pilot circle low so he could point out to his companions the route his party had taken in 1917.[57]

His tour was interrupted by a cryptic wireless message from Daniels recalling him to Washington. Radio messages had informed the embassy there that Germany had announced its intention to resume unrestricted submarine warfare as of February 1, but Franklin and his party sailed on the fourth with no clear knowledge of the exact situation. Secretary of State Robert Lansing (1864–1928) had called for a break in relations with Germany immediately upon the news of the resumption of submarine warfare.[58]

Franklin, as hawkish as any prominent member of the administration, champed at the bit and tried to push matters as best he could. He recounted the following story on several later occasions.

> I was Acting Secretary of the Navy [that is, Daniels was out of town] and it was the first week in March. It was perfectly obvious to me that we were going to get into the War within the course of two or three weeks, depending entirely on when the first ship flying the American flag was sunk by the unlimited submarine warfare of Germany. I went to see the President and I said, "President Wilson, may I request your permission to bring the Fleet back from Guantanamo, to send it to the Navy Yards and have it cleaned and fitted out for war and be ready to take part in the War if we get in?" And the President said, "I am very sorry, Mr. Roosevelt, I cannot allow it." But I pleaded and he gave me no reason and said, "No, I do not wish it brought north." So, belonging to the Navy, I said, "Aye, aye, sir" and started to leave the room. He stopped me at the door and said, "Come back." He said, "I am going to tell you something I cannot tell to the public. I owe you an explanation. I don't want to do anything, I do not want the United States to do anything in a military way, by way of war preparations, that would allow the definitive historian in later days—these days—to say that the United States had committed an unfriendly act against the central powers."[59]

War came some two months after Franklin's return from Haiti. Wilson, with the unanimous support of his cabinet for war, called Congress into special session on March 21 and when it convened on April 2 asked Congress to declare war because German submarine warfare was "warfare against mankind" and the "world must be made safe for democracy." Congress deliberated and agreed: on April 4, the Senate approved, 82–6, and two days later the House followed suit, 373–50. For the first time in just over a century, the United States was involved in a European war.

The reactions of the two leaders of the navy were, of course, quite different. After the crucial March 20 cabinet meeting, Daniels wrote in his diary, "It was a supreme moment in my life. I had hoped & prayed this cup would pass. . . . Having tried patience, there was no course open to us except to protect our rights on the seas. If Germany wins, we must be a military nation."[60]

Franklin, the hawk par excellence, chafed at the delay after the cabinet decision and was relieved when war finally came. Both Franklin and Eleanor were present in the Capitol when Wilson asked for war. She later remembered, "Everyone wanted to hear this historic address and it was with the greatest difficulty that Franklin got me a seat. I went and listened breathlessly and returned home still half dazed by the sense of impending change."[61]

The war marked, for Eleanor, an important period of transition toward the intensely public life that she was eventually to lead. Unable to join a Red Cross motor corps because she "could not drive a car," Eleanor worked in a Red Cross canteen and "helped Mrs. Daniels to organize the Navy Red Cross." She also had much official entertaining to do, as many of the representatives of America's allies "found their way at times into our home."[62]

Eleanor, who later became adroit at using the press to her advantage, had an unfortunate first brush with publicity in July 1917. Named by Herbert Hoover's War Food Administration as an exemplar for large households, she gave an interview to a *New York Times* reporter headlined:

HOW TO SAVE IN BIG HOMES
Food Administration Adopts Mrs. F.
D. Roosevelt's Plan as Model

The story described her household of seven persons with ten servants and quoted Eleanor: "Making the ten servants help me do my saving has not only been possible, but highly profitable. . . . Since I have been following the home-card instructions prices have risen, but my bills are no larger."

By the time the story ran, Eleanor had left for Campobello. Franklin twitted her in a letter: "I am proud to be the husband of the Originator, Discoverer and Inventor of the New Household Economy for Millionaires! . . . All Washington is talking of the Roosevelt plan. . . . Uncle Fred[63] says 'It's fine, but gee how mad Eleanor will be!'" Uncle Fred was right. Eleanor wrote Franklin, "I do think that it was horrid of that woman to use my name in that way and I feel dreadfully about it because so much of it is not true and yet some of it I did say. I will never be caught again that's sure and I'd like to crawl away for shame."[64]

Franklin, as assistant secretary, did contribute significantly to winning the war. Like Theodore, Franklin was anxious to be a serving officer, but both Daniels and Wilson insisted that he remain at his post. In addition to getting things done—a good portion of it done by Louis Howe, who became a surprisingly efficient administrator—Franklin pushed for two major innovations and eventually got each adopted. The first was for 50-foot motorboats for antisubmarine defense in and around U.S. harbors. Daniels and most naval officers were skeptical, to say the least, preferring 110-foot boats.[65] In retrospect, it is clear that the small patrol boats met no real need in World War I and were irrelevant, though similar more powerful vessels became legendary in the Pacific during World War II.

Franklin's second innovation, however, was highly relevant. Known as the North Sea Mine Barrage, it called for separate minefields from the Orkneys to Norway and from Dover to Calais, to prevent German submarines from entering the Atlantic proper; it was the kind of innovative and ambitious project that often fired Franklin's imagination. Both the British Admiralty and the American naval commander in Europe, Admiral William S. Sims (1858–1936), regarded the scheme as "quite unfeasible." Franklin, however, had presented a plan, drawn up by an American admiral, Frederic R. Harris,[66] to the president, who ordered the matter pursued, as he had long wanted to "shut up the hornets in their nests." Because of Wilson's insistence, the undersea mines, some fifty-six thousand of them, were laid. Once in place, the mine barrage was a major success: it not only penned up the hornets but destroyed or damaged a number of them. This sapped the morale of German U-boat crews and was undoubtedly a contributing factor in the German naval mutiny that began on November 3, 1918. No less an authority than former first lord of the Admiralty Winston S. Churchill (1874–1965) wrote that "the mine . . . proved to be the most effective killing weapon" in the war against submarines.[67]

Franklin, frustrated in his attempts to become a serving officer, was also anxious to inspect U.S. naval forces in Europe. Blocked for a time by Daniels's insistence that he remain at his desk, eventually he prevailed and made two overseas inspection trips, one during the war and one after. During the wartime trip, July 9 to September 19, 1918, he ventured close enough to the front lines to be able to pull the lanyard on a French 155mm artillery piece so he could say that he fired at the enemy. For the rest of his life, as was his wont, he dramatized and magnified this personal experience for political purposes. This was never more apparent than in his famous speech at Chautauqua, New York, just before the onset of his first campaign for reelection as president.

I have seen war. I have seen war on land and sea. I have seen blood running from the wounded. I have seen men coughing out their gassed lungs. I have seen the dead in the mud. I have seen cities destroyed. I have seen two hundred limping, exhausted men come out of line—the survivors of a regiment of one thousand that went forward forty-eight hours before. I have seen children starving. I have seen the agony of mothers and wives. I hate war.

I have passed unnumbered hours, I shall pass unnumbered hours, thinking and planning how war may be kept from this Nation.[68]

These remarks should be compared with his extensive contemporary diary of the 1918 trip in which he speaks of "my partially successful efforts to see the real thing."[69]

During visits to London, Paris, and Rome, Franklin met and spoke with many of the allied leaders, including David Lloyd George (1863–1945) and Georges Clemenceau (1841–1929), and had an audience with Britain's George V (1865–1936). He had also met Winston Churchill previously in Washington and saw him again in London in an affair at Gray's Inn, but neither seems to have made much of an impression on the other.[70]

Franklin's homecoming was not a happy one. To begin with, he caught pneumonia in Europe just before embarking. While still incapacitated during what must have been a miserable Atlantic crossing, he contracted influenza, becoming one of the first American victims of the so-called Spanish flu, which killed some 450,000 Americans in 1918–19 and perhaps 20 million worldwide.[71] He was stretchered off the ship on September 19, 1918, and taken directly to the Sixty-Fifth Street houses on Manhattan's East Side. He was not fit enough to return to his Washington office until mid-October. This was the most serious of several episodes of respiratory and throat ailments that plagued him during his Washington years. Yet outwardly, he was a picture of health. After his return to Washington, all five Roosevelt children caught the flu, and their father got a second and apparently milder dose.

Walter C. Camp (1859–1925), the Yale football coach and administrator who virtually invented American college football, had come to Washington partially at Franklin's behest to become director of the U.S. Navy Training Camps Physical Development Program. He conducted morning workouts for cabinet members and other ranking government executives and hailed Franklin as "a beautifully built man, with the long muscles of an athlete."[72] Daniels, twenty years older and paunchy, who adamantly refused to exercise, enjoyed "perfect health," whereas, as he remarked privately in the 1930s, Franklin "seemed to catch every bug that came along."[73]

During her husband's first convalescence, Eleanor helpfully unpacked his luggage and discovered a packet of "love letters" between Franklin and her onetime social secretary Lucy Mercer, who had enlisted as a yeomanette in the navy and had been assigned to the Navy Department's executive offices. Apparently, the letters no longer exist, and we have only hearsay accounts of the consequences of the discovery. None of the four major figures, Franklin,

Eleanor, Lucy, or Franklin's mother, Sara, ever said a public word. It is widely believed that Eleanor offered him a divorce, stipulating that if the marriage were to continue, he must agree never to see Lucy again. Also, Eleanor would no longer share his bed, though there are some reasons to believe that sexual relations between them had ceased after her sixth delivery in March 1916. There is no evidence that Franklin ever considered divorce, which would have meant political suicide. Supposedly, Sara threatened to cut off the financial aid she had been giving him; reports that she threatened to disinherit him are probably not credible, given the terms of James Roosevelt's will. A major distributor of the rumors was Theodore's daughter, Alice Roosevelt Longworth (1883–1980), a persistent source of ill-will toward Franklin and Eleanor and all their works.[74]

Beyond doubt, the affair was a devastating experience for Eleanor Roosevelt, so much so that in all her self-revealing autobiographical writing the name of Lucy Mercer never occurs. The best indications of the depth of feelings that Franklin and Lucy had for each other is their behavior during World War II, which is documented in the final chapters of this book.

Shortly after Franklin returned to the office, Daniels finally agreed to let him get a naval commission and told him to take his request to Wilson. When he saw the president, sometime after October 29, Wilson explained that because he had received the first suggestions of an armistice from Germany Franklin's request was no longer viable.[75]

Franklin did, however, manage to get back to Europe after the Armistice, and though that trip did not advance his political prospects as frontline military service would have done, it helped prepare him for the presidency. The primary purpose of the trip was to close down American naval facilities in Europe, renegotiate contracts, and dispose of surplus property. Eleanor went too: the dubious rationale was that Franklin was still convalescing and needed her assistance.[76] He took a support staff with him: his Harvard classmate Livingston Davis (1882–1932) was special assistant; Thomas J. Spellacy (1880–1957), a Connecticut lawyer-politician who had represented trade unions and was an assistant attorney general, handled legal matters; and Commander John M. Hancock (1883–1956), a Republican industrial banker who had run navy purchasing, did much of the contract work. In addition, once in Europe, various U.S. Navy and Marine Corps officers were assigned as Franklin's aides.

The party sailed from New York on New Year's Day 1919 aboard the *George Washington,* the navy-run liner that had taken the president and his party to Europe. Six days at sea, they learned of Theodore's death at his home, Sagamore Hill; he was only sixty-one. In a letter to Daniels, Franklin noted, "My cousin's death was in every way a great shock, for we heard just before leaving that he was better—and he was after all not that old. But I cannot help but think that he himself would have had it this way and that he has been spared a lingering illness of perhaps years."[77]

Franklin handled the navy's business well, and his constant concern for both efficiency and cost saving is at variance with the stereotype of him as a careless spender. His most important negotiation was with the French government over compensation for a not yet completed, very powerful radio transmitter being erected on French soil. He eventually got full payment, which military negotiators had failed to achieve. After he and appropriate European officials had reached a general agreement on this and other matters, Hancock would work out the details with his opposite numbers.[78]

Letters to Sara from both Franklin and Eleanor show that each of them not only attended almost daily official functions but saw as many sights as they could. They again met friends and relations everywhere in both France and England.[79] Franklin would have liked an official role at the peace conference then going on at Versailles, but he was only an interested bystander. On the trip home on the *George Washington,* Woodrow Wilson was a fellow passenger. To Franklin's delight, he was summoned to the presidential cabin on one occasion to listen to Wilson talk about the League of Nations. That meeting seemed to cement Franklin to Wilsonian principles—if not methods—for life. Earlier, in addressing the Chinese and Mexican delegations to the peace conference at a luncheon he had hosted for them on the eastward crossing aboard the *George Washington,* Franklin had spoken as strongly about peace as he had earlier supported preparedness.[80] On another occasion, both Roosevelts attended a small shipboard luncheon at which the president used a phrase that both of them always remembered. Speaking of the League of Nations, Wilson said, "The United States must go in or it will break the heart of the world, for she is the only nation that all feel is disinterested and all trust."[81]

The *George Washington* docked in Boston on February 24. Franklin held a press conference explaining the navy's role in Europe and his mission there, but the big news was Wilson's triumphal parade—Franklin and Eleanor were in the fifth car of his motorcade—and the first of his speeches calling for ratification of the Treaty of Versailles and joining the League of Nations. They then traveled on the same train to Washington with the president and were impressed by the enthusiastic crowds that greeted him at every station.[82]

While there was much to do in further winding down the navy's wartime activities—while placing orders for steel to construct four authorized battleships before the newly elected Republican-controlled Congress majorities could meet and perhaps cancel the authorization—Franklin faced "unemployment" at the end of Wilson's term.

He had not, of course, been politically dormant while assistant secretary, but after the fiasco of his 1914 run for the senatorial nomination he was more cautious. In 1916 he had campaigned, as expected, for the Wilson ticket. By 1917 he had made enough of an accommodation with Tammany that he was chosen as the main speaker at its 128th annual Fourth of July festivities. It was a kind of audition, and Franklin clearly passed, getting a laugh with his opening comment that if Tammany could stand to have him, he could stand to come.[83]

For 1918 there was discussion of Franklin running for governor with Tammany backing. He discouraged it by asserting that his duty was at his Washington post. In mid-1918, shortly before he left for his first trip to France, President Wilson passed the word, through Daniels, that Franklin "ought not to decline to run" for governor of New York if it were tendered to him.[84] Franklin later wrote the president to ask that he not support any move to get him the nomination.[85] The matter was complicated by the fact that Franklin had earlier released a letter supporting the anti-Tammany candidacy of one William C. Osborn, who, in the event, unsuccessfully challenged Al Smith for the Democratic nomination for governor. As Franklin was in Europe during the primary campaign, he did not have to choose between the candidates. After Smith won the primary, he endorsed him strongly, further strengthening his relationship with Tammany.[86] Smith went on to win his first term as governor in what was otherwise a Republican year, further demonstrating to Tammany leaders the usefulness of having Franklin, an upstate Protestant, in their man's corner. Roosevelt and Smith were never close, but each was valuable to the other in the period between 1918 and 1930, when one or both of them were candidates in every election and in need of support outside of their geographic and ethnic areas of greatest strength. During that period, of course, Smith was by far the more powerful figure.[87]

Nationally, the 1918 election gave the Republicans control of both houses of Congress. Daniels and Franklin now expected to be grilled about their leadership of the wartime navy by more hostile congressional committees, but they were blindsided by attacks from Admiral Sims, which were at bottom an attempt to substitute professional military leadership for traditional civilian control. On February 1, 1920, in a speech in Brooklyn, Franklin foolishly, and probably inadvertently, supported some of Sims's charges, which had to do with the relative unpreparedness of the navy at the outbreak of the war. The real subject of the speech, at least according to the *New York Times* account, was Franklin's war effort.

BROKE LAW FOR NAVY
F. D. ROOSEVELT SAYS
Committed Enough Illegal Acts
to Put Him in Jail for 999
Years, He Adds

The headlines merely repeated boasts he had made at least as early as March 1919. And earlier the same day, in a debate with his Hyde Park neighbor Republican stalwart Ogden L. Mills (1884–1937) at New York's Colony Club, he had defended the administration's conduct of the war, praising Wilson's "progressive idealism," which represented "the best aspirations of the American people." But in the Brooklyn speech, he also complained, as he had done in private letters during the war, of the navy's prewar unpreparedness, telling the story of his urging Wilson to mass the fleet in the days before the declaration of war and Wilson's refusal on the grounds that he did not wish to commit an overt act.[88]

Not for the first or last time, Franklin's glib braggadocio and egotism—qualities he shared with Theodore—got him into trouble. He quickly realized, or was made to realize, that his speech was inappropriate. In Washington the next day, he issued a lame statement in which he argued that his remarks about unpreparedness merely reflected the fact that the nation was "at peace." He denied that he had criticized the president. He also dismissed those of his acts that he had often claimed threatened him with nearly a millennium of jail time as a mere "technical illegality."[89] It was probably the Brooklyn speech in particular that caused Daniels to remark about Franklin's seeming to join his enemies. But the optimistic Methodist quickly forgave him; Wilson, the dour Presbyterian, was slower to do so.[90]

With that settled, Franklin could continue winding down his official duties and concentrate on politics. Any sophisticated observer understood that the Republican victory in the 1918 off-year election probably presaged a Republican victory in 1920. Wilson's failure to persuade the Senate to accept the League of Nations, plus his physical collapse and invalid status for the final seventeen months of his presidency, only strengthened that probability. Franklin's strategy was, despite the swing to the right in public opinion, to position himself as the standard-bearer of the progressive wing of the party. His chief rival for that role was Wilson's second attorney general, A. Mitchell Palmer (1872–1936). While Palmer is remembered today, if at all, only as the chief instigator of the first "Red Scare," he was, first and foremost, an urban progressive and an early front-runner for the 1920 Democratic nomination.[91] He was Franklin's senior by ten years, in addition to outranking him in the Wilson administration.

Yet when they both spoke at a national Democratic dinner in Chicago at the end of May 1919, Franklin's then friend, the egomaniacal publisher of the *Chicago Tribune*, Robert R. McCormick (1880–1955) was so impressed that his paper's headline was "Palmer Loses Place in Sun to Roosevelt." Freidel calls it "the first of Roosevelt's great political addresses."[92] In it Roosevelt, like Palmer, placed himself in the progressive tradition in the party but somewhere to the right of Bryan, whom he argued may have gone too far but was on the right track. Unlike Bryan, Franklin strongly supported the League of Nations and predicted, accurately as it turned out, that the Republicans, if returned to power, would raise tariff barriers and reduce the income tax for the benefit of millionaires. He criticized the press as too much controlled by rich men, which gave "a Republican color to the news." And, in a notion he would return to late in his presidency, he predicted that "within a year," there would be a "political smashup" and all the Tories would wind up in the Republican Party, while all

"Progressives" would unite "under the Democratic emblem."[93] The speech made Franklin someone to consider for the vice presidency and even sparked some far-fetched talk about the presidency among a few of his supporters.

In the discussion of Roosevelt's nomination for vice president that follows, it is important to remember that in 1920, no incumbent vice president since Thomas Jefferson had been elected president, and none would be elected until the first George Bush achieved it in 1988.[94] By the time of the Democratic convention in San Francisco at the end of June, the Republicans had already nominated a weak candidate, Warren G. Harding, a one-term senator from Ohio, after three stronger candidates had killed one another off. As had been the case eight years before at Baltimore, Franklin went to San Francisco prepared for any eventuality, but this time he was a member of the New York delegation, a known quantity with an assigned role. On the convention's eve, press stories spoke of him as a possible candidate for New York's open U.S. Senate seat.

On the first day of the convention, when, alone of all the delegations, the Tammany-dominated New York delegation remained seated during a demonstration for Woodrow Wilson, Franklin seized the standard from a Tammany stalwart and, with others, joined in. Whether or not the *New York Times* headlines ("New Yorkers in Fist Fight," "F. D. Roosevelt and Small Group Join Procession," "After Battle for State Standard") overdramatized the event is a matter of conjecture, but it was one of the things that made Roosevelt, according to the historian of the 1920 campaign, "a star of the convention."[95] The next day, he reiterated his longtime support for ending the unit rule in the New York delegation, which would weaken Tammany's power.[96] Both actions confirmed his position as a reformer in the party.

But other events showed that his arrangement with Murphy and Tammany, while not a full-blown alliance, was still in effect. On July 1, he was chosen to give one of the seconding speeches for Al Smith's nomination for president. This was both a favorite-son tribute and a predicate for future action: all knew that Smith would be a candidate for reelection as governor in 1920. Smith was nominated by the golden-voiced Bourke Cockran (1854–1923), the noted political orator, in his final appearance at a national convention. Since his half-hour tribute to Smith was eloquent and thoughtful, Franklin, the first seconder, had a tough act to follow. His speech was brief—three paragraphs—direct, and cogent. He praised Smith; took a potshot at the GOP, assuring his audience that "the nominee of this convention will not be chosen at 2 a.m. in a hotel room"; and reminded the delegates of his own wartime role: "In the Navy we shoot fast and straight."[97] It was an effective and promising introduction on a national stage and a public sign that he and Tammany could work together on some issues while disagreeing on others. By July 1, the word was out, as the *Times* headline put it: "Franklin D. Roosevelt Talked of for Senator Even among Tammany Delegates."[98]

The convention's major business was, as usual, a tedious process. The first ballot was completed just before midnight on Friday, July 2, and no result was achieved until the wee hours of Tuesday morning, July 6. The two chief candidates, the dry McAdoo and the wet Palmer, in effect knocked each other out, and Ohio governor James M. Cox (1870–1957), who had a respectable 159 votes on the first ballot, as opposed to McAdoo's 289 and Palmer's 264, eventually took the lead on the thirteenth ballot, but could not get the necessary two-thirds until the forty-fourth ballot, when, in the midst of postballot switches to Cox, McAdoo's floor leader surrendered and moved, successfully, that the nomination of Cox be made unanimous.[99]

When the delegates returned, bleary-eyed, at noon, they made short work of the vice presidential nomination. On the surface, it seemed that Tammany had little to do with the result, although there had been talk in the New York delegation three days previously about Roosevelt as a vice presidential candidate.[100] Apart from Franklin, seven other candidates were nominated; none was well known nationally, though one, Edward L. Doheny (1856–1935), would soon become notorious. Franklin's nomination was made by one of Cox's managers, and the first two seconding speeches were by other midwestern delegates. After an interval, Al Smith made an additional nominating speech for Roosevelt, "instructed by the delegation," making it seem that Tammany was bowing to the will of the convention or to the wishes of the presidential nominee.

Murphy contributed to this version. Asked by Cox's man after the Ohioan had been nominated whether Roosevelt would be acceptable to him, the Tammany boss replied, "I don't like Roosevelt . . . but . . . this is the first time a Democratic nominee for the presidency has shown me the courtesy. . . . I would vote for the devil himself if Cox wanted me to. Tell him we will nominate Roosevelt on the first ballot as soon as we assemble."[101]

His account, except for its last sentence, does not hold water. Murphy had thrown Tammany's support to Cox on the seventh ballot, putting him ahead of Palmer but not McAdoo, so the obligation was the other way around. Because Tammany had not given significant support to a successful presidential nominee since 1880, there was no reason for any of the recent presidential candidates to have cleared a vice presidential nomination with Murphy.

Cox wrote in his memoirs that, after a dawn phone call to him in Ohio informed him of his nomination, only then was he asked about his choice of a running mate. "I told him I had given the matter some thought and that my choice would be Franklin D. Roosevelt of New York. . . . [S]o far as I knew, I had never seen him, but I explained . . . that he met the geographical requirement, that he was recognized as an Independent and that Roosevelt was a well known name."[102]

The press reaction was predictable—the *New York Times* headlined a sidebar story "Roosevelt Career Like That of Cousin." Unlike every other major-party vice presidential nominee since Theodore in 1900, Franklin was regarded as a nominee with a future rather than a past.[103] The nomination had come as a surprise to Eleanor, who was with the children at Campobello; she learned of it from a telegram sent by Daniels the day after the nomination.[104]

It is an open question whether Roosevelt had any real expectations of a victory; all the omens proclaimed the near certainty of a Republican victory that was more a repudiation of Wilson and progressivism than enthusiasm for Harding. But, intent on making a good impression now that he had a place on the national scene, he acted as if he thought that victory was within the Democrats' grasp. Right at the outset, in his first friendly meeting with Cox at the governor's home outside Dayton, he asked the Ohioan to announce that the vice president would sit in on cabinet meetings. Cox turned him down; Roosevelt made that innovation himself thirteen years later. The pair then journeyed to the nation's capital for a courtesy call and a symbolic laying on of hands by the enfeebled Woodrow Wilson. Franklin wrote Eleanor that it was "a very wonderful experience."[105] Years later Roosevelt described the scene: "The President was in a wheel chair, his left shoulder covered with a shawl which concealed his left arm, which was paralyzed. . . . Wilson looked up and in a very low, weak voice said, 'Thank you for coming. I am very glad you came.' [After Cox declared that they were "a million percent" for him, his administration and the League of Nations] The President looked up again, and again in a voice scarcely audible he said, 'I am very grateful' and then repeated, 'I am very grateful.'"[106]

Franklin then went back to Dutchess County to welcome-home ceremonies in both Poughkeepsie and Hyde Park; Eleanor came down from Campobello to attend. From the veranda of Springwood, the local state senator introduced him to the crowd with "Here's our boy."[107] Then Franklin went on to Columbus to attend a Democratic National Committee (DNC) meeting held there to accommodate Cox and then back to Washington to answer some of what he estimated were twenty-five hundred messages about his nomination. After a brief vacation visit to Campobello aboard a destroyer to join the family, he, Eleanor, and daughter Anna, aged fourteen, went to Washington in August heat so he could resign formally from the navy and Eleanor could make arrangements for giving up their house. Howe, who had not gone to San Francisco, stayed on in the Navy Department until the end of September. Daniels turned down Franklin's request that Louis replace him, though he did serve briefly as acting assistant secretary.[108] Franklin, Eleanor, and Anna then went on to Dayton for Cox's formal notification and acceptance ceremony, and then the three returned to Hyde Park, where, two days later, Franklin's formal notification took place. His neighbor and new friend Henry Morgenthau Jr. (1891–1967) chaired the notification ceremonies, beginning a public relationship with the Roosevelts that would be lifelong.

The candidate spoke to a crowd estimated at three thousand studded with many Democratic notables, including Al Smith, three Wilson cabinet members

(Daniels, McAdoo, and William C. Redfield, secretary of commerce), and Democratic National Committee chairman Homer S. Cummings (1870–1956). Roosevelt's short speech, some three thousand words, praised his running mate and addressed the two major themes of the campaign, support for the League of Nations and continuation of the progressive modernization begun by the Wilson administration. It was an effective address, if not a great one, and was marked by what would become a Roosevelt trait—ad libs to a prepared advance text. After reading the sentence "Some people—some little people—have been saying of late: 'We are tired of progress, we want to go back to where we were before, to go about our own business: to conditions; to restore "normal" conditions,'" he broke up the politically sophisticated audience by adding, "I mean conditions of normalcy," a clear shot at Harding, whose acceptance speech had promised "not nostrums but normalcy."[109]

The formalities accomplished, Franklin began the first of three extensive campaign tours that took him to the West twice, where progressive sentiment ran strong, and once to New England. He traveled in a private railroad car, as he had done with his father, with a small entourage that included two former journalists, both southerners, who would serve him in the White House. Marvin H. McIntyre (1878–1943), a former publicity man in the Navy Department, handled his publicity and wrote speeches, while Stephen T. Early (1889–1951), who had covered the Navy Department for the Associated Press (AP), was the advance man who scouted political conditions in the places where the candidate would speak. Along with five others, they became the "Cufflinks Club" of veterans of the campaign, so named for the gold cufflinks Roosevelt gave them.[110] By the time of the second trip to the West, both Louis Howe and Eleanor joined the party. At this point in her life, Eleanor's role as a candidate's wife was essentially passive: she reported that her days were spent "going on and off platforms, listening with apparently rapt attention to much the same speech, looking pleased to see people no matter how tired I was or greeting complete strangers with effusion."[111] But it was also while on this largely tedious trip that Louis Howe began tutoring her about politics, a tutoring that later, as James Kearney noted, "ushered [her] into politics as a full-time participant."[112]

Franklin threw himself into the campaign with a vigor that Theodore would have admired. He made close to a thousand speeches of various lengths, which largely rang changes on the two themes of his acceptance address, with shadings for local circumstances. But on a few occasions, as happens even in the most cautious campaigns, he made statements that were unfortunate or worse. In Montana, while explaining, quite accurately, how politics would work inside an international organization, in attempting to gain support for the League of Nations, he dismissed the notion that votes for members of the British Commonwealth gave Great Britain an advantage. In practice, he argued, the United States could control the votes of several small nations in the Western Hemisphere. He went on to say, in one of his less fortunate personal asides, "Until last week I had two of them myself and now Secretary Daniels has them. You know I have had something to do with the running of a couple of little republics. The facts are that I wrote Haiti's Constitution myself and, if I do say it, I think it is a pretty good constitution."[113] It was not true. While drafts of the Haitian constitution may have come across his desk in the Navy Department, he did not write it. Of course, he denied that he said that he had done so, but the evidence is clear that he not only said it, but had made a similar statement at least once previously.[114] On other occasions, he pandered to local prejudices, favoring development of local resources over conservation before certain western audiences, even though he clearly believed the opposite, and, most blatantly, referring to American Legionnaires killed while conducting a vigilante raid on a radical meeting in Centralia, Washington, as "martyred . . . in the sacred cause of Americanism."[115]

Nothing Roosevelt said or did affected the result. Harding won in a landslide. Eleanor believed, seventeen years later, that "campaign trips by anyone except the presidential candidates themselves are of little value."[116] This was a particularly shortsighted view. Had someone else been chosen as the vice presidential nominee in 1920, or had Franklin, once chosen, not campaigned seriously (Calvin Coolidge, his Republican counterpart did not), it is highly unlikely, given the disabling polio attack that struck less than a year after the campaign, that he would have ever become governor of New York, much less president. His campaign swings left an image of a vigorous and buoyant extrovert in the minds of many thousands of political activists from Maine to California. And it also provided the names and addresses of persons he met that were entered on file cards and formed the basis of the extensive political correspondence that Roosevelt and his staff conducted throughout the years in which he held no public office. In fact, the campaign for the vice presidency was surely a step up for Roosevelt's political career. In the months after the November debacle, he regarded it as such, even though he could style himself, in one letter, as "Franklin D. Roosevelt, Ex. V.P., Canned. (Erroneously reported dead.)."[117]

3 Roosevelt and the Old Order
1921–28

ROOSEVELT'S RESIGNATION FROM THE GOVERNMENT meant that he was an outsider during the sad last four months of the Wilson administration and free to begin a career in the private sector. It was a given that he would eventually seek elective office again and that the White House remained his ultimate goal. Roosevelt took on two jobs. In March 1920, while still in the government, he arranged a new law practice, Emmet, Marvin, and Roosevelt, a firm specializing in estates and personal trusts. At the same time, he arranged with Van-Lear Black (1875–1930), a venturesome Baltimore capitalist and Democrat, to become a vice president of the Fidelity and Deposit Company of Maryland and take charge of its New York office at an annual salary of twenty-five thousand dollars. Fidelity issued surety bonds, and, as was the case with the law firm, the Roosevelt name and contacts were expected to bring in business. The arrangement was that he would spend mornings in his law office and afternoons at the Fidelity. Both offices were in the financial district, the Fidelity at 120 Broadway and the law firm a block and a half away, at 52 Wall. Thus, at this stage of his career, Franklin D. Roosevelt was, of all things, a Wall Street lawyer. And like other Wall Street lawyers, he participated in a number of activities that can be categorized as business and public service. These will be only summarized here, but the press depicted him as a well-known public figure offering effective pro bono public service.

The Fidelity gave him a flashy welcome—a 1921 banquet honoring him addressed by a Federal Reserve Board (FRB) governor. Roosevelt hired Marguerite (Missy) LeHand (1898–1944), who had worked in his campaign, as his secretary and later that year brought Louis Howe into the bonding company as his assistant. Howe was able to use contacts made with labor unions during his years in Washington, while Roosevelt could ply his stature as a national figure with a famous name to steer public business to the bonding firm. By 1928 the business of the New York office had doubled.[1]

Roosevelt's legal practice was less effective. He would not handle cases against the federal government but was not averse to using his and Howe's navy contacts with businessmen and labor leaders to drum up bonding contracts for Fidelity. He seems to have brought little business into his new law firm and can hardly be described as actually practicing law. He and his partners came to an amicable parting of the ways in late 1924. That December the new and enduring law partnership with Basil O'Connor (1892–1972) was created. The new firm, Roosevelt and O'Connor, met the requirements that Roosevelt had explained to Van-Lear Black three months earlier. "The other partners are dear delightful people, but their type of law business . . . is mostly estates, wills, etc. all of which bore me to death. . . . Also I get not one red cent out of my connection with them . . . [adding that he wanted a partnership] with my name at the head instead of at the tail."[2]

O'Connor, the younger man, was to do the bulk of the work and guaranteed his partner ten thousand dollars annually from the new firm. One factor in the change was that Roosevelt, after his polio attack in 1921, could no longer get into his law office. As one of his partners later explained, "After the infantile [paralysis], when he was able to come downtown, he could not come to our office which [had] a high front stoop."[3] Access to the Fidelity offices was not a problem, so, for a time, Roosevelt had conducted his law work from there. That O'Connor's practice was in the same building as Fidelity was another factor in the new partnership.

But Roosevelt did not practice much law in his new firm, either; making investments in new business ventures was much more interesting. Until he became governor, Roosevelt regularly risked modest sums of money—modest for him, anyway—in a variety of speculative endeavors. No one has made a systematic audit of his ventures, but it is clear that he was using disposable income and that, even in the prosperity decade of the 1920s, Roosevelt lost more times than he won. At least two gambles were quite successful: an investment in a firm speculating in depreciating German marks netted more than a 200 percent return, and one five-hundred-dollar investment made for him by Henry Morgenthau Jr. turned a quick profit of three thousand dollars for each of them. Something of Roosevelt's attitude toward these ventures may be gathered from his proposal that each of them donate half their profits to the patients' aid fund at Warm Springs, as "this will cost us nothing and enable us to deduct" fifteen hundred dollars from their income tax.[4] Roosevelt was not a successful investor, and Louis Howe, who joined him in some schemes, could tease him about buying "white elephants."

Somewhere between business and public service were Roosevelt's brief connection with the National Civic Federation and his more lasting association with the American Construction Council. The former had begun as an early Progressive Era attempt to mediate strikes. It had included Samuel Gompers and the American Federation of Labor, but during World War I it had begun to focus on antiradicalism. Roosevelt accepted an appointment to its executive committee but had little to do with it.[5]

The American Construction Council, apparently dreamed up by Roosevelt and Howe, was what John Kenneth Galbraith might have described as a "no business organization." Before it actually began, Howe planted a five-column story in the *New York Times* that laid out the council's hopes. Under the headline "INDUSTRY'S NEW DOCTORS" were photos of the three "doctors": Kennesaw Mountain Landis, Will H. Hays, and Franklin D. Roosevelt. The first two already had well-established practices: Landis drew a salary of fifty thousand dollars as commissioner of Major League Baseball, and Hays was paid one hundred thousand dollars to keep the movies clean. Created at a Washington meeting some days later presided over by Secretary of Commerce Herbert Hoover, the council elected Roosevelt its president. It was supposed to create greater efficiency in the entire building industry, but no salary was provided for Roosevelt, who told his board a year later that it had "not done one darned thing." That was essentially the case when he left it, five years later.[6]

It is all too easy, as critics on both the Right and the Left have done, to paint the Roosevelt of these years and largely unsuccessful schemes as someone caught up in the hedonistic ethos of the 1920s.[7] That this is part of the truth is impossible to deny. But it seems to me that there are good reasons to modify that appraisal, reasons that will be set forth at the end of this chapter.

Roosevelt was also a very active public man, lending his name to many nonprofit organizations and campaigns and playing a role in some. The following were among his publicized activities, large and small, in the first eight months of his new life. In addition to fulfilling his notions of civic duty, they were a good way of keeping his name before the public. They included heading the Manhattan Navy Club, which provided a USO-type facility for sailors on leave; a term on Harvard's Board of Overseers; service on the Greater New York Council of the Boy Scouts of America represented a lifelong interest, as did his vice presidency of a newly formed Netherland-America Foundation; he had long since taken over his father's role as church warden and in early 1921 was elected a trustee of Manhattan's Episcopal cathedral and later supervised its fund drive; a staunch conservationist, he was also a vice president of the state's forestry association and had one to four thousand trees planted every year at Hyde Park.[8]

Some minor activities involved both Roosevelts, and Eleanor was frequently mentioned as a sponsor in her own right, invariably described as Mrs. Franklin D. Roosevelt.[9] Not noted in the press was the more significant fact that Eleanor Roosevelt had joined, almost as soon as the couple resumed their New York residence, two feminist organizations, the League of Women Voters and the Woman's City Club, and began her personal involvement in New York politics.[10]

One activity initiated by Roosevelt early in 1921 was of enduring significance. He was the key figure in the creation of the Woodrow Wilson Foundation, established to memorialize Wilson and his ideals, particularly in regard to international affairs. Wilson was at first a little chary of the organization and of its most active organizer. Roosevelt's injudicious postwar comments about prewar unpreparedness had left a bad taste in Wilson's mouth, and, judging from the correspondence published in the sixty-nine-volume Woodrow Wilson Papers, the relations between the two had never been close. Even after the invalided former president had given his consent to the organization, the correspondence—mostly brief notes—remained cool and correct. All that would change on September 16, 1921, when Wilson opened his morning paper and read of Roosevelt's illness. He immediately sent a get-well note to "My dear Roosevelt" and signed it, "Your sincere friend."[11] The remaining nine short notes or telegrams are often touched with similar warmth.[12] For Roosevelt, the foundation was not only a way of paying homage to his former chief but a means of keeping internationalist goals alive in a time of isolation. Roosevelt would, in seeking the presidency, trim his internationalist sails in public, but he remained, even then, a closet Wilsonian.

Other evidence of his 1920s internationalism was Roosevelt's chairing of the committee that, largely thanks to funds provided by lawyer-industrialist Owen D. Young (1874–1962), led to the establishment of the Walter Hines Page School of International Relations at Johns Hopkins University.[13]

Roosevelt soon found himself under attack by Republicans who sought to discredit the Democrats' conduct of the war. The most dangerous for Roosevelt's reputation was an investigation of homosexuality at the naval training facility at Newport, Rhode Island, a personnel matter and thus in his bailiwick.

What became the Newport scandal resulted from a typically progressive morality crusade.[14] After war was declared, both the army and the navy conducted attempts to eliminate organized prostitution in areas adjacent to military establishments. Roosevelt had announced routinely in June 1917 that an investigation of unspecified unwholesome conditions in Newport was under way. In June 1919, after being told that conditions in Newport had not materially improved, Roosevelt authorized the establishment of a small undercover investigative unit that bypassed the normal chain of command and was responsible directly to him: "Section A—Office of the Assistant Secretary." When, in September 1919, he learned that, in order to gain evidence that would stand up in court, enlisted men on the squad were told to participate in homosexual acts, he ordered the unit to cease operations. There is no credible evidence that Roosevelt had known earlier what methods were being used. Had he simply admitted what seems to be the case, that he had not exercised proper supervision, the resulting scandal probably would not have caused him much concern.

Instead, he reacted as public officials often do in such instances, by denying any responsibility for those methods and calling for investigations by both the navy and the Senate Naval Affairs Committee. Because some of those entrapped by Roosevelt's investigators were upper-class citizens of Newport, a local furor arose that centered on the arrest, indictment, and two trials of a local Episcopal priest, the Reverend Samuel Neal Kent, for sodomy with a member of what the press called the navy's vice squad. It must be noted that throughout his career,

Franklin Roosevelt was often less than scrupulous about violations of the rights of individuals when he was convinced that they were guilty of something.

Protests to Daniels and Roosevelt by a group of Newport citizens and to President Wilson by the Episcopal bishop of Rhode Island eventually triggered a second naval court of inquiry: Roosevelt, as an "interested party," did not sit on it. The matter attracted attention outside of New England only when a nationally known Providence newspaper editor, John R. Rathom,[15] charged that with Secretary Daniels's knowledge, "many seamen in the navy have been used in vile and nameless practices in order to entrap innocent men." Then, when he learned that Roosevelt was the person in authority, he made the same charge against him. By the end of January 1920, there were two investigations in progress, an official Navy Court of Inquiry in Newport and a closed-door investigation by a subcommittee of the Senate Naval Affairs Committee—two Republicans and a Democrat—in Washington.

Rathom, called as a witness before the Court of Inquiry at Roosevelt's insistence in early 1920, admitted that he had no evidence, as he had previously claimed, that either Daniels or Roosevelt had prior knowledge of the methods used by the squad.[16] Then, ten days before the November 1920 election in what we now call an "October surprise," the Republican National Committee released a letter from Rathom to Roosevelt whose gravamen was that Roosevelt and in some cases Daniels had caused the return to active duty of eighty-three men who had been convicted of what the press would only call "unnatural acts." Rathom claimed to have eighty-three sets of personnel records that, if they existed, could have been furnished only by enemies of the Daniels-Roosevelt regime within the Navy Department.

Roosevelt asked Francis G. Caffey, the federal attorney for New York City, to institute a suit for criminal libel. Two days later, Roosevelt got a little help from his friends in the Department of Justice. Caffey announced that because Rathom's letter had been hand delivered and never sent through the mails, there was no federal jurisdiction, although in his opinion it was "clearly libelous." At the same time, he released the text of a previously unrevealed "confession" by Rathom made to the Department of Justice in February 1918, admitting that his claims about investigations made by him and his papers being responsible for arrests of German spies were untrue. He had made the signed and sworn statement in order to avoid having to testify before a grand jury. Caffey said that he was releasing the 1918 statement by authority of Attorney General A. Mitchell Palmer in order to show that Rathom's record did not entitle him to "credence." Roosevelt then filed a libel suit against the editor for five hundred thousand dollars in state court, but once the election was over nothing further was heard of it.[17]

The Newport scandal had a longer life. Roosevelt had testified briefly before the congressional subcommittee in February 1920 and said that he had been told that he would be called back after the Newport Court of Inquiry report was available. The report reached Daniels only in February 1921: it held that Roosevelt was "unfortunate and ill-advised," which Roosevelt thought was unfair. This was a relatively mild rebuke. It was sent to the Senate subcommittee in March, which then called a number of witnesses but never called Roosevelt. On July 13, 1921, while vacationing at Campobello, a telegram from Daniels summoned Roosevelt: "COMMITTEE READY TO REPORT [JULY 18]. LIBELOUS REPORT OF MAJORITY. CAN YOU GO TO WASHINGTON AT ONCE. ANSWER."[18] He exchanged telegrams with the subcommittee chair, Senator Lewis H. Ball (R-DL), crying foul and demanding to be heard. Ball denied any previous agreements, said that Roosevelt's testimony was unnecessary, but agreed to allow him to testify if he was in Washington on the eighteenth. Roosevelt came and was denied the promised opportunity. After he protested that he had not seen the testimony against him and wished to have the opportunity to rebut it, Ball allowed him to examine the previously unavailable six thousand pages of testimony and agreed to publish his denial, *if* Roosevelt got the statement to him by eight o'clock that evening when the delayed subcommittee meeting would open. The Democrat on the subcommittee, Utah's William H. King, thought that the report could be amended to include Roosevelt's rebuttal before its release.

Roosevelt, borrowing an office in the Navy Department, and with the help of Steve Early, then covering Washington politics for the Associated Press, and his secretary, Missy LeHand, managed to put together not only his own denial but a draft for the use of his ally Senator King in his minority report. Well before the eight o'clock deadline, they were told that Senator Ball had released a copy of the majority report to the press with an embargo until the following afternoon. Roosevelt and his helpers finished their rebuttal in time for the subcommittee meeting and got it to reporters. Outside of Rhode Island, it was not a big story. The *New York Times* put it on page 4 in three columns, which contained the charges of the majority, Roosevelt's rebuttal, and Ball's rebuttal of Roosevelt as well as, adjacent to it, a summary of King's minority report supporting Roosevelt. What readers made of it is not clear: the words *sodomy, homosexual,* and even *sex* were not then fit to print; as the *Times* subhead proclaimed, "DETAILS ARE UNPRINTABLE."[19] The majority could not believe that: "Franklin D. Roosevelt . . . a man of unusual intelligence and attainments, and after three days of conversation on the subject must have known the methods used and to be used to secure evidence."

After complaining about the subcommittee's broken promises, Roosevelt's rebuttal countered, reasonably, that he and the admiral who participated in the meetings authorizing the special investigating unit were busy men, but failed to concede that either of them should have inquired about methods. King's minority report agreed that Roosevelt "erred" in approving the creation of the squad but found, "The inferences and statements and innuendoes that Mr. Roosevelt or Mr. Daniels knew of these methods are wholly without justification."[20]

Roosevelt was both furious and distraught. He directed most of his anger not at Chairman Ball but at his colleague Henry W. Keyes, a New Hampshire Republican serving the first of three undistinguished terms. Keyes was Harvard '87, and Roosevelt wrote him a brief letter headed *Personal* and with the salutation "Sir:" concluding, "I have had the privilege of knowing many thousands of Harvard graduates. Of the whole number I did not personally know one whom I believed to be personally and willfully dishonorable. I regret that because of your recent despicable action I can no longer say that. My only hope is that you will live long enough to appreciate that you have violated decency and truth, and that you will pray to your maker for forgiveness." He never mailed it, but kept it in its envelope, annotated "Not sent—what was the use? FDR" and filed it for historians.[21] He was quite upset, but his habitual optimism soon returned. The same day, he wrote "Dearest Babs" that "since no papers have taken it up it may seem best to drop the whole thing."[22] We now know that he suffered no serious political damage. But, almost certainly, the scandal did put him very much in harm's way.

In late July, Roosevelt left New York for Campobello in style aboard Van-Lear Black's yacht, arriving on August 8. Sometime during his absence from Campobello, he had contracted the polio virus, whose effects he began to feel only after his return there. It is impossible to know exactly where or when this occurred: a likely guess is sometime during his July 27 visit to the Boy Scout camp at Bear Mountain, New York, a visit documented by a photograph of Roosevelt routinely published in the press. It is the last picture of him walking.[23]

Roosevelt himself never made a connection between that trip and his malady. The narrative he and his handlers developed emphasized his previous exhaustion before returning to Campobello and his physical exertions and immersions in the frigid waters of the Bay of Fundy after he arrived. Three years later, after he discovered how much he could move when immersed in warm water, he remarked that "the water put me where I am and the water has to bring me back." For years he spoke and acted as if he believed that his recovery was just around the corner. Exactly when he stopped believing that he would eventually walk again is, like so much about his inner life, unknowable. My own guess would be that by 1928, almost seven years after the onset of his paralysis, he was reconciled to what must have been apparent to those closest to him for some time: he would never walk again. Roosevelt could achieve, with crutches or the assistance of others, some forms of self-locomotion, but Roosevelt's legs were so weak that they could not even support him in a standing position unless his braces were locked at the knee.

Roosevelt's illness, even before its true nature was diagnosed, represented two sets of problems for his family and close associates, one medical and one political. The first medical problems were to find out what was wrong with him and to meet his increasing physical needs. No one on Campobello kept a medical diary, and much of what has been written comes from accounts Roosevelt himself supplied the authors of two campaign biographies published in 1931 and 1932.[24] We do have three August 1921 letters from Eleanor Roosevelt to her brother-in-law, Rosy (James Roosevelt Roosevelt), that show her growing awareness. I have constructed a brief chronology from them and Eleanor's 1937 autobiography.[25]

August 10—Roosevelt has "chill" and goes to bed.

August 11—He has "much pain in back and legs." "Our faithful friend" Dr. E. H. Bennett is sent for from the mainland and finds nothing serious.

August 12—He has lost the ability to walk or move his legs.

August 13—Dr. Bennett suggests sending for a specialist. He and Howe go to the mainland and find one on vacation, Dr. W. W. Keen, who first misdiagnoses the malady as a blood clot on the spine and predicts recovery in "some months."

August 17—Dr. Keen, in a long letter, without ever seeing the patient again, says he now thinks that a lesion on the spinal cord is more likely and that recovery might be longer than his previous "some months."

August 23—In a letter to Rosy, Eleanor explains that Franklin's "Uncle Fred" (Frederick A. Delano), using information provided by her and Howe, had consulted some specialists, who advised Delano that Roosevelt's illness might be infantile paralysis and that the man to consult was a Boston specialist, Dr. Robert W. Lovett, a leading authority on the disease.[26] Informed of this, Keen dissents but agrees to call in Lovett.

August 25—Lovett arrives, makes a positive diagnosis of infantile paralysis (poliomyelitis), and, while hedging his opinion, says that the attack is mild and that Roosevelt might recover. It is decided to hospitalize him in New York City, but not to move him until mid-September, when the worst of the summer heat should have dissipated.

The most immediate nonmedical problem to be faced was how to tell Sara, who was in Europe. Uncle Fred and a sister met her ship on August 31 with a letter from Eleanor explaining only that "Franklin has been quite ill."[27] Sara went straight to Campobello and described the scene to her brother:

I got here yesterday at 1:30 and at once . . . came up to a brave, smiling, and beautiful son, who said: "Well I'm glad that you are back Mummy and I got up this party for you!" He had shaved himself and seems very bright and *keen*. Below his waist he cannot move at all. His legs (that I have always been proud of) have to be moved often as they ache when long in one position. He and Eleanor decided at once to be cheerful and the atmosphere of the house is all happiness, so I have fallen in and follow their glorious example. . . . Dr. Bennett just came and said "This boy is going to get all right." They went into his room and I hear them all laughing. Eleanor in the lead.[28]

What she did not say was that she was determined that her son, whose health had long concerned her, should return to his rightful place in Hyde Park and commence the kind of life his father had lived as the local squire, with some outside interests but no political career. His son might have been able to resist her all by himself, but he had two strong allies, his wife and his political manager, Louis Howe. Together, they prevailed over his strong-willed mother. Roosevelt, as part of his persona, always ascribed his stubborn streak to his Dutchness, but, to the degree that such a characteristic is heritable, it surely came from his mother, who had no trace of Dutch ancestry.

The political problems began on August 26—the day after Lovett's polio diagnosis had been made—when Louis Howe, who according to Eleanor "had been the greatest help" in tending to Roosevelt's physical needs, began what Hugh Gallagher has called the "splendid deception," the concerted campaign to minimize public awareness of the true nature of Roosevelt's physical condition.[29] Howe put out information that the *New York Times* ran at the bottom of page 7. Its story, with an Eastport, Maine, dateline headed FRANKLIN D. ROOSEVELT ILL, said, in two sentences, that he was "seriously ill" and "improving."[30]

Getting Roosevelt off the island and safely away to New York without having him photographed helpless was more difficult. Loading him onto a launch on Campobello without public scrutiny was relatively simple, but to get him from the launch, unnoticed, into the private railroad car that Uncle Fred, a former railroad president, had arranged took some doing. Howe had a rumor circulated that Roosevelt would be brought to the public dock at a certain time and took him to a different dock. He then got his stretcher onto a baggage cart and into his berth on the car before the reporters arrived to find a cheerful Roosevelt smiling and joking with them through the window.[31] Dr. Bennett and a nurse sent up from New York by Dr. Lovett accompanied the Roosevelts to New York City, where the patient was checked into Presbyterian Hospital. Only then was the press told that he had polio.

That story—the one that Wilson had read—made the front page of the *New York Times,* headlined "F. D. ROOSEVELT ILL OF POLIOMYELITIS."[32] In it his new doctor, George Draper (1880–1959),[33] one of Dr. Lovett's associates and, as it happened, a schoolmate of Roosevelt's at both Groton and Harvard, was quoted: "I cannot say how long Mr. Roosevelt will be kept in the hospital but you can say definitely that he will not be crippled. No one need have any fear of permanent injury from this attack." Draper soon came to realize that the senior physician's diagnosis had been far too optimistic; eight days later, he wrote Lovett that he was "much concerned" about his patient's lack of progress, and when he signed Roosevelt's discharge chart in late October, he wrote "not improving."[34]

A man of exceptional psychological insight, Draper understood his patient. After a week of treatment, he wrote Lovett about his strong feeling that the psychological factor was most important: "[Roosevelt] has such courage, such ambition, and yet at the same time such an extraordinarily sensitive emotional mechanism that it will take all the skill which we can muster to lead him successfully to a recognition of what he really faces without crushing him."[35]

Treatment in the months that followed, some of it quite painful, was designed not to "cure" Roosevelt but to enable him to manage his disability. Draper pushed Roosevelt to get out of his Manhattan town house at a time when the patient was self-conscious about being seen helpless in public. Perhaps a turning point came in June 1922, when Roosevelt went to Boston to be fitted by Dr. Lovett for the metal braces that he would have to use for the rest of his life. He stayed in a suite at Phillips House, part of Massachusetts General Hospital, for two weeks getting physiotherapy and relaxing, which may have provided one of those "refueling" periods that he sometimes felt the need of. The braces became a semipermanent part of his equipment, except when he was in bed or in a swimming pool. For him to stand, unaided, the braces, which were hinged at the knees so that he could sit, had to be locked straight by someone else. Without them he was confined to a wheelchair. He never referred to them in public until the month before he died. He began his last appearance before a joint session of Congress on March 1, 1945, "I hope that you will pardon me for this unusual posture of sitting down during the presentation of what I want to say, but I know that you will realize that it makes it a lot easier for me not to have to carry about ten pounds of steel around on the bottom of my legs; and also because of the fact that I have just completed a fourteen-thousand-mile trip."[36]

Although I will treat aspects of Roosevelt's disability here and there, the reader must remember, on every page, in every circumstance, that this is the story of a man who could not move freely and had to be transported almost everywhere he went. As president he did not often use a normal wheelchair in which he could propel himself with his powerfully developed arms. Instead, he had small wheels placed on an ordinary kitchen chair with no arms—but with an ashtray under the seat on a swivel!—which someone had to push to move him from one room to another. On arrival he could use his arms to transfer himself from his wheeled chair to a normal chair. During his presidency, every schoolchild knew that Roosevelt was physically handicapped, but his public appearances were stage-managed so that there was no visible reminder of his infirmity. His twice-weekly press conferences, for example, were usually held in the Oval Office, with the reporters entering to find the president behind his large littered desk, a cigarette glowing at the end of his ivory holder and very much in charge. Using the Oval Office made it seem natural that he was sitting and provided a very different visual impact than its alternatives—being wheeled onto a stage or laboring to a podium on crutches with braces locked.

I will treat briefly here not what polio did to Roosevelt, but what Roosevelt did for polio. It is not for nothing that medical historian Naomi Rogers subtitled her history of the early years of the disease *Polio before FDR*.[37] She argues that by the end of the 1930s, the image of polio had been transformed from a disease associated with immigrants and urban slums to one associated with cleanliness and occurring largely among those children—and occasionally adults—who had been protected from contact with the virus in early infancy. Physicians and researchers who had believed that polio was a disease of the central nervous system came to understand that it was a systemic viral infection centered in the intestines and to attribute the periodic epidemics to the infection of previously unexposed individuals and to mutations of the virus itself.

Roosevelt contracted the disease at the beginning of a subepidemic polio outbreak. Two days after he was admitted to the hospital, the *New York Times*—in a story that referred to Roosevelt's illness—quoted the city's heath commissioner's statement that so far that year, 269 poliomyelitis cases had been diagnosed, of whom 53 had died. Although these were much higher than normal numbers, they paled when compared to the 1916 epidemic in which some 27,000 cases and 6,000 deaths were reported in twenty-six states. New York City alone had tallied 8,900 cases and 2,400 deaths between June and December 1916. The health commissioner could only advise parents to have their children avoid "contact with those who had colds and . . . keep out of crowds."[38]

After Roosevelt became president, the annual Birthday Balls honoring him, which began on his first birthday as president (January 30, 1934) and were dedicated to benefiting polio, netted millions of dollars with the slogan "Dance so that others may walk." In 1937 he announced the establishment of the National Foundation for Infantile Paralysis, only the third major foundation dedicated to the eradication of a single disease. Through its March of Dimes campaigns, additional millions were collected and funneled to scientific research, leading to the development of the Salk and Sabin vaccines in the 1950s. Almost certainly, without the associated glamour of Roosevelt's presidency that helped raise the funds to finance the search for the vaccines that virtually rid America and other modernized societies of the once dread disease of infantile paralysis, the vaccines would not have been developed nearly as soon as they were.

Even before the polio attack, Eleanor Roosevelt had been creating an independent public life for herself, though she did so as Mrs. Franklin D. Roosevelt, the wife of an increasingly prominent public figure. By the mid-1920s, she and other feminist activists—what Al Smith called "lady politicians"—were exercising a growing influence. As her major biographer, Blanche Wiesen Cook, has observed, the Roosevelts operated largely in "separate spheres" during those years and were often physically separated.[39] Eleanor did not understand what a vacation was and was always ill at ease when she visited her husband on various vessels or at Warm Springs, perhaps guiltily so. She was particularly uncomfortable in her mother-in-law's house when her husband was away. Eventually understanding this, Roosevelt built the "cottage" called Val-Kill for her during 1925–26 on

Hyde Park land that he had purchased. He did much of the designing—in Dutch colonial style—himself.[40]

Although the June 1922 visit to Massachusetts General seems to mark a turning point in Roosevelt's coming to grips with his malady, his political career was being managed even during the darkest days of his illness. Press releases from Howe continued to generate stories that mentioned Roosevelt. Between the *New York Times'* story about the Newport scandal (July 20) and its first mention of Roosevelt's illness (August 27), at least three *Times* stories included his name, two of them concerning the Woodrow Wilson Foundation.[41] The very day the *Times* ran its front-page story about Roosevelt's illness, the patient signed a cheerful, flattering note to its publisher, Adolph Ochs, pretending that while his doctors had assured him that he "was not going to suffer any permanent effects," reading that diagnosis in the *Times* relieved him "immensely . . . because I know of course that it must be so." This was the beginning of what became a largely covert seven-year enterprise.

To effect this, Louis Howe became, for long periods of time, a member of the Roosevelt New York City household. From the very first days out of the hospital, the town house at East Sixty-Fifth Street was filled with politics and political visitors as well as some from the Fidelity office downtown. This added to the tensions that already existed within the family. Of her own role in her husband's illness, Eleanor admitted to a single instance of several hours of uncontrollable sobbing, but Draper noted in a report to Lovett toward the end of March 1922 that "Mrs. R. is pretty much at the end of her tether."[42] It is apparent that the strains on both the patient and his wife were more than either of them ever admitted or any of their acquaintances and most of those who have written about them seem to have realized. In their own very different ways, each of them wore a mask appropriate to their needs at any given time. For illness, both of them felt that denial was most appropriate, particularly denial of psychological stresses and fears. If Al Smith was, in a phrase that Roosevelt would later use, the Happy Warrior, Franklin Roosevelt succeeded in presenting himself as the Happy Patient.

The relationship between Roosevelt and Smith, who was eight years his senior, continued to evolve. In 1922, without ever seeming to be working together, Roosevelt and Smith collaborated in thwarting Hearst's gubernatorial designs, in a noncampaign campaign that ended with Roosevelt publishing a "Dear Al" letter that was the previously agreed-upon method of unleashing Al's successful bid for the nomination and subsequent reelection. Roosevelt and Howe used support of Smith as a vehicle to demonstrate that, despite his illness, Roosevelt remained a force in state Democratic politics.[43] One of Hearst's backers, New York City mayor John F. Hylan, remarked to reporters that he could not "figure out who Frank Roosevelt represents."[44] Any keen observer of New York politics could have told him that Roosevelt represented himself: backing Al Smith was simply the best way of doing so in 1922 and later. Eleanor played her part: as

Louis Howe reported from Syracuse, "Al nominated . . . Morgenthau and your Missus led the Dutchess delegation with the banner three times around the hall."[45] A week after the convention, Smith, whose wife took no active part in politics, wrote Roosevelt: "I had quite a session with our lady politicians as Mrs. Roosevelt no doubt told you. . . . I am really sorry that you could not be there but take care of yourself—there is another day coming.[46]

Two years later, strengthened by persistent exercise, Roosevelt had an even bigger role to play, although it was not yet his day. Smith's second election as governor, with coattails strong enough to pull in the whole state ticket, made him a serious contender for the Democratic nomination for president in 1924, as opposed to his complimentary nomination in 1920. Although Smith and most of his advisers consistently underrated Roosevelt, the Hyde Park patrician would be an important element in their political plans for the next six years. For their part, Roosevelt and Howe were committed to Smith's candidacy, seeing it as a necessary stepping-stone to their own goals, which increasingly concentrated on somehow keeping lines open to Democrats of every persuasion.

As 1924 approached, divisions in the country and within the Democratic Party seemed more and more irreconcilable.[47] One can speak of four different struggles going on simultaneously: dry versus wet, Protestant versus Catholic, rural versus urban, and native stock versus immigrant stock. Al Smith was, unambiguously, on the second-listed team in each of those contests. Roosevelt, while supporting Smith, could, as an old-stock Protestant, maintain relations with most major elements within the party. He was an active Protestant who spoke out for tolerance, a supporter of programs for city dwellers who nevertheless had rural roots, and old stock without being nativist. He could thus stay in touch with party politicians who were bitterly opposed to Smith; eventually, the support of some of them would be crucial to his own presidential nomination in 1932. Smith could never be a force to unify the Democratic Party and lead it to a national victory. I believe that Roosevelt always understood this. But since his presumed road to the White House led first to Albany, and since Smith and Tammany could block that road, continued support for a doomed Smith presidential candidacy was crucial for his strategy.

On most substantive issues of the 1920s, Smith and Roosevelt more or less concurred. Their chief disagreement was a tactical one about how to deal with Prohibition. Roosevelt's political position on liquor can best be described as "damp." He chose a number of not-quite-wet political stances, such as advocating a national referendum or shifting enforcement to the states. All this equivocation, while leaving him open to charges of opportunism, would pay off in 1932. He tried to get Smith, who was, as people said, "dripping wet," to temporize, but to no avail.[48]

In the early run-up to the national convention in 1924, Eleanor Roosevelt was featured in two political news stories instead of merely mentioned deep in the text. The first told of DNC chairman Cordell Hull appointing her to chair "an advisory subcommittee of Democratic women to formulate planks on social welfare legislation for the Democratic platform."[49] Then an Albany story reported that a committee of "Up-State women," headed by "Mrs. Franklin D. Roosevelt," met with Governor Smith and won an agreement that Democratic women should select the female delegates and alternates to the state convention, rather than having them named by men, which in practice had meant boss Murphy.[50]

The battle within the Democratic Party in 1924 began over where to meet: the choice of New York's Madison Square Garden as the convention site was made over the objections of the party's dry wing whose candidate was William Gibbs McAdoo, the transplanted Georgian. His political base had been New York, but now he was running from strongly Protestant Southern California. Smith's campaign took a hard hit before it even began. Charles Murphy, the Tammany boss who had encouraged urban progressives like Smith and Robert F. Wagner to assume leadership roles in the state party, died suddenly on April 25, 1924, in his sixty-sixth year. No one in Tammany could replace him: Roosevelt and Howe were able to fill some of the leadership vacuum and play important roles in the organization and operation of the Smith campaign, even if they could not control major policy decisions.

Five days after Murphy's death, Smith announced that Roosevelt, "an independent Democrat," would head his campaign committee for the Democratic presidential nomination. Roosevelt met the press twice that day, first at his downtown office and then at his home. He was vague about precise plans—he said committee membership might be thirty or three hundred—and expressed confidence that Smith would win the nomination at the June convention and be elected in November. As we now know, neither he nor Howe expected that to occur.[51] A *New York Times* editorial hailed Roosevelt's appointment, calling him "one of the finest types of independent Democrat [whose] character and national reputation and acquaintance make him particularly fit" for the job. The *Times* also praised "Mrs. ROOSEVELT . . . a highly intelligent politician," and quoted at some length her praise of Smith at the recent state convention.[52]

For much of May, while Smith tended to business in Albany, culling the bad bills the legislature had passed, Roosevelt was the major voice for the campaign. But in the latter part of the month, Smith took over as his own chief spokesman, insisting to skeptics that he would be the party's nominee. Roosevelt was to be the convention floor manager and, more important, make the nominating speech in Madison Square Garden on June 26. A text, largely written by Smith adviser Judge Joseph M. Proskauer, had been presented to Roosevelt, which, as he could do so well, he made his own.[53] He reluctantly accepted the judge's phrase "the Happy Warrior"—from Wordsworth's poem—which became Smith's epithet thereafter.[54]

The physical problems involved in delivering the speech—getting to the podium on crutches, wearing both the heavy leg braces and a corset, with the help of his sixteen-year-old son, James—were an ordeal. Elmer Davis, later Roosevelt's director of the Office of War Information (OWI), described it in the *New York Times:* "Mr. Roosevelt, who has been crippled since an attack of illness three years ago, had been brought to the podium in a wheeled chair. He walked forward on crutches . . . placed both hands on the speakers' desk and stood with head erect, a vigorous and healthful figure, except for his lameness."[55] Davis's report highlights the paradox that Roosevelt's physical presence presented: even when observers could see and describe the means by which he moved and was moved, he so exuded confidence and power that his limitations were often put to one side.

What is not usually pointed out is that in 1924, Roosevelt took his normal place on the convention floor with the rest of the New York delegation every day for two weeks. His son James, who acted as his father's page throughout, remembered that "he was absolutely determined that he would not be wheeled onto the convention floor, and it was my job to get him in early. . . . We practiced the awkward business of standing together by a chair, with me supporting him and taking his crutch as he lowered himself into his seat. . . . After his first few entrances he was greeted regularly with applause [from the galleries] as he entered the hall."[56] Of course, once he was president, his preliminary movements were almost always screened from public view, and self-censorship by press photographers aided the continuing impression of vigorous health. By the time he was president, his affliction was well known—his opponents had made it so—and from 1934 the Birthday Balls were an annual reminder, if one were necessary.

Roosevelt's nominating speech, while platitudinous, was a triumph. It was timed by Elmer Davis at just thirty-four minutes. His performance impressed individuals as diverse as columnist Walter Lippmann and Kansas City boss Tom Pendergast: the latter predicted to one of Roosevelt's friends that the New Yorker would get the nomination himself in 1928.[57]

But while the convention was a triumph for one Democrat, it was a disaster for his party, a shambles unmatched until 1968. Neither Smith nor McAdoo could achieve the two-thirds majority necessary for nomination, and the fratricidal convention dragged on for 103 bitter ballots over an unprecedented fourteen days in un-air-conditioned July humidity before naming a cockeyed ticket. The nominees were, for president, conservative Wall Street lawyer John W. Davis (1873–1955), who in his last appearance before the Supreme Court would champion segregation in *Brown v. Board of Education* (1954), and, for vice president, William Jennings Bryan's brother Charles (1887–1945), then serving as governor of Nebraska.[58] The election was the nadir for the national party, which won only 28.8 percent of the popular vote in a three-way contest won by incumbent president Calvin Coolidge with 54 percent. Wisconsin's progressive Republican Robert M. La Follette (1855–1925) garnered 16.6 percent, still a post–Civil War high for third parties.

The importance of the 1924 campaign in Roosevelt's political career cannot be overemphasized. When added to the prestige of name, wartime service, and 1920 vice presidential campaign, his showing before the assembled Democrats made him a person who could not be ignored when possible presidential candidates were discussed. For any politician only forty-two years old, this would have been a considerable accomplishment. For one who was crippled and had been out of office and largely out of sight for almost four years, it was an amazing situation. It cemented, for a time, his relationship with Al Smith, who, had he won the nomination, would have never achieved it again. He would, with Roosevelt's help, win that prize in 1928. In doing so, he would lever a reluctant Roosevelt into making what many thought was a premature grasp for power in Albany. As Smith lost the presidency and while Roosevelt won the governor's chair and was reelected in 1930, the younger man became an unconquerable impediment to Smith's continuing ambitions, which were probably unattainable in any event.

Eleanor Roosevelt campaigned vigorously for Smith and with uncharacteristic vehemence against his opponent, her first cousin Theodore Roosevelt Jr. She had deeply resented the nature of "young Ted's" campaign against her husband in 1920. In speech after speech, he had pronounced Franklin a "maverick" without "the brand of our family." Ted's reward was the all but traditional family appointment as assistant secretary of the navy. But for him, that post led not to glory but to the scandal of Teapot Dome: he was not directly implicated in the improper transfer of the navy's oil, but he had worked for oilman Harry F. Sinclair, who got the oil. Eleanor's revenge was to campaign against Ted in a car mounted with a large "teapot" that could emit steam. She dismissed the Republican candidate who was three years her junior as a "young man whose public service record shows him willing to do the bidding of friends."[59] Ted never again sought elective office.

At the height of the 1924 campaign, Roosevelt went to Georgia to investigate a mineral spring that philanthropist and Democratic Party activist George Foster Peabody (1852–1938) had written him about. Peabody gave a *New York Times* reporter a partly mythological account of Roosevelt and Warm Springs sometime during the New Deal. He recalled that in mid-1924, an associate had told him of a young polio sufferer who had found that swimming in the warm mineral springs on Peabody's Georgia property had so improved his condition that he could dance.

> At once, before eating supper . . . I wrote to Franklin Roosevelt advising him to drive down to Georgia and try the swimming in the pool. . . . He was

able to discard crutches, ride horseback, drive a motor after a blacksmith under his direction arranged that he not use his feet on a Ford car. When the Governorship was forced upon him by Alfred E. Smith the campaign was made possible by reason of Warm Springs. Furthermore, the Presidential nomination was much assured by his adoption of Georgia—strategic center of the South—as a second home state.[60]

Roosevelt went by train, arriving on October 3, 1924, accompanied by Eleanor and a small entourage. The next day, he found the eighty-eight-degree water "really wonderful and will I think do great good."[61] In the pool's buoyant mineral-laden waters, he could stand unaided and move about, which he called "walking." The myth that he propagated, and may have come to believe himself, was that his condition was greatly improved by Warm Springs. This was not the case. Warm Springs and his role in the institution he created there helped him to manage his disease by making him more comfortable with it, both physically and, perhaps more important, psychologically. Over the objections of his law partner, Basil O'Connor, in April 1926 he purchased the property from Peabody. He invested some two hundred thousand dollars—two-thirds of his capital—in Warm Springs and set about improving and publicizing it.[62] As was his optimistic wont, he often spoke of making money from his investment in the decrepit resort, but he gained only psychic income from it. Facilities were improved, and patients were attracted by newspaper stories, one of which, widely syndicated, was headlined "Franklin Roosevelt Will Swim to Health."[63] In the early days at Warm Springs, Roosevelt was, in effect, the "doctor" and general impresario. The man who would later describe himself as "Dr. New Deal" and "Dr. Win-the-War" devoted hour after hour to helping the dozens of "polios" who were attracted by newspaper stories and word of mouth. "Dr. Roosevelt" really functioned as an amateur physiotherapist: he helped his "patients" use the pool and explained the details of their musculature and so forth. Later, full-time professional staff was added, beginning with one physician and two physiotherapists.

Roosevelt's restless energy and insatiable curiosity caused him to explore and become familiar with the impoverished Georgia countryside and its people as he spent increasing amounts of time there. These experiences provided him with stories and examples that he used to make political points for the rest of his life and were clearly his most thorough encounters with the economic underside of American life. He established a farm that he hoped would serve as a model: it raised cattle, not cotton. When, as president, he spoke of the South as "the nation's No. 1 problem," he knew whereof he spoke.[64]

In January 1927, he set up the Georgia Warm Springs Foundation. The legal work was done by Basil O'Connor, who, despite himself, became drawn into the complex of organizations that flowed out of Roosevelt's investment. He ran the business side of the foundation, then of the Birthday Balls, and, eventually, the March of Dimes. By the time of O'Connor's death in 1972, his obituary headline described him simply as "Polio Crusader" and reported that he had overseen the collection of "seven billion dimes" (seven hundred million dollars), though much of it came in more substantial amounts. The first large donation was from Edsel Ford and his wife: twenty-five thousand dollars to improve the pool.[65]

Although in some ways the focus of Roosevelt's life seemed to have switched to the South, it must be remembered that Missy LeHand was there to take care of his large correspondence and that Louis Howe continued to make sure that his name was frequently kept before the public. In addition, he entertained a steady stream of visitors and guests on his houseboats and at Warm Springs. Above all, Roosevelt continued to be an effective and necessary presence in New York Democratic politics.

The 1926 political year began in late January with Governor Smith's announcing, as he had done in 1922, that he would not be a candidate for governor in November.[66] Few were fooled; the next month, bookies had Smith an odds-on favorite—nine to five—to be the Democratic nominee and listed Roosevelt at five to one.[67] An even better indicator of Roosevelt's continuing influence was his attendance at a small dinner at the Washington home of Montana's Democratic senator Thomas J. Walsh in which a few select party leaders mapped strategy.[68] By late June, Smith was still insisting that he would return to private life and was pushing Roosevelt as the party's candidate for the U.S. Senate seat long held by Republican James W. Wadsworth. Papers printed an unattributed statement, clearly circulated by Howe, saying that Roosevelt would not run, "in order to complete his full recovery from a long illness."[69]

Although Smith continued to insist that he was retiring, the announcement at the end of August that Roosevelt would be temporary chair of the state convention and give the "keynote" radio address for the party meant, as journalists assumed correctly, that Smith would run. Roosevelt and the Republican keynoter made their addresses on the air, showing the growing importance of radio in American politics.[70] Smith and the entire state Democratic ticket won.[71] In retrospect, the most important convention decision, dictated by Smith, was the nomination of Robert F. Wagner (1877–1953) for U.S. senator: he served until 1949 while becoming the New Deal's most important legislator. Roosevelt took no further part in the campaign, leaving for an extended stay at Warm Springs. Eleanor Roosevelt campaigned vigorously for Smith and Wagner and was active throughout the year, pushing women's issues and their status within the party.[72]

No sooner had Smith been reelected than maneuvering about the 1928 presidential campaign began. Most pundits, within and without the Democratic Party, believed that Smith could not be denied the nomination in 1928 and that a McAdoo candidacy was no longer viable.[73] Roosevelt's plans were a subject of much speculation. In late March 1927, the *Atlanta Constitution* suggested that Roosevelt "would be an ideal [presidential] candidate."[74] More plausible suggestions were made from other quarters: that Roosevelt should be a candidate to succeed Smith as governor or for a Senate seat.

But Roosevelt and Howe had a different timetable. They expected Smith to get the nomination and lose the election. As Roosevelt wrote Josephus Daniels in June 1927, "Between ourselves, I'm doubtful whether any Democrat can win in 1928 [assuming] the present undoubted general prosperity of the country continues."[75] Once Coolidge announced in early August 1927 that "I do not choose to run for president in 1928," Howe and Roosevelt assumed that Herbert Hoover would be nominated by the GOP and become president.

Their target was the White House—probably in 1936—and they believed that Roosevelt's road to the White House ran through Albany's statehouse, not the U.S. Senate. But getting elected governor in 1928 would be too soon. New York governors then served two-year terms, so Roosevelt, if he ran and won in 1928, would have to be reelected thrice if he wanted to run as an incumbent governor in 1936 and not run against a probably incumbent Republican president. Thus, an initial run for governor in 1932 seemed the ideal choice. We now know that, had they persisted in their strategy, Roosevelt might never have become president.

But the major thrust in 1927–28 had to be to work hard for Smith as the best way to get the presidential nomination for Roosevelt at some future date. In addition, however, Roosevelt had to demonstrate leadership within the party. His role in Smith's campaigns made him a familiar figure to Democrats of all persuasions. He had long staked out a position for himself as a spokesman for internationalism within the party, beginning with his enthusiastic support for the League of Nations in the 1920 campaign and continuing with his role in the Woodrow Wilson Foundation. In 1923 he published an article, "Shall We Trust Japan?," answering that question much more positively than most American leaders.[76] By the later 1920s, his views had evolved so that he no longer favored the kind of imperialism that he had once advocated in Haiti. The fullest statement of his views came in July 1928 when he published a statement in *Foreign Affairs* that he hoped would help shape the party platform plank. He gave a strong endorsement for joining the World Court, an endorsement he would repudiate in his successful effort to get the presidential nomination four years later. His comments on Latin America were a far cry from his braggadocio in 1920. Admitting that he had had "a slight part" in Wilson's foreign policy in the Caribbean, he praised the ends of intervention in Haiti and Santo Domingo but felt that "we seem to have paid too little attention to making the citizens of [Haiti and Santo Domingo] more capable of reassuming control of their own governments." He recognized that these interventions, for which they "ought to thank us," were in fact "disapproved almost unanimously" by the other American republics. Thus, he argued, in a preview of his as yet unnamed "Good Neighbor policy," that the United States needed to respect the sovereignty of these nations and that any future hemispheric intervention should be in consort with other New World nations.[77]

Many of Roosevelt's critics, then and later, have argued that, as Richard Hofstadter put it, "His mind, as exhibited in writings and speeches of the 1920s, was generous and sensible, but also superficial and complacent."[78] Perhaps in an ideal world, where politicians were social scientists with a philosophical bent, such a criticism would have merit, but if we compare Roosevelt with his contemporaries, men such as McAdoo, John W. Davis, and Al Smith among the Democrats, and Harding, Coolidge, and Hoover among the Republicans, a different judgment follows. The only one of them who could be said to have had any kind of a rounded view of America's problems was Herbert Hoover. Among the others, Al Smith had a good grasp of the problems of New York, but the country west of the Bronx or the world beyond the nation's borders was terra incognita. Hoover and the others assumed that the nation had entered a "new era" in which economic depressions were a thing of the past. Roosevelt never shared that assumption and, as noted, on a number of occasions after 1920 speculated privately that the Democrats might have to wait for a depression before recapturing the White House.

Roosevelt's closest approach to a statement of fundamental beliefs came in a 1926 commencement address he gave at Milton Academy, a Massachusetts prep school not unlike his own Groton but with less éclat. It can be argued that his talk, quickly published in book form, was a collection of bromides, but they were progressive bromides.

He looked to the future—"I ask the question: 'Quo Vadis—Whither Bound?'"—and gave his audience a simplified version of the Whig interpretation of history, which he called the "laws of the history of progress." He hailed, among other things, the emancipation of women and the blurring of class lines but was silent about race. He explained why "the government of our own country . . . is conservative by far the greater part of the time," and argued, "Our national danger is . . . not that it may for four . . . or eight years become liberal or even radical, but that it may suffer from too long a period of the do-nothing or reactionary standards." He insisted that internationalism was necessary: "True service will not come until all the world recognizes all the rest of the world as one big family." He was, typically, full of optimism and assured the graduates, as many commencement speakers do, that their generation would do better than his own, and he insisted, as he would always insist, that he represented modernity.[79]

Both Roosevelts actively supported Smith's presidential candidacy: in terms of actual campaigning before the national convention, Eleanor did more than he, as had been the case since 1921. In January she invoked her uncle Theodore's 1908 letters to show his hopes for a day when a Catholic or a Jew could become president.[80] In February Franklin was chosen as one of four at-large male members of the party's delegation to the Democratic National Convention in Houston in mid-June, but Eleanor was not among the women similarly chosen.[81]

In March Eleanor Roosevelt published a forthright magazine article on women in politics; an accurate summary appeared on a news page of the *New York Times*. It drew wide press comment and gave her more publicity than she had ever had. Its theme was simple: in important matters, "women have no voice or power whatever."[82] Some weeks later, Eleanor was the subject of a laudatory feature article in the *New York Times Sunday Magazine* by S. J. Woolf, accompanied by his sketch of her drawn from life.[83] Clearly, she had become a personage in her own right. When the New York Democrats formally launched Smith's presidential candidacy, she made the seconding speech after George R. Lunn nominated him, and when in May the Southern Women's National Democratic Organization endorsed Smith's candidacy, she gave the major address.[84]

Despite a claim late in April that New York City mayor Jimmy Walker (1881–1946) would nominate Smith at Houston, a week later the decision was made that Roosevelt would again make the key speech.[85] There was not the drama of his experimental 1924 appearance, and his polio management skills had improved so that he needed only a cane and son Elliott's arm as he moved to the podium. As *New York Times* correspondent Richard Oulahan described it: "Crippled in body and limb, that picture of him changed quickly. . . . Pink cheeked, full of glow of health, Mr. Roosevelt offered an attractive appearance. . . . Everyone knew why he was standing there, leaning heavily on a cane. Then another yell as he took the few steps forward and leaned on the reading desk before him."[86]

The speech itself was conversational rather than oratorical; a complimentary editorial described it as "a gentleman speaking to gentlemen." There was no attempt by Smith's advisers to provide a text, although Roosevelt again used Proskauer's "Happy Warrior" tag in his closing.[87]

Before the convention, Roosevelt had written his mother that "I plan *not* to do any work to amount to anything after Sept. 1st," but, the convention over, he was drawn into more and more activity. He steadily resisted efforts to get him to run for governor or become chairman of the Democratic National Committee.

But the pressures were continuous. He told his mother, "I have had a difficult time turning down the Governorship, letters and telegrams by the dozen begging me to save the situation by running, but I have been perfectly firm. I only hope that they don't try to stampede the convention tomorrow and nominate me and then adjourn."[88]

Adjournment could have left Smith looking ridiculous if Roosevelt had refused to run. Roosevelt, on his part, never went so far as to make a Shermanesque refusal. (The Civil War general had stopped all talk by avowing, "If nominated I will not run; if elected, I will not serve.")

At the convention in Rochester, the Tammany leaders were desperate to have Roosevelt on the ticket. They feared losing the governorship, which meant losing state patronage, because the Republicans had nominated the state attorney general, Albert Ottinger (1878–1938), a vigorous candidate and the first Jew to get such a place on a state ticket; he would surely draw the votes of many Jewish Democrats. There was already some talk in GOP circles about urging such voters to mark their ballots for "Al and Al." After arriving at the convention on October 1, Smith tried other gambits. He got Herbert Lehman (1878–1963), a prominent investment banker, to agree to run for lieutenant governor and be willing to fill in for Roosevelt if he needed rest at Warm Springs. When he learned from Roosevelt's friend Edward J. Flynn, the cultured boss of the Bronx, that Roosevelt might run if his financial problems at Warm Springs could be taken care of, Smith persuaded John J. Raskob (1879–1950), the multimillionaire who had just become chairman of the Democratic National Committee, to guarantee the financial health of Warm Springs.[89]

Roosevelt refused to take phone calls from Smith, so Smith got Eleanor Roosevelt, a convention delegate, to place the call, which involved telephone tag across rural Georgia. Once she got a clear line, she handed the phone to Smith and left to catch a train to New York City, where she was teaching. After problems with the connection, Smith and Roosevelt finally got to talk. He told Roosevelt about the guarantees, and both Lehman and Raskob came on the line and confirmed what Smith had said. Roosevelt still said no. Smith then asked him what he would do if nominated. Roosevelt replied that he did not know. That was enough for Smith, who handed the phone to Lehman, who finished the conversation.[90]

The next day, Jimmy Walker nominated Roosevelt for governor; the delegates, who had been told in advance what was going to happen, cheered for a perfunctory two minutes, approved the nomination by acclamation, and went home.

Why did he give in? Of those closest to him, only daughter Anna urged him to run; he wired back, "You ought to be spanked." One can only speculate, but Roosevelt probably felt that, after all, as he had been saying for years, anyone who was governor of New York had a good chance of becoming president and there would probably never be another situation in which he could have the nomination without lifting a finger. In addition, turning it down under those circumstances might well create lasting animosities, especially if the Democrats lost the state. Always flexible, he quickly shifted gears. His final refusal to say no to Smith meant, in the language of politics, yes. In this instance at least, instinct was superior to planning.

4 Running the Empire State
1929–31

IN ROCHESTER THERE WAS JUBILATION AT ROOSEVELT'S nomination. The delegates felt that they had put together the strongest possible state ticket. Smith was elated. On the train back to Albany, he spoke to reporters and met the health issue head-on: "Frank Roosevelt today is mentally as good as he ever was in his life. Physically he is as good as he ever was in his life. His whole trouble is his lack of muscular control in his lower limbs. . . . A Governor does not have to be an acrobat. We do not elect him for his ability to do a double back-flip or a handspring. The work of the Governorship is brain work. Ninety-five percent of it is accomplished at a desk. There is no doubt about his ability to do it."[1]

Republican papers shed crocodile tears for the drafted candidate: three examples will suffice. The *Albany Knickerbocker Press* argued that Roosevelt would be "a first class Governor in the remote contingency of Democratic success . . . were it not for . . . the candidate's health." The *New York Evening Post* found the nomination "both pathetic and pitiless. . . . Even his own friends will hesitate to vote for him now. [Being Governor] is killing hard work . . . for a man struggling out of one of the most relentless of modern diseases." And the GOP flagship *Herald Tribune* claimed that "the nomination is unfair to Mr. Roosevelt [and] to the people of the State, who, under other conditions, would welcome [his] candidacy for any office." But the *New York World,* in a striking simile, insisted that the candidate was as qualified for the job as a "war veteran who has lost an arm or a leg."[2]

From Warm Springs, Roosevelt pretended that he was "amazed" at the Republican charges: "Let me set this matter straight at once. I was not dragooned into running by the governor. . . . I am in this fight not to win personal honor, but for carrying forth the policies of Governor Smith."[3] He went on to say that he not only wanted his friends to vote for him but to get others to do so. He said nothing at all directly about his physical condition.

Before Roosevelt left the South, he gave a speech for Smith in Columbus, Georgia, whose major theme was a denunciation of religious prejudice. He claimed that for "generations we Americans have lived side by side in harmony—Protestants, Catholics, Jews. . . . Yet this year of 1928 has seen . . . a flare-up during the months of July and August of an old passion that we thought was dead." Claiming that prejudice was dead anywhere in the United States in 1928 was, on its face, curious, but to say it near the border between Georgia and Alabama was ridiculous. Roosevelt's strategy throughout the campaign was to argue that religious prejudice was something that had not flourished in America since colonial times and even in 1928 was practiced by only a "handful of Americans."[4] In his Cleveland speech before an overflow crowd in Masonic Auditorium, he placed the locus of bigotry on activities of Republicans in the South and elsewhere who were using "vile slanders" against Smith, even though there was plenty of prejudice in Ohio, the home of the Anti-Saloon League and other aspects of militant Protestantism.[5] Later, during his own gubernatorial campaign, he often discussed prejudice. Two of Smith's key advisers, Judge Proskauer and Belle Moskowitz, felt that Roosevelt should not stress prejudice, an attitude then common for middle-class American Jews.

Roosevelt pledged himself to a continuation of Smith's policies with a particular emphasis on the public control of electric power. This would be a key issue in the campaign, since Ottinger, very much a proponent of laissez-faire, opposed that aspect of Smith's program. In remarks to reporters, Roosevelt ridiculed his opponent as a "promising man" whose promises included "all manner of public works on a gigantic scale at the same time reducing taxes."[6]

The next morning, the candidate went across the Hudson to catch a train to Binghamton. On the ferry, he was introduced to a young lawyer, Samuel I. Rosenman (1896–1973), who had been assigned by the Smith leaders to help him with speeches. The son of Russian Jewish immigrants, Rosenman had graduated from Columbia summa cum laude in 1915 and spent two years in its law school before enlisting as a private shortly after the United States entered World War I.[7] Mustered out as a second lieutenant in 1919, he completed his law degree in 1920, passed the bar, and affiliated himself with Tammany. Elected to the state assembly in 1921, he so distinguished himself that he was appointed legislative commissioner on Governor Smith's staff. His job was to analyze pending and proposed legislation for the governor. Roosevelt soon folded him into his entourage, dubbing him "Sammy the Rose."

Rosenman, whose memoir is the best participant account of Roosevelt's gubernatorial campaigns, tells us that he came with low expectations, having absorbed the unflattering characterization of the candidate that prevailed among Smith's official family. He had envisaged "a playboy and idler," weak and ineffective, but he was soon disabused. For the first three days of the campaign tour, he had nothing to do while Roosevelt gave brief extemporaneous talks along New York's southern tier, mostly standing up in an open car, reminiscent of his 1910 campaign. He often asked the crowds if he looked like a sick man.[8] But when they got to Buffalo, Roosevelt said that he planned to make a formal speech on labor the next evening. Rosenman had packed two suitcases filled with speech material organized by subject in large manila envelopes and handed over those dealing with labor. "[Roosevelt] looked through the material for some time, calmly smoking his cigarette, his chin resting in his hand in a position I was later to see many times. . . . He could read fast; sometimes you wondered if he was reading at all, he flipped the pages so quickly. But when he started to talk about what he had read, you knew that had he had absorbed most of it."

Rosenman was surprised that Roosevelt had taken no notes. He quickly learned why. Roosevelt told him, "I've got to run now," a favorite phrase despite his obvious inability to do so. "Suppose you knock out a draft of what you think I ought to say and let me have it in the morning."

Rosenman produced a draft, which he felt was pretty dull, and slipped it under the candidate's door in the small hours of the morning. Reporting back at breakfast time, he found Roosevelt in bed. The nervous author watched as Roosevelt read. Then, as they ate room-service breakfasts, Roosevelt allowed that there was good material, agreed with his ghost's appraisal that much of it was dull, and added that it needed something to hold it together. A stenographer was called in, and Roosevelt, still in bed, dictated inserts and corrections, giving Rosenman his "first lesson in how to pull a speech together and pep it up." To introduce the material on Republican promises to labor—Rosenman describes it as "long and boring"—the candidate dictated the following:

> And so tonight I am going to tell you all about it, tell you the facts, go back in my own mind and in your mind into the history of this State. Somewhere in a pigeonhole in the desk of the Republican leaders of New York is a large envelope, soiled, worn, bearing a date that goes back twenty-five or thirty years. Printed in large letters on this old envelope are the words, "Promises to labor." Inside the envelope are a series of sheets dated two years apart and representing the best thought of the best minds of the Republican leaders over a succession of years. Each sheet of promises is practically the duplicate of every other sheet in the envelope. But nowhere in that envelope is a single page bearing the title "Promises kept."

It was a technique Roosevelt would use time and again. He would denounce "Republican leaders," but never "Republicans." Roosevelt wanted—and got—votes from Republicans, so he never assailed them. If one compares this paragraph from a little-known 1928 campaign speech with the corresponding passage of his most famous campaign speech, the "Fala" speech of 1944, the parallel structure is immediately apparent. The "Republican leaders" had evolved into "Republican fiction writers," but the basic claim—the falsity of Republican promises to labor—remained the same.

Rosenman reports that the speech went through several drafts that day and then explains how speechwriters react when their efforts are performed: "When applause came I was more uplifted than the speaker." Rosenman says that he never really lost that initial excitement and reports watching a later Roosevelt speechwriter, playwright Robert E. Sherwood, "actually forming the words with his own lips as they were being spoken by Roosevelt."[9]

After Buffalo came major speeches, put together in the same way, at a rate of almost one a day. In Rochester the focus was on "human functions of government," in Syracuse it was on "water power," and in Utica it was on "Prohibition and state enforcement." In Troy he spoke of the "typical day of campaigning by the 'sick' candidate," in Queens he talked about "state parks" and defended Smith from President Hoover's charge that he was a "socialist," in the Bronx he spoke about "prison Reform," and in his last major campaign stop, at Yonkers on November 1, he devoted much of his talk to the ideological differences between Hoover and Smith. And throughout the campaign, there had been dozens of extemporaneous talks, mostly from his car.

Most of his remarks broke no new programmatic ground and largely advocated a continuation of Smith's popular reforms. But in speaking about providing aid to crippled children and adults—calling the latter "wheelchair cripples"—he used himself as an example: "Seven years ago I came down in the epidemic in New York, I came down with infantile paralysis, a perfectly normal attack, and I was completely, for the moment, put out of any useful activities. By personal good fortune I was able to get the very best kind of care, and the result of having the right kind of care is that today I am on my feet." And after reminding his audience—the speech was broadcast across the state—that he was "quite capable of going on to Albany and staying there two years," he took an extremely advanced position on health care. Pointing out that most of those who had become incapacitated could not afford the "cost and the time necessary for rehabilitation," he argued, "It seems to me that that it is the clear duty of the State and local governments[10] to make up what is needed to bring the splendid definite results that medical science can now provide. And I promise to do all in my power to make available to others that which I myself have been fortunate enough to obtain."[11]

Roosevelt campaigned vigorously up to election day; he made five speeches in his old senatorial district on the last day of the campaign. The afternoon before that, he held a kind of press conference in his home for reporters and two hundred supporters—his mother had cake served—and reviewed the campaign with great optimism. He also insisted that he was "feeling much fitter and walking much better than when the campaign began."[12]

Roosevelt's campaign may have been the most intensive speaking tour of the state by any previous candidate for governor. In the process, he left Ottinger looking inept. The New York bookies, who had listed Roosevelt as a two-to-one underdog at the campaign's beginning, had him an almost two-to-one favorite at its end.[13] On election day, he voted in Hyde Park and then took the train to Manhattan to get returns at campaign headquarters.

By early evening, it became apparent that Smith would lose in both the nation and his home state, and it seemed that Roosevelt would go down with him. He trailed Smith in the early returns, which were mostly from New York City and other urban areas. But when all the votes were tallied, Roosevelt prevailed by a very narrow margin, so narrow that Ottinger delayed his concession for almost two weeks.

No single factor can explain Roosevelt's victory. Final tabulations gave him a 25,000-vote margin over Ottinger out of some 4.25 million votes cast, while Smith lost the state to Hoover by 103,000. In the city returns, it is clear that some voters—presumably Jews—voted for Al and Al, but upstate many voters, presumably Protestants, voted for Herbert and Franklin. In Chautauqua County in far western New York, for example, the results were as follows:

President		Governor	
Hoover	38,320	Ottinger	35,183
Smith	13,223	Roosevelt	15,128

Of the 50,000 who voted for governor, nearly 2,000 voters, about 4 percent, split their tickets to vote for the two Protestants. But some of those voters were also opposed to Tammany, and Roosevelt, though running with Tammany support, still had an anti-Tammany aura. To complicate the analysis further, looking at just the New York City vote, Smith won the city by 448,000 votes, 42,000 more than Roosevelt's margin there, while Herbert Lehman, the Jewish investment banker running for lieutenant governor, did better than either, winning the city by 515,000 votes. Some 67,000 voters opted for Herbert and Herbert. Clearly, religion was important in Roosevelt's election, but so were his vigorous campaign and the fact that Ottinger was a conservative Republican, and, of course, Roosevelt's name counted for something. It was a victory, but a very near thing.[14]

Smith carried only six southern states plus Massachusetts and Rhode Island for a total of 89 electoral votes. Hoover carried the other forty states with 444 electoral votes, becoming the first Republican to win electoral votes in the Deep South since Reconstruction. Smith, and most contemporaries, attributed the magnitude of his defeat to his religion. As Smith put it, bitterly, on election night, "The time just hasn't come when a man can say his beads in the White House."[15]

Modern interpretations of the 1928 election take a different view. Although everyone agrees that Smith's Catholicism was the key factor in the Democrats' temporary loss of much of the South, most now argue that nationally Smith's candidacy was not the backward step for the Democratic Party it seemed to be in 1928. For the first time, there was a net Democratic plurality in the twelve largest American cities. Smith garnered a larger share of the popular vote than the two previous Democratic nominees: he received almost 41 percent as opposed to Cox's 34 percent in 1920 and Davis's mere 28 percent in the three-way 1924 race. Some have argued that in terms of the popular vote, Smith's Catholicism got him as many votes as it cost him. And, finally, there is a clear consensus that no Democrat could have defeated Herbert Hoover, billed as the advance agent of greater prosperity.[16]

Many contemporaries and later historians have treated Roosevelt's four years in Albany as significant only because the governorship provided such an excellent launching pad for a presidential campaign. But those years had other importance. They enabled him to hone his skills at management and conciliation, to learn about many issues with which he would have to deal as president, and, after the Great Depression began to set in, to gain the kinds of knowledge of and contact with the problems of mass poverty and its relief that were invaluable in his early years in the White House.

In early December, the governor-elect summoned the leaders of the Democratic minority in both houses of the legislature, the chairman of the state Democratic Party, Lieutenant Governor–elect Lehman, and Sam Rosenman for a series of conferences in Warm Springs. The agendas included planning a legislative program and strengthening the state party organization, especially upstate. Roosevelt told Rosenman that he wanted to appoint him counsel to the governor. This took Rosenman by surprise; during the Smith years, that job was a meaningless sinecure, as Smith took advice from a small group of advisers, including the formidable Belle Moskowitz (1877–1933), one of the first women to exercise this kind of political power.[17] Roosevelt explained that "I do not expect to continue to call on these people whom Al has been using. I shall expect the Counsel to do much of the [that] work." Rosenman told his boss that he wanted to think it over; while he was thinking, he read in the papers that he had been appointed. Roosevelt told him that his mind had been made up for him.[18]

As counsel Rosenman functioned as the administrative hub of the governor's office. This made him and Louis Howe rivals. Louis stayed in New York City, running the office that handled Roosevelt's national political correspondence. Rivalries within Roosevelt's entourage were more the rule than the exception. Those around him resembled nothing so much, in some ways, as courtiers vying for favor. As president Roosevelt, like an American Louis XIV, would become the sun around whom all revolved. He insisted on having multiple sources of information both in Albany and in Washington.

But his problem in Albany was that he was displacing a former star, a star who fully expected to continue his domination of state government. Al Smith's expectations were dashed even before the new administration took office. What became the great falling-out between the two men began when Roosevelt refused to take his predecessor's suggestion that he appoint Mrs. Moskowitz as his secretary. Both Eleanor and Louis had warned him about her. The governor-elect understood that Smith expected him to be a weak, largely absentee governor resting at Warm Springs and leaving Lehman in charge to do the heavy lifting during the legislative sessions. Instead of Moskowitz, Roosevelt appointed a minor member of Smith's staff, Guernsey Cross, as his secretary. Cross functioned largely as a gatekeeper, while Rosenman exercised administrative power as counsel.

Smith was further disappointed when Roosevelt refused to reappoint the imperious Robert Moses (1888–1981) as secretary of state. Instead, Roosevelt appointed the one New York City political leader he trusted, Bronx party leader Edward J. Flynn (1891–1953). Flynn, whose parents were middle-class Irish immigrants, was a 1912 graduate of Fordham Law School who enjoyed both political and social relations with Roosevelt and would serve him in one capacity or another until 1945. A modest boss who avoided the limelight, he became, after Howe, the most important member of the small team that guided Roosevelt's quest for the Democratic presidential nomination.[19]

Roosevelt made Frances Perkins (1880–1965) industrial commissioner, the administrative head of the state's labor department. Smith, who had broken precedent by naming her chair of the Industrial Commission, felt that her promotion was a mistake because the male administrators would not accept female leadership.[20]

The now unhappy warrior had planned to spend Mondays and Tuesdays in Albany while the legislature was in session, to "help out." Clearly, Smith had expected to be the real power in Albany. Despite their long association, he had no understanding of Roosevelt's character. Smith left Albany shortly after the inaugural ceremony.[21] His most recent biographer claims that, in 1928, Al "had no idea that Roosevelt was planning to run for president."[22] If that is true, it was a blind spot in a canny political brain.

Eleanor told interviewers, shortly after the election, that she would be a part-time first lady of the state, spending part of each week in New York City, where she was vice principal of the Todhunter School for Girls and taught American history and English, and that "in spare moments" she would help run her Val-Kill furniture factory at Hyde Park, serve on various boards of directors and committees, keep up with current affairs, and, as the mother of "four boys away at school," be available "to go at a moment's notice to Groton or Cambridge." In this and other interviews, she ignored the fact that she had become one of the most important leaders of the growing network of women in New York's Democratic Party.[23]

At the New Year's Day inaugural, Roosevelt went out of his way to honor Smith's past achievements, even while thwarting his present attempts to keep his hands on the levers of power. Breaking precedent, he invited the outgoing governor to address the statehouse throng before his own speech. Smith, directing some of his remarks to his chosen successor, said, "I am turning the government over to you, not perfect—no human instrumentality reaches perfection—but as good as it can be made." Toward the end of his brief talk, he clasped the new governor's hand, saying, "A personal word, Frank, I congratulate you. I hope you will be able to devote that intelligent mind of yours to the problems of this State."[24]

Roosevelt, after the formal oath taking, opened with a generous tribute to his predecessor: "No Governor in the long history of the State has accomplished more than he . . . a public servant of true greatness." His brief and eloquent speech deliberately challenged current conventional wisdom. In an era that hailed American isolation, he insisted that "our civilization cannot endure unless we, as individuals, realize our personal responsibility to and dependence on the rest of the world." Instead of praising rugged individualism, he pointed out that "it is literally true that the 'self-supporting' man or woman has become as extinct as the man of the stone age." He insisted, contrary to Smith's claim of near perfection, that although state government had made progress, "we have far to go." Then he spoke of three major issues—water power, the proper administration of justice, and the relative poverty of the state's farmers—that would be featured in the following day's message to the legislature.[25] All three were topics likely to appeal to upstate voters and many Republicans.

Roosevelt's annual message the next day included an ambitious list of additional objectives: most striking were his promises to labor and a pledge to do something for the physically disadvantaged. He called for an eight-hour day, a forty-eight-hour week for women and children, and the establishment of an advisory minimum or fair wage board for them. (Supreme Court decisions still barred states from regulating the labor of men.) He also proposed extending workmen's compensation to cover all occupational diseases, barring temporary injunctions in industrial disputes without a hearing, and to provide a trial by jury for any alleged violations of injunctions. These were all traditional advanced progressive reforms; truly innovative was his call for a commission of experts to study "old-age security against want."

His proposals for the disabled—he referred to them as "cripples"—called for state financing of both care and rehabilitation. Estimating that some fifty thousand New Yorkers were so seriously disabled that they required "constant attention" by some "able-bodied person," Roosevelt argued that it was "the duty of the State to give the same care to removing the handicaps of its citizens as it now gives to their mental development. Universal education of the mind is, after all, a modern conception. . . . We must recognize the same obligation of the State to restore to useful activity those children and adults who have the misfortune to be crippled." He ended the message with an appeal for nonpartisanship, hoping that there would be another "Era of Good Feeling" in the state. Then, ignoring the legislators before him, he thanked the radio audience for electing him.[26]

The nonpartisan guise was a necessity: Roosevelt, like Smith before him, was predestined to face a Republican legislature because provisions in the state constitution, adopted in 1894, were written so that New York City's representatives, no matter what population it achieved, would be unlikely to dominate the legislature. They provided that only citizens counted for purposes of apportionment, fixed the size of the assembly at 150, allotted at least one assemblyman to each of sixty counties, and specified that no two adjoining counties, or those divided by a river, could have as many as half the seats. Thus, during Roosevelt's terms as governor, New York City, which had 52 percent of the state's people, elected only 41 percent of the members of the assembly. From 1918 through 1940, Democrats elected a governor in every election except 1920, yet they won a majority in the legislature only once, in 1934.[27]

Roosevelt never enjoyed a legislative majority in Albany. He had to cajole rather than direct and constantly needed to appeal to the people over the heads of the legislature. In Albany he developed those conciliatory skills that were so useful to him as president; such skills had been singularly lacking during his navy days. Huey Long's famous 1933 fable about Roosevelt's arts of co-optation—he claimed that Roosevelt was like a "scrooch owl" who "slips into the roost and scrooches up to the hen and talks softly to her . . . and the next thing you know, there ain't no hen"[28]—describes tactics that Roosevelt practiced and honed in Albany as a chief executive forced to deal with a hostile legislature.

Any semblance of an "Era of Good Feeling" disappeared near the end of the governor's first month in office. The issue involved was not a new initiative but the consummation of one of the last great accomplishments of Smith's regime. In 1927 Smith had persuaded the voters to adopt a constitutional amendment requiring the executive to submit an annual budget for the state. Such budgets were still a relative novelty in the United States: the first federal budget was submitted by Warren G. Harding in 1921. Because the New York amendment came into effect only in 1929, Roosevelt's budget was the first under the new dispensation. Such budgets have become common and have served to increase the power of presidents and governors and consequently diminish the power of legislators. That Roosevelt chose the budget for his first battle with the legislature is a mark of his superior sense of political tactics, which rarely failed him.

The Republican leaders tried to maintain control by passing a statute providing that a committee of three—the governor and the chairs of the Finance Committees in both houses of the legislature—had to approve the actual allocation of funds within the budget. Roosevelt decided to take the matter to the courts. The struggle between the governor and the legislature could have led to a virtual cessation of government activities, but Roosevelt agreed to go along with what he considered an unconstitutional statute, pending a final court decision. He and the two designated legislators agreed on the actual allocation of funds within departments without significant differences. On November 19,

1929, almost ten months after Roosevelt submitted his budget, the state's highest court upheld his position, ruling that the law was unconstitutional because it gave "administrative powers" to members of the legislature.[29] From this first battle on, Roosevelt regularly wrong-footed the legislative majority, as he, not they, chose the battlegrounds on which to fight.

He understood that he would get few innovative measures passed, but he resorted to a favorite device of progressives, the use of independent experts, to win the battle of public opinion. That forced the legislature to move part of the way along the road he wished it to travel. A good case in point was the struggle over the development of hydroelectric power in New York, which began long before Roosevelt's governorship, continued long after it, and in many ways foreshadowed the national battles over public power that arose during the New Deal. Roosevelt's fight for public power and lower rates would be a plus factor in his 1930 reelection, and public power would be a major focus of his presidency.

Roosevelt's basic point, as he put it in his inaugural address, was that the hydroelectric power potential of the St. Lawrence River had to be developed as efficiently as possible. He did not advocate full public ownership but insisted that "it is our power; and no inordinate profits must be allowed to those who act as the people's agents in bringing this power to their homes and workshops."[30]

Al Smith had struggled with the legislature over the issue during his terms as governor. After Smith's defeat in 1920, the Republican administration moved to grant a fifty-year lease of St. Lawrence sites to private interests. This was blocked by Smith after his return to power in 1923. He and the legislature remained at loggerheads for the rest of his tenure. The issue was further complicated by the fact that New York shared the St. Lawrence with Canada, and any agreement with Canada was a federal matter. Under American law, the navigation of the St. Lawrence and other border or interstate rivers was under federal jurisdiction, but the water power was owned by the states that controlled the riverbanks.[31]

Roosevelt spelled out his program in a special message to the legislature, delivered in person on March 12, 1929. It differed from Smith's chiefly in bypassing the existing state Public Service Commission, filled with political appointees with fixed terms, and creating a Board of Trustees, to be appointed by the governor. Roosevelt held that the state should own the dams and powerhouses in perpetuity and that, ideally, it should make arrangements with private utilities for cheap transmission of that power. In a move that he would often repeat as president, Roosevelt sent along the text of a bill that he wished the legislature to adopt. Although he did not mention it, he had consulted with experts, most notably James C. Bonbright (1892–1985), a professor of finance at Columbia and a strong advocate of public power.[32] Thus, from the beginning of his governorship, Roosevelt utilized academic experts extensively. Roosevelt used these experts not only to help shape and sometimes to testify or lobby, but also as part of his own education. His habit was to invite them to Albany to brief him, have dinner, and spend the night at the executive mansion.

Rosenman describes the procedure at some length, using a February 1929 visit by power expert Leland Olds (1890–1960) as a typical example. Joining the governor and Olds were Rosenman and Missy LeHand, sitting in for Eleanor Roosevelt as she often did. During dinner and the coffee taken separately in the governor's study, everything but electric utility rates was discussed. Only later was business done. Roosevelt began, as he liked to do, by describing people whose problems he had observed, often in and around either Hyde Park or Warm Springs. In this case, it was a real farm family living about ten miles from Hyde Park, too isolated to be able to get power from the local utility, and how this made many aspects of their daily lives more difficult. Sometimes he invented individuals to make a point, and Rosenman notes that sometimes the invented examples became real to him after a while. Harsher observers have pointed out that this was a form of lying.

After a fairly long recital, Roosevelt switched to a searching interrogation of Olds, while Rosenman took detailed notes for his speech file. A customary final question came, in this instance, after midnight: "Tell me, what would you recommend if you were Governor?" After that Roosevelt would bid his visitor "good night" and invite him to come to see him in his bedroom the next morning before leaving.[33] Those who take Roosevelt's undistinguished performance at Harvard as evidence of limited intellectual ability should consider how remarkable it was that in his late forties, he should arrange for postgraduate tutorials.

This was the way that Roosevelt preferred to get his information. On a crucial question, such as public power, he would grill a variety of experts until he felt that he had a thorough understanding of the problem and the ramifications of this or that policy. When in 1931 the legislature finally agreed to let the governor appoint a power commission, Olds was one of three outstanding authorities he named to the five-man body.[34] The larger power issues in New York State were not resolved during Roosevelt's governorship, but his fight for public power and lower rates would be a plus factor in his 1930 reelection, and public power would be a major focus of his presidency.

Most of his first-year proposals suffered a similar fate. The fact is that except for some laws to improve the lot of the state's rural population—an interest group that Smith largely ignored—about which Roosevelt and the legislative generally agreed, very few of Roosevelt's early proposals were adopted by his first legislature. His 1930 annual message repeated a number of requests that had not been acted upon.

In June 1929, he used his new clout as governor to convoke a lunch meeting at the Bankers Club to raise money for the Warm Springs Foundation. William H. Woodin (1868–1934), a Republican industrialist who was a Roosevelt supporter and adviser, served as toastmaster and assured the governor that support would come and announced the formation of a New York fund-raising committee, which he headed. That year $369,000 was raised for the foundation.

Roosevelt spoke at the lunch about his experiences at Warm Springs and about the state's limited plans for expanded health care. His remarks illustrate nicely what he then saw as the limits of public health policy. After announcing his appointments to a state commission, headed by financier Bernard M. Baruch (1870–1965), to establish state-owned Saratoga Springs as an efficient health resort, he went on to discuss how the state, in cooperation with New York City and various agencies, planned to discover how many "cripples" needed care. He estimated that there were perhaps fifty thousand who could be rehabilitated. "We have got to dig them out. . . . We believe that the great majority can with proper help be put back on their feet. But this must be done largely through private enterprise. . . . [It is] impossible to take care of this number, all we can do is send them to clinics, look them over and see what treatment is necessary."[35]

He also spent a good part of the summer of 1929 touring upstate New York by car and in a state canal boat that was adapted for his uses. That fall, during a visit to a regional fair in Atlanta, he was introduced as "the next President of the United States," and what the *Times'* stringer called "pandemonium" erupted. Obviously relishing the demonstration, Roosevelt shrugged it off. He told the crowd that while he traveled around New York that summer, at one point a crowd of two or three hundred was gathered around his car and one old man asked, "What's all the fuss about." "It's Governor Roosevelt," he was told. "Pshaw," the old man replied. "I thought it was Lindbergh." After the inevitable laugh, Roosevelt added, "Only to tell the truth, he did not say 'pshaw.'"[36]

Although Roosevelt had occasionally speculated that the Democrats might not get back into power until after some kind of economic collapse, his reactions to the first episode of that collapse, the stock market crash that began in late October 1929, were almost interchangeable with those of Herbert Hoover. The president, in a statement immediately after Black Thursday, October 24, had insisted that "the fundamental business of the country, that is the production and distribution of commodities, is on a sound and prosperous basis. The best evidence is that although production and consumption are at high levels, the average prices of commodities as a whole have not increased and there have been no appreciable increases in the stocks of manufactured goods. Moreover, there has been a tendency of wages to increase, the output per worker in many industries again shows an increase, all of which indicates a healthy condition."[37]

On November 5, in an off-the-record news conference, the president told reporters, "The sum of it is, therefore, that we have gone through a crisis in the stock market, but for the first time in history the crisis has been isolated to the stock market itself. It has not extended into either the production activities of the country or the financial fabric of the country, and for that I think we may give the major credit to the constitution of the Federal Reserve System."[38]

Roosevelt, speaking in Poughkeepsie the day after Black Thursday, condemned "a fever of old fashioned speculation" but argued that "business and political morality was improving."[39] A month later, he responded to a telegram from Hoover that was sent to all governors suggesting that they expedite spending in public works. Roosevelt promised that his first message to the legislature in January would ask for funds to build hospitals and prisons. But he added that the construction program would be limited "by estimated receipts from revenues without increasing taxation," showing that he too felt no sense of urgency.[40]

In late January, Roosevelt began to separate himself from Hoover, thanks in part to his labor commissioner, Frances Perkins. As she tells the tale, while reading the *New York Times* on the train from Albany to Manhattan, she was outraged to find a front-page story headlined "Employment Turns Upward, Hoover Reports; Changes for First Times since Stock Slump." She knew better, and as soon as she got to her office she put her statistical people to work. The following morning, she called in reporters and contradicted what the president had said. Published under headlines such as "Disputes Hoover on Employment," the story provoked immediate controversy, including telephone calls and telegrams both pro and con. The reaction, she says unconvincingly, "astonished" her.

One of the positive calls came from her boss, with whom she had not cleared the statement. "Bully for you!" he told her. "That was a fine comment and I am glad that you made it." When she apologized to him about not clearing her statement with him, he replied, "Well, I think it was better that you didn't. If you had asked me, I would probably have told you not to do it, and I think it is much more wholesome to have it right out in the open."[41] Roosevelt's style already gave trusted subordinates a long leash; it also gave him deniability.

Hoover, his secretary of labor, and various tame committees of industrial leaders such as the newly formed National Business Survey Conference all had a shot at refuting Perkins, the latter group arguing that "business had returned so far toward normal that no emergency measures are required."[42]

By early March 1930, unemployment was a growing concern not only in the United States but throughout the Western world. So-called red rallies coordinated with Communist Party rallies in New York City, Detroit, Cleveland, Pittsburgh, Boston, Milwaukee, Buffalo, New Haven, and Seattle, while in Madison there was a student riot. Philadelphia, Chicago, San Francisco, and several New Jersey cities had demonstrations without disorder. Coordinated rioting took place throughout Europe, with two deaths reported in Germany.[43] In the United States, these and subsequent demonstrations were crucial in the formation of the Communist-led Unemployed Councils, which soon mobilized hundreds of thousands at a time when the American Communist Party had perhaps ten thousand members under banners calling for "work or wages." These results forced traditional labor leadership to at least make some demands.[44]

For example, a group of largely American Federation of Labor union leaders, specifically disassociating themselves from the "antics" of the Communists, announced the formation of the Emergency Conference on Unemployment and petitioned New York's mayor for palliatives previously used: speeding up public works, free distribution of food and clothing, and free employment agencies.[45] In Washington three bills on unemployment sponsored by New York's junior senator, Robert F. Wagner, were reported out of committee. They called for steps long advocated by reformers: advanced planning for unemployment, a system of federal-state employment agencies, and the collection of more accurate data on unemployment.[46]

At the end of March, Roosevelt was ready to take limited action. He appointed Henry Bruère (1882–1958), a Progressive Era municipal reformer and officer of a savings bank who had been concerned about joblessness since the winter of 1914–15, to head a committee to coordinate public- and private-sector efforts to stem unemployment. Similar committees had been formed in previous depressions; within a year, thirty-one other states had followed New York's example.[47] Bruère's group was a coordinating and cheerleading body similar to those that would soon be created by President Hoover, but with a more realistic awareness of social conditions. Initially, it urged employers to emulate the work-spreading plans of such exponents of welfare capitalism as Cincinnati's Procter and Gamble.[48]

It is noteworthy that Roosevelt did not call for a federal role at this time or for any relief program. But his rhetoric was a far cry from Hoover's. Without directly criticizing the president, the governor insisted that the situation was "serious," as "bread lines are increasing in our great cities." "Unemployment is a problem for the entire community. It is a major social tragedy for the individual who is denied the opportunity to work and earn, but it does not stop there, and if not soon corrected will have a long-time depressive effect on business and trade in the state."[49]

Bruère's committee, initially consisting of two other businessmen and a labor leader, with Commissioner Perkins as an ex officio member, issued a preliminary report in less than a month. It stressed planning and the kinds of managerial strategies that reformers had been urging for years.[50] Its short-term suggestions for the reduction of unemployment included such palliatives as "working the full force part-time" as opposed to "working a reduced force full time," "the manufacture of stock to the limit of economic wisdom," and a dismissal wage "or at least two weeks notice."

Five days after Bruère's report, President Hoover pooh-poohed the unemployment problem in a decidedly unfunny off-the-record talk to Washington's Gridiron Club: "Not long ago it was demanded that the miseries of unemployment from speculative crashes should be cured by Government doles or unemployment insurance, yet today we see them being cured before our eyes by voluntary cooperation of industry with the Government in maintaining wages against reduction, and the intensification of construction work. Thereby, we have inaugurated one of the greatest economic experiments in history on a basis of nationwide cooperation, not of charity."[51]

Unlike the situation in 1929, when the governor had few legislative accomplishments to report, the 1930 session saw some of his important proposals enacted. Speaking in Albany after the session adjourned and in two radio talks—of a kind that would be called Fireside Chats during his presidency—he was able to list fourteen accomplishments. The two most significant were the acceptance by the legislative majority of the principle of state primacy in the development of water power and its grudging acceptance of the court decisions on the executive budget.[52] On the issue of old-age pensions, Roosevelt got only part of what he asked for. He had called for a pension system in which workers could make voluntary contributions during their working years. The legislature appointed a committee, dominated by Republicans, which passed a bill that was in some ways a continuation of the old poor law. It provided for noncontributory pensions, based on need, for persons beginning at age seventy and ranging from $5 to $50 a month. Eligibility was largely determined by local rather than state authorities. Roosevelt argued that the law was a "distinct and definite step" toward the "great purpose" of real old-age security. The assumption was that the average pension would be $232 a year, less than 70 cents a day.[53]

With the legislature adjourned, Roosevelt and his team turned overtly toward the twin goals that appeared increasingly attainable: winning reelection in November and becoming the front-runner for the Democratic presidential nomination in 1932. A resounding victory in the election was necessary for there to be a realistic chance at a dominant preconvention position. Even before he finished dealing with the 750 bills that the legislature passed—he had a month to do so— Roosevelt spoke on a radio hookup to thirty Jefferson Day luncheons across the nation. His basic theme was that Jefferson and the Democratic Party were for majority rule, while Republicans were not. Without a specific reference to current issues, he assured his listeners that Democrats were waging "an age old conflict for the square deal for the average man and woman" and that they "were on the side of right and right would prevail."[54] The April issue of the Catholic publication *Commonweal*, taking his reelection as given, predicted his nomination for president in 1932 for a variety of reasons, including his presumed opposition to the "centralization of government."[55] More politically potent was an endorsement that came at New York's Jefferson Day dinner at the end of April. Roosevelt spoke early in the proceedings and attacked the concentration of wealth and corporate power in general terms, but he ignored deteriorating economic conditions. He left after speaking, pleading fatigue.[56] Apparently, he learned at the eleventh hour that his nomination for president was going to be proposed at the dinner and, following contemporary custom, left the premises for that reason.

The "nominator" was Burton K. Wheeler (1882–1975), a fiery Montana Democrat who served in the Senate from 1923 to 1947 and had been Robert La Follette's vice presidential running mate on the Progressive ticket in 1924. Wheeler told the New Yorkers that if they reelected Roosevelt governor, "the West will demand his nomination for President and the whole country will elect him." He gave as his reasons the governor's stands on the tariff and public power. Wheeler later wrote that when he returned to Washington, Jouett Shouse (1879–1968), whom Raskob had made chairman of the Democratic National Committee, and others complained that he had "upset the applecart." They were planning to nominate a liberal industrialist such as Owen D. Young or Myron C. Taylor.[57]

A few days later, just before leaving to spend most of May in Warm Springs, Roosevelt used a routine communication from Secretary of Commerce Robert P. Lamont to challenge, personally, the Hoover administration's continued downplaying of the unemployment situation. Lamont had been sending monthly queries to governors, asking them to report on unemployment in their state. Roosevelt, as he had done before, sent a serious answer but chose to make it public. After insisting that there was no way to answer the question adequately "on the basis of present information," he insisted that "it is safe to say that there is now more than usual unemployment [and that] such unemployment has increased rather than decreased since the middle of January. . . . The index of factory employment has declined steadily since October 1929, and is now at its lowest point since the series was begun in June, 1914."[58]

Roosevelt came back from his month at Warm Springs primed for national politics. Fortuitously, the 1930 governors' conference was in the West, where Roosevelt was presumably strong, and he prepared to open his campaign for the presidency there, though he would not admit it. Since he had boned up on unemployment and had followed the work of Bruère's committee closely, he arranged with the meeting's organizer to open the conference with a speech on that topic.[59]

Probably tipped off by Louis Howe that Roosevelt would make real news at the conference, *New York Times* Albany correspondent A. J. (Baron) Warn, who had written the paper's first profile of Roosevelt back in 1911, joined the governor and his party. They left Albany in a private railroad car for the ten-day round-trip. Roosevelt made his strategy clear to Warn, whose first story, filed from Syracuse, began, "The unemployment problem . . ." The second story, filed from Missouri, made a point of noting that Roosevelt "walked" from one train platform to another in St. Louis.

In Salt Lake City, Roosevelt got an unexpected accolade when its Republican mayor in his welcoming remarks noted that one of the twenty-eight governors present, if elected, "might make one of the great presidents of the United States." Most assumed that he meant Roosevelt, which the mayor later confirmed. Roosevelt's unemployment speech called for a system of unemployment insurance and for old-age pensions, but he treated these as state rather than federal problems. He made no direct mention of Hoover but did criticize attempts by "government officials and leading financiers" to "juggle figures" and "distort facts" about the nature and extent of unemployment.

The contrast between the governor and the president was thrown into focus that evening when the delegates listened to a radio greeting by Hoover. He thanked the governors for their cooperation with his program of accelerating public works to combat unemployment and claimed that its success was an event "of the first importance."[60] Later in the conference, Roosevelt, who often in these years took a states' rights position on certain issues, joined the western governors in criticizing the federal government's "invasion" of state prerogatives by barring the products of prison labor from interstate commerce.

The notion that Roosevelt's first term as governor was "the genesis of the New Deal," put forth by Sam Rosenman and others, is unconvincing.[61] As late as May 1930, he could write in a personal letter that "it would be misunderstood if I were to tell the public that I regard the present business slump as a great blessing," but it might cause the "average citizen" to think about "fundamental principles."[62] The Roosevelt of mid-1930 was, in essence, still a progressive reformer with what now seem parochial horizons. At the trip's end, Warn filed a long wrap-up piece hailing Roosevelt as a future presidential candidate with strong western support.[63]

Given his presidential ambitions, Roosevelt needed more than just success in his reelection bid; he needed to win big. Although we think of him now as a champion campaigner, in mid-1930 his won-lost record was only three and two, and each of his three wins had been close. He repeatedly used his official position to campaign without seeming to do so, again spending much of the summer making inspection trips, often aboard the glass-roofed *Inspector,* a state vessel refitted for his special needs, which cruised at less than ten miles an hour.

Roosevelt, clearly the favorite, wanted the campaign to stress his record as an able and attractive governor noted for his advanced progressive reforms. He understood that his "damp" views on Prohibition were becoming more and more popular and that the issue would cause the Republicans real problems. Republicans wanted to embroil him in the growing scandals involving Tammany graft in New York City, which, under the popular but venal mayor Jimmy Walker, were a continuing embarrassment to reform-minded Tammanyites like Smith and Wagner. Roosevelt, despite his deserved reputation as a reformer, needed Tammany support in the city to achieve the majorities he wanted.

The Republicans constantly sought to exploit this chink in the governor's electoral armor. The legislature passed a bill requiring him to appoint a commission to investigate corruption in the city. Roosevelt's veto called it "a pity, for the sake of orderly government," that the legislature was trying "to foist upon the Governor . . . [a] new and unheard of function": supervising an investigation of "the [city's] vast governmental machinery." He described his constitutional duties to investigate formal and specific charges and gave four recent instances in which he had done so. He invited the legislature to conduct its own investigation, a suggestion he knew would be ignored.[64] That round went to Roosevelt, but the problem of Tammany would continue to plague him well into 1932. To point up this issue, the Republicans chose Charles H. Tuttle (1880–1971), the U.S. attorney for the southern district of New York, to run against Roosevelt. His successful prosecutions of political and judicial corruption made him a logical choice. But there was little enthusiasm in the state Republican camp: shortly after Wheeler's speech had set off a "Roosevelt Boom," some GOP leaders were reportedly already doubting that their party could recapture the governor's chair in 1932 if Roosevelt was a presidential nominee that year.

As the summer progressed and the long slide into depression continued, 1930 looked more and more like a Democratic year. Even before his informal acceptance speech to the state convention at the end of September, Roosevelt demonstrated that he was in charge. Unlike his passive role in 1928, he dominated every aspect of the convention and ensuing campaign. Three weeks before the convention opened, he sent a public letter to Senator Wagner, setting forth the matters that should be stressed: "the serious unemployment situation," what his administration had done in terms of "social welfare," the "great strides" made to control water power and utility rates, the "notable achievements in farm relief," and the first measures for "old age security." All this progress, he claimed, was made despite the "determined opposition" of Republican leaders. (Actually, Republicans had generally supported his farm relief program, if nothing else.)

The real news in the letter was Roosevelt's direct attack on Prohibition. He told Wagner that people should no longer "beat around the bush"—a phrase that describes his own previous "damp" positions quite well—but that the Eighteenth Amendment itself should be repealed and the resulting amendment should "restore the real control of liquor to the states." Thus, Roosevelt, and subsequently the state Democratic platform, avoided being "dripping wet": that position, held by Raskob and many longtime opponents of Prohibition, was that Prohibition and other sumptuary laws were infringements on personal liberty. The letter ignored the issue of Tammany corruption.[65]

Waiting in the wings while Al Smith and Caroline O'Day (1875–1943) made spirited nominating speeches, and with his mother, wife, and daughter on the stage, the governor was renominated by acclamation. His appearance was greeted by a cry of "Three cheers for the next President of the United States." His reference, in his brief informal acceptance speech, to "these dark hours of 'Republican Prosperity'" made it clear that the Depression would be a major issue in the campaign.[66] His control of the party machinery was solidified by the elevation of James A. Farley (1888–1976) from secretary to chair of the Democratic state committee. (Roosevelt would have preferred Bronx boss Flynn, who turned it down.) Farley, a Rockland County businessman, had been secretary of the committee and in 1928 had done impressive work in organizing the upstate Democratic vote for Roosevelt. Although he and Roosevelt were never personally close—Farley would complain bitterly in his second memoir about repeated slights—he ran the reelection campaign and remained an important cog in the Democratic political machinery until he broke with Roosevelt over the third-term issue in 1940.[67]

Formally accepting the nomination four days later in Manhattan, the governor devoted most of his speech to a review of the accomplishments of his administration and belittling the corruption charges of his opponent without mentioning his name. In his closing remarks, he attacked "the lack of leadership in Washington," which had resulted in "unemployment and financial depression." But he concluded that "each state must meet this situation as best it can."[68]

The degree to which Roosevelt actually believed in October 1930 that state as opposed to federal policy was chiefly responsible for economic health is impossible to measure. But the claim that Roosevelt was in 1930 an incipient New Dealer, ready to reverse almost a century and a half of state primacy, is difficult if not impossible to demonstrate from anything he had done or said up to that time.

For the next two weeks, Roosevelt remained in Albany, working on the executive budget for the coming year. During that time, he made three separate radio "reports to the people" that served as campaign speeches and granted a filmed interview at his desk in Albany, shown by Movietone news in theaters through the state as the campaign began.[69]

Until the last day of campaigning, Roosevelt ignored Tuttle and the Republican message of corruption: instead, he systematically cataloged his administration's record while spicing his talks with comments on the Depression and the failings of national leadership in Washington. Tuttle, the former prosecutor, spent almost all of his time on corruption in New York City and Roosevelt's failure to do anything about it. In addition, the Hoover administration sent three high-ranking officials—Secretary of State Henry L. Stimson, Secretary of War Patrick J. Hurley (1882–1963), and Undersecretary of the Treasury Ogden L. Mills—to buttress Tuttle's weak campaign. Many liberal commentators, such as Walter Lippmann, also criticized Roosevelt's failure to discuss the corruption charges. Roosevelt explained to Rosenman that one should "never let your opponent pick the battleground on which to fight. If he picks one, stay out of it and let him fight all by himself." In addition, Roosevelt's carefully nurtured image as an anti-Tammany Democrat stood him in good stead with the voters.

Roosevelt saved corruption and the stumping Republicans for the last speech. Toward its end, before five thousand partisans in Carnegie Hall, he first focused on Hurley, an Oklahoman, and claimed that New Yorkers resented this federal interference in their affairs, "as would the people of Oklahoma if the tables were turned."

Stimson and Mills, however, were both New Yorkers. Roosevelt pointed out that their credentials were, in one sense, identical: each had previously run for governor, and each had been "*defeated* by the people of this state." Then, in a series of paragraphs beginning "They tell the 12,000,000 people of this state . . . ," he derided their message and ended by telling them to "return to your posts in Washington, and bend your efforts" to solving the nation's problems. Only then did he respond to the corruption charges, insisting, as he had done before the campaign, that he had acted on any formal charges and that any official proven corrupt would be removed. Roosevelt's formal request to the appellate court, which under New York law had the sole power to remove magistrates, resulted in the court's appointment of Samuel Seabury (1873–1958)—whom Roosevelt had privately suggested—as a referee to investigate charges of corruption against certain Tammany-appointed judges. This began a chain of events that drove Tammany from power.[70]

In the event, Roosevelt carried the state by a record 725,000 votes, almost double Al Smith's best showing. One reason was his strength outside of New York City: he actually carried upstate New York with a plurality of 167,000 votes, winning forty-three of fifty-seven upstate counties. This astonishing result was due not just to Roosevelt's attractiveness and Tuttle's inept campaign. A Prohibition ticket garnered more than 180,000 votes. Had they been cast for Tuttle, he would have had a narrow win upstate. In addition, many thousands of upstate Republicans simply stayed home. It is also clear that thousands of normally Republican voters went for Roosevelt.

*　*　*

On election eve, speaking to the voters of his home county in Poughkeepsie, the governor was humble. He reminisced about his first election, twenty years before, as a "green" politician, and claimed that "little did I dream" of victory in this "Republican senatorial district. . . . Nor did it, of course, enter my head that I would be called on to be Governor."[71] We know, of course, that hopes and dreams of the White House had been in his mind for at least a quarter century.

5 Winning the White House
1931–32

THE 1930 ELECTION WAS NOT JUST A VICTORY for Roosevelt; by the time the new Congress met in December 1931, the Democrats had taken control of the House of Representatives, 220 to 214, and while the Senate remained Republican by the narrowest of margins, the presence of a potent bloc of progressive Republicans meant that the Hoover administration had lost effective control of Congress. The two previous such changes of control, in 1910 and 1918, had each presaged a change of party in the White House two years later. Unlike Roosevelt's success, which was chiefly due to his record and the lackluster opposition, the gain by Democrats nationally was largely due to the increasing seriousness of the Depression, though business leaders and much of the nation's press remained in denial. Only during the winter of 1930–31 did a general awareness develop that what was happening to the nation's economy was far beyond a normal business-cycle downturn.

In Washington President Hoover's postelection "press conference" was limited to a two-sentence statement: "I have a number of inquiries from you gentlemen upon contentious questions, but the job for the country to concentrate on now is further measures of cooperation for economic recovery. And that is the only suggestion I have for you on this occasion."[1] In Albany, where the governor's return was greeted by a cheering throng of five thousand despite a heavy rainstorm, a spokesman made the traditional disclaimer that the governor "would stick close to his job . . . and avoid any thought of 1932." When Albany reporters found out that Jim Farley had bragged in a Manhattan press conference that he "did not see how Mr. Roosevelt can escape becoming the next presidential nominee . . . even if no one should raise a finger to bring it about," they asked the governor about it. Roosevelt wrote out before them a statement that he was giving "no consideration . . . to any candidacy . . . in 1932." But no serious observer believed either Farley's hyperbole or Roosevelt's denial, and neither man expected to be believed.[2] Capturing the White House in 1932, which had seemed an impossible dream even to a romantic realist like Louis Howe, now seemed within grasp. Despite Will Rogers's postelection-day quip that "the Democrats nominated their President yesterday, Franklin D. Roosevelt," Howe and his boss knew that even winning their party's endorsement, which required collecting the votes of two-thirds of the delegates, would involve many difficulties.[3]

Behind the scenes, Howe was setting up a letter-writing operation from offices on Madison Avenue, with funds supplied by Ed Flynn and others. As opposed to the gigantic war chests politicians need today, Flynn acknowledged fifteen persons in his memoirs, including himself and the candidate's mother, who gave as much as two thousand dollars to the preconvention war chest.[4] From both New York and Albany, a barrage of letters went out to Democratic leaders and to editors of all persuasions across the country, while Howe kept an eye on what the Democratic National Committee and other potential intraparty rivals were doing.

Before leaving for Warm Springs, Roosevelt received the report of Henry Bruère's committee on unemployment, accepted its palliatives as if they were a solution, and asked the legislature to continue its existence as an "Emergency Commission" to coordinate reemployment efforts "until the emergency is abated." He promised to ask the legislature to fund the future work of the committee—whose expenses had been paid by its members—and to establish "loan funds" for the unemployed, "if they are set up on a sound basis with the participation of banking and business interests."[5] He also offered the state's armories as shelters for the "homeless unemployed" and sent a letter to mayors throughout the state, telling them to report to him when their resources for the homeless had been exhausted.[6] Instead of a call to action, he announced a conference on unemployment with six other governors of industrial states to be held in January.[7] Speaking to the annual convention of the National Grange in Rochester, he went so far as to predict that in the near future, farmers' mutual cooperation and enlightened state policies "would lift agriculture to the splendid level it used to have."[8]

Although it is easy to be dismayed by the inadequacy of Roosevelt's responses, it is important to remember what low levels of expectation about social legislation prevailed even in an advanced state such as New York. When Abraham Epstein (1892–1942), a major figure in the long battle for old-age security, successfully urged a conference to recommend that New York drop the age limit in its newly established pensions for the needy to age sixty-five from seventy, Roosevelt ignored it.[9] The governor may have been aware of the need for decisive action to stem the ever-worsening unemployment crisis and the endemic problems of American agriculture, but nothing he did or said publicly in 1930 can be cited to support that possibility.

Although the failure of two independent New York City banks—the Bank of the United States (BUS) on December 11, 1930, and the Chelsea Bank and Trust Company twelve days later—were ominous signs, the governor's brief second inaugural made no mention of economic matters. The views expressed are not those of an ebullient New Dealer in embryo but of a somewhat grumpy progressive. Most startling, in view of his expansion of federal power as president, is the following passage: "Let us get this picture clearly before us. We have three main branches of government: first, the Federal, operating, at least in theory in the national field and in accordance with strictly limited powers of control ceded to it by the sovereign states. . . . When States become indifferent to their duties, the natural tendency is for the national government to grasp for more power."[10]

Roosevelt followed his own precepts when reacting to the failure of the BUS. At the time, it was the largest such failure in American history: some 450,000 depositors lost access to $200 million in deposits; the average account had about $450. Founded as a bank run by and for Jewish immigrants in 1914—Wall Streeters sneered at the "pants presser's bank"—it grew spectacularly in the 1920s and had fifty-seven branches. Like the City Trust Company, a similar but much smaller bank that catered to Italian immigrants, and had failed before the crash in early 1929, the BUS shutdown involved not just mismanagement but criminal fraud. The City Trust fraud was committed with the complicity of Al Smith's superintendent of banks, who eventually went to jail. In Roosevelt's absence, Acting Governor Lehman, himself a banker, appointed Robert Moses to investigate. Moses's able report recommended needed reforms, but it was ignored by Roosevelt and the legislature and opposed by the banking community. Over the years, Roosevelt has been sharply and properly criticized over this misfeasance, but few critics have recognized the woeful lack of leadership in the banking community itself.

In the Wall Street panic of 1907, the elder J. P. Morgan (1837–1913) had assembled the city's solvent bankers in the huge library of his midtown Manhattan residence and eventually assessed each a prorated fee calculated by him to bail out endangered banks.[11] His son, also J. P. Morgan (1867–1943), was no such leader: though Roosevelt and Lehman had met secretly with representatives of the major New York banks in an effort to get them to save the BUS, the big bankers eventually refused to act. As for Roosevelt, it is important to remember that he was not only a Wall Street lawyer but also a member of New York's Bankers Club, who, like the rarely criticized Lehman, took the conventional wisdom of the banking community at its inflated face value. Roosevelt did urge the Manhattan district attorney to "prosecute vigorously": top BUS leaders were sent to jail.[12]

In his annual legislative message, Roosevelt spoke neither of depression nor of Hoover's "further . . . economic recovery," but rather talked of "a decline in prosperity." He assured the legislators accurately that the state's finances were "in good condition" and claimed falsely that "we have done and are doing all within our power to relieve the emergency and to build against the future." He did propose continued initiatives that the Republican majority would largely ignore: the adoption of "insurance [based on] a system of contributions commencing at an early age" so that "all men and women will . . . be assured . . . enough income to maintain life . . . in accordance with the American standard of living." As opposed to this almost utopian proposal—remember that the new means-test pension law just taking effect provided the average pensioner just seventy cents a day—his agenda for labor was to call for measures previously submitted by Al Smith and himself.

Four paragraphs on unemployment stressed the "present abnormal situation," but despite the steadily rising numbers of unemployed, he insisted that New York was "doing and will do what it can in the way of emergency relief" and asked only that Bruère's committee be funded. He did speak of his coming conference, noting that he would submit any worthwhile recommendations the conference might make.[13]

That gathering, held in Albany on January 23–24, predictably produced no worthwhile recommendations, but it was remarkable in two ways. First, it was more like an academic seminar than a political gathering. To brief the six visiting governors and their representatives, Perkins had brought in a stellar cast of progressive economists and experts, including Paul H. Douglas, William Leiserson, Bryce M. Stewart, and Leo Wolman.[14] Douglas (1892–1976), secretary of Bruère's commission, had been recruited to bring Roosevelt up to speed on unemployment insurance, which was the major subtopic. He reported in his memoir that he had converted Roosevelt to support it. Second, when pickets from the communist Trade Union Unity League showed up outside the executive mansion, Roosevelt sent them an invitation to appear before the conferees. Their demands, presented by two delegates, were practical: they wanted cash relief and an end to evictions. Roosevelt replied that the state constitution did not allow such payments.[15] None of the other governors was yet prepared to endorse unemployment insurance, or anything else.

It is not clear what Roosevelt expected from the conference, but I believe that if other governors had agreed to support unemployment insurance, he would have recommended such a measure to the legislature. Rather than go out on a limb alone, he recommended only that the legislature create a commission to investigate the problem and to report during the 1932 session on "a plan for accomplishing some kind of scientific unemployment insurance," which it did while refusing to fund the Bruère committee.[16] Nothing the governor asked for would have put a single person back to work or provided aid to any of the hundreds of thousands of New Yorkers then unemployed through "no fault of their own." Unemployment insurance was an idea whose time had not quite come. Wisconsin would enact the nation's first state unemployment insurance law in January 1932.

In the spring of 1931, Roosevelt was not prepared to propose anything significant to help the jobless. In his now traditional post-legislative-session radio address to the people, he mentioned the governor's conference as if it were an accomplishment. The states' study of unemployment insurance, he said, would produce "something safe and sound . . . so that in the event in the days to come we pass through another period of depression like this one, the real suffering and the real want . . . will not be nearly as serious as the period we are now going through."[17]

In a ceremonial address of little substance at a dinner celebrating the centennial of New York University's charter, the governor used an academic metaphor that was revealing of both his self-confidence and the way in which he wished to be perceived. Describing the just-ended legislative session, he called himself a professor who had just graded the 1,120 examination papers of 201 students and had failed—that is, vetoed—about a third of them. He would often use similar metaphors. I do not think that he ever described himself as a politician in a public address.[18]

At the end of April, a cable and a transatlantic telephone call from Paris informed Roosevelt that his seventy-six-year-old mother had been stricken with influenza and hospitalized. He sailed aboard the Cunard liner *Aquitania* with only his son Elliott on May 6 and arrived in Paris a week later. Finding his mother convalescing nicely, he sailed back on the North German Lloyd liner *Bremen,* arriving home three weeks after he left. It would be his last trip to western Europe.

A fellow passenger, Charles G. Dawes (1865–1951), the Chicago banker who had been Coolidge's vice president and was then the American ambassador in London, who dined with Roosevelt twice in the governor's stateroom, wrote in his journal, "Roosevelt is only 49 years of age. . . . I feel that if he is the next President of the United States, he will serve with honor to his country and credit to himself. He seems to have strength and equipoise, clarity of mind with soundness of judgment, and to steer his course by the compass of common sense."[19]

Four days after landing, Roosevelt was in French Lick, Indiana, for the annual Governors' Conference. Roosevelt's speech there served his political purposes, but offered little that was new. The blunt postconference headline—"Not Much Was Done at Indiana Meeting"—was accurate, but the gathering served Roosevelt's political purposes quite well. The New Yorker likened the state of the nation to a fleet of forty-eight ships with serious navigational problems, but he had no national solutions. His address concentrating on his state's agricultural and land-utilization policies was well designed to appeal to midwestern leaders. In his conclusion, he called for "national planning," but planning done not in the nation's capital but in forty-eight separate laboratories. What he required from the national government was that it be "an information gathering body" and "act as a clearing house for all of us Governors to work through and I think that is [its] correct and most useful function . . . instead of trying to run the whole works."[20] This message of decentralized reform was calculated to appeal to those elements in the Democratic Party who adhered to states' rights; it was not a sailing direction to the New Deal.

Despite his public words persistently denying a key role for the federal government, there is evidence that Roosevelt's private thoughts entertained other possibilities. But given what we know about his thought processes, we can surmise that the late-August plan to create the nation's first statewide relief program had a long gestation period.

While a few other leaders, such as Pennsylvania's Republican governor, Gifford Pinchot (1865–1946), and Detroit's mayor, Frank Murphy (1890–1949), agitated for various action to aid the unemployed, Roosevelt, who had said virtually nothing about unemployment, seemed preoccupied with both his still unannounced but active campaign for the presidential nomination and the revelations and repercussions of the ever-widening Seabury investigations of Tammany. After the legislative committee investigating Tammany corruption headed by Senator Samuel H. Hofstadter, a silk-stocking Republican from Manhattan, was stymied by a court decision denying it the right to grant immunity to witnesses without statutory approval, it formally requested the governor to call a special session to enact such legislation. Roosevelt promptly acceded, despite the disgust of some Tammany diehards.[21]

Roosevelt sought to appear as the fair, impartial arbiter independent voters demanded, yet not offend Tammany by leading a crusade against it, as some reformers and their journalist allies demanded. He needed Tammany support to ensure large majorities in New York City, as he would need the support of other urban political machines as president.[22]

New York law restricted a special session to acting only on matters that the governor brought to its attention. Roosevelt let it be known that he would sign the immunity bills that Seabury was to draft, and it was assumed to be a done deal and would be the only business of the session.[23] But Rosenman relates that as soon as he called the special session, the governor summoned him to Hyde Park, telling him, "This is the time to get some direct action on unemployment relief. Suppose you take a try at a first draft of such a message." Rosenman knew that Roosevelt was opposed to the payment of money by dole, as was done in Great Britain and which was the bugaboo of those opposed to relief.[24] President Hoover and his supporters repeatedly inveighed against the dole, as did Roosevelt, both as governor and as president. But Hoover used the term to denigrate not only unemployment insurance but any kind of direct relief, while Roosevelt supported unemployment insurance and differentiated sharply between work relief and merely handing out money.

Roosevelt's opening message called for legislation giving the Hofstadter committee the power to grant immunity. Two days later, the governor sent a second message, requesting investigations of a number of upstate communities, which everyone knew that the Republicans would reject. Only then did Roosevelt let it be known that a request for a large-scale state relief program was on the way.[25]

That message came the next day, August 28: it is the first evidence, it seems to me, that Roosevelt was something more than an advanced progressive. Delivering it in person, he began with a philosophical statement, arguing that "the duty of the State toward the citizen is the duty of the servant to its master. . . . One of these duties . . . is that of caring for those of its citizens who find themselves . . . unable to obtain even the necessities for mere existence without the aid of others." He then described the levels of suffering that large numbers of New York's thirteen million residents faced in what would be the third winter of the Great Depression and the obvious inability of either municipal relief or private charity to meet their needs. Noting that "it is true" that the federal government might come up with an effective program or programs, the governor insisted that "the State of New York cannot wait for that [but] must itself make available at once a large sum of public moneys to provide work for its residents." He called for the creation of an emergency three-person commission, the Temporary Emergency Relief Administration, to oversee the distribution of twenty million dollars. TERA's initial mandate to May 31, 1932, established that no money would be paid in the form of a dole, that relief would be restricted to persons with at least two years' residence in the state, and that no employment or relief would be given except in accordance with rules and regulations that TERA would set. To demonstrate his conservative tendencies, Roosevelt proposed a pay-as-you-go device by roughly doubling the existing steeply graduated New York State income tax rates, in a manner calculated to raise the twenty million dollars. Because only some three hundred thousand tax returns had been filed in 1931, this would affect only a tiny portion of the state's 12.6 million people. Single persons and families of four would pay additional taxes according to the following table:[26]

New York State income tax, 1932

Income	Additional tax	
	Single person	Family of four
$3,000	$2.50	no tax
$5,000	$12.50	$1
$10,000	$37.50	$26
$20,000	$125.00	$102
$100,000	$1,162.50	$1,128

Source: GPA, 1931, 178.

To no one's surprise, the Republican majority, while praising the purpose, refused to go along and called for a different kind of bill. The Socialists, who were no longer represented in the legislature, insisted that the amount was not nearly enough.[27]

After the recess, the Republicans introduced bills providing for a relief program located in the existing state welfare department, legislative control of the appointed commissioners, funding by a bond issue, and more control by local governments. They intended to pass the bills and adjourn. Roosevelt made it clear that he would not only veto the bills but also immediately call the legislature back into another special session. This latter was a serious threat, because it was clear that there was a need for more relief funds and that Roosevelt's radio talks and public appearances explaining and pushing for his version of relief had been effective. That and the fact that an election loomed in November (New York still elected its assembly and half of its senate every year) were factors the politicians had to consider. Finally, on September 19, the Republicans caved in and in essence gave the governor what he had asked for. From the beginning of the controversy, Roosevelt had insisted that he had an open mind on the topic, but it is clear that he was determined not to make significant concessions.[28] He stipulated, even before he signed the bill, that in addition to the pick-and-shovel type of labor, there would be clerical tasks available for older white-collar unemployed.[29]

The victory over the legislature demonstrated Roosevelt's increasing political savvy. He and Lehman put together a balanced—for New York—group of three high-minded citizens to oversee TERA. The chairman was Jesse I. Straus (1872–1936), a Jew, president of Macy's (the world's largest department store), an active Harvard overseer, and a lifelong Democrat. His two colleagues were John Sullivan (1870–19??), an Irish-born former streetcar conductor and a Catholic who was president of the state AFL, and Philip J. Wickser (1887–1949), scion of a prominent Protestant Buffalo family, a Republican lawyer, and spokesman for the insurance industry whose activities included pro bono service with the National Urban League, an African American organization.[30] Eight days later, Chairman Straus announced the appointment of Harry L. Hopkins (1890–1946) as his executive director. Roosevelt played no part in this fateful appointment of the man who, apart from his wife, would become his most important political associate.[31]

A lanky Iowan who had followed his older sister into New York social work immediately after his 1912 graduation from Grinnell College, Hopkins is usually described as a social worker. But by 1931, he was managing director of the New York Tuberculosis and Health Association and the second-highest-paid social work executive in the country. He ran TERA from the beginning and in April 1932 became its third chairman.[32]

Roosevelt got the 1932 legislature to add $5 million more for relief, extend TERA's life until November 15, 1932, and authorize a $30 million bond issue that was successively extended into 1937. During its life, the agency disbursed about $739 million, of which some $503 million came from the federal government. These funds first came in the Hoover administration as a result of the Emergency Relief and Construction Act of 1932 and then from various New Deal relief acts.[33] And, obviously, TERA became a kind of model for all of the federal work relief once the New Deal got under way, from the CCC through the Works Progress Administration (WPA).

In mid-1931, Roosevelt's still undeclared presidential campaign picked up steam. He dispatched Jim Farley on a nineteen-day delegate-hunting expedition to Seattle and back.[34] Roosevelt's front-runner status was clear, but the continuing disaffection of Al Smith remained the chief cloud on the delegate horizon. Although Smith had publicly said never again in 1928, now that it seemed likely that any Democratic candidate could defeat Hoover, Smith's presidential ambitions again surfaced. Encouraged by Belle Moskowitz and his daughter, Emily, he began to believe that the party owed him a second presidential nomination. In mid-October 1931, he attended a Tammany Hall rally at which he was hailed as the "next president."[35] He, John J. Raskob, and Democratic National chairman Jouett Shouse began to organize a stop-Roosevelt coalition within the party.

Roosevelt formally announced his candidacy on January 22, 1932, in replying to a letter from the chairman of the North Dakota Democratic Party asking permission to place his name on the state's March 15 presidential primary ballot, as state law required. Roosevelt, in a letter of seven paragraphs, pretended that he was following the path of "simple duty of every American to serve."[36] In 1932 presidential candidates did not campaign in person in the relatively few state primaries, even important ones like California's.

Just over two weeks later, Smith issued a three-paragraph statement affirming his willingness to run if nominated. But he claimed that he would "not make a pre-convention campaign for delegates" and insisted that he would not "in advance of the convention either support or oppose" any candidate.[37]

Nevertheless, he soon entered primaries and won delegates. The long-submerged struggle between Smith and Roosevelt was now overt. Given the human tendency to believe what one wants to believe, a failing to which politicians are particularly vulnerable, Smith may well have believed that he had a good chance to get the nomination, but few astute persons outside of his entourage thought so. There were simply too many leaders and delegates, some of them Roman Catholics, unwilling to risk a repetition of the 1928 defeat. What the Smith candidacy did was to make Roosevelt's nomination more difficult, and we can now see that the July nomination was a much riskier struggle than the November election.

As Roosevelt's attention would focus on the national scene in 1932, this is a good place to assess his performance as governor. For his virtues, it is hard to improve upon the 1963 judgment made by historian Allan Nevins, who witnessed it as a New York City journalist. After describing Al Smith's accomplishments, Nevins wrote:

> Roosevelt showed greater social vision and thrust, a special skill in appealing to the plain man, whether farmer or urban dweller, and striking ability to out-maneuver Republican leaders of the legislature. In a long battle with the finance committees of the two houses, he finally vindicated his special powers over the state budget. He was ceaselessly busy; [although often] absent from the state, he spent most of his time there and even when away gave hard study to its problems. Not only did he have a hundred ideas, on tax relief, on old-age insurance, on state development of St. Lawrence water power, on farm betterment, on schools, but he knew how to drive them home to the public consciousness.[38]

To those positives should be added that Roosevelt, with the help of his wife and such devoted and effective organizers as Molly Dewson (1874–1962), was in the forefront of contemporary national politicians who understood how to appeal to women. And, like his cousin Theodore, he had demonstrated that he was a champion of the environment.[39]

At the other extreme, Nevins's former journalistic colleague Walter Lippmann wrote the most famous—and perhaps the most fatuous—prepresidential criticism of Roosevelt, dismissing him in January 1932 as "a highly impressionable person, without a firm grasp of public affairs . . . a pleasant man who, without any important qualifications for the office, would very much like to be President."[40]

More reasonable criticisms of Roosevelt's two gubernatorial terms should note his slowness to understand that the post-1929 downturn was not a mere crack in the economic system but a deep chasm. Only in January 1932 did he invoke what William Leuchtenburg has called the "analogue of war," arguing that not since the Civil War "have the people of this State and of this Nation faced problems as grave, situations as difficult, suffering as severe."[41]

Even as he recognized the seriousness of the situation, the measures he proposed in 1932, apart from the extension of TERA and the bond issue that stretched it further, were not at all of an emergency nature. Among his contemporaries, Senator Robert F. Wagner saw the seriousness of the Depression earlier and proposed sounder remedies some two years before. Nor can one find a recognition by Roosevelt that his state's four hundred thousand black citizens might have some special problems—but this could be noted about almost any mainstream American politician of the time.

That said, most seasoned political observers saw him as a credible candidate with solid leadership credentials, as well or better qualified for the presidency than any of the other aspirants. And, of course, there was the magic of the Roosevelt name. Along with his prominence as New York's governor and the continuous public relations campaign that he and Howe had conducted, it made him a front-runner long before he declared his candidacy.

As Roosevelt announced his candidacy, Farley publicly claimed 678 delegate votes, fewer than 100 shy of the 770 votes necessary for nomination.[42] Smith's candidacy, which by itself probably could not attract enough delegates to block Roosevelt, inspired a number of favorite-son candidates, most of whom had no hope of gaining the nomination, but whose votes at the convention might be worth something. The most important of these was Texan John Nance Garner (1868–1967). A small-town banker first elected to Congress in 1903, Garner became, through seniority and diligence, minority leader in 1929 and speaker of the House in 1931. Garner had no illusions about the likelihood of his gaining the nomination.[43]

Even before the Smith and Garner candidacies had materialized, but after he had been attacked by the Hearst papers for his support of the League of Nations, Roosevelt abandoned his long-standing support for the league. In a brief Albany talk to the New York State Grange on February 2, after calling for reciprocal tariff reduction as a way to export more farm products, he assured his listeners that this need not "involve the United States in any participation in political controversies in Europe or elsewhere." After recounting his previous support for American membership in the league, he said, "If today I believed that the same or even similar factors entered into the argument, I would still favor America's entry into the League; and I would go so far as to seek to win over the overwhelming opposition which exists in this country today."

But after noting that the present-day League of Nations was "not the League conceived by Woodrow Wilson," and summarizing some of its failings, he announced that "I do not favor American participation."[44] This apostasy served its purpose as a sop to Cerberus: Hearst's attacks ceased. But it not only disturbed some Wilsonians, such as Colonel Edward M. House, but disappointed Eleanor and many of his supporters. Yet it was probably reassuring to most of the few voters who paid attention to such matters: in 1932 foreign policy was not a major issue.

Some historians have argued that Roosevelt went through an isolationist phase in the later 1920s and most of the 1930s. Prominent among them is Robert A. Divine, who titled the first of his 1968 Albert Shaw lectures "Roosevelt the Isolationist."[45] The most cosmopolitan American president since John Quincy Adams, Roosevelt was never an isolationist. And from the time of his conversations with Wilson aboard the *George Washington,* he was a devoted Wilsonian who, as president, endeavored to avoid Wilson's mistakes while adhering to his chief's purposes as he understood them.

Sometime in March 1932, as Sam Rosenman tells the story, he mentioned to his boss one evening that they needed to develop a way to get all the necessary speeches on national topics written during the coming campaign. Roosevelt was immediately interested. "It was easy to tell when he was listening out of politeness and when he really wanted to listen. There was always something about the eyes, about the tilt of the head, the outthrust of the jaw, that seemed to say, 'Go ahead, I'm listening.'"

What his counsel proposed and he quickly accepted was to set up a panel of experts whom they could call upon for speeches, memoranda, and other written documents. Varying groups or even individual advisers would meet with and without Roosevelt to draft or redraft public papers. Thus was born what Roosevelt privately called his "Privy Council" but the press soon christened the "Brains Trust."[46]

Rosenman's proposition seems like an expansion of the use of intellectuals, such as Bonbright, Olds, and Douglas, who had counseled Roosevelt on electric power and unemployment, but the two chief brain trusters, Columbia University professors Raymond Moley (1886–1975) and Rexford G. Tugwell (1891–1979), would each became important members of Roosevelt's presidential administration. Later, a third Columbia professor, Adolf A. Berle (1895–1971), was added. Roosevelt and Rosenman liked the convenience of having advisers a short train ride away from Albany and even closer to Hyde Park and Roosevelt's city home off Fifth Avenue. When asked about the Brains Trust, Roosevelt quipped that he did not have one but that he "trusted in brains."

To be sure, Roosevelt took advice from other intellectuals. None had more influence than the Vienna-born Harvard law professor Felix Frankfurter (1882–1965). After the 1932 election, when the existence of a "Brains Trust" began to be known, what was startling to the public was that Roosevelt took so much of his advice from intellectuals—often very young intellectuals—rather than from the captains of industry, political insiders, or even occasional university presidents, as had been the wont of previous residents of 1600 Pennsylvania Avenue. In the conservative attacks on Roosevelt and his ways, few negative stereotypes would be more enduring and effective than "New Deal professors."

The first artifact of the Brains Trust was a ten-minute radio speech culminating in this striking passage: "These unhappy times call for the building of plans that rest upon the forgotten, the unorganized but the indispensable units of economic power, for plans like those of 1917, that build from the bottom up and not from the top down, that put their faith once more in the forgotten man at the bottom of the economic pyramid."[47]

Six days later, Al Smith, speaking at a Jefferson Day Dinner in the nation's capital, used the appeal for the "forgotten man" as an excuse to break his February pledge not to oppose any candidate before the June convention. Smith declared, "I will take off my coat and fight to the end against any candidate who persists in any demagogic appeal to the masses of the working people of this country to destroy themselves against class and rich against poor."[48] Smith immediately denied to reporters that his threat was directed against any candidate, but everyone understood that Roosevelt was his target. As dark-horse–hopeful Albert Ritchie told reporters, Smith's speech marked the "reopening of the fight for the nomination."

Realistic hope for a Roosevelt first-ballot victory was dimmed by Smith's speech. Subsequent primary victories in Massachusetts by Smith and in California by Garner were evidence that a stop-Roosevelt coalition was forming. It was essentially unstable. The Garner forces, largely southwestern and dry, would never support Smith, and vice versa. Roosevelt remained a front-runner, but a front-runner with growing problems.

Most serious, apart from Smith's cutting into what should have been Roosevelt's New York power base, was the continuing exposure of Tammany corruption. Roosevelt was against corruption but needed Tammany support to win elections. He also needed the support of independents who took a dim view of his inaction in the wake of Seabury's investigations that were producing shocking evidence of Tammany corruption. The most blatant single example in a Seabury investigation came when Manhattan's sheriff, Thomas M. Farley, confronted with evidence that during seven years when his total legitimate income did not exceed $37,000, he managed to deposit $396,503.66 into his bank account, could only refer to "the good box I had . . . a wonderful box" in which he kept money before depositing it.

On December 30, 1931, Seabury forwarded Farley's testimony along with some two thousand pages of other testimony and evidence to Roosevelt, who sent it to Farley and his attorneys. Then, using the semijudicial powers New York law gave the governor, he summoned Farley to Albany to face two days of public examination that Roosevelt conducted personally in mid-February. A week later, he removed Farley from office. His opinion set forth "as a matter of sound public policy" that public officials—especially elected ones—had to give "a credible explanation" of the sources of their income.[49] As one headline put it: "Unexplained Funds Sole Basis of Action."[50] Roosevelt was walking a tightrope: he could neither ignore Tammany corruption nor risk committing political suicide by becoming an unrelenting foe of political bossism.

Many New York reformers, including the Committee of 1,000 that had also filed charges against Farley, were satisfied with Roosevelt's performance. Seabury, however, in a radio address from Cincinnati, criticized Roosevelt for not ousting Sheriff Farley earlier in October when his testimony about his little tin box became public. The severest tests of Roosevelt's struggle with Tammany were yet to come. Despite the verdict, Seabury and his closest allies still felt that Roosevelt gave corrupt officials too much leeway.

On June 8, Seabury and others filed charges against debonair and highly popular mayor James J. Walker. Walker, a college dropout, had a successful career as a songwriter but, following his immigrant father's wishes, took a law degree at New York Law School in 1904, entered politics in 1909, and passed the bar in 1912. Boss Murphy had tapped him for the state assembly in 1909; in 1914 he went to the state senate and in 1921 became its minority leader. In the senate, he supported Al Smith's programs until he was elected mayor of New York City in 1925. His flamboyant lifestyle made him an iconic figure of the Roaring Twenties.[51] Seabury and his allies had reached the top of the Tammany food chain.

Both national conventions met in Chicago in June. Meeting first, the Republicans renominated Herbert Hoover and, by adopting a platform that called for a modifying constitutional amendment to be submitted to state conventions, essentially took the sting out of the liquor issue. The Democrats followed, sweltering in an un-air-conditioned city from June 27 to July 2. Roosevelt remained in Albany; his convention forces were managed by Jim Farley and Ed Flynn. Howe, arriving later, arranged for a direct telephone line to Roosevelt's Albany residence and installed Louise Hackmeister (1911–2006), head operator at the executive mansion, to supervise it, as she would later supervise the White House telephone switchboard.[52]

Once the convention began, the Roosevelt forces got their man, Senator Thomas J. Walsh of Montana, installed as permanent chairman. The delegates voted overwhelmingly for outright repeal of the Prohibition amendment and demanded that Congress submit it to state conventions. This deprived Smith of his biggest issue.

The Roosevelt forces had secretly planned to remove the two-thirds rule, which could be done by a simple majority vote of the convention, before the balloting started, but an error of judgment by Farley, who convoked a private meeting of several dozen important Roosevelt delegates, which adopted, over Farley's objections, a public resolution urging the convention to repeal the two-thirds rule. This upset most southern delegates, who knew that the two-thirds rule enabled them to block any candidate likely to interfere with segregation. This created a furor of discussion, and Roosevelt, from Albany, issued a statement announcing that, although he had long opposed the two-thirds rule, since its removal had not been discussed publicly, it would be unfair to take it up before the selection of a candidate. The rule would be allowed to survive. He gave notice that if he gained the nomination, he would push for its removal for subsequent elections, which is what occurred. This became crucial in 1948; had it still been in effect then, the Dixiecrat revolt might had had an earlier success. That it was in effect in 1932 forestalled a first-ballot Roosevelt victory.

On that ballot, which began at 4:28 a.m., July 1, Roosevelt, as expected, had an absolute majority, 666 votes, but was just over 100 votes shy of the necessary two-thirds, 770 votes. No one else was even close: Smith had 201, Garner had 90, and 196 votes were divided among seven others, mostly favorite sons. The deadlock continued unabated, for two more ballots, without significant change: Roosevelt had inched up to 682, with Smith down a little and Garner up 10 to 101. At 9:15 a.m., the exhausted delegates agreed to adjourn.

The slight changes in numbers made Garner's votes enough to push the Roosevelt tally beyond the two-thirds point. The crucial negotiation was between Farley and Garner's manager, Sam Rayburn (1882–1961): in return for the votes of Garner's delegates, the Texan would become vice president.

When the fourth-ballot roll call arrived at California, William Gibbs McAdoo, who had been denied the nomination by Smith in 1924 even though he had a clear majority, came to the rostrum with Farley at his side. "California," he proclaimed, "came here to nominate a president" and cast California's 44 votes for Roosevelt. Everyone knew that the deal was done. Smith, unlike the other failed candidates, refused to allow his name to be withdrawn so that the vote would not be unanimous.

As planned, Roosevelt broke precedent and flew to Chicago to accept the nomination, rather than waiting for a committee from the convention to come to Albany and notify him personally. The nine-hour flight from Albany to Chicago in a trimotor Ford required two refueling stops. Roosevelt's party included Eleanor, two sons, Sam Rosenman, three secretaries, two New York policemen, and John F. Kieran of the New York Times. The latter wrote that one of the reasons for the flight was to demonstrate that the nominee, despite "his physical condition," could perform his presidential duties.[53] By the time Roosevelt reached Chicago, the convention had adjourned, reconvened, nominated Garner for vice president by acclamation, and was waiting for its candidate.

Greeted and jostled by a cheering crowd at Chicago's airport, and without the Secret Service support a nominee would have today, Roosevelt's glasses were knocked off but returned to him unbroken. His acceptance speech to the convention was filled with glittering generalities and focused on economic issues. Its peroration promised "a new deal for the American people." Without intending to do so, the candidate and his writers had christened an era.[54]

Before returning to Albany by train, the nominee attended a meeting of the Democratic National Committee, graciously thanking Raskob and Shouse for their work in rebuilding the party after the 1928 defeat, even though their most recent efforts had been aimed at stopping him. Jim Farley was installed as the new national chairman. Tammany leaders were backing the ticket, but Smith's support would remain in doubt for some time.[55]

Once back in Albany, Roosevelt faced two major New York problems even while he planned his second national campaign: the matter of Mayor Walker and securing the gubernatorial nomination for Herbert Lehman. Each involved further conflict with Tammany.

Charges against Walker involved misfeasance and malfeasance: that he failed to see that the public's business was conducted honestly and efficiently and that he had accumulated assets, both in cash and in bearer bonds, that he could not properly account for.[56] Walker sometimes called the latter "benefices." Although the mayor had promised to answer the charges fully when he returned from the convention, only on July 28 did he and his attorneys make filings that denied any wrongdoing. Seabury filed a rebuttal on August 2, Walker responded on August 4, and on that day Roosevelt summoned the mayor to hearings before him in Albany beginning on August 11.

Aided by special counsel, most notably Martin Conboy, a well-known New York City attorney who was an independent Democrat and a prominent Catholic layman, Roosevelt not only attended fourteen days of hearings but by his active and informed participation in questioning Walker showed that he had mastered the details of Seabury's complex charges. In addition, as he had done in the case of Sheriff Farley, he made it clear that removal from office did not require the same kind of evidence as would a conviction for a crime. It was enough, he said, to show that a public official had income for which he could not or would not account. Walker and his attorneys were obviously trying to extend the proceedings as long as possible—they understood that Roosevelt had an election campaign to fight—when, unexpectedly, on the evening of September 1, Walker formally resigned. He wrote a one-sentence note to the city clerk and issued a vituperative statement claiming that his resignation was on advice of counsel because Roosevelt was treating him unfairly.

A more fortunate result for Roosevelt's candidacy is hard to imagine. It seems almost certain that eventually he would have had to remove Walker, but the mayor's political swan song achieved that result without inflaming Tammany partisans as much as a removal would have. While mutterings about "knifing the ticket" emanated from Tammany supporters, that was mere wind. John Curry and the other party leaders had no suicide pact with Walker.[57] The disgraced ex-mayor spoke boldly about a reelection campaign, but soon went off to Europe with his mistress and never again ran for public office.[58]

Apart from Tammany bitter-enders, praise for Roosevelt was all but unanimous.[59] Even Seabury conceded that "the elimination of Mr. Walker as Mayor of this city is a distinct victory for higher standards of public life, and in the elevation of this standard Governor Roosevelt did much to contribute, by reason of the manner in which he conducted the hearings."[60]

Tammany and its boss, Curry, while supporting Roosevelt for president, foolishly tried to get even by attacking his friends. First they went after Sam Rosenman, who, as a gubernatorial appointee to the state supreme court, had to run for the seat in the November election. Despite a long-standing practice of supporting the candidacy of any judge appointed by a Democratic governor, Curry had someone else put on the ticket for Rosenman's seat. (Rosenman could have mounted a campaign as an independent, but that would have been expensive and unlikely to succeed.) In less than a year, Lehman appointed Rosenman to the first vacancy.[61]

Next, Curry and company went after bigger game and sought to deny Lieutenant Governor Lehman the nomination to succeed Roosevelt as governor, for which he was already campaigning. The seemingly divisive fight over Lehman resulted, curiously enough, in greater Democratic unity. Al Smith, who had no quarrel with Lehman, came to the Democratic state convention in Albany to fight for Lehman's nomination. There was no way that Tammany, which had lost most of its political allies outside of Manhattan, could withstand the combination of Roosevelt and Smith. In the customary preconvention negotiations, Curry tried to get Lehman to agree to run for Robert F. Wagner's seat in the United States Senate with Wagner running for governor, but Lehman refused. Curry and company surrendered just before the convention opened, and a full state slate, headed by Lehman, was agreed to.[62]

The postconvention banquet was wonderful ethnic political theater: in their first meeting since before the convention, Smith and Roosevelt shook hands,[63] the Catholic and Protestant paladins reconciled by a fight for a Jewish candidate. Roosevelt's New York State political career, which began by annoying Tammany, ended by humiliating it. The tiger's claws would never be the same.

The fight over Lehman was Smith's final political triumph. He went on to stump effectively for the Roosevelt-Garner ticket in the northeastern urban centers where he was most beloved, but his later collaboration with wealthy conservatives in a futile effort to defeat Roosevelt in 1936 seemed to mock his earlier acute social vision.[64]

Roosevelt's formal campaign for president began in September. He stumped in every national region, including even the Deep South, even though no electoral vote was in doubt there. He enjoyed himself, using his favorite form of transportation, the private railroad car. The trip allowed him to show himself to large numbers of voters and to touch base with, however briefly, many of the congressional leaders he would have to depend on to get his programs through Congress.

The campaign and the election need not detain us much. Almost certainly, any possible Democrat nominee—except perhaps Al Smith—would have been elected. The 1932 election was not so much a Roosevelt triumph as a Hoover defeat. Although this had been conventional wisdom—which is not always wrong—an anecdote told by Rex Tugwell gives a clear view of Roosevelt's mindset. As it happened, on July 29, 1932, Tugwell, who had an early-morning appointment with Roosevelt in Albany, entered his bedroom about seven thirty to find him in bed with the *New York Times* spread out before him. He was reading about the ouster of the Bonus Army of war veterans from Washington by federal troops commanded by General Douglas MacArthur the previous day and night. After expressing his disgust that such a thing could happen, "Roosevelt went on to say that his own political problem was smaller than he would have believed before this incident happened. MacArthur and the army had done a good job of preventing Hoover's re-election. . . . If Roosevelt had had any doubt about the outcome of the election, I am certain he had none after reading *The Times* that day."[65]

Although Roosevelt and Rosenman later made the argument that not only his terms as governor but also his 1932 campaign speeches were a kind of blueprint for the New Deal, even a cursory reading of those speeches shows no such thing. The most notorious example is the Pittsburgh speech in which Roosevelt attacked Hoover for his deficit spending and pledged himself to enforce the Democratic Party platform plank that called for reducing the expenses of the federal government by "not less than 25 percent."

Rosenman tells us that as the 1936 election campaign opened, Roosevelt told him that he intended to return to Pittsburgh and make a speech in the same ballpark and asked him to provide "a good and convincing explanation of it." After rereading the speech, the judge reported back, "Mr. President, the only thing you can say about that 1932 speech is to deny categorically that you ever made it."[66]

This oft-quoted joke conceals two significant facts. First, Roosevelt and Rosenman did provide a first-person explanation in his published papers that tried to be convincing.[67] Second, there was a side of Roosevelt that was fiscally conservative. He believed in balanced budgets, even though, as president, he never achieved one. As time passed, more and more New Dealers became some kind of Keynesian, including ultimately the president himself, but Roosevelt always kept by his side at least one key economic adviser—most prominently budget director Lewis Douglas and his second secretary of the Treasury, Henry Morgenthau—who rarely strayed from essentially nineteenth-century economic beliefs despite running up deficits that seemed massive to them.

Various campaign speeches did treat almost all of the major problems of American society—with the exception of race relations—but the comments provided on such vital matters as agricultural policy, unemployment, and banking practices, while criticizing the actions of "Republican leaders," presented no clear picture of what the new administration would propose. Despite constant instruction by assorted advisers and his own observations of what was happening, there is no evidence that Roosevelt had any clear notion of how he would proceed. But he was supremely confident that he would find answers for the nation's problems.

The election results, though not a landslide, were a clear and indisputable victory for Roosevelt and for his party. He received 22.8 million votes to 15.8 million for Hoover. Almost 3 million more people voted in 1932 than in 1928, but Hoover's vote total fell by 5.6 million votes, while Roosevelt attracted 7.8 million more voters than Smith had in 1928. While minor-party candidates almost tripled their votes, the 1.2 million minor-party voters in 1932 were not quite 3 percent of the electorate. Three out of four such voters chose Socialist Norman Thomas, who drew nearly 900,000 votes, while Communist William Z. Foster polled just over 100,000. Roosevelt carried every section of the country and won in forty-two states with 472 electoral votes, while Hoover carried only six eastern states—four in New England plus Pennsylvania and Delaware—with 87 electoral votes, all by margins greatly reduced from 1928. In Pennsylvania Hoover's advantage fell from almost 1 million to just over 150,000 votes.

Roosevelt carried his home state easily, topping Hoover by nearly 600,000 votes, but, unlike his 1930 reelection as governor, he failed to carry most upstate counties: his 870,000-vote margin in the city elected him. Lehman was again the most popular Democrat, topping Roosevelt's vote total in the city by some 75,000. Roosevelt, in turn, led Bob Wagner, who held his Senate seat, by 15,000. Clearly, the feared Tammany knifing of the ticket did not materialize.

Roosevelt's sweeping victory was paralleled by large Democratic gains in Congress, beginning a period of dominance by his party that endured throughout his lifetime, as the table here shows. In addition, Democrats were elected or reelected in twenty-four of twenty-eight governor's races, as opposed to three Republicans and one Farmer-Laborite, Minnesota's Floyd B. Olson.[68]

Political representation in Congress, 1929–47

| Year | House of Representatives | | | Senate | | |
	Dem.	Rep.	Other	Dem.	Rep.	Other
1929	167	267	1	39	56	1
1931	220	214	1	47	48	1
1933	310	117	5	60	35	1
1935	319	103	10	69	25	2
1937	331	89	13	76	16	4
1939	261	164	4	69	23	4
1941	268	162	5	66	28	2
1943	218	208	4	58	37	1
1945	242	190	2	56	38	1
1947	183	245	1	45	51	0

Note: Table does not reflect vacancies.
Source: U.S. Department of Commerce, *Historical Statistics of the United States: Colonial Times to 1957,* Series Y 139-145, 691.

As opposed to the tensions of 1928, the Roosevelts had a fairly stress-free election day, if a long and busy one. Franklin and Eleanor voted at the Hyde Park Town Hall a little after lunch and then were driven to their Manhattan home. The Roosevelts hosted a buffet supper for a small group of friends and the correspondents who had covered his campaign, and then Franklin was driven to Democratic headquarters at the Biltmore Hotel, where he received selected guests for congratulations. Al Smith, the most celebrated visitor, arrived about nine thirty for a ten-minute visit, able to announce early that "the returns show a Democratic victory. I am delighted." When Roosevelt returned home in the wee hours, his mother greeted him at the door, and before it closed he was heard to say, "This is the greatest night of my life."[69]

It certainly was not Eleanor's greatest night, though she, too, savored the victory of her husband and their party, a victory to which she had made no small contribution. She worried, as she put it in her post–White House memoir, that "this meant the end of any personal life of my own." She noted that she had seen what Theodore Roosevelt's wife had to put up with and was not pleased at the prospect.[70] One suspects that she was already planning how she could continue to play an active role in political life. A week later, she was on message, telling eight hundred guests at the annual dinner of the New York State Federation of Women's Clubs that no leader could go far unless he had intelligent and enthusiastic backing, and she thought that "the women of this country are going to give that backing."[71]

The next day, the president-elect returned to Hyde Park and on the following day to the governor's mansion, where he took to his bed for nearly a week with what was announced as a "slight cold." He told President Hoover that it was the "flu." The truth was probably somewhere in between. One suspects that he was, to use Harry Hopkins's word, "refueling" as well as recuperating.

He held his first postelection press conferences at their normal four o'clock time slot in his bedroom while recuperating on November 15 and 16. For the first, he was propped up in bed wearing pajamas and smoking a cigarette; for the second, he was dressed and seated at a bridge table, appearing "fully recuperated" and talking mostly about balancing the state budget.[72] The White House was more than a hundred days away, and for about half of that time he would be governor of a great state in the grip of the third winter of the Depression, so while he was planning how to create a team to manage a nation, he still had to govern a state. But already things were different. The halo effect had begun.

The *New York Times,* which had often treated Roosevelt's disabilities realistically, now glossed over them. Its postelection-morning biographical sketch of the new president baldly stated what its editors, or some of them, knew was an untruth. Retelling the now familiar story of the 1921 polio attack, the *Times* concluded the discussion of his health with the following: "He was paralyzed from the waist down and his disability was doubly difficult for one who had been a crack tennis player, a swimmer, and a general outdoor man. He recovered and gradually regained the use of his legs. Mr. Roosevelt is today in excellent health. He has benefited from the waters of Warm Springs, Ga., and he has discarded his crutches."[73]

This was no mere aberration: it was clearly policy. Four days later, the *Times* published a profile by W. A. Warn, its chief Albany correspondent who had written the paper's first profile of Roosevelt back in 1911. Warn, who knew well the true state of Roosevelt's mobility, used nearly identical language: "Paralyzed from the waist down [in 1921] . . . he has gradually recovered the use of his legs."[74]

6 The Interregnum
1932–33

ROOSEVELT INTENDED TO FOCUS MAINLY ON New York state matters while planning for and staffing his administration, but he was sidetracked by Hoover's efforts to involve him in ongoing negotiations about the Allies' war debts and other fiscal issues. The president, who had voted at his Palo Alto, California, home, did not even wait until he had returned to Washington, but sent the president-elect a telegram as his train passed through Yuma, Arizona, on the Sunday after election day. Hoover's timing was triggered by an unexpected note from the British government—in his diary Secretary of State Henry L. Stimson called it a "bombshell"—announcing a suspension of payments on its war debts to the United States, beginning with the installment of ninety-five million dollars due on December 15.

It is clear that Hoover wanted a meeting or meetings at which he hoped to get Roosevelt to endorse his policies. The president-elect wisely rebuffed these efforts, although he did participate in three face-to-face meetings at the White House before inauguration day, which only heightened bad feelings between the two men who had once been friendly.[1] Roosevelt insisted that he could not take responsibility for anything while he remained, as he put it, a "private citizen," though a president-elect is something more than that. In fact, by late January, more than a month before he took the oath of office, he had held discussions that approached negotiations with the British ambassador and reached some understandings with Stimson about other aspects of foreign policy in conversations that had Hoover's prior approval.[2] But there should have been no misapprehensions on Hoover's part about Roosevelt's position. He had indicated in his pajama-clad November 15 news conference, as the *New York Times* reported, that "he does not intend to commit himself to any policy with regard to the debt question."[3]

Hoover, for his part, remained convinced that his rejection by the electorate had been a serious error. His memoirs insist again and again that he had beaten the Depression until the election of Roosevelt deprived the markets and the country of the confidence needed for continuing recovery. In a private discussion with a White House correspondent, Hoover revealed a humbler, more human side: "[Every] new man that comes to this job thinks he can fix things up right off. We all come into it with the idea the other fellow was mostly wrong and with our own ideas of what should be done. But it doesn't work out always the way we think it will."[4]

In dozens of little ways, the governor and president-elect stayed on message: for a routine Thanksgiving proclamation, he took from the Book of Common Prayer a selection that included "Remember in pity such as are this day destitute, / Homeless, or forgotten of their fellow-men." The papers, naturally, called it a prayer for the "forgotten man."[5]

Roosevelt, adept at multipurpose travel plans, arranged it so that his first post-election visit to the White House on November 22 was folded into his regular Thanksgiving trip to Warm Springs. He went from Albany to Hyde Park for a night and then motored to Manhattan, where he visited a hospital to greet a new grandson, the Elliott Roosevelts' first, and at the town house conferred with Herbert Lehman about the upcoming budget hearings.[6] The special train to the capital arrived a half hour before the 3:30 p.m. appointment with Hoover, for which Roosevelt was ten minutes late, delayed by the unexpectedly numerous cheering crowds.

Roosevelt was seconded by Raymond Moley, a function that Treasury Secretary Ogden Mills performed for the president. As noted, Hoover wanted Roosevelt to endorse his policies, not only about the war debts but also about fiscal and monetary matters.[7] The meeting resulted in only a three-sentence press release claiming that "progress has been made."[8]

Leaving the White House, Roosevelt checked into the Mayflower Hotel and then went to a dinner in his honor at the National Press Club, where he talked, off the record, to an audience of journalists and dignitaries. Back in his hotel suite, a meeting with Democratic congressional leaders arranged by Speaker Garner to discuss the upcoming lame-duck session went on until after midnight. The next morning, his visitors included his cousin Warren Robbins, his uncle Frederick A. Delano, Associate Justice Louis D. Brandeis, Minnesota governor Floyd B. Olson, and a host of others. So busy that he ate his lunch during a press conference, Roosevelt found time to speak to a young woman polio victim who had been a patient at Warm Springs. When the special train left for Georgia in the early afternoon, Eleanor, daughter Anna, and Missy LeHand had arrived from New York to join the party, as did a number of newsmen.[9]

The Democratic Party had been out of power for twelve years, and the quest for major and minor offices was unremitting. Farley, and to a lesser extent Louis Howe, oversaw many of the secondary appointments, while cabinet and other high-level positions were managed by the president-elect.[10] At Warm Springs, where he held court until December 6, Roosevelt continued to meet with office seekers, many of whom he had no intention of appointing, and listened to much advice he was prepared to ignore, all the time nodding that he understood, which the naive took as agreement. His objective was to form an administration that represented something more than a traditional presidential cabinet of the usual suspects. Unlike today, it did not involve the Federal Bureau of Investigation (FBI) or other security checks.

While he was at Warm Springs, Roosevelt's first postelection preview of his program for the nation appeared in a brief article he had written for the mass-circulation magazine *Liberty*. It was then summarized in most newspapers. He claimed "a mandate, truly national in scope . . . to meet the depression boldly and give the American people a new deal in their political and economic life." He laid out a broad outline of a legislative program beginning with unemployment relief and steps to prevent the recurrence of depression, followed by debt relief for the farmer, rehabilitation and reconstitution of the railroads, the cheapening of electric power through government development of the nation's unutilized power resources, federal regulation of security and commodity exchanges, tariff agreements to restore the normal flow of foreign trade, and an international monetary conference. He proposed to achieve these goals by legislation he would draft. "The Constitution," he wrote, "clearly contemplated that the Presidency *might, without overstepping* its proper functions, provide a degree of leadership for the varied points of view represented in the Congress."[11]

At the end of the first week of December, the governor returned to Albany, finished work on the state budget, and with great satisfaction opened the new year by saluting his handpicked successor. Herbert Lehman's inauguration was a Democratic lovefest: page 1 of the *New York Times* carried a photo of Lehman flanked by his two predecessors. In his valedictory, the president-elect praised Lehman and presaged a new era of federal-state cooperation. "I shall have a friend in Albany, and he will have a friend in Washington."[12]

His second meeting with Hoover took place on January 20, 1933, and focused on war debts and the forthcoming London Economic Conference, which the president-elect caused to be pushed back to June. It was again a pause on the way to Warm Springs. Roosevelt was seconded not only by Moley but also by Norman H. Davis (1878–1944), an old Wilsonian who was currently a Hoover appointee to a disarmament conference. In addition to Mills, Hoover was seconded by Secretary Stimson. This meeting also came to naught; a joint statement, hammered out by aides, was all but meaningless.[13]

When Roosevelt headed south, his party included Nebraska senator George W. Norris, the outstanding progressive Republican who had supported him in 1932. The first stop of his special train was near Muscle Shoals, Alabama, on the Tennessee River, the site of a federally built nitrate plant and dam created in 1917–18 as part of the war effort and idle since then. Norris had long struggled for federal development of the rest of Muscle Shoals, a thirty-seven-mile stretch of rapids with a combined fall four-fifths that of Niagara. After Roosevelt had seen the still largely wild river, he renewed his campaign pledge to do something about it, promising to "make Muscle Shoals a part of an even greater [Tennessee River] development." It would become the Tennessee Valley Authority (TVA). At each of his five stops in Alabama, Roosevelt made brief speeches and was greeted by large crowds. Jim Hagerty, the usually hard-boiled *New York Times* reporter who later became Dwight Eisenhower's press secretary, wrote: "At every stop . . . a sea of faces turned upward, gazing at him with the hope that he would be the Moses to lead the American people out of the wilderness of the economic depression. . . . Mingled with the applause there could be felt, rather than heard, a note of trust that [he] would be able to bring back the 'happy days' promised in his campaign song."[14]

The planning continued at Warm Springs, punctuated by numerous visitors and a public celebration of Roosevelt's fifty-first birthday, attended by 150 patients and staff members of the Warm Springs Foundation.[15] Docking in Miami after an eleven-day fishing cruise on Vincent Astor's yacht *Nourmahal* on February 15, Roosevelt was driven in an open car to Bay Front Park in downtown Miami, where thousands of people were waiting to see him. His bodyguard Gus Gennerich (1887–1936) adeptly boosted him to a sitting position atop the back of the open car, and he spoke very briefly—seven sentences—telling the crowd that he was no stranger, having been in Miami several times and had a wonderful time.[16]

Moments later five shots rang out, as Giuseppe Zangara, thirty-two, a naturalized Italian American, attempted to kill Roosevelt. He was standing on a bench, two or three dozen feet away, and opened fire with a cheap .32-caliber revolver bought in a Miami pawn shop two days before. Impeded by a brave woman who grabbed his arm and hung on, he missed Roosevelt, who, by this time, had slid back down to the car seat, but did hit five others; two of them, Chicago mayor Anton Cermak, who had briefly shaken Roosevelt's hand just after the talk and was walking away from the car, and Mrs. Joe H. Gill, wife of the president of a local utility, were in critical condition. Cermak would eventually die.

Roosevelt himself was the epitome of cool. A telegram of thanks he sent to the woman who may have saved his life included the following passage: "It now appears that by Divine Providence the lives of all the victims of the assassin's disturbed aim will be spared."[17] If he believed that—and there is every reason to think that he did—he must also have believed that God had spared him. He gave his own account to reporters the next morning:

> After I had finished speaking . . . I slid off the back of the car into my seat. Just then Mayor Cermak came forward. I shook hands and talked to him for nearly a minute. Then he moved off around the back of the car. Bob Clark (one of the Secret Service men) was standing right beside him to the right. As he moved off a man came forward. . . . While he was talking to me, I was leaning forward toward the left side of the car. Just then I heard what I thought

was a firecracker, then several more. The man talking to me was pulled back and the chauffeur started the car. I looked around and saw Mayor Cermak doubled up and Mrs. Gill collapsing. Mrs. Gill was at the foot of the band stand steps. . . . I called to the chauffeur to stop. He did—about fifteen feet from where we started. The Secret Service men shouted to him to get out of the crowd and he started forward again. I stopped him a second time, this time at the corner of the bandstand, about thirty feet further on. I saw Mayor Cermak being carried. I motioned to have him put in the back seat of the car, which would be the first out.

Roosevelt held Cermak all the way to the hospital, telling him, at one point, "Tony, keep quiet—don't move. It won't hurt you if you keep quiet."[18]

Back in New York, Eleanor was informed of the event and that her husband was safe. She put through a call to Miami's Jackson Memorial Hospital and reached Franklin at Cermak's bedside. "These things are to be expected," she told reporters. "He's all right. He's not the least bit excited." Her real concern was for Franklin's mother. She went next door to give her the news personally and then left to catch a late-night train for Ithaca so she could deliver a speech at Cornell University the next day.[19]

Zangara had emigrated from his native Calabria in 1923, had worked as a bricklayer in New Jersey where he was a member of an AFL union—he earned good wages, twelve to fourteen dollars a day—and was a registered Republican. He had no criminal record. Although there was no evidence that Zangara was a member of any anarchist organization, he gave traditional anarchistic reasons for his deed and, police reported, had in his wallet a clipping describing Czolgosz's assassination of McKinley—the event that brought the first Roosevelt to power thirty-two years earlier. As he told it, he had come early to the park to get a front-row seat, but not early enough, as those were all taken. He had to settle for a seat in a second row of benches facing the bandstand. When Roosevelt's car arrived, everyone stood up, and Zangara, who was just over five feet tall, could not see his target. When the speech quickly came to an end, he became desperate that his quarry would escape, and he stood on the bench. Perhaps he got the idea from seeing that a woman was standing on the bench they shared. She, Mrs. Lillian Cross, forty-eight years of age and the wife of a local physician, saw him aiming his pistol and said to herself, "all in a flash, 'Oh! He's going to kill the President.'" Shifting her purse from her right hand to her left, she seized his arm and pushed it up and away from the president just as Zangara opened fire. She hung on until a bystander and police overwhelmed him.[20]

In a trial that began and ended less than ninety-six hours after the shootings, Zangara pleaded guilty to all four counts of attempted murder and refused to allow his court-appointed lawyers to plead insanity. He freely stated in response to an interrogation:

I just went there to kill the president. The capitalists killed my life. I suffer, always I suffer. I make it 50–50—some one else must suffer.

Q: Do you think that Mr. Roosevelt is responsible for your suffering?

A: Yes I think like that.

Sentenced to twenty years on each of the four counts, to run consecutively, Zangara shouted at the judge, "Don't be stingy. Give me more—give me 100 years."[21]

Two weeks later, Cermak died, and Zangara, who had been kept in the city jail for just such an eventuality, was indicted for murder the same day. Tried three days later before a different judge, he again pleaded guilty and made statements consistent with what he had said at his first trial. The next day, the judge preceded his sentencing with remarks calling for federal gun control and then ordered Zangara put to death in the electric chair. The switch was thrown on March 20, just thirty-three days after the crime. Zangara was defiant to the end. He seated himself in the chair, looked around the room, and asked, "No cameraman? No movie to take a picture of Zangara?" Told that none were there, he shouted, "Lousy capitalists—no picture—capitalists, no one here to take my picture—all capitalists lousy bunch of crooks." After he was strapped in and the headpiece adjusted, he cried out, "Adios to all the world." His last words were "Push the button."[22]

*   *   *

After spending much of the day following the assassination attempt in Miami, Roosevelt boarded an evening train and arrived in New York City on the afternoon of February 17. It was time to get the cabinet slots filled, and, as he did repeatedly, he had used his northbound train as a mobile office, pulling major figures aboard for personal contacts and conferences. Some got on for a handshake and a word and got right off, while others stayed on for a stop or two. On this trip, the most significant talks were with three important senators, each a possible cabinet member. Cordell Hull (D-TN) boarded in Richmond and got off at Washington, where Carter Glass (D-VA) and Bronson Cutting (R-NM) got on to go as far as Baltimore. Philadelphia was a family stop: Anna and Elliott got on with Missy LeHand and traveled to New York with Franklin. At an onboard press conference, the president-elect told reporters that the cabinet might be announced earlier than the March 2 or 3 dates he had posited earlier. At each of the stops, there was visibly enhanced security, while in New York there was a ridiculous overreaction: "Roosevelt Here Guarded by 1,000." Happily for her, "Mrs. Roosevelt Left Unguarded All Day."[23]

On the day after Roosevelt's return to New York, at a banquet given by New York political reporters in a downtown hotel, a Secret Service agent handed him a ten-page handwritten letter from the president, warning him of an impending banking crisis. Hoover's analysis blamed it on the actions of the Democratic

Congress and the fear created by the results of the presidential election. He called upon "My Dear Mr. President-elect" to "give prompt assurance that there will be no tampering or inflation of the currency; that the budget will be unquestionably balanced, even if further taxation is necessary; that the Government credit will be maintained by refusal to exhaust it in the issue of securities." Roosevelt made no reply but carefully wrote on the back of the envelope when and where it was received.[24]

In other words, the president wanted his successor to bind himself further to the policies that had in fact led to the dire situation in which the nation now found itself. Hoover knew exactly what he was asking. In a letter to a senior Republican senator, Pennsylvania's David A. Reed, the president wrote, "I realize that if these declarations be made by the President-elect, he will have ratified the whole major program of the Republican Administration; that is, it means the abandonment of 90% of the so-called new deal."[25]

Hoover was not crying wolf. The long deflationary cycle that had begun before the 1929 stock market crash had finally reached the point where it was impossible for many banks of all kinds to allow depositors access to their own money. The failure of unsound banks naturally led to runs on banks that were sound. Beginning in October 1932, the governors of several thinly populated western states declared banking "holidays" of varying duration. The more places that restricted depositors access to their funds, the more people decided to take their money out of banks that were still unrestricted. The event that turned the growing trickle of bank failures into a flood was the decision of the governor of Michigan to close all the banks in that large industrial state on Valentine's Day. This set off a domino effect of bank failures and statewide closings that continued right up to the last hours of Hoover's presidency. These holidays were all called by state governors. Many of Hoover's advisers had urged him to close all the banks, but Hoover doubted his authority. Roosevelt also urged Hoover to close the banks but made it clear that he himself would not act or join any action before he became president.[26]

It was in that atmosphere that Roosevelt revealed his cabinet choices. The most convoluted appointment was at Treasury, where a drawn-out, complex minuet took place over the nonappointment of Carter Glass, renowned as the father of the Federal Reserve System and a rock-ribbed conservative. Roosevelt did not really want him, as he expected to resort to unorthodox fiscal measures to raise prices, a strategy that was anathema to Glass. Glass did not really want it because he feared that Roosevelt would inflate the currency. Yet each had to pretend that the appointment was a possibility long after both understood that it was impossible. At one point, Glass had insisted that he wanted to bring in a J. P. Morgan and Company partner as undersecretary, and Roosevelt made it clear, through Moley, that no Wall Streeters were acceptable. Eventually, the seventy-five-year-old Glass refused, ostensibly because of the strain on his wife.[27]

But part of the accommodation was that if Glass was not in the cabinet, the other Virginia senator, seventy-year-old Claude Swanson, would be appointed to something, freeing a seat to which a Glass protégé, Harry F. Byrd, age forty-five, would be appointed. Byrd would hold the seat until 1965, when he stepped down so that his fifty-year-old son, Harry Jr., could be appointed. He would fill the seat until 1982.[28]

The first two announcements of cabinet members were made on February 21, though some cabinet members were told of their appointments well before that. Jim Farley, for one, knew that he would be postmaster general fairly early in the process, and Utah governor George Dern had a letter early in February from Roosevelt saying that he would have an unspecified seat in the cabinet. The two senior chairs, State and Treasury, were filled by Cordell Hull and William H. Woodin, respectively; by the end of the month, the cabinet was complete. Roosevelt appointed nine men and the first woman to sit in the cabinet; all were white, of course. Only Jim Farley and Henry Wallace, at forty-five, were younger than the president, and the group averaged sixty-one years of age. Originally, it consisted of seven Protestants and two Catholics; six were Democratic politicians of the kind usually appointed; the four untraditional appointments were the most interesting of the bunch. Each appointment satisfied a particular need or paid a debt (or both).

FDR's First Cabinet

Name	Life span	Age	Left	State	Department
Cordell Hull	1871–1955	63	1944	TN	State
William H. Woodin	1866–1934	65	1934	NY	Treasury
George H. Dern	1862–1936	71	1936[a]	UT	War
Thomas J. Walsh[b]	1859–1933	74	—	MT	Justice
Homer S. Cummings	1870–1956	62	1939	CT	Justice
James A. Farley	1888–1976	45	1940	NY	Post Office
Claude A. Swanson	1862–1939	71	1939[a]	VA	Navy
Harold L. Ickes	1874–1952	59	1946	IL	Interior
Henry A. Wallace[c]	1888–1965	45	1946	IA	Agriculture
Daniel C. Roper	1867–1943	66	1939	SC	Commerce
Frances Perkins	1880–1965	53	1945	NY	Labor

[a] Died in office.

[b] Died March 2, 1933, and never served. His replacement, the Protestant Cummings, left Farley as the sole Catholic, reduced the average cabinet age to sixty, and gave New England a seat.

[c] Wallace left the cabinet in 1940 after his nomination for vice president. In 1945 he returned to the cabinet as secretary of commerce.

Three of the six politicians—Hull, Swanson, and Walsh—were sitting senators. Hull, a devout free trader, would work to lower tariff barriers and was effective in establishing the Good Neighbor policy with Latin America, but was largely bypassed by Roosevelt on many crucial matters after his disastrous performance at the London Economic Conference.[29] Swanson was a capable administrator but had no important policy impacts. Tom Walsh, able and highly respected as the hero of the Teapot Dome investigation of the 1920s that revealed much of the corruption in the Harding cabinet, might have become an important force in the administration and had been promised eventual promotion to the Supreme Court. But Walsh, who had been a widower since 1917, remarried a wealthy Cuban widow in Havana on February 25 and died of a heart attack in their train compartment en route to the inauguration.[30] Roosevelt, who knew that he would need an attorney general in place to give rulings on some of his planned executive actions before Congress returned, replaced him immediately with Homer S. Cummings, an unusual Bryan Democrat in that he was a graduate of Yale and its law school. His prior officeholding had been restricted to multiple terms as mayor of Stamford, Connecticut, and as state's attorney for its county. Long a wheelhorse of the Democratic Party and a stalwart of Roosevelt's campaign who rendered good service at the Chicago convention, he had been slated to become governor-general of the Philippines. He proved to be an undistinguished attorney general best remembered as the exponent of the ill-fated Court-packing plan of 1937.

The other Democrats were a mixed group. Jim Farley, the glad-handing small-town politician who had ably managed Roosevelt's campaign, was postmaster general and would be concerned with patronage and not issues. Daniel C. Roper at Commerce was an old political ally of Roosevelt's as far back as the Wilson administration, in which both served. As first assistant postmaster general in the first Wilson administration, he helped Roosevelt get some of his supporters appointed as postmasters in upstate New York. The Commerce Department, which had grown enormously during the 1920s, particularly during Hoover's long tenure as secretary, was destined to shrink in importance.[31] Utah governor George Dern, a longtime Roosevelt supporter, was an old progressive who as secretary of war would oppose certain of Roosevelt's policies involving resource use. Of the six, only Cummings could be properly called a New Dealer.

The senior of the four who were not politicians was Treasury Secretary William H. Woodin. He was what the press then styled a captain of industry. He had worked his way up from the middle ranks to become, by 1916, the president of American Car and Foundry, the nation's largest maker of railroad cars. A lifelong Republican, he became involved with a number of charities in the 1920s, including the Warm Springs Foundation, where he met and became friendly with Roosevelt. He supported him for governor in both his races, served as an adviser on banking matters, and was a significant financial contributor to his presidential campaign. An amateur composer, he played a mean guitar and enjoyed awful puns. Although largely unknown even to professional historians, Woodin bore much of the burden of the reanimation and management of the banking system, which had ground to a sputtering halt on March 4. He was always described as a fiscal conservative, but he executed Roosevelt's inflationist policies without a public murmur.

The other three cabinet members became important New Dealers, each of whom stayed the course for the entire Roosevelt presidency and are well-known historical figures. Their multiple contributions to the Roosevelt era will be assessed in appropriate places. Two of their appointments were widely anticipated, but one was totally unexpected.

Harold L. Ickes was Roosevelt's wild card, an appointee whom no one, not even the self-styled curmudgeon himself, could have possibly predicted as a cabinet member. A Chicago lawyer and Bull Moose Republican progressive, he had, along with many others of his persuasion, supported Roosevelt over Hoover in 1932. He hoped for an appointment as commissioner of Indian affairs, and his best chance for that job seemed to depend on California Republican senator Hiram Johnson getting the Interior post, for which he was highly touted. Ickes had been Johnson's campaign manager in his ill-fated quest for the Republican presidential nomination in 1920. But Johnson turned the cabinet post down, and it fell to Ickes. His long tenure and many accomplishments, some of them unrelated to his cabinet post, were coupled with a biting political wit and a near-paranoid feeling of persecution. A proponent of "clean" politics, he could never forget that he was a successor to Albert Fall, one of the disgraced members of Harding's cabinet for his culpability in the Teapot Dome scandal.[32]

Ickes's fellow midwestern progressive Henry A. Wallace was the odds-on favorite for secretary of agriculture and came to the job with an impressive agrarian pedigree. His grandfather Henry Wallace (1836–1916) was a Presbyterian minister, scientific farmer, and journalist who, with two of his sons, took over an existing weekly farm journal in 1895 and soon renamed it *Wallace's Farmer.* It quickly became a major voice for midwestern agriculture. Wallace was a member of Theodore Roosevelt's Country Life Commission and, along with his son and grandson, supported TR's Bull Moose candidacy in 1912. His son Henry C. Wallace (1866–1924) practiced and taught scientific agriculture as a professor at Iowa State College and worked for the family paper, succeeding as editor at his father's death. He also was permanent secretary of the Corn Belt Meat Producers Association (1905–21), an organization representing the interests of corn farmers and hog raisers. During World War I, he clashed with "food czar" Herbert Hoover and in 1920 lobbied against his presidential candidacy. Appointed to Harding's cabinet along with Hoover and Charles Evans Hughes as one of the "best minds," he and Hoover clashed over farm policy within the cabinet. The accession of Calvin Coolidge in 1923 doomed whatever chance there might have been for the adoption of Wallace's policies, best represented by the successive McNary-Haugen bills that Coolidge (and Hoover) opposed. It was expected that he would be replaced when Coolidge became president in his own right in 1925, but he died shortly before the 1924 election of complications following gallbladder surgery. When he entered the cabinet, in 1921, his son Henry A. Wallace, aged thirty-three, took over the editorship of the family paper.

The third Wallace had gone to work on the family paper upon graduation from Iowa State in 1910 and helped to develop a breed of hybrid corn and founded a company to market it that would make him a millionaire. He studied genetics, mathematics, and economics after leaving college.

He was enough of an economist to be included in a high-powered group that offered advice to the nation on economic matters and to appear on the program of the American Economics Association.[33] He had a better understanding of science than anyone else in Roosevelt's cabinet and was the only one who could be considered an intellectual. Although a registered Republican, he supported Robert M. La Follette's third-party presidential bid in 1924 and Al Smith in 1928. He visited Roosevelt at Hyde Park during the election campaign and at Warm Springs in December. He was clearly a candidate to fill the post his father had held, and his candidacy had the support of many farm organizations.[34]

The appointment of Frances Perkins as secretary of labor not only rewarded her excellent performance in Roosevelt's New York administration and satisfied the growing demands of women for greater political recognition but also gave the new president a chance to demonstrate his independence of organized labor's hierarchy. Since the creation of a separate Department of Labor in 1913, all four department heads had come from the ranks of labor. By 1933, as Perkins warned the president-elect in advising him not to appoint her, the AFL chiefs thought that they owned that seat in the cabinet. The labor leaders reacted to her appointment as she had foretold: AFL chief William Green, who had gone to Hyde Park to lobby for the appointment of Daniel Tobin of the Teamsters, insisted that "the Secretary of Labor should be representative of Labor . . . and one who enjoys the confidence of labor. . . . [T]he newly appointed Secretary of Labor does not meet these qualifications. Labor can never become reconciled to the selection made."[35]

Perkins was seemingly unperturbed by Green's rancor. Asked about his statement at her farewell New York City press conference the next day, she described him as "a man of great integrity, and patriotism." Speaking of the special session of Congress that Roosevelt had promised, she noted that "there will be many matters to talk over with Mr. Green" and other labor leaders. "If they cannot find the time to see me, I will hasten to see them." Questions about her family—husband Paul Wilson and daughter Susanna—clearly put her off, and she complained about "exploiting" those who were not in public life. At her retirement banquet on June 27, 1945, at which Green and other labor leaders lauded her, she drew a laugh from her knowing audience by observing that, after twelve years, labor was finally reconciled to her appointment.[36]

One other major appointment, that of Lewis W. Douglas (1874–1934) as budget director, should be considered here. Some press commentators described him as the eleventh member of the cabinet, which, while technically incorrect—he did not meet with the cabinet—indicates both his importance and his self-importance. The son of a wealthy Arizona family who was sent east for prep school and college, he served in France as a second lieutenant during World War I. After briefly teaching history at his alma mater, Amherst, and chemistry at his prep school, he returned to Arizona, where he developed interests in copper mining and citrus growing. After two years in the Arizona Legislature, he was elected to Congress in 1926 as a Democrat and was reelected three times. A man of both intellect and personal charm, he preached economy in government and had opposed such projects as the great dam on the Colorado and the development of the Tennessee River, projects that Roosevelt later made his own.

In 1932 Douglas became a supporter of FDR and began work on drafting memorandums that evolved into the Economy Act of 1933. He appealed to that side of Roosevelt's approach to government that had always called for efficiency, economy, and a balanced budget, as pledged in his Pittsburgh speech. Douglas's appointment initially gave hope to conservatives in both parties, but since he was not only not a New Dealer but an anti–New Dealer as well, his appointment was doomed to lead to frustration, and it surprised few in Washington when he became the first major figure in Roosevelt's inner circle to walk away.[37]

Many contemporary observers, assessing the cabinet appointments as a whole, were struck by the seeming conservatism of the body and by its apparent deference to the Democratic heritage of Wilsonian progressivism. They predicted—some with relief and others with disgust—an administration of little innovation, with a subservience to Congress and tradition. Few grasped what Rex Tugwell had noted in his diary early in the interregnum: "The formal set up of government structure will, I imagine, never mean much to Mr. Roosevelt."[38]

While a few cabinet members would be key players in the coming New Deal, a few of Roosevelt's appointees to head special agencies and projects outshone, for a time, many cabinet members. The most flamboyant of those appointees was Hugh Johnson of the ill-fated National Recovery Administration (NRA), while the most enduring and influential was Harry Hopkins. Unlike cabinet officers, there would be a large turnover of such high-level advisers.

In addition, there was an amazing influx of talented and often idealistic younger people who came to Washington to fill lower-echelon posts in established departments and temporary positions in agencies not covered by civil service regulations. Two among them, Adlai Stevenson, who filled a legal slot in the deciduous-fruits division of the Agricultural Adjustment Administration (AAA), and Lyndon Johnson, who headed the Texas organization of the National Youth Administration (NYA), would lead the Democratic Party and carry on the Roosevelt heritage, or parts of it, from the end of the Truman administration until the debacle of 1968 when Hubert H. Humphrey, the last candidate to carry the unabashed New Deal standard into a race for the White House, lost the narrowly decided election in which Richard M. Nixon triumphed.

The cabinet completed—except for the unanticipated replacement of Walsh—Roosevelt went to Hyde Park to work on his inaugural address. At noon on March 1, seventy-two hours before his inauguration, a second letter from Hoover was hand-delivered in the same manner as the first. Alarmed by the growing banking crisis, Hoover wrote that "a declaration even now" along the lines he had suggested in his first missive "would save losses and hardships to millions of people."

Roosevelt hastily dictated a reply, claiming that he was "dismayed" to discover that an answer to the first letter had not been sent due to a secretary's error. He enclosed that letter, which Freidel believes was hastily drafted, misdated, signed, and handed to Hoover's waiting messenger, along with a briefer direct response to the letter received that day. Both letters rejected the president's call for the president-elect to make a pledge of what steps he would take about banks and the currency, which Roosevelt assumed ended the matter, but he did say that Secretary of the Treasury–designate Woodin would be in touch with Secretary Mills.[39]

The pace of the tumbling banking dominoes increased in the last week of Hoover's presidency. The Associated Press reported as of March 2 that some kinds of banking restrictions were in force in twenty-three states and the District of Columbia. When banks were open, there were many restrictions on how much cash individuals or businesses could withdraw from their own accounts: no more than 5 percent was a common figure.[40] In the next two and a half days, every state in the nation had put some restriction in force. The last holdout, New York's Governor Lehman, announced a two-day holiday at 4:30 a.m. on March 4 after an all-night conference during which word arrived from Chicago that all Illinois banks would be closed for three days. Massive amounts of gold had been withdrawn from the Treasury to meet both domestic and overseas demands. The last financial panic in American history, so far, caused the banking system of the richest nation in the world to grind to a halt some eight and a half hours before Roosevelt took the oath of office.[41] The stock exchange and the commodity markets, which usually worked a half day on Saturday, also closed on their own accord.

The first shocking disclosures of the United States Senate's so-called Pecora investigation were reported in the same late February and early March papers that chronicled the growing banking panic. President Hoover had called for a committee to investigate one of his favorite conspiracy theories: that Democratic "bears" had artificially pulled the market down. Over two years and two chief counsels, the investigation had turned up nothing of consequence, and in January 1933 the committee chair, Peter Norbeck (R-NJ), appointed as the investigation's third chief counsel Ferdinand Pecora (1882–1971), a Sicilian-born Protestant New York lawyer, to wind up the investigation.

Pecora, who had spent a dozen years in the New York district attorney's office investigating investment fraud, knew just where to look. In early February, he sent a team of lawyers to New York's powerful National City Bank to examine and seize records and then subpoenaed its president, Charles E. Mitchell. Testifying under oath, Mitchell admitted that he had sold stock in his own bank short while he was exhorting customers to buy it and that he had concocted phantom sales and repurchases of stock to create nonexistent losses that enabled him to avoid paying income taxes despite a multimillion-dollar annual salary and bonuses. None of these actions was then illegal, but they were clearly unethical and infuriated many "shorn lambs" as well as the president-elect, who would pay his respects to such bankers in his inaugural address. Pecora so impressed the Senate and the nation that the incoming Democrats kept him in charge of a continuing investigation.[42]

Further animosity against the bankers, if any was needed, was created by congressional reports listing the huge amounts of cash that had been loaned to specific big-city banks by the Reconstruction Finance Corporation (RFC). These loans were both legal and proper but, when coupled with the lack of direct federal relief for individual sufferers, enabled critics to sneer that Hoover had put the bankers on relief while ignoring the poor.

Roosevelt, his family, and a considerable entourage arrived in the capital by special train on March 2. He had learned of Walsh's death before he left New York, and the decision to appoint Cummings was made on the train and announced in Washington, as was the appointment of his close friend and adviser Henry Morgenthau Jr. to head the Federal Farm Board.

The death of Walsh caused a dampening of festivities. The following day, as planned, Franklin and Eleanor, accompanied by their oldest son and daughter-in-law, paid the customary courtesy call on the president and Mrs. Hoover. Jimmy was there to provide physical support for his crippled father. We now know that the longtime chief usher at the White House, Ike Hoover—no relation to the president—had been concerned that the outgoing chief executive was violating long-standing protocol by refusing to invite Roosevelt and his family to dinner at the White House. The president eventually issued an invitation to tea. Apparently, Roosevelt believed that his letters to Hoover two days earlier had ended their negotiations, but he had underestimated the dogged persistence of the outgoing president.

When the four Roosevelts arrived for tea on the afternoon of March 3, Ike Hoover greeted them with "It's good to have a Roosevelt in the White House again" and whispered that Secretary Mills and Federal Reserve Board governor Eugene I. Meyer were waiting for them. Roosevelt sent for Ray Moley, who interrupted his nap at the Mayflower Hotel across the street and quickly joined them. These final talks were fruitless, but allowed each leader to exhibit testiness. Roosevelt recalled later, perhaps creatively:

> I decided to cut it short. It is the custom for an outgoing President to return the call of an incoming one. I knew that Hoover didn't want to go through the strain involved in this custom, so I tried to give him a way out. I mentioned the custom to him, and then said, "I realize Mr. President, that you are extremely busy so I will understand completely if you do not return the call." For the first time that day, he looked me squarely in the eye and said: "Mr. Roosevelt, when you are in Washington as long as I have been, you will learn that the President of the United States calls on nobody." That was that. I hustled my family out of the room. I was sure that Jimmy wanted to punch him in the eye.[43]

After the family returned to their hotel, Roosevelt, uncharacteristically, had no comment. The new presidential press secretary, Steve Early, released a one-sentence account in Roosevelt's name: "President Hoover and I talked about a number of matters, all of which will have to be taken up by the new administration."[44]

Five years later, in a note written for the first volume of his presidential papers, Roosevelt felt it necessary to enter a justification for his refusal to cooperate with Hoover during the banking panic. He concluded that "it was abundantly clear to me . . . that appeals for confidence and minor legislative changes could not during that period stop the downward spiral and turn its course upward. . . . No participation by me as a private citizen would have prevented the crisis; such participation in details would have hampered thoroughgoing action under my own responsibility as President."[45]

On inauguration day, Saturday, March 4, Roosevelt arose early and was joined by his cabinet in services conducted by his Groton schoolmaster, Endicott Peabody. After the brief service, Roosevelt returned to his hotel and met with aides, and at 11:00 a.m. he and Eleanor drove to the White House. They and the Hoovers, in open cars, segregated by gender, made the short ride to the Capitol. There they separated, as the president entered the President's Room in the Capitol to sign his last presidential documents, while the president-elect waited in an adjoining room. Then all entered the inaugural podium, Roosevelt on the arm of son James, as usual—the *New York Times* story says that he "marched" in. After listening to "Hail to the Chief" played for him for the first time, Franklin Delano Roosevelt repeated the oath of office after Chief Justice

Charles Evans Hughes, his left hand on the old family Dutch-language Bible opened to First Corinthians, the key verse of which is "And now abideth faith, hope and charity, these three; but the greatest of these is charity."

The crowd of many thousands that the new president turned to face—and the millions listening on radios throughout the nation—knew well that the country was in desperate shape. Only Abraham Lincoln's first inaugural, seventy-two years before, had seen the nation in a more perilous condition. The political crisis of Lincoln's America—the dissolving Union—called for conciliation. The economic crisis of Roosevelt's America clearly had other imperatives. He began his address—some eighteen hundred words, only half the length of Lincoln's— with a line partially ad-libbed: "This is a day of national consecration."[46] He then spoke phrases avowing confidence: "This great Nation will endure as it has endured"; "the only thing we have to fear is fear itself."

Not mincing words and avoiding statistics, he went on to provide a realistic description of what had befallen the nation:

> Values have shrunken to fantastic levels; taxes have risen; our ability to pay has fallen; government of all kinds is faced by serious curtailment of income; the means of exchange are frozen in the currents of trade; the withered leaves of industrial enterprise lie on every side; farmers find no markets for their produce; the savings of many years in thousands of families are gone. More important, a host of unemployed citizens face the grim problem of existence, and an equally great number toil with little return. Only a foolish optimist can deny the dark realities of the moment.

But any trace of Pauline charity was lacking:

> Yet our distress comes from no failure of substance. We are stricken by no plague of locusts. . . . [The] rulers of the exchange of mankind's goods have failed through their own stubbornness and their own incompetence, have admitted their failure, and have abdicated. Practices of the unscrupulous money changers stand indicted in the court of public opinion, rejected by the hearts and minds of men. . . . Faced by failure of credit they have proposed only the lending of more money. Stripped of the lure of profit by which to induce our people to follow their false leadership, they have resorted to exhortations, pleading tearfully for restored confidence. . . . They have no vision, and when there is no vision the people perish. The money changers have fled from their high seats in the temple of our civilization. We may now restore that temple to the ancient truths. The measure of the restoration lies in the extent to which we apply social values more noble than mere monetary profit.

Then came a homily about the importance of happiness as opposed to material goods, followed by a brief discussion of priorities, goals, and methods. Using again "the analogue of war,"[47] the president declared: "Our greatest primary task is to put people to work. This is no unsolvable problem if we face it wisely and courageously. It can be accomplished in part by direct recruiting by the Government itself, treating the task as we would treat the emergency of a war, but at the same time, through this employment, accomplishing greatly needed projects to stimulate and reorganize the use of our natural resources." Roosevelt was inveighing not against a class but against a whole era of the nation's recent past, an era in which he had participated, for a time, without any apparent awareness of its now flagrant flaws. "Finally, in our progress toward a resumption of work we require two safeguards against a return of the evils of the old order: there must be a strict supervision of all banking and credits and investments, so that there will be an end to speculation with other people's money,[48] and there must be provision for an adequate but sound currency."

Yet it was clear that the "war" was at home, not abroad. Only fifty-four words, none of them belligerent, were devoted to foreign affairs. "In the field of world policy I would dedicate this Nation to the policy of the good neighbor—the neighbor who resolutely respects himself and, because he does so, respects the rights of others—the neighbor who respects his obligations and respects the sanctity of his agreements in and with a world of neighbors."

Although one passage insisted that his program was not "narrowly nationalistic," some critics sensed that his administration might resort to undemocratic means, as many foreign leaders had done. In Europe and Asia in particular, it was becoming clear that rather than making the world safe for democracy, what contemporaries called the Great War had made parliamentary democracy an endangered species. After arguing that "our Constitution is so simple and practical that it is possible always to meet extraordinary needs by changes in emphasis and arrangement without loss of essential form," Roosevelt posited a scenario in which the president and Congress would, together, lead the nation out of the economic wilderness:

> It is to be hoped that the normal balance of Executive and legislative authority may be wholly adequate to meet the unprecedented task before us. But it may be that an unprecedented demand and need for undelayed action may call for temporary departure from that normal balance of public procedure. I am prepared under my constitutional duty to recommend the measures that a stricken Nation in the midst of a stricken world may require. These measures, or such other measures as the Congress may build out of its experience and wisdom, I shall seek, within my constitutional authority, to bring to speedy adoption.

However, in case that cooperation did not occur, Roosevelt returned to the war metaphor in a form that alarmed many thoughtful persons. "But in the event that the Congress shall fail to take one of these two courses, and in the event that the national emergency is still critical, I shall not evade the clear course of duty that will then confront me. I shall ask the Congress for the one remaining instrument to meet the crisis—broad Executive power to wage a war against the emergency, as great as the power that would be given to me if we were in fact invaded by a foreign foe."

Although retrospectively, one can annotate the address by associating the names of future programs—an FERA or WPA here, an FDIC or SEC there—the address was, in fact, largely devoid of specifics. And one of the few specifics that many Americans, including their new president, thought was most vital, a pledge to make "income balance outgo," was never redeemed. It was, in essence, an attempt to bolster confidence, the same kind of speech that Herbert Hoover had been delivering, with diminishing success, for more than two years. But Roosevelt delivered his speech with consummate skill. And, by almost every contemporary and historical judgment, it transformed the mood of a nation.

As we know to our sorrow, presidential inaugurals are almost always times of relative confidence and hope, all too often misplaced. It was not at all clear what kind of crisis President Roosevelt would be facing, but he began on a note of triumph.

7 Improvising the New Deal
1933

THE NOTION THAT WHEN FRANKLIN ROOSEVELT became president he had a plan in his head called the New Deal is a myth that no serious scholar has ever believed. But to ordinary people in 1933 and after, the whirlwind of events that came whistling out of Washington from the very beginning of his presidency, combined with the superb self-confidence that Roosevelt projected, created the illusion of mastery. In fact, the president and his closest advisers seriously underestimated the difficulties of restoring the stricken nation to prosperity, and none of the nostrums of the man who delighted in calling himself Dr. New Deal produced anything like prosperity.

The real cure for the Depression came instead from the tonic of global warfare, most of which, happily for Americans, took place far from American shores. What Roosevelt did accomplish in peacetime was to preside over the reversal of the steep downward economic decline and to transform the nature of American government so that once an economic equilibrium had been achieved in the early 1940s, nothing even resembling a depression, as opposed to a recession, took place for some six decades. This was no mean feat. And, toward the end of his life, as evidenced by his great State of the Union speech of January 1944, he had a fairly clear vision of what John Maynard Keynes had called, in 1930, "economic possibilities for our grandchildren."[1] But in 1933, the new president had no such vision.

Roosevelt wasted little time in getting started. On Sunday, March 5, while the moving-in process at the White House was still under way, he issued a proclamation summoning Congress for a special session beginning that Thursday; when its last major accomplishments were signed into law, a hundred days later on June 16,[2] the president and his government had been granted sweeping powers unprecedented in peacetime. At the beginning, neither he nor Congress knew what would be taken up by the special session or how long it would last. As he explained, "on background," in his March 17 press conference, he had originally thought that Congress would sit briefly to take care of a few matters, adjourn for perhaps a month, and come back in April to address matters that could not wait until January. But after talking to congressional leaders, the brief recess was scrubbed.[3] Nothing better indicates the improvisational nature of the early

New Deal. Roosevelt and his advisers were making it up as they went along. And, as the account above indicates, Congress had more influence than some scholars allow.

Even before Congress reassembled, Roosevelt, as he had promised, took power. On Monday he proclaimed a four-day bank holiday based on the 1917 Trading with the Enemy Act that authorized the president to "prohibit any transactions in foreign exchange and the export, hoarding, melting, or earmarkings of gold or silver coin or bullion or currency."[4] It was clearly a stretch of authority, a stretch that some of Hoover's Treasury officials had unsuccessfully urged the outgoing president to take. Since banking everywhere had pretty much come to a halt, the only real change was that the "holiday" was now supervised by the federal government. The presidential holiday expired the day Congress met, placing pressure on the lawmakers to act expeditiously. Later on Monday, Roosevelt spoke extemporaneously to a governors' conference in the White House and called for federal-state cooperation. The governors, representing thirty-seven of the forty-eight states, gave the president an extraordinary vote of confidence, urging Congress to grant him "such broad powers as may be necessary to enable [him] to meet the challenging emergency."[5]

The hectic activity was part of the charged atmosphere that Roosevelt, his family, and his entourage brought to Washington. On inauguration day, the head of the White House Secret Service detail personally escorted the Hoovers to Union Station and put them on the train taking them to New York. When he returned later that day, he found "a gay place full of people who exuded confidence."[6] Many of those people were Roosevelt's support group from Albany, augmented by others who had served Roosevelt during his political campaigns.

Louis Howe, though his role was much diminished once Roosevelt was nominated in Chicago, remained, as long as he lived, secretary to the president. Missy LeHand and her assistant, Grace Tully, continued in the secretarial roles they had played in Albany, as did the telephone expert Louise Hackmeister. Additional functions were divided between press secretary Steve Early and appointments secretary Marvin H. McIntyre, who had been associated with Roosevelt during his days in the Navy Department. The one newcomer to that group was his military aide, a serving army officer, Colonel Edwin M. (Pa) Watson (1883–1945), who had been a military aide to President Wilson at the Versailles Conference. Watson quickly became so useful to the president that he was appointed secretary in 1939 and served until his death on his way back from the Yalta Conference in 1945.

During the first weeks in the White House, Roosevelt established a kind of routine that, with variations, continued throughout his presidency. At 8:15 he normally began with breakfast in bed, which came with six morning newspapers; in the evening, he would go over five afternoon papers.[7] His physician, Ross T. McIntire, would look in before the president was dressed.[8] At 9:30 he would meet with his secretaries. His appointments normally began at 10:30 or 11:00. They were scheduled in fifteen-minute blocks, although his staff understood that their garrulous boss would, as often as not, prolong some of them despite efforts to keep to the schedule. At about 1:00 or 1:30, lunch was usually brought in on a food cart for the president and his lunch guest(s). After lunch was normally the period for answering mail, usually by dictation to Grace Tully. In the late afternoon, he would often have a swim, a massage by physiotherapist Lieutenant Commander George Fox, and his daily sinus treatment from Dr. McIntire. Before dinner Roosevelt liked to have a cocktail hour—he called it the children's hour—at which he mixed martinis.

Two periodic meetings regularly interrupted this schedule. Cabinet meetings were usually on Friday afternoons at 2:00, and press conferences were initially held on Wednesday mornings and Friday afternoons, but later were changed to Tuesday afternoons and Friday mornings.[9]

The first press conference was on held Wednesday, March 8. There would be more than a thousand others during the 4,403 days of his presidency, many more than the combined number of press conferences of *all* his predecessors and successors. Usually, correspondents were ushered into the Oval Office to find him seated behind his desk cluttered with papers, a telephone, and a growing number of knickknacks and mementos. This was an ideal setting for a man who did not want to emphasize his physical disabilities. He would be flanked by aides and a shorthand reporter. It was informal. Early in the first conference, Eleanor came in, whispered in his ear, and stayed for a while to watch the proceedings. Then John and young Franklin popped in to say their good-byes before leaving for Arizona. On many occasions, the president would have guests. Above all, there was news. Roosevelt talked freely, answered questions, exchanged wisecracks, and generally enjoyed himself.

The nearly 125 correspondents loved it. Gone were the "White House spokesmen" of the Coolidge administration and the taciturn Hoover, who rarely went beyond the bare bones of a brief press release.[10] To be sure, the ground rules, which Roosevelt spelled out, seem restrictive today—no direct quotation was allowed except by special permission, and much was "off the record"—but there was all but unanimous agreement among the press that the new format was a great improvement. Roosevelt himself, in a note in his *Public Papers* written in 1937, said that although most of the newspaper owners were opposed to the New Deal, "the great majority of newspaper correspondents who cover the White House are personally friendly to the Administration."[11]

Later that busy afternoon, both Franklin and Eleanor, acting on Felix Frankfurter's suggestion, visited with retired justice Oliver Wendell Holmes in his home on K Street to mark his ninety-second birthday. They had known him during their Wilson administration days, and perhaps Franklin wanted to demonstrate to Herbert Hoover that some presidents do make calls. Holmes, famously, later described Roosevelt as "a second-class intellect" but "a first-class temperament." The one-hour visit was a small matter—page 17 in the *New York Times*—but it further demonstrated that the new president would be his own man.[12]

The next morning, Roosevelt sent a blunt, brief first message—427 words—to the new Congress limited to the banking crisis. "On March 3 banking operations in the United States ceased. . . . Our first task is to reopen all sound banks. This is an essential preliminary to subsequent legislation directed against speculation with the funds of depositors and other violations of positions of trust." He asked for immediate ratification of his actions and for new powers to control banks, expand the currency, and reopen sound banks at the discretion of the executive branch. Admitting that these actions would not "prevent the recurrence of the evils of the past," he promised "at an early moment" to send two other measures of "particular urgency." Once Congress passed those, "we can proceed to the consideration of a rounded program of national restoration."[13]

Although some would soon speak of a "Roosevelt revolution," there was nothing revolutionary in what the president proposed. Congress passed the bill he sent over that day, and Herbert Hoover quickly endorsed the result, as well he might since much of its substance had been worked out by holdover treasury officials led by former treasury undersecretary Arthur A. Ballantine.[14] Once Roosevelt had signed the new statute, he issued a proclamation extending the bank holiday until further notice.[15] The next day, an executive order (EO) set procedures for reopening banks after they had been examined and found sound, differentiated between banks in the Federal Reserve System and those operating under state authority, and codified the restrictions on gold and silver.[16] On the seventh day of his presidency, Roosevelt announced that banks found sound would begin reopening in two days and that he would explain it all the next day—a Sunday—at 10:00 in the evening.

He established a new principle of presidential responsibility. Pointing out that the Constitution required the president to report to Congress on the condition of the country—(Article 2, Section 3, puts it: "He shall from time to time give to the Congress Information of the State of the Union")—Roosevelt argued that "I have a like duty to convey to the people themselves a clear picture of the situation at Washington." He would in his Sunday talk "explain clearly and in simple language to all of you just what has been achieved and the sound reasons which underlie this declaration to you." Thus began the not yet named "Fireside Chats," an innovation so successful that it has been emulated in one way or another by each of Roosevelt's successors.[17] Roosevelt's style, unlike most politicians who used the airways, was relaxed and conversational. He spoke slowly—about 100 words a minute as opposed to a radio standard of 175, while some professional practitioners such as newsman Walter Winchell (1897–1972), spoke in staccato bursts at an even faster pace.

In his Sunday-evening remarks, Roosevelt explained that he was speaking to "the overwhelming majority who use banks for the making of deposits and the drawing of checks." But the average American of the 1930s did not use banks in that way; most workers were paid in cash in weekly pay envelopes. He explained carefully why banks had been closed and the process by which most of them would soon reopen. His treatment of bankers was much gentler than in the inaugural. One cynic remarked that the money changers had been driven out on March 4, but were back a week later.

> We had a bad banking situation. Some of our bankers had shown themselves either incompetent or dishonest in their handling of the people's funds. They had used the money entrusted to them in speculations and unwise loans. This was, of course, not true in the vast majority of our banks, but it was true in enough of them to shock the people for a time into a sense of insecurity and to put them into a frame of mind where they did not differentiate, but seemed to assume that the acts of a comparative few had tainted them all. It was the Government's job to straighten out this situation and do it as quickly as possible. And the job is being performed.

And, as he would always do, he ended on a positive note: "Confidence and courage are the essentials of success in carrying out our plan. You people must have faith; you must not be stampeded by rumors or guesses. Let us unite in banishing fear. We have provided the machinery to restore our financial system; it is up to you to support and make it work. It is your problem no less than it is mine. Together we cannot fail."[18]

Critics on the Left have argued that during the banking crisis, Roosevelt could have instituted a truly national banking system, but the president was not interested in that.[19] His chief concern was to stop the bleeding, get the old system working, purge some of its more flagrant abuses, and strengthen the regulatory powers of the government, especially its ability to control the export and import of specie. Once liquidity had been established, he would proceed to protect depositors.

His activist conservative course continued as, even before the banks began to open, he asked Congress for the authority to effect "drastic economies in government." The message was largely the handiwork of budget director Lew Douglas and marked the beginning of his brief heyday. Roosevelt argued that the budget deficits of the Hoover administration constituted a drag on the economy and claimed that "too often in recent history liberal governments have been wrecked on rocks of loose fiscal policy." Roosevelt called for budget cuts and targeted veterans and government employees. He asked Congress to grant him authority to administer unspecified cuts. There was significant congressional resistance, focused on veterans' benefits, but steamroller tactics by congressional leaders stifled that. The House approved the bill after debate limited to two hours by a "gag rule." Resistance was more effective in the Senate, but it crumbled after four days of debate. The result was an unprecedented peacetime grant of budgetary authority to the executive. The president was empowered to cut benefits and salaries at his pleasure, stipulating only that all pensions fall within a $6–$275 range. All pension legislation since the Spanish-American War was repealed.[20] In memorandums Douglas and General Frank T. Hines, the holdover head of the Veterans Administration (VA), estimated savings at between $400 and $460 million of the nearly $900 million annual expenditure on veterans.

A minor aspect of the economy drive continued an injustice first perpetrated by the Hoover administration whose 1932 Economy Act provided that if a married couple worked for the federal government, one spouse—in practice almost always the woman—had to be dismissed. The Hoover administration dismissed some fifteen hundred women under this law, which the Roosevelt administration continued to enforce.

The administration's 1933 Economy Act provoked the first of many public policy disagreements between the president and his wife. Eleanor Roosevelt thought that the government ought to spend more money on veterans rather than less, and she joined Frances Perkins in public complaints about the ban on working couples. Extraordinary as this may seem, it is merely one example of the latitude that Roosevelt not only tolerated but encouraged among members of his administration. In this instance, after Eleanor continued her criticism in a Democratic Party newsletter, her husband responded with a guest editorial justifying the cuts.[21]

Although liberal complaints about the Economy Act cuts had no visible effect, continuing complaints from Congress bolstered by effective lobbying by the American Legion resulted in a series of administrative actions modifying the cuts significantly. By early May, the White House announced its retreat. A formal statement summarizing conferences between Roosevelt, legion commander Louis Johnson, and Lew Douglas claimed, falsely, that the cuts in service-connected disabilities had been "deeper than was originally intended" and promised a review that restored many cuts, including announced closings of VA hospitals and offices. At least half of the announced savings never took place. The major actual cut was the almost total elimination of compensation for non-service-connected disabilities.[22]

A final skirmish in which a majority of senators voted to restore even more of the actual cuts continued into the closing hours of the special session. The possibility of a veto was openly discussed at each end of Pennsylvania Avenue, but at the last minute enough senators backed down to give the president a victory.[23]

A little-recognized aspect of the Economy Act gave the president power to eliminate government jobs without reference to Congress. One target was the Commerce Department, which had grown fat under Hoover's aegis as its secretary and as president. Its budget was cut by a third, and it lost all of its commercial attachés: "There are two hundred and fifty of them running all around the world having a grand time," Roosevelt complained at a press conference. He and Douglas axed two hundred attachés and transferred the rest to the State Department. However, the Economy Act's impact on total federal employment was minuscule and fleeting. After the first four months of the new administration, there were almost two thousand fewer employees than there had been a year before, one-third of 1 percent of the total; a year later, however, federal employment had increased some 15 percent.[24]

The foregoing demonstrates that even at a time when Roosevelt seemed to be able to push anything through Congress, he was, in reality, subject to all kinds of pressures. In what political scientists call the broker state, this kind of give-and-take goes on almost perpetually. And, ironically, one of the New Deal's first acts was to cut much of veterans' health care, the only effective federal program providing health care to civilians.

In addition, Roosevelt, like most old progressives, had deeply ingrained notions about public debt that economists like Tugwell and Paul Douglas regarded as archaic. And, of course, when the New Deal expansion of the government began in earnest, the deficit soared. In one of the extreme examples of the barefaced casuistry that Roosevelt was capable of mustering, he explained, in an infamous 1937 note, that he had cut spending and balanced the budget "exclusive of the extraordinary relief expenditures which began with the new Administration."[25]

Since the process for state ratification of the Twenty-First Amendment repealing national Prohibition was a little slow, Roosevelt remarked to a group of associates that "it was a good time for beer." He sent Congress a terse message recommending that it modify the Volstead Act, which still enforced Prohibition, "to legalize the manufacture and sale of beer and other beverages of such alcoholic content as is permissible under the Constitution" and to tax those sales. Congress was delighted to comply because its members knew that it would be popular and also provide employment and painless tax revenue. With straight faces, members passed the Beer Revenue Act, decreeing that beer and wine with a 3.2 percent alcohol content were "non-intoxicating beverages" on March 22. The 164 breweries federally licensed to sell "near beer" could start at once adding alcohol, and real if weak beer could be sold after midnight on April 7. The law had no effect in states with Prohibition laws, but most Americans could drink beer legally in April. Five minutes after midnight on April 7, a truck carrying two cases of new beer and a band playing "Happy Days Are Here Again" arrived at the White House. Roosevelt's theme song was still a mirage, but beer, at least, was real.[26]

"Our greatest primary task," the president had proclaimed in the inaugural, "is to put people to work." But speaking "just for background" in a March 15 press conference, he admitted that the first three measures he had proposed—controlling the banks, the Economy Act, and beer—had done nothing "on the constructive side." He promised that two measures would be forthcoming to aid farmers and workers and that he would attend to agriculture first, because "if it does not go through at this time it might as well wait until next winter."[27] In what is arguably the beginning of the New Deal, Roosevelt sent a message to Congress on March 16 proposing what became the Agricultural Adjustment Act.

He had indicated the broad outlines of his farm policy speaking at Topeka, Kansas, during the 1932 campaign. Two basic approaches had long been debated among agricultural reformers and farm-bloc leaders: one allowed unlimited production to continue while trying to keep domestic prices relatively high and dumping the surplus abroad at whatever the market would pay; the other sought to keep prices high by instituting controls on domestic production. At Topeka Roosevelt supported the latter policy by backing, without naming it, the domestic allotment approach developed by Milburn L. Wilson (1885–1969), a Montana agricultural economist, who had, in consultation with Henry Wallace and others, written the basic draft of the speech. One of Wallace's first acts as secretary of agriculture was to call a conference of fifty farm-bloc leaders for March 10. These men were desperate: Ed O'Neal of the powerful American Farm Bureau Federation, the umbrella group representing large commercial farmers, had testified before a lame duck–session Senate committee that "unless something is done for the farmer, we will have a revolution in the countryside within less than 12 months." The bloc leaders quickly approved a domestic allotment plan put forth by Secretary Wallace; the next day, he and Rex Tugwell, now Wallace's assistant secretary, took them to the White House for a ceremonial meeting with the president.[28]

After a complex bill was drafted in the U.S. Department of Agriculture (USDA), Roosevelt sent it to Congress with a brief message merely stating its importance and purpose: "It . . . seeks to increase the purchasing power of our farmers and the consumption of articles manufactured in our industrial communities, and at the same time greatly to relieve the pressure of farm mortgages and to increase the asset value of farm loans made by our banking institutions." Admitting that the proposal took "a new and untried path," he insisted that the proposed legislation "is necessary now for the simple reason that the spring crops will soon be planted and if we wait for another month or six weeks the effect on the prices of this year's crops will be wholly lost."[29]

Although Roosevelt eventually got what he wanted, and more, he had to wait until May 12 to sign a farm bill. Thus, crops already in the ground would have to be plowed under, which gave enemies of regulation a propaganda field day. Roosevelt had miscalculated in his belief that a farm bill—something that many members of Congress had decided opinions about—could be rushed through.

In addition, the president never devoted much time to explaining the farm problem to the people: no Fireside Chat was devoted to it.

And Roosevelt himself, though willing to be guided by Wallace and Tugwell, had serious misconceptions about national as opposed to New York State farm problems. In the inaugural address, for example, he had coupled the need to raise agricultural prices and inhibit foreclosures with a call to "recognize the overbalance of population in our industrial centers," a kind of back-to-the-land notion to which he returned time and again.[30] Although he did not anticipate it, his farm program would accelerate the exodus from the South and Midwest to the North and the Southwest, an exodus not of ambitious strivers, but of those defeated by capitalist agriculture.

The delay in Congress was understandable for a number of reasons. First of all, the idea of curtailing production was, for most of its members, counterintuitive. The glory of American agriculture had been ever-increasing production. The notion that government should limit the number of acres individual farmers could plant, and, as reward for leaving acres fallow, give cash payments to the farmers, made no sense to many of them. But most commercial farmers and their organizations had come to understand that overproduction resulted in ruinous marketing situations in which crops had to be sold at prices below the cost of production and in extreme situations could not be sold at any price.

In addition, there were ideological objections from the Right and the Left. Conservatives were appalled by the collectivism that seemed to Congressman Frederick A. Britten (R-IL) "more Bolshevistic than any law or regulation existing in Soviet Russia."[31] This did not disturb most agrarian radicals, whose more politically serious opposition complained that the bill did nothing about the mortgages, contracted in relatively prosperous times, whose payments more and more farmers could not meet: they wanted both a moratorium on foreclosures and monetary inflation. Roosevelt eventually accommodated the demands for debt relief, but the persistent attempts of radical inflationists to attach various schemes to the farm bill remained a serious problem. Some simply wanted to print more currency, while others wanted to cause inflation by raising the price of silver in relation to gold, often using the same sixteen-to-one ratio espoused by the Populists and William Jennings Bryan some forty years earlier. While Roosevelt clearly favored a more measured inflation—he liked to call it "reflation"—he was concerned, if not frightened, about too much inflation, as we have seen in his remarks about "loose fiscal policy" in the inaugural.[32]

By mid-April, with his farm bill still stalled, he met with the most prominent inflationist, Senator Elmer Thomas (D-OK), and agreed to accept his amendment as long as it was couched in language that gave the president permission to expand the currency but did not require him to do so. He then met with his advisers and shocked some of them—including budget director Douglas and banker Felix Warburg—by telling them that the United States would leave the gold standard. While the startled Douglas moaned about "the end of western civilization," from Wall Street the realistic House of Morgan gave its blessing, as did many other bankers.[33] Roosevelt could be flippant about such things as the gold standard, which drove some of his less perceptive advisers to distraction, but he had a good understanding of the basic problem. For a variety of reasons, continued adherence to the gold standard was deflationary and would further reduce commodity prices in the United States, and Roosevelt pursued, erratically, an inflationary policy. His problems in this regard were complicated by the fact that many of his congressional supporters, like Oklahoma's Thomas, were in what can be described as the William Jennings Bryan wing of the Democratic Party. They had an essentially religious belief in the moral as well as the economic superiority of a silver-based or a bimetallic-based currency. Although Roosevelt listened to a wide variety of economic theorists, I suspect that he took none of their theories to heart. It seems to me that his remarks—very much off the record—at his April 19 press conference, when he told reporters what he wanted them to tell the public, give an inkling about his real views:

> THE PRESIDENT: If I were going to write a story, I would write it along the lines of the decision that was taken last Saturday, but which actually goes into effect today, by which we, the Government, will not allow the exporting of gold, except for earmarked gold for foreign governments of course, and balances in commercial exchange. That is for straight movement. If you want to know the reason why, I think the best explanation of it was by Walter Lippmann yesterday morning.
>
> In other words, the whole problem before us is to raise commodity prices. For the last year, the dollar has been shooting up and we decided to quit competition. The general effect probably will be an increase in commodity prices. It might well be called the next step in the general program.
>
> Q: In other words, let the dollar take care of itself?
>
> THE PRESIDENT: Yes, let the dollar take care of itself and seek its own natural level instead of trying artificially to support it.[34]

That last colloquy is a classic example of Roosevelt's technique. His whole policy was *not* to let the dollar take care of itself but to take care of the dollar by deliberate manipulation. Instead of correcting the reporter, he realized that he could use the misleading phrase to his advantage, and did so adroitly.

These matters evoked violent passions. Many conservatives were particularly outraged at the Gold Clause Act of June 5, 1933, which abrogated the clauses in existing private and public contracts, including federal government bonds, that stipulated payment in gold. Almost two years later, when the Supreme Court, in a five-to-four decision, upheld Roosevelt's law, the chief dissenter, Justice James C. McReynolds, denounced the act and compared Roosevelt to "Nero at his worst."[35]

While Congress debated, many farmers, particularly Corn Belt farmers, took radical action. The most prominent of these was Iowa's Milo Reno (1866–1936), a former preacher and longtime exponent of agrarian reform. Reno created the Farmers' Holiday Association, whose strategy was to have farmers withhold their crops until prices rose. If bankers could have a holiday, he reasoned, why not farmers? The holiday supporters, a minority of Iowa's farmers, tried to stop produce from moving to the cities, using first persuasion, then intimidation, and finally violence directed mostly against farmers and truckers trying to move produce and livestock to market. As had long been the case in industrial disputes, this rural violence resulted in Iowa's governor calling out the National Guard.

On April 27, in Le Mars, Iowa, a crowd of five hundred farmers, many of them farm-holiday supporters and some of them masked, surged into the courtroom of state district judge Charles C. Bradley (1880–1939), demanding that he stop signing foreclosure orders. When he refused, they pulled him from the bench, drove him into the countryside, and put a noose around his neck as if to lynch him. When he still refused to agree to their demands, they reviled him, threw dirt and mud on him, and took off his trousers, leaving him filthy and disheveled but essentially unharmed. If such things could happen in Iowa—where it was long held that the state would go Democratic only after Hell had been converted to Methodism—could the revolution that Ed O'Neal feared be far away?[36] From neighboring Minnesota, its Farmer-Labor governor, Floyd B. Olson (1891–1936), telephoned the White House on May 9, warning that the Farmers' Holiday Association there was planning to resist any attempts at foreclosures.[37]

Fear of more rural violence was a factor in breaking the impasse between what the president wanted and what Congress was willing to agree to. Roosevelt's real struggle was with Democrats who wanted mortgage relief and general inflation. The administration's farm bill, passed on May 10, contained three separate titles.[38] Title I created a new agency, the Agricultural Adjustment Administration, within the Department of Agriculture to administer the domestic allotment plan. It financed most of its costs through a "processing tax." Ostensibly levied on the processors of agricultural products such as mills and dairies, but in fact universally passed on to consumers, it exemplifies how the early New Deal advantaged rural citizens over less well-organized urbanites.[39]

Title II of the bill amended existing legislation to provide for the refinancing of farm mortgages, 90 percent of them held by banks and other private lenders. Its provisions were shrewdly and efficiently administered by the president's friend Henry Morgenthau. Roosevelt originally named him head of the Federal Farm Board and then abolished that body, transferred its funds and equipment to the newly created Farm Credit Administration (FCA), and made Morgenthau its head in a March 27 executive order. Thus, Morgenthau was able to refinance some farm mortgages even before Congress passed the Farm Credit Act, which funded the FCA and gave it legislative recognition.

The refinanced mortgages gave farmers lower interest rates and usually reduced the amount of their indebtedness as well. Morgenthau achieved this by insisting that any mortgage refinanced by the FCA could not have a principal of more than twice the current assessed value of the property. Because land prices had fallen drastically, most banks and other institutions accepted the paper losses that these refinancings represented because the government paid cash, which most farmers were not able to do. This part of the act provided relief for bankers and other lenders as well as for farmers.[40] Similar procedures would later be used to refinance home mortgages.

Title III—a.k.a. the Emergency Farm Mortgage Act of 1933—was an inflationist's wish list arrayed in constitutionally fundamentalist language. It authorized the president to use most of the known ways of inflating the currency except counterfeiting. Roosevelt had no intention of using most of them. While the farm bill was clearly an achievement, both as a reform and as a demonstration of Roosevelt's ability to manage Congress, it ignored the millions of farmers, small producers and tenants, who would get no relief from its provisions except in the general raising of prices that accompanied it. Raising farm prices, of course, while good for farmers, increased the problems of the ill-nourished urban and rural poor.

Amid this emergency activity, Roosevelt, who as a boy had collected and mounted a specimen of each type of bird nesting at Springwood, found time to issue an executive order establishing the Rio Grande Wild Life Refuge on 73,000 acres of public lands in New Mexico, the first of 136 such refuges covering approximately 5.74 million acres he would create by July 1, 1937. Most were on existing public lands, but in that period 1.588 million acres were purchased for about ten million dollars in public funds.[41]

The creation of the Civilian Conservation Corps sprang from the president's brain and became, in the memory of most Americans, the most popular of all New Deal programs. Historians have dubbed it a "new deal for youth," but that was not what Roosevelt intended. He initially envisaged a program putting unemployed men to work at conservation projects in the woods. The TERA program in New York had done that, and he mentioned such a possibility during the campaign. In his March 15 press conference, he spoke of emergency conservation work being done by unemployed men at a dollar a day. Five days later, he asked Congress for authority to establish the "Office of Federal Relief Administrator." He explained that there was enough money left from appropriations for the RFC made in the lame-duck session to last until May. He used strikingly personal language: "I propose to create a civilian conservation corps

. . . confining itself to forestry, the prevention of soil erosion, flood control, and similar projects." He noted existing machinery in four departments—Labor, Agriculture, War, and Interior—could handle "control and direction of the work" and speculated that if Congress acted within two weeks, "250,000 men can be given employment by early summer." (During the campaign, he had talked about a million being so employed and then scaled it back to a half million.) He admitted that it was "not a panacea for all the unemployment but . . . an essential step."[42]

The division of authority for the CCC seemed a bureaucratic nightmare. Frances Perkins tells us that when she protested, the president overrode her, and she managed to get her part—recruiting the workers—done. Her comment about this awkward arrangement in her memoir is one that all students of Roosevelt should keep in mind: "It was a technique of administration which drives professors of political science almost mad—but government in a representative democracy has to be adapted to human feelings."[43]

The brief bill that accompanied the president's message included important details. The president could select "unemployed citizens" to enroll for one year and to be paid "at a rate fixed by the President"—but not more than thirty dollars a month—and provided with "quarters, subsistence, clothing, medical attendance and hospitalization." Wives and other dependents would get an involuntary allotment of recruits' pay. Enrollees had to agree to abide by any rules and regulations the president established but were not obliged to bear arms. No gender was specified, but everyone understood that it was for men only. Nothing was said about age.[44]

AFL chief William Green (1873–1952), soon joined by other labor leaders and Norman Thomas, immediately attacked both the pay scale and what he saw as military control, although he was ready to support using the unemployed to work in the forests at prevailing wages. (The base pay for such Forest Service workers was about three dollars a day.) Three days later, in prepared testimony, Green denounced the president's plan as "smacking of fascism, Hitlerism and in some respects of sovietism." William P. Connery of Massachusetts, chair of the House Labor Committee, attacked it as "a virtual labor draft act," opposed the low wage, and eventually proposed a fifty-dollar limit, well below Green's prevailing wage criterion.[45] Both budget director Douglas and army chief of staff General Douglas MacArthur testified in favor of the bill, but the burden of defense rested upon Labor Secretary Frances Perkins. (Roosevelt told his press conference, off the record, that Green was talking "utter rubbish" and gave a detailed refutation. But he insisted that the reporters' stories not be written as if he were answering "Bill Green.")[46]

The small woman in a black dress topped by a tricorne hat—virtually a uniform for Madame Secretary—delivered her testimony standing while the newsreel cameras rolled. She explained that her department, not the military, would recruit the men, working through local social welfare agencies. They would be processed somewhat like recruits at existing army bases and then shipped to facilities run by the Forest Service of the Department of Agriculture or the National Park Service of the Interior Department. She also pooh-poohed the fears expressed by Green and Connery about a dollar-a-day wage becoming standard, telling the latter to his face that his statement "didn't make sense. If all common labor were reduced to $1 a day we would have a complete national collapse. . . . [The plan is] primarily a relief measure to provide honest occupation to self-respecting Americans who have been forced to panhandling and similar practices against their will."[47]

Congress tinkered with the bill, made some of it even vaguer, and gave the president even more authority, allowing him "under such rules and regulations as he may prescribe and by utilizing such departments as he may designate" to put unemployed to work on conservation projects mostly on public lands and to provide them with food, clothing, shelter, medical attendance, and hospitalization. The bill specified only that recruits be "citizens of the United States" and that "no person under conviction for crime and serving sentence therefor" was eligible. A last-minute successful amendment by Chicago Republican representative Oscar S. De Priest (1871–1951), then the only black American in Congress, provided that "no discrimination shall be made on account of race, color, or creed . . . under the provisions of this act."[48] It was the first federal statute barring any kind of racial discrimination enacted since Reconstruction. It must be remembered that, according to the constitutional interpretation that prevailed until *Brown v. Board of Education* in 1954, the mere fact of segregation was not deemed discriminatory. A number of later statutes, most significantly the Selective Service Act of 1940, contained similar nondiscriminatory provisions, which were similarly interpreted. Although the subject could not have been avoided, dealing with this stipulation was the first episode in President Roosevelt's awkward wrestling with race that evolved throughout his presidency.

Once the bill passed, a great deal of ad-lib planning took place, much of it at a meeting on April 3 of second- and third-echelon bureaucrats—no cabinet members or senior advisers—with the president in the White House at which Roosevelt sketched a rough organizational chart headed by his not yet appointed director of the CCC, whose name he misspelled. Below the chart, he wrote, "I want *personally* to check on the location scope etc. of the camps, assign work to be done etc."[49] He signed it with the soon to become familiar FDR.[50] This meant that hundreds of minor decisions had to be submitted to the White House. There was no way the president could handle even a tiny fraction of them, so the chore devolved on Louis Howe and occasioned much delay. Howe would be involved with the CCC as with no other presidential project.[51]

The day after Green's criticism, Roosevelt or Louis Howe or both had remembered Robert Fechner (1876–1939), a labor leader they had known from their navy days, who agreed to head the CCC after a phone call from Howe. He had union business to attend to and did not come to Washington until just before his appointment on April 5 with the title of director of emergency conservation work.

Fechner announced recruiting goals, stipulated that the first twenty-five thousand recruits would come from sixteen eastern and midwestern cities, and only unmarried men aged eighteen to twenty-five would be accepted. The rationale for the restrictions was explained to state and federal forestry officials at a Washington conference convened by Secretary Wallace on April 6. W. Frank Persons (1877–1955), a veteran social work executive who had been recruited by Frances Perkins to run the selection process, told them that places in the CCC would be allotted to the states on the basis of their 1930 population. Persons commented, "Young unmarried men have had the greatest difficulty in recent years in securing either work or work and relief, and this group have both need themselves and numbers of people dependent upon them. Therefore, in the first selections of people for this work, we will make the work available for unemployed, unmarried men, 18 to 25 years of age, who desire to allot a substantial amount of the cash allowance for the benefit of their families and dependents."[52]

It is not clear when and how the CCC became a youth program, and most historians who have written about it simply assumed that Roosevelt so conceived it. One distinguished historian even wrote, "In his acceptance speech, Roosevelt advocated a reforestation program which would employ the nation's youth, an obvious anticipation of the Civilian Conservation Corps."[53] Roosevelt did call for reforestation in that speech, but only said that it could provide employment "for a million men," with no specification as to age.[54] One can speculate that the rationale given on April 6 about the difficulties young unmarried men had in gaining employment or relief was crafted by an experienced social worker, and the only person of that description at the April 3 meeting was the Department of Labor representative W. Frank Persons.[55] Thus began the "New Deal for Youth."

Robert Fechner, the corps director until his death in 1939, was Tennessee born and Georgia bred, a journeyman machinist who had plied his trade in Mexico and South America before returning to Georgia to work for a railroad. Elected in 1914 to the executive board of his important union, the International Association of Machinists (IAM), he was based in Boston when his skill as an arbitrator first brought him to Roosevelt's attention during his stint in Wilson's administration. Although not a college graduate—he had attended Georgia Tech—Fechner had been a visiting lecturer at Harvard and had spoken at other New England universities. At the time of his appointment, he was general vice president of the IAM. Efficient and modest, he once described himself during the New Deal as "a potato bug among dragonflies" and avowed that most of his clerks were better educated than he was.[56]

Although Fechner has been described as a "felicitous" choice for the CCC, his views on African Americans were consistent with his southern upbringing and the practice of his union, which barred black members until well into the civil rights era.[57] Historian John Salmond has documented the struggle that took place within the government over the admission of southern blacks into the corps and their role in it once selected. Persons, in charge of initial selection, quickly found that most southern states were either not enrolling black men or letting only a very few enroll. He effectively pressured state officials to do better by threatening to transfer their allotments to other states if they did not.

The vast majority of the almost two hundred thousand black men enrolled in the CCC were in segregated camps. The placement of those camps was often difficult because many communities, North and South, protested their presence. (Similar difficulties would arise for Job Corps camps during Lyndon Johnson's administration.) Fechner, unlike Persons, was unsympathetic to demands for equality of treatment, opposed appointing black staff members, and decreed restrictive regulations that prevented assignment of black men to camps outside their home states and sought to minimize their enrollment, positions that army officers and War Department officials supported. Persons got only limited support from Perkins, who silenced her appointee when she felt that his protests might embarrass the president.[58]

Secretary of the Interior Ickes tried to prod Fechner into providing more opportunities for blacks and wrote him, without effect, in 1935: "I have your letter of September 24 in which you express doubt as to the advisability of appointing Negro supervisory personnel in Negro CCC camps. For my part, I am quite certain that Negroes can function in supervisory capacities just as efficiently as can white men and I do not think that they should be discriminated against merely on account of their color. I can see no menace to the program that you are so efficiently carrying out in giving just and proper recognition to members of the Negro race."[59]

The disputes about the role of black men in the corps eventually had to be settled by Roosevelt, who sided with Fechner in August 1935 but asked that his name not be drawn into the subject. Salmond's judgment that "the Negro never gained the measure of relief . . . to which his economic privation entitled him" is clearly just, as is his caveat that despite its failings, the CCC "did fulfill at least some of its obligations toward unemployed Negro youth."[60] Perhaps nothing is more indicative of how the CCC administrators regarded black Americans than the way they treated its "Negro adviser" Edward G. Brown. (Such advisers appointed to many departments and agencies eventually became known as the "Black Cabinet," although that informal group began to meet only in 1936.) Ralph Bunche (1904–71), in a massive 1940 report aiding Gunnar Myrdal's research, surveyed "Negroes and the New Deal agencies." His paragraph on the

CCC pointed out that adviser Brown's office was the smallest and least equipped of all those he visited: "it was formed by a panel placed across a space at the end of a corridor."[61]

The CCC got up and running very quickly, and by August Roosevelt was ready to make an inspection trip to five of the nearby camps of the forty-nine already established. Not only did the visit provide an opportunity for the press and the newsreel cameras, but Roosevelt also took pains to invite the CCC critic in chief to join him. More than a week before the trip, he told Marvin McIntyre that he "would like to have Bill Green, President of the Federation of Labor, join me down there and come back to Washington with me." Green came, saw, and was conquered.[62]

Vast public works became a hallmark of the New Deal. None was more ambitious than the plan to create a Tennessee Valley Authority that grew out of Roosevelt's postelection pledge at Muscle Shoals. In planning for the Tennessee Valley, he was working with an icon of American reform, the Republican senator from Nebraska George W. Norris. On the first day of the special session, Norris, for the seventh time, introduced a joint resolution to create a public corporation to operate the government's Muscle Shoals facility as part of the development of the Tennessee Valley. Four days later, Roosevelt wrote him that "as soon as this rush of emergency legislation is over, I hope you will come and have a talk with me about Muscle Shoals and Tennessee Basin development."[63] On April 1, Norris, Ickes, Wallace, and two members of the House had a two-hour meeting with the president to discuss Norris's proposed legislation.[64] Norris and the president had another long meeting on the evening of April 7, at which Roosevelt told him that he would send a message to Congress on April 10 dealing with their joint project. Roosevelt's conception was even more sweeping than Norris's, embracing the entirety of the watershed of the river and its tributaries, a region including parts of seven states that was home to some of the most disadvantaged white people in the nation. Perhaps it was the sweep of the president's vision that caused Norris to fret that Roosevelt did not understand the "power trust"; had he known more about Roosevelt's experience in New York, he might have been less nervous.[65]

The president's message to Congress proposed the creation of the Tennessee Valley Authority,

> a corporation clothed with the power of Government but possessed of the flexibility and initiative of a private enterprise. . . . The Muscle Shoals development is but a small part of the potential public usefulness of the entire Tennessee River. . . . [It] transcends mere power development; it [includes] flood control, soil erosion, afforestation, elimination from agricultural use of marginal lands, and distribution and diversification of industry. In short, this power development of war days leads logically to national planning for

a complete river watershed involving many States and the future lives and welfare of millions. It touches and gives life to all forms of human concerns.[66]

The measure passed without much difficulty over the objections of the power companies, whose chief spokesman was Wendell L. Willkie (1892–1944), then a Democrat and head of one of the power companies. Willkie testified that he supported the idea of regional planning but wanted the power companies to control the transmission lines, which meant control of price and profit. At the May 18 signing ceremony, Roosevelt, perhaps twitting Norris for his concern, in mock seriousness asked him, pointing to the bill, "George, are the transmission lines in here?" Assured that they were, the president signed the bill.[67]

The TVA was directed by a three-person board, appointed by the president and subject to Senate confirmation. Although Roosevelt consulted Norris about the legislation, publicly honored him, approved naming one of the large dams on the Tennessee River after him, and said that he was consulting him about board members, in fact Norris was informed rather than consulted about the appointments. The chair, Arthur Morgan (1878–1975), an outstanding hydraulic engineer without any post–high school education, had headed Ohio's Miami (Valley) Conservancy District, the nation's largest flood-control district, before becoming president of Antioch College. Apparently, James M. Cox suggested him to Roosevelt—Morgan had voted for Hoover—and the appointment was not one of the president's happier ones.[68] Morgan chose, with Roosevelt's approval, the other two board members, Harcourt Morgan (1867–1950), no relation, an agricultural scientist and former president of the University of Tennessee, and David E. Lilienthal (1899–1981), a brilliant lawyer who had studied with Frankfurter at Harvard and chaired the Wisconsin Public Service Commission. Arthur Morgan took chief responsibility for dam construction and social and educational planning, Harcourt Morgan for fertilizer, and Lilienthal for electric power policy. The work went well, but, as is often the case with triumvirs, a division arose as early as August 1933, with Lilienthal and the elder Morgan more and more opposing the chairman. By 1935 the breach became open, a development that will be discussed later.

In 1959 Arthur Schlesinger argued, "The Tennessee Valley authority . . . became [one of many] battlefield[s] in the struggle which divided the early New Deal—the struggle between the social planners, who thought in terms of an organic economy and a managed society, and the neo-Brandesians, who thought in terms of decentralization of decision and the revitalization of choice."[69] That is, it seems to me, at least a part of the truth, but I doubt if Franklin Roosevelt ever saw it that way. He is rightly criticized for being Hamlet-like in his reluctance to make certain choices. He was, I believe, rarely able to understand why people who were really on his side of the great divide that separated the friends and foes of the New Deal could not just compromise and settle their differences. In many instances, they could, but when they would not or could not, he often found it difficult to make the decisions that he needed to make. In the case of the TVA, he wanted Morgan to remain as the planner and Lilienthal as the fighter against the power companies. But some five years after the split occurred and three years after it became public, he finally summoned all three directors to the White House and, after hearing them out, fired Arthur Morgan and replaced him with the other Morgan. Three years later, Lilienthal became chairman, and it is his name that is most associated with the TVA.[70]

Composed of some thirty dams and thirteen large power plants, plus a whole array of essential infrastructure, the TVA successfully transformed one of the more underdeveloped regions of the United States and remains the largest example of regional planning in American history. Initially, it drew all but unanimous support among liberals and only minor complaints from conservatives.[71] Years later it became a prime target not only for free marketers like Barry Goldwater, who in 1961 spouted, "I think TVA should be turned over to free enterprise, even if they could only get one dollar for it," but also for environmentalists, who complained that the TVA was just another polluter.[72]

The remaining major initiatives of the hundred days, some of the most important actions of the early New Deal, will be treated briefly in the following pages in a kind of chronological order. Some, like the National Recovery Administration, are examined further in later chapters. Others, like the Federal Deposit Insurance Corporation (FDIC), one of its clearest successes, will get little or no further attention.

In early May 1933 came a pale reprise of what had been a tragedy the year before: some 3,000 World War I veterans, a minor fraction of them organized by Communist Party forces, again "marched" on Washington in another attempt to get their bonus paid early. Before any "marchers" arrived, VA chief General Frank T. Hines recommended that bonus marchers be housed in an army facility across the Potomac at Camp Hunt and that the age limits for the new CCC be raised to accommodate any veterans who wished to enroll. Roosevelt accepted both suggestions, even though CCC director Fechner objected. Eventually, the president issued an executive order authorizing the enrollment of up to 25,000 world war veterans in special CCC units; nearly 2,700 of the 3,000 veterans who registered at Fort Hunt signed up for the CCC. Throughout its life, more than 250,000 veterans were among the 3.25 million plus in the forest army.

Soon after Camp Hunt was in operation, Eleanor Roosevelt visited the veterans, led then in song, and spoke to them about her wartime volunteer work and her hopes for peace. Later Franklin had 3 of 3,000 brought to the Oval Office for a thirty-five-minute meeting. He explained why he could not advance their bonus payments. He told them frankly that he would veto a bonus bill if one were passed, explained that some of the cuts in veterans' benefits would be restored, hoped that many of them would sign up for the CCC, and commended them for their excellent behavior in Washington. The contrast with Hoover's actions, just ten months past, could not be missed. What had been a disaster for his predecessor was a small plus for Roosevelt.[73]

Roosevelt's second Fireside Chat on May 7, another Sunday night, turned out to be almost the midpoint of the hundred days. Because not very many of the major bills had been enacted, the president stressed the continuities rather that the changes. After painting a grim picture of the state of the nation as his presidency began—"the country was dying by inches"—he stressed the need for a "prompt program applied as quickly as possible." He denied that anything constitutionally improper had occurred. He insisted that Congress, which he praised, "still retained its constitutional authority" and said that this would not change. He insisted, "The only thing that has been happening has been to designate the President as the agency to carry out certain purposes of the Congress."

The legislation already passed, he argued, "can properly be considered as part of a well-grounded plan" and claimed only that "we have reason to believe that things are a little better than they were two months ago." He continued, "We are working toward a definite goal, which is to prevent the return of conditions which came very close to destroying what we call modern civilization. The actual accomplishment of our purpose cannot be attained in a day. Our policies are wholly within purposes for which our American Constitutional Government was established 150 years ago."

Despite the earlier praise for Congress, he emphasized that it was his program and his responsibility. Indulging in the fanciful role playing he delighted in to make his power seem commonplace, he freely admitted, "I have no expectation of making a hit every time I come to bat. What I seek is the highest possible batting average, not only for myself but for the team. Theodore Roosevelt once said to me: 'If I can be right 75 percent of the time I shall come up to the fullest measure of my hopes.'" He closed with a typical upbeat sentence: "In the present spirit of mutual confidence and mutual encouragement we go forward."[74]

On the same day, May 12, that the farm bill was approved, Roosevelt also signed the act establishing the Federal Emergency Relief Administration (FERA). Why it took more than two months to make significant provision for those who had lost their jobs, when Roosevelt had declared in the inaugural that "our greatest primary task is to put people to work," is one of the largely undiscussed anomalies of the hundred days. Unemployment, as then defined, included only those who had lost jobs; their number in early 1933 has been estimated at between 13.3 and 17.9 million, more than a quarter of the labor force. Other workers had had their hours of work drastically reduced. The CCC bill had also created the position of federal relief administrator, but it had not been filled. Morgenthau told his biographer that at some point, Roosevelt offered to make him relief administrator, but he turned it down.[75]

In contrast to the CCC bill that Roosevelt literally handcrafted, the bill for unemployment relief had its origins elsewhere. Shortly after the inauguration—probably on March 14—Harry Hopkins and William Hodson (1891–1943),[76] a lawyer and social worker who was executive director of the Welfare Council of New York City, came to Washington to see the president. Unable to get an appointment, they met Frances Perkins at the Women's University Club, where she was living. Unable to meet in her rooms either by house rules or by Perkins's sense of propriety, they held their conference "in a hole under the stairs." Impressed with their plans and their practical approach, even though she had more than two thousand plans for unemployment relief on her desk, she pressured Marvin McIntyre to give the New Yorkers an immediate appointment. This began a series of meetings after which Roosevelt met with the three senators most responsible for the 1932 relief bill, Democrats Robert F. Wagner (NY) and Edward P. Costigan (CO) and Republican Robert M. La Follette Jr. (WI). They in turn met with Perkins to draft a bill. Their handiwork passed easily—55 to 17 in the Senate and 326 to 42 in the House. But the process took almost two months: it was signed into law on May 12.[77]

The relatively brief and simple statute stipulated an unemployment emergency calling for federal action. It authorized the RFC, which began funding loans to the states for relief in 1932, to transfer $500 million to the FERA administrator. It expanded RFC borrowing authority by a similar amount and took that agency out of the relief business by transferring any unobligated relief funds to FERA. An administrator was to be appointed by the president subject to Senate confirmation with a salary not to exceed $10,000 a year. Its lesser employees were exempted from civil service regulations, as most New Deal agency employees would be. The administrator was given the authority, with the consent of the president, to "assume control" of relief in any state or states to secure "more effective and efficient cooperation between the State and Federal authorities," empowered him to make investigations, and ordered him to make regular reports. Grants were to be made to the "several states," the District of Columbia, Alaska, Hawaii, the Virgin Islands, and Puerto Rico. No provision was made for the Philippines, the Pacific dependencies, or the Panama Canal Zone.

Unlike the 1932 law, the New Deal act made grants, not loans, to the states. States had to apply for them and say how the money would be spent. No state could receive more than 15 percent of the funds. Half the $500 million was to be allocated to states on a matching basis, one federal dollar for every three spent by the state and its lesser units on relief. Knowing that many states were broke, Congress provided that the other $250 million could be allocated to the states according to the judgment of the FERA administrator with no matching requirement.[78] A provision allowing the federal government to override state authority proved very important; the lack of such authority in Lyndon Johnson's War on Poverty was a serious impediment to the success of some programs.[79]

That Roosevelt was not enthusiastic about getting into relief is further demonstrated by comparing his signing statements for farm relief and unemployment relief, which became law on the same day. He said that the farm bill was "in the interest of all the people" and in line with "public duty and private interest." By contrast, on the unemployment relief bill, Roosevelt challenged "governors, legislatures and local officials . . . to provide for their own citizens." Sounding like Herbert Hoover, he insisted that "the giving of life's necessities by the Government, in ratio to contributions made by States and local communities, should lead to the giving of generous contributions to community chests and welfare organizations throughout the country."[80]

Four years later, when Roosevelt and Rosenman wrote explanatory notes for the first volumes of his *Public Papers,* they sang a different tune. By 1937, establishing a system of public relief—not yet generally called welfare—was an achievement the president was proud of. Their account made it seem that the bill was timed to meet the exhaustion of the money appropriated in the Hoover administration, but many states had long since exhausted their share of those funds.[81]

Roosevelt had yet to select a relief administrator. Asked during his March 17 press conference if he was going to name a relief administrator and take relief out of the RFC, he responded, as if he had made a decision, "That is a secret. Wait until next Monday or Tuesday." Two months and two days later and a week after signing the relief bill, a reporter asked if "Harry Hopkins is going to head this five hundred million dollar relief organization?" Roosevelt explained that Governor Lehman wanted to keep Hopkins in New York and that "I am looking for somebody else but if I cannot find someone else I am asking him to come down here."[82] Perkins remembered that Hopkins and Hodson had come up with a list of six or eight names, including their own, and they argued that either of them, because of their New York experience, would be a better choice than any of the others. Ironically, in 1930 Hodson had been offered the TERA job, turned it down, and suggested Hopkins. Had Hodson taken the TERA job, it is difficult to imagine a scenario in which Hopkins becomes Roosevelt's right-hand man. Roosevelt soon wired Lehman that he had just talked to Hopkins, who had agreed "to take over for a month or so."[83] The month or so was a dissimulation of the kind Roosevelt often used to soften a blow.

On Monday, May 22, Hopkins came to Washington, was appointed federal relief administrator, set up shop in a hallway until an office could be cleared for him, and began "to put people to work" eighty days after the inaugural promise. Phoning and wiring governors and other administrators, he authorized disbursement of $5 million that day; by the time he resigned, five years later, he would have spent $9 billion, an enormous sum for that era, about 20 cents of every dollar spent by the New Deal during that time.[84]

In a mid-June 1933 meeting for state relief representatives, including eight governors, Roosevelt lectured them about their responsibilities.

It is essential that the States and local units of Government do their fair share. They must not expect the Federal Government to finance more than a reasonable proportion of the total. It should be borne in mind . . . that there are four million families in need of the necessities of life. . . . The Federal Relief Administrator should put as much responsibility as possible on the State Administration. This means a competent set-up in each State . . . [that] will not only administer the relief in a business-like way but entirely apart from partisan politics.

After explaining his hopes for recovery and increased employment, the president closed with an exhortation: "And so all I can tell you now is, 'Go to it, and God bless you. We will help you all we can.'"[85]

Roosevelt's inaugural call to supervise "investments, so that there will be an end to speculation with other people's money," was partially redeemed by the Securities Act of 1933, signed at the end of May. As early as 1844, Britain and other European nations had regulated the issuance of securities, but there was no such federal legislation in the United States prior to the New Deal. The law, sometimes referred to as the Truth in Securities Act, required all issuers of securities to file applications disclosing all relevant information. No securities could be marketed or issued until twenty days after applications had been approved by the Federal Trade Commission (FTC) and made available to investors. Providing incorrect or incomplete information could result in criminal prosecutions with fines up to $5,000, five years in jail, or both and subjected issuers to civil suits in federal court as well. Roosevelt said that it gave him "much satisfaction" to sign the bill, but admitted that the act corrected only "some of the evils which have been so glaringly revealed in the private exploitation of the public's money. This law and its effective administration are steps in a program to restore some old-fashioned standards of rectitude. Without such an ethical foundation, economic well-being cannot be achieved."

The FTC, a creation of the Wilson administration, had become dominated by Republican appointees who disapproved of its regulatory purposes. In addition to its obvious weaknesses, it proved to be an inappropriate mechanism for securities regulation. More thorough regulation would be legislated in 1934.[86]

The very end of the special session—Congress would adjourn in the wee hours of June 16—saw the passage of four important initiatives. First, Congress approved the administration's bill to create a Home Owners' Loan Corporation, which would provide protection and refinancing for homes valued up to $14,000. The HOLC soon refinanced about a fifth of all American homes, and its existence substantially lowered mortgage costs for all home owners. In asking

Congress for the legislation, the president made "a declaration of national policy . . . that the broad interests of the Nation require that special safeguards should be thrown around home ownership as a guarantee of social and economic stability, and that to protect home owners from inequitable enforced liquidation in a time of general distress is a proper concern of the Government."[87] In signing it, he explained that it "extends the same principle of relief to home owners as we have already extended to farm owners. Furthermore, the Act extends this relief not only to people who have borrowed money on their homes but also to their mortgage creditors."[88]

Although the Glass-Steagall Act, a.k.a. the Banking Act of 1933, is properly regarded as an iconic piece of New Deal legislation—it established the Federal Deposit Insurance Corporation that insured individual depositors for up to $2,500 per account and created a wall between commercial and investment banking, as the Pecora investigation had suggested—Roosevelt signed it in silence. No statement about it emanated from the White House. The insurance went into effect on January 1, 1934, and was slated to expire six months later. The only mention of it was in a 1933 press conference six months after its signing when the president allowed that "the only thing . . . tentatively decided on is that this insurance fund should probably be pretty well left alone during this session of Congress so that we could see how it works."[89]

But in less than two months, Roosevelt recommended—and Congress agreed—to extend the experiment until July 1, 1935, and the Banking Act of 1935 made the FDIC permanent. The published *Public Papers* for the first term in 1937 included a comment on an October 1933 document to claim the act for Roosevelt. The note traced the evolution of FDIC coverage, saying that coverage had been doubled to $5,000 and that losses to uncovered depositors had been negligible. "This record amply justifies the confidence which we placed in deposit insurance as an effective means of protecting the ordinary bank depositor."[90]

Among the final accomplishments of the hundred days was the passage of the National Industrial Recovery Act (NIRA), creating the National Recovery Administration, which was designed to manage economic recovery and sustainable economic growth through industrial self-government by a variety of codes. The law also appropriated $3.3 billion for a public works program. That program, something many in Congress had been calling for, was attached to make the NRA more palatable. Historian Ellis Hawley describes the aims of the NRA concisely: "to establish and administer a series of industrial codes which, through appropriate controls over pricing, production, trade practices, and labor relations in codified industries was supposed to check the contraction of the national economy."[91]

Favored by many businessmen and some labor leaders, the NIRA also called for suspending the antitrust laws to allow price- and wage-fixing as well as production controls. The rationale was that if national control of the economy had worked during the war crisis of 1917–18, it ought to work in the crisis of the Great Depression. It was not difficult to sell this idea to Franklin Roosevelt, who often used the war analogy; a proximate cause of his original espousal of the plan seems to have been the passage by the Senate of the bill championed by Hugo Black (D-AL) that would have established a thirty-hour workweek in manufacturing, which Roosevelt and most of his advisers opposed.[92]

There were many New Dealers, some of them influenced by the ideas of Justice Louis D. Brandeis, who opposed such controls. Many thinkers on the Left, largely outside the government, saw an ominous parallel with the corporate state of fascist Italy, while others on the Right welcomed the seeming parallel. It must be remembered that, at the time, Mussolini was seen as the man who made the trains run on time rather than the "sawdust Caesar" that he was.

Roosevelt hailed the notion of industrial self-government in a message to Congress urging passage of the NRA legislation, calling it "the machinery necessary for a great cooperative movement throughout all industry in order to obtain wide reemployment, to shorten the working week, to pay a decent wage for the shorter week and to prevent unfair competition and disastrous overproduction. Employers cannot do this singly or even in organized groups, because such action increases costs and thus permits cut-throat underselling by selfish competitors unwilling to join in such a public-spirited endeavor." He justified the suspension of the antitrust laws, arguing that "the public interest will be served if, with the authority and under the guidance of Government, private industries are permitted to make agreements and codes insuring fair competition. However, it is necessary, if we thus limit the operation of antitrust laws to their original purpose, to provide a rigorous licensing power in order to meet rare cases of non-cooperation and abuse. Such a safeguard is indispensable."[93]

·Congress debated the NRA bill long and intensely, particularly in the Senate, where the bill prevailed by a mere seven votes, forty-six to thirty-nine.[94] Roosevelt hailed the result, predicting in his signing statement that "history probably will record [the NRA bill] as the most important and far-reaching legislation ever enacted by the American Congress."[95] The verdict of history has been otherwise. The NRA and its codes would represent the most dismal failure of the early New Deal, though the public works program eventually created many of its most enduring and impressive achievements.

To administer the NRA, Roosevelt chose Hugh S. Johnson (1881–1942), a West Point graduate who was sent to law school at the University of California in 1914 and then assigned to headquarters staff. As a serving officer, he helped to organize the World War I draft and then became the key army representative on the War Industries Board, run eventually by Bernard M. Baruch. (The WIB would become a kind of model for the NRA.) After the Armistice, Johnson left the army as a brigadier general and pursued a not very successful business career in the 1920s. By the early 1930s, according to his biographer, his only reliable income came from Baruch, who kept him on retainer to investigate and analyze companies whose stock Baruch wished to buy or sell short. Baruch also loaned him to the Smith presidential campaign in 1928 and to the Roosevelt campaign after the Chicago convention for various chores. Despite his analytical brilliance, energy, and imagination, Johnson was an unstable personality, given to bouts of alcoholic excess.[96] Although some regarded his appointment as a result of Baruch's influence, the speculator had sent word to Roosevelt, via Perkins, warning that although Johnson was a valued subordinate, he was not a good "number one man." But since he had been deeply involved, with others, in drafting the legislation that created the NRA, his appointment was expected.

As the story is often told, at the June 16 cabinet meeting, just hours after Congress had adjourned and with Johnson, not yet officially appointed, waiting outside, Roosevelt raised the possibility of separating the public works functions from the NRA. There was general approval. The president then asked, "Who shall it be?" Perkins suggested Ickes, who agreed. Then Johnson was called in and told he was appointed. After Johnson had responded appropriately, Roosevelt added that it would be too much work for one man to administer both the NRA and the public works projects, so he had decided to make other arrangements. Johnson, thunderstruck, could only mutter, "I don't see why. I don't see why." The president, noting Johnson's distress, told Perkins to calm the general. She did so, although Johnson initially told her that he would resign. This, in essence, is the story told by Arthur Schlesinger in 1957, based largely on Frances Perkins's 1946 memoir and used to a greater or lesser degree by many subsequent narrators.[97]

Contemporary documents and later memoir accounts make it clear that the story is more complex. An executive order, drafted that day, created the Public Works Administration and placed a Corps of Engineers bureaucrat, Colonel Donald H. Sawyer, in charge as temporary federal emergency administrator of public works. It also named a Special Board for Public Works, with Ickes as chair, to oversee the PWA.[98] Only twenty-two days later, another executive order named Ickes to the position Sawyer held temporarily.[99] Probably Roosevelt had Ickes in mind all along, but perhaps Ickes did not know that. Perkins appears to have helped orchestrate the narrowing of Johnson's control.

The most important thing about this episode is what it shows us about Roosevelt. There was, in much that he did, a certain deviousness, a deviousness in which he sometimes gloried. One of his favorite cartoons about himself showed the Sphinx in the Egyptian desert with Roosevelt's face. Warren Kimball's titular description of him as "the juggler" or William S. White's attribution of "majesty & mischief" each in its own way helps us to understand him.[100] It is also instructive in both Perkins's scenario and a somewhat different one described in Ickes's diary—someone else does the dirty work or cleans up the mess. It is not a pretty picture, but presidents, even the greatest of them, do many things that are not pretty.

By the time of the cabinet meeting that dealt with Johnson, the hundred days were over. Roosevelt, obviously pleased with the results, deferred his public appraisal of the hundred days for more than a month, but an analysis here is appropriate.

First, the president demonstrated an ability to dominate Congress and did so with relative ease. Only in the matter of veterans' benefits did Congress have much of its own way. Even there, the president had his victories, and his threatened veto caused the proveteran forces in the Senate to retreat.

Second, a tremendous amount of important legislation was drafted, mostly in the executive branch, enacted, and acted upon, in many cases with great efficiency. Most notable were the examination and reopening of most of the nation's banks and the enlistment of three hundred thousand men into the CCC by the end of July.

Third, it is clear that the bulk of the legislation was aimed not at uplifting the "forgotten man" but rather at helping members of the middle class, those with a clear stake in society, keep or regain their former levels of security. Help for farmers but not sharecroppers or farm laborers, succor for home owners but not renters, and insurance for those who still had money to put in banks not only took priority but were actually effected. Those who had only their labor to sell, whether in the country or the city, got few direct benefits in those early months and suffered somewhat from the gradual rise in prices caused by the gradual inflation that New Deal measures caused.

Even more important, it seems to me, are the various evidences that Franklin Roosevelt had, so very quickly, won the hearts and minds of most Americans. His popularity was nowhere more apparent than in those very large segments of American society that in 1933 had little or no tangible stake in it. In mid-1933 Roosevelt had not yet justified their faith with works, nor had he yet earned the sobriquet "a traitor to his class."

8 Getting the New Deal Moving
1933–34

AFTER THE JUNE 16 CABINET MEETING, ROOSEVELT prepared for an eighteen-day seafaring vacation. He would have months to govern without having to deal with Congress on a day-to-day basis, a situation that persisted until World War II.[1] As he explained to the National Emergency Council (NEC): "When Congress is here, I probably have on the average of between three and four hours a day of conferences with congressional leaders, with committees, with individual senators and congressmen who want something for their districts, and so forth, and during that time I cannot devote to the administrative end of the government quite the same time I can devote when Congress is away."[2]

After he had signed papers, sent congratulatory messages to congressional leaders, seen his last visitor, and taken a swim in the newly opened White House pool, the president dined with his secretaries and staff and boarded his special train for Boston about eight thirty. There, a motorcade took him past cheering crowds and on to Groton, where his plans to see his son Franklin graduate the day before had been thwarted by the extended congressional session. He greeted his mother and Eleanor, had lunch with Endicott Peabody, spoke briefly to his son's classmates, and was driven to Marion, on Buzzards Bay, where he spent the night aboard the forty-one-foot schooner *Amberjack II*. With a crew consisting initially of his eldest son, James, two of his friends, and a professional mariner, Captain Eldon Coldbeth,[3] as backup, the president navigated a leisurely twelve-day cruise of some four hundred miles up the Maine coast to Campobello, his first return since he was stricken with polio. He stayed aboard the entire trip.[4] An odd flotilla following in *Amberjack*'s wake, the destroyers *Ellis* and *Bernadou* plus the Coast Guard cutter *Cuyahoga* carrying Secret Service men, was protective and provided services; smaller vessels were hired by the wire services, newspapers, and newsreel companies for journalists who covered the president from a distance, though they were able to speak to him and even film him during most overnight stops. Steve Early and Marvin McIntyre rotated aboard the *Ellis* and wrote out received radio messages and had them taken to Roosevelt by the ship's cutter.

Near Portland the president picked up sons Franklin and John, plus one of their school friends. On the next day's run to Pulpit Harbor, he took the inshore route between many rocky islands, forcing the larger "protecting" vessels to veer off to the main channel out of sight of the president's vessel. Norman Davis, the American delegate to the Geneva disarmament conference, was summoned to report to the president. Roosevelt was demonstrating that the real seat of government—a kind of virtual White House—was wherever he happened to be.

After a delay caused by weather, Davis reported to the president for a two-hour conference aboard *Amberjack II*. Then Roosevelt had the waiting reporters called in. When the eight correspondents came aboard, as the *Times*' Charles Hurd wrote, "crowding into a cabin about seven by eight feet, the President, dressed in gray trousers and sweater, and with a day's growth of beard, lounged in a corner of a settee-berth and left most of the talking to Mr. Davis."[5] In describing a similar scene, two days later on Campobello, in his 1965 memoir Hurd would comment, "He was not wearing his braces," and describe how "the President pushed back his wheel chair," but in his dispatches there was not even a hint that the president was crippled or disabled in any way.[6]

Off Campobello Roosevelt was met by the American cruiser *Indianapolis*, which gave him a twenty-one-gun salute. A small Canadian fleet with scarlet-clad Mounties and a kilted highland band provided a quieter greeting. Once ashore he was welcomed formally by the premier of New Brunswick, lesser Canadian officials, his wife and mother, Missy LeHand, Louis Howe, and Henry Morgenthau. After his two-night, one-day stay at the family home on the island,[7] Roosevelt, with Howe and Morgenthau, boarded the *Indianapolis* for a fast run south to Washington. He so enjoyed shipboard life and its privacy that he stayed aboard and convoked a floating minicabinet meeting while anchored off Annapolis.[8]

Roosevelt was back in the White House on Independence Day; Eleanor, having flown back from Campobello, greeted him but soon took her own vacation.[9] Separate vacations, like separate bedrooms, were long-standing features of the Roosevelt marriage. The Roosevelts' vacations and other absences from Washington were more than recreational. They enabled them to see much of the country and for many thousands to see them. The whole process was more than today's endless and often mindless junketing and photo ops: their trips, combined with radio talks and constant appearances in the newsreels that were shown in most motion picture theaters, were an essential part of the Roosevelts' uncanny ability to connect positively with a substantial portion of the American people.

Although the president's major domestic concerns were the recovery program in general and the AAA, NRA, and public works in particular, both the unprecedented amount of important legislation involving new programs and agencies plus the concomitant administrative duties and responsibilities delegated to him meant an extraordinarily heavy workload. In addition, most patronage appointments had deliberately been put in abeyance until after the session. Jim Farley had at least a thousand appointments to take up with him, and, of course, the wishes of some members of Congress had to be considered. In the first nine months of the New Deal, some one hundred thousand jobs were added outside of the Civil Service, most, but not all, going to "deserving Democrats."[10]

Two of the midyear appointments demonstrate that while the New Deal was an innovative regime, it still practiced patronage politics as usual. One of the more cynical appointments was the naming of Theodore G. Bilbo (1877–1947), a venal, unscrupulous, out-of-office Mississippi politician, to an executive position in the AAA for which he had no qualifications, in order to meet the political needs of Mississippi's Byron P. (Pat) Harrison (1881–1941), chair of the Senate Finance Committee. Given a secretary, Bilbo's only task was to maintain scrapbooks of clippings about the agency; he was derided as the "pastemaster general." Elected to the U.S. Senate in 1934, Bilbo became its most vociferous racist.[11]

The deal to appoint Bilbo was worked out between AAA administrator George Peek and Harrison, apparently without direct recourse to Roosevelt. But the president reveled in telling of a 1934 patronage deal in which he appointed a man he described as "Cotton Ed Smith's favorite murderer"—South Carolina senator Ellison D. Smith (1864–1944), chair of the Senate Committee on Agriculture and Forestry—as a U.S. marshal so that Smith would let Rex Tugwell's promotion to undersecretary of agriculture be confirmed.[12]

On the other end of the racial divide, the president appointed Robert L. Vann (1879–1940), a Pittsburgh lawyer, publisher of the *Pittsburgh Courier*, and sometime assistant city solicitor, as an assistant to the attorney general. This would have been an unexceptional appointment except for the fact that Vann was a black man. While Republican presidents had been appointing a few African Americans to minor offices since Rutherford B. Hayes named Frederick Douglass federal marshal of the District of Columbia, no Democrat had ever done so. The most recent, Woodrow Wilson, had imposed strict racial segregation in federal employment that led to the dismissal of many black employees.

Vann's appointment was a reward for services rendered. Joseph F. Guffey (1870–1959), a Pennsylvania Democratic leader and later senator, who was one of the first Democrats to see the possibility of capturing black votes, had persuaded Howe and Farley to create the Negro Division of the Democratic National Committee and name Vann to head it. One of the few black leaders to support Roosevelt then, Vann campaigned before black audiences, urging them to "turn Lincoln's picture to the wall. . . . [T]hat debt is paid." The story goes that when Guffey, who was the chief patronage dispenser in Pennsylvania, asked the president to appoint Vann, Roosevelt responded, "Will I have to get him confirmed by the Senate?" When Guffey told him no, the president answered, "The job's yours, Joe."

In the Justice Department, Vann was given no significant tasks; the department would have no civil rights division until 1939. Frustrated, he resigned in 1936. As late as 1938, he was participating in Democratic politics in Pennsylvania, but in 1940 he endorsed Roosevelt's opponent, Wendell Willkie.[13]

Busy with hundreds of details, chief of which were working out the first NRA codes with Hugh Johnson, AAA processing taxes with Henry Wallace, and hundreds of public works projects with Harold Ickes while coordinating everything with budget director Lew Douglas, Roosevelt waited almost five weeks after adjournment before reporting to the people about the beginnings of the New Deal. His third Fireside Chat examined the "events of the hundred days [that turned] the wheels of the New Deal." He insisted that its programs were not "just a collection of haphazard schemes, but rather the orderly component parts of a connected and logical whole." First came "foundation stones": getting the banks reopened, refinancing home and farm mortgages, appropriating "half a billion dollars" to "meet the needs of hundreds of thousands who were in dire straits," putting "300,000 young men [to] work in our forests," and creating the "great public works program [of more than] three billion dollars."

Then came "links . . . to build us a more lasting prosperity." These were "the Farm and the Industrial Recovery Acts [that] will work if people understand their plain objectives." He devoted some two-thirds of the chat to them. His gloss on the AAA was that "the Farm Bill gives [farmers] a method of bringing their production down to a reasonable level and of obtaining reasonable prices for their crops."

When the president got to the NRA, his touch was less sure, despite allotting it the broadest coverage. He argued that "democratic self-discipline" in industry would produce increases in wages and shortening of hours sufficient to enable industry to "pay its own workers enough to let those workers buy and use the things that their labor produces." "The essence of the plan is a universal limitation of hours of work per week for any individual . . . and a universal payment of wages above a minimum . . . by common consent. I cannot guarantee the success of this nationwide plan, but the people of this country can guarantee its success." He would soon learn, if he did not already know, that enlightened self-interest was not a common trait among American business leaders of that era. While some critics, then and later, have likened this aspect of the NRA to the corporate state of fascism, a more relevant matter is whether the realistic, pragmatic Roosevelt really believed that this kind of sweet reasonableness, a veritable industrial Peaceable Kingdom, would ever prevail. The bulk of his chat was an attempt to sell this improbable idea. His one tangible claim—that "child labor has been abolished" by the cotton textile and other codes—was a gross overstatement, though it was a stated goal.[14]

The president made no mention at all of the one aspect of the NRA that would endure, the famous "Section 7(a)," which trade unionists claimed guaranteed the right of workers to organize.[15] When he did get around to talking about workers, the result was strangely flat. He first placed the onus of possible failure not on himself, his administrators, or business leaders, but on the people themselves. "I cannot guarantee the success of this nationwide plan, but the people of this country can guarantee its success." His final words seemed to separate workers from the American people. "That is why I am describing to you the simple purposes and the solid foundations upon which our program of recovery is built. That is why I am asking the employers of the Nation to sign this common covenant with me—to sign it in the name of patriotism and humanity. That is why I am asking the workers to go along with us in a spirit of understanding and of helpfulness." For him, it was a lame appeal that perhaps suggests his reservations. There was, however, within the message a pledge that "we are not going through another winter like the last."[16] To redeem that pledge, Roosevelt, as winter approached, created the Civil Works Administration.

In the pages that follow, the course of three key innovative programs—the NRA, the AAA, and the CWA—will be analyzed through mid-1934. During most of that period, the NRA seemed the paramount New Deal measure. Both of the men atop its sprawling structure made the cover of *Time*, Johnson as 1933's "Man of the Year" and, nine months later, Donald R. Richberg, each described as "Assistant President."[17]

Roosevelt, while orchestrating the recovery efforts, was also engaged in a continuing effort to create an institutional framework to control a mushrooming federal government with the White House as the command-and-control center. While his major concerns were with the existing departments and the new agencies, he also sought to reshape inherited independent regulatory agencies by removing appointees before their terms expired. In October 1933, for example, he secured the resignation of George Otis Smith, a Hoover appointee to the Federal Power Commission, who favored private power, and removed William E. Humphrey, a Coolidge appointee to the Federal Trade Commission, when he refused to resign.[18]

The effort to control fell heavily on the NRA and its flamboyant leader, Hugh Johnson, beginning by transferring public works from Johnson to Ickes and shifting his agricultural function to Wallace.[19] In July Roosevelt created the Executive Council, the first of many institutions designed to effect overall control, and, four months later, the National Emergency Council. The more important NEC aimed to give its members, including the president, a clearer notion about such things as the levels of industrial and agricultural production, wage rates, and employment.[20]

Roosevelt often had more than one person in an organization reporting directly and independently to him. For example, after Johnson named Chicago lawyer Donald Richberg (1871–1960) as NRA's general counsel and his chief subordinate, Roosevelt granted the Chicagoan regular access. This afforded him an inside view of the agency distinct from what Johnson and official reports told him. Naturally, Richberg came to consider himself the president's watchdog within the NRA. These various checks on Johnson are evidence of Roosevelt's wariness of the NRA chief, and they are often pointed to as an unfortunate aspect of the president's administrative style. Most critics fail to note that when Roosevelt had confidence in an administrator, such safety valves were either removed or not installed in the first place. In addition, strong and shrewd administrators did everything they could to remain, relatively speaking, masters in their own houses.

Jesse H. Jones (1874–1956) of the RFC was one such master. A hard-as-nails Houston banker and magnate who mistrusted Wall Street, Jones, unlike most conservatives of the era, was a strong advocate of government investment in business enterprise. Installed by Hoover in the pre–New Deal RFC in 1932, he strongly advocated deposit insurance for sound banks and exercised important influence on business recovery. While Harry Hopkins and his relief agencies expended some nine billion dollars by 1939, the overwhelming majority of it in wages to the otherwise unemployed, in the same period Jones's RFC made loans totaling thirteen billion dollars to businesses and states, the vast majority of which were profitable.

Roosevelt allowed the NRA to pursue its basic goal of recovery by getting businesses to agree on standards of "fair competition." Eventually, 557 codes plus 189 supplements were approved. They included not only major industries such as auto- and steelmakers and coal and copper producers but also such "industries" as burlesque shows: its code, among other things, regulated how many times a stripper might take off her clothes each "day." And famously, the Supreme Court case that eventually delivered the coup de grâce to the NRA stemmed from an attempt to regulate the "kosher chicken industry" in New York City.

A general or blanket code—officially the President's Reemployment Agreement (PRA)—was delivered by mailmen to every business in the nation in July 1933. This was a necessary expedient. Eventually, some 2,383,000 employers with 16 million employees accepted the PRA. While the word *boycott* never appeared in official literature, patriotic producers and consumers were supposed to patronize firms that displayed an NRA placard with a blue eagle and the slogan "We Do Our Part," what the president had called a "bright badge."[21] Even individual consumers could sign up: one who did was former president Herbert Hoover, who would later denounce the NRA as "fascism."[22]

The president's message "To Every Employer" began: "This agreement is part of a nationwide plan to raise wages, create employment, and thus increase purchasing power and restore business. That plan depends wholly on united action by all employers. For this reason I ask you, as an employer, to do your part by signing."[23]

The PRA itself, a mere eleven hundred words, limited child labor, established maximum hours and minimum wages, attempted to stabilize prices, and admonished entrepreneurs to "refrain from taking profiteering advantage of the consuming public." No one under sixteen was to be employed full-time, but fourteen- and fifteen-year-olds could work as much as three hours a day. White-collar work was limited to forty hours a week, and most stores were to be open at least fifty-two hours a week. Blue-collar work was generally limited to thirty-five weekly hours and to an eight-hour day. Minimum white-collar wages, set according to city size, ranged between fourteen and fifteen dollars weekly, and blue-collar wages were generally set at forty cents an hour, but in no case less than thirty cents an hour. Individual industry codes, when adopted, could change any of those standards up or down. There was, however, no significant enforcement mechanism, partly because Johnson and most of his lawyers feared that the whole program would be declared unconstitutional.[24]

Instead of legal sanctions, the NRA relied upon a campaign of patriotism and ballyhoo, modeled in part on the Liberty Bonds campaigns of the world war, including speeches by "Four Minute Men." Parades were organized in most major cities, culminating in one up New York's Fifth Avenue involving perhaps 250,000, who marched well into the night.[25] Even before the first code was approved, the AFL had embarked on what its officials called the biggest organizing drive in its history; the United Mine Workers alone claimed 300,000 new members.

Thus, both business and labor found the NRA useful for a time. Businesses were allowed to fix prices without fear of antitrust prosecutions, while labor unions translated the key phrase of Section 7(a) into the slogan "The President wants you to join a union." Roosevelt had said no such thing but never publicly denied it.

Richberg, as counsel for the railroad brotherhoods, had helped draft the Railway Labor Act of 1926 and the Norris–La Guardia Act of 1932 that sought to eliminate injunctions from labor disputes. He helped draft the NIRA and was apparently responsible for writing Section 7(a), which guaranteed workers the right to "bargain collectively" with their employers through "representatives of their own choosing," language taken from the 1926 act.[26] AFL leaders, perhaps naively, believed that the inclusion of Section 7(a) meant that the NRA codes would be a "charter of liberties": William Green compared it to the Magna Carta, while the miners' John L. Lewis evoked the Emancipation Proclamation.[27] But employers were also signing up their employees—often by fiat—into what are usually called company unions. In the early months of the NRA, these largely tame unions grew faster than traditional unions included in the AFL and the railway brotherhoods.

Not surprisingly, the honeymoon between the AFL and the NRA was short-lived. By Labor Day 1933, there were serious criticisms of Johnson, and by June

1934 AFL leaders would denounce the general as the ringmaster of a "National Run Around."[28] Business leaders and middle-of-the-road newspapers also criticized Johnson, whose remarks were often over the top. He had complained that the gangster Al Capone was a "piker" compared to some businessmen and that many "captains of industry" were really "corporals of disaster." By November the U.S. Chamber of Commerce, once a great NRA booster, was complaining that the codes were "unenforceable." The *New York Times,* in a scathing editorial, quoted Johnson's remark that the NRA would never result in "plunging over any abyss" by commenting, "If it did, General JOHNSON would go up and down the land assuring the people that an abyss was the very thing they needed, and if they did not like it, he would ram it down their throats."[29]

Perhaps the root of labor's quick disenchantment with the NRA may be found in what Johnson's biographer called his two basic beliefs about labor: "workers . . . had the right to organize" and "workers should not strike."[30] It soon developed that, when push came to shove, Johnson and most of his staff would side with management. Some labor representatives had expected more from Richberg, but despite his previous advocacy for organized labor, he sided with management on almost all crucial matters. Like so many other former progressives, he wound up opposing the New Deal.[31]

Roosevelt appointed, at the suggestion of the labor and management advisory boards of the NRA, a seven-man part-time National Labor Board (NLB), chaired by Senator Robert Wagner, with three businessmen and three labor representatives. Roosevelt saw this board as a way to ensure labor peace, and in announcing it he mentioned Samuel Gompers's world war no-strike pledge.[32] If such a result—few or no strikes—was Roosevelt's expectation, he was mistaken. The outstanding labor historian of the period tagged the New Deal era as "turbulent years."[33] The NLB, like the NRA, had no powers of enforcement. Thus, it could help mediate and even settle disputes among those truly willing to bargain, but much of American industry was resolutely against sharing any power with its workers.

The submission of a draft code in mid-July by the steel industry, which had a long-standing antiunion tradition, exposed the gulf between capital and labor in some industries. A provision that all voting in representation elections "shall take place on the premises of the employer" was vehemently rejected by labor representatives.[34] A crucial issue in industries like steel, which had no tradition of collective bargaining, was the question of majority rule. Labor's position was that, after an election for representation, the organization that received a majority of the votes should be the bargaining agent for all the workers. And, of course, being compelled to bargain did not mean being compelled to agree.[35]

By October many if not most AFL leaders felt that Johnson and Richberg were far too favorable to employers who preferred to deal with tame company unions.[36] Aware of the deteriorating relations between the AFL leaders and the NRA, Roosevelt used a ceremonial occasion—the unveiling of a memorial to Samuel Gompers (1850–1924) in downtown Washington—to promote his vision of a community of interest between labor and capital. Recalling his own contacts with Gompers during the world war, which typically he magnified, Roosevelt quoted President Wilson's homily on the roles of capital and labor in wartime—"The horses that kick over the traces will have to be put in the corral"—and added his own gloss: "That sermon is just as good today as it was in 1917. We are engaged in another war, and I believe from the bottom of my heart that organized labor is doing its share to win this war. . . . Just as in 1917 . . . we must put and we are putting unselfish patriotism first."[37]

Belatedly, in mid-December Roosevelt issued the first of two executive orders clarifying the role of Wagner's NLB. It was "to settle by mediation, conciliation, or arbitration all controversies between employers and employees" and establish regional boards. Since it had no statutory authority, it could not enforce its recommendations or even subpoena witnesses or documents. Wagner, frustrated, drafted a statute giving the NLB subpoena power and the ability to go to the federal courts to have its orders enforced, as other regulatory agencies could do. Roosevelt gave it no support, and the measure never came to a vote in the 1934 congressional session. Yet, showing his ambivalence, he ignored suggestions from business leaders and their organizations that he do away with the NLB.[38]

Sometime in the closing months of 1933, Roosevelt realized that the NRA was not the desired great engine of recovery. There had been an economic bounce in the early weeks of the NRA's existence, but by the end of September the economic reports sent to Roosevelt and the Executive Council began to show negative progress. Marriner S. Eccles (1890–1977), the Utah banker who came to Keynesian conclusions independently and without higher mathematics, refers in his memoirs to a "Roosevelt depression" in the fall of 1933.[39] Harry Hopkins, privy to the same economic reports as the president plus information gathered by his own people, decided to push for a massive program of work relief. He and his staff, with input from a number of social work specialists, proposed a program to spend $600 million and put 4 million unemployed to work in a matter of weeks. Sometime during the last week of October, Hopkins got a tentative okay for his program from Roosevelt, who supposedly said that 4 million jobs should require $400 million. That would come, as Hopkins suggested, from Ickes's PWA funds, paring down Hopkins's request by a third. (In the event, the new program would cost almost $834 million during its five-month existence.)[40]

Over the weekend of November 4–5, Hopkins and a group of aides and consultants brainstormed in a marathon session at Washington's Powhatan Hotel and at FERA headquarters and drew up a detailed plan for what became the Civil Works Administration.[41] On Monday, at Roosevelt's request, Hopkins met with Ickes, Perkins, and Wallace and received their endorsement. Ickes, whose

PWA kitty provided the first $400 million, while noting that the plan would put "a serious crimp" in his program, recorded in his diary that "there was a general feeling that we really are in a very critical condition and that something drastic and immediate ought to be done."[42]

On Wednesday Roosevelt announced the creation of the CWA at his press conference and issued an executive order establishing it. A week later, in a speech to CWA administrators in Washington—they were, essentially, the same persons who had been administering the FERA—the president backed the program of work relief and admitted, for the first time, that the 2 million persons on the FERA rolls were "on what we might just as well call, frankly, a dole. When any man or woman goes on a dole, something happens to them mentally and the quicker they are taken off the dole the better it is for them during the rest of their lives." And although the program proposed to include those 2 million plus 2 million other unemployed, Roosevelt also admitted that the bulk of the unemployed—"twelve or fourteen or sixteen million or whatever you like"—could not be included in the program.

He pledged that no one would "ask whether a person needing relief or work is a Republican, Democrat, Socialist or anything else." He closed with an exhortation: "Speed is essential. I am very confident that the mere fact of giving real wages to 4,000,000 Americans who are today not getting wages is going to do more to relieve suffering and to lift the morale of the Nation than anything that has ever been undertaken."[43]

Roosevelt's acceptance of this radical program of work relief signals a little-remarked change in his approach. From the inception of his presidency—and before that in his campaign—the stated purpose was "to put people to work," but his emphasis had been on restoring the economic health of employers so that what we now call the private sector could provide the jobs. The failure of the NRA to reach its reemployment goals impelled Roosevelt to try something else, as he had promised.

Hopkins's plan actually produced results in an amazingly short time. On November 23, just fifteen days after the CWA was created, the first government paychecks were issued to 814,511 workers; two weeks later, 1,975,615 workers were paid, and by January 18 the goal of 4 million jobs had been surpassed, as 4,263,644 workers were paid. And while the emphasis was on putting men to work, Eleanor Roosevelt, who presided over the White House Conference on the Emergency Needs of Women, and Harry Hopkins, the only man present, both insisted that women would get, for the first time, an appropriate share of the CWA's jobs. Hopkins had already appointed Ellen S. Woodward (1887–1971), a former Mississippi legislator and social work executive, as head of the FERA's Women's Division. He now spoke of employing as many as 400,000 women—10 percent of the CWA's goal—and, in the event, Woodward's division put 375,000 women to work. But the jobs were all "women's work"—sewing rooms and the like—and conservative contemporary estimates were that women were 18 percent of the unemployed.[44]

The basic difference between the CWA and earlier relief programs can be best illustrated by a report from Frank C. Walker (1886–1959), the executive secretary of the NEC, who informed Roosevelt that in his home state of Montana:

> I saw old friends of mine—men I had been to school with—digging ditches and laying sewer pipe. . . . wearing their regular business suits as they worked because they couldn't afford overalls and rubber boots. If I ever thought, "There, but for the grace of God—," it was right then. One of his friends pulled some silver coins out of his pocket and said, "Do you know, Frank, this is the first money I've had in my pockets for a year and a half? Up to now I've had nothing but tickets that you could exchange for groceries." Hopkins and his associates are doing their work well. . . . During Christmas week many of [those on CWA] were standing in a payroll line for the first time in eighteen months. You have every reason to be proud of C.W.A. and its administration. It is my considered opinion that [the CWA] has averted one of the most serious crises in our history. Revolution is an ugly word to use, but I think we were dangerously close at least to the threat of it.[45]

Hopkins quickly became a celebrity, appearing on the cover of *Time* in mid-February.[46] The key member of his staff urging the program was Aubrey W. Williams (1890–1965), an Alabaman with more advanced civil rights views than any other white person who had access to Franklin and Eleanor Roosevelt during the New Deal. He was a trained social worker with a decade of experience when Frank Bane (1893–1983)[47] hired him to persuade governors to apply for federal loans made available through the RFC by the Hoover administration. Soon Williams was placed in charge of overseeing relief in several southern states, and Hopkins, when he took over relief in May 1933, hired him to do the same for the FERA. In both capacities, he stepped on a lot of toes; when in August 1933 he had publicly praised striking Arkansas cotton pickers, the state's senior senator, Majority Leader Joseph T. Robinson (1872–1937), demanded that Roosevelt fire him. Hopkins summoned him to Washington, and Williams, who had voted for Norman Thomas in 1932, feared the worst. But Roosevelt, intrigued, invited him to dinner at the White House, called him Aubrey, and won his lifelong support.[48]

The major goals of the New Deal for agriculture—reducing output and increasing prices—were clearly being met. But unlike much of the rest of Roosevelt's other programs, its focus was on products like corn, cotton, and tobacco rather than on the people who produced them. Overall New Deal agricultural policy provided only few benefits to the smaller producers, hardly any to most sharecroppers and other tenants and none at all to farm laborers, who were also denied the protections of New Deal labor legislation. The president rarely spoke of the millions of surplus farmers who were, in John Steinbeck's phrase, simply "tractored off the land." Although agricultural prices in peacetime never reached the statistical nirvana of "parity," that is, the same purchasing power they had in the boom years of 1909–14, prices were raised significantly from the drastic lows that had produced the rural disorders in Iowa and elsewhere. That those subsidized prices had a negative effect on the lives of the urban poor was a matter that few in the Department of Agriculture and even fewer of the Democratic leaders in Congress had serious concerns about.

The AAA, the prime New Deal agency for agriculture, did not stand alone but was inserted, awkwardly, into the existing conservative bureaucracy of the USDA, the largest and most prestigious department in Washington. And despite the relative success of New Deal agricultural policy, clashes over policy and culture wracked the AAA from its earliest days. The initial major clash involved George N. Peek (1873–1943), an advocate of the failed McNary-Haugen bills of the 1920s, aimed at raising domestic prices of farm goods, who remained convinced that the answer to America's agricultural problems was an aggressive agricultural export program. He was opposed to the notion of curbs on production, which was the heart of the program Wallace and Tugwell supported. Yet Roosevelt appointed him as initial administrator of the AAA, an indication of his own ambivalence about production controls. Peek's differences with Wallace and Tugwell were well known. After seven months during which Roosevelt denied, against the evidence, that there were any differences between Peek and the Wallace-Tugwell duo, Peek was shifted to an inconsequential post in the State Department, which he soon resigned. By that time, December 1933, Roosevelt's support for production controls and compensatory payments to commercial farmers was secure.[49]

In a letter read at the Farm Bureau's December convention, Roosevelt admitted that the problems of agriculture "cannot be corrected overnight," but argued:

> In a few short months the whole complexion of the agricultural outlook has been changed. Money is getting into the hands of the people who need it; it is coming from higher prices for the things farmers have to sell; it is coming in the form of Government checks for those cooperating producers who are willing to swap a hazardous present for immediate improvement and a stable future. . . . But, in all candor, I think a brief moment of gratification is enough; we seem to be on our way, but we are not yet out of the woods and it is of the utmost importance that we guard against letting a rise in farm income tempt us to forget the realities of supply and demand.

In response, the Farm Bureau's president, Ed O'Neal, hailed the government's program as the farmers' "magna charta."[50]

The president was correct about the improvement. End-of-year figures showed that though the size of the 1933 harvest was 18 percent smaller than the 1932 harvest, farmers received 42 percent more for their crops, $4.1 billion as opposed to $2.9 billion. In addition, a substantial portion of the $534 million in AAA subsidies paid to farmers by the end of 1934 for plowing up or not planting crops was paid in 1933, and many if not most had their mortgage payments reduced.[51]

But Roosevelt's claim that his policies had put money "into the hands of the people who need it" ignored the facts: almost all of the benefits went to the least-needy farmers. And the diminished need for farm labor actually reduced the income of many of the neediest inhabitants of rural America. It would be years before Roosevelt even began to face the most intractable problems of American poverty. The early New Deal focused almost exclusively on getting the once prosperous back on their feet.

The resolution of the fight over basic policy did not end internal disputes over agricultural policy. An even more fundamental split occurred between the longtime agricultural bureaucrats in and out of the USDA—men like M. L. Wilson, the Montana agricultural economist who was an architect of the domestic allotment plan—and a group of more thoroughly radical thinkers, most of whom were in the office of the AAA's dynamic general counsel, Harvard-trained Jerome Frank (1889–1957). These two very different sets of authentic New Dealers represented different cultures. The USDA men, largely midwesterners who, like Wallace, had attended land-grant colleges, resented the predominantly Ivy League lawyers who reported to Frank. A widely circulated canard had Frank asking in a meeting, "What about the macaroni growers?" Although the fight over Peek was, at bottom, a challenge to Wallace's authority, some journalists saw the Peek ouster as a victory for Rex Tugwell, soon to be promoted to undersecretary of agriculture, and it was to Tugwell, rather than to Henry Wallace, that many of the Frank group looked for leadership.[52]

Frank, one of those recommended to the president by Felix Frankfurter, was not shy about his ideas. In a speech at a scholarly meeting, he speculated;

> If force ever undermines the present American system it will be because of the stubborn and blind refusal of a few powerful beneficiaries of the old order to accept improvements and of their attacks on and obstruction to needful revisions of traditional business practices.
>
> Although the profit system . . . seems to have worked poorly, most Americans believe that, properly controlled, it can work well. As long as the majority of the American people continue to cherish that system, it would be impossible, even if it were considered desirable, to abandon it completely.

Describing the New Deal as an elaborate system of experiments, Frank argued that the real threat to the system came from "rock-ribbed standpatters" who had forgotten capitalism's "disastrous adventures . . . the closing of banks and the horrors of unemployment" that accompanied "the old system of drunken prosperity."[53]

Coupled with and fundamental to the rise in agricultural prices were the inflationary monetary policies (which Roosevelt termed "reflation") that the administration pursued fairly consistently. In agriculture these policies favored producers as opposed to consumers, but in the larger economic picture, coupled with lower interest rates on property as well as money, they also favored debtors rather than creditors. This not only was good for home and farm owners, but also favored the largest debtor of all, the federal government, which could finance and refinance much of its debt, old and new, at much more favorable rates. Much contemporary attention was devoted to government purchases of gold and silver, often paying a premium. In late December, for example, the president ordered the annual purchase for the next four years of at least 24.4 million ounces of silver at 64 cents an ounce, 2.5 cents above the current market price but only half of the former statutory rate of $1.29. This was in line with both the Democratic platform of 1932 and an agreement reached at the London Economic Conference earlier in the year, but was a far cry from the unlimited coinage that western inflationists wanted. As Roosevelt later explained, the primary purpose was "to help increase and then stabilize the commodity price level."[54]

Central to these policies and their relatively smooth application was the work of Treasury Secretary William H. Woodin, one of the unsung heroes of the New Deal. But Woodin had been ill since early summer 1933 and on leave in Arizona. Roosevelt told reporters, "I talk to him over the telephone almost every day."[55] Despite Roosevelt's optimism, Woodin's "strep throat"—today cured almost routinely by wonder drugs—was persistent and life threatening.

Woodin's leave required the appointment of someone to take charge of the Treasury. The incumbent undersecretary, Dean G. Acheson (1893–1971), son of an Episcopal bishop and a wealthy mother, was a graduate of Groton, Yale, and Harvard Law School, where he studied with Felix Frankfurter, who arranged for his clerkship with Justice Louis D. Brandeis. Acheson then became a prominent Washington lawyer. A sound money man, his job as undersecretary was to manage the department. It would have been inappropriate for him to be in a policy role, so he resigned and Roosevelt's friend, Henry Morgenthau, became undersecretary and acting treasury secretary.

Roosevelt and Acheson each put his own spin on the resignation. Roosevelt told his press conference, explicitly off the record, "Dean is a fine boy: he has done awfully good work but, of course he has not had the kind of experience in both government and finance that I really should have in the next few months. So he is retiring with the affectionate regards of all of us and Henry Morgenthau, Jr. becomes Undersecretary of the Treasury and acting Secretary during the next few months while Woodin is away."

On his part, the forty-year-old "boy," who would return to Roosevelt's administration as assistant secretary of state during World War II and become secretary of state under Truman, eventually let it be known that he "resigned in protest over Franklin D. Roosevelt's gold policy." But if it was a protest, it was a very silent one. Apparently, Woodin spoke to him and told him that his resignation was required.[56]

Woodin retendered his resignation from Tucson, Arizona, on December 13: Roosevelt accepted it with "great sorrow" and assured "Dear Will" that when "wholly well," he was "wanted and needed. Your calm, practical and courageous action in the difficult days of last Spring and Summer will always be remembered." The resignation was made effective December 31 but not announced until after Morgenthau had been sworn in on January 1; Woodin died on May 3, 1934.[57]

By normal standards, which called for a successful entrepreneur, Morgenthau was the least-qualified secretary of the treasury in modern American history, "a post of dignity beyond his legitimate expectation." Just two years older than the "boy" he replaced, he was without previous financial experience apart from his brief but successful stint as governor of the FCA. He was, after all, a rich man's son who had used his inherited wealth to live as a gentleman farmer, and had he not been Roosevelt's personal friend he would never have been appointed to either job. Woodin, although no banker, had the gravitas of a captain of industry. Such was Roosevelt's authority that Morgenthau's confirmation was routine and unanimous. He became a most successful secretary who, after a couple of minor stumbles, ran the department well and chose capable subordinates.[58]

Morgenthau was only the second Jewish cabinet member in American history.[59] Although Roosevelt never took public notice of the incidence of Jews in the administration, many others did. Four months after Morgenthau's appointment, *Time* published an article about Jewish influence in the New Deal, noting that "a section of U.S. public opinion" blamed "the more radical measures of the New Deal" on Roosevelt's "Jewish advisers." As if to refute this attitude, the magazine summarized findings reported in the *American Hebrew*: that there were one Jew in the cabinet, none in either the subcabinet or the Senate, ten in the House, and two on the Supreme Court and that, overall, just thirty of the top one thousand jobs were held by Jews, roughly the putative percentage of Jews in the American population.

After noting that Roosevelt had nothing to do with either the Jews in the House or on the Supreme Court, *Time* then took up the question of Jewish advisers. It found relatively few in the higher ranks, with some, like Baruch and Warburg, not presently in favor. The bulk of the article then focused on Felix Frankfurter as a talent scout rather than as an adviser and concluded, in lurching *Time* style: "No hierarchy, indeed, are the Jews of the Administration, but they are by no means insignificant. Their power rests not upon their jobs but upon their great industry, their extraordinary mental ability and their crusading fervor for what they conceive to be the high and remote ideals of the New

Deal."[60] Of course, the notion that Jews were, somehow, a cohesive bloc within the New Deal is nonsense. The staid Herbert Feis, "Secretary Hull's leading Jew," had little else in common with the AAA's Lee Pressman, later revealed as a member of the Communist Party.

Two years later, Roosevelt, in a letter he knew would be made public, answered an inquiry from the editor of a Detroit Jewish weekly about the persistent rumors that he had Jewish ancestors. He explained that he had no knowledge of the religion of his ancestors in Holland and added, "In the dim past they may have been Jews or Catholics or Protestants. What I am more interested in is whether they were good citizens and believed in God. I hope they were both."[61]

Although Morgenthau was in many ways an advanced New Dealer—one of his last acts at the FCA had been to appoint a black educator to run a campaign to make black farmers aware of the available federal credit opportunities[62]—he continued to adhere to the traditional shibboleth of a balanced budget. Although he served Roosevelt faithfully and well, he gave him terrible advice, urging him to curtail spending after the 1936 electoral triumph, which helped produce the steep "Roosevelt recession" of 1937. Even after the obvious prosperity following the massive spending of World War II, as his biographer points out, "Morgenthau argued that a balanced budget had never been tried and might have worked."[63]

Morgenthau began his stewardship at the Treasury ineptly. In his first days acting for Woodin, he issued two foolish fiats. First, he ordered that only he and one specified subordinate could speak to reporters, even on background—which set off a justified howl from the press. And he instructed guards and other attendants to snap to attention when he and other departmental dignitaries walked by—which produced snickers all over town, especially since the underlings seemed to pay no attention to it. When a somewhat chastened Morgenthau went to Warm Springs for the traditional Thanksgiving dinner, the president reportedly greeted him, "Well Henry, you have certainly begun at the bottom. The only direction you can go is up."[64]

Appeals for the president to intervene in the already famous Scottsboro case—the alleged gang rape of two young white women on a freight train in Alabama by nine teenage black "Scottsboro Boys" in 1931—were, predictably, brushed aside by press secretary Steve Early, claiming that the president "cannot interfere in any case" in a sovereign state.[65] But when in the following week California's Republican governor, James Rolph (1869–1934), praised a San Jose mob that broke into jail and lynched two white men who had confessed to kidnapping, Roosevelt joined a nationwide chorus of disapproval by denouncing "that vile form of collective murder—lynch law. . . . We do not excuse those in high places or the low who condone lynch law."[66]

Back in the White House, Roosevelt proclaimed the adoption of the Twenty-First Amendment to the Constitution, repealing national Prohibition. Not a

New Deal measure, it was one of the few accomplishments of the final lame-duck session of Congress, which on February 20, 1933, had approved submitting it to state conventions. The amendment is doubly unique: it repeals a previous amendment and was ratified by state conventions rather than legislatures. It both repealed the "eighteenth article of amendment" as its second section and prohibited the "transportation or importation . . . of intoxicating liquors" into any dry state. Since Congress was not in session, a special NRA code was issued and a Federal Alcohol Control Administration created to levy federal taxes and enable state taxation and other regulation until appropriate statutes could be enacted. Although the New Deal era transformed American government, this was its only experience with formal constitutional change.[67]

Apart from a brief speech to the Protestant Federal Council of Churches, in which he defined the New Deal as a "collective effort on broad lines of social planning . . . wholly in accord with the social teachings of Christianity," Roosevelt devoted most of December to planning for his first budget and the coming congressional session.[68] Both he and Eleanor found time to plunge wholeheartedly into both public and private Christmas celebrations. She presided at parties for needy children at the capital's Central Union Mission and Salvation Army, relating her version of the story of Tiny Tim and Scrooge at the latter; he issued pardons restoring citizenship to fifteen hundred war resisters and evaders convicted under the Espionage and Selective Service Acts during the period 1917–19. Roosevelt's Christmas greeting to the nation expressed a "deep conviction that this year marks a greater national understanding of the significance in our modern lives of the teachings of Him whose birth we celebrate. To more and more of us the words 'Thou shalt love thy neighbor as thyself' have taken on a meaning that is showing itself and proving itself in our purposes and daily lives."[69]

On Christmas Eve, both Roosevelts hosted two celebrations. The first was for children of the White House police and servants and their parents. Each child was given an individually wrapped present by the president. The second was the family celebration at which Franklin read *A Christmas Carol* to a four-generation gathering stretching from his mother, Sara, to daughter Anna's two small children. On Christmas morning, family members—not just the little ones—came to Franklin's bedroom to find what was in their stockings hanging from his mantle.[70]

The Roosevelts received a flood of Christmas greetings and gifts. Although the volume of mail that Franklin and Eleanor received—and which they and their staffs answered—had been extremely large from the beginning, the number of Christmas letters and gifts was extraordinary: fifty thousand letters in two days, ten times greater than normal.[71] This outpouring is but one indicator of the extraordinary affection that the president, and eventually his wife, received from many millions of Americans. Lorena Hickok, reporting to Harry Hopkins about conditions in Alabama, was struck by "the number of letters you see around over the President's and Mrs. Roosevelt's signatures. They are seldom anything more than the briefest and most formal acknowledgment of a letter. . . . These people take them all very seriously, as establishing a personal relation."[72]

As he prepared his first annual and budget messages, Roosevelt could justly feel proud of the accomplishments of his first three hundred days. The downward spiral had ended, and some recovery had occurred. His task was to continue that momentum and prepare for the off-year congressional elections in which his party had to expect to lose some of its huge majorities. He felt that reform must continue, but there was no question of a program of legislation to rival that of the first few months.

The president personally delivered a relatively brief annual message to Congress and broadcast it as well; it was the first presidential speech there since Harding's.[73] Without a great deal of specifics and containing nothing like an agenda, Roosevelt made it clear that reforms would continue—one headline read that the New Deal was "here to stay"—and that he expected, with Congress, "to build on the ruins of the past a new structure designed to meet the present problems of modern civilization."

Just before a final paragraph extolling the legislators before him rather than his radio audience, Roosevelt summarized what he thought he had accomplished, his valedictory for the year past, phrased in one of the rural metaphors he loved: "We have plowed the furrow and planted the good seed; the hard beginning is over. If we would reap the full harvest, we must cultivate the soil where this good seed is sprouting and the plant is reaching up to mature growth."[74]

The budget message was sent to Congress and released to the press the next day. It was only slightly longer than the annual message and contained just three tables. It could not conceal the facts, not mentioned in the broadcast message, that the deficit for the current year was estimated at $7.3 billion, that the Treasury planned to borrow $1 billion a month for the six months remaining in the fiscal year, or that an additional deficit of almost $2 billion was predicted for the following year.[75]

Roosevelt tried to cushion the shock in his closing sentence: "If we maintain the course I have outlined, we can confidently look forward to cumulative beneficial forces represented by increased volume of business, more general profit, greater employment, a diminution of relief expenditures, larger governmental receipts and repayments, and greater human happiness."[76]

The notice of continuing deficits alarmed both Wall Streeters and many members of Congress. Most of them had not been paying attention, or they would have realized that, despite the emphasis on economizing, the New Deal programs were expensive: even small weekly paychecks for four million CWA workers would mount up. Roosevelt was able to calm most of his party, but awareness of the deficit stimulated fiscal conservatives in both parties to oppose the New Deal aggressively and paint Roosevelt as a reckless spender, a point of view that gained organizational focus with the formation of the American Liberty League seven months later. Some even accused him of taking advice from John Maynard Keynes.[77]

Keynes had indeed given Roosevelt advice, but in 1934 the president was no Keynesian. In a stunning public letter, sent privately beforehand to him via Felix Frankfurter, the Cambridge economist offered friendly but sharply critical comments on the president's program, softened by an adulatory beginning and conclusion. After calling Roosevelt "the trustee for those in every country who seek to mend the evils of our condition by reasoned experiment within the framework of the existing social system," he warned that if you "fail, rational change will be gravely prejudiced throughout the world, leaving orthodoxy and revolution to fight it out." Keynes closed by telling the president that if he followed the advice about "adaptations or enlargements of your existing policies, I should expect a successful outcome with great confidence" that would contribute "not only to the material prosperity of the United States and the whole world, but in comfort to men's minds through a restoration of their faith in the wisdom and power of Government!"

Keynes's basic message, taking up almost a page in the *New York Times,* was spend much more, spend it quickly, and spend it on useful public works. "The set-back American recovery experienced this past Autumn was the predictable consequence of the failure of your administration to organize any material increase in new loan expenditure during your first six months of office. The position six months hence will depend entirely on whether you have been laying the foundations for larger expenditures in the near future."

It is the most trenchant friendly criticism of the early New Deal economic program offered by any contemporary. Roosevelt clearly did not "get it," writing "Dear Felix" smugly to "tell the professor [Keynes] that in regard to public works we shall spend nearly twice the amount we are spending in this fiscal year."[78]

Liberals within the administration were most alarmed by a threat in the budget message to existing and future programs. Roosevelt, noting that there had been "no coordinated control over emergency expenditures," announced an executive order "prohibiting the further obligation of emergency funds prior to . . . approval" by the budget director. As this gave Lew Douglas, who disapproved of deficits, a means of delaying and perhaps aborting important programs, Ickes, Hopkins, Perkins, Tugwell, and others made strong remonstrances, resulting three days later in a second executive order canceling the first. Thus, what had seemed to be a triumph for Douglas became a bitter defeat. He and other opponents of spending would later have some victories, but until 1937 the most important wins went to the spenders. The budget-message episode was merely a skirmish in an ongoing battle within the administration as well as evidence of Roosevelt's desire for control.[79]

A separate set of struggles over spending involved Roosevelt and Congress: though the stereotype of the spendthrift executive and the tightwad legislators prevails, in many instances it was the other way around. To be sure, Roosevelt's restraints were most often objections to what Congress wanted to spend money on rather than to total outlay. In the first term, for example, it was veterans' benefits that Congress often pushed for.

Roosevelt's legislative tactics in 1934 were more relaxed than those of the hectic hundred days. After pushing through the Gold Standard Act, which ratified earlier emergency actions and gave statutory sanction to Roosevelt's monetary fiats,[80] he deliberately took his foot off the accelerator. More than a month was devoted to unfinished and continuing business such as another six-month extension of the Economy Act's federal pay cut, reauthorizations and funding for the CCC and RFC, guarantees for the FCA mortgages already refinanced, and support for the administration's monetary policies.[81] The Senate did reject the 1932 St. Lawrence Treaty with Canada, which dealt with both navigation and public power. Its rejection, forty-six to forty-two, was thirteen votes short of the required two-thirds. Although this was Hoover's treaty, Roosevelt had supported it since his gubernatorial days. The vote reflected perceived regional economic advantage. Midwesterners supported it; easterners opposed it regardless of party.[82] On January 30, Roosevelt and the nation celebrated his first presidential birthday in spectacular fashion. Among his private visitors during Thanksgiving at Warm Springs had been the utility magnate Henry L. Doherty (1870–1939) and his publicist Carl Byoir (1888–1957). On leaving, Doherty, cryptically, asked the press "to remind the people that the President has a birthday on January 30." He and Byoir had come to discuss plans for the first of the president's Birthday Balls to benefit the Warm Springs Foundation. A torrent of ballyhoo followed, with most of the work done by Byoir, his staff, and Keith Morgan, a successful insurance salesman recruited by Basil O'Connor in 1928. Using a slogan coined by newspaper and radio reporter Walter Winchell—"Dance so that a little child can walk"—the thousands of Birthday Balls, large and small, all across the country drew, according to an Associated Press tabulation, a paid attendance of 737,067 persons.[83] Eleanor Roosevelt attended the several balls in the capital, while the president used what was described as the largest coast-to-coast radio hookup yet to thank the participants for "the happiest birthday I have ever known." The 1934 balls netted $1,003,030.08 and became an annual event.[84]

The key item in the new legislative agenda was for effective regulation of securities; it aroused primitive passions on Wall Street. Less controversial measures included the establishment of sugar quotas and control of the cotton crop, creation of the Federal Communications Commission (FCC), expansion of the HOLC, loans to medium and small businesses, a National Housing Act, Philippine independence, a request for presidential power to make trade agreements, and unemployment insurance.[85]

Before any of these matters were resolved, Roosevelt delivered the first major veto of his presidency and suffered his first override. His target was the Independent Offices Act, which according to White House arithmetic would add $228 million to the budget: $125 million was to restore half of the 10 percent pay cut approved in 1933 and extended a few days earlier; the rest, a $103 million increase in military pension benefits, established principles that could cost many times that amount in years to come. The great danger was the creation of a pension for service—not disability—for veterans of the Spanish-American War, which could later be used to justify extending that privilege to the millions of World War I veterans.[86]

The next-day veto was immediately and overwhelmingly overridden, by 310–72 in the House and by a comfortable margin in the Senate.[87] In both houses, a majority of Democrats deserted the president, while only two Republicans in the House and none in the Senate voted for economy. Leaders of the American Legion called it their greatest victory. The pundit Arthur Krock argued that Congress had reclaimed its power: "The President's supreme control of the parliamentary arm lasted a year and twenty-four days."[88]

Although the temptation to denounce Congress must have been strong, Roosevelt's usual superb sense of tactics prevailed. Instead of complaining, he went fishing! The night the House overrode, he was on his special train heading for Florida without commenting on his reversal. Unlike the summer trip to Campobello, he was not roughing it as a navigator but relaxing in plutocratic luxury aboard Vincent Astor's *Nourmahal,* escorted by the destroyer *Ellis.* The president embarked at Jacksonville, while the White House press contingent went on to Miami and saw the president only once in the fifteen days he was at sea. In response to a rumor that Roosevelt was seriously ill, they were taken sixty miles to a rendezvous off Bimini to see a suntanned president.

Roosevelt's all-male party was made up of either fishing cronies or family, sons James and Elliott plus cousin Kermit; no staff was aboard, but the Secret Service was. The president put in a little work, signing two bills, approving a message to Congress, and receiving one official visit. At Nassau Harbour, he got a twenty-one-gun salute from the British cruiser *Danae,* which fired a seventeen-gun salvo when the Bahamas' governor came aboard to greet the president. On Easter Sunday, in his role as commander in chief, Roosevelt conducted Easter services for the sailors on the *Ellis* as well as the yacht's complement, using the Book of Common Prayer. This and other "news" was radioed daily by Vincent Astor to McIntyre in Miami, distributed to the press, and duly printed. Back in Washington, Eleanor presided at the annual White House Easter Egg Roll.[89]

On his arrival in Washington, Roosevelt was treated as if an emperor returning from some foreign triumph. The day before, the House decided to greet him officially, and the Senate demanded to be included. Some two hundred members of the House, accompanied by their sergeant at arms and the Marine Corps band, actually "marched" the several hundred yards downhill from the Capitol to Union Station; some thirty senators came individually. The vast majority were Democrats doing public penance for overriding his veto and other sins. As one bystander observed to Eleanor Roosevelt, "It's too bad that the President hasn't a bowl of water to sprinkle these men with to wash away their sins." The first lady laughingly agreed. Her husband, who claimed that he was not advised of what to expect, delivered brief bantering remarks, which he later said were an allegory. Telling the crowd that while he had a good time fishing, "I gather also that both houses of Congress have been having a wonderful time in my absence." Aware that even some of his own leaders in Congress had been talking about early adjournment, he remarked:

> I hope you will stay here just as long as you like to. For you younger members . . . I want to point out the advantages of the Washington climate in July and August. It rarely gets over 110° here; there is no humidity and I don't mind if I stay here all summer. . . . I have come back with all sorts of new lessons learned from barracuda and sharks. I am a tough guy. So if you will come down and see me as often as you possibly can, I will teach you some of the stunts I learned.[90]

Although some of the less sophisticated members were mystified by the president's humor, the subtext was clear: Roosevelt was back in the driver's seat, and he expected his agenda to go through if it took all summer. What he did not say was that Congress would have more significant input than in the previous session. The next day, the vice president, Majority Leader Joseph T. Robinson (1872–1937) of Arkansas, and fourteen leading Senate Democrats were summoned to the White House to strategize; Speaker Henry T. Rainey (IL), Majority Leader Joseph W. Byrns (TN), and fourteen other important House Democrats came the following day to meet with the president and Morgenthau. On leaving the White House, the two House leaders told the press that the president wanted them to finish their business by May 15, that the securities bill would have to be worked out, that perhaps $1.5 billion would have to be appropriated for relief, and that there would be, as the phrase went, "something for silver."[91] Most of Roosevelt's original agenda—and more—passed with relatively little fuss.

Nothing better demonstrates Roosevelt's effective control than his supplemental budget request of mid-May. Although actual expenditures had been slower than anticipated in January, he asked for an additional $1.3 billion, more than 90 percent of it for relief. He asked Congress to appropriate a lump sum and allow him to make the allocations. Congress complied.[92]

That Roosevelt was willing to let Congress fill in some of the details is demonstrated by the history of the securities legislation. His goal was to place controls on the stock market, which was left untouched by the 1933 law. Two bills developed, one from a Senate committee headed by Florida's Duncan U. Fletcher (1859–1936), who had been in the Senate since 1909, the other from the corresponding House committee chaired by Sam Rayburn, who had come to Congress in 1913 and was on his way to becoming one of the century's most important legislators.[93]

The final bill, which went through thirteen versions, each polished by Ben Cohen, faced two kinds of opposition, outside and inside. The outside opposition was led by Richard Whitney (1888–1974), whose seventeenth-century ancestry and early career—Groton and Harvard—resembled Roosevelt's. A broker who had represented J. P. Morgan, he was in his fourth term as president of the New York Stock Exchange. He and most Wall Streeters were opposed to many of the provisions of both the Senate and the House bills. The inside struggle focused on whether the securities industry should continue to be regulated by the FTC or by a new commission and whether the Federal Reserve Board or the securities regulatory body should control the margin requirements that were a major provision of all versions of the bill.

None of the most powerful actors managed to get everything he wanted. The president indicated his preference for having the FTC continue in charge. Senator Glass, the legislative father of the 1913 Federal Reserve Act, did not want "his" FRB contaminated by contact with the stock market. Whitney, though he strongly preferred to have the stock exchange regulate itself—he told Pecora committee investigators in 1933 that "the Exchange is a perfect institution"— eventually favored both FRB regulation of margin and the creation of a new regulatory body. In the event, the 1934 Securities Act created such a body, the Securities and Exchange Commission (SEC), and divided control of margin requirements between it and the FRB. In retrospect, Whitney should have been more careful about what he wished for. The SEC, especially under its second and third chairmen, law professors James M. Landis and William O. Douglas, became one of the most powerful and professional of all New Deal regulatory agencies.

Whitney fell afoul not of the SEC but of a New York Republican prosecutor, Thomas E. Dewey, who in 1938 got him indicted and convicted for fraud—the outright theft of money entrusted to him. It turned out that this iconic figure of capitalism had been, in the hyperbolic language of John Kenneth Galbraith, "one of the most disastrous businessmen in modern history." He managed to lose money during the boom of the 1920s: so, as we have seen, did Franklin Roosevelt. But Roosevelt lost a little of his discretionary income; Whitney lost not only his shirt but also large amounts of money borrowed from his brother

George, a Morgan partner, and then used securities owned by the customers of his brokerage firm as collateral for other loans. He pleaded guilty and went to Sing Sing prison, where he served three years and four months of a five-year sentence. His brother and wife eventually restored his embezzlements.[94]

A second new regulatory commission, the Federal Communications Commission, was established without much controversy and received authority to regulate telephones, telegraph, and radio.[95]

The Civil Works Administration, a great success, was always intended as a short-term winter stopgap. It gradually closed shortly after it reached its peak employment in mid-January with a weekly payroll of $64 million. The initial cut was not in personnel but in hours worked: most of those working a thirty-hour week were cut to twenty-four or fifteen hours. Asked what would happen to the four million CWA workers, Roosevelt answered "on pure background" with the hope that most of them would be absorbed into the economy. He admitted that some would not be, but insisted that "we are not going to let people starve." Concurrent with the "demobilization" of the CWA, Roosevelt announced a new relief program that would be for three groups "in want through no fault of their own": distressed families in rural areas; "stranded populations," that is, people living in single-industry communities in which there was no hope of future reemployment, such as miners in worked-out fields; and the unemployed in large cities.[96]

This curious compromise was difficult to justify. Why, for example, were unemployed in large cities more deserving than those in medium-size and small cities? The compromise reflected the simple fact that, until the economic boom set off by World War II, there was never enough money appropriated to cover even half of the nation's unemployed. Hopkins and his staff had to create a patchwork dual system. The federal government never stopped funding traditional relief—what Roosevelt called a dole—most often through the states. Direct FERA grants to supplement state relief continued in the era of World War II. Like every part of the New Deal programs that dealt with the poor, relief programs could deal with only a part, usually a minor part, of the problem of poverty.

No one was more aware of this or deplored it more than Aubrey Williams, but in a signed feature article in the *New York Times* he spoke of the end of the CWA. "In abandoning Civil Works and embarking upon his new tripartite policy, the President has abandoned a tentative program of relief for a quasi-permanent one. I say quasi, for it is believed that the new program holds greater possibilities than did the old of aiding those now on relief to regain a foothold in the economic order."[97]

Why did Williams, who was "bitterly disappointed" by the termination of most work relief, which he believed was its "only morally legitimate form," support Roosevelt's action? It was not just a matter of being a loyal subordinate.

Williams, like his chief, Hopkins, realized that despite Roosevelt's retreat, a retreat that was influenced both by his continuing fiscal conservatism and by a reluctance to incur an even bigger deficit before the November elections, he was the only conceivable political leader who could get even part of the reforms that he and Hopkins wanted. Supporting Roosevelt seemed the only viable choice, so he embraced a result he had struggled against.[98]

In midwinter 1934, Alabama's Hugo Black told Roosevelt about his Senate investigation of collusion between Hoover's postmaster general and struggling airline companies in awarding federal contracts for delivering airmail. The president, remembering that the army had briefly flown the mail in 1918, asked the air corps chief, Major General Benjamin D. Foulois (1879–1967), if the army could do it again. Foulois rashly answered yes. Roosevelt then ordered the contracts canceled and the army to fly the mail. The result was unmitigated disaster. Inadequate preparation, continued poor operational misjudgments, and miserable winter weather resulted in many crashes, which killed twelve pilots and injured others in a little more than a month. Roosevelt ordered the flights suspended; they were soon resumed on a reduced and more prudent basis until June 1, when new and lucrative contracts were awarded. Many personages connected with aviation criticized the army; Charles A. Lindbergh (1902–74), renowned for his solo New York–Paris flight in 1927, criticized Roosevelt for canceling the contracts, in which the aviator had a personal stake. The episode was not, in itself, important to the careers of either, but it surely made subsequent conflicts between them intractable.

A quarter century later, with sensitivities deadened by global carnage, the loss of twelve pilots seemed mere incidental to some. In his 1951 memoir, General H. H. (Hap) Arnold, World War II air corps commander, who in 1934 had been a major in charge of West Coast airmail flights, emphasized the "wonderful experience" gained and "more sophisticated equipment" acquired as a result of having to fly the mail. General Foulois, in a 1954 memo for scholars, argued that the flights marked a "turning point" in the development of American military aviation.[99]

Amid increasing complaints about the NRA from labor, members of the public, congressional critics such as Senator Gerald P. Nye (R-ND), a progressive who supported much of the early New Deal, and consumer advocates within and without the NRA, Hugh Johnson desperately tried to find ways to counter them. At a December meeting with consumer activists, he and Leon Henderson (1895–1986) engaged in a shouting match. The general immediately appointed the economist, then working for the Russell Sage Foundation, as a special assistant and two months later made him chief of the NRA's Division of Research and Planning. From within, Henderson charged accurately that, as he told a reporter, "American industry is slipping into a cartel form of organization." Johnson, under pressure, announced a committee to investigate the NRA and agreed, in what he later called "a moment of total aberration," to have it headed by the flamboyant Clarence Darrow, the nation's most famous trial lawyer. Johnson clearly intended that Darrow's board, as the press came to call it, report to him, but the cagey lawyer got Roosevelt to make a formal appointment, which meant that he, not Johnson, would get the report.[100]

On May 29, Darrow's report was released by the White House, followed by choleric responses from both Johnson and Richberg. "A more superficial, intemperate and inaccurate document, I have never seen" was Johnson's capsule summary. Roosevelt's more measured response came only in his defensive 1937 note to his *Public Papers:* "Unfortunately, the [Darrow] Board . . . proceeded rather as a prosecuting agency to prove a case against big business, than as an impartial investigating body."[101] After the furor over the Darrow report, the NRA clearly had lost whatever impetus it had, and critics on the Left were increasingly joined by business leaders and others on the Right.

Although drought is endemic in much of the arid and semiarid western United States, conditions in much of the Midwest and Great Plains in the first half of 1934 were described by the chief meteorologist of the U.S. Weather Bureau as "the driest of which we have any record." Roosevelt called it "the great drought of 1934." One manifestation of its seriousness was that cities as far east as New York felt its effect. On May 12, the *New York Times* reported: "A cloud of dust thousands of feet high, which came from drought-ridden States as far west as Montana, 1,500 miles away, filtered the rays of the sun for five hours yesterday and New York was obscured in a half-light similar to the light cast by the sun in partial eclipse."

The earliest of a series of giant dust storms had come in the previous November; they continued for years, removing millions of tons of topsoil from the plains. Interviewees in Cincinnati in the 1970s and 1980s remembered vividly having to close windows on hot summer Ohio Valley days in vain efforts to keep the fine dust out.

While the Hoover administration had responded to drought largely through the Red Cross, Roosevelt used federal agencies already in place to administer relief and to begin countermeasures. On May 14, he conferred with Hopkins, Chester Davis of the AAA, and W. I. Myers, Morgenthau's successor at the FCA. Roosevelt recalled, "It is fortunate that . . . the Government [was] better prepared [because] emergency agencies . . . had been created by Congress with broad and flexible powers to meet critical situations as they developed." He never mentioned, publicly, the ironic truth that the drought helped achieve two of the objectives of his program for agriculture: it further reduced the harvest and contributed to a rise in prices.

Nearly a month later, Roosevelt met with members of Congress from the affected areas and told them that, "of course, the Government has to take care of a disaster of that size." He asked for and received from Congress $525 million for an expanded drought-relief program: Hopkins's FERA, for example, not only added jobs in the drought region, but also bought large numbers of cattle that could not be fed and arranged for their slaughter and the distribution of the resulting products among families on home relief. Even before the legislation was approved, FERA had purchased nearly a quarter of a million cattle; by year's end, about 8 million head had been purchased, plus 3.6 million sheep and 354,000 goats. The CCC received $50 million to increase enrollment of youth from the drought area.

Back in March 1933, Roosevelt had asked chief forester Robert Y. Stuart about the possibility of planting trees on the Great Plains and learned, if he did not already know, that the Forest Service had been involved in tree-planting projects in Nebraska and Kansas under Gifford Pinchot in Theodore Roosevelt's administration. An executive order in June 1934 allocated $15 million to the USDA for planting "forest protective strips in the plains region as a means of ameliorating drought conditions." Thus began a gigantic conservation project, planting shelterbelts. (The word was used as early as 1833; the first shelterbelts on the Great Plains had been planted by German Mennonites in the nineteenth century.)

The shelterbelt idea—officially the Prairie States Forestry Project—was often greeted with skepticism and ridicule: a Texas editor wrote that "only God can make a tree. . . . [I]f He had wanted a forest on the wind-scoured prairies . . . He would have put it there." But in fact, the project survived and was largely accepted in the region. It not only provided immediate income for the destitute but also limited soil erosion, preserved moisture, and increased agricultural yields in protected fields. By 1942, when war priorities ended the project, more than 220 million trees had been planted, largely by WPA and CCC labor, in noncontiguous strips around the ninety-ninth meridian, from North Dakota to the Texas Panhandle. Roosevelt continued to be interested even after the project's termination. Overall, the effective response to disaster gave the nation, and especially the residents of the drought area, a splendid example of their government in effective action.[102]

When great men meet, the expectation is that the results will be important, but such meetings are often a disappointment to all concerned. The first meetings between Keynes and Roosevelt in May 1934 fall into that category. The economist and his ballerina wife were invited to the White House for tea, and an hour's talk between the men followed. No spark was struck. Each participant, but particularly the economist, was disappointed. He remarked to Frances Perkins immediately afterward that he had "supposed the president was more literate, economically speaking." Sometime later, Roosevelt told her, "I saw your friend Keynes. He left a whole rigmarole of figures. He must be a mathematician rather than a political economist."[103]

Although we cannot know what Keynes said to Roosevelt, we can get a good notion of his basic message from a little-noted essay he published in the *New*

York Times less than two weeks after their conversation. In it he calculated that the cost of the CWA program had raised emergency expenditure from about $90 million to some $300 million monthly, with good effect. But even that level, he thought, was not enough to sustain recovery, and he suggested that $400 million monthly would be needed until the private sector took up the slack. Keynes maintained, then and later, that for full recovery, business confidence had to be restored.[104]

Despite the failure of Roosevelt and Keynes to have a meeting of the minds, the English economist had an increasing impact on New Deal thought, or, to be more precise, on some New Dealers. Writers as diverse as John Kenneth Galbraith and the hacks of the right-wing Veritas Foundation have created the impression that Keynes's influence came to America chiefly through Harvard. Although that is certainly true after publication of Keynes's *General Theory* in the spring of 1936, before then his influence came through other avenues. Keynes had been publishing articles in American journals such as the *New Republic* since 1919; it had not been American economists but public intellectuals such as Felix Frankfurter and Walter Lippmann who helped spread his early influence. By 1934 he had received strong support from economists at the University of Chicago, and the proximate cause of his 1934 trip was to receive an honorary degree from Columbia.[105]

In Washington Rex Tugwell, a professional economist, was "more or less host" to Keynes during his week in Washington. Tugwell introduced him to a number of midlevel New Dealers and sat in on some of his interchange with Roosevelt. Tugwell gives Roosevelt more credit than most in economic matters and argues that the "extraordinarily secretive mind of" the president "was in process of making transition from what I have called the First New Deal to the Second New Deal."[106] What is clear is that even before 1936, what we now call Keynesian notions were influential among some mid- and lower-level New Dealers, although "the boss" remained immune to Keynes's blandishments: before 1938–39 Roosevelt spent when he had to but remained committed to the ideal of a balanced budget, which as president he never achieved.

By the time of congressional adjournment in mid-June 1934, it was clear that Roosevelt's "tough guy" tactics had paid off: the legislation passed in 1934 would be deemed exceptional except that it followed and preceded sessions that were even more fruitful. As Turner Catledge of the *New York Times* noted, "Congress . . . fulfilled with but few exceptions every desire of the executive" and "wiped the legislative slate as clean as" anyone in Washington could remember.[107] Yet there were important matters—none of them on the president's "must list"—that were drafted and discussed but left to future Congresses. The most important were matters to which Roosevelt was, in principle, committed: Wagner's labor-disputes measure plus bills on old-age pensions and unemployment insurance. In addition, two of the carryover bills—Senator Black's thirty-hour workweek bill and Representative Wright Patman's (D-TX) bill to pay the bonus—were opposed by the president.[108]

Apart from January's monetary bill and the stock exchange bill, the major pieces of legislation dealt with housing, American Indians, and the management of the public domain. The HOLC legislation of the preceding session had stemmed the tide of housing foreclosures but had not done much for either the real estate market or the larger economy. Most of those whom Roosevelt chose to advise him had favored a large-scale public housing program, which meant even larger deficits, and which he rejected. Instead, the National Housing Act further expanded the HOLC and created the Federal Housing Administration (FHA) to insure mortgages for new homes and the refurbishing of existing housing. By assuming risks, it was able to force lenders to reduce rates and generally liberalize the rules of the game for white home owners. At the same time, through the practice of redlining in which the FHA participated, the agency contributed to the further segregation of urban and suburban neighborhoods and in effect denied support to most housing owned or occupied by persons of color. While Roosevelt stressed the reforms enabling home ownership for "the family of moderate means," he never discussed redlining. Public housing—which during the Roosevelt era was primarily for poor whites—would be largely left to Harold Ickes's slow-moving PWA.[109]

The law that changed significantly how the government dealt with American Indians—the Wheeler-Howard bill, which became the Indian Reorganization Act—was largely the work of Ickes and his commissioner of Indian affairs, John Collier (1884–1968). It was a major reform of government policy toward the American Indian, the first statute that can be regarded, in retrospect, as encouraging cultural pluralism. It replaced what has been called the "missionary protectionism" that had long prevailed in the management of Indian lives with a "social science protectionism" that had respect for Indian culture. Indians were encouraged to develop their own self-government under the guidance of white federal officials. Nevertheless, Indians, as a group, remained the poorest and least long-lived of all Americans. Roosevelt said he was "primarily interested in the principles of the bill" and emphasized, then and later, the New Deal's reversal of the long decline in Indian landholding. Most of what came to be regarded as "the Indian New Deal" was effected by executive actions that gave reservation Indians separate versions of various relief programs, beginning with the CCC.[110]

The Taylor Grazing Act was about much more than grazing. It did establish cooperative grazing districts on public lands, and by 1937 forty-nine had been set up on 110,000 acres of western public land under the supervision of the Interior Department. More important, the law gave the president discretionary powers to withdraw public land from entry or purchase for the purposes of conservation. By 1937 Roosevelt, using executive orders, had withdrawn some

166 million acres. The practice became a cornerstone of federal land management. The passage of the Taylor Act was also a part of the internal struggle between the Agriculture and Interior Departments to control conservation. This skirmish was won by Interior: Ickes had urged the president to sign the bill, while Wallace had urged him to withhold his approval. Roosevelt made sure that neither department achieved total victory.[111]

Among the other notable administration measures enacted were the following:

> The Deficiency Appropriation Act, which authorized more than $2 billion for "relief" to be spent largely at the president's discretion, including the $525 million for drought relief.[112]
>
> Limited gun-control legislation affecting machine guns and sawed-off shotguns and a variety of other statutes federalizing many kinds of criminal activities formerly left to the states as part of what Roosevelt called the "war on crime."[113]
>
> The Reciprocal Tariff Act, which authorized the president to negotiate bilateral trade agreements raising or lowering existing tariffs by up to 50 percent. Secretary of State Hull, who saw these agreements as a panacea, negotiated eighteen of them. They had little overall effect on the Depression economy but did largely remove what had been one of the most contentious issues from the annual legislative agenda.[114]
>
> The Vinson Act, which authorized naval construction up to the limits set by the naval limitation treaties of 1922 and 1930. In a public statement about the bill, Roosevelt explained, correctly, that the bill was merely an authorization and did not actually start construction. In a specifically off-the-record statement to reporters, he explained that his statement was in response to "appeals from pacifist organizations." It did not mention that, as he spoke, some 30 naval vessels were under construction. During 1933–36, often using PWA funds, work was begun on 115 vessels: 2 battleships, 3 aircraft carriers, 2 heavy and 9 light cruisers, 75 destroyers, 22 submarines, and 2 gunboats.[115]

Roosevelt signed one measure about which he had serious doubts. The Frazier-Lemke Farm Bankruptcy Act allowed courts to grant farmers a five-year mortgage moratorium under certain circumstances. His action was clearly an attempt to keep western agrarian radicals on the reservation in the upcoming elections.[116]

While he was still signing and vetoing bills, issuing executive orders implementing the new laws, making appointments to fill newly created positions and old vacancies, and otherwise tidying up after Congress departed, Roosevelt delivered the first Fireside Chat of 1934. Unlike the relatively full account at the end of the hundred days, a paragraph sufficed to describe "a few of the major accomplishments" of Congress. Most of the rest of the talk was devoted to a defense of the New Deal and was really a prelude to the looming off-year elections, which the president chose not to mention. In describing his basic priorities—relief, recovery, and reform—the president avowed, for the first time, that relief was going to be a long-term proposition. "Relief was and continues to be our first consideration. It calls for large expenditures and will continue in modified form to do so for a long time to come. . . . It comes from the paralysis that arose as the after-affect of that unfortunate decade characterized by a mad chase for unearned riches, and an unwillingness of leaders in almost every walk of life to look beyond their own schemes and speculations."

Here, and elsewhere, Roosevelt was campaigning not against a party or individuals, but against recent unhappy history. As he was wont to do since writing *Whither Bound?* in the midtwenties, he identified himself with the future; his unnamed opponents were men of the past. "We have recognized the necessity of reform and reconstruction—reform because much of our trouble today and in the past few years has been due to a lack of understanding of the elementary principles of justice and fairness by those in whom leadership in business and finance was placed—reconstruction because new conditions in our economic life as well as old but neglected conditions had to be corrected." Recognizing the criticisms that were beginning to mount, he insisted that "the simplest way to judge recovery" was to ask, "Are you better off than you were last year? Are your debts less burdensome? Is your bank account more secure? Are your working conditions better? Is your faith in your own individual future more firmly grounded?"

Note that these questions are largely addressed to a middle-class audience; Roosevelt knew that the working class was already on his side. He also knew that the mounting attacks on the very real regimentation required by much of the recovery program—controls over both business and agriculture—had to be met, as did the more easily countered bugaboos of dictatorship and communism. For the former, he asked another "simple question":

Have you as an individual paid too high a price for these gains? Plausible self-seekers and theoretical die-hards will tell you of the loss of individual liberty. Answer this question also out of the facts of your own life. Have you lost any of your rights or liberty or constitutional freedom of action and choice? Turn to the Bill of Rights of the Constitution, which I have solemnly sworn to maintain and under which your freedom rests secure. Read each provision of that Bill of Rights and ask yourself whether you personally have suffered the impairment of a single jot of these great assurances. I have no question in my mind as to what your answer will be. The record is written in the experiences of your own personal lives.

His anonymous opponents—he called them "Doubting Thomases"—were those who sought either "special political privilege" or "special financial privilege." His own program—the words *New Deal* were not used—sought "the security of the men women and children of the Nation" and involved three principles:

1. Added means for providing better homes for the people of the Nation.
2. To plan the use of land and water resources of this country . . . to meet [the] daily needs of our citizens.
3. To use the agencies of government . . . to provide sound and adequate protection against the vicissitudes of modern life—in other words social insurance.

He then spoke of "a few timid people" who were putting "new and strange names" on "what we are doing[—]'Fascism,' 'Communism,' 'Regimentation,' 'Socialism.' . . . [T]hey are trying to make very complex and theoretical something that is really very simple and very practical." Proclaiming himself a believer "in practical explanations and in practical politics," he used a homely example. He described the renovations that were planned for the White House during his summer vacation—the addition of some rooms, modern electrical connections, modern plumbing, and "modern means of keeping the offices cool." But, he explained, the basic structure would remain.

> The artistic lines of the White House buildings were the creation of master builders when our Republic was young. The simplicity and the strength of the structure remain in the face of every modern test. But within this magnificent pattern, the necessities of modern government business require constant reorganization and rebuilding.
>
> If I were to listen to the arguments of some prophets of calamity who are talking these days, I should hesitate to make these alterations. I should fear that while I am away for a few weeks the architects might build some strange new Gothic tower or a factory building or perhaps a replica of the Kremlin or of the Potsdam Palace. But I have no such fears. The architects and builders are men of common sense and of artistic American tastes.

The analogy with the New Deal was obvious. "All that we do seeks to fulfill the historic traditions of the American people. Other Nations may sacrifice democracy for the transitory stimulation of old and discredited autocracies. We are restoring confidence and well-being under the rule of the people themselves. We remain, as John Marshall said a century ago, 'emphatically and truly, a government of the people.' Our Government 'in form and in substance . . . emanates from them. Its powers are granted by them, and are to be exercised directly on them, and for their benefits.'"[117]

In one brief talk—some twenty-five hundred words, less than thirty minutes of airtime—Roosevelt not only brilliantly laid out the basic tactics for the 1934 and 1936 electoral campaigns but also gave notice of where the New Deal was headed. If the Roosevelt presidency was, in essence, one long improvisation, by mid-1934, and not, I believe, very much before that time, relatively specific objectives had been set.

Clearly, there were important matters left unaddressed. Only an implicit justification for spending was offered, perhaps representing the president's own ambiguity about deficits. Even more glaring was the failure to discuss labor problems—at a time when the San Francisco waterfront strike, begun in May, was about to erupt into violence—and the continuing failure to deal with taxation. And, of course, the appeal to John Marshall would, after conflicts with the Supreme Court became a major issue, be succeeded by appeals to his great enemy, Thomas Jefferson.

9 Advancing Reform
1934

ROOSEVELT MANAGED VERY DIFFERENT KINDS of reforms in a variety of ways. To initiate the work of the Securities and Exchange Commission, he chose as its first chair not a dedicated reformer, but an experienced speculator, Joseph P. Kennedy (1888–1969). He was controversial in his own right even before the election of his second son as our only Catholic president gave him an almost mythical significance. A tough Harvard-educated, third-generation Irish American Boston businessman—his father was a banker—by 1934 he was a multimillionaire. Much of his fortune came from his part in arranging the merger that created RKO Pictures. His insider profits then and his participation in a "pool" that drove up the price of the large glass manufacturer Libby-Owens-Ford in 1933 were precisely the kinds of legal abuses the SEC was created to regulate. Harold Ickes, disapproving, complained to his diary that Roosevelt had "great confidence in [Kennedy] because he has made his pile . . . knows all the tricks of the trade" and assumed that he wanted "to make a name for himself for the sake of his family."

There were good political reasons for the appointment. Unlike most eastern Irish American Democrats, Kennedy was a "before Chicago" Roosevelt supporter who had made significant cash campaign contributions, helped get William Randolph Hearst's convention support, and been of minor assistance to the brain trust during the 1932 campaign. He was also a useful connection to the conservative bishops of the East Coast Catholic hierarchy as well as to the political priest Charles E. Coughlin.[1]

Kennedy proved Roosevelt's judgment correct by getting the SEC off to a good start. He declared that the commissioners were not "coroners sitting on the corpse of financial enterprise" but a means of bringing "new life" into the securities industry. The new life was a long time coming, but the SEC soon grew into a large and successful administrative bureaucracy. It became, as regulatory bodies usually do, an important adjunct of the industry it was designed to reform. Kennedy, who stepped down as planned the next year, was succeeded in the next three years by three true New Deal reformers—James M. Landis, William O. Douglas, and Jerome Frank—each of whom moved on to bigger jobs.[2]

Another newly created agency, the Federal Communications Commission, was part of a reforming tidying up and modernization that went on during the New Deal. The Communications Act of 1934 merged functions into the FCC that had been divided between the Interstate Commerce Commission and the Federal Radio Commission, abolishing the latter body. It produced few noticeable changes until Roosevelt moved another of Frankfurter's protégés, James Lawrence Fly (1898–1966), from the legal department of the TVA to become its chairman in 1939. Three somewhat conflicting sections of the new law created controversy and, eventually, litigation about what could be said on radio stations. Section 309 provided for revocation of a station's license if it did not provide "public interest, convenience, or necessity," while Section 326 barred censorship except in cases of "obscene, indecent, or profane language." The act also laid down in Section 315 the so-called Fairness Doctrine, requiring broadcasters to offer equal time to political candidates. All three provisions were in potential conflict with the First Amendment. (In 1959 Congress exempted news programs from the equal-time provision, which has since enabled, among other things, two-party presidential debates and openly partisan radio and television stations and networks.)[3]

On the labor front, amid a pyramiding number of strikes and lockouts—historian Irving Bernstein's chapter about labor during the spring and summer of 1934 is titled "Eruption"[4]—Roosevelt had held back from endorsing a comprehensive labor measure drafted by Senator Wagner. Instead, he had the majority leaders in both houses introduce Public Resolution No. 44, approved at the very end of the session on June 19, empowering the president to appoint "a Board or Boards" to investigate labor disputes and conduct representation elections "for the purpose of collective bargaining as provided in Section 7(a)" of the NRA act. After adjournment Roosevelt took three separate actions based upon it. First, he issued a pair of orders about a dispute in the steel industry, assigning it to Labor Secretary Frances Perkins by empowering her "to represent me in taking whatever action seems appropriate," and a few days later he created a separate board for the steel industry to report to him through Perkins.[5]

The next day, the president created the first National Labor Relations Board (NLRB), a body independent of the Labor Department. The order establishing it reemphasized the determination of the president to support workers' rights: "Nothing in the order shall prevent, impede or diminish in any way the right of workers to strike or engage in other concerted activities." Like its predecessor, the NLB, the new board's authority rested in part on the NRA act, and it lacked subpoena power or an effective means of enforcing its decisions. Its appointees no longer represented interest groups but were "impartial persons," government employees at ten thousand dollars a year. Two skilled lawyers headed the first NLRB during its short life. Lloyd K. Garrison (1899–1991), dean of Wisconsin's law school, took a summer's leave to get the board started and persuaded Francis Biddle (1886–1969), of the Philadelphia Biddles, to succeed him in November.[6]

Biddle, a new boy at Groton when Franklin Roosevelt was a sixth former, earned undergraduate and law degrees from Harvard and served as Oliver Wendell Holmes's law clerk. Although Biddle was a Republican who supported Roosevelt's candidacy in 1932, the AFL's William Green protested his appointment because he and his firm had many corporate clients. Biddle became a quintessential New Dealer, rising to become Roosevelt's last attorney general.

The major achievement of the first NLRB was to settle the vexed question of who should represent workers who had not supported the winning union in an election to decide representation held under 7(a) in the NRA statute. In the 1934 *Houde* case, later affirmed by the Supreme Court, Biddle's board ruled: "When a person, committee, or organization has been designated by the majority of the employees . . . it is the right of the representatives so designated to be treated by the employer as the exclusive bargaining agency of all the employees in the unit."[7] Roosevelt, speaking off the cuff at his June 15 press conference, had given a diametrically opposed interpretation of 7(a), probably acquired from Richberg or Johnson:

THE PRESIDENT: Section 7-A says that the workers can choose representatives. Now if they want to choose the Ahkoond of Swat they have a perfect right to do so. If they want to choose the Royal Geographic Society, they can do that. If they want to choose a union, of any kind, they can do that. They have free choice of representation and that means not merely an individual or a worker, but it means a corporation or a union or anybody. And that has to be made absolutely clear in this legislation.

Q: How do you feel on the point of minorities?[8]

THE PRESIDENT: The question of minorities is not a tremendously serious one, because that has to be worked out in each individual case. If there is a substantial minority, it seems fair and equitable that that minority should have some form of representation, but that is a matter of detail depending on the individual case. In some industries it is possible that neither side may want to have it.

Q: Suppose they do choose the National Geographic Society, then do the employers have to trade with them?

THE PRESIDENT: Absolutely.[9]

Roosevelt quietly abandoned this view and came to support the principle established by the NLRB.

Among other postadjournment actions, Roosevelt created the Committee on Economic Security to plan for the measures promised in the Fireside Chat. Although headlines called the CES a "Cabinet Committee," its four cabinet members—Perkins (chair), Morgenthau, Cummings, and Wallace—were joined by Hopkins, an indicator of his growing importance. The real work was done by a group of advisers and an executive secretary. In the note to the order in his published papers, Roosevelt called it "a first step toward the adoption of the Social Security Act of 1935."[10]

A look at how the CES was assembled provides further insight into the ways the New Deal was staffed. Just as a significant percentage of its lawyers came from Harvard, funneled to Washington by Frankfurter and others, and large numbers of economists and agronomists came from land-grant agricultural colleges and universities, the University of Wisconsin and some of the reform institutions of its very progressive state were an important source of reform-minded social scientists. In staffing the CES, and later the Social Security Administration, the key figure was Arthur J. Altmeyer (1891–1972). A student of Wisconsin labor economist John R. Commons (1862–1945) who helped run the state Industrial Commission for eleven years, Altmeyer was hired by Perkins on Senator La Follette's recommendation to coordinate matters with state labor departments. In 1934, when he had become second assistant secretary of labor, she tasked him with heading the CES advisory committee. In turn, Altmeyer looked back to Wisconsin for the CES's executive secretary and recruited another Commons Ph.D., Edwin E. Witte (1887–1960), head of Wisconsin's fabled Legislative Reference Service. Witte, often called the "father of Social Security," in turn brought with him from Wisconsin as his research assistant Wilbur J. Cohen (1913–87) with a fresh B.A., who in 1935 became the Social Security Board's first employee and thirty years later was crucial to the enactment of Medicare. John Kennedy dubbed him "Mr. Social Security," and he became one of Lyndon Johnson's secretaries of health, education, and welfare. Senator Paul Douglas once quipped that "an expert on Social Security is a person who knows Wilbur Cohen's telephone number." Not all the key Social Security planners, of course, were of the Wisconsin school. The chief drafter of the Social Security Act, Thomas H. Eliot (1907–91), the assistant solicitor of the Labor Department and executive secretary of the CES, was Harvard '28, Harvard Law '32, but not a Frankfurter protégé.[11]

In the final analysis, what was crucial to the success of these and other networks was the attractive force of the New Deal and of Roosevelt himself, who was simply "the Boss" to thousands of mostly very young and often talented people who flocked to Washington, hoping to make history and a better world. John Kenneth Galbraith (1908–2006) described the mood in Washington in the summer of 1934 when he, with a freshly minted Ph.D. from Berkeley, had a minor temporary job in the Department of Agriculture.

> I did not meet F.D.R. that summer. He was, nonetheless, the major, indeed the dominant, figure in my life. So he was for all the others I knew. We talked

of him all day and every night, there was no other topic of conversation. We were responding to a central part of Roosevelt's political personality. . . . He was a man of intelligence and a deep sense of social responsibility, but he was also without a controlling personal ideology, social belief, of his own. That meant that he was available to be persuaded, he was open to any well-stated solution to the great and painful problems of the time. No one ever said, "You can't sell the President on that"; it was possible that you could.[12]

In a burst of work that the White House claimed was record setting, in the five days after Congress adjourned Roosevelt attended to some 200 bills and saw about the same number of visitors. Roosevelt, during his presidency, would veto 635 bills, 9 of which were overridden.[13]

Even as he disposed of bills, issued orders, and selected officials, Franklin Roosevelt was thinking about his summer voyage, remarking at the close of the June Fireside Chat that "it is a good thing for everyone who can possibly do so to get away at least once a year for a change of scene." The fact that millions of his listeners were in no position to travel did not seem to bother him or them. Just before he took his vacation, he ordered cabinet members and other top officials to take vacations of at least thirty days.[14]

The 1934 postsession vacation was a far cry from his relatively spartan trip in 1933. He sailed on the USS *Houston*, a 9,050-ton vessel commissioned in 1930, 600 feet long with a top speed of 33 knots and specially adapted for his convenience; he utilized it again in 1935, 1938, and 1939. A reporter who visited the *Houston* in Annapolis before the president boarded described his quarters on the "floating White House":

> The suite lies on the port side . . . a little aft of the bridge. There is a large sitting room, a smaller bedroom, a bath and an adjoining kitchen. . . . Deep-cushioned divans and chairs are scattered around the sitting room, jaunty with brightly covered slip-covers. There is a large writing desk, pigeonholes neatly stuffed with paper of all sizes, and pens and pencils. Near the desk stands a glass-doored bookcase . . . with volumes especially selected . . . detective stories, humor, history, books on the places Mr. Roosevelt will visit [and] on the navy and its heroes.

The 1934 trip of thirteen thousand miles began when the *Houston* headed for the Caribbean on July 1; it would transit the Panama Canal and sail to Hawaii and then return the president to the continental United States at Portland, Oregon, on August 3. From there his train took him east with stops to view, firsthand, results of the New Deal, reaching the White House on August 10.[15]

Many questioned how, despite his ability to keep in touch by radio, the president could leave the capital at such a crucial time. The answer was that Roosevelt, unlike many in and out of government, felt that given the changes that were taking place, a certain amount of turmoil on the labor front was inevitable. His clearest statement of this came in an explicitly off-the-record sequence in a press conference, in which he explained why he had not made the Wagner bill—essentially the same bill that became the Wagner Act the next year—an administration measure.

It would be perfectly all right to say I am in favor of [Wagner's bill] and hope it will go through; but, off the record, you all know that in any period of this kind, with a return of prosperity and reemployment and with an increase in values, you are bound to have more strikes. I look for a great many strikes in the course of this summer, a good many more. It is a normal and logical thing. I think I have said this before at a strike conference. They are brought about by a great many causes.

For instance, keeping this again entirely off the record, in this Toledo case the strike originated with only 400 employees in one factory, but there are a lot of other factors involved. They had pretty serious political trouble where a lot of graft and misgovernment, etc., was shown in the city. The result was that the population as a whole "got sore." It wasn't just these 400 men.

Yesterday, when this crowd of between 5,000 and 10,000 people started, they were, as a body, "sore" at certain definite people. As they went along, they would throw stones at one particular factory or shop, and then they would go along past several other factories or shops they were not "sore at," and then they would pick out the next fellow at whom they were "sore."

Charlie Taft[16] telephoned to Miss Perkins about two hours ago and made the point that it is not an indiscriminatory strike; it is a strike against people they are "sore at," and it is not just the 400 strikers; it is a very large element of the population.

So each case really has to be taken up on the merits of that particular, individual case. There is no general statement that can be made relating to it. Miss Perkins used a parallel which, of course, has got to be entirely off the record. She said in conference today that it is not a general revolutionary feeling but a feeling against certain old-line politicians and a feeling against certain industrialists. It is a pretty discriminating opposition. It is based on reason of some kind.

In the Toledo situation, of course, the one thing that all of us ought to appreciate and write about is that there are methods of settlement, and that the attitude of employers in many cases has been so autocratic. Take, for instance, the man who said, in one of the papers this morning, that he would consider that he was demeaning himself if he sat in the same room with William Green. Now that kind of autocratic attitude on the part of a steel company official does not make for working things out. On the other hand, there are [labor] people who are just as autocratic.

Those who write about Roosevelt's initial naïveté about labor matters have obviously not read this transcript.[17]

The *Houston*'s first landfall was at Cap Haitien, where Roosevelt came ashore to be greeted by Haiti's president, who returned the call on the *Houston* the next day. Roosevelt's brief remarks spoke of his previous visit in 1917, the pending withdrawal of the last of the U.S. Marines, and future friendship. In a letter to Eleanor, the president explained that his speech started in French, "but when I got to the serious part I shifted to English!" Still the benevolent colonial administrator, he continued, "Perhaps the Haitians will recognize the vast amount of good things we have done for them in these 18 years. The *people* do, but the ruling mulatto class doesn't, I fear." He reported that their boys were "really interested," "movies in the well deck every night," and that "the [Filipino] mess boys from the 'Sequoia' take very good care of us."[18]

Eleanor had preceded him to the next stops, American possessions Puerto Rico and the Virgin Islands, and had briefed him about the abysmal social conditions in both. Landing at Mayagüez, the president motored nearly the length of the island to San Juan, some 136 miles, with fifteen brief stops. "The trip across the island via Ponce was thrilling. I drove with [Governor Blanton] Winship but others got in from time to time and I drank in all kinds of information. Cheering crowds all the way and really pathetic *faith* in what we are trying to do."

He dined with federal officials—no Puerto Ricans had been invited—and spent the night. The next morning, he saw "the forts and then those vile slums," and then boarded the *Houston* for a quick run east to St. Thomas and, in fewer than twenty-four hours, visited both main islands and the three chief towns of the American Virgin Islands. He wrote Eleanor about being greeted and driven to the square, "where the whole population paraded. What nice children they are." He also saw some new two-room houses that the PWA had built, which he liked. The two-day leg to Cartagena was, even the seasoned sailor reported, "quite a rough trip."[19]

The state visit to Colombia was a little touchy, as public opinion there still deeply resented the U.S.-backed coup in 1903 that had separated Panama from Colombia. This had created a client state that gave carte blanche to Theodore Roosevelt's government to build and operate the Panama Canal in the zone ceded to it. That the first American president to visit the country was also named Roosevelt and that he was passing by on his way to utilize that canal were ironies that all parties understood. After a successful visit, Franklin pointed out to Eleanor that "in a sense this was a test visit to a South American Republic, especially in view of the bitter feeling about the Panama Canal episode." In contrast to his remarks in Haiti, Puerto Rico, and the Virgins, his remarks in Cartagena, though labeled "extemporaneous," clearly had been worked up to flatter his audience by showing the American's knowledge of Colombia's origins and early history.[20]

The *Houston* took Roosevelt through the canal with a brief stop to allow him to meet with Panamanian and American officials and then, with escorts from the Pacific fleet, sailed to Hawaii, with a brief fishing stop off Cocos Island. A rare wire story revealing the president's physical helplessness described an incident of the Cocos Island fishing. Quoting a letter by a chief petty officer on the *Houston*, "[The president wanted to go ashore] in water up to our chins. . . . We lifted him out of the boat and tried to keep him out of the water, but somehow we dropped him a little and he got wet. He just laughed and said for us not to worry." When such accidents happened out of public sight, Roosevelt bore them with equanimity and great patience; if they happened at a public event, that was another matter.[21]

Back aboard the *Houston*, Roosevelt could not escape involvement in one of the few general strikes of American workers.[22] The dispute that led to it had a long history. Back in March, Roosevelt had received a telegram from George Creel (1876–1953), an old Wilsonian who was the California director of the NEC, about the seriousness of a pending strike of Pacific Coast longshoremen. Roosevelt asked for a suspension of the strike and appointed an ad hoc Federal Mediation Board whose hearings delayed the strike but settled nothing.[23] The dispute that led to it had a long history. On May 9, longshoremen from Bellingham, Washington, near the Canadian border, to San Diego went out on strike. Other seafaring unions soon walked off their jobs, transforming it into a maritime strike. After May 15, no freighter sailed from any American Pacific port for more than two months. In San Francisco, where the dispute was centered, the city's business elite had long sought to destroy all but company unions and create an open-shop city, hired a public relations firm, and sought to brand the strike a Communist plot. The new longshoremen's leader, a previously unknown Australian, Harry R. Bridges (1901–90), was a radical and may have been a Communist Party member, although the Supreme Court eventually rejected the charge that he was. The longshoremen struck over basic trade union issues, union recognition, working conditions, and pay.

After more than a month and a good deal of violence, Roosevelt had appointed a National Longshoremen's Board, which had jurisdiction only on the Pacific Coast, before leaving on his holiday. San Francisco's Roman Catholic archbishop, Edward J. Hanna (1860–1944), chaired the board. The strike continued with sporadic violence, as strikebreakers were used to move the backlogged cargoes.[24]

On "Bloody Thursday"—July 5—a pitched battle between a thousand police, mostly using tear gas and clubs, and a greater number of pickets, using rocks and clubs, left two men, a striker and a sympathizer, shot dead and dozens on each side seriously injured. The governor called out the National Guard, which deployed on San Francisco's largely deserted Embarcadero that evening, but they had no one to confront and little traffic to control. Bridges understood that it was useless to try to resist well-armed troops. The next day, the San Francisco Labor Council, seeking to forestall a general strike that some radicals were calling for, set up a committee of seven AFL union leaders to investigate the strike situation and denounced the employers and state and local officials. But numbers of union locals of all kinds in the Bay Area and northward as far as Seattle voted to strike. The bodies of the two workers were laid out at union headquarters in San Francisco over the weekend, and on Monday a massive funeral procession of many thousands marched behind trucks carrying the open coffins up the city's main thoroughfare, Market Street, to an undertaker's parlor two miles away while a union band played Beethoven's funeral march. Not a policeman was in sight, by prior agreement, and armbanded trade unionists directed traffic.

Continuing efforts at mediation by the president's board bore no fruit. But its chairman, Archbishop Hanna, one of the several ranking leaders of the Catholic Church who provided important support to the New Deal, made an appeal for labor peace broadcast by three local radio stations the day after Bloody Thursday.

> We believe in the right of the working man to organize within their vocations, and to choose their representatives and to bargain collectively with their own employers.
>
> We believe in the principles of collective bargaining, we believe that workingmen have the right to be represented by men of their own choice, we believe workingmen may organize within a craft, and have a right to deal directly with their employers.
>
> We think that both the employers and the workingmen involved in the disputes before us must be prepared to approach this problem in the interests of justice, which our board is determined shall be the basis of settlement.[25]

This statement, which did not end the strike, was valuable since it came from a trusted figure in a largely Catholic city and gave many of the union delegates a reason to believe that any arbitration would be largely in their favor.

By the time the Central Labor Council met on that Friday night, San Francisco was already shut down. Delegations from 115 unions met, debated, and, despite the opposition of most of the leadership, voted overwhelmingly in support of a general strike to begin Monday morning, July 16. Exceptions to the strike were ordered: public utility workers were kept on the job, deliveries of bread and milk were not interrupted, nineteen restaurants were kept open, and the newspapers were printed, all by union members exempted by the strike committee. Nonunion establishments—food markets, department stores, and hotels—were also open. Violence, which had been endemic before the general strike, was all but nonexistent during the four days it lasted.

It is clear that most union workers and most employers did not want a general strike, but both radicals and extreme conservatives welcomed it, including the editors and publishers of some of the most influential newspapers in the state. A prominent San Francisco businessman put it this way: "This strike is the best thing that ever happened to San Francisco. . . . When this nonsense is out of the way and the men have been driven back to their jobs, we won't have to worry about them any more. . . . I don't think that we'll have a strike of any kind in San Francisco during this generation. Labor is licked."[26]

Numerous appeals were made to Roosevelt to send in federal troops or come to San Francisco and settle things himself. In Washington Cordell Hull, who considered himself acting president, and Attorney General Cummings joined in the cry, but Frances Perkins, who understood the issues, after trying to talk sense to her colleagues went to the White House to have a radio message sent to the president late Saturday, explaining the situation. Louis Howe, vacationing in Massachusetts, who probably felt that Franklin had much to lose and little to gain in returning, urged him not to come.

Roosevelt's radioed reply to Perkins was consistent with his notion that strikes were to be expected and endured. He refused to be stampeded. After thanking her for her estimate of the situation, he ordered:

> If other means fail you might offer complete arbitration all employers and all unions involved. . . . If you think advisable you can issue any statement or offer as coming from me or with my approval. . . .
>
> Confidential: please consult with Hull and Cummings as to our ability to maintain food supply in affected areas, and with this concurrent maintenance of traffic and order.
>
> I am inclined to think after Howe's radio today it is at present best for me not to change my itinerary. Keep Howe in touch. Wire me Monday.[27]

Clearly, Roosevelt wanted Perkins left in charge: citing Howe as a factor was a face-saving gesture for the senior male cabinet members so they did not have to feel that the president preferred the advice of a mere woman to theirs. In the event, Perkins did not find it necessary to use the president's name.

Nearly three months later in a brief press conference at Hyde Park, Roosevelt gave an account of his part in the affair; as was often the case, it lost nothing in the telling. Triggered by a mention of the British General Strike of 1926 by his guest, a visiting London press lord, Roosevelt mused: "In the San Francisco strike a lot of people completely lost their heads and telegraphed me, 'For God's sake come back; turn the ship around.' . . . Everybody demanded that I sail into San Francisco Bay, all flags flying and guns double shotted, and end the strike. They went completely off the handle." Roosevelt divided the blame between the intransigence of the "old, conservative crowd" in California and "hot-headed young leaders who had no experience in organized labor whatsoever." For the former, he had no hope, but of the latter he remarked: "They have got to go through the actual processes, actual examples, and not interference from the Federal Government or the President or the United States troops. People will learn from a certain number of examples. We have to conduct the country and essentially conduct labor to their responsibility."[28]

No federal official went further off the handle than Hugh Johnson, who was staggering through his last months as head of the NRA, often in an alcoholic haze. As fate would have it, he was scheduled to give the Phi Beta Kappa lecture at the University of California across the bay from San Francisco on Tuesday, July 17. He was flown into San Francisco on Monday in an army plane. After drinking with management representatives at San Francisco's Plaza Hotel until three in the morning, Johnson delivered a rambling diatribe Tuesday afternoon in Berkeley, calling the strike "civil war" and insisting that denying "milk to children . . . is bloody insurrection"—even though the unionized milk drivers were still delivering.

As he spoke, the strike was unraveling. That evening, against the wishes of Bridges and other radicals, the Labor Council voted 270–180 to submit all issues to binding arbitration. On Wednesday the president's Longshoreman's Board hailed the council's action as a basis for ending the strike. The next afternoon, Thursday, July 19, the Labor Council voted 191–174 to accept the board's terms if the employers did. The strike was effectively over when the Labor Council agreed to arbitrate, though it took time for the Pacific Coast longshore locals to ratify the agreement. The board's award, along the lines that Archbishop Hanna had indicated, along with a pay boost, was not handed down until October 12. Roosevelt was surely gratified at the result, but he made no public comment.[29]

By the time the *Houston* arrived in Hawaiian waters late in July, the strike was off the front pages. The president—the first to visit Hawaii—made two shore visits, a brief one at Hilo, where he was driven to the edge of the Kilauea volcano, and a longer one at Honolulu, where sixty thousand people greeted him. He reviewed troops at Schofield Barracks and visited Ford Island, the heart of the navy's anchorage at Pearl Harbor. We have no evidence of what he was told there by naval officers, but it would be surprising if the presumed dangers stemming from the large numbers of Japanese immigrants and their American citizen children in the islands did not come up. We do know that in October, Roosevelt, after seeing a military report on Japanese espionage in Hawaii and the fact that the ethnic community there often visited Imperial Japanese Navy vessels calling there and feted officers and men ashore, wrote the chief of naval operations: "One obvious thought occurs to me—that every Japanese Citizen or non-citizen on the Island of Oahu that meets these Japanese ships or has any connection with their officers or men should be secretly but definitely identified and his or her name be placed on a special list of those who would be placed in a concentration camp in the event of trouble."[30]

Although Roosevelt had ignored race in his talks in the Caribbean, he spoke of it in Hawaii. The big public event for him in Honolulu was a parade that the *New York Times* correspondent called "a scintillating picture of life in a 'melting pot.'" It featured native Hawaiians, Chinese, Japanese, Filipinos, and Koreans. It was introduced by the city and county attorney of Honolulu, Wilfred C. Tsukiyama (1897–1966), "an American citizen of Japanese ancestry."

While some of Roosevelt's brief departing remarks the next day—which spoke of the nation's wish for peace and denied "imperialistic aims"—were obviously directed toward Japan, most were addressed to the people of Hawaii. They were assured that they were

> in very truth an integral part of the Nation. In a fine old prayer for our country are found these words: "Fashion into one happy people those brought hither out of many kindreds and tongues." That prayer is being answered in the Territory of Hawaii. You have a fine historic tradition in the ancient people of the Islands and I am glad that this is so well maintained. You have built on it—built on it wisely—and today men and women and children from many lands are united in loyalty to and understanding of the high purposes of America.
>
> You are doing much to improve the standards of living of the average of your citizenry. This is as it should be, and I hope that you will put forth every effort to make still further progress.
>
> There are indeed many parts of the mainland where economic and educational levels do not come up to those which I find here.[31]

Despite this, Roosevelt did not hold out the hope of statehood, probably because he knew that Congress was not likely to grant it to a place where whites were but a small minority. Congress held hearings on statehood in Honolulu in 1937 with the administration's blessing. Ernest Gruening (1887–1974), whom Roosevelt appointed director of the Division of Territories and Island Possessions, knowing that Gruening believed that "a democracy shouldn't have any colonies," remembered that during those hearings, after several Japanese Americans had testified, John Rankin, the Mississippi congressman, turned to him and said, "Mah Gawd, if we give them folks statehood we're lahkley to have a senator named Moto."[32]

The *Houston* anchored off the mouth of the Columbia River on the afternoon of August 2. The next day, in Portland, the president was met by family, officials, and staff. A drive through cheering crowds downtown paused only to be greeted by crippled children at the local Shrine hospital before continuing upriver through the Columbia Gorge, where the Bonneville Dam was under construction. From a cliff above the dam, he spoke very briefly—"I have to go to the train"—about the development of public power and the growth of the Northwest to some five thousand people, most of whom had come a good distance to see and hear him.[33]

Roosevelt's special train took the party to the site of another New Deal project, Grand Coulee Dam on the upper Columbia in central Washington. After touring the area by car and inspecting the work in progress, the president spoke briefly just after noon, again from bluffs overlooking the river, to a crowd estimated at forty thousand that had been gathering since before daylight. Introduced as "the master builder of our time," he focused his remarks on electric power. After establishing that he had talked about power during his 1920 campaign there, he predicted that the region would experience significant population growth: "We are going to see, I believe, with our own eyes electricity and power made so cheap that they will become a standard article of use, not merely for agriculture and manufacturing, but for every home within the reach of an electric transmission line."[34]

As the train rolled toward the next stop at Glacier National Park, Harold Ickes, invited to dinner in the president's car, joined the first couple and three sons, along with Louis Howe, War Secretary George Dern, Montana senator Burton K. Wheeler, and a young friend of one of the boys, and recorded his first experience with the Roosevelts unbuttoned.

> . . . a most interesting dinner. It resolved itself into a debate between the members of the Roosevelt family, with all of them frequently talking at one and the same time. Mrs. Roosevelt precipitated the discussion by raising some social question and her three sons at once began to wave their arms in the air and take violent issue with her. . . . The President joined in at intervals, but he wasn't President of the United States on that occasion—he was merely the father of three sons who had opinions of their own. They interrupted him when they felt like it and all talked at him at the same time. . . . At one stage when they were all going on at once, I raised my voice and observed to the President that I now understood how he was able to manage Congress. Senator Wheeler followed my remark with the observation that Congress was never as bad as that.[35]

In Montana the next day, Roosevelt made a 157-mile tour of Glacier National Park, had lunch there, and gave a brief formal radio report to the nation on his trip. He directed most of his talk to the national parks and the struggle for the environment. "The fundamental idea behind the parks," he said, "is, in brief, that the country belongs to the people. He spoke of the "constant struggle . . . to protect the public interest . . . from private exploitation [by] the selfish few." The president went on to link more controversial measures to the all but universally appreciated national parks, suggesting, without using the phrase, national planning: "The splendid public purpose that underlies the development of great power sites, the improving of navigation, the prevention of floods . . . erosion . . . forest fires, the diversification of farming . . . the distribution of industry . . . [is that] the Nation must and shall be considered as a whole and not as an aggregation of disjointed groups."[36]

As the president's train descended from the Rockies to Montana's high plains, he entered a region that government scientists were describing as the secondary drought area and part of what demographers would later speak of as the triangle of depopulation, a large area of the nation's intermountain central plains in which two out of three counties had steadily lost population since 1920. Harry Hopkins had dispatched FERA's Lawrence Westbrook to tell the president and accompanying press that the drought now affected twenty-four states, covering 60 percent of the nation and containing 27 million persons, more than one American in five. It was worst in Montana, both Dakotas, and Wyoming, with twelve other central states heavily affected. Recognizing this, Roosevelt's celebratory tone changed. In a rear-platform talk at Havre, he said that he had come "to learn something at first hand both by talking to the people, and by seeing conditions with my own eyes." At the site of the giant earthen dam under construction at Fort Peck on the Missouri River, the president spoke not only about the project but also about rumors circulating about the Subsistence Homesteads Program, though he did not name it.

> I understand that some people . . . have suggested that . . . we are . . . saying to the families on marginal lands . . ."You have to leave your homes tomorrow morning and get out."
>
> Of course no person who thinks twice will believe silly tales of that kind. . . . On the other hand, your Government believes in giving [such families] a chance to go to better places—a voluntary chance. That is why this very broad national planning is seeking to provide farms . . . where they may be able I hope, to make not only both ends meet [but also] may come to own their farms free and clear of debt.[37]

Later that day at Devils Lake, North Dakota, after having been driven to see the now largely dried-up lake bed that had until recently supplied water for irrigation, Roosevelt spoke to several thousand, many of them once prosperous farmers and cattlemen now on relief. They hoped to hear him announce a seventy-five-million-dollar dam project to bring Missouri River water to refill their lake. The *Times* correspondent wrote of a "visibly moved" president: "His seersucker suit was splotched with dust and perspiration. Sweat ran down his face and made rivulets in the dirt on his cheeks. He stood alone while he talked. . . . He seldom smiled and his words came slowly."

The president began by saying that he had come to see "with my own eyes" the problems caused by the drought and said that he would be frank and "not try to fool you by saying we know the solution. . . . We do not." Then he addressed the specific problem of Devils Lake. "I saw some signs along the road that said: 'You gave us beer, now give us water.' Well, the beer part was easy." He explained what most of his audience must have heard before, that engineers reported that there was no safe place to erect a dam and offered no easy answers. His blunt answers drew cheers.[38]

In neighboring Minnesota, his major appearance was to participate in a tribute to the Mayo brothers, William J. (1861–1939) and Charles H. (1865–1939), physicians who with their father had established what became a world-class medical center in Rochester, an otherwise unexceptional prairie city of twenty thousand. Consistent with his new policy of letting his experts handle labor disputes, Roosevelt refused to intervene in a violent strike of teamsters in Minneapolis, despite requests from both a citizens committee and his sometime ally Farmer-Labor governor Floyd B. Olson, who came to Rochester to see him. When a delegation of labor leaders also showed up, they had to settle for an interview with Louis Howe. The strike was settled later that month, one of the first major successes of the new NLRB.[39]

His Rochester talk, where he was greeted by a crowd estimated at twice the city's population, not only hailed the Mayos and their institution but also provided him an opportunity to draw an analogy between medical progress and social progress. "Those of us who are concerned with the problems of government and of economics are under special obligation to modern medicine. . . . [I]t has taught us that with patience and application and skill and courage it is possible for human beings to control and improve conditions under which they live [and] how science may be made the servant of a richer, more complete common life. . . . Modern medicine has set an exalted example. It has shown the way for us all." Had he been so inclined, the Rochester remarks could have been a time to talk about the provision of medical care to all Americans, but such a prospect seems not then to have been part of his agenda or his consciousness.[40]

The final stop was in Green Bay, Wisconsin, to participate in the tercentenary of the arrival of the first white pioneer there. Although everything a president does is "political" by definition, at Green Bay, for the first time since he had left the capital, Roosevelt made an overt move in the year's congressional elections. In a talk that was broadcast nationally, he praised both of Wisconsin's senators, Francis Ryan Duffy (1888–1979) and Robert M. La Follette Jr. (1895–1953). The praise for Duffy, a Democrat who had been elected in 1932, was a given, but his plaudits for La Follette, who was running for reelection against a Democrat, were another matter. A sitting Republican senator who was often "left" of the New Deal, La Follette had recently formed a statewide Progressive Party. Roosevelt's endorsement was a political coup that delighted independents as it upset Wisconsin's Democratic Party leadership. La Follette, for his part, said later that he would support the president "as long as he is right." Roosevelt was the most effective presidential party leader in our history, but there were times when seeming to be nonpartisan was the best politics. Of course, Roosevelt insisted, before and after Green Bay, that he made no primary endorsements, which would be the general rule until 1938.

The theme of his Green Bay talk was a pledge that he would continue the New Deal: "In one year and five months, the people of the United States have received at least a partial answer to their demands for action; and neither the demand nor the action has reached the end of the road." Using a favorite device, he spoke of an influential man—quite possibly imaginary—who had written to tell him that the way to restore confidence

> was for me to tell the people . . . that all supervision by all forms of Government, Federal and State, over all forms of human activity called business should forthwith be abolished. . . .
>
> In fact, my friends, if we were to listen to him and his type, the old law of the tooth and the claw would reign in our Nation once more. . . .
>
> We who support this New Deal do so because it is a square deal and because it is essential to the preservation of security and happiness in a free society such as ours.[41]

The speech was an effective August kickoff for the more formal campaign, which, in those days, did not begin until Labor Day.

Although there were no speeches between Green Bay and Washington, the president did say a few words from the rear platform to a crowd of fifty thousand as his train paused in Milwaukee and waved to crowds as his train was switched in Chicago. More remarkably, in what was called a "triumphal procession," crowds along the route gathered just to see the train, with a sleeping president, pass by even in the wee hours of the morning. Only a few hundred greeted his arrival in Washington about noon on August 10. He had been gone forty-one days. At the White House, where renovations were still in progress, he went right to work in his office, which had been moved temporarily upstairs.[42]

It is difficult to overestimate the importance Roosevelt placed on his contacts with people during his travels. A few days after returning, he remarked in a colloquy with AAA head Chester Davis at an NEC meeting in the White House, "This is the first time I have been west of the Mississippi since 1932. The difference was perfectly apparent in the faces of the people. You could tell what that difference was by standing on the end of the car and looking at the crowds. They had courage written all over their faces. They looked cheerful. They knew they were 'up against it' but they were going to see the thing through; whereas, in 1932 there was a look of despair."[43]

As part of the run-up to the fall election, conservative Democrats figured prominently in creating the American Liberty League, which claimed to be nonpartisan but was in fact aimed directly at the New Deal. Its founding president was Jouett Shouse, whom Roosevelt had removed from party leadership just after the Chicago convention and who, with his wealthy wife, Katherine, a daughter of liberal Boston magnate Lincoln Filene, maintained a largely anti-Roosevelt salon at their Wolf Trap Farm in northern Virginia. In an outward show of courtesy, Shouse had called on the president immediately before announcing the league's formation, and he made special mention of the visit in his initial press conference, while denying that the league was anti-Roosevelt. But the league's five-man executive committee—the two most recent losing Democratic presidential candidates, John W. Davis and Al Smith, two New York Republicans long opposed to Roosevelt, plus the multimillionaire industrialist Irénée du Pont (1876–1963)—made clear its anti–New Deal orientation. Shouse's windy one-sentence definition—"a non-partisan organization formed . . . 'to defend and uphold the Constitution . . . and to gather and disseminate information that (1) will teach the necessity of respect for the rights of persons and property . . ., and (2) will teach the duty of government to encourage and protect individual and group initiative and enterprise, to foster the right to work, earn, save and acquire property, and to preserve the ownership and lawful use of property when acquired"—can be reduced to, in modern jargon: an organization for stakeholders.[44]

Roosevelt understood. Asked at his next press conference about it, he confirmed Shouse's story and commented that he had read a story on the financial page of the morning's *New York Times:* "I laughed for ten minutes . . . one paragraph started off like this—I forget the exact phraseology—The speculative fraternity in Wall Street regards the new American Liberty League as a direct answer from Heaven to their prayer." The exact phraseology was "Talk in Wall Street yesterday indicated that the announcement of the new American Liberty League was little short of an answer to a prayer."[45]

The emergence of the Liberty League, significant in itself, was also indicative of a larger trend: the gradual erosion of the once significant business-sector support for Roosevelt and at least some of his policies. Just when Roosevelt became, for so many of the well-to-do, "a traitor to his class," "that man in the White House," or "that damned cripple" is a matter of debate among scholars. Some have placed it as early as the end of the hundred days, others as late as the passage of the 1934 Securities Act. My own choice would be the late fall or early winter of 1933, as confidence in the NRA fell and anxieties about spending on relief grew. In any event, the nodal point in that process was clearly sometime before the formation of the league in August 1934. The short-term political result of the league's activity was probably counterproductive; in the political campaigns to defeat the New Deal and Roosevelt in the 1934 and 1936 elections, however, the massive disaffection of what would later be styled the American business elite from the recovery program would have both a short- and a long-term negative impact on American economic development.

The president's desire to stay out of primary battles was sorely tested by the ultimately successful challenge of the well-known writer and socialist Upton

Sinclair (1878–1968) for the Democratic nomination in the California governor's race. Few politicians had paid much attention in 1933 when Sinclair self-published a book, *I, Governor of California,* but Sinclair switched his registration from Socialist to Democratic, developed a plan to "End Poverty in California" (EPIC), organized a mass movement to support it, and challenged the state organization's candidate, the old Wilson progressive journalist George Creel, in the Democratic gubernatorial primary. Although it became clear that Creel's candidacy was in danger, Roosevelt maintained his policy of noninterference in primaries. Sinclair won the primary with 436,000 votes to Creel's 288,000. In his memoirs, Creel wrote that his campaign in "Northern California offered no problem, for hardheaded, hard-working native sons and daughters were in a majority, but when I crossed . . . into Southern California, it was like plunging into darkest Africa without gun bearers."[46]

Thus began Southern California's now well-established national reputation as a region with often kooky politics. As late as 1928, its largely white Protestant population, many of them recent migrants from the Midwest, had made Los Angeles the only large city outside the South to give Hoover a substantial majority; unlike San Francisco, it was very much an open-shop town. Sinclair's new status as the Democratic nominee provided further problems for the president, who normally supported Democrats. But Sinclair, who desperately wanted Roosevelt's seal of approval and who embraced him and the New Deal with enthusiasm, would not renounce his EPIC plan. Its key provisions involved a pension plan that would award fifty dollars a month to every Californian aged sixty and over and provide for full employment by acquiring vacant lands, settling unemployed persons on them to raise their own food and put them to work in "production for use" workshops that the state would build. They would be paid scrip valid only for foods and goods produced within their cooperative system.

The California press reacted hysterically to Sinclair's primary victory. The Chandler family's *Los Angeles Times* was perhaps the most extreme of the major papers, claiming, two days after Sinclair's primary win:

> The nomination of Upton Sinclair creates a crisis for California—and for America.
>
> Mr. Sinclair is not the ultimately important factor. What is eating at the heart of America is a maggot-like horde of Reds who have scuttled to his support.
>
> He is opening the gate of our defenses to a vicious horde who have every intention of turning to rend him with the others at the first opportunity—in favor of a complete and violent revolution.
>
> By a twist of fate it is for California to decide for America.[47]

This "big lie" was given a boost later when fake newsreels, apparently filmed on the MGM lot, showed ragged, bearded Bolsheviks streaming into California to vote for "Comrade Sinclair." But the left-wing myth that the forces of reaction in California stole the election with these and other smear tactics is overdrawn. Although Sinclair had overwhelmed Creel, he garnered only about a third of the total vote cast in the primary, and the chances of his election in November were slim indeed.

Right after his primary victory, Sinclair came to Hyde Park to meet Roosevelt, with a prior understanding that no politics would be discussed. He emerged, after a one-hour appointment that had been stretched to two, pleased with himself. Pledged not to reveal what they discussed, he praised his host extravagantly—"one of the kindest . . . most genial . . . frank . . . open minded . . . lovable men"—but blurted out that the president "talked for two hours." This was one of Roosevelt's standard ploys when he did not want to hear what his visitor might say. In his next day's press conference, Roosevelt refused to comment, but when asked what Sinclair had during the visit—which took place between five and seven o'clock, the president's traditional cocktail time—he responded, "two long glasses of iced tea."[48] In the event, Sinclair managed to get almost 38 percent of the vote in a three-man race, but was badly defeated by a conservative Republican.[49]

Meanwhile, in the weeks before the election, two of the most influential figures during the first year and a half of the New Deal quit their jobs: Lewis Douglas resigned as budget director on August 31, and Hugh Johnson stepped down as head of the NRA almost a month later. The later careers of the two defectors were somewhat different. Douglas supported Roosevelt's opponents in both the 1936 and the 1940 presidential elections, while Johnson did so only in 1940. Johnson became an isolationist, supporting the America First Committee, while Douglas backed interventionist groups. After Pearl Harbor, he held secondary administrative positions dealing with allocation of shipping. In the Cold War era, he was an adviser to General Lucius D. Clay in Germany and served as Truman's ambassador to Great Britain (1947–50). In those years, Douglas, always an enemy of deficit spending for the welfare state, had no problems with such spending for a warfare state.

Douglas was replaced by Daniel W. Bell (1891–1971), who had come to the Treasury as a bookkeeper in 1911 and worked his way up, telling the Associated Press that he "had no politics." The traditional formalities about Douglas's departure were not observed: Marvin McIntyre simply announced that the budget director had submitted his own resignation and that of his assistant along with news of Bell's appointment. Bell was acting budget director for four years and retired from the Treasury at the end of 1945 as undersecretary, one of the rare civil servants to reach the subcabinet level.[50]

The only surprise about Hugh Johnson's departure was that it had not come sooner. He was never replaced. Although unwieldy, the NRA had become a machine that could, after a fashion, run by itself. In reality, if anyone ran the NRA in its final months, Leon Henderson did.[51]

Roosevelt did not campaign in any formal sense in the run-up to the No-vember elections, which served as the first national referendum on the New Deal. He did, however, give a Fireside Chat at the end of September that should be considered his one campaign speech, even though it was a good five weeks before election day and he never mentioned the election. Its message was that Roosevelt was a man in the middle. Although the speech's real news was Roo-sevelt's call for "a period of industrial peace," when he and Rosenman had to supply a headline for it in his *Public Papers*, they chose to emphasize a minor theme, that the New Deal was providing "Greater Freedom [and] Greater Se-curity for the Average Man." The reason for the switch in emphasis is clear. The president had said that he would "confer within the coming month with small groups of those truly representative of large employers of labor and of large groups of organized labor, in order to seek their cooperation in establishing what I may describe as a specific trial period of industrial peace." And although the AFL's William Green and a number of industrial leaders hailed this approach, and Roosevelt did confer as he proposed, there was little real slackening of the industrial turbulence. Within a month, the *Times'* crack labor reporter Lou Stark noted that "the industrial truce . . . has all but vanished." He accurately predicted that the coming months would see more strikes, especially in the mass-production industries.

In his peroration, Roosevelt did talk about liberty and security:

I believe with Abraham Lincoln, that "The legitimate object of Government is to do for a community of people whatever they need to have done but cannot do at all or cannot do so well for themselves in their separate and individual capacities."

I am not for a return to that definition of liberty under which for many years a free people were being gradually regimented into the service of the privileged few. I prefer and I am sure you prefer that broader definition of liberty under which we are moving forward to greater freedom, to greater security for the average man than he has ever known before in the history of America.[52]

Later in October, he continued his emphasis on being a man in the middle by calling for an "an alliance of all forces intent upon the business of recovery" in an address to the American Bankers Association.[53]

Although Roosevelt did not campaign, members of his family did. Eleanor and his mother, Sara, were prominent in the successful campaign to elect the socialite reformer Caroline O'Day to Congress. O'Day, whose leadership in New York's Democratic Party went back to 1916, had become a good friend of Elea-nor's in the 1920s.[54] The president himself, as a resident of New York, endorsed his successor, Herbert Lehman, for reelection as governor and after casting his ballot in Hyde Park said that he had voted the straight Democratic ticket.[55]

Commentators had agreed beforehand that the elections would be a national barometer of support for Roosevelt and his New Deal, and only a die-hard few had predicted significant Republican gains. But even dyed-in-the-wool New Dealers were astounded by the magnitude of the Democratic victory in the face of the rule of thumb that in an off-year election, the party in power will lose seats. Instead, the Democrats made significant gains, particularly in the Senate: the seats that were contested in 1934 were those that had been filled at the high tide of Republican prosperity in 1928. Jim Farley had predicted "substantial gains" in the Senate but had not expected that 9 seats would be added to the 60 the party already held. The Republicans, reduced to 25 in the new Senate, actually lost 10 seats, as La Follette switched to his own one-state Progressive Party. (Roosevelt's support of La Follette substantially weakened Wisconsin's Democrats: the senator's brother, Phil, defeated an incumbent Democratic governor, and in congressional races Progressives took seats from both parties, unseating 5 Republicans and 2 Democrats.) Senate newcomers who became prominent included Pennsylvania's Joe Guffey and Missouri's Harry Truman.

In the House, where Farley had been "satisfied" that his party would maintain its advantage and might "possibly make some gains," the Democrats had a net gain of 9, giving them 319 seats; the Republicans lost 17, dropping them to 103 seats. Thus, in both houses Roosevelt's party had more than a two-thirds majority.[56] Results in state races were less lopsided. Democrats unseated Republican governors in four states but lost three to them and, as noted, one to a La Follette in Wisconsin. The Democrats continued to control thirty-eight statehouses and had independent allies in Madison and St. Paul, with the GOP in control in only eight.

Political theorists now describe the 1934 contest as a transformative election, that is, one that changed the nature of American politics for decades. Unlike the shift in 1912 to Wilson, which proved to be merely a two-term interruption, the election of Roosevelt in 1932 set off a long period in which most voters generally supported Democratic candidates.

Who were the voters who swung to support the New Deal in 1934? In Pennsylvania, a state that Hoover had carried in 1932 by 150,000 votes, Republicans lost 12 seats in Congress, presaging Roosevelt's triumph there in 1936. In the Keystone State, all of the elements of what came to be known as the "Roosevelt Coalition" were in place: traditional Democrats, intellectuals, working people, ethnic minorities, and blacks.

It can be argued—and was argued at the time—that Roosevelt did not deserve the support of many in the underclass. Socialists like Norman Thomas and many labor leaders complained that much of the New Deal largely benefited the middle class, and most black leaders and their white supporters like Oswald Garrison Villard insisted, justly, that Roosevelt was not a paladin of black Americans. As Villard, a founder of the National Association for the Advancement of Colored People (NAACP), wrote in the organization's journal just after the election, "Whatever the New Deal has done for the white workman it seems to have done less than nothing for the Negro. . . . Mr. Roosevelt is frankly not interested in the Negro problem."[57]

Villard's comment would have been accurate for Governor Roosevelt, who, unlike Herbert Lehman, seems to have had no meaningful contact with New York's African American leaders, but as president he was surely aware of the political potential of the northern black vote. And, although Villard ignored it, black voters were switching their allegiance. This was nowhere clearer than in Chicago, where Arthur W. Mitchell (1883–1968), "wrapped in the already magic mantle of Roosevelt and the New Deal," took Oscar De Priest's seat away from him and became the nation's first black Democrat elected to Congress. Some elite blacks, especially in the South, had great difficulty in leaving the Republican Party: Martin Luther King's father never voted for a Democrat until 1960, and did so only after the Kennedys had been instrumental in getting his son out of jail. In the North, the transition was generally made quickly but was still painful. In far-away Seattle, Revels Cayton, grandson of Hiram Revels, the nation's first black U.S. senator, remembered coming home on election day in 1932 to find his father, who edited a local newspaper, sitting dejectedly on their front steps:

> "Hey Dad, what's wrong?" he asked.
> His father answered, "I just voted for a Democrat, son."
> "Well," the son answered, "Roosevelt's going to feed ya."
> "Yes, that's true," the father said, "but the Republican Party *freed* me."[58]

Roosevelt had an appeal—later generations would call it charisma—that transcended rationality and reached persons not normally touched by American politics. A *corrido,* a traditional Mexican form of political protest, written in Anaheim, California, sometime in 1935, idolized Roosevelt:

> When Hoover left office
> we were convinced:
> What did he do for the
> people of the United States?
> Roosevelt appeared
> like a resplendent sun
> assumed his administration
> and met his senators
> One month as president
> He dreamed a profound dream:
> We all have the right
> to live in this world.[59]

Roosevelt himself understood, though he did not refer to it publicly, the class aspects of much of his early program. Meeting with the NEC in December after much of the planning for the 1935 agenda had taken place, he delivered a long, apparently ad-libbed disquisition, showing an acute awareness of whom his housing program had and had not helped and did so, as he put it, "in words of one syllable." It showed an awareness and a mastery of the subject that was beyond anything previously demonstrated by him.

There are in this country about 120,000,000 people. The government is doing something for three groups . . . in the way of housing. The richest group . . . are those who have borrowing capacity. . . . For various reasons banks and other lending agencies have shown a disinclination to come forward as fast as we hoped they would. . . . The Housing Administration has made excellent progress . . . guaranteeing a percentage of the loan . . . the insurance method. They have been lending money . . . under Title I of the Housing Act to people . . . with average income of about $2,750 a year. In almost every case, those people already have their own homes and they are borrowing money [for improvements]. People in this country with an average of $2,750 a year income are rich people. They are far above the average in respect to income; and we are doing a fine job for them.

Next come the people a little lower down the scale [who have] some form of security to offer to private capital . . . who already had their homes or their farms. Bill Myers and John Fahey are looking after their wants. In other words the Farm Credit Administration is extending government credit to people who already have property . . . in the form of loans or . . . reduced interest rates on existing mortgages. . . . There may be 10,000,000 men women and children who have taken advantage of the Housing Administration . . . and perhaps 20,000,000 people—who would take advantage of the [FCA or HOLC]. This is about 30,000,000 million people in this country.

Below them is the largest mass of the American population—people who have not got enough, either in earning capacity or . . . tangibles to go to Moffett or Fahey or Myers. These are people who are living—most of them—in un-American surroundings and conditions. . . . The question comes up, are we licked in trying to help them in their living conditions? A good many real estate people consider we are. . . . We say, "Will private capital help them?" They say, "No it can't . . ." Are we licked in trying to help these people—forty million of them, men, women, and children? Their answer is, "Yes, we are licked, we must not do anything to help them, because we might interfere with private capital." The answer is, "No, we are not licked! We are going to help them!" . . . [W]e are going to help those forty million people by giving them better houses—a great many of them, all we possibly can. . . . [W]e will kill two birds with one stone; we are going to provide better housing, and put a lot of people to work.[60]

A little more than two years later, in his second inaugural, Roosevelt would make his most celebrated attack on poverty—"I see one-third of a nation ill-housed, ill-clad, ill-nourished."[61] A third of the nation was forty million people, the same figure he had used in lecturing the NEC. But the unstated but patent arithmetic of the talk to his most trusted advisers clearly left some fifty million people unaccounted for. A few were in the top income brackets, but most were below that $2,750 line. They were, the unvoiced logic of his 1934 argument suggests, beyond the range of what the government might be expected to do. One-third of a nation—forty million people—was a target that Roosevelt thought might be attained. If achieved, that would make poverty a minority phenomenon. Nathan Straus (1889–1961), Roosevelt's first U.S. housing commissioner from 1937 to 1942, gave a more accurate estimate of poverty in his 1952 book analyzing America's housing, post–New Deal: he called it *Two-Thirds of a Nation*.[62]

Roosevelt devoted the nearly two months between the elections and the opening of the new Congress largely to planning and the continuing attempt to coordinate the rapidly expanding federal bureaucracy. In retrospect, it is clear that the mid-November promotion of the maverick Utah banker Marriner S. Eccles to chair the Federal Reserve Board was a victory for the spenders within the New Deal. Eccles was a successful Mormon entrepreneur who had expanded the business interests inherited from his father who had twenty-one other children from plural marriages. He never completed high school. His banks remained sound during the banking crisis in a region with many defaults.

Eccles first appeared on the national scene in testimony given before the Senate Banking Committee in February 1933, advocating a five-point program of the sort that would later be called "Keynesian" without the intellectual baggage that the Cambridge economist would bring to his advocacy. Eccles's early-1933 proposals included $500 million in outright grants to the states for relief, a $2.5 billion public works program, the domestic allotment system, relief for farm mortgages, and settlement of the war debts, preferably by cancellation. This brought him to the attention of Rex Tugwell and then other New Dealers. Although almost a year would pass before he took a government job, during the hundred days he did contribute to the drafting of the Emergency Banking Act and the HOLC legislation. In January 1934, he was taken on as a special assistant to Henry Morgenthau in the Treasury Department, after which he became the major draftsman of the National Housing Act. When Morgenthau, among others, suggested Eccles to the president for the Federal Reserve post, he apparently had no notion that his former assistant would become his rival for Roosevelt's ear on fiscal matters and economic policy generally. Eccles would serve as chair until Truman replaced him in 1948, but he stayed on the board until 1952. During his tenure, the board's powers were greatly expanded.[63]

Roosevelt's annual Thanksgiving visit to Warm Springs was also an inspection trip: his private train made stops, and he spoke in Kentucky, Tennessee, Mississippi, and Alabama before reaching his destination. Neither race nor race relations were mentioned in his talks, but during a visit to Nashville he and Eleanor did drive to Fisk University to hear a brief outdoor recital by its famous singers. Perhaps twenty-five thousand turned out to see the president make his first appearance at a black institution. When viewing the partially built dam named for Senator Norris, he assured those working on it and other TVA projects that they would "be known as veterans of a new kind of war, the kind of war that is going to improve conditions for millions of our fellow American citizens."[64]

The only real news generated on the trip was the announcement of a second set of Birthday Balls at the end of January. As the president put it in a letter to Doherty, who again footed some organizational expenses, he was happy "to lend my next birthday" to his committee. A formal announcement by the Warm Springs trustees explained that the receipts from the 1935 balls would be divided in a new way: 70 percent of the funds raised would go to provide polio treatment facilities in the places where the balls were held; the other 30 percent would be devoted to funding basic medical research, seeking "to develop preventatives of and immunization against Infantile Paralysis with the purpose of eradicating this scourge."[65]

Franklin and his mother, Sara, seen here in an 1893 photo when he was eleven, had an intense, enduring relationship until her death in his sixtieth year. She was surely an important source of his progressive social outlook, while his concern for the environment can, in part, be attributed to the influence of his father.

Although the childhood photos Eleanor Roosevelt chose to illustrate her autobiographies all feature a glum young girl, this charming school portrait done in New York City in 1898, the year she turned fourteen, presents an alternate view.

FDR's class portrait as chair of his Class Committee, Harvard University, 1904. Although his grades and the courses he enrolled in were respectable, Roosevelt seems to have been more interested in the extracurricular side of college life.

Eleanor and Franklin Roosevelt during their honeymoon, Hyde Park, March 1905. That summer, after Franklin's first year in law school, they took a second honeymoon in Europe.

A family portrait in post–World War I Washington on June 12, 1919. The standing older children are Anna, James, and Elliot. Seated are FDR Jr., FDR, Eleanor, Sara, and John.

FDR seated at the edge of the swimming pool at Warm Springs in 1924. This is one of the few images of the wasted legs that his mother was once "so proud of."

FDR welcoming John W. Davis, the recently nominated Democratic candidate for president, to Hyde Park on August 7, 1924, with his fellow New York Democrats George Lunn and Al Smith. Smith would win the 1928 nomination and, like Davis, lose the election. FDR would win the nomination and the presidency in 1932.

FDR in his specially engineered Ford Model A Roadster in Hyde Park, 1928. It was the first automobile equipped with hand controls so that a paraplegic could operate it. His friend Edsel Ford had it produced at his family's factory. FDR drove it mostly on the grounds of his estate and Warm Springs, but sometimes used it for short trips on public streets and highways.

Governor Roosevelt and Al Smith in the Albany office Al had worked in for three two-year terms. Their attire proclaims their class difference. Note the cuspidor, lower right.

Governor Roosevelt seated at his desk in Albany with Eleanor, Missy LeHand, Grace Tully, Dorothy and Sam Rosenman, and, in FDR's lap, the Rosenmans' son in 1930. The Roosevelts treated their closest staff members as family.

New York's first lady, Eleanor Roosevelt, and state labor commissioner Frances Perkins flank Mrs. Percy Pennypacker, president of a local woman's club, in New York City, January 1931, at a public occasion. Eleanor did not enjoy such duties but performed them most effectively.

Governor Roosevelt in his special car at Warm Springs in 1931. Pictures like this, suggesting that FDR could perform functions associated with physical ability that he did not have, were an important part of his legend. (Another version of this image shows the New York publisher Bernarr Macfadden [1868–1955] standing beside the car.)

President-elect Roosevelt in his Hyde Park study, February 27, 1933. The large volume before him is the family Dutch-language Bible. Five days later, and on three subsequent occasions, he would place his hand on that volume and swear the presidential oath. Presumably, he is pointing to First Corinthians, the place at which the volume would be opened on those occasions. Its key phrase is "And now abideth faith, hope and charity, these three; but the greatest of these is charity."

President Franklin Delano Roosevelt in his first year in the White House. Similar portraits over his four terms show clearly, as he told the Teamsters in 1944, that he was "twelve years older" than when he became president.

A very informal vacationing President Roosevelt in the cockpit of the schooner *Amberjack II* during a cruise from Marion, Massachusetts, to Campobello, June 16, 1933.

President Roosevelt and federal officials during a tour of five CCC camps near Washington, D.C. This is Camp Big Meadows in Virginia's Shenandoah Valley. Seated around the president are General Paul Malone, Louis Howe, Harold Ickes, Robert Fechner, Henry Wallace, and Rex Tugwell, while the young men of CCC Company 350 are behind him. This is the trip during which the AFL's William Green, not shown, ceased his opposition to the CCC.

President Roosevelt and newly appointed treasury secretary Henry Morgenthau seated in FDR's car at Hyde Park, February 9, 1934. Morgenthau was the only member of Roosevelt's cabinet who was his personal friend before Roosevelt returned to politics. The president wrote on what was Morgenthau's copy, "For Henry from one of two of a kind," and signed his name.

First Lady Eleanor Roosevelt, an enthusiastic Democrat, emerging from a curtained voting machine in Hyde Park's town hall on November 2, 1936, surely voted for her husband and the entire Democratic ticket. FDR swept the nation and all but two small states, but never carried Hyde Park in a presidential election.

President Roosevelt, eating lunch sitting on the backseat of an open touring car wearing an overcoat, at the Grand Coulee Dam site on the Columbia River in central Washington on October 2, 1937. Roosevelt, on tour, was a virtual prisoner in whatever vehicle he was using. He could not get in or out of a car without considerable assistance from more than one person. At a place like this dam site, he was in full view of the public. No wonder a private railway car was his favorite mode of transportation.

President Roosevelt speaking at Queen's University, Kingston, Ontario, Canada, on August 18, 1938. In this first speech by an American president in Canada, Roosevelt pledged that "the people of the United States will not stand idly by if [Canada] is threatened by any other Empire."

10 The Triumph of Reform
1935

ALTHOUGH IT HAS BECOME TRADITIONAL TO SPEAK of the reforms of 1935 as marking a second New Deal, Roosevelt himself never suggested that there was more than one New Deal.[1] Strengthened in his resolve by the results of the midterm elections and with a steadily growing awareness of fundamental flaws in the structure of American society, he began the year with a broadcast annual message that laid out more fully than any previous manifesto the expanding purposes of the New Deal. He identified three kinds of security: "the security of a livelihood," "security against the major vicissitudes of life," and "the security of decent homes."

He promised "to submit to the Congress a broad program designed ultimately to establish all three," but in fact no new housing program materialized in 1935. The Home Mortgage Relief Act passed in May expanded the authority and scope of the HOLC and largely benefited those who were already home owners. The major emphasis in the message was on a work program—which became the as yet unnamed Works Projects Administration under the direction of Harry Hopkins—with a second message focusing on "security against the major hazards of life" promised in "a few days."

Returning to his pledge in the inaugural address to "put people to work," Roosevelt admitted that in spite of some government successes in that regard, "the stark fact before us is that great numbers still remain unemployed." Noting that a "large proportion of these unemployed and their dependents have been forced on the relief rolls," Roosevelt insisted that the "Federal Government must and shall quit this business of relief."

Some contemporary conservatives and latter-day free marketers have misunderstood this statement. The far-right *Los Angeles Times,* for example, hailed it as the message's "most important point [representing] an abandonment of the program which his party launched [in] 1930 and has carried on."[2]

What Roosevelt proposed and executed most scholars have called "work relief," a term the president did not use. Although he would call for a huge appropriation for work relief—$4.8 billion—there would never be enough funds appropriated to eliminate massive unemployment in peacetime; it would continue until the halcyon days of World War II. Roosevelt's argument for work relief was a moral one.

> I am not willing that the vitality of our people be further sapped by the giving of cash, of market baskets, of a few hours of weekly work cutting grass, raking leaves or picking up papers in the public parks. We must preserve not only the bodies of the unemployed from destitution but also their self-respect, their self-reliance and courage and determination. This decision brings me to the problem of what the Government should do with approximately five million unemployed[3] now on the relief rolls.
>
> About one million and a half of these belong to the group which in the past was dependent upon local welfare efforts. Most of them are unable for one reason or another to maintain themselves independently—for the most part, through no fault of their own. Such people, in the days before the great depression, were cared for by local efforts—by States, by counties, by towns, by cities, by churches and by private welfare agencies. It is my thought that in the future they must be cared for as they were before.[4]

Thus, despite his daring innovations, Roosevelt remained bound by his notions of the appropriate division of responsibility between federal and state governments. Had all state governments been as conscientious about their responsibilities as New York had been under Smith and Roosevelt, and continued to be under Lehman and Thomas E. Dewey, relief—eventually called welfare—would not have been the continuing problem it became. In effect, Roosevelt's decision left millions of Americans, and a majority of black Americans, at the mercy of state governments that had neither the ability nor the desire to care for their most disadvantaged citizens.

Almost coeval with the annual message was the budget message. Roosevelt delivered what is now usually called the State of the Union message on Friday; the budget message was distributed to members of Congress on Monday. It so happened that on Monday, the Supreme Court, for the first time, struck down a New Deal measure. Thus, Tuesday's newspapers headlined two topics that would plague the president for the next two and a half years: the growing deficit and the Court's disapproval of New Deal legislation.[5]

Despite his previously expressed hope that a "definitely balanced budget" would occur by fiscal 1936, the budget message predicted a gross deficit of $4.5 billion. The largest single item was the unprecedented recommendation that "$4 billion be appropriated by the Congress in one sum, subject to allocation by the Executive, principally for giving work to those unemployed on the relief rolls."[6]

In a special budget briefing for the press with acting budget director Bell at his side, Roosevelt was relatively frank about the budgetary predictions.

Q: A year ago you looked forward to 1936 as being the year when the Budget might possibly be balanced?

THE PRESIDENT: Ought to if we could and we couldn't.

Q: Are you looking forward to another year when it might well be?

THE PRESIDENT: I hope so. Hope springs eternal. We hope this year, having shown a smaller deficit for 1936 than for 1935, [that further reductions will follow]. . . . There is always the hope . . . that this deficit for 1936 will [be smaller than present estimates].[7]

Asked if he had any fixed notion of a limit beyond which "the public debt ought not be permitted to rise," he responded with a question of his own.

THE PRESIDENT: Suppose, in 1937, we should find this country in a situation where there were five million people starving—starving—what would you do if you were president? Would you let them starve in order to keep the public debt from going beyond a specific amount of debt in 1937?

Q: Of course not, Mr. President.

THE PRESIDENT: There you are; I don't know.[8]

Thus, when in the *Hot Oil Case*—*hot oil* was the term for oil produced beyond limits set by the oil-production code of the NRA—the Court in its first decision of 1935 declared by a vote of eight to one that Section 9(c) of the National Industrial Recovery Act of 1933 was unconstitutional,[9] Roosevelt's initial reaction was one of nonconcern. Asked in his Wednesday press conference if he would like to comment on the case, he answered no and then suggested that reporters read a story in that morning's *Wall Street Journal*. It concluded that the Court had not made "a blanket ruling against the delegation of power by Congress to the Executive which would justify one in concluding that the whole NIRA and perhaps the Agricultural Adjustment Act as well are flatly unconstitutional."[10]

Roosevelt then recounted an anecdote about a probably mythical "certain village in up-State New York" whose protracted efforts to solve a dangerous traffic problem ran into legal snags. Eventually, a proper ordinance was drafted, but in the meantime the village's solution—a traffic light and a constable—continued to operate. He expected an analogous result from the *Hot Oil Case*.

THE PRESIDENT: Now of course you and I know that in the long run there may be a half a dozen more court decisions on oil before they get the correct language. . . . But this country is headed for the control of the great natural resource which is called "oil." That's about the beginning of it and the end of it.

Q: Doesn't this rather circumscribe your actions as quarterback of the New Deal?

THE PRESIDENT: No. . . . We can go as far as Congress can possibly go. There is good intent on all sides if you try to do things the right way.[11]

In this instance, the "right way" was a relatively routine statute, the so-called Hot Oil Act, in which Congress provided legislative authority for the practices that had been banned by the Court when stemming solely from executive action. Roosevelt then issued an executive order empowering Ickes to administer the statute in the same way as he had been doing.[12]

If Roosevelt was not then worried about the legal status of his recovery program, he and many other New Dealers were seriously concerned about what the Court might do in the *Gold Clause Cases,* which were being argued that week. They arose from a statute passed during the hundred days at Roosevelt's behest, abrogating clauses existing largely in public and private bond issues calling for payment in gold. At immediate issue were $100 billion in outstanding government Liberty Bonds that would be worth $169 billion if redeemed at the current statutory price of gold. But the total windfall to bondholders would far surpass that and place the government's entire fiscal program at risk.[13]

After arguing the government's case in the morning, Attorney General Cummings reported at Friday's cabinet meeting that he expected a split decision in the government's favor.[14] Nevertheless, Roosevelt and the Treasury Department made detailed arrangements for, in effect, nullifying an adverse decision if the Court ruled against the government. On February 18, the day the Court's decision was expected, Roosevelt, Morgenthau, and key Treasury officials with "Plan B Variations" in their briefcases sat waiting in the Cabinet Room for a telephoned result from the Court. They soon learned that the gold clause had been allowed to stand by the margin of one vote. Morgenthau's biographer John Morton Blum describes the result:

> As the group at the White House talked the cases over, Morgenthau saw from the President's questions that Roosevelt knew no more than he about the legal details. [Herman] Oliphant had to interpret the meaning of the decisions for both of them. . . . [15] [T]hose around the cabinet table . . . sat and talked for about an hour with the atmosphere "very jolly." Roosevelt was "very natural, laughing and smiling practically all the time. . . . It certainly was one of the big moments of my life," Morgenthau later reflected, "and it was an experience to be with him."[16]

Chief Justice Hughes, speaking for a five-man majority in the *Gold Clause Cases,* had ruled that Congress had undoubted power to regulate the monetary system and could override private contracts that were at odds with that authority. But he also ruled that, by canceling the gold clauses in government bonds, it had unconstitutionally impaired its own obligations. Still, he also held that bondholders could recover only nominal damages for breach of contract, and thus their suit in the Court of Claims was invalid. In other words, Congress—at Roosevelt's behest—had acted illegally, but nothing tangible could be done about it.

A formal dissent by Justice McReynolds, joined by Justices Van Devanter, Sutherland, and Butler, argued that letting the government off scot-free was scandalous and shameful. It concluded: "Loss of reputation for honorable dealing will bring us unending humiliation; the impending legal and moral chaos is appalling."[17]

In the courtroom, McReynolds, instead of reading the written opinion, delivered a tirade that castigated the majority opinion, claimed that the Constitution was "gone," and invoked Nero as an appropriate predecessor to Roosevelt. The White House restricted itself to a terse statement of gratification at the result. Roosevelt made no public reference to either the decision or McReynolds's antics, and the stock market and other exchanges reacted positively.[18]

Privately, Roosevelt was cock-a-hoop. Writing the next day to Joe Kennedy, who as chair of the SEC would have issued an edict closing the stock exchanges had the decision gone the other way, the president referred to "an historic day." "The Nation will never know," he noted, "what a great treat it missed in not hearing the marvelous radio address the 'Pres' had prepared for delivery . . . Monday night if the cases had gone the other way." But his comment, "As a lawyer it seems to me that the Supreme Court has at last definitely put human values ahead of the 'pound of flesh' called for by a contract," suggests that he had not read Hughes's decision carefully.[19]

At this point, it seems to me, Roosevelt felt that he was home free with the Supreme Court. He surely expected setbacks about this or that administrative detail, but like the town board of his "certain upstate village," he and his aides would make the necessary adjustments.

Roosevelt sent his Social Security message to Congress on January 17, accompanied by a formal recommendation from his cabinet-level Committee on Economic Security that had been meeting since June. It was a careful, conservative approach, which fell well short of what advanced social reformers had wanted. As the president warned:

> It is overwhelmingly important to avoid any danger of permanently discrediting the sound and necessary policy of Federal legislation for economic security by attempting to apply it on too ambitious a scale before actual experience has provided guidance for the permanently safe direction of such efforts. The place of such a fundamental in our future civilization is too precious to be jeopardized now by extravagant action. It is a sound idea—a sound ideal. Most of the other advanced countries of the world have already adopted it and their experience affords the knowledge that social insurance can be made a sound and workable project.

Three principles should be observed in legislation on this subject. First, the system adopted, except for the money necessary to initiate it, should be self-sustaining in the sense that funds for the payment of insurance benefits should not come from the proceeds of general taxation. Second, excepting in old-age insurance, actual management should be left to the States subject to standards established by the Federal Government. Third, sound financial management of the funds and the reserves, and protection of the credit structure of the Nation should be assured by retaining Federal control over all funds through trustees in the Treasury of the United States.

The first two of those principles can be regarded as compromises that limited the effectiveness of the program. The insistence that funds from general taxation not be used did not come from the experience of other advanced nations—which universally used such funds—and has created a seemingly endless series of crises about the impending bankruptcy of the Social Security system. Leaving most of the program to be managed by the states left large numbers of the poor at the mercy of authorities who despised them. As one of Mississippi's leading newspapers editorialized in opposing the act, "The average Mississippian can't imagine himself chipping in to pay pensions for able-bodied Negroes to sit around in idleness on front galleries, supporting all their kinfolks on pensions, while cotton and corn crops are crying out for workers to get them out of the grass."[20]

Roosevelt called for four separate kinds of security legislation: unemployment compensation, old-age benefits, federal aid to dependent children, and additional federal aid to state and local public health agencies as well as the strengthening of the federal Public Health Service. But, in the biggest single disappointment for advanced reformers, there was no health insurance associated with Social Security. As the president explained: "I am not at this time recommending the adoption of so-called 'health insurance,' although groups representing the medical profession are cooperating with the Federal Government in the further study of the subject and definite progress is being made."[21]

In addition to that weakness—and others—in the initial proposal, the dozens of compromises that occurred in getting a Social Security bill through Congress have made it possible for some on the Left to argue that, in the final analysis, the creation of the flawed Social Security system was an impediment to real reform. Roosevelt understood full well most of the limitations and flaws of the act he would sign into law in August. It was, in many ways, far from his own vision of "cradle to the grave" coverage for all Americans.[22] But it established a baseline and a principle—as conservative leaders from Ronald Reagan to George W. Bush discovered—that have endured.

In June 1941, when social scientist Luther Gulick told Roosevelt that it had been a mistake to finance Social Security with payroll taxes, the president responded, "I guess you're right on the economics. They are politics all the way through. We put those pay roll contributions there so as to give the contributors a legal, moral, and political right to collect their pensions and their unemployment benefits. With those taxes in there, no damn politician can ever scrap my social security program. Those taxes aren't a matter of economics, they're straight politics."[23]

Following his two major initiatives, Roosevelt sent such a steady stream of proposals to Congress that some scholars have written of a "second hundred days" in 1935. Analyzing the session's work, the New York Times listed fifty-seven statutes as "the Principal Acts of Congress" for 1935.[24] These included new initiatives, expansions and continuations of previous New Deal measures, and statutes necessitated by actions of the Supreme Court.

Despite his absorption with recovery and his legislative program, Roosevelt was constantly taking a longer view of things. Nothing better illustrates the protean nature of his presidency than a message he sent to Congress at the end of January. On its face a mere transmittal of a report, it shows Roosevelt to be not just a supporter of conservation but an environmentalist who saw the need for national planning. After the end of the 1934 session, he had established the National Resources Board (NRB) to recommend "public policies for the development and use of land, water, and other natural resources." He ordered that its first efforts be directed toward "saving those lands in the country now being rapidly turned into virtual deserts through wind and water erosion, and the relocation of those trying to wrest a living from this rapidly deteriorating land."[25] But the massive and often desperate internal migration that John Steinbeck immortalized in The Grapes of Wrath had already begun, and the orderly relocation that Roosevelt envisaged never took place.

But the plan his NRB submitted was what the president called a "comprehensive [report] dealing with problems of land, water and minerals, the organizing and timing of public works programs, and made available many basic data for State regional and national planning." It was the first attempt in our national history to make an inventory of our national assets and of the problems related to them.[26]

Unlike many of the special bodies created in the early New Deal, the NRB had a respectable shelf life, morphing into the National Resources Planning Board (NRPB), which lasted until 1943.[27] It also had a remarkably consistent membership: its chair, Charles W. Eliot II (1899–1993), and two of the three original members—the president's uncle Frederick A. Delano (1863–1953) and political scientist Charles E. Merriam (1874–1953)—stayed the course; economist Wesley C. Mitchell (1874–1946) resigned in 1936 and was replaced by two business executives with Keynesian attitudes, Beardsley Ruml (1894–1960) and Henry S. Dennison (1877–1952). In its heyday, the board met with the president once a month and during its life produced some 370 reports with a total length of forty-five thousand pages. Its influence declined in the World War II years, as Roosevelt concentrated on military problems. By the time Congress abolished the NRPB in 1943, its staff, which peaked at 271 in 1935, had been reduced to 50. From its beginnings, it was opposed by cabinet members such as Harold Ickes,[28] who thought that such bodies ought to be located in regular departments and resented Roosevelt's insistence that the board report directly to him. But the board was also frustrated, as it aspired to be the president's chief adviser, but Roosevelt always insisted on having multiple sources of information and counsel.[29]

As the 1933 statute had authorized the NRA for only two years, reauthorization by the 1935 Congress was necessary. That legislation had not only created the vast regulatory apparatus but also provided for public works programs. It and Jesse Jones's RFC were the two major money pots of the early New Deal. The NRA was also the legislative authority for Roosevelt's various labor boards. A February message to Congress called for an extension of the NRA for another two years. "The fundamental purposes and principles of the Act are sound. To abandon them is unthinkable. It would spell the return of industrial and labor chaos."

Roosevelt envisaged some changes, recommending that "the policy and standards" for administering the law be clarified by Congress. He thought that "voluntary submission" of codes should be continued but insisted that if an industry did not create an acceptable code, the government must have "unquestioned power" to set fair standards of competition and labor standards: "'child labor' must not be allowed to return," and "fixing of minimum wages and maximum hours is practical and necessary. The collective bargaining rights of employees should be fully protected."

And in response to one of the most persistent criticisms of the NRA, the president affirmed that "the fundamental principles of the anti-trust laws" ought to apply and that "monopolies and price fixing" were impermissible. But he argued that government "supervision" of certain natural resources—coal, oil, and gas were specified—was needed.[30]

The Senate soon passed a one-year extension, and the House was expected to pass a two-year extension; given Roosevelt's political potency, it is reasonable to assume that he might well have gotten most of what he wanted from Congress. But on May 27, the Supreme Court settled the matter in a sweeping decision that simply ended any question of reauthorization. There could be no quick fix as had been done in the *Hot Oil Case*.[31]

Before analyzing the Court's decision and its broad impact, it is important to understand that it did not otherwise significantly interfere with the progress of the president's program in the spring of 1935. Not everything he suggested got immediate action. Among important measures sent to Congress in March were proposals for the merchant marine, for utility regulation, and for a revised pure food and drug act. Only utility regulation would be passed in 1935; the other two were enacted only in 1937 and 1938.[32] At the same time, Congress was not only picking apart the NRA but preparing to present the president with a bonus bill that he would have to veto. Amid newspaper speculation about the difficulties the president's program was having—a "critical situation," according to the *New York Times*—Roosevelt, as he had done the year before, announced that he was going on vacation.[33] He left Washington on March 25 for thirteen days of fishing off Florida, again on Vincent Astor's *Nourmahal*, accompanied by personal rather than political companions.

When he returned to shore at Jacksonville on April 8, the $4.8 billion measure for work relief he had asked for in his annual message was waiting for his signature; it was the largest single appropriation in American history. The funds were to be allocated at the president's discretion, though there were some earmarks, such as $600 million for the CCC. It had been finally agreed to on Saturday; he signed it Monday afternoon as his northbound train passed through South Carolina and immediately allocated the initial $155 million so that relief programs could continue. Funds from the original 1933 PWA appropriation had been used to keep the FERA and CCC going after the appropriations for them had run out, which meant that some authorized projects had to be canceled or reallocated.[34] The president's train took him to New York so he could attend the funeral of his cousin Warren Delano Robbins, the son of his mother's sister, Katherine, whom he had made minister to Canada. Just three years FDR's junior, Robbins began a career in the foreign service after graduation from Harvard. In 1932–33, then the State Department's chief of protocol, he had welcomed the president-elect to Washington. Roosevelt also used his two hours in New York to visit the sickbed of Claudette Roosevelt, the daughter of his fishing companion Kermit Roosevelt. That Roosevelt added ten hours to a long trip at a busy time provides some notion of his sense of family obligation.[35]

While Roosevelt was away, Louis Howe's health took a dramatic turn for the worse. Howe—but not his family—had long lived in the White House and since January had been largely confined to his room in an oxygen tent. The president spent the first half hour of his return at Louis's side. Howe's influence, which had been in decline since the Chicago convention, was all but nonexistent from this point. By August he had to be removed to the naval hospital in Bethesda, where he died, eight months later. But as long as he lived, only he was secretary to the president. No one in the inner circle, ever again, could tell Franklin to his face to "go to Hell!"[36]

Leaving Howe, Roosevelt met with two House leaders he had summoned, the new speaker, Tennessee's Joseph W. Byrns (1869–1936) and North Carolina's Robert L. Doughton (1863–1954), chair of the Ways and Means Committee. On emerging they told the press that the president wanted the Social Security bill passed and that they would speed it through the House. But New York's

John J. O'Connor (1885–1960), chair of the Rules Committee and a thorn in the president's side, assured a reporter that there would be no "gag rule," suggesting that passage would be neither swift nor sure.[37]

Executive action was swifter and surer. In the following weeks, while Congress debated, the president created three agencies crucial to the aims of the New Deal, the Works Projects Administration, the Resettlement Administration (RA), and the Rural Electrification Administration (REA). The WPA, which lasted until 1943, became Roosevelt's chief work relief agency; the RA, which endured until 1946, sought, with only slight success, to improve the lives of America's rural proletariat, white and black. But at the same time, FERA's responsibilities to alleviate rural poverty were transferred to the RA, which meant that the landless rural poor were largely beyond the reach of the major relief agency. Both of the relief agencies were associated with a controversial Roosevelt lieutenant, the WPA with Harry Hopkins and the RA with Rex Tugwell.[38] By contrast, the REA, so successful that it became a permanent part of the government, was run by administrators largely unknown except among those concerned with the electrification process. Even most American history professors cannot name a single REA administrator. A simple statistic summarizes its—and Roosevelt's—success. The census before Roosevelt's presidency found that just 10 percent of American farm families had electricity. The census after his presidency found that only 10 percent of such families did *not* have it. Like Federal Deposit Insurance, once enacted and understood, rural electrification was quickly enfolded into the American consensus.[39]

The work relief program was first described in three White House statements that seemed to give its oversight to a committee of twenty-four headed by Harold Ickes. Then a Fireside Chat, discussed below, explained it to the people, and finally, two weeks after the first announcement, an executive order created the WPA and stipulated the National Emergency Council as its supervisory body.[40]

In reality, Harry Hopkins, who remained federal emergency relief administrator, ran the WPA with essentially the same staff that had run the FERA and the short-lived CWA. Its key members were his number two, Aubrey Williams, who had occasional access to the president; Jacob Baker (1895–1967); Corrington Gill (1898–1946); and Ellen Woodward (1887–1971).[41] Hopkins and Ickes oversaw and often fought about whose organization would build what; when they disagreed, the president decided.

The Fireside Chat on Sunday evening, April 28 (the first in seven months), began with a claim—essentially false—that events were evolving according to a blueprint, "like the building of a ship." The New Deal was never like that. Roosevelt spoke briefly about the Social Security bill before Congress, emphasizing its job-creating potential, as its "old age pensions [would] help those who have reached the age of retirement to give up their jobs" to the younger generation.

The most detailed part of the talk was about the new "work relief program." Roosevelt described the criteria for projects that were to be "useful," labor intensive, and likely to provide some return to the Treasury; funds should be spent promptly and not held over; projects should employ those on the relief rolls and were to be allocated to cities and states in relation to the numbers of workers actually on relief. Warning that "there may be occasional instances of inefficiency, bad management, or misuse of funds," the president called upon "my fellow citizens" to exercise "eternal vigilance" and "tell me of instances where work can be done better, or where improper practices prevail." As was his habit, he did not name any of those who ran his programs.

He then ticked off the most important other pending legislative measures: the renewal of the NRA, the elimination of "unnecessary holding companies in the public utility field," and measures to regulate transportation and to strengthen the Federal Reserve Act. He closed on a positive note: without claiming that the Depression was over, he suggested that "the darkest moments" had passed, that "fear is vanishing and confidence growing. . . . For that we can be thankful to the God who watches over America."[42]

Before any of the measures Roosevelt advocated were enacted, the House again took up the soldiers' bonus question, which could expect even more support—perhaps enough to override a veto—since the conservative American Legion, which had previously opposed early payment, had reversed its position, arguing that the old economy argument was no longer valid, as government policy was "committed to the policy of spending" for recovery.[43] There were two major bonus bills in the House. Wright Patman (1893–1976), a Texas Democrat and devout inflationist, sponsored a dual-purpose bill providing "for immediate cash payment . . . and for controlled expansion of the currency," while the bill of Kentucky Democrat Frederick M. Vinson (1890–1953) carried no such inflationist baggage. The Patman version prevailed over the Vinson measure in the House, 207–204; the vote on its passage was 319–90 and clearly veto proof. A similar struggle took place in the Senate, and again the Patman version prevailed, 52–35. But a number of those who voted for the Patman version, including the majority leader, Arkansas's Joseph T. Robinson, did so because they believed that it would be easier to get votes sustaining a veto of the more radical version.

Roosevelt directed this strategy and was determined to make a big thing of his veto. He summoned Sam Rosenman from New York to help draft his carefully crafted veto message, which, in an unprecedented personal appearance, he read before a joint session of Congress in the House chamber. His basic arguments—that the bill was inflationary, unsound, and special interest legislation—were the same ones he had been using since his gubernatorial days. On finishing the message, he theatrically handed the unsigned bill back to Speaker Byrns. The House immediately overrode the veto, 322–98, but it was sustained in the Senate the next day, as 40 of 94 voting senators upheld the president; a vital 12 nays had come from Republican senators. Roosevelt assured his press conference that if a bonus bill were attached to the still pending Social Security legislation, he would veto that, too.[44]

As Roosevelt certainly knew, the bonus issue was far from dead. A conservative measure would be all but irresistible in 1936, an election year. Why, then, did Roosevelt make such a production of his veto? There is no clear answer. It did enable him to be seen as more fiscally responsible than Congress and to demonstrate that he was in charge. But any impact of the veto, which was delivered on a Wednesday, was eclipsed the following Monday, May 27, 1935, by the Court's action on the NRA.[45]

As has often been true of the quarrels that have shaped the American Constitution, the issue involved was trivial: a fine assessed against the Schechter brothers, New York City kosher poultry butchers, for violation of the NRA code regulating their particular trade. While many of those connected with the NRA had feared that it would be struck down, in whole or in part, by the Court, and Roosevelt was aware of those fears, the totality of the decision and its 9–0 unanimity provided a real shock. It is true that a decision earlier that month had nullified a minor measure, the Railroad Retirement Act. The opinion written by Justice Owen J. Roberts was supported by the Four Horsemen, but countered by Chief Justice Hughes in a biting dissent. William Leuchtenburg has written of that May 6 decision: "From that moment on neither Roosevelt nor his aides would rest until they had found a way to overcome the obstacle to their plans presented by the Court."

This seems to me an overstatement. Not only was May 1935 an exceedingly busy month, but there is no evidence of Roosevelt's concern beyond an entry in Rex Tugwell's diary saying that the president had agreed with his notion that "the Courts will declare the NRA unconstitutional."[46] I believe that Roosevelt, habitual optimist that he was, continued to believe that minor adjustments could be made, as the administration had done in response to the *Hot Oil* decision, that would bring the NRA into line with what the Court might accept. He had been asked about it just after the Roberts ruling came down and seemed not particularly concerned.

> Q: Has your study of the Justice Department report on the Railroad pension (Retirement?) Act made you change your mind about N.R.A.?
> THE PRESIDENT: No, not a bit.[47]

But the totality of Hughes's denunciation of the NRA in *Schechter*, its unanimity, and the accompanying furor made it clear to him that he had a major problem. At the first post-*Schechter* press conference, rather than criticize the Court directly he used a device with which the reporters were familiar.

If I were going to write the story . . . I would write it something like this: The spot news is not in Washington! . . . The real spot news in the present situation is what is happening as a result of the Supreme Court decision in every industry and in every community in the United States. Are there any people in the garment industry in the city of New York who cut their wages from twelve dollars minimum to eight dollars today? . . . Are there factories anywhere in New York or anywhere else this morning that said to the girls, "Instead of going home at five o'clock this afternoon, we have a lot of rush work on. You are going to stay until nine o'clock tonight."

Asked whether he had talked to anyone about "congressional action to limit the power of the Supreme Court," he answered, "No. Oh, I have had—this is the batch since nine o'clock this morning, but I suppose that we have had about fifty different suggestions. They go all the way from abolishing the Supreme Court to abolishing the Congress, and I think abolishing the President. That is so as to make it complete. (Laughter)."[48]

The next press conference lasted a record hour and twenty-five minutes, most of it an uninterrupted presidential monologue. After the routine beginning— Roosevelt asking the reporters if they had any news for him while fitting a cigarette into his holder—the president spoke without a manuscript but with a sheaf of telegrams and the text of the *Schechter* decision before him. After reading excerpts from the telegrams, all asking him to do something, he launched into his analysis of the Court's decision, which he called "more important than any decision probably since the Dred Scott case." He argued that more important than the question of delegation of power, which he thought could be taken care of, was the very narrow redefinition of interstate commerce. Harking back to the *E. C. Knight* decision of 1895, which had, for a time, virtually nullified the Sherman Antitrust Act, he read a key passage from Hughes's opinion:

Were these transactions "in" interstate commerce? Much is made of the fact that almost all the poultry coming to New York is sent there from other states. But the code provisions, as here applied, do not concern the transportation of the poultry from other states to New York, or the transactions of the commission men or others to whom it is consigned, or the sales made by such consignees to defendants. When defendants had made their purchases, whether at the West Washington Market in New York City or at the railroad terminals serving the city, or elsewhere, the poultry was trucked to their slaughterhouses in Brooklyn for local disposition. The interstate transactions in relation to that poultry then ended. Defendants held the poultry at their slaughterhouse markets for slaughter and local sale to retail dealers and butchers who in turn sold directly to consumers. Neither the slaughtering nor the sales by defendants were transactions in interstate commerce.[49]

Roosevelt read Hughes's strictures on emergency power—"Extraordinary conditions may call for extraordinary remedies. But . . . [e]xtraordinary conditions do not create or enlarge constitution power"—and observed that wartime legislation had gone further than anything that the New Deal had done. The memorable quotation from the conference—which an alert correspondent got explicit permission to use—was that the Court had taken the country back to "the horse-and-buggy definition of interstate commerce."

Nothing better shows Roosevelt's wonderful ear for the right phrase than appropriation of "horse-and-buggy." As he was about to be taken to the press conference, Steve Early had remarked that his brother-in-law said to him that the justices "think that this is still the horse-and-buggy age." Roosevelt made no response, but in the middle of a long conference he used the phrase, which became iconic.[50]

More revealing of Roosevelt's basic strategy, however, was the following colloquy at the conference's close.

> Q: You referred to the Dred Scott decision. That was followed by the Civil War and by at least two amendments to the Constitution.
> THE PRESIDENT: Well, the reason for that . . . was the fact that the generation of 1856 did not take action during the next four years.
> Q: You made a reference to the necessity of the people deciding within the next five or ten years. Is there any way of deciding that question without voting on a constitutional amendment or the passing of one.
> THE PRESIDENT: Oh, yes; I think so. But it has got to come in the final analysis.
> Q: Any suggestion as to how it might be made, except by a constitutional amendment?
> THE PRESIDENT: No; we haven't got to that yet.[51]

Contemporary speculation was that the Court would be the big issue in the 1936 presidential election, but that was not Roosevelt's strategy. He wanted the focal issues of the campaign to be his leadership and the New Deal itself. Thus, after a pause to recover and adjust, he continued to push his program forward and, in his public statements, largely ignored the Supreme Court. Although toward the end of the long press conference he speculated that it might take "five years or ten years" to settle the question of the scope of federal regulatory power, it is reasonable to assume that he hoped and expected to get it done during the next five years, which he then expected to be the limit of his presidency.[52]

A week and a day after the *Schechter* decision, 350 reporters, more than twice the usual complement, showed up for the Tuesday-afternoon press conference. Many expected to learn of impending constitutional change; they got mostly housekeeping details. Emerging from a meeting with Democratic congressional leaders, Roosevelt announced the actions planned as a consequence of the NRA's demise. The leaders had agreed to a joint resolution continuing a skeleton NRA that would continue to gather statistical data and to monitor all government purchases. Most of the NRA's fifty-four hundred employees were terminated.

New legislation had been agreed on to resurrect the Federal Alcohol Control Administration, the Electric Farm and Home Authority (an adjunct of the TVA), the Petroleum Board, and the Central Statistical Board, which had been included in the NRA for funding purposes. Two other agencies, the National Emergency Council and the National Resources Board, would be continued by executive order, as they could be charged to the Work Relief Act.

But the most important of the collateral consequences of the NRA's demise was that the only legislative authority protecting labor's right to bargain collectively through representatives of their own choosing had been contained in its famous Section 7(a). This more or less forced Roosevelt to get behind the bill backed by New York senator Robert F. Wagner, a step he had refused to take earlier, though he had never actively opposed the bill. The resulting legislation, the National Labor Relations Act of 1935, is universally regarded as one of the crown jewels of the New Deal and, with Social Security and the WPA, one of the three greatest achievements of 1935.[53]

Although the consequences of the *Schechter* decision took up a great deal of time and effort, and undoubtedly extended the congressional session, other aspects of the administration's program continued to evolve. Getting the WPA going was a massive task. Both in his press conferences and in his remarks to the state directors of the WPA, Roosevelt simplified the complex problems of putting 3.5 million unemployed men and women to work with a $4 billion fund. On average, he told both groups, the annual costs had to be about $1,100 to $1,200 per person employed. That meant that most of the projects had to be labor intensive and that each more expensive project—he specifically mentioned grade crossings and dams—would have to be balanced by projects with minimal costs in materials and planning. To the state administrators, he stressed four points:

> We want to get rid of the dole [which] is destructive of all that is best in our citizenship . . . we want to make people feel that they are no longer in the bread line—no longer getting something for nothing. We want them to feel that they are getting work. . . .
>
> We want . . . to have every relief administrator make every effort to get the unemployed into private industry. . . .
>
> [W]e have to be extremely careful not to make any kind of discrimination. We cannot discriminate in any of the work we are conducting because of race or religion or politics.
>
> [W]e want [the projects] to be as useful as possible.

The warning against racial discrimination in employment, the first such of his political career, is noteworthy even though most of the emphasis in that part of the talk was about avoiding political discrimination—that is, hiring deserving Democrats—which turned out to be one of the besetting sins of the federal relief program.[54]

What Roosevelt never discussed publicly was how Hopkins and his staff developed a wage scale below the "prevailing wage" standard that had been applied in many federal contracts. The WPA ideal was a "security wage," which workers received, even when, as was often the case in outdoor work, weather conditions or other problems made work impossible or impractical. As long as they showed up, workers would be paid. The amount a WPA worker received depended on skill level, the geographical region of employment, and the size of the work site's county. Thus, a worker of the highest of four skill levels, in a large county of the most expensive of the four regions, could receive $94 a month, while a worker of the lowest skill level, in a very small county of the least expensive region, could get only $19.[55]

In July, after meetings with Ickes and Hopkins, Roosevelt issued a much misunderstood statement establishing the relative "jurisdictions" of the PWA and WPA. The first part of the statement assigned construction projects costing more than $25,000 to the PWA, while those costing less than that were assigned to the WPA, as were all "non-construction projects" that employed clerical, professional, and white-collar workers. At the press conference where the order was handed out, a reporter asked:

Q: So there won't be any projects under Hopkins' Division, individually more than $25,000 each?

THE PRESIDENT: There will be quite a number. . . . You had better read this order.

What the reporter had missed was a provision deep in the order that "applications rejected by [Ickes] shall be submitted immediately to the WPA." Which federal agency sponsored a project could be crucial for the sponsoring local government. For PWA projects, the sponsoring city or county would have to provide 55 percent of construction materials; in some instances, the WPA could provide 100 percent of those costs if the sponsoring agency did not have the needed funds. But many journalists and later historians have ignored this sometimes crucial detail and stressed the ongoing "feud" between Hopkins and Ickes.[56]

A month later, Roosevelt announced, "I have determined that we shall do something for the Nation's unemployed youth because we can ill afford to lose the skill and energy of these men and women. They must have their chance in school, their turn as apprentices and their opportunity for jobs—a chance to work and earn for themselves."

Using the broad authority provided in the $4.8 billion work relief bill, an executive order established the National Youth Administration as a freestanding division within the WPA and named Aubrey Williams as its executive director. (Williams remained Hopkins's principal aide in running the WPA.) Youth was defined as persons between the ages of sixteen and twenty-five. In addition to providing jobs and job training, the NYA took over the existing FERA college aid programs and added one for high school students initially supported by an allotment of $50 million of WPA funds. By the end of 1936, five hundred thousand young people were enrolled, more than five times the number that had been assisted under the FERA programs. Some of the funds were used to create projects, largely nonresidential, for training and employment of out-of-school youth.[57]

Largely because of Williams's advanced social views, the NYA gave more scope to women, blacks, and other persons of color than any other New Deal relief organization. Precise data are hard to come by, and gender is better documented than race, but throughout its existence about 45 percent of those in its out-of-school work program were female. Less complete data for the work study programs show women an absolute majority of the high school program, 53 percent, and 40 percent of the college program for 1939–40. Scantier data on race suggest that in 1939, about one in eight of those in both the high school and the out-of-school programs was black, as was one of eighteen in its college programs.[58]

Only in mid-June 1935 did Roosevelt sent his first general tax message to Congress. Unlike more recent conservative governments, the Hoover administration had raised taxes significantly and, with the assistance of what was in effect a Democratic Congress, passed the largest peacetime tax increase of the pre–World War II era in 1932. But under both Hoover and Roosevelt until the war came, more than 90 percent of Americans paid no income tax. An absolute majority of the money raised from the personal income tax came from the fewer than twenty thousand annual individual tax returns reporting $50,000 or more. Although the 1932 measure did raise income and estate tax rates and narrowed exemptions on the former, most of the new money raised in Hoover's administration came from federal excise taxes on many manufactured goods and electricity, all regressive imposts that were passed on to consumers. Similarly, consumers also paid, one way or another, the major new taxes approved by Roosevelt in 1933–34: the processing tax of the AAA and the taxes on newly legalized beer, wine, and liquor. Although it did not take effect until 1937, the same was true, with much greater consequence, of the 1 percent tax on the first $3,000 of the wages of employees covered by Social Security. Morgenthau, with Roosevelt's support, had insisted that this tax was fundamental to the Social Security program, whose general benefits began five years after that. (A similar

1 percent was assessed against their employers, who could deduct it from their taxes.)[59]

But Roosevelt's populist rhetoric about tax loopholes and tax avoidance by the very rich, which began with his tax message in June 1935, and the overreactions to that rhetoric by his opponents have created the myth of him as an earnest tax reformer foiled by Congress. Like most myths, it has some basis in reality. Roosevelt did call in peacetime for a number of reforms and got some of them approved by Congress, often in modified form. But they did not materially affect income distribution and benefited the middle class—home and farm owners—as opposed to renters and tenants. Roosevelt called for increased taxes on large inheritances, increased gift taxes to limit evasions, increased rates on very large incomes, and a graduated tax rate for corporations, changing a flat 13.75 percent rate to one that ranged from 10.75 percent to 16.75 percent—which lowered the taxes on many small businesses. (Congress narrowed the corporate range to 12.5 percent and 15 percent.) The raising of the top rate on the richest Americans from 63 to 79 percent affected very few persons. The very top rate in 1936 affected only one taxpayer: John D. Rockefeller. These 1935 reform proposals, largely enacted in that year, contributed only $250 million to total federal tax receipts in 1936 of more than $4 billion. Much more important, in terms of government revenue, was Roosevelt's successful request that Congress renew a number of excise taxes that were about to expire.

Modest as they were, these "wealth taxes" raised the hackles of conservatives, who were further agitated by Roosevelt's soak-the-rich rhetoric. In his press conferences and later speeches, the president resounded a note that had been largely muted since the metaphor about the money changers in the inaugural. An example of the way Roosevelt used the issue of wealth came in a press conference while his tax proposals were working their way through Congress.

He talked about—and allowed the correspondents to quote the phrase—"the 58 thriftiest people in the United States . . . so thrifty that they had a million dollars in income or more and . . . paid no tax to the Federal government whatever on 37% of their net income." He defined the difference between tax evasion and tax avoidance: "Tax avoidance means that you hire a $25,000 fee lawyer and he changes the word 'evasion' into the word 'avoidance.'" He reported cases of millions of dollars being given as gifts just before death, greatly reducing the tax liability of large estates. He cited one case in which a $100 million estate was reduced to $8 million and one family that had 197 different family trusts.[60]

Roosevelt would return to this mode occasionally during the next three years, but he often disavowed it. In a comic passage in a speech to an appreciative audience on a university campus toward the end of 1938, he commented on his image in some quarters.

You undergraduates who see me for the first time have read in your news-papers and heard on the air that I am, at the very least, an ogre—a consorter with Communists, a destroyer of the rich, a breaker of our ancient traditions. Some of you think of me perhaps as the inventor of the economic royalist, of the wicked utilities, of the money changers of the Temple. You have heard for six years that I was about to plunge the Nation into war; that you and your little brothers would be sent to the bloody fields of Europe; that I was driving the Nation into bankruptcy; and that I breakfasted every morning on a dish of grilled millionaire.

Actually I am an exceedingly mild mannered person—a practitioner of peace, both domestic and foreign, a believer in the capitalistic system, and for my breakfast a devotee of scrambled eggs.[61]

By that time, after the 1938 elections, the tone of presidential rhetoric had largely moderated. The initial shift was, in part, a reaction to some of the ex-treme criticism leveled against him and his works, in part a tuning up for the 1936 election. Perhaps equally or even more important, it was a way of counter-ing what some have called "Thunder on the Left," particularly the "Share Our Wealth" program of Huey Long, the Townsend Plan, and the radio rantings of the Michigan Catholic priest Charles E. Coughlin.

Long, nominally a U.S. senator but in effect the dictator of Louisiana, had a "Share Our Wealth Plan" that promised every family a "$5,000 homestead" and an income of $2,500 a year. The "plan" was unworkable. Long called for steep income and inheritance taxes to scale down large fortunes and redistributing the surplus wealth. But even confiscating all the great fortunes would not have garnered nearly enough to provide what Long promised.

Francis E. Townsend (1867–1960) was a retired physician in Southern California with a socialist background who in September 1933 hatched a plan to give every citizen over sixty years of age $200 a month, with the proviso that it all be spent in the month it was received. The program was to be financed by a 2 percent transaction tax, a kind of super sales tax. Such a tax could not have supported the costs of the scheme, but it attracted a growing army of supporters, organized into a nationwide network of social clubs, who submitted petitions with twenty million unaudited signatures to Congress. The movement drew support from a good-size congressional bloc, largely Republican, most of whom understood that it was impossible but backed it in an effort to derail Social Security. Such schemes flourished in the same atmosphere that fostered Upton Sinclair's EPIC program.

Father Charles E. Coughlin (1891–1979), born, educated, and ordained in Canada, emigrated to the United States in 1923 and three years later became a parish priest in Royal Oak, Michigan, a Detroit suburb, where he remained. He quickly joined the growing ranks of radio preachers and became one of the most successful. Beginning on one powerful Detroit station, by 1930 he was broadcasting weekly on the CBS network with an audience estimated by some at more than forty million. As the Depression deepened, his once chiefly moral sermons became more and more political, and he soon began attacking Hoover and eventually supported Roosevelt in 1932: one of his slogans was "Roosevelt or Ruin." A supporter of extreme inflation, an isolationist, and an opponent of "international bankers," he eventually founded an overtly anti-Semitic secular organization by mid-1935 and was drifting away from Roosevelt. The priest never had even the semblance of a plan, but he did support the hopeless third-party candidacy of William Lemke in 1936.[62]

All these nostrums concerned Roosevelt, but in the summer of 1935 his attention was focused on the progress of his legislative proposals. He gave up all thought of a Fourth of July holiday and spent the day in the White House, much of it with leaders of the House Ways and Means Committee on the tax bill.[63] The next day, he was able to sign the National Labor Relations Act; in addition to relegislating the 7(a) guarantee of the right of collective bargaining, it established a new NLRB whose members were appointed with the advice and consent of the Senate and whose major tasks were to prevent unfair labor practices, supervise representation elections, and certify their results. Unlike many of the special labor boards, the NLRB was not charged with settling labor-management disputes.

One significant achievement of the 1935 session went unremarked in Roosevelt's *Public Papers,* perhaps because it was associated with the destruction of the NRA. When the *Hot Oil Case* was originally argued before the Court in December 1934, counsel for the litigants, a Texas oil company, had complained to the Court that he had been unable to find a copy of the particular regulation his client had been fined for violating until he discovered it "in the hip pocket of an agent sent down to Texas from Washington." This brought a smile even to the Jovian countenance of the chief justice.[64] But the problem was serious. Although during World War I there had been a system for publication of government regulations, there had been no such publication since. Roosevelt had discussed the need at a National Emergency Council meeting, and a number of legal scholars, including Justice Brandeis, arranged for an article in the *Harvard Law Review* by Erwin R. Griswold, deploring "government in ignorance of the law," just as the *Hot Oil Case* was being argued. Even before the decision came down, Roosevelt put a committee to work on solving the problem. The result was a statute creating the *Federal Register,* a daily publication for the "prompt and uniform printing of public documents." The first issue appeared on March 16, 1936. It was a fundamental element in the revolution in government procedure that accompanied the New Deal. And although the president never publicly discussed the *Register,* he and Rosenman did include a complete list of the numbers and titles of the 1,468 executive orders and 882 proclamations of the first term in an appendix to the 1935 volume of his personal papers.[65]

Still in Washington in the mid-August heat, Roosevelt was able to sign the Social Security bill on the fourteenth. His signing statement closed by noting that if Congress "had done nothing more than pass this bill, the session would be regarded as historic for all time."

> This social security measure gives at least some protection to thirty millions of our citizens who will reap direct benefits through unemployment compensation, through old age pensions and through increased services for the protection of children and the prevention of ill health.
>
> We can never insure one hundred percent of the population against one hundred percent of the hazards and vicissitudes of life, but we have tried to frame a law which will give some measure of protection to the average citizen and to his family against the loss of a job and against poverty-ridden old age.[66]

Since the population was about 125 million, using Roosevelt's arithmetic Social Security would, in the near future, benefit less than a quarter of the population. No old-age benefits would be paid until 1942, but aid to dependent children and grants to the states for relief began shortly after passage. And, as Roosevelt understood, the act provided—and still provides—a base for American social policy.

Other significant late-1935 bills included important amendments to the Agricultural Adjustment Act, the Banking Act (which reorganized the Federal Reserve System and made the FDIC permanent), the Tax Bill, the first Neutrality Act, the Bituminous Coal Conservation Act,[67] and the Public Utility Holding Company Act. The utility bill was somewhat weakened in that it delayed the "death sentence" on second-degree holding companies for five years in a compromise worked out between Felix Frankfurter, acting for the president, and Senator Alben Barkley (D-KY). It gave the Federal Power Commission authority to regulate interstate transmission of electric power, enabled the Federal Trade Commission to regulate the transmission of gas, and assigned the SEC authority over the financial operations of such utilities. The large utility combines fought against the regulations in court for years: Wendell L. Willkie, a Wall Street lawyer who became president of the mammoth public utility holding company Commonwealth and Southern in 1933 and was not yet a public figure, won his spurs as an opponent of the New Deal in this eventually futile struggle.[68] By 1952 more than 750 affiliates with assets of more than $10.3 billion had been divested by public utility holding companies.

Congress did not go home until the wee hours of August 27, though the House had stopped its clock at midnight on the twenty-sixth in accordance with a joint resolution to adjourn that day. Huey Long was filibustering in the Senate, blocking both adjournment and the ensured passage of a deficiency appropriation already agreed to by the House. He had started at 6:30 p.m. and was apparently prepared to go on for hours when, just seconds before midnight, a senator raised a parliamentary inquiry and Vice President Garner took the opportunity to bang down his gavel, shouting, "The Senate of the United States stands adjourned *sine die*." The waiting House adjourned moments later. Long, notoriously a physical coward, dashed out a side door, not wishing to face angry colleagues.[69] It was an oddly appropriate end to his sterile legislative career. Fourteen days later, the man Roosevelt had privately called one of the two most dangerous men in America[70] was dead, gunned down by an outraged constituent in the capitol of the state he dominated.[71]

As the session was ending, Roosevelt sent letters to the appropriate congressional committee chairs, asking that during the recess they and their staffs consider creating "further industrial legislation" to preserve gains won by the NRA, including "minimum wages, maximum hours, and prohibition of child labor," but nothing came of it. By year's end, Roosevelt would issue a final executive order that, in effect, buried the major creation of the hundred days and divided its remaining effects and personnel between the Commerce and the Labor Departments. The objectives he sought would be achieved by the 1938 Fair Labor Standards Act, but there would be no new bureaucratic organization created to administer them.[72]

The adjournment, as usual, left Roosevelt with much to do. Appointments had to be made to staff the new boards and agencies, executive orders had to be issued, and ways had to be found to fund temporarily the agencies left without the means to operate by the failure to pass the deficiency appropriation. He had planned to travel to Milwaukee and address the national convention of the Young Democratic Clubs of America, but because the congressional session ran so long, he spoke to the delegates by radio. Talking to this partisan group, he assumed the role of "President of the whole people" and insisted, improbably, that "what I am about to say to you, members of the Young Democratic Clubs, is precisely—word for word—what I would say were I addressing a convention of the young of the Republican Party."

In this guise, he gave a talk that can be considered as the opening gun of his 1936 reelection campaign, fifteen months before election day. He harked back to his own youth: "Party or professional leaders who talked to us twenty-five or thirty years ago almost inevitably spoke to us in a mood of achievement and of exultation. . . . I did not know then of the lack of opportunity, the lack of education, the lack of many of the essential needs of civilization which existed among millions of our people." Speaking, as he loved to do, of his first days in the New York State legislature, he aid:

> In 1911, twenty-four years ago . . . a number of the younger members . . . called for laws governing factory inspection, for workmen's compensation and for the limitation of hours of work for women and children to fifty-four hours,

with one day's rest in seven. [We] were called reformers, socialists, and wild men. . . . The reforms . . . for which we were condemned twenty-four years ago are taken today as a matter of course. And so, I believe, will be regarded the reforms that now cause such concern to the reactionaries of 1935. . . .

Let me emphasize that serious as have been the errors of unrestrained individualism, I do not believe in abandoning the system of individual enterprise. The freedom and opportunity that have characterized American development in the past can be maintained if we recognize the fact that the individual system of our day calls for the collaboration of all of us to provide, at the least, security for all of us. Those words "freedom" and "opportunity" do not mean a license to climb upwards by pushing other people down.[73]

In the speech, the president casually mentioned "the cruel suffering of the recent depression," and in a September press conference he spoke similarly of "the five years of the depression." Clearly, by mid-1935 the nation's economy had recovered much of its lost ground, but the continued existence of very large numbers of unemployed, not to speak of other economic indicators, was evidence that real recovery had not arrived. Yet from August 1935 to October 1937, the economy did expand significantly: the Bureau of Labor Statistics showed a total employment rise of nearly 10 percent, from almost 42.3 million to 46.3 million. But from 1935 through 1937, there was still an average of 7.7 million unemployed. It is easy to see now that this was a false dawn—and a few like Keynes saw it very clearly then—but Roosevelt and most of his advisers greatly overestimated the vigor of recovery, with very painful results. Roosevelt himself

Unemployment in the Great Depression

Year	Number (millions)	Percentage
1930	4.3	8.7
1931	8.0	15.9
1932	12.0	23.6
1933	12.8	24.9
1934	11.3	21.7
1935	10.6	20.1
1936	9.0	16.9
1937	7.7	14.3
1938	10.4	19.0
1939	9.5	17.2
1940	8.1	14.6
1941	5.6	9.9

Source: U.S. Department of Commerce, *Historical Statistics of the United States*, Series D, 46–47, 73.

was more cautious than most. Even when speaking of the Depression in the past tense, he recognized that employment lagged behind other indicators.[74]

Morgenthau, the most economically traditional of Roosevelt's key advisers, actually brought him a speech, drafted in the Treasury in August 1936, that began: "We have today reached the point where we can say with real meaning, wasn't the depression awful."[75] Roosevelt was too cautious to give that speech. After all, he regularly received unemployment figures and had a growing realization of the actual misery that still existed. Although one of the New Deal's little-noted accomplishments was the upgrading of the federal government's statistical apparatus, Roosevelt in some of his off-the-record remarks in his press conferences seemed to be denying the validity of his own government's figures. Eventually, he came to understand the counterintuitive truth that the random sample method was the most reliable way to get a grip on such matters as the true extent of unemployment.[76]

Roosevelt's long-delayed "summer" vacation began only on September 26. After a cross-country rail trip to Southern California, during which he made four formal speeches and twelve short talks, most of them end-of-the-train whistle-stops, he boarded the now familiar USS *Houston* on October 1 in San Diego for brief naval maneuvers, fishing in the eastern Pacific, and a long cruise through the Panama Canal to Charleston, South Carolina.[77] Unlike his previous voyage, his companions were all part of his administration: two of his closest advisers, Harold Ickes and Harry Hopkins; his two military attachés "Pa" Watson, now a colonel, and navy captain Wilson Brown; and physician Ross McIntire. The inclusion of Hopkins was an overt demonstration that, though he did not have cabinet rank, he was in the first echelon of Roosevelt's subordinates. Eleanor Roosevelt and a number of others were in the party that went to California, and, as Ickes complained in his diary, politicians kept getting on and off the train to see and be seen with the president, many of whom insisted on lobbying the PWA boss.[78]

The trip's first formal talk, also broadcast to the nation, took place in the railroad yards at Fremont, Nebraska. The president was quick to remind his listeners that the last time he had been in Nebraska was campaigning in 1932: "I saw farmers threshing thirty-cent wheat and shelling twenty-cent corn." He did not have to tell the crowd that faced him that wheat was currently selling at $1.12 and corn at $1.05. Nor did he need to go into a detailed defense of his AAA; that day, speaking in Topeka, Kansas, Republican stalwart senator Arthur Capper, while claiming that Roosevelt had lost much support among farmers, made it clear that "the AAA" was not an issue with midwestern farmers but a "Godsend."[79]

In the Nevada desert two days later, Roosevelt spoke at the dedication of what is now called Hoover Dam,[80] at the time the largest dam in the world. Standing on a platform above the dam, the Colorado River, and Lake Mead, he spoke through amplifiers to perhaps twenty thousand persons who had come to the site in their cars and to a nationwide radio audience. Recognizing that planning for the dam had begun ten years before, he paid tribute to two Republican California lawmakers, his quondam ally Senator Hiram Johnson and former representative Philip D. Swing (1884–1963), the dam's chief legislative sponsors, but ignored the roles of his predecessors.[81] After hailing the multipurpose facility—flood control, irrigation, and the creation of cheap electric power, a prototype for many New Deal projects to come in the Tennessee Valley and elsewhere—Roosevelt went on to praise lesser projects of the kind his PWA and WPA were beginning to produce. "Can we say that a five-foot brushwood dam across the head waters of an arroyo, and costing only a millionth part of Boulder Dam, is an undesirable project or a waste of money? Can we say that the great brick high school, costing $2,000,000, is a useful expenditure but that a little wooden school house project, costing five or ten thousand dollars, is a wasteful extravagance? Is it fair to approve a huge city boulevard and, at the same time, disapprove the improvement of a muddy farm to market road?" He went on to argue that the projects completed since the beginning of the New Deal had not only "helped mankind by the works themselves" but also "created the necessary purchasing power to throw in the clutch to start the wheels" of private industry. "It is a simple fact that Government spending is already beginning to show its effect. . . . [P]utting people to work by the Government has put other people to work through private employment. . . . [W]e have come to the point where private industry must bear the principal responsibility of keeping the processes of greater employment moving forward with accelerated speed."[82]

In Los Angeles the next day, Roosevelt received, unexpectedly, the "largest reception of his career," as crowds totaling a million persons cheered as his motorcade traveled a total of fifty-seven miles of city streets from the downtown Union Station to the San Fernando Valley and back in a two-and-a-half-hour procession. After a ticker-tape reception downtown, he paused on the campus of the University of Southern California (USC) just long enough for its president to confer a drive-through honorary degree on Roosevelt as he sat in the open car in which he and Eleanor rode. In the adjacent Los Angeles Coliseum, more than seventy-five thousand were waiting for what turned out to be a five-minute address. The president spoke from his car at about the fifty-yard line.

Expecting, as was apparently the case, a large number of Sinclair's EPIC followers in the audience, Roosevelt touched on the nature and problems of liberalism. After avowing that "we have come through stormy seas into fair weather," he related:

Years ago President Wilson told me a story. He said that the greatest problem that the head of a progressive democracy had to face was not the criticism of reactionaries or the attacks of those who would set up some other form of government, but rather to reconcile and unite progressive liberals themselves. The overwhelming majority of liberals all seek the same end, the same ultimate objectives. But because most liberals are able to see beyond the end of their own noses, they are very apt to want to reach their goal by different roads. People who do not want to move forward in the improvement of civilization are perfectly content to stand in one spot, and these people find it easy to remain united in demanding inaction. Liberals, therefore, must find common ground and a common road, each making some concession as to form and method in order to obtain the substance of what all desire.

Roosevelt made three more brief stops—at a veterans hospital, a CCC camp, and a camp for transient youth—before returning to his train for lunch and a meeting with leaders of three different factions of the state's Democrats.[83]

The next day in San Diego, he delivered a longer, more complex speech to an audience of forty-five thousand in a local stadium. It began with another summary of old-order disaster and New Deal achievement: after summarizing the dire economic situation he confronted on taking office, he described the improvement his administration had wrought and claimed. "We stand upon an economic plateau. We have therefore the right to look forward to the brighter future, while at the same time, we remember the mistakes of the past." Then, in a transition brought about in part by Mussolini's invasion of Ethiopia, Roosevelt cited "the greatest writer in history" who had spoken of two great dangers to humanity—"malice domestic and fierce foreign war"[84]—but assured his audience that they need not fear them. "'Malice domestic' from time to time will come to you in the shape of those who would raise false issues, preach the gospel of hate, and minimize the importance of public action to secure human rights or spiritual ideals." More serious, he thought, was "the second cloud—'foreign war.'" Without referring directly to the Italian invasion, he drew loud cheers by declaring:

> Despite what happens in continents overseas, the United States of America shall and must remain, as long ago the Father of Our Country prayed that it might remain—unentangled and free.
>
> This country seeks no conquest. We have no imperial designs. . . . As President of the United States I say to you most earnestly once more that the people of America and the Government of those people intend and expect to remain at peace with all the world. . . . I hope from the bottom of my heart that as the years go on, in every continent and in every clime, Nation will follow Nation in proving by deed as well as be word their adherence to the ideal of the Americas—I am a good neighbor.[85]

Before his speech, Roosevelt had inspected several military and naval installations. Afterward, he and his party boarded the *Houston* to observe a brief naval display that navy public relations called "the largest tactical maneuvers" in American history, involving 129 ships just off San Diego. In early evening, the *Houston,* accompanied by the cruiser *Portland,* headed for Cocos Island, in Mexican waters off Baja California, where the fishing holiday began. Unlike the previous fishing vacations, three wire-service reporters were aboard the *Houston.*[86]

Despite the president's absence, official business continued to get done. While in Mexican waters, he signed two proclamations effecting American neutrality in the war in Ethiopia: one forbade the export of "Arms, Ammunition and Implements of War" to either side; the other warned against but did not prohibit Americans from traveling on belligerent vessels and issued a statement saying that "any of our people who voluntarily engage in transactions of any character with either of the belligerents do so at their own risk."[87]

As a fishing trip, the cruise was a huge success. Roosevelt landed two large sailfish, one of which, a nine-and-a-half-footer weighing 134 pounds, he described as "the perfect specimen. . . . The sail of the first one I caught was cut by the line. This one was gaffed four miles from where it was hooked after exactly 2 hours and 20 minutes. I had 400 yards of line out."[88]

Harold Ickes, a keen if often self-centered observer, was particularly impressed with how Roosevelt accepted the realities of his condition.

> It was a marvel to me to see the way the President was gotten into and out of his fishing boat. . . . Captain Brown and a sailor who had been especially detailed to the *Houston* because he had had a lot of experience in deep-sea fishing stood on the top of the roof that sheltered the stern of the launch. When the *Houston* anchored, a companionway was lowered [and the] launch was brought [alongside. Then] two men would carry him sideways down the companionway [and] hand him over to Captain Brown and the other man . . . who would swing him around into his armchair. . . . [E]specially when the water was rough . . . I was worried about this transshipment of the President to and from the launch. Any misstep or any sudden lurch of the launch might have caused an accident resulting in serious injury to him. But he never seemed to mind. . . . I marveled again and again at his high cheer and at his disposition. Never once did he act self-conscious; on no occasion did he seem to be nervous or irritated. Cheerfully he submitted to being wheeled up and down the special ramps . . . or to being carried like a helpless child when he went fishing. . . . [W]ith his strong arms and shoulders, he was able to give a good account of himself . . . once he got a fish on his hook.[89]

At the end of the twenty-two-day cruise, Roosevelt lunched with his son James and Jim Farley in Charleston Harbor, conducted a brief shipboard press conference, debarked to the usual greetings from local officials, and went to the Citadel to make brief remarks to a crowd of twenty thousand on the college parade ground. There, typically, he reminisced about his visit to Charleston during the Wilson administration and bragged about recovery: "We are on our way back—not just by pure chance, not just by a turn of the wheel, of the cycle. We are coming back more soundly then ever before because we are planning it that way. Don't let anybody tell you differently." Then, in a note that would be repeated several times as the war in Ethiopia continued, he reminded his audience of what he had said in San Diego, "that it shall be my earnest effort to keep this country free and unentangled from any possible war that may occur across the seas."[90]

After returning to Washington by train, he spent the first day in the White House after a four-week absence in conferences, the longest with Secretary of State Hull. In late afternoon, he was driven to the Naval Hospital in Bethesda to visit Louis Howe, something he would do often as long as Howe lived.[91] After dinner he made a radio address for a national charity headed by General Electric's Gerard Swope (1872–1957), the Mobilization for Human Needs, in which he continued his upbeat reports on the economy.

Citing figures from the Labor Department, he reported that in September, "350,000 men and women were returned to private employment in the reporting industries [bringing] payrolls back to the level of May 1931." In addition, the president assured the nation that by the end of November, a "majority" of the 3.5 million relief jobs would be filled, a tacit admission that the combined WPA and PWA reemployment had been at a slower rate than had been promised. Why, he asked his radio audience, if unemployment was decreasing, should they give more to charity? He answered that "as you and I know [there are] hundreds of thousands of men, women, and children who require the kind of assistance which private charity and not Government should give. . . . It is with them that our private social agencies are primarily concerned. We know that medical care needs to be extended to thousands who have not the means to pay for it. We know that great numbers of children still suffer from malnutrition." Roosevelt would later expand his notion of what government should do in providing services to the poor. In just fifteen months, after his electoral triumph, his definition of who was poor would expand from "hundreds of thousands" to "one third of a nation," that is, some 42 million people.[92]

Probably no large group of Roosevelt constituents was served as well as the established commercial farmers who survived the Depression. The various programs of the Department of Agriculture, particularly those of the AAA, won the support of the majority of those farmers who voted heavily in favor of the crop limitation, price supports, and the subsidies that came with those programs. For example, in late October, on the eve of the AAA election by corn and hog farmers across the nation but centered in the midwestern Corn Belt, Ed O'Neal of the American Farm Bureau Federation urged a "huge vote" to answer critics of the AAA. The nearly 600,000 farmers who voted accepted the government's conditions for another year by a six-to-one margin. The terms included not only curbs on production but an insistence on farmer participation in soil enrichment and other conservation programs. To be sure, there was organized opposition from more radical farmers like those in the farm-holiday movement, who claimed that the AAA was putting farmers "under dictatorship" and demanded Secretary Wallace's removal, while from the other end of the political spectrum came similar complaints from the American Liberty League. The AAA was also under attack in the courts, and a case challenging the processing tax that financed the subsidies was about to be heard in the Supreme Court.[93]

In this charged atmosphere, a confident Roosevelt argued that the achievements of the two-year-old emergency program not only aided "millions of farmers" but also, through farmers' increased purchasing power, promoted better business conditions everywhere. He proposed to make the AAA permanent, with two principal objectives: "First, to carry out the declared policy of Congress to maintain and increase the gains thus far made, thereby avoiding the danger of a slump back into the conditions brought about by our national neglect of agriculture. Second, to broaden present adjustment operations so as to give farmers increasing incentives for conservation and efficient use of the Nation's soil resources."[94]

But for millions of farmers, sharecroppers, and farm workers, white, black, and Latino, there were no such benefits. Large numbers of small farmers lost their land, some of them, like Steinbeck's Joads, "tractored off," while others were foreclosed or otherwise forced to sell. Between 1935 and 1945, while farm acreage increased slightly from 1.06 to 1.14 billion acres, one American farm in eight disappeared.[95] Farm laborers, unlike most other American workers, were excluded from the benefits of Social Security. The attempt by some New Dealers in the AAA—most of them lawyers hired by Jerome Frank, the AAA's general counsel—to have AAA benefit checks prorated between landowners and their tenants in the same ratio as their crops was turned down by AAA administrator Chester Davis. The ensuing protests resulted in the so-called purge in early 1935 in which Frank and many of the lawyers he had hired were fired, while others resigned. Some returned to or found better-paying jobs with leading law firms, some found other posts within the New Deal, and Frank himself, at Roosevelt's request, worked part-time as special counsel for the RFC. The president appointed him a member of the SEC in 1939 and in 1941 gave him a seat on the U.S. Court of Appeals for the Second Circuit. When asked about the "purge" at a press conference, Roosevelt unconvincingly claimed ignorance.[96]

Much of the late fall and early winter was taken up with work on the 1936 budget, which had to be presented at the beginning of January. The budget director brought the president a blue pencil to use in his markups every year, and Roosevelt liked to show it to the press; someone teased him by suggesting that a red pencil (for deficit) might be more appropriate. Since extensive renovations, including some air-conditioning, were going on at the White House, a good deal of his time that fall was spent at Hyde Park.[97]

Work on the budget continued during the traditional Warm Springs Thanksgiving trip, which, as usual, involved speaking engagements: he spoke to a rally in Atlanta, at a Farm Bureau meeting in Chicago, and as part of an honorary degree ceremony at Notre Dame. One of the obligatory daily stories about the president's doings described how, after a morning of work, he drove Grace Tully in his small open car, especially equipped for a paraplegic, alongside the adjacent golf course, making disparaging remarks about the play of some of his press corps, suggesting loudly to one reporter that he might do better with a billiard cue. The irony that this president watched reporters play rather than the other way around was not mentioned. It would have violated the code that then prevailed. After several days of predominantly soft "news," mostly about young polio patients and turkeys, on the day after Thanksgiving an advertised presidential motorcade took him, Eleanor, and son James seventy-five miles to Atlanta, slowing down in each small town so that waiting crowds could at least glimpse the president passing in his closed car.

In Atlanta, after a half-hour rest stop at Fort McPherson, he participated in three scripted events. First, in a public park, he was serenaded by several thousand flag-waving schoolchildren who recited the Pledge of Allegiance and sang "America." Then he visited two PWA slum-clearance projects. The first, University Homes, for blacks, was at Atlanta University, where he made brief unrecorded remarks to perhaps twenty thousand assembled on the university's athletic field who, like the schoolchildren, were equipped with flags.[98] At the second, the larger, more elaborate Techwood Homes for whites, he simply unveiled a plaque and went on to the football stadium, a block away.

There, before a cheering crowd of fifty thousand, with another fifty thousand listening via amplifiers outside, and a national radio audience, Roosevelt in effect kicked off his campaign for reelection. Introduced by Senator Walter F. George (1878–1957) as "the next president," Roosevelt gave a detailed defense of his program, punctuated with sharp attacks on critics.

He reprised the "four years of disaster" of the old order and hailed the accomplishments of the "past two and a half years." In nine pithy paragraphs, each beginning "You and I," he reminded his listeners of the lows of the Hoover years and the relative highs of his own administration. He ticked off ending child labor, establishing the right of collective bargaining, creating Social Security, and beginning conservation programs "to cooperate with Nature and not to fight her." As was usually the case, he attacked no individual but, in a telling passage, referred to "gentlemen in well-warmed and well-stocked clubs [who] tell me that a dole would be more economical than work relief." He acknowledged that this was true, but he argued, "The men who tell me that have, unfortunately, too little contact with the true America to realize that in this business of relief we are dealing with properly self-respecting Americans to whom a mere dole outrages every instinct of individual independence." He went on to report that "on Wednesday, two days ago, by actual figures," 3.125 million were at work on "useful projects." This was still 375,000 jobs short of his goal.

He granted that these efforts had been accomplished by deficit spending and recounted that the gross national debt under "the last Administration" had risen from $17 billion to $21 billion and that his administration had increased it to $29.5 billion. He insisted that the government was solvent and could incur a much greater debt, but he predicted, incorrectly as it turned out, that "as things stand today, in the light of a definite and continuing improvement, we have passed the peak of appropriation . . . and we can look forward with assurance to a decreasing deficit."[99]

While the president was still at Warm Springs, he responded to a memo titled "AMERICA'S CHOICE—Which Shall It Be?" from the McNary-Haugenite George Peek, repeating and sharpening his decided differences with basic administration policies while he clung to his posts as president of the Export-Import Bank and as a foreign trade adviser in the State Department. In response, Roosevelt, who did not like to fire people, provoked his resignation. Pretending that he did not know who wrote the memo, Roosevelt wrote Peek that the memo was "rather silly. It sounds like a Hearst paper." He went on to refute its eight major points, one by one. Peek, in reply, avowed his authorship and said privately that, in view of fundamental differences, he was resigning. In his public announcement, he stressed differences over the recently signed reciprocal trade agreement with Canada.[100]

After sixteen mostly restful days in Georgia, Roosevelt's train took him directly to Chicago's Union Stockyards, where he spoke to fourteen thousand members of the Farm Bureau in the auditorium, defending his farm policy and attacking speculators, profiteers, and, in a phrase that could have been aimed at George Peek, "dispensers of discord" who claimed that American farmers would be victimized by the new reciprocal trade agreements with Canada. He pointed out that the country exported more agricultural products to Canada than it imported.[101]

More significant than the speech or its setting was the fact that although Illinois's Democratic governor, Henry Horner (1878–1940), was present, it was Chicago's mayor, Edward J. Kelly (1876–1950), who took precedence, presiding over the lunch for the president at the stockyard's Saddle and Sirloin Club. Symbolically, this marked the alliance between Roosevelt and big-city political machines that became crucial for the political survival of each and a central part of the New Deal coalition.[102]

The president's train then made the short trip to South Bend, Indiana, where what seemed like the entire population of one hundred thousand turned out to line the four-mile drive to the Notre Dame campus. The event there was a kind of pendant to the one in the Union Stockyards, as it enabled Roosevelt to touch base with another element in his electoral coalition.

In sharp contrast to his drive-through degree from USC, Roosevelt's *honoris causa* from Notre Dame was part of a great occasion, a convocation to celebrate the granting of a deferred independence to the Philippines. Degrees were awarded to Roosevelt as the grantor and to Carlos P. Romulo (1899–1985), a Notre Dame alumnus and a rising figure in the islands' politics.

It apparently came as a surprise to Roosevelt when he received what was, despite denials, a virtual blessing of him and his New Deal from a prince of the Roman Catholic Church on the cusp of a presidential election year. George Cardinal Mundelein, archbishop of Chicago, after a disclaimer—"We are not in politics, neither the church nor I"—proceeded to welcome Roosevelt into the house of his friends, lauding him as a leader and praising not only his courage in overcoming "a great physical handicap that would have laid low almost any other man" but also "the courage to set aside the traditions of his class, the friendships of his youth, the pressure of the money-power, to come to the aid of the forgotten man in the more equal distribution of wealth."[103]

The president's brief talk was appropriately nonpartisan. Like most American presidents since 1898, he denied any imperialism in the almost forty-year American occupation of the Philippines and quoted the statement about "free exercise of religion" from George Mason's Virginia Declaration of Rights (1776), an important forerunner of the First Amendment.[104]

After the convocation, the president's train went directly to Washington's Union Station, with one whistle-stop talk in Toledo. He had reason to feel satisfied that the year was ending well. The WPA program was under way, the economic indicators were slowly rising, and if he seemed less and less able to command the support of business, other constituencies were providing stronger backing.[105]

In addition, as the brief visit to Atlanta University indicated, he was beginning to notice what was then called the Negro vote. In his four years as governor and in the first two years of the New Deal, he had not paid any official attention to black causes and institutions, save for receiving a musical tribute at Fisk. He had refused, through his secretaries, to meet with black leaders and ignored petitions about injustice to blacks, as in the ongoing Scottsboro trials.

In 1935, after he became aware of the shift in the African American vote in the 1934 congressional elections, Roosevelt for the first time told subordinates publicly that there should be no racial discrimination in relief. And, at year's end, he made two token gestures, claiming interest in issues that concerned some in the black community. He issued a formal presidential statement "as an adopted citizen of the South," praising its "white people" for funding a new agricultural building at Tuskegee Institute, since "the success of Southern agriculture is dependent in great part on the industry, intelligence and thrift of the Negro farmers." And he wrote a letter to a former publicist for Booker T. Washington, lauding the progress made by "the Negro people" since Lincoln's Emancipation Proclamation of 1863. Copies were provided to black churches and read in many of them as part of the anniversary observances of the 1863 event in January. This new show of interest almost certainly reflected not only his increased awareness of black voters but also the fact that northern black political leaders were beginning to strive for more significant participation in the political process.[106]

For most of the rest of December, Roosevelt continued to work on the budget and his speech for the opening of Congress. He celebrated Christmas with a large family gathering at the White House: someone informed the press that on Christmas morning, the president had been awakened by his four-year-old granddaughter, Sara, "who burst into his bedroom eager to learn what Santa Claus had put in her stocking."[107] He terminated what remained of the once powerful NRA with an executive order, sending some employees, equipment, and supplies to the Commerce Department, while its former Consumers Division, always a stepchild within the NRA, survived and was transferred with its remaining personnel, effects, and records to the Labor Department.[108]

Earlier in the month, speaking extemporaneously to state superintendents of education, Roosevelt could be charitable about the safely dead Huey Long, praising his accomplishments "in teaching adults to read" in the course of bragging about the "more than five hundred thousand men and women" taught to read and write by his FERA. Referring to Long was as close as he came to a public discussion of the looming 1936 campaign and election, in which Huey would surely have been a significant actor, but privately, as early as November, Roosevelt said in cabinet, "We will win easily next year but we are going to make it a crusade."[109]

11   Landslide

1936

WANTING TO CAMPAIGN WITHOUT CAMPAIGNING, Roosevelt persuaded congressional leaders to meet to hear his annual message at 9:00 p.m. Twenty-three years after Woodrow Wilson personally delivered his address, breaking the tradition set by Jefferson of having it read by a clerk, Roosevelt transformed the once staid event into a political rally aimed largely at millions of listening constituents rather than the five hundred–plus legislators or the twelve hundred packing the Capitol's galleries. The address was a preview of Roosevelt's strategy for 1936. He wanted to make himself and the New Deal *the* issue in the November election and run against not an opposing candidate or even a political party but what he called the "old order" and "a generation of self-seekers."[1]

He spoke of his increasing concern about international affairs for almost half of the message. Then, moving effortlessly into domestic politics, the president claimed that "within our borders, as in the world at large, popular opinion is at war with a power-seeking minority," a struggle that was "no new thing" but had been "fought out in the Constitutional Convention [and] since then . . . under Thomas Jefferson, Andrew Jackson, Theodore Roosevelt and Woodrow Wilson." From that point, the message became not an agenda for the future but a spirited defense of the New Deal, though that phrase was never mentioned.

Hailing what he and Congress had done in "thirty-four months of work" as an "effort to restore power to those to whom it rightfully belong[s]," he asserted that government had operated in "the public interest" and "returned the control of the Federal Government to the City of Washington." As a result, he had "earned the hatred of entrenched greed." After describing aspects of the New Deal program that had enraged his opponents, he said of them:

> Our resplendent economic autocracy does not want to return to that individualism of which they prate, even though the advantages under that system went to the ruthless and the strong. They realize that in thirty-four months we have built up new instruments of public power. In the hands of a people's Government this power is wholesome and proper. But in the hands of political puppets of an economic autocracy such power would provide shackles for the liberties of the people. Give them their way and they will take the

course of every autocracy of the past—power for themselves, enslavement for the public.

Their weapon is the weapon of fear. I have said, "The only thing we have to fear is fear itself." That is as true today as it was in 1933. But such fear as they instill today is not a natural fear, a normal fear; it is a synthetic, manufactured, poisonous fear that is being spread subtly, expensively and cleverly by the same people who cried in those other days, "Save us, save us, lest we perish."

Roosevelt closed the long attack section of his message with an expression of confidence in the legislators before him and devoted the final tenth of the speech to a positive assessment of the nation's condition. National income was up for the third straight year, "agriculture and industry are returning to full activity," and "we approach a balance of the national budget." He believed that "no new taxes" were either advisable or necessary. He repeated several more phrases from his inaugural, the last of which insisted that "we do not distrust the future of essential democracy." For the peroration, he chose an inspirational and vaguely religious passage from "a wise philosopher [Josiah Royce] at whose feet I sat many, many years ago."[2]

The president's Friday-night spectacular was followed by the prosaic budget message presented at noon Monday: it called for expenditures of at least $6.75 billion for fiscal 1937, some $893 million below the revised estimates for the current year, resulting in a deficit of almost $1.7 billion. This was greatly reduced from the more than $3.2 billion for fiscal 1936. In addition, it insisted that Congress provide "additional taxes" for any new spending not contained in the budget.[3]

But the message's note of cautious economic optimism was becoming obsolete even as it was being read by the clerk. Also meeting at noon that day, the Supreme Court invalidated the AAA in a way that called the entire New Deal regulation of the economy into question.[4]

Unlike the unanimous *Schechter* decision, this second AAA case, *U.S. v. Butler,* found the Court bitterly divided, six to three. Justice Roberts's majority opinion, supported by the Four Horsemen and Hughes, not only killed the remodeled AAA but seemed to rule out any federal farm program at all by insisting that the AAA was unconstitutional because the Tenth Amendment had reserved for the individual states the regulation and control of agricultural production. To many observers, it also seemed to presage a similar fate for other vital New Deal statutes, including the Social Security Act and the Wagner Act. Justice Stone, speaking for himself, Brandeis, and Cardozo, called Roberts's decision "a tortured construction of the Constitution," a judgment that is now all but universally recognized.

In Congress most Democrats were livid, and many Republican senators, such as Kansas's Arthur Capper and Oregon's Charles McNary, immediately declared that Congress would continue to aid the farmer.[5]

At his press conference the next day, Roosevelt repeatedly refused to comment on the AAA decision except to say that the government had a moral obligation to pay wheat farmers what was due them under contracts signed in 1935 for winter wheat, which had been planted but would not be harvested until the spring, and that he would ask Congress for a special appropriation for that purpose, which was rapidly enacted.[6] Unlike the NRA, the AAA was not allowed to die. Secretary Wallace immediately convoked national and regional meetings of farm groups and, with largely bipartisan support in Congress, refocused benefit payments to farmers to center on the soil conservation practices that had always been part of the program. By mid-January, the alternate path for agriculture had been worked out.[7]

Speaking to the annual Jackson Day Dinner in Washington and a national radio audience two days after the Court's latest blow, the president pretended that he had not made up his mind about the *Butler* decision. But he assured his listeners that he was still examining "two of the most momentous opinions, the majority opinion and the minority opinion." He defined "the basic issue" before the nation as "the retention of popular government," named "our enemies" as "the forces of privilege and greed," and concluded that "we will not retreat."[8]

In less than two weeks, Roosevelt beat a strategic retreat, not from his economic adversaries but from most of the Democrats in Congress. Predictably, a simple bill for immediate payment of the soldiers' bonus at a cost of $2.49 billion breezed through Congress, 74–16 in the Senate, 346–59 in the House. It was obviously veto proof: the only real question was how Roosevelt would react. Would he make a desperate attempt to change votes or allow the bill to become law without his signature? He chose a third option and sent back a handwritten veto message of barely two hundred words. Reminding Congress of his previous veto and its rationale, he ended: "My convictions are as impelling today as they were then. Therefore I cannot change them."[9]

Ironically, in the final analysis, Roosevelt was the great gainer from the bonus bill. On the one hand, he got credit from moderates for sticking to his convictions; on the other, the administration's rapidity in getting the bonus payments to the veterans—the Veterans Administration had worked out the regulations and printed and begun distribution of the appropriate forms even before Roosevelt executed the veto—was a talking point in election materials aimed at veterans. And the infusion of what is now called a "stimulus" of some $2 billion into the economy was a significant contribution to the relative recovery in the summer of 1936, which boosted Roosevelt's chances in November.[10]

While prevailing opinion holds that Roosevelt lost not only the bonus battle but also his touch in early 1936, it seems to me that this is not the case.[11] If one assumes that he was deliberately deferring the inevitable fight over the Court until after the election, and that his primary goal was reelection, his decision not to make a real fight over the bonus, a fight that he could not win, makes perfect sense. Nor did he want unnecessary fights with Congress in an election year. But his carefully hedged no-new-taxes statement in his message to Congress, issued before the expected bonus-veto override, suggests that he knew in January that he would have to ask for some new taxes. It also seems clear that, unless his hand were forced by events, the president was quite willing to let most new initiatives pass over to the new Congress that would meet in January 1937. As he assured a gathering of Baltimore young Democrats in early April, "the period of social pioneering is only at its beginning."[12]

By then he had sent a supplementary budget message to Congress asking for a $620 million addition to the annual tax bill to replace the voided processing tax and provide funds for paying the bonus. In what became the most controversial part of the tax package, he called for a new tax on undistributed corporate profits, arguing that this practice was a form of tax evasion. It would prove to be a difficult measure in an election year.[13] The public announcement of planning for reorganization of the executive is further evidence of Roosevelt's long view.[14]

The annual end-of-January Birthday Ball for the fifty-four-year-old president involved some 5 million persons in more than six thousand individual events. Although nonpolitical, it nevertheless contributed to the aura that now surrounded him. As usual, he addressed the nation by radio from the White House and announced the formation of a research committee headed by Jeremiah Milbank (1887–1972), a financier and philanthropist, and Paul H. de Kruif (1880–1971), a bacteriologist and an important writer about science, "to carry on the fight against infantile paralysis until the dread disease is brought under definite and final control." This presaged a move from a concentration on care to a search for a cure.[15]

In mid-February, the Supreme Court refused to inhibit the government's plan to sell and distribute power from the dams being built in the Tennessee Valley by an eight-to-one majority. McReynolds, the only justice from the region, was the dissenter. The majority opinion by Chief Justice Hughes, while not ruling on all aspects of the TVA, found that the government could build dams and sell a by-product—electricity.[16]

In March extremely heavy rains coupled with snow runoff produced major flooding from New England to Virginia and extending westward into the Ohio River valley. With the papers full of flood news—"Pittsburgh in Darkness; Thousands Marooned"; "Large Vermont Dam Breaks"; "Seven Towns in Potomac River Valley Inundated"; "Transportation Facilities from New York to the West Tied Up"—Roosevelt formed and met with a committee chaired by War Secretary Dern and other officials, including Harry Hopkins, the CCC's Robert Fechner, and American Red Cross chairman Cary Grayson, to plan flood relief. He publicly described the government's response and called for public donations for the American Red Cross, which had a goal of $3 million. Roosevelt reallocated more than $43 million of already appropriated relief funds for reconstruction and gave the WPA "blanket authority to restore roads, streets, bridges, sewers, water and electric plants, and other damaged public properties." This eventually involved some 250,000 workers. The Red Cross estimated that 500,000 individuals received substantial emergency assistance.[17]

These events gave evidence that the federal government could respond quickly and effectively in disaster situations. Three subsequent statutes appropriated nearly $600 million for flood control and authorized interstate agreements if approved by their legislatures.[18] The performance of CCC workers during the flood emergency was probably a factor in Roosevelt's cancellation of some previously announced cuts in the CCC program, though pressure from Congress to preserve a popular program was surely more important.[19]

Roosevelt took an extended fishing trip that had been delayed by the floods. Only toward the end of the trip was there any hard news. Responding to aid requests from the Red Cross after a series of severe tornadoes hit thirty counties in six southern states, killing 425 persons, seriously injuring some 1,700, and destroying 3,200 homes, the president allocated $2.5 million of relief funds to the WPA for reconstruction.[20]

Roosevelt chose an indirect route back to Washington so he could meet with tornado victims. His train was met at 10:30 p.m. by 2,000 residents of the hard-hit small North Georgia town of Gainesville. After a brief talk from the rear platform, he invited a group of 10 citizens into his car to learn about their experiences firsthand. He spent a few hours the next day at Warm Springs and returned to the capital the following afternoon.[21]

A memorandum to Jim Farley dated when Roosevelt was at sea, but obviously dictated earlier, shows him supervising the party's preparations for the campaign quite closely.

1. All speech material, replies [in the] press, . . . attacks on our opponents, direct answers to them, etc., to clear through Charlie Michelson.
2. All pamphlets [and arrangements about them] to clear through Stanley High [who] will cooperate with Michelson and Halsey and keep them advised every two or three days. . . .
3. Radio policy [to be handled by] a committee of three—Michelson, High and the head of the Speakers Bureau.
4. Plans for organizing business men—I suggest the Chairman arrange with Forbes Morgan, Michelson, and High for names of the committee . . . statements . . . and letters. . . .

I should like to glance personally at this publicity before it is decided upon.
F.D.R.[22]

In mid-April, while Republican presidential aspirants were still struggling through primary contests, Roosevelt and Farley were planning to cap their

June convention with an outdoor extravaganza in a football stadium where Roosevelt would make his acceptance speech.

Roosevelt used two April speeches to get his message out. Like most of his 1936 political speeches, they shared two unarticulated major premises: the president would be reelected, and the nation would continue to recover and be reformed under his leadership. To an audience of Young Democrats, he stressed expanding both educational and work opportunities. In New York, speaking before the city's Democrats with neither Al Smith nor Jimmy Walker present, he answered complaints about the cost of government by noting that while the year's deficit was "about three billion dollars, the national income . . . has risen from thirty-five billion dollars in . . . 1932 to sixty-five billion dollars in . . . 1936." He insisted that "the only burden we need to fear is the burden that our children would have to bear if we failed to take these measures today." His prescription was "nationwide thinking, nationwide planning and nationwide action . . . to prevent nationwide crises for future generations to struggle through."[23]

A week before the New York speech, the architect of the 1932 victory—and much more—was gone. Louis Howe died in Bethesda Naval Hospital late in the evening of April 18. Roosevelt had paid what turned out to be a last visit that afternoon. He canceled all his appointments for two days, and after a White House funeral Franklin and Eleanor took Howe's body and his family back to Fall River, Massachusetts, on the presidential train for the burial, which the Roosevelts silently attended. Although Howe's direct impact on Roosevelt had been on decline since the Chicago convention, no one, apart from Eleanor, had been of greater importance in shaping Roosevelt's career after 1921.[24]

In May the pace in Congress quickened. The majority wanted adjournment before the Democratic convention, which would begin in Philadelphia on June 23. Early in the month, Roosevelt announced his support for the principles of Wagner's housing bill, aimed primarily at replacing the worst urban slums, but weakened that support by refusing to label it "must" legislation. He reserved that designation for his tax bill and the further funding of work relief.[25]

Adjournment was complicated by further Supreme Court rulings, as each of the term's last three decision Mondays brought further judicial intervention against government regulation of the economy at every level. First, in a six-to-three decision, Hughes and Roberts plus the Four Horsemen struck down the Guffey Coal Act of 1935, which regulated wages and fixed prices and had been enacted in response to the Court's destruction of the NRA. In a separate opinion, the chief justice held that only that part of the act which regulated wages should have been struck down and accused the five-man majority of attempting "to amend the Constitution by judicial decision." Cardozo, for the dissenters, argued that both price and wage regulations were within the power of the federal government.[26] Roosevelt, in his press conference the next day, could have used Hughes's statement to support his own views. Instead, he made no direct comment except to note that the opinion indicated divisions in the judiciary and that the government needed to find a way to bring stability to a troubled industry.[27]

The following week, the Court voided a minor New Deal statute, the Municipal Bankruptcy Act of 1934, in a five-to-four decision written by McReynolds for the other Horsemen and Roberts; the chief justice, Brandeis, and Stone joined a dissent written by Cardozo. The law had been little used, and Roosevelt took no public notice of the decision.[28]

The *Tipaldo* decision was a real shocker that Roosevelt could not ignore. The Court struck down, five to four, a 1933 New York state law that set minimum wages for women and children, arguing that it violated the due process clauses of the original Constitution and its Fourteenth Amendment. Court watchers were surprised that this decision attracted the vote of Justice Roberts, who just two years earlier in *Nebbia* had written that "a state is free to adopt whatever economic policy may reasonably be deemed to promote public welfare." Hughes, joined by the three liberals, in a measured dissent could "find nothing in the Federal Constitution which denies to the State the power to protect women from being exploited by over-reaching employers through the refusal of a fair wage."[29]

Roosevelt, in his press conference, complained: "It seems to be fairly clear, as a result of this decision and former decisions . . . that the 'no-man's-land' where no government can function is being more clearly defined. A state cannot do it and the Federal Government cannot do it. . . . [T]hat is . . . about all we can say on it."[30]

The *Tipaldo* decision drew very little support. Even Herbert Hoover, on his way to the GOP convention in Cleveland, thought something should be done to give the states the "power they thought they had." He called for a constitutional amendment, if necessary, to enable them to establish minimum wages and hours, and this thought was reflected, almost verbatim, in his party's platform the following week, except that the plank claimed that it could be done "within the Constitution as it now stands."[31] When it came time to draft the Democratic platform, Roosevelt paid particular attention to the passage labeled "The Constitution." It pledged, without using the words *Supreme Court,* that if important matters could "not be solved by legislation within the Constitution, we shall seek such clarifying amendment" to enable state legislatures and Congress to act.[32] Had that scenario been followed, the history of Roosevelt's second term would have been substantially different.

Congressional adjournment planned for June 8 was delayed by the sudden death of Speaker Joseph W. Byrns on June 4. Within hours the House unanimously elected Alabama's William B. Bankhead (1874–1940), and both houses recessed until June 15 to accommodate Byrns's interment in Nashville and the Republican convention in Cleveland. Roosevelt took his special train to Nashville for the funeral, returned, met briefly with congressional leaders on a tax bill compromise, and got back on his train for a weeklong trip meant to keep him on the front page during the Republican convention.[33]

Officially, the trip was to attend state centennial celebrations in Arkansas and Texas; he also spoke to support the reelection of two legislative leaders, Majority Leader Joe Robinson and Sam Rayburn, chair of the House Committee on Commerce. While the Republican convention was listening to Hoover denounce the New Deal as "socialism," adopting an attack platform that claimed that the New Deal had placed America "in peril," and nominating a ticket of Kansas governor Alfred M. Landon (1887–1987) and Chicago newspaper publisher Frank Knox (1874–1944), the president spoke in four states. His eleven crowded hours in Arkansas included an automobile tour of the Hot Springs area and a visit to a reenactment of a camp meeting at which he urged Arkansans to keep "spiritual faith and to remember the early days when your ancestors brought religion across the Mississippi." Roosevelt delivered his major Arkansas address in Little Rock's football stadium, where he spoke about the state's early history. In explaining Jefferson's Louisiana Purchase, which brought Arkansas into the nation, he noted that while some had questioned Jefferson's constitutional authority to make the purchase, he did it, and when Congress appropriated the money to pay for it, "nobody carried the case to the Supreme Court." Reaching modern times, he insisted that "we can march forward, believing, as the overwhelming majority of Americans believe, that the Constitution is intended to meet and to fit the amazing physical, economic and social requirements that confront us." Without mentioning that Robinson was a candidate for reelection, he hailed him for his "loyal devotion to a great cause of humanity." Even more impressively, Roosevelt broke the custom that the president does not dine with individuals by having dinner at Robinson's home.[34]

The president's two Texas days began with an open-car drive through Houston before large crowds undeterred by blistering heat. He then sailed down Houston's Ship Canal to a point near the San Jacinto battlefield, where he interpreted Texas's rebellion against Mexico as a struggle for "civil liberties," without mentioning that a chief liberty sought was the right to maintain slavery. In San Antonio, he visited the Alamo, noting that, "unlike them, we do not need to take up arms. . . . [W]e can carry on a national war for the cause of humanity without shedding blood."

A Dallas motorcade took him through packed streets to the Cotton Bowl. His speech in the stadium stressed the danger to American democracy posed by the concentration of economic power, a theme used in six subsequent campaign speeches, including the acceptance speech and the final one in Madison Square Garden. "The net result of economic and financial control in the hands of the few [means treating] labor as a commodity. If labor is to be a commodity in the United States, in the final analysis it means that we shall become a Nation of boarding-houses, instead of a Nation of homes. If our people ever submit to that, they will have said 'good-bye' to their historic freedom. Men do not fight for boarding-houses. Men do fight and will fight for homes."

The president's remarks at a subsequent luncheon touched again on his concern about the way things were going in Europe and Asia and reiterated his intention to avoid getting "tangled up with their troubles."

On his way north, Roosevelt gave an endorsement of Sam Rayburn at a whistle-stop in the Texan's district; he would become House majority leader in January. In the final speech of the trip, at Vincennes, Indiana, Roosevelt described the wasteful land use of earlier generations and emphasized the increasing importance of sound conservation practices to repair some of their damage. He then went, by train and auto, on a pilgrimage to Lincoln's birthplace in Kentucky and spoke of renewing "the faith which Lincoln had in the common man."

On his midday return to Washington, a visibly tired president had lunch with Henry Morgenthau but did nothing of a public nature; he seemed refreshed by the time of his brief press conference the next afternoon. Congress had come back from its recesses, and Roosevelt was waiting to deal with the final batch of bills.[35]

Sam Rosenman, summoned from New York, checked into a White House bedroom on the Sunday of Democratic convention week. In a meeting with Roosevelt, he and Stanley High were assigned to write drafts of the party platform and Roosevelt's acceptance speech scheduled for that Saturday. The president, who had rejected several previous platform drafts, felt that the Republican attack platform fitted in nicely with his plan to make himself and the New Deal the focus of the campaign. After a brainstorming meeting that went on until a little past midnight, he told Rosenman and High that he wanted the platform to be based on Jefferson's words—"We hold these truths to be self-evident"—in the Declaration of Independence. He handed them several existing drafts and said that he wanted to see their version in the morning. The two speechwriters did an all-nighter in a White House office and got their product onto the president's breakfast tray. With some additions, it was adopted by the party convention four days later.

The platform began with five one-sentence paragraphs, each beginning "We hold this truth to be self-evident." The first said "the test of a representative government is its ability to promote the safety and happiness of the people." The next two compared "12 years of Republican leadership" and "surrender to the dictatorship of the privileged few" with "three years of democratic leadership" that had put the nation "back on the road to restored health and prosperity" and "returned the people themselves to the places of authority." The last stated that the "inescapable obligations of government" included "protection of the family and the home," "establishment of a democracy of opportunity for all the people," and "aid to those overtaken by disaster." The remainder was a detailed list of things that the New Deal had done for the nation and for various interest groups within it.

The Rosenman-High duo then went to work on the acceptance speech, without being aware that another version had been commissioned from Ray Moley and Tom Corcoran. Roosevelt was already notorious for giving the same assignment to more than one individual or group. In this instance, the president asked for, and got, two very different speeches. The Rosenman-High version gave him a "militant, bare-fisted statement," while Moley-Corcoran provided a "a very moderate, conciliatory" text that would appeal to independents.[36]

While the two versions were being melded and other last-minute convention arrangements refined, Roosevelt dealt with the usual postadjournment rush of business. The accomplishments of the six-month session, while dwarfed by the breakthroughs of 1935, were substantial. Roosevelt got his two "must" bills: the additional relief funds—$1.425 billion to be spent at "the direction and discretion of the President"—and a tax bill, the Revenue Act of 1936, which raised taxes on corporations and included a tax on undistributed profits. Similar to the effect of the 1935 statute, the new taxes fell short of closing the gap between income and spending. They would provide less than $800 million annually at a time when federal spending was some $7 billion annually, with roughly half of that representing deficit. Regressive taxes, including the new ones on Social Security that would kick in on January 1, continued to be the government's largest source of income by far. While the press and many later commentators have emphasized three important measures that had passed the House but not the Senate—Wagner's slum-clearing housing bill, a proposed pure food and drug bill, and a replacement for the Court-nullified Guffey Coal Act—Roosevelt was clearly content to let them come up again in 1937. Many journalists who looked at the overall accomplishments of the Seventy-Fourth Congress—that is, everything done in 1935 and 1936—tagged it a "$20-billion Congress," while noting that it was an all-time record.[37]

Among the more important pieces of 1936 legislation not discussed earlier were the Walsh-Healey Public Contracts Act, which reimposed NRA-type wages, hours, and working conditions on private firms with government contracts, and the Robinson-Patman Act, a Canute-like anti–chain store addition to antitrust legislation that was a sop to the populist wing of the party. Increased expenditures for national defense effected a small increase of personnel and a more significant increase in the number of planes for each service. These defense bills reflected Roosevelt's increasing concern about events in Europe and Asia.[38]

Shortly before leaving to accept his renomination, Roosevelt granted one of his infrequent interviews to newspaper columnist Anne O'Hare McCormick (1882–1954). A skillful interviewer, McCormick drew from him the famous self-description that he was "a little to the left of center," but her own description of his personality is even more compelling: "Mr. Roosevelt is a unique figure in the modern world; the one statesman this writer has seen who is able to relax. . . . He talks well, not so much in terms of ideas as of concrete cases. Collectivist he may be, but he reduces all general problems to individual instances, the experience of this banker, that manufacturer, one homesteader, a particular relief worker. He sounds rather like the head case worker in a tremendous social service organization."[39]

At about the same time, Roosevelt had an hour-long meeting with John L. Lewis, who emerged to tell reporters of his support of the president's reelection "to the fullest degree." His miners' union would use its "influence and resources" to that end. Lewis's union later gave almost $500,000, not quite a quarter of the $2.2 million collected and spent by the Democratic National Committee. This was the first time that union funds had been so important in a political campaign. Not surprisingly, contributions from Wall Street shrank. Bankers and brokers had provided about 25 percent of the $1,000-plus contributions to Democratic campaign funds in 1932; in 1936 the comparable figure was less than 4 percent. We can now see that this meeting between Roosevelt and Lewis marks the enfolding of organized labor into what would become the triumphant New Deal coalition that had begun with the creation of Labor's Non-Partisan League (LNPL) in April.[40]

Unlike the chaotic and nerve-racking 1932 Chicago convention, the 1936 conclave was carefully scripted from the White House, and Roosevelt sent Marvin McIntyre to Philadelphia to keep order. The delegates dutifully adopted the amended Rosenman-High platform and, without significant ado, got rid of the two-thirds rule that had given the South a veto power over Democratic candidates since the era of Andrew Jackson. Despite preconvention bravado about making a floor fight over it, the party's southern leaders came prepared to bargain and did so. They agreed not to have a floor fight in exchange for a resolution promising to change the basis for allocating delegates to the next convention from population to votes cast for the Democratic candidate. Scrapping the two-thirds rule had no effect on Roosevelt's renomination: that was assured. But had it remained in effect, the history of the Democratic conventions in the 1940s might have been significantly different.[41]

Although Roosevelt and other party leaders were making plans to mobilize northern black voters, the Democratic platform contained no challenge to Jim Crow. The one-sentence plank labeled "Civil Liberties"—"We shall continue to guard the freedom of speech, press, radio, religion and assembly which our Constitution guarantees; with equal rights to all and special privileges to none"— was a meaningless formula. There were, however, a few visible sops for black voters. For the first time, an African American minister, the Reverend Marshall Shepard, was added to the rota of local divines who routinely opened each convention session. Apparently to provide "balance," his invocation was followed immediately by the band playing "Dixie." By that time, one major southern politician, South Carolina's Cotton Ed Smith, followed by a few members of his state's delegation, had stalked out in protest, complaining that Shepard was "as black as melted midnight." Smith repeated his temporary walkout the next day when Chicago's black congressman, Arthur Mitchell, one of thirty-two black delegates or alternates, spoke briefly.[42]

The unprecedented black presence was an advertisement that there was now space in the rear ranks of the national Democratic Party for black leaders; in addition, throughout the 1936 campaign, major New Deal figures, such as Harold Ickes and Aubrey Williams, actively sought the black vote. Two days after the convention closed, Ickes spoke at the annual conference of the NAACP and argued that "Roosevelt realized as no other president since Lincoln" that the "mere existence" of the Thirteenth, Fourteenth, and Fifteenth Amendments was no guarantee of their enforcement. He went on describe how blacks had benefited from particular New Deal programs.[43] On the other hand, Smith's histrionics were a harbinger of the Dixiecrat split in 1948 and the slow but relentless transition of white southern voter allegiance from one party to the other. Roosevelt was the last Democrat who could count on the electoral votes of the "solid South."

The rest of the convention followed Roosevelt's script for each of its three days. The president was renominated by acclamation without a roll call, as was Vice President Garner. The convention adjourned in midafternoon.[44]

While the convention sat, Roosevelt remained in Washington, signing and vetoing bills into the wee hours. While refusing to acknowledge that the platform had been written in the White House, he admitted making phone calls to keep in touch. He boarded his presidential train early that evening and arrived at Philadelphia's Twenty-Fourth Street station just thirty-five minutes before his speech was scheduled to begin. He was whisked through closed-off streets past empty sidewalks to Franklin Field, where more than one hundred thousand spectators had waited for him, some of them for more than five hours, despite intermittent rain showers and one "deluge." His car entered the stadium and went up an uncovered but curtained-off ramp, stopping just short of the large temporary platform. Out of sight from all but those in the platform party, the president was taken out of his car, his braces locked, and he began his slow upward progress on the arm of his son James. Near the top, he leaned or reached out his hand to greet someone he knew and, still unseen by the crowd, lost his balance and was allowed to fall, facedown, on the wet, muddy ramp, his speech pages scattering. "Clean me up," he barked furiously, and as his security people got him quickly to his feet and retrieved the now mud-daubed pages, he resumed his slow ascent up the ramp. Seeing none of this, Arthur Krock wrote, "One hundred thousand people rose and roared unmistakable acclaim as Mr. Roosevelt entered."[45] After listening to a brief notification speech by Senator

Joe Robinson, the president went to the rostrum on James's arm and began to speak. Even today, listening to his cool, measured delivery, it is difficult to accept that just minutes before, he had been badly shaken and "the damnedest, maddest white man . . . you ever saw."[46]

The acceptance speech effectively laid out the themes for the campaign, comparing the three-plus years in which, under his leadership, the nation had "conquered fear" with what had gone before. He noted that "Philadelphia is a good city in which to write American history . . . to reaffirm the faith of our fathers . . . to restore to the people a wider freedom; to give to 1936 as the founders' gave to 1776—an American way of life." The founders' struggle against the "tyranny of . . . eighteenth century royalists" was likened to the struggle against contemporary "economic royalists," who "carved new dynasties" and built "new kingdoms" based on "control of material things."

> Through new uses of corporations, banks and securities, new machinery of industry and agriculture, of labor and capital—all undreamed of by the fathers—the whole structure of modern life was impressed into this royal service. . . . It was natural and perhaps human that the privileged princes of these new economic dynasties, thirsting for power, reached out for control over Government itself. They created a new despotism and wrapped it in the robes of legal sanction. In its service new mercenaries sought to regiment the people, their labor, and their property. And as a result the average man once more confronts the problem that faced the Minute Man. . . . Against economic tyranny . . . the American citizen could appeal only to the organized power of Government. The collapse of 1929 showed up the despotism for what it was. The election of 1932 was the people's mandate to end it. Under that mandate it is being ended.

Roosevelt rode the "royalist" theme hard—"royalist," "economic royalist" (twice), and "royalists of the economic order."[47] But toward the end, he dropped the attack and emphasized the positive, using the Pauline triad of faith, hope, and charity:

> Faith—in the soundness of democracy in the midst of dictatorships.
> Hope—renewed because we know so well the progress we have made.
> Charity—in the true spirit of that grand old word. For charity literally translated from the original means love, the love that understands, that does not merely share the wealth of the giver, but in true sympathy and wisdom helps men to help themselves. . . . In the place of the palace of privilege we seek to build a temple out of faith and hope and charity.

In closing he humanized his own role and, in almost the next breath, indicated that he might already have a notion of becoming a world leader:

Governments can err, Presidents do make mistakes, but the immortal Dante tells us that divine justice weighs the sins of the cold-blooded and the sins of the warm-hearted in different scales.

Better the occasional faults of a Government that lives in a spirit of charity than the consistent omissions of a Government frozen in the ice of its own indifference.

There is a mysterious cycle in human events. To some generations much is given. Of other generations much is expected. This generation of Americans has a rendezvous with destiny.

In this world of ours in other lands, there are some people, who, in times past, have lived and fought for freedom, and seem to have grown too weary to carry on the fight. They have sold their heritage of freedom for the illusion of a living. They have yielded their democracy.

I believe in my heart that only our success can stir their ancient hope. They begin to know that here in America we are waging a great and successful war. It is not alone a war against want and destitution and economic demoralization. It is more than that; it is a war for the survival of democracy. We are fighting to save a great and precious form of government for ourselves and for the world.

I accept the commission you have tendered me. I join with you. I am enlisted for the duration of the war.

Tumultuous waves of cheering rolled on and on; Arthur Krock called it "a personal triumph of a kind given to few men." After a rendition of "Auld Lang Syne," Franklin and Eleanor circled the field twice in an open car, accompanied by more cheers, and were sped back to the train; he had been gone just ninety minutes.[48]

At Hyde Park, two days later, he solved a political problem that had been troubling him for months. New York governor Herbert Lehman, just fifty-eight years of age, had announced that he would "not be a candidate for reelection." In a three-hour meeting, Roosevelt persuaded Lehman to change his mind. Two days later, Lehman relented publicly, citing his long fight "for equal opportunity and social security." Then, from Washington, the White House released an agreed-upon letter, dated on the day of their meeting, in which the president urged the governor to reconsider, pointing out that if he did not run, Roosevelt feared that his successor might not have his "heart . . . in the right place" about the "social legislation" for which they both had worked. Your "reconsideration would make me very happy . . . would make millions of people all over the United States very happy."

Roosevelt's concern was not, as has often been written or implied, about his own ability to carry New York but about the absence of a good Democratic successor. He had earlier asked Morgenthau to put pressure on the governor, because "you and I know what a mess would be caused by trying to find a successor."[49]

The macropolitical arrangements made, Roosevelt was ostentatiously "presidential" rather than "political" for almost three months. He deferred his overt campaigning to well past the traditional Labor Day opening, resulting in just a five-week formal campaign. To be sure, behind the scenes he continued to manage—and occasionally micromanage—the overall Democratic campaign. When, for example, Jim Farley had referred publicly to the Republican nomination going to "the governor of a typical prairie state," Roosevelt chided him—"I thought we had decided that any reference to Landon or any other Republican candidate was inadvisable." He told Farley to pass the word "down the line to all concerned with speech material" not to refer to any section as "typical," because "coming from any New Yorker," the word "is meat for the opposition."[50]

After completing work on the remaining legislation—giving him a first-term box score of 2,694 bills signed and 221 vetoed—and a heavy period of postsession conferences, Roosevelt planned to take a July cruise and generally relax, but very quickly reports about the western drought and New England flooding caused him to add inspection trips to both regions. He would spend very little time in Washington in the next four months and less in Hyde Park than he had intended.[51]

With remodeling continuing at the White House, Eleanor made Hyde Park her summer headquarters. In a predeparture press conference, she announced that she would make no campaign speeches but would go along on one campaign trip and would continue visiting WPA and NYA projects. She also offered statistics about what an irreverent reporter called the White House "tourist trade": during the Roosevelt tenure so far, 10,628 guest meals had been served, and in the six months just past there had been 242 overnight guests.[52]

Roosevelt spent the Fourth of July weekend in Virginia, dedicating the Shenandoah National Park, whose facilities had been built by the CCC. He called it an example of what his administration was doing to end "the tragedy of waste—waste of our people, waste of our land," and promised that other young men would create other parks. The next day, at Thomas Jefferson's self-designed mountaintop home on the 160th anniversary of the Declaration of Independence, he ended a short speech praising the man rather than the third president. Asking if Jefferson and his era represented "a Golden Age, gone now and never to be repeated," he answered, "That is not my belief." He was sure that there were "no limitations on the Nation's capacity to obtain and maintain true freedom."

It was not necessary for him to make the obvious comparison: that had been done by Virginia's leading political figure, Carter Glass, often a severe critic of New Deal measures who might have been more at home at a Liberty League meeting. Glass told the small crowd and the nationwide radio audience that Roosevelt had shown "incomparable patience and courage" and "professes the same love of humanity and love of the plain people as was manifested by Thomas Jefferson." Despite the politics of upheaval that disturbed them, Glass and most conservative southern leaders stood by the party and its president in election years. The *Times'* Charles Hurd noted that many in the enthusiastic crowds greeting the president's motorcade waved both the American and the Confederate flags.[53]

Back at the White House, Roosevelt concentrated on coordinating the government's ongoing efforts to deal with the drought. It had assumed crisis proportions on the northern Great Plains: centered in the Dakotas, it reached into parts of Minnesota, Montana, and Wyoming, accompanied by heat as high as 119 degrees. The Southeast and adjoining parts of Oklahoma and Arkansas also experienced significant drought. Meeting with Rex Tugwell and Aubrey Williams, the president rejected any notion of large-scale relocation of families and authorized already appropriated WPA funds to be used for relief. At his press conference, with Williams on hand to provide backup, he explained with an impressive command of detail that the winter wheat crop would be only some 15 percent of normal and that 240,000 families "need some form of immediate cash relief." Fifty thousand new WPA jobs were being created to do useful work, chiefly "digging wells," "building earth dams" to catch and store rainwater, and paving "farm to market roads" at wages averaging fifteen dollars a week. Seventy thousand families had already received subsistence loans, and another 50,000 would soon get them. Relief plans were pending to take care of the remaining 34,000 families. A cattle purchasing program bought still healthy animals that could no longer be fattened for market in areas where the grass had burned up, and a soil conservation program paid farmers to turn cropland into pastureland.

When asked about a rumored drought-created food shortage, Roosevelt pointed out that since the current reduced crop estimates called for a 600-million-bushel wheat crop, normal annual consumption was some 625 million bushels, and stored surplus amounted to 150 million bushels, there would be no shortage.[54]

On July 10, he closed down his White House office and headed north; Hyde Park would be his summer headquarters, even though there was still no airconditioning there. In Manhattan briefly, he held a series of meetings. The most significant was with Hopkins, Aubrey Williams, and the WPA's point man for the drought area, Howard Hunter, who provided a firsthand report. Roosevelt then went to dedicate the massive Triborough Bridge, the largest project built with PWA funds in the East during Roosevelt's first term. It was really four bridges in one, serving as what Robert Caro calls "a traffic machine, the largest ever built." Mayor Jimmy Walker had broken ground in 1929, but after spending some $4.5 million on land acquisition and preliminaries, the city, broke, had to abandon the project; in 1933 PWA funds enabled its resumption. Eventually, the federal government put up more than $45 million of the bridge's $60 million cost, but the wily Robert Moses, now New York City's commissioner of parks, made sure that the funds went to the Triborough Bridge Authority, which he controlled. This led to public feuding between Moses and both Ickes and Roosevelt. The long-standing mutual animosity between Moses and Roosevelt had intensified in 1934 when Moses, in his only attempt at electoral politics, was foolish enough to accept the GOP nomination for governor and run against Herbert Lehman in a campaign that flopped dismally.

Although Moses was the impresario of the dedication and introduced all the other speakers, Roosevelt insisted that someone else introduce him, so La Guardia did it. Roosevelt's speech invoked a family connection: "Not much more than a hundred years ago my own great-grandfather owned a farm in Harlem, right across there [indicating], close to the Manhattan approach of this bridge. But I am quite sure, Bob Moses, that he never dreamed of the bridge."[55] A later passage—"People require and demand up-to-date government in place of antiquated government"—had a political subtext in a presidential election year.

After the brief ceremony, the president's motorcade took him home to Hyde Park, where he stayed for two nights. A conference on flood control with officials from several eastern states in his home was followed by his departure by train for the Maine coast, where his cruise would begin.[56]

The trip was, in some ways, a less spartan reprise of the 1933 cruise, aboard a much larger vessel, the five-year-old, fifty-six-foot schooner *Sewanna*, which had broad decks, a roomier cockpit, and much more space below. Eldon Coldbeth was again captain, but with two paid crewman to assist the president and sons James, John, and Franklin; Eleanor's brother Hall joined the party for a few days. The official part of Roosevelt's party was on the presidential yacht *Potomac*; the Secret Service men were aboard the destroyer *Hopkins* from which they deployed in motor launches for picket duty around *Sewanna* during anchorages. A fourth vessel, the large schooner *Liberty*, had been chartered for seven accompanying press. On several occasions, the Roosevelts visited the *Potomac* for more elaborate meals than could be had on their vessel.[57]

Roosevelt's meandering cruise took two weeks, during which Landon formally accepted the nomination in Topeka and began campaigning. In Cleveland Father Coughlin managed to put together an unstable coalition of Townsendites and former partisans of Huey Long in support of the third-party candidacy of William Lemke (1878–1950), an Independent North Dakota congressman who had initially supported Roosevelt but broke with him when he would not support his radical bankruptcy legislation and extreme inflationary measures. The headlines went to the popular radio priest, who tore off his clerical collar and appeared in shirtsleeves to denounce the president as a "great betrayer" and a "liar."

Harold Ickes, Jim Farley, and many other New Deal notables were growing antsy. As Ickes put it, "Our private polls show an alarming falling off in the President's vote [but he] smiles and sails and fishes and the rest of us worry and fume." The crusty Ickes, who had an unblemished record of failure in managing the campaigns of reform candidates in Chicago—admittedly a thankless task— told his diary that "I would not want [Roosevelt} to be managing my campaign." Eleanor, with similar worries, fired off a detailed memo to Farley, with copies to Franklin and a number of party and White House insiders, complaining of inaction and warning that the Landon campaign had "the spirit of a crusade." Roosevelt remained supremely confident. He sent a note to Garner in Texas about his own plans, observing that "the Republican high command is doing altogether too much talking."[58]

Roosevelt thoroughly enjoyed the two weeks of his vacation. Although much of it was in Canadian waters, it had been agreed that no official notice of his presence would be taken before his arrival at Campobello. He wore old clothes and did not shave. When the flotilla put in for an overnight anchorage in the harbor of Shelburne, Nova Scotia, the president, accompanied only by his son Franklin, made a tour of the harbor in a small motorboat, waving at spectators who came down to see the flotilla. *Times* man Hurd reported that "apparently none knew that the bewhiskered man in oilskins was President of the United States."[59]

Informality came to an end at the family's private wharf on Campobello, where forty red-coated Mounties were lined up to greet and guard him. In two weeks at sea, the *Sewanna* had traveled nearly 450 miles in ninety hours of actual sailing. During two days, the president dealt with some paperwork, attended a large reception at the house for locals who had been invited by his mother, and held a brief press conference, largely devoted to his further summer travel plans. When asked to comment on Landon's acceptance speech, which he had listened to, he replied, "Off the record, if it would stay off the record, I might."[60]

The president left the island on the existing ferry to make a tour of the Maine towns adjacent to the island. Some there resented his failure to visit them in 1933. He and Sara made amends in Lubec and Eastport, where he said good-bye to his mother and boarded the *Potomac* to rejoin his official party for the short run to meet his train at St. Andrews, New Brunswick, for the overnight trip to Quebec City.

In Quebec the next morning, Roosevelt began the eight hours that constituted the first official visit of an American president to Canada. (Before Franklin, only Theodore and Wilson had left the country while president; each of his successors has done so.) He was welcomed by the governor-general, Lord Tweedsmuir— John Buchan, the right-wing politician and thriller writer—as well as the prime minister, William Lyon Mackenzie King, and provincial officials. Tweedsmuir, speaking for Britain, hailed Roosevelt as "one of the major forces in the statesmanship of the world" and went on to express the hope that the United States and the British Commonwealth "may help to restore the shaken liberties of mankind."

Roosevelt's brief address to the dignitaries and "my friends and neighbors of Canada" insisted that he was "not a stranger," as he had spent most of his summers since he was two in New Brunswick. He spoke of the trade agreement he and Mackenzie King had recently signed as further evidence of friendship and expressed the hope, in a speech that was broadcast to Britain, that the new king, Edward VIII, whom he had met during the war, might make an official visit, an invitation that was accepted by his brother three years later. He then delighted the Francophones in the audience with three mundane paragraphs in French, responding to the greetings from provincial and municipal leaders. The speech was followed by private discussions about trade, tourism, and cross-border hydroelectric projects.[61]

From Quebec his train took him through three New England states for a one-day examination of flood-prevention work in the oft-stricken Connecticut River valley, where ten new dams were planned. Accompanied by Major General Edwin M. Markham, chief of the Corps of Engineers, he left the train to visit two dam sites in Vermont. The trip was in keeping with the president's electoral strategy, as it showed the New Deal in action. The first stop was at the Little River Dam site near Waterbury, where sixteen hundred CCC workers on three six-hour shifts were building an earthen dam. Then, atop the completed Winooski Dam near Wrightsville, he held an impromptu press conference. Calling the reporters to gather around his car, Roosevelt pointed out that the dam, begun as a CCC project in 1933 and completed the previous November, had already more than paid for itself by preventing property damage in the March 1936 floods. General Markham supplied figures. The dams were joint federal-state projects: Vermont paid for land acquisition; the federal government financed the construction.

After conferences with Vermont's governor and other officials in Montpelier, Roosevelt rode over into New Hampshire, rejoined his train, and met on board with that state's officials. He repeated the process in Springfield for Massachusetts. In between, he held a more formal press conference as the train ran south. After Roosevelt finished providing more details about past and future flood control, a reporter volunteered:

Q: That speech went swell with the crowd yesterday (at Quebec).

THE PRESIDENT: Wasn't it funny when the Prime Minister of Quebec switched from English to French, how a round of applause went up?

Q: We saw King later in the Citadel and met the chap who writes King's French speeches. He said, "It is too bad we haven't Roosevelt running up here because he would carry Quebec any time."[62]

The train took the president home to Hyde Park late that evening. The three women who handled personal correspondence—Missy LeHand and Grace Tully for Franklin and Malvina Schneider for Eleanor—were already settled in Springwood, while a larger staff, including the telephone operators who kept the president in direct touch with Washington, were in downtown Poughkeepsie, a few minutes away by car under Steve Early's management.

Some public business was done. Secretary Wallace and Chester Davis, now a member of the Federal Reserve Board, came to discuss the drought and helped plan the president's trip to the stricken area later in the month.[63]

Much of Roosevelt's time that summer was seemingly not spent on politics but being an activist president seen to be doing the people's business, which was, of course, the best politics. In terms of objectives, the president wanted to win a sweeping victory, a victory surpassing that of 1932. He wanted to attract voters and potential voters who had not previously voted for Democrats and, at the same time, maintain the loyalty of previous Democratic voters.

In three parallel approaches, the president sought to reach out to voters not likely to be attracted to the Democratic Party: Labor's Non-Partisan League, the White House–organized Good Neighborhood League (GNL), and, in New York State, the American Labor Party (ALP) had all been created for that purpose. On the national scene, the drive for labor votes was clearly the most important of these efforts. There was also a labor bureau within the Democratic National Committee, headed throughout the Roosevelt era by Daniel J. Tobin (1875–1955) of the Teamsters Union. Two of the most important leaders of the CIO, John L. Lewis, a Republican, and the Amalgamated Clothing Workers' Sidney Hillman (1887–1946), a Socialist, had created the LNPL in April and put George L. Berry (1882–1948), head of a relatively small printing trades union with long-established Democratic Party connections, in nominal charge. Roosevelt, who was at great pains to ignore the growing split in the ranks of labor, sent Berry a public letter, thanking the league for supporting his candidacy. These kinds of connections to the labor movement became a vital part of the Roosevelt coalition. The American Federation of Labor had a traditional policy of supporting friends and opposing enemies; AFL president William Green personally endorsed Roosevelt, and in an early October visit to Hyde Park he assured the president of the enthusiastic support of American workers. At least twenty-three of the twenty-six state federations endorsed him as well. On the other hand, some important AFL leaders, like the Carpenters' Union head, William Hutchinson, were avowed Landon supporters.[64]

Next in importance among the 1936 nonparty organizations was the Good Neighbor League, which aimed to attract liberal Protestant clergy and others who favored Roosevelt's ideals but as Republicans or independents were leery of the Democratic Party. The GNL was unveiled in late April after its cochairs, George Foster Peabody and Lillian Wald, called on Roosevelt at the White

House and later told the press that Stanley High would be in charge, without mentioning that High had been on the payroll of the Democratic National Committee since mid-February. They also announced an all-white board of directors featuring prominent Protestants, Catholics, and Jews.

As things played out, however, the GNL's major impact was in attracting black voters. In August the DNC had begun the distribution of a million copies of a photograph showing two handsome black Reserve Officers' Training Corps cadets escorting Eleanor Roosevelt during a visit to the Howard University campus, despite the certainty of its raising the ire of white southerners. In early September, High announced a drive to capture "some two million [northern] Negro votes," and Eleanor Roosevelt, in her first overtly political appeal for those votes, spoke to the forty black leaders of the GNL's efforts under the leadership of two African Methodist Episcopal church bishops, Philadelphia's R. R. Wright Jr. and Harlem's Dr. Adam Clayton Powell Sr.

The group's most important event was the staging of twenty-six rallies across the northern states on the seventy-fourth anniversary of the Emancipation Proclamation. The largest was a "Monster Tribute . . . to Negro Progress" held in Madison Square Garden on September 21, sponsored by the "Colored Committee of the Good Neighbor League."

The climax of the rally, attended by sixteen thousand blacks, suggested that Roosevelt, like Lincoln, was a bestower of freedom. A huge poster was unfurled depicting a standing image of the president, some twenty feet high, his hands outstretched as if bestowing a blessing, with a group of Negroes kneeling at his feet, while in the background the spirit of Abraham Lincoln hovered. Crude and unconvincing as this symbolism will seem to twenty-first-century readers, it was mimetic of familiar statues of Lincoln and kneeling freed blacks, which had been erected in black neighborhoods all through the northern states. It sent the same message that Robert Vann had emphasized in 1932. In addition, the Colored Division of the DNC "spelled out" the black participation in the New Deal's relief programs, but especially the WPA, a significance that was only highlighted by the incessant attacks made on the WPA by Republican campaigners.[65]

Toward the end of the campaign, Roosevelt made his first and only visit to the Howard University campus, a brief drive from the White House, to dedicate a new chemistry building.[66] Although it was labeled a nonpolitical appearance, Harold Ickes, whose PWA provided the money for the building, preceded the president's speech by recounting the many other benefits black Americans had received from the New Deal. Roosevelt's address, broadcast nationally, was his first real speech aimed at a black audience, unless one counts his talks in Haiti in 1917. In it he recognized publicly, for the first time as president, the existence of race discrimination and claimed, extravagantly, that "as far as it was humanly possible, the Government has followed the . . . policy that among

American citizens there should be no forgotten men and no forgotten races. It is a wise and truly American policy. We shall continue faithfully to observe it." A preelection poll of Howard students overwhelmingly favored Roosevelt, who got 289 of 452 straw votes; Landon had 91, Communist Earl Browder 62, Socialist Norman Thomas 4, and 6 votes went to a Prohibition candidate.[67]

Of much less significance in 1936 was the creation of the American Labor Party in New York State, founded in that year by Hillman and the International Ladies' Garment Workers' Union's David Dubinsky (1891–1982) as a means of attracting left-wing voters who identified the Democratic Party with Tammany Hall. Since both men resigned from the Socialist Party, it also contributed to the decline of that party. Although it is sometimes written that the ALP vote was crucial in carrying New York for Roosevelt, that was not the case in 1936. In that election, as opposed to 1940 and 1944, the president's vote total on the Democratic line alone was an absolute majority of votes cast in the state. How many ALP voters would have voted for Roosevelt if that option had not existed is a question that cannot be answered, but certainly many would have done so. Roosevelt also collaborated with two midwestern third parties, Wisconsin's Progressives and Minnesota's Farmer-Laborites. The former, as noted, mitigated against the Wisconsin Democrats then and for years to come, while the latter collaboration led to a Minnesota Democratic Farmer-Labor Party that would dominate the state for decades. The party's leader, Governor Floyd Olson, dictated a strong letter of support for Roosevelt from his hospital bed just four days before his death on August 22. Olson's letter also deplored the candidacy of his former ally William Lemke.[68]

Roosevelt went out of his way to support an occasional Republican or independent candidate for office, even though that candidate had a Democratic opponent. His endorsement of George Norris's reelection to the Senate in Nebraska was, like the 1934 endorsement of Robert La Follette in Wisconsin, an exception. In addition, as had been the case in 1932, some important Republicans either endorsed Roosevelt, as Michigan's James Couzens and North Dakota's Peter Norbeck would do, or sat out the campaign without endorsing anyone, as Senate minority leader Charles McNary of Oregon and three other sitting Republican senators would do. In September Norris, La Follette, and Fiorello La Guardia convoked a Chicago conference of progressives to endorse Roosevelt.[69]

As important as all these and similar activities were, most of the organized campaign effort was under the banner of the Democratic Party. Central to Roosevelt's strategy, however, was his conviction that, in the final analysis, what he himself said and did on the campaign trail—and before—was crucial to victory.

The two planned "presidential" inspection trips were laid out by the president in press conferences, the first to eastern flood areas, the second to the midwestern drought region.

Again accompanied by General Markham plus representatives of the WPA and CCC, he left for the three-day eastern flood-area tour. At perennially flooded Johnstown in western Pennsylvania, Roosevelt took a two-hour inspection drive. In remarks later, he emphasized the importance of seeing the damage "with my own eyes." Tours of other flood areas in Ohio, western New York, and eastern Pennsylvania followed. Although Roosevelt drew crowds everywhere, the *Times'* Hurd was impressed with both the size and the intensity of those along the Susquehanna River in eastern Pennsylvania: "Persons of all ages and types fought good-naturedly to get as close to the President as possible, in a manner which those who travel habitually with the President have rarely seen."[70]

After a restful week at home and two days catching up on paperwork in the White House, Roosevelt's western trip began on August 25. Despite Roosevelt's insistence that this was not a political trip, the many whistle-stops on the day and a half it took to get to the first drought-area destination in Bismarck, North Dakota, were "a series of political demonstrations." At Gary, Indiana, for example, Governor Paul McNutt set off cheers by introducing him as "the man who . . . will continue to be . . . president." Between stops, there were ongoing conferences with Henry Wallace, Harry Hopkins, and a half-dozen second-rank federal officials who accompanied him.

At Bismarck Roosevelt, after an inspection trip, told a crowd that the drought situation "really comes down to three problems . . . immediate relief for those who have lost their crops and livestock . . . keep[ing] them going . . . until next year, when we hope we shall have more rain [and] working out a plan of cooperating with Nature instead of . . . trying to buck Nature."

Aware that many opponents of New Deal planning in the region had criticized some of the federal informational campaign about the Great Plains as demeaning both the region and its people, Roosevelt made a point of praising the spirit of his listeners.

> There was another reason for my coming out here, and that was to look at you people. Back East there have been all kinds of reports that out in the drought area there was a widespread despondency, a lack of hope for the future, and a general atmosphere of gloom. But I had a hunch and it was right that when I got out here I would find that you people had your chins up, that you were not looking forward in despair to the day when this country would be depopulated, but that you and your children fully expected to remain here.[71]

Roosevelt's main message was a simplified version of the Cooke Committee's report summary, which was released to the press that day. It recounted the money already spent on the Great Plains under the New Deal—nearly $500 million—and observed that "the agricultural economy of the Great Plains will become increasingly unstable and unsafe" unless poor agricultural practices were prevented. It prescribed a number of methods for changing farming and grazing practices and ended with a blunt warning: "We endanger our democracy if we allow the Great Plains or any other section of the country to become an economic desert."[72]

Roosevelt spent his second day touring WPA projects and various conservation activities and observing, at one stop, that what he had learned confirmed his belief in a three-word solution for the Great Plains' problems: "better land use." At another stop, he noted that "the word 'planning' is not popular with some people, but one reason why the water table has sunk as low as it has is that we did not think about the future twenty years ago."

At his last stop in the Dakotas, Roosevelt was able to see Mount Rushmore for the first time since Gutzon Borglum had begun his massive project in 1927. He dedicated the bust of Jefferson, the second of the four to be completed.

At that point, Roosevelt's travel plans were disrupted by the death of War Secretary George Dern. Roosevelt rerouted the train to Salt Lake City for the funeral. Pausing for a hastily scheduled inspection trip and a conference in western Nebraska, Roosevelt attended the funeral but took no personal part in it or other public activities during his seven hours there. Unlike his cousin Theodore, of whom it was said that he wanted to be the bride at weddings and the corpse at funerals, Franklin felt that funerals were a place to evince grief and nothing else. He soon promoted Harry H. Woodring (1887–1967), a Kansas Democrat who had been assistant secretary since 1933, to the cabinet post.[73]

The detour caused the scrubbing of planned stops in Minnesota and Wisconsin. After typical whistle- and inspection stops in Wyoming, Colorado, and Iowa, the president's train arrived in Des Moines shortly before a meeting with midwestern governors. Originally planned for four, inclusion of Minnesota and Wisconsin executives made it a sextet, with host Iowa, Missouri, Oklahoma, and Kansas in the other chairs. Media attention focused on the face-to-face meetings between Landon and Roosevelt, as no other president had ever had such an encounter with a nominated challenger. Despite the media hype, there was little to report. Their two encounters—a lunch and a dinner on the president's train—were both closed to the press. Roosevelt made no rear-platform or other public remarks, telling newsreel cameramen who filmed his arrival, "No mikes today. This is silent."[74]

In his last public remarks of the trip, still after claiming that he was "not talking politics," he told an Indianapolis audience:

This trip . . . is a tremendous contrast to the trips that I made . . . in the autumn of 1932. I shall always remember . . . not only the garb, the clothing of people, but the faces of people. It was a harrowing experience as I campaigned in that year, because there was such obvious want in almost every part of the country. . . . Those were difficult years that we went through. I am thankful, as an American, that today the faces of the people and the clothing they wear show that their mental condition and their physical condition are a whole lot better than they were at that time. . . . It is not a question, in my judgment, that ought to be brought into politics, into the partisan give and take of a campaign—it is a fact. Today the people of the country, of all parties and in every section, are looking forward to the future with a great deal more hope than they could possibly have looked forward to in 1932.

Despite Roosevelt's disclaimer, that passage contained the real message of his 1936 campaign: Roosevelt and the New Deal had inherited a broken country and made it work again.[75]

Returning to Washington, Roosevelt made the first Fireside Chat in seventeen months. After describing what he saw and heard—five of the first seven paragraphs began with the personal pronoun—he insisted that there would be no surrender to the drought. "No cracked earth, no blistering sun, no burning wind, no grasshoppers are a permanent match for the indomitable American farmers and stockmen and their wives and children who have carried on through desperate days, and inspire us with their self-reliance, their tenacity and their courage. It was their fathers' task to make homes; it is their task to keep those homes; it is our task to help them with their fight."

For almost two-thirds of his chat, he continued to talk about agriculture and what the New Deal had done and would do for farmers, underlining the economic interconnectedness of all elements of American life. In the last third, he concentrated on labor, stressing again the economic dependence of "all American workers . . . and all the rest of us whose well-being depends on theirs." He had earlier criticized "those who fail to read both the signs of the times and American history. They would try to refuse the worker any effective power to bargain collectively, to earn a decent livelihood and to acquire security. It is those shortsighted ones, not labor, who threaten this country with that class dissension which in other countries has led to dictatorship and the establishment of fear and hatred as the dominant emotions in human life."

He closed with a homily about Labor Day, which "belongs to all of us. . . . Anyone who calls it a class holiday challenges the whole concept of American democracy. The Fourth of July commemorates our political freedom—a freedom which without economic freedom is meaningless indeed. Labor Day symbolizes our determination to achieve an economic freedom for the average man which will give his political freedom reality."[76]

Never before had any president placed this kind of emphasis on the importance of labor in a talk addressed to the nation. Many of those, inside the organized movement and without, who had doubted Roosevelt's commitment now had these doubts eased, if not removed. Ironically, the day before Roosevelt spoke, the AFL council suspended the ten rebellious Lewis-led unions for persisting in what was still called the Committee for Industrial Organization. A permanent rift seemed likely, but the president made no public comment.

In September Roosevelt's major appearance was at Harvard's tercentennial. It was no secret, of course, that most men of Harvard, past and present, opposed the New Deal; a later newspaper poll reported that barely a quarter of Roosevelt's own class of '05 supported him, while Landon had the support of nearly 90 percent of his classmates, Kansas '08. During Roosevelt's October campaigning, Harvard students booed the president from university buildings as his motorcade passed. The largest tercentenary outdoor ceremony took place under leaden skies and a steady drizzle. When Yale's president, James R. Angell, opened his remarks by observing that the rain was Harvard president Conant's "method of soaking the rich," Roosevelt, sitting on the exposed stage, joined in the laughter.

That afternoon in an indoor speech, he related some Harvard history. Pointing out that on Harvard's two hundredth birthday, "many of the alumni of Harvard were sorely troubled concerning the state of the Nation. Andrew Jackson was President. On the two hundred and fiftieth . . . alumni again were sorely troubled. Grover Cleveland was President." Then, his voice dropping almost to a whisper, he concluded the passage: "Now, on the three hundredth anniversary, I am President," to much laughter and resounding applause. The rest of the speech was an urbane defense of the right of free inquiry and in praise of Harvard men "Charles William Eliot, William James, and Justice Holmes who made their minds swords in defense of freedom."[77]

Only at the end of September, at the state Democratic convention in Syracuse, did Roosevelt formally open his campaign. His opponents had been in full cry for some time; their three main spokesmen, Landon, Knox, and John D. M. Hamilton (1892–1973), the Kansas lawyer whom Landon made party chairman, had been on the stump for months along with Herbert Hoover and two former Democrats, Al Smith and Bainbridge Colby (1869–1950), Woodrow Wilson's last secretary of state. All were financed by the Republican National Committee. Landon's biographer argues convincingly that it was a dysfunctional campaign that Landon could not control, which obscured his relatively moderate Republicanism and frustrated any chance the Kansan had of making a decent showing in the election. All but Landon denounced almost every aspect of the New Deal and labeled Roosevelt as a socialist and advocate of communism. Even worse, from Landon's point of view, were the wild charges of the Hearst press and the American Liberty League, which Landon called privately "the kiss of death."

Yet in mid-September, many leading Democrats were still quite nervous about the results, and many conservatives were relatively sanguine about Landon's prospects. When the results from Maine, which still voted in September, produced a Landon victory, the old bromide—"As goes Maine, so goes the nation"—was repeated mindlessly. The actual figures were virtually identical with those of 1932, when it was one of six states that Hoover won; the 1936 results would be "As goes Maine, so goes Vermont." Most newspapers outside the South supported Landon, as did many of the pundits. Walter Lippmann wrote that "I am going to vote for Governor Landon." He reasoned that there were no great issues between the two parties except what remained of the New Deal after the Court decisions and that Roosevelt had alienated business, while Landon, if elected, would be checked by a Democratic Senate and would have to constitute a government of "national union," which Lippmann thought the times demanded.[78]

In Syracuse Roosevelt, speaking in the same armory where he had accepted his second gubernatorial nomination, took the occasion to place himself in the context of charges that had been laid against past presidents—Washington wanted to become a king, Jefferson wanted to set up a guillotine, Jackson soaked the rich; Lincoln was called a Roman emperor, Theodore Roosevelt a Destroyer, and Wilson a self-consumed Messiah.

This campaign's red herring was communism. "Desperate in mood, angry at failure, cunning in purpose, individuals and groups are seeking to make Communism an issue in an election where Communism is not a controversy between the two parties." Roosevelt pointed out that he had a long record of public service, demonstrating a devotion to the American form of government. "I have not sought, I do not seek, I repudiate the support of any advocate of Communism or of any other alien 'ism' which would by fair means or foul change our American democracy."

He added that while "there is no difference between the major parties as to what they think about Communism," there was a great difference between what they would do about communism. Pointing out that communism thrived on widespread economic maladjustment, he blamed Republican mismanagement for the economic disasters of 1929 to 1933, "a crisis made to order for all those who would overthrow our government." After a litany of those disasters, he noted, "Most people remember . . . that starvation was averted, that homes and farms were saved, that banks were reopened, that crop prices rose, that industry revived, and that the dangerous forces subversive of our form of government were turned aside. A few people—a few only—unwilling to remember, seem to have forgotten those days." Then, as he often did, he lightened up and told one of his stories: "In the summer of 1933, a nice old gentleman wearing a silk hat fell off the end of a pier. He was unable to swim. A friend ran down the pier, dived overboard and pulled him out, but the silk hat floated off with the tide. After the old gentleman had been revived, he was effusive in his thanks. He praised his friend for saving his life. Today, three years later, the old gentleman is berating his friend because the silk hat was lost." When the laughter died down, Roosevelt returned to the attack: "Conditions congenial to Communism were being bred and fostered throughout this Nation up to the very day of March

4, 1933. . . . Discontent and fear were spreading throughout the country. The previous national Administration, bewildered, did nothing."

His campaign finally started, Roosevelt left the cheering convention to be driven to the train to return to Hyde Park. At the station, he found the local American Legion Glee Club waiting to serenade him; after listening to several numbers while he sat in his car, he got out and joined them for one last song, "Pack Up Your Troubles in Your Old Kit Bag," which he rendered while wearing "a Legion cap perched jauntily over one ear," before boarding his train for Hyde Park.

As if on cue, that very day, John D. M. Hamilton, opening the Republican campaign in Kentucky, charged that the New Deal was "communistic." He and others continually repeated the charge throughout the campaign. For Roosevelt, the issue was settled. He never mentioned communism again during the campaign. The rest of the Syracuse speech, in petto, prefigured his entire campaign scenario: the Republicans had caused the Depression and brought misery and danger to the nation, and he, his party, and the New Deal had come to the rescue.[79]

During October Roosevelt made nineteen "campaign addresses," two of them just for radio audiences; six "addresses," mostly ceremonial; fourteen "informal extemporaneous remarks"; twenty-four "extemporaneous rear platform remarks," all printed in his papers; plus twenty-nine other brief remarks listed but not printed. Although all had their place in the campaign and served a real purpose, they each delivered the same fundamental message—Roosevelt had assumed command of what seemed to be a sinking ship that had lost its way, and, once he had assumed the helm, great improvement could be felt by all.[80]

In a long first-person note on the 1936 campaign, Roosevelt, in reaction to some of Stanley High's published claims of authorship, gave his own take on speeches and ghostwriters. "Naturally the final draft will contain some of the thoughts and even some of the sentences submitted. I suppose it is human that two or three of the many persons with whom I have consulted in the writing of the speeches should seek to give the impression that they have been responsible for the writing of the speeches, and that one or two of them should claim authorship or state that some other individual was the author. Such assertions, however, are not accurate." I think the fairest single statement about Roosevelt's ghosts is Sam Rosenman's caveat that no matter who worked with the president, "the speeches were always Roosevelt's."[81]

Speaking in Pittsburgh's Forbes Field, where in 1932 he had attacked Hoover for spending too much money, Roosevelt met the deficit question, on which GOP speakers were concentrating, head-on. "A baseball park," he began, "is a good place to talk about box scores," and he proceeded to discuss the national economy and the election as if they were part of a ball game. "When the present management of your team took charge . . . you [had] voted for a change . . . to give the country a chance to win the game. And we are winning it." When the "Democratic administration came to bat," the "box score" showed a net deficit of $3 billion incurred "under my predecessor." "To balance our budget in 1933 or 1934 or 1935 would have been a crime against the American people. . . . When Americans suffered, we refused to pass by on the other side. . . . My administration has increased the [net] national debt . . . eight billion dollars. Put that . . . eight billions . . . on the scoreboard, and let me tell you where the dollars went." He first ticked off $1.5 billion for the soldiers' bonus, which removed a government obligation, and then $6.5 billion that went for CCC camps, work relief, and conservation of natural resources: "billions for security and a better life."

After pointing out that in the year just ended, not a single national bank had failed—something that had not happened in fifty-five years—he invited the crowd

> to compare the scoreboard . . . now with the scoreboard . . . when I stood here at second base . . . four years ago. At that time, as I drove through these great valleys, I could see mile after mile of this greatest mill and factory area in the world, a dead panorama of silent black structures and smokeless stacks. Today as I came north from West Virginia, I saw mines operating, I found bustle and life, the hiss of steam, the ring of steel on steel—the roaring song of industry.

He closed by noting that since the national income had risen from $38 billion in 1932 to $53 billion in 1935 and was still rising, it was likely that government receipts would, without new taxes, take care of both ordinary and relief expenditures and thus balance the budget.[82]

The next day, in New York, Roosevelt went to a real ball game, throwing out the first pitch at the Polo Grounds in the second game of the World Series. When he left in the seventh inning to preside at the groundbreaking for the Queens-Midtown Tunnel, the Yankees were well ahead in a record-breaking game they won eighteen to four on the way to a six-game triumph.[83]

The presidential train was the largest ever, with eleven cars including two diners and a club car to accommodate more than one hundred passengers, some forty of them journalists, for ten days. Eleanor and Betsey Cushing accompanied the president, whose staff included Marvin McIntyre, Missy LeHand, Pa Watson, Dr. McIntire, and Sam and Dorothy Rosenman. As it was mainly a midwestern route, Secretary Wallace was aboard and held conferences with farm leaders throughout the trip. Three western senators, Nevada's Key Pittman, Wyoming's Joseph C. O'Mahoney, and Montana's Burton Wheeler, were on board from the beginning, and dozens of others got on and off along the way.[84]

Each of the major speeches, and many of the minor ones, had a single theme. In St. Paul, the chief topic was reciprocal trade agreements; in Omaha, after formally endorsing the reelection of Senator George W. Norris, Roosevelt talked about farm policy; while in Denver, he spoke of his water projects.[85]

Speaking in Wichita in Alf Landon's Kansas—he never mentioned the names of his opponents—he spoke of the "bedtime stories" of the opposition, which tried to peddle a "gospel of fear" about the future. At a whistle-stop at Emporia later that day, one of six he made in Kansas, he began his rear-platform remarks by noting that he did not see "Bill White [who] is a very good friend of mine for three and a half years out of every four." As Roosevelt must have suspected, William Allen White (1868–1944), America's most celebrated small-town journalist and one of Landon's liberal advisers, was covering the president's appearance, as shouts from the crowd demonstrated. White sheepishly came forward to be greeted amid much applause and laughter. "Now that I see him," the president remarked, "I shall not say anything about the other six months."[86]

In a Kansas City speech at which young people were given preferred seating, Roosevelt spoke of what historians call the "New Deal for Youth"—the CCC and NYA—in which "we are trying to keep young people at useful work or in useful education." In Chicago, speaking to a national radio audience from the same platform on which he had accepted the nomination in 1932, he told how his administration had "saved the system of private profit and free enterprise" so that for the first time in seven years, most businesses were profitable. Using a medical metaphor—he the doctor, the nation the patient—he claimed, "Some of these people don't remember how sick they were. . . . They came to Washington in great numbers. Washington did not look like a dangerous bureaucracy. . . . Oh, no! It looked like an emergency hospital. . . . Now most of the patients seem to be doing very well. Some of them are even well enough to throw their crutches at the doctor."[87]

In Detroit, where two days earlier Landon had been "cooly received" by a crowd of 20,000 and charged that the New Deal was "akin to fascism," Roosevelt spoke to 150,000 massed in the same city square. He talked of matters of direct concern to many in his audience: he related meeting an autoworker, who told him that he made $1.25 an hour, $10 dollars a day. When Roosevelt responded that it was "a pretty good wage scale," the worker agreed but pointed out that "last year I worked only sixty-eight days." The president concluded, "It is my belief that manufacturers of automobiles and [others] must, by planning, do far more than they have done to date to increase the yearly earnings of their employees."[88]

In Cleveland he compared his administration's help for every level of society with the theory of the "previous Administration . . . that if you lend some money to the few financial interests at the top of the economic pyramid, it will trickle down." The problem with that, he explained, was that the trickle never got more than halfway down the economic ladder.

By the last day of the trip, which took the president from Niagara Falls to Hyde Park, those in Roosevelt's circle agreed that the campaign was well in hand. Most polls now pointed to a Roosevelt triumph, although the soon to be notorious *Literary Digest* poll continued to tout a Landon victory.[89] At the last stop, in Albany, "throngs" were so dense that the president's car had to be stopped several times and a path cleared. On the grueling ten-day western trip, he had logged more than five thousand miles, made sixty speeches, and shaken the hands of innumerable supporters in twelve states.[90]

A day or two after the western trip ended and the speeches for New England were being written, Rosenman remembered that at a White House cocktail hour, Roosevelt speculated about what he would do if he were running against Franklin D. Roosevelt. "You know, boys . . . I don't know whether I could [win, but I would give] him a close race—a darned sight closer than Landon is doing." His alter ego's strategy would have been to shed the extreme right-wing support and say, "I am for social security, work relief, etc., etc. But the Democrats cannot be entrusted with the administration of these fine ideals. I would cite chapter and verse on WPA inefficiency—and there's plenty of it—as there is bound to be in such a vast, emergency program." The president's enthusiasm grew as he speculated. He concluded his fantasy by remarking, "The more I think about it, the more I think I could lick myself."[91]

The two-day campaign swing through southern New England culminated in Roosevelt's main address at Worcester, which was broadcast nationwide. His major theme was a democratic tax policy in which he quoted Justice Holmes on taxes as the necessary price of civilization. He also responded to a widespread Republican tactic of providing employers with political messages to be placed in employees' wage packets. "I want to say a word also to the wage earners who are finding propaganda about the security tax in their pay envelopes. I want to remind them that the new social security law was designed for them, for the greater safety of their homes and their families. The fund necessary to provide that security is not collected solely from workers. The employer, too, pays an equal share. And both shares—yours and the employer's—are being held for the sole benefit of the worker himself."

It is clear that, despite the confusion of the campaign, Roosevelt often gained vivid impressions of the realities of Depression life and drew lessons from some of its incidents. Months later, discussing the problems of working people in a press conference, he spoke of an experience "on that hectic ride from Providence to Boston" that reporters did not see because they were "half a mile back."

> We got into New Bedford and in that park there was the most awful jam . . . around my car [and] a girl six or seven feet away . . . was trying to pass an envelope to me. . . . [O]ne of the policemen threw her back into the crowd and I said to Gus (Generich), "Get the note from that girl." . . . It said, "Dear Mr. President: I wish you could do something to help us girls. You are the only recourse we have got left. We have been working in a sewing factory

". . . and up to a few months ago we were getting our minimum pay of $11 a week (I think it was $11) and even the learners were getting $7 or $8 a week. Today the 200 of us girls have been cut down to $4 and $5 and $6 a week. You are the only man who can do anything about it. Please send somebody from Washington up here to restore our minimum wages because we cannot live on $4 or $5 or $6 a week."

Roosevelt wound up the campaign in New York City, leaving his train in Bayonne, New Jersey, and was driven some thirty miles through city streets with every block's sidewalks jammed with enthusiastic crowds—though there was some booing as he passed Wall Street. Landon was also campaigning in the city that day; the two did not meet, but Roosevelt tipped his hat as his motorcade passed Landon's headquarters on Murray Hill.

After laying a cornerstone for a PWA building at Brooklyn College, Roosevelt crossed over to lower Manhattan to take a ferry to the military post on Governors Island for lunch with its commander. The cruiser *Indianapolis* and the gunboat *Erie* were standing by in the harbor to provide twenty-one-gun salutes, as did the battery at Fort Jay. After lunch he was ferried to the Statue of Liberty for ceremonies commemorating the fiftieth anniversary of its opening.

Roosevelt, whose New Deal had made no significant changes in the nation's restrictive immigration laws, hailed the "steady stream of men, women, and children [who] brought to one new country the culture of a hundred old ones." Back in Manhattan, for a celebration of the anniversary at a park on the Lower East Side named for his mother, he told an audience who were largely immigrants and their children:

I am inclined to think that in some cases the newer citizens have discharged their . . . obligations to us better than we have discharged our obligations to them. For example, their coming helped to intensify the housing problem in many of our great cities. . . .

We have spent large sums of money on parks, on highways, on bridges, on museums and other projects . . . but we have not yet begun adequately to spend money in order to help the families in the overcrowded sections of our cities to live as American citizens have a right to live.

The notion that decent housing was a right and a responsibility of government was not yet a part of the national consensus. Making the speech overtly political, he promised that, if reelected, "the next Congress will start us on our way with a sound housing policy."[92]

On the next day's swing through Pennsylvania, a speech at Wilkes-Barre, where John L. Lewis introduced him, was devoted to labor. At Harrisburg he spoke about consumer issues and expressed confidence that "the American people will not return to power those leaders who emptied the national market-basket." There was no formal address in Philadelphia, but the massive street-blocking turnout—it took his motorcade an hour to travel four miles—persuaded Democratic leaders there, correctly, that he would carry the city, something they had not previously claimed. In Camden, New Jersey, he defined the "great objectives . . . greater permanence for employment, safety for earnings, protection for the home, and a better security for the average man and his family."

By this time, professional bookmakers made the president a three-to-one favorite, and one consensus of two hundred political observers was that Roosevelt would likely win with at least 406 electoral votes. At a meeting of a Manhattan Democratic club, Jim Farley made what seemed to almost everyone—including, as he later admitted, Franklin Roosevelt—a rather outrageous prediction, claiming that the president would carry forty-six of the forty-eight states. The enthusiasm of the occasion inspired Jimmy Walker to make his first public speech in four years, an hour-long denunciation of Al Smith and other "Jeffersonian Democrats" for walking out on their party, while hailing Roosevelt as "the man who saved the nation from destruction." Smith, for his part, addressed a nationwide audience under the auspices of the Liberty League to accuse Roosevelt of "preparing the way for a Communist controlled America."[93]

The major event of Roosevelt's return to New York was the traditional closing speech in Madison Square Garden, which was, in Sam Rosenman's judgment, the best of that campaign. It certainly pleased its partisan audience. The president wanted a speech with "the gloves off," and it included an uncharacteristically strident passage, one of the few in any of Roosevelt's formal addresses that can be described as ugly. After tagging the old order as "government by organized money," he went on to boast:

> Never before in all our history have these forces been so united . . . against one candidate as they stand today. They are unanimous in their hate for me—and I welcome their hatred.
>
> I should like to have it said of my first administration that in it the forces of selfishness and of lust for power met their match. I should like to have it said [at this point, the responsive roar of the crowd became so intense that Roosevelt had to hold up his hand and shout "Wait a minute!" to hush them] of my second Administration that in it these forces met their master.[94]

There was enough contemporary criticism of that strident passage that Rosenman in his memoir defends his chief—and, of course, himself—arguing that there was nothing for him to retract or explain: that he intended to carry out his program "until reactionary political thinking" was conclusively rejected. It is worth observing that a more appropriate metaphor paints the president as the people's servant and that in no subsequent campaign was the offending metaphor—or anything like it—repeated.[95]

The speech itself ended positively, as the president told the crowd that "of course we will continue" to work for various specific public goals, all of which "spell peace at home." Noting that "today there is war and rumor of war," he insisted that "democracy cannot live without that true religion which gives a nation a sense of justice and a moral purpose." After quoting the prophet Micah—"do justly . . . love mercy . . . walk humbly with thy God," he explained: "That is why the recovery we seek, the recovery we are winning, is more than economic. In it are included justice and love and humility, not for ourselves as individuals alone, but for our Nation. That is the road to peace."

From the Garden, he went directly to his train for a quick run up to Hyde Park, where, in what became a tradition, he spent the forty-eight hours before election day. Sunday he went to church and relaxed, while on Monday he made a seventy-five-mile tour of his old three-county state senatorial district, as he had done in elections he was contesting since 1910. He had expressed the hope that he would carry Dutchess County, which he had carried in 1930 but not in 1928 or 1932, but it was not to be, though he did improve his showing: he got 46 percent of the vote in 1936, up from 40 percent in 1932. But the tour was not to gain votes, not just a customary action, but his visible effort to show that he had a decent respect for the opinions of his neighbors and that he remained a member of their shared community. That night, speaking from his twelve-by-twelve-foot study at Springwood, Roosevelt made a truly nonpartisan nationwide radio address: it contained an appeal to vote without specifying candidate or party and underlined the fact that whoever was elected would "become President of all the people."[96]

On election morning, he voted at the Hyde Park town hall, as he had done since 1903, and spent the day quietly at home. That evening, surrounded by family and a few members of his personal staff, he settled down with pencils and pads and two press-association news tickers to tabulate results. Rosenman reports that when early results showed him ahead in New Haven by 15,000 votes, he insisted that someone get on the phone to check the figures. He had carried the city only narrowly in 1932. When the vote was confirmed, "he leaned back in his chair, blew a ring of smoke at the ceiling, and exclaimed 'Wow!'" By ten thirty, he abandoned his tally even before any West Coast votes were in and joined the larger party in the library for sandwiches and, almost certainly, a cocktail. Landon waited until one thirty in the morning to send a telegram of concession, by which time the president had greeted a torchlight parade of his neighbors and gone to bed.[97]

When all the results were in, it was and remains the greatest electoral triumph in modern American history. Roosevelt had carried all the states, save Maine and Vermont, receiving in the process 60.8 percent[98] of the vote, up from 57.4 percent in 1932. Landon received 1 million more votes than Hoover, but since almost 6 million more people voted his percentage of the popular vote shrank to 36.5 percent from Hoover's 39.7 percent.

The total third-party vote remained almost identical, 1.14 million in 1932, 1.20 million in 1936. But in the earlier election, the bulk of it came from urban easterners: 882,000 for Socialist Norman Thomas, 103,000 for Communist William Z. Foster, and 33,000 for a Socialist Labor candidate. In 1936 the bulk of the third-party vote was from rural midwesterners: William Lemke garnered 882,000 votes, while the left-wing vote in the East shrank to 268,000, 188,000 for Thomas and 80,000 for Communist Earl Browder.

Roosevelt's coattails continued strong: in the Senate, whose incumbent candidates had been elected in 1930, the Democrats picked up 6 seats, for a total of 75, while the Republicans lost 9, dropping to just 16 of the 96. The already lopsided House added 11 more Democrats, for a total of 331, while Republican numbers shrank to 89, the lowest figure since 1891. Most of the independents—4 in the Senate and 13 in the House—usually voted with the Democrats and included such iconic former Republicans as Norris and La Follette.

Because of the seniority system, most of the key congressional committees were still controlled by largely conservative southern Democrats, but the great increase in the number of Democrats in Congress meant that southerners were a shrinking minority. During the years of Republican ascendancy after 1920, the 26 senators from the former Confederate states were an absolute majority of the Senate's Democrats; by the time the Seventy-Fifth Congress convened in January 1937, they were barely a third of the 75 Democrats in the upper chamber, though the seniority system gave them disproportionate power.

The election of 1936 was what many students of politics describe as a "transforming election" in that it made the Democratic Party the majority party in the nation for many elections to come. It welded disparate groups of voters into an effective bloc. As opposed to the mid-1920s, when Roosevelt's wartime chief, Josephus Daniels, described the Democratic Party as composed chiefly of "southerners, Catholics, and Jews, none of whom can be elected president," by 1936 what came to be called the Roosevelt Coalition retained all those traditional Democrats plus the urbanites whom Smith had drawn into the party, while adding most trade unionists, most ethnic groups and blacks, and the professoriate. If only college professors had voted in 1932, Hoover would have been reelected; a similarly restricted ballot in 1952 would have seen Adlai Stevenson defeat Dwight Eisenhower. And though Republican candidates would prevail in seven of the next fifteen presidential elections, from 1940 to 1996, the GOP controlled both houses of Congress in only two years, 1953–55, between the Roosevelt era and 1995.

The lopsided result amazed the nation and its president. In Roosevelt's first press conference after his triumphal return to Washington, the correspondents were eager to learn the Electoral College results that he had privately predicted on four occasions, which they knew had been dated and stored in a sealed envelope in his safe. Pretending reluctance because his results were "so far off," he read out his predictions: January 30: Democrats 325, Republicans 206; June 5: Democrats 315, Republicans 216; August 2: F.D.R. 340, A.M.L. 191; and November 1: F.D.R 360, A.M.L. 171. In apologizing for being so wrong, he did not point out that all four predictions were not only well below the true result, 523 to 8, but also the 1932 tally, 472–59. When asked, "What frightened you?" he replied, "Oh, just my well known conservative tendencies," evoking much laughter.[99]

In a move that his biographer says was voluntary, Rex Tugwell, who had become a major target of anti–New Deal critics, submitted his request "to be permitted to resign from the government," which Roosevelt accepted with the caveat that "later on I fully expect you to come back to render additional service."[100]

Administratively, Tugwell's Resettlement Administration lost its independent status and became a part of the Department of Agriculture, which probably would have happened in any event. Although the agency's philosophy remained the same as Will Alexander (1884–1956), a loyal Tugwell associate, was named as its new head, Secretary Wallace made it clear that collective approaches to the problem of tenancy would no longer be stressed. As had been the case with the purge of the AAA radicals, the major focus of the department would remain the nation's commercial farmers. Naturally, Tugwell's departure stimulated press and insider speculation about cabinet changes for the second term—Frances Perkins was a favorite candidate—but none would be forthcoming.[101]

Most of the time between the election and Christmas was taken up by the long cruise to Buenos Aires and back to kick off the Inter-American Peace Conference there on December 2, which is discussed in the next chapter. The trip meant that the otherwise sacrosanct Thanksgiving at Warm Springs was canceled, but the by now traditional large Roosevelt family Christmas at the White House continued, with, as the press noted, one minor innovation. After Franklin made his annual Christmas greeting to the nation and formally "lit" the national yuletide tree in Lafayette Park, Eleanor, in an activity not previously reported, "went to speak at another Christmas tree set up in an alley in Washington's Negro district."[102]

At Christmas dinner, Uncle Fred Delano, who had long been chairman of the National Capital Park and Planning Commission, handed Franklin a letter from the multimillionaire Pittsburgh magnate Andrew W. Mellon (1855–1937), who had been secretary of the treasury during the three Republican presidencies of the 1920s. Mellon not only offered the people of the United States his collection of old-master paintings, which art dealer Joseph Duveen called "the greatest ever assembled by any individual collector," but also provided money to build what became the National Gallery of Art in the nation's capital. Mellon's offer included the stipulation that the new museum not bear his name.

Roosevelt, himself a serious collector of naval prints, conferred with Attorney General Cummings and replied the next day, expressing his delight in accepting Mellon's "very wonderful offer." He said that he had long felt the need for a "national gallery of art" and, practical man that he was, noted that "your offer of an adequate building and an endowment fund means permanence in a changing world." He invited Mellon "or whoever you may care to designate [to] come to see me next week." Mellon came to the White House with his lawyer and met with the president and Cummings on the afternoon of the last day of the year. Tea was served in the library, and while various grandchildren wandered in and out, the basic details were agreed to. Roosevelt must have turned on his vaunted charm, as Mellon remarked to his lawyer on the way back to his apartment, "What a wonderfully attractive man the President is."

As gentlemen, neither party mentioned that Roosevelt's government was prosecuting Mellon for income tax delinquencies; Mellon had called it "persecution." The Department of Justice had tried, and failed, to get a criminal indictment against Mellon, but a civil suit for underpayment of his personal income tax was still in the courts. The government had asked for $3 million in back taxes and penalties. After Mellon's death, the Board of Tax Appeals ruled that he had not been guilty of fraud. A settlement reached between his lawyers and the Bureau of Internal Revenue resulted in what one Mellon biographer called a "token payment" of $644,588. The Pittsburgh millionaire had practiced strenuous tax avoidance. It was Morgenthau, not Roosevelt, who had pushed the prosecution.[103]

Much of the last weeks of the year were devoted to preparing the various documents necessary for the opening of the second term—the State of the Union message, the budget message, and the second inaugural, all of which would occur in less than a three-week span. In addition, as Roosevelt explained to the press, work on a reorganization of the government would continue. There was a small rearrangement of his personal staff. Steve Early moved into Louis Howe's old office—but did not assume his title—and the president's son Jimmy moved into Early's and was assigned Howe's former secretary. About the legislative agenda for the New Year, however, the president continued to say nothing.[104]

12 Foreign Affairs

1933–36

ROOSEVELT CAME TO THE PRESIDENCY CONVINCED THAT his immediate primary tasks were domestic, but that should not blind anyone to his long-standing fascination with foreign policy.[1] After all, not only was he the most cosmopolitan president since John Quincy Adams, but much of his postpolio prominence as an independent leader of the national Democratic Party had come as a foreign policy spokesman. As noted, the continuing negative public reactions to Wilsonian internationalism—an attitude usually called isolationism—so dominated American public opinion in the post–World War I era that Roosevelt in his quest for the presidency found it politic to reject joining the League of Nations and not to mention his support for the World Court. Whatever political damage these retreats cost him among internationalists was more than compensated for by the support they won him from William Randolph Hearst. His major biographer, Frank Freidel, argues that without those disavowals, "he probably would not have won the nomination."[2]

As opposed to the cold shoulder he turned to Hoover during the interregnum, when the defeated president tried to tie him to what Roosevelt considered failed policies, his fateful warm conversations with Hoover's secretary of state Henry L. Stimson signaled the foreign policy establishment that the president-elect remained an internationalist. Stimson was particularly pleased with Roosevelt's acceptance of the so-called Stimson doctrine of January 7, 1932, which declared that the United States would not recognize Japan's creation of a puppet regime in Manchuria and its installation there of the "last emperor," the Manchu Henry Puyi (1906–67).[3]

After a Washington leak reported that Stimson had notified European governments that the new administration would continue the policy of nonrecognition in the Far East, reporters at a press conference in his East Sixty-Fifth Street town house asked the president-elect if this was the case. Roosevelt borrowed a pencil and wrote out a one-paragraph statement for them, confirming the rumors. Stimson was so delighted that he immediately sent a copy to Ambassador Joseph C. Grew in Tokyo. The Japanese, naturally, were not pleased, while Britain and France indicated approval.[4]

On other matters, Roosevelt's responses—or, in some cases, lack of response—were less satisfactory to Stimson. The question of war debts, Roosevelt understood, was insoluble. Even before his meetings with Stimson, he had met with the representatives of both of the nation's major wartime allies. He had the British ambassador come down to Warm Springs during the Thanksgiving Day break and subsequently spoke with the French envoy about a possible arrangement to settle the war debts at some discount, but he knew that any such action would be unpopular. Most Americans agreed with President Coolidge's blunt "They hired the money, didn't they?" Nothing Roosevelt said publicly disagreed with that view. He collaborated with the arch-isolationist senator Hiram Johnson by sending amendments to the so-called Johnson Act of 1934 that barred loans to nations in default. The press regularly reopened the wound by reporting that little Finland was making its tiny annual debt payment while all other wartime borrowers remained in default.[5]

The war debts would be invoked as a reason not to become positively involved in foreign affairs right up to Pearl Harbor, and with only marginal effect after that. In 1940 Roosevelt would make sure that no such issue would arise after World War II by inventing Lend-Lease, one of the ways he improved on Wilson's wartime and postwar actions in hopes of establishing a more lasting peace.

Roosevelt gave further indication of continuity with many of his diplomatic appointments. The key post of undersecretary of state went to William Phillips (1878–1968), who had filled that post in the Harding-Coolidge administration. Phillips, Harvard '00, was in many ways typical of the striped-pants set. A rich man's son who entered the foreign service rather than his father's business, he had served under every president since the first Roosevelt and would continue into the Truman years.[6] Many other key policy makers were also kept on.

Although personnel changes throughout the rest of the federal bureaucracy during the Roosevelt era made it much more representative of the nation at large, new appointments to the foreign service remained almost entirely restricted to sons of the existing elites. Even in choosing his ambassadors, Roosevelt did not often stray far from the old orthodoxy. Many important assignments went to career men or to those who had previous diplomatic experience. Like most of his successors, Roosevelt was highly critical of the State Department bureaucracy, but he did little to change it until late in his presidency. He did appoint some liberal Democrats who had no previous connection with diplomacy. In the president's initial round of filling major slots, Robert W. Bingham (1871–1937), owner of two Louisville newspapers and an early supporter of Roosevelt's presidential candidacy, got the London embassy; history professor William E. Dodd (1869–1940), who had a degree from Leipzig, was sent to Berlin; Paris went to Jesse I. Straus of Macy's Department Store, who had business ties there and was fluent in French; and Claude G. Bowers (1878–1958), a journalist and historian who got the Madrid embassy, had no ties to Spain. All four men were, at the time of appointment, noncontroversial, as was Roosevelt's choice of William Jennings Bryan's daughter Ruth Bryan Owen, a former Democratic congress-woman, as minister to Denmark. She was the first woman named chief of mission and the only such action by Roosevelt. The most important ambassadorial holdover was career man Joseph C. Grew (1892–1965), Groton and Harvard '02, who had been named ambassador in Tokyo in 1932, knew Roosevelt, and kept his post until he came back home on the exchange ship *Gripsholm* in 1942.[7]

Roosevelt's appointment of his old chief Josephus Daniels was a very different matter. Josephus had angled for the navy again, but Roosevelt did not want a strong-minded pseudopacifist in charge of the fleet. He offered Daniels the United States Shipping Board with a mandate to expand it to include other forms of transportation. Daniels, a longtime foe of independent agencies, not only turned the job down, but suggested abolishing the board and turning its functions over to the Department of Commerce. He let it be known, through Dan Roper, that he would like to be ambassador to Mexico, which the president quickly arranged, even though Daniels would be remembered by many Mexicans as the secretary of the navy responsible for the 1914 American naval incursion that killed 195 Mexicans. Incredibly, when Daniels's wife, Addie, asked him and Roosevelt how they could even contemplate sending her and her husband to a country he had ordered bombarded, both men claimed to have forgotten it!

The Mexican government, not wishing to offend a new American president, quickly agreed to receive Daniels and tried to quiet the inevitable criticism from its opposition. But Daniels, a self-styled "shirt-sleeve diplomat," quickly overcame most Mexican resistance with his folksy, open ways and his vigorous application of the Good Neighbor policy. Among his severest critics was most of the American business community in Mexico, who felt, with some justification, that he did not put their interests first.

The impropriety of the Daniels appointment did not escape American notice. One skit at the May 1933 Gridiron Dinner invented a 1914 scene:

DANIELS (BROAD HAT, STRING TIE, ETC.): I've ordered the fleet to take Veracruz!

ROOSEVELT: Mexico will love you for that.

DANIELS: If necessary I'll march the Marines to the Halls of Montezuma.

ROOSEVELT: I can hear the Mexicans shouting "Viva Daniels!"

DANIELS: I'll drive Victoriano Huerta and the whole Mexican government out of business.

ROOSEVELT: (laughs aloud.)

DANIELS: What are you laughing about?

ROOSEVELT: I was just thinking how funny it would be if I ever get to be President and sent you as Ambassador to Mexico.

DANIELS: I can't imagine anything as funny as that ever happening.[8]

Appropriately under the circumstances, foreign affairs received short shrift in the inaugural address: as we have seen, he devoted just one long, chatty sentence to the rest of the world that included a Good Neighbor policy. Later that spring, he made what could have been a routine talk—a speech on Pan American Day—into an important statement of American policy.

The president reiterated his Good Neighbor message and insisted that the Monroe Doctrine "was and is directed at the maintenance of independence by the peoples of the [Americas and] against the acquisition . . . of additional territory in this hemisphere by any non-American power." In addition, "each Republic must recognize the independence of every other Republic." He also called for the mutual reduction of artificial barriers to trade. Spanish and Portuguese versions of the speech were recorded and distributed throughout the hemisphere. It was a far cry from both the attitude of the first Roosevelt—that the United States could exercise police power in the hemisphere—and his own position in 1920, when he boasted inaccurately about having written the Haitian constitution.[9] In none of his many references to the Good Neighbor policy did Roosevelt ever give credit to what most historians regard as its minor precursors initiated by the Coolidge and Hoover administrations in Nicaragua and Mexico.

The first significant test of the new policy began a few days later in a series of attempts to bring stability to Cuba. It had been, in effect, an American protectorate since its "independence" in 1898. The immediate problems in Cuba were economic, stemming from the collapse of the world market for Cuban sugar, and political, as the autocratic government of President Gerardo Machado (1871–1939) used increasingly repressive measures to stifle dissent. As conditions in Cuba worsened in late April, Roosevelt chose Sumner Welles (1892–1961), who would be a significant player in American diplomacy for a decade, to be his ambassador in Havana; he behaved more like a proconsul.

A Roosevelt family friend, Welles carried Eleanor's train when she and Franklin married. He was Harvard '14 and joined the State Department after scoring highest score in the 1915 foreign service examination. Initially assigned to Japan, he chose to specialize in Latin American affairs and became fluent in Spanish. Displeasure about his scandalous divorce and quick remarriage led to his resignation; he then published a critical account of American relations with the Dominican Republic,[10] which ended with an appeal for a more liberal approach to all of Latin America. Formerly a Republican, he advised Roosevelt on foreign policy as early as 1928, supported his presidential campaign, and was appointed an assistant secretary of state.

When named ambassador to Cuba three weeks later, Welles publicly disavowed any intention to pressure Machado to resign, but once there and observing the deteriorating economic and political conditions, he did just that. On July 1, Roosevelt sent a message urging conciliation, which Welles read to a conference of Cuban leaders he had organized. Following a mid-August army coup, Machado fled to Miami and was replaced by the pro-American Carlos Manuel de Céspedes, who had little support among the Cuban people. His government was toppled in less than a month by another coup, this one led by sergeants rather than generals and with the support of university students. Welles asked Washington to send in marines to restore Céspedes, but neither Hull nor Roosevelt approved. Roosevelt did send U.S. Navy and Coast Guard vessels to evacuate any endangered Americans, but there were none.

Welles's recommendation not to grant formal recognition to the replacement government of Dr. Ramón Grau San Martín was followed. Welles returned to his former post in the State Department in mid-December after what had to be considered a failed mission. The next month, the Grau San Martín government fell; the former president reported, "I fell because Washington willed it."[11]

Roosevelt had justified nonrecognition in a formal statement in late November 1933, arguing that it would be an injustice "to the Cuban people" for the United States to recognize any government that did not have "the support and approval of the people of the republic." In a note to his *Public Papers* written in 1937, Roosevelt claimed that "our government was unwilling to accord recognition to the Grau San Martin administration in Cuba because of the lack of general support of public opinion in Cuba and also because it seemed unable to maintain order or to carry out many other normal and necessary functions of government."

In his 1933 statement, the president indicated what benefits Cuba would accrue once recognition occurred. A month and a half later, Colonel Carlos Mendieta was installed as provisional president of Cuba; American recognition followed five days later.[12]

Once Roosevelt saw a government in Havana that he felt he could do business with, the reform aspects of the Good Neighbor policy began to take effect. In May a treaty renouncing the Platt Amendment was negotiated and quickly agreed to by the Senate. The Platt Amendment, initially a rider to a U.S. military appropriations bill in 1901, was included in the Cuban constitution of 1903 as the price of independence and the removal of American troops.[13] In August the first of the bilateral reciprocal trade agreements, authorized by the Trade Agreements Act of 1934, allowed a significant portion of the Cuban sugar crop to be sold in the American market by lowering the prohibitory rates imposed by the Smoot-Hawley tariff of 1930.[14]

Formal American renunciation of the right to intervene in Cuba was the crown jewel of the Good Neighbor policy, along with subsequent troop withdrawals from Haiti and the Dominican Republic. It facilitated more friendly relations with most Latin American nations and would pay dividends in the cooperation the United States received from most of them during World War II. But it had a downside, largely unremarked for a time. As it had done in Cuba, the United States recognized—and often, in the name of Pan-Americanism, hailed as democracies—cooperative regimes in such places as Nicaragua, Haiti, the Dominican Republic, and Panama; in fact, they were brutal dictatorships.

At the height of American triumphalism during and after World War II, many American historians followed the lead of the then preeminent historian of American foreign relations, Samuel Flagg Bemis: they spoke of the succession of U.S. military interventions in the hemisphere, from the Spanish-American War until the late 1920s, as the "great aberration" in American foreign policy. From the point of view of the early twenty-first century, it seems that, rather than setting a new standard, it is the period from late Coolidge to early Eisenhower, with the Roosevelt-Truman years at its center, that is the aberration. Continuing intervention, covert and overt, not only in Latin America but globally became the true norm from 1954 on.[15]

In Cuba Fulgencio Batista (1901–73), one of the sergeants who, along with university students, had helped oust the Céspedes government, became Cuba's strongman until driven out by Fidel Castro at the close of 1958. Other notorious beneficiaries of American support in the circum-Caribbean in the Roosevelt era included the Somozas in Nicaragua and the Trujillos in the Dominican Republic, both inherited from previous American administrations and remaining in power well into the Cold War era.

*   *   *

The London Economic Conference (June–July 1933) stemmed from Hoover's futile efforts, beginning in 1931, to restore financial equilibrium by international accord. Plans for the conference began in October 1932; after the election, the efforts of Hoover and Stimson persuaded Roosevelt to agree to participate. At his initiative, in early spring he held a number of insubstantial bilateral discussions with European leaders and ambassadors. The one with British prime minister Ramsay MacDonald required five brief joint statements filled with bromides claiming a unity of purpose that did not exist. Britain held to its recently established policy of not making scheduled repayments of its war debts.[16]

In mid-May, Roosevelt issued an "Appeal" for "Peace by Disarmament and for the End of Economic Chaos" to fifty-four fellow heads of state—from King Zog of Albania to King Alexander of Yugoslavia, and including President Mikhail Kalinin of the Soviet Union, which the United States did not recognize. It is extremely doubtful that Roosevelt had any real hope that his appeal, which called for the abolition of all offensive weapons, would be adopted, but it did show that he already had a pretty clear notion of what future wars might be like: "frontier forts" and other "fixed fortifications" were vulnerable to attacks by "war planes, heavy mobile artillery, land battleships called tanks, and poison gas." A little more than a month earlier, the French ambassador reported to Paris that the president had told him, "The situation is alarming. . . . Hitler is a madman. . . . *France cannot disarm now and nobody will ask her to.*"[17]

Similarly, one must doubt that Roosevelt had serious hopes for the economic conference, but he went through the motions. He sent a delegation headed by his secretary of state, though Hull was not consulted in choosing it. Roosevelt eventually put together what commentators have agreed was a weak delegation. It was based on a tactic he would employ for vital conferences during World War II, that is, involving members of Congress and other persons representing both political parties to avoid the fate of Wilson's failed postwar diplomacy. Strong leadership might have held such a delegation together, but Roosevelt did not even try to provide it, and Hull was incapable of doing so. A more prudent subordinate leader would have insisted on formal instructions or at least a brief, but Hull went off on his first diplomatic mission without either. A wiser president would not have sent an uninstructed delegation to represent the United States, and Roosevelt never did it again.

On June 14, press reports from London about the American delegation agreeing to some kind of currency stabilization set off alarm bells in Washington. Treasury Secretary Woodin made a blunt two-paragraph statement that "such reports cannot be founded in fact," because any such proposal "would have to be submitted to the President and to the Treasury. . . . [A]ny agreement on this subject will be reached in Washington, not elsewhere." The statement was released by the White House, so it should have been a warning to Hull that he was in very deep waters.

Roosevelt was just tidying up after the adjournment of the hundred-days Congress and was soon off on his vacation cruise to Campobello. At this point, Raymond Moley, who had been foisted on Hull as an assistant secretary of state and left behind in Washington, enters the story. Moley, his ego inflated by his sudden prominence, infuriated Hull as he stepped out from behind the scenes and thrust himself into the public eye. Roosevelt allowed him to report personally aboard *Amberjack II*. Moley could have done so unobtrusively, but he came, in full view of the correspondents covering Roosevelt's cruise, via navy seaplane and destroyer, had a brief talk with the president, and was soon off to the London conference with a message from Roosevelt. Although the message he carried was routine, he encouraged press speculation that he was sent to save the conference.

Actually, Roosevelt, as he had told his last prevacation press conference off the record, planned to send Moley to London as his cousin Warren Delano Robbins returned. Robbins sent reports directly to Roosevelt, and Moley would do the same. Such irregular procedures were par for the course for Roosevelt, part of his much-deplored administrative style. The style was messy, and it drove some subordinates, like Hull and Ickes, to distraction. But it worked for Roosevelt and for wise subordinates, like Frances Perkins, who understood it. Complaining about it was about as useful as complaining about the weather. One of the important aspects of Roosevelt's style was that it usually ensured that he got a broader range of opinions, which would not have been the case if everything came to him through bureaucratic channels. In foreign affairs, he relished his personal communications with many key ambassadors. The important thing to remember is that in the final analysis, Roosevelt got more accomplished in less time than any other president.

Moley sailed to London on June 21 "to aid London delegates," as he told the press, and was so eager to be there that when the liner docked temporarily in Northern Ireland, he got off and took a plane to London on the twenty-seventh. Once there he chose to stay in the embassy rather than at the hotel with Hull and the delegation and insisted on meeting privately with the British prime minister, which outraged an already angry Hull. The delegation continued to struggle ineffectively to get something accomplished. Then on July 3, in a message fired from the radio shack of the cruiser *Indianapolis*, Roosevelt sank the conference, although he later tasked Hull with keeping it going for a time in a doomed effort to avoid having the United States blamed for its collapse.[18]

Roosevelt's message, often called a "bombshell," made it clear that he regarded the efforts toward merely temporary monetary adjustments, rather than working for "permanent financial stability and a greater prosperity to the masses of all Nations," as a "catastrophe." He saw the direction of the conference as "an excuse for the continuation of the basic economic errors that underlie so much of the present world-wide depression"—in other words, the same old order he had been struggling against at home. The message meant that he would continue the policies of inflation and currency manipulation that he had been pursuing since he took charge, which had also raised the domestic price of agricultural products.

Roosevelt's own postmortem on the conference came in a press conference when he gave an extended account "off the record." "They . . . seek to have us enter into something which is not really on the agenda at all—an agreement between five or six nations out of the sixty-six present to set up some kind of fund temporarily to control the exchange fluctuation [which would obligate us] to let down the bars on the export of gold that we have in this country. Well, we are not willing to do that at this time."

Roosevelt omitted from his account any mention of the necessity, from his point of view, of retaining his ability to inflate—or, as he would put it, reflate—the currency and raise prices. Readers familiar with the monetary history of World War II will recognize that the kinds of international control that Roosevelt rejected in 1933 were at the heart of the 1944 Bretton Woods agreements.

Most Americans were probably pleased to see their president tell off European leaders, but conventional elite opinion, at home and abroad, saw the president's actions as irresponsible. A few Europeans, including John Maynard Keynes, hailed Roosevelt's stance as an effective break with old failed policies, and Roosevelt's prestige continued to grow. But most sophisticated observers probably agreed with the French journalist who described the conference even before its demise as an "interminable comedy."[19]

* * *

Whatever problems Hull had helped to create in London, he and the State Department were crucial elements in the events that seemed, almost magically, to transform the image of the United States in much of Latin America that made the presidential visit to Colombia in 1934 such a public relations success.[20] Somewhat to the surprise of both the president and the State Department, the Pan-American Conference in Montevideo in December 1933 was a clear success for American policy, a success attributable both to the effects of the Good Neighbor policy and to the earnest efforts of Cordell Hull. Ironically, the secretary had wanted to cancel the conference, but Roosevelt insisted it be held. Hull, a petulant man much given to complaining, had been upset that in the rush of the hundred days, there had been no time for legislation authorizing bilateral trade treaties and furious about his humiliation in London. He had taken to complaining to intimates about "that man . . . who never tells me anything." While literally untrue, this reflected the fact that Hull and his bureaucratic department were never the only source of diplomatic advice and often were out of the loop on important matters that Roosevelt arrogated to himself or outsourced. In addition, Sumner Welles and others among Hull's subordinates had regular direct access to the president.[21]

But once the decision had been made to go to Montevideo, Hull persuaded the president that even though trade treaties could not yet be negotiated, it was good policy for him to talk them up. Hull worked very hard to ingratiate himself, personally calling on each delegation. He thus made striking contrast to the austere Charles Evans Hughes, his predecessor at the previous conference in 1928, who had the task of defending the interventionism that was then still U.S. policy. Roosevelt publicly gave Hull credit for his efforts. He seems to have decided that Hull could be effective in minor league diplomacy in the Americas, if not on the vaunted scene of Europe. All in all, the conference, which reemphasized the pledges of respect for the sovereignty of other republics in the hemisphere, contributed to the success of the Good Neighbor policy and helped to create a positive atmosphere.

* * *

The recognition of the Soviet Union was an example of the unorthodox diplomacy that Roosevelt loved. He had wanted to initiate relations with the USSR from the beginning of his administration and largely conducted the negotiations himself in Washington. In the spring of 1933, he bypassed the State Department and began to explore possibilities by having Morgenthau speak with Soviet representatives at Amtorg, the New York–based trading company that handled what little commerce there was between the two countries, but the effort came to naught. One comment, reported by Morgenthau in his "diary," could serve as an epigraph for all of Roosevelt's personal diplomacy: "If I could only, myself, talk to some one man representing the Russians, I could straighten out this whole question." This extreme self-confidence never left him, and he would, eventually, in 1943 and 1945, talk to that one man.

In the fall, informal negotiations continued with Morgenthau, now seconded by William C. Bullitt (1891–1967), who had been sent to Moscow by Woodrow Wilson in early 1919. He was an old friend of Roosevelt's who had supported and advised him during the 1932 campaign. Roosevelt placed him in the State Department as an assistant to Hull; unlike Moley, Bullitt, while also reporting directly to Roosevelt, made himself useful to Hull. Part of Hull's staff at the London Economic Conference, he met with Soviet foreign minister Maxim Litvinov (1876–1951) on routine conference business and learned that Boris Skvirsky, who headed a Soviet information office in Washington, could provide what is now known as a back channel. Roosevelt had Morgenthau and Bullitt meet with Skvirsky, who assured them that discussions would be welcomed. On October 10, Roosevelt formally invited Soviet president Kalinin to send a representative to discuss "outstanding questions." A week later, Kalinin accepted, saying that he would send Litvinov to conduct negotiations. Three days later, Roosevelt made the exchange of letters public.[22]

Meanwhile, Roosevelt had informal talks with Father Edmund A. Walsh (1885–1956), a Jesuit priest who had founded the School of Foreign Service at Georgetown University. Walsh, a major foreign affairs spokesman for American Catholicism, gave a kind of imprimatur for recognition after Roosevelt assured him that he would get from the Soviets some concessions on religious freedom. A State Department survey of newspaper opinion confirmed what Roosevelt had assumed: there was little opposition to recognition and much support for it. Hull came to approve recognition, and the State Department prepared for a long period of negotiations.

Litvinov arrived in Washington on November 7. After two days of conferences with the State Department that went nowhere, he made it clear that he wanted to negotiate with Roosevelt. After all, Bullitt had told Skvirsky that whoever negotiated would "sit down with the President of the United States." Litvinov would not want to report to Stalin that he had settled for less than that.[23]

Roosevelt and Litvinov met three times for a total of nearly nine hours over six days. The crucial breakthrough came after the first hour, in which Litvinoff agreed to consider topics he had refused to consider at the State Department the day before. Roosevelt then said he wanted to have a "man-to-man" talk with the Russian alone, so he "could call Mr. Litvinoff names if he wanted to" and hoped that Litvinov would do the same. At a cabinet meeting later, Roosevelt gave a spirited account of the private meeting, knowing that it would be told and retold. According to one version, Roosevelt began by telling Litvinov that "every man in his deepest heart knows the existence of God.... You know, Max, your good old father and mother, pious Jewish people, always said their prayers. I know they must have taught you to say prayers.... Now you may think you're an atheist [but] when you come to die ... you're going to be thinking about what your mother and father taught you." The president reported that "Max was red as a beet" from embarrassment, but the tough old Bolshevik may simply have been trying to contain his laughter. After a few more hours of meetings, the deal was sealed, as the two principals signed the several documents a little before one in the morning of November 17; the Russian had been in the United States less than ten full days.[24]

Roosevelt, in announcing the agreement, had refrained from comment, but on his way to Warm Springs for Thanksgiving, he told a Savannah audience that the "most impelling motive" for the agreement was "the desire of both countries for peace."[25]

What, objectively, had been accomplished and what was its significance? The sixteen-year hiatus in relations was ended. Both nations agreed not to interfere in each other's domestic affairs or harbor those seeking the overthrow of either government. The USSR promised to permit Americans in the Soviet Union the right to exercise religion and to give consular officials access to imprisoned Americans. The Soviets also agreed not to ask for reparations for what American troops had done during their post–World War I incursion into Siberia. A verbal gentlemen's agreement that the USSR would make at least a token payment on the czarist war debt to the United States was like so many such, not kept.

Each of the parties had unmet expectations. Roosevelt had hopes for economic gains from greatly increased trade, but they were chimerical. Bullitt, who went to Moscow as the first American ambassador to the USSR, soon became frustrated by broken promises and was totally disillusioned well before the end of his mission in 1936. The Soviets felt that recognition of the United States might reduce the likelihood of a Japanese armed expansion into Siberia and increase the likelihood of effective collective security on their western front, but eventually they had to fight Japan in inner Asia in 1938–39, and their hopes of collective security in the West collapsed after the 1938 Munich agreement.[26] The historical consensus has been that, in 1933 and for years afterward, recognition was no big deal. But in 1941, after the German invasion of the Soviet Union, the fact that normal diplomatic relations existed facilitated the delivery of armaments and other aid to the USSR.

The American public's reaction to recognition was muted. A few, like Representative Hamilton Fish (R-NY), whose district included Hyde Park, predicted dire results, but only after the Liberty League began to attack Roosevelt as "communistic" did recognition figure in the charges made by other zealots. It produced much more negative discussion during the Cold War than there was while Roosevelt was alive, but the deal worked out in 1933 remained in place. And despite the obvious lesson that such relations could be useful even with a seemingly implacable foe, a similar inflexible nonrecognition policy was in effect toward the People's Republic of China from its creation in 1949 until Richard Nixon used a back channel arranged by Henry Kissinger to visit China in 1972 and jump-start a major policy shift, although full recognition did not come until the Carter administration. In this one regard, Nixon was more Roosevelt's heir than Truman, Kennedy, or Lyndon Johnson.

* * *

Philippine independence seemed a settled matter by the time Roosevelt took power. It had been supported in every Democratic Party platform since 1920, and in the lame-duck session during the interregnum an independence bill passed Congress. After Hoover vetoed it, there was enough bipartisan support to override it. But the bill required the concurrence of the Philippine Congress, which rejected the terms offered on October 17, 1933. A major complaint was the retention, after independence, of military and naval bases in the islands by the United States. When the U.S. Congress reconvened in January 1934, its leaders, resentful about the rejection, told Filipino commissioners that there would be no time to reconsider independence that year. But Roosevelt, who had debated in favor of independence as a Groton schoolboy, and his new governor-general, Frank Murphy, were both independence advocates.

By March 2, 1934, having worked out details with congressional leaders, Roosevelt sent a message to Congress recommending that the military bases be relinquished simultaneously with the accomplishment of independence and that the status of the naval bases be settled later by mutual agreement. The subsequent Tydings-McDuffie Act, enacted and signed in just over three weeks, provided for a commonwealth form of self-government for ten years to be followed by independence. The Philippine Congress accepted the act, and a convention wrote a constitution that Roosevelt approved in March 1935. He pretended that relations between Americans and Filipinos had always been friendly and of mutual benefit, a myth he repeated at Notre Dame in December 1935. The transition to independence was more rapid that that of any other colonial power in Asia.[27] In the event, of course, independence had to be delayed because of the invasion and occupation of the Philippines by Japan during World War II.

* * *

Roosevelt's continuing support for what can be called "antiwar measures" not only was designed to cater to the isolationist bloc of politicians, including many western progressives of both parties who were strong supporters of most of his New Deal programs, but also represented his sincere desire for peace. But unlike perhaps a majority of Americans, he was never prepared to say that American entry into World War I had been a mistake. And in the first months of his administration, he resumed a naval construction building program that aimed to reach the limits imposed by the multilateral treaties of the 1920s that the United States had signed.[28]

The search for peace took many forms. Its first important manifestation was the Good Neighbor policy and its promotion of the peaceful settlement of hemispheric disputes. More challenging were Roosevelt's always careful dealings with the politically potent American peace movement, which at its height in the 1930s claimed twelve million adherents and an audience, largely through religious organizations, of nearly half the American population. The political point person for the movement was Dorothy Detzer (1893–1981), executive secretary of the American section of the Women's International League for Peace and Freedom and a most effective Washington lobbyist. She and others had been trying since early in the Hoover administration to get a congressional investigation of munitions makers whose activities, many then felt, had been instrumental in American intervention in World War I.[29] She finally succeeded in persuading Senator Gerald P. Nye (1892–1971), a North Dakota Republican with a Non-Partisan League background who, like many other progressive Republican westerners, had supported most of Roosevelt's New Deal, to introduce a resolution in February 1934 calling for an investigation. It was combined with another pending resolution by a more conservative midwestern Republican senator, Michigan's Arthur H. Vandenberg (1884–1951), which supported a "take the profits out of war" proposal sponsored by the American Legion. The new resolution, offered by Nye, in April gained Senate approval without debate or recorded vote. It called for an investigation of all aspects of the munitions industry and authorized Congress to consider a government monopoly in the manufacture of munitions.[30] Nye received help from the administration, and without publicity the State Department's expert on the munitions trade, Joseph Green, was delegated to advise the committee, which started work in September.

In May Roosevelt quickly got on the right side of the issue, sending a message, drafted by Green, to the Senate reporting his "gratification" that the inquiry was afoot. He pointed out that a convention for supervising the arms trade had been signed in 1925 and was still pending in the Senate and recommended that it be approved. He denounced the "mad race in armament" as a "grave menace to peace" and supported the "supervision and control of the merchants of the engines of destruction."

Roosevelt was taking advantage of the current fascination with the conspiratorial notion that not governments but international arms dealers, "merchants of death," were the real threat to peace, a notion that the Nye Committee's often sensational hearings emphasized during its eighteen-month headline-grabbing investigation. The president encouraged the committee by meeting with its members more than once and ensuring that it had the cooperation and support of the State Department and other executive branch agencies.[31]

In December 1934, he went so far as to support publicly one of the more quixotic proposals of the peace movement, using words in a press conference that sounded strange coming from one who had been an early war hawk in the Wilson administration.

> Those of us who served in the World War know that we got into the war in a great hurry . . . and did a lot of things we should not have done. . . .
>
> We have decided that the time has come when legislation to take the profit out of war should be enacted. . . . Everybody in the country knows what munitions profits meant during the World War. Not only our country but the world as a whole is pretty thoroughly alive to these profits of munitions makers in time of war and in time of peace.

He went on to say that he expected to send a message to Congress "on this general subject."

It developed that the president had not been well briefed or perhaps had not fully absorbed the briefing papers. A better-informed reporter pointed out:

> Q: You have a complete report on this line as a result of the report of the War Planning Commission. Will that serve as a basis?
> THE PRESIDENT: I don't know that.
> Q: They studied it here for about two years and brought out a very exhaustive report.
> THE PRESIDENT: I have got to confess, off the record, that I never heard of it.[32]

He must have learned later that day that his Quaker predecessor had appointed a War Policies Commission—six cabinet officers, four senators, and four representatives—to study the promotion of peace, the equalization of the burdens of war, and the minimization of war profits. Its March 1932 report to Congress called for a constitutional amendment empowering wartime Congresses to stabilize prices and to tax war profits—defined as profits in excess of average profits for three years before the war—at a 95 percent rate.[33] The report was, almost literally, never heard of again until the reports of Roosevelt's press conference were published.[34] The proposed message to Congress was never sent. When war did come, its profits resuscitated American capitalism after Roosevelt had taken it off life support.

Clearly, in 1934 and later, Roosevelt was anxious not to seem to be out of touch with the broad swath of American opinion that, in reaction to the slaughter in the trenches, opposed war and preparation for war. There is some justice in the judgment of Wayne Cole, the sympathetic historian of American isolationism, speaking not of the evanescent proposal just discussed but of the investigations of the Nye Committee and the constituencies that it represented: "The attitudes, interests, and strength that the [Nye Committee] represented were more formidable than President Roosevelt was prepared to challenge head-on during his first term in the White House."[35]

But it should also be noted that just at that time—December 1934—aggressive signals were being received from both Europe and Asia. The more immediately disturbing were the beginnings of what became, in October, the Italo-Ethiopian War of 1934–35. The other, Japan's formal notice that at the end of 1936 it would renounce the existing naval limitation treaties of 1922 and 1930, was, in retrospect, the more important. Both helped to focus American attention on neutrality legislation, which would be central to foreign policy debates until the attack on Pearl Harbor made it irrelevant.

In 1935, as the neutrality debates took center stage, interest in the Nye Committee waned. As what turned out to be its last set of hearings—an investigation into the wartime activities of J. P. Morgan and Company—was winding down in mid-January 1936, Nye himself, in an unwise speech on the Senate floor, denounced Wilson and his secretary of state for claiming that they had not known about the secret treaties between the European allies until after the United States entered the war: "Both the President and Secretary Lansing falsified." Although Congress had repudiated Wilsonian objectives, such language directed at a revered former president was considered impermissible, and Nye lost so much status that further funding of the committee's activities became impossible. The committee quickly published a long report and went out of business. No legislation resulted from its inquiries. It had raised public consciousness and, unlike many congressional investigations, had been conducted with decorum and essential fairness, though Nye and others had made reckless and inaccurate predictions in Congress and elsewhere about what the inquiry would reveal.

As internationalism became the leitmotiv of American foreign policy during World War II and after, the Nye Committee became a convenient whipping boy for both defenders and attackers of Roosevelt's policies. President Truman, for example, in his *Memoirs,* wrote that the "committee made it appear that the munitions manufacturers had caused World War I, and as a result the Neutrality Act was passed." As a senator, however, he had found the committee's reports useful in preparing for his investigation of wartime industry, which was his chief claim to fame before 1944. During the Cold War, Whittaker Chambers testified in 1949, apparently falsely, that Alger Hiss, a committee legal assistant who had been a minor participant in sixteen of ninety-three hearings, had used that position to gain access to classified State Department documents, which he copied and passed on to the USSR. Ironically, the Nye Committee's most lasting contribution was that its hearings and subsequent report put a quietus to the misconception on which it was based: that the "merchants of death" had caused World War I. By 1938, at the height of the struggles over neutrality, "what everyone in the country" had known in 1934 no longer figured significantly in the debates.[36]

Roosevelt's 1935 annual message devoted only five sentences to foreign affairs, but for the first time included a negative comment about the state of the world—"I cannot with candor tell you that general relationships outside the United States are improved"—but it was quickly coupled with an assurance that there was "no ground for apprehension that our relations with any Nation will be other than peaceful."[37]

In a small step toward internationalism, Roosevelt finally decided to act on American membership on the World Court,[38] which had been pending since Hoover submitted it to the Senate in December 1930. Roosevelt had instructed the Senate leadership not to act in 1933 and 1934, but at the beginning of the 1935 session, after a meeting that included Hull and key senators, he decided to move for its ratification. After the membership treaty had reached the Senate floor with a positive recommendation from the Foreign Affairs Committee, Roosevelt asked the Senate to give its consent so that "the United States has an opportunity once more to throw its weight into the scale in favor of peace." After acrimonious debate, the measure failed by a vote of fifty-two to thirty-six, seven votes short of the necessary two-thirds; twenty Democratic senators voted no, as did the western progressives who usually supported Roosevelt's proposals. Conversely, he had the support of many conservative eastern Republicans. It was widely believed that a blizzard of forty thousand telegrams instigated by Father Coughlin and the Hearst newspapers opposing approval had been crucial in the measure's defeat. Three days earlier, Senate leaders on both sides of the aisle had predicted acceptance. Roosevelt, still angry a day after his defeat, wrote thanking Joe Robinson for his efforts and said of the "36 gentlemen" who refused their consent: "I am inclined to think that ~~when~~ if they ever get to Heaven ~~or go the other way whichever it may be~~, they will be doing a lot of apologizing ~~for a good many centuries~~—that is if God is against war—and I think He is."[39]

Ten days later, in a private postmortem to ninety-year-old Elihu Root, the Republican elder statesman who had labored long for American membership, the president explained that "as the check-up on votes progressed we thought we should win, but we had at all times twelve or fourteen Senators who would not commit themselves. . . . The deluge of letters, telegrams, Resolutions of Legislatures, and the radio talks of people like Coughlin turned the trick against us."

He did not comment on the fact that he had not, himself, made any effort to arouse the public. It was his first major defeat in Congress since the bonus vote had gone against him, and there was no way to veto the Senate's turndown.[40]

The defeat made him even charier about foreign policy initiatives that required congressional action. For a time, as had been the case with the Johnson Act in 1934, he let Congress take the initiative while he reacted.

Although neutrality legislation had been debated in Congress as early as the hundred days, none would be enacted until mid-1935 when an Italian invasion of Ethiopia seemed imminent.[41] By that time, a growing revisionist consensus among many if not most historians and public intellectuals held that American entry into World War I had been an error; some argued that an improved legal definition of neutrality and American neutral rights could prevent involvement in future foreign conflicts. Walter Millis's best-selling, oversimplified account, *The Road to War* (1935), exemplified what had become an article of unfaith for millions of Americans.[42]

The passage of four neutrality acts—one each in 1935, 1936, 1937, and 1939—laid down limitations on national action that, had they been in place, might well have prevented American entry into the war that Europe blundered into during the summer of 1914 and the United States entered in 1917. They were largely irrelevant to the conditions that prevailed after Hitler went to war in September 1939, but they placed certain limits on presidential action before December 7, 1941, that tested the president's ability to operate within the limits of the law. By the time of the first neutrality act, Roosevelt, more than any of his counterparts in the other Western democracies, was alive to the threat that Hitler presented, though this was not yet apparent from his public statements.

Despite his claims, then and later, of a "consistent . . . clear policy" about neutrality, Roosevelt's words about it reflected a consistent ambiguity. It stemmed from the tensions inherent between his closet internationalism and his notions about the domestic dangers of revealing too much of his real foreign policy views. In 1935 he would clearly have preferred to have no neutrality legislation so as to allow him freedom of action. But, faced with a significant demand from Congress and the public for some kind of legislation, he instructed Assistant Secretary of State Phillips and others dealing with Congress in late July to work for legislation that would permit him, if he wished, to discriminate between aggressors and victims. This the isolationist bloc on the Senate Foreign Affairs Committee would not accept, and the president reluctantly acquiesced. He rationalized that, in the only likely new conflict on the horizon, there would be no practical way to send help to Ethiopia, whose limited access to the outside world could easily be blocked by Italian forces. He thus approved a bill that left him no real options in case of war. It is interesting that neither Roosevelt nor his isolationist opponents thought much about neutrality legislation in terms of the conflict in East Asia. Attention was riveted on Europe, and Asian wars seemed unlikely to involve the United States.

The 1935 act's basic provision was that once a president proclaimed that a state of war existed, Americans could no longer export arms, munitions, and implements of war to belligerents, nor could American vessels carry them to belligerents. In approving it, Roosevelt explained that he was signing because its purpose—avoiding war—was "wholly excellent," but since "no Congress and no Executive can foresee all possible future situations," its very inflexibility might "drag us into a war instead of keeping us out." Pointing out that much of the legislation expired in six months, he called for further study and clarification.[43]

When the expected Italian invasion came on October 3, 1935, Roosevelt was aboard the USS *Houston,* fishing in the Pacific. The appropriate proclamation of neutrality was drafted and issued by the State Department, as were subsequent warnings from the president that Americans who traveled on vessels of either belligerent or made transactions of any character with them did so "at his/ their own risk." Since the three wire-service reporters covering him were on an accompanying vessel, the president had a brief radio message sent to them for guidance in filing their stories.[44]

Roosevelt's annual message in 1936 for the first time took detailed notice of the state of the world as well as that of the nation. He insisted that, if the world was in fact again on the verge of another era of conflict, "The United States and the rest of the Americas can play but one role: through a well-ordered neutrality to do naught to encourage the contest, through adequate defense to save ourselves from embroilment and attack, and through example and all legitimate encouragement and assistance to persuade other Nations to return to the ways of peace and good-will."

But the disconnect between this statement of one of the classic themes of American isolationism, sometimes called a Fortress America policy, and Roosevelt's overall approach is jarring. The declaration failed to convince isolationist leaders, particularly since the president immediately followed it with a sentence more consistent with what most scholars are convinced were his true beliefs: "The evidence before us clearly proves that autocracy in world affairs endangers peace and that such threats do not spring from those Nations devoted to the democratic ideal." Logically, that sentence should have led to a discussion of policies to support democracy abroad, but instead Roosevelt moved on to safer political ground by using it to attack "a power seeking minority" within the United States.[45]

The war in Ethiopia was proceeding toward the inevitable Italian victory. Roosevelt, realizing that Italian imports of American oil at triple the prewar rate in the last months of 1935, unaffected by the expiring law, were fueling Mussolini's war machine, had a bill drafted in the State Department adding two new provisions to the exiting expiring statute: barring loans to belligerent governments and authorizing the president to limit exports of essential war materials other than armaments (such as oil and scrap iron) to "normal quantities." Two competing measures by isolationists in Congress opposed one or the other of those new provisions. A stalemate resulted, and no new bill passed. Instead, the old law was reenacted as the Neutrality Act of 1936, adding only the provision prohibiting American loans to belligerents and a new expiry date of May 1, 1937. Roosevelt's signing statement expressed his regret that the broader prohibition had not been adopted, and he renewed a previous exhortation that Americans in trading with belligerents not "give aid to the continuance of war," an exhortation he knew would fall largely on deaf ears.[46]

Throughout 1936 the news from Europe grew more menacing. In March Hitler smashed what was left of the Versailles Treaty's restrictions on Germany by a military reoccupation of the Rhineland, increasing fears of a European war. In mid-July, the Spanish Civil War broke out, creating another challenge for American neutrality since the act contained no provisions applicable to civil wars. Traditional diplomatic usage called for nonrecognition of any such rebellion until after it had gained at least de facto control of a government and its institutions. Had Roosevelt and Hull wished to pursue such a policy, they could have cited in support the protests of Lincoln and Seward when Great Britain recognized the belligerency of the Confederacy early in the American Civil War. But the State Department was concentrating on avoiding any action that might embroil the United States in European hostilities, and Roosevelt took no initiative. Also a factor—never mentioned by the State Department or the president—in what was a failure to support the Spanish Republic was the hostility of American Catholics toward the Madrid government's conflicts with the Spanish Catholic hierarchy.

Roosevelt's first public comments came nine days after the war began in a brief press conference at Campobello as he ended his summer cruise there. Asked about Spain, he merely referred reporters to Secretary Hull's statement in the newspapers that, for the moment, the department was concentrating on the safety of Americans in Spain. After about a month, the State Department let it be known that it had declared a "moral embargo" in letters to "munitions makers," asking them not to send shipments to either side in the Spanish conflict: the most important letter had resulted from an inquiry by the Glenn Martin aircraft firm asking about an order for planes it had received from the Spanish government; as a result, it declined to fill the order. Roosevelt, who had approved sending the letters on August 10, made it clear, in an off-the-record press conference at Hyde Park, that this was his policy.[47]

Thus, in effect, the United States had recognized the rebellion led by a then obscure Spanish general, Francisco Franco (1892–1975), and denied to the legitimate, freely elected government of Spain the right to purchase arms in the United States. This fell into line with the policy of "nonintervention" being promulgated by the British government. In later years, conventional wisdom often ascribed great significance to the Spanish Civil War as a rehearsal of sorts for World War II, but at the time most Americans who thought about it in 1936 feared that, somehow, any involvement with it could ensnare the United States in another European war.

Perhaps the best way to understand Roosevelt's views at the time is to look at his speech at Chautauqua, New York, four days after his approval of the moral embargo. Clearly, the Chautauqua speech was part of his reelection efforts, but since his words and his deeds are coordinate, they should be taken seriously. In putting together his speech, planned long before the war in Spain began, Roosevelt resisted requests that he talk specifically about the war. But immediately after its most famous and parodied passage—"I have seen war . . . I hate war"—he declared: "I have passed unnumbered hours, I shall pass unnumbered hours, thinking and planning how war may be kept from this Nation. I wish I could keep war from all Nations; but that is beyond my power. I can at least make certain that no act of the United States helps to produce or to promote war. I can at least make clear that the conscience of America revolts against war and that any Nation which provokes war forfeits the sympathy of the people of the United States."[48]

Congress had not been in session when the Spanish Civil War began, so, perhaps to avoid even more extensive congressional action, his 1937 annual message asked Congress to add to the existing Neutrality Act provisions covering "specific points raised by the unfortunate civil strife in Spain." The administration's bill wrote Roosevelt's moral embargo into law but made it applicable only to the Spanish conflict. It passed both houses that day, unanimously in the Senate and with just one dissenting vote in the House.[49] Roosevelt's most extensive contemporary public defense of his Spanish policy came in a letter to Norman Thomas at the end of January, responding to the Socialist leader's criticisms. The president argued that "the civil conflict in Spain involves so many non-Spanish elements and has such wide international implications that a policy of attempting to discriminate between the parties would be dangerous in the extreme."[50]

Although Franklin Roosevelt would by his later actions well earn the accolade that James Macgregor Burns has given him, "the Soldier of Freedom," the president who could describe the main object of his foreign policy as assuring that "no act of the United States helps to produce or to promote war" was not yet that warrior.

Another event in the second half of 1936 that increased concerns about war was the establishment through bilateral treaties of the so-called Berlin-Rome-Tokyo Axis—though the signatories called it the Anti-Comintern Pact and claimed that it was directed only against the Soviet Union. In discussions with advisers and in internal documents, Roosevelt would soon be referring to the three "bandit powers," but for a time these sentiments were not shared with the public.

*   *   *

In the weeks after his triumphant reelection, Roosevelt concentrated on the Western Hemisphere, the one region in which he could claim significant foreign policy success. In addition to the renunciation of the Platt Amendment and other Cuban developments, the State Department had completed reciprocal trade agreements with Brazil, Colombia, Haiti, and Honduras and was in the process of negotiating pacts with nine other American nations. A new 1936 treaty with Panama relinquished the right of unilateral American intervention imposed in 1903 and gave Panama some of the responsibility for defending the Panama Canal and, more important, a larger share of the profits from its operation.

The only aspect of Roosevelt's Latin American policies that created significant domestic political problems was his refusal to criticize actions of the Mexican government in its long-standing dispute with the Catholic Church in Mexico that had opposed the Mexican Revolution from its outset in 1909. Protests by some American Catholics, led by Martin H. Carmody (1872–1950), grand knight of the Knights of Columbus, opened a public dispute between him and the president, with Roosevelt defending his policy in a 1935 public letter. After noting that the right of Americans overseas to be able to worship freely was desirable and stating that the past year had seen no complaint by an American citizen in Mexico about restrictions there, he reaffirmed that "I decline to permit this government to undertake a policy of interference in the domestic concerns of foreign governments and thereby jeopardize the maintenance of peaceful conditions." The issue was taken up by some of Roosevelt's political opponents, including Al Smith and Protestant senator William E. Borah (R-ID), who introduced a resolution calling for withdrawal of diplomatic recognition from Mexico. The public embrace of Roosevelt by Cardinal Mundelein some months later had this dispute as one of its hidden but understood subtexts.[51]

Since at least early 1935, Roosevelt had wanted to stabilize relations between the American republics but had decided that it would be appropriate to wait until the end of the Chaco War of 1932–35 between Bolivia and Paraguay in which perhaps one hundred thousand were killed. At the end of January 1936, Roosevelt suggested to all the other republics what became the Inter-American Peace Conference in Buenos Aires in December 1936. As late as mid-September, Roosevelt told reporters that he would not go, but immediately after the election he said that he would. This meant that the almost sacrosanct Thanksgiving visit to Warm Springs would be canceled and that Vice President Garner would be in Washington rather than at his Texas ranch.[52]

Those who remember only the era of *Air Force One* have difficulty comprehending what an undertaking Roosevelt's trip to Buenos Aires was. The twenty-eight-day, twelve-thousand-mile voyage was, by far, the longest trip taken by a sitting president. It involved a three-vessel flotilla plus an airborne relay system to get crucial papers needing signature to the president. Roosevelt took no political advisers with him aboard the USS *Indianapolis:* his personal party consisted of son James and one of his friends; two military aides, Colonel Watson and Captain Paul Bastedo; and his physician Ross McIntire. Secretarial duties would be taken care of by a navy yeoman. The three wire-service reporters aboard the escorting cruiser USS *Chester* had to depend on radioed reports from the president's vessel for most of their "news."[53]

His South American itinerary put him in three capitals: Rio de Janeiro, Buenos Aires, and Montevideo, with a formal and an informal address in each. At Rio he was welcomed by Brazil's president, Getulio Vargas (1883–1954), with whom he rode in an open car through streets lined with flowers, flags, and three hundred thousand enthusiastic citizens shouting "Viva la democracia! Viva Roosevelt!" Franklin wrote Eleanor later that when Vargas told him during the ride that "perhaps you have heard that I am a dictator," he responded that it had been said of him as well. Locals were impressed that both men wore business suits rather than formal dress or uniforms.

In all of his formal addresses, Roosevelt stressed the twin themes of the Good Neighbor policy in general and Western Hemisphere peace in particular. After being introduced at a ceremonial joint session of the Brazilian Congress and its Supreme Court as "the Man—the fearless and generous man who is accomplishing and living the most thrilling experience of modern times," Roosevelt began by describing his "first introduction to Brazil": "Nearly half a century ago a little boy was walking with his mother and father in a park of a city in Southern France. Toward them came a distinguished looking elderly couple— Dom Pedro II and his Empress."[54]

After some flattery about Rio—"A visit—even of a single day—is one of the outstanding experiences of my life"—Roosevelt moved on to his main theme, insisting that "the more firmly peace is established in this hemisphere . . . the better it will be for all the rest of the world." He urged that, having learned "the glories of independence, let each one of us learn the glories of interdependence." In the more relaxed format of a banquet in his honor, he remarked that "two people . . . invented the New Deal—the President of Brazil and the President of the United States." Writing to Eleanor, he observed that "I really believe that the moral effect of the Good Neighbor Policy is making itself definitely felt."[55]

The reception in Buenos Aires was even more spectacular. President Augustín Justo met him at the foot of the gangplank and enfolded him in an *abrazo,* smothering Roosevelt's planned Spanish-language greeting so that only his "Mi amigo" could be heard. They then traveled in an open car through the city with ten thousand soldiers posted along the way and before crowds of perhaps two million. A dinner with Cordell Hull and the other members of the U.S. delegation ended his day.[56]

When the president was awakened the next morning, he learned that after he had gone to bed, his bodyguard Gus Gennerich had died of a heart attack in a local café. Shaken by the loss of the fifty-year-old former New York City policeman who had not only been his bodyguard since being assigned to him during his first campaign for governor in 1928, but often assisted the president in bathing, dressing, and dozens of other ways, Roosevelt canceled most of the day's scheduled events. He arranged for a brief funeral service at the embassy, conducted by the *Indianapolis*'s chaplain. Writing to Eleanor the next day, he asked her to arrange for a second service in the East Room, explaining that Gus's body would come back with him.[57]

But he did make a brief appearance in the embassy's garden to greet three hundred pupils from the local American school and held a Roosevelt-style press conference for local reporters before driving with his host and an escort of just two motorcycles. Another large crowd awaited them in the square before the Congressional Palace.[58] Roosevelt's opening address, while praising peace in the Americas, spoke of the armaments race and the dangers of war elsewhere: "The madness of a great war in other parts of the world would affect us and threaten our good in a hundred ways. And the economic collapse of any Nation or Nations must of necessity harm our own prosperity. Can we, the Republics of the New World, help the Old World to avert the catastrophe which impends? Yes; I am confident that we can."[59]

In his peroration, Roosevelt spoke of the "fifth century" of the "Western World" and went through a kind of checklist of secular common goals: a wider distribution of culture, greater economic opportunity, fostering commerce, "true justice . . . hope for peace and a more abundant life to the peoples of the whole world."

Then, perhaps shaken by Gus's premature death, he inserted into his prepared text an unusually strident avowal of faith. "But this faith of the Western World will not be complete if we fail to affirm our faith in God. In the whole history of mankind, far back into the dim past before man knew how to record thought or events, the human race has been distinguished from other forms of life by the existence, the fact, of religion. Periodic attempts to deny God have always come and will always come to naught."[60]

When a lone heckler in the front row had shouted "Abajo con el Imperialismo!" (Down with imperialism) and was quickly hustled away, the incident only served to emphasize the flood of what seemed to observers to be genuine enthusiasm for the American president. Roosevelt ignored him; he had been heckled before. Police later revealed that the protester was Liborio Justo, a son of the Argentine president who had previously been deported from Brazil as a Communist. He had visited the United States in 1930 on a scholarship from the Argentine-American Cultural Institution.[61]

The American president encountered a different kind of untoward event at the following banquet at Argentina's Casa Rosada (Pink House). After he and the other guests were seated, the band played "The Star-Spangled Banner"; Roosevelt, unattended, was unable to rise with the others. Bernice Berle, a guest, noted the incident, apparently not recorded by the press, in her diary. "Roosevelt blushed and remained seated; by the time the Argentine anthem started, James Roosevelt and some one else had arrived to help him up. President Justo toasted Roosevelt [who was] seated and rose to his feet to answer which was received with great applause. We are all used to his infirmity and take it for granted—to impose oneself thus on a new people and a new country takes great courage and he did it very well."[62]

The next day, after a luncheon for the Justos at the American embassy, Roosevelt returned to the *Indianapolis*. Again soldiers lined the streets, and despite a steady summer downpour thousands of civilians waited for as long as two hours to see him pass, many throwing flowers at his car.[63] A short run down the Rio de la Plata put Roosevelt in Montevideo the next morning, where President Gabriel Terra met him, provided a brief tour of the city, and gave him lunch at the Presidential Palace, where he held another press conference for local reporters. Some two hundred thousand persons turned out to see him off late that afternoon. As had been the case in Rio and Buenos Aires, an official holiday had been declared.[64]

The trip was a triumph for the president but something less than that for American foreign policy. The real business of the conference in Buenos Aires became a duel between Cordell Hull and his Argentine opposite number, Carlos Saavedra Lamas (1878–1959). The Argentine, a veteran scholar and diplomat who had been involved with the International Labor Office since its inception, led Argentina back into the League of Nations, and had just won the Nobel Peace Prize for his role in settling the Chaco War, was effusive in his praise of Roosevelt. In a speech opening the working sessions of the conference as the *Indianapolis* sailed away, he called his presence a "godsend" and explained his impact: "The great throngs which cheered him as he passed saw in him the triumphant expression of democracy. He was proof that there still exists in all its grandeur the constitutional regime invented by great American statesmen. . . . The masses . . . wear [his] image . . . in their hearts . . . because he is the symbol this hour demands."[65]

At the same time, Saavedra opposed, and eventually thwarted, Hull's attempts to bind the American republics to nonintervention, as he supported the league's position of differentiating between aggressors and victims. He also probably saw himself as following earlier Argentine diplomats such as Luis María Drago (1859–1921), who sought to organize Latin American opinion against the policies of earlier American presidents. The argument became heated; Hull eventually was so annoyed that he developed a diplomatic illness and left the final formal American speech to Sumner Welles.[66]

Roosevelt, as he usually did, emphasized the positives in assessing the conference results. Essentially, these were a reaffirmation of previously agreed-upon principles, particularly consultation when peace was threatened and what he called the fundamental principle: "no nation has the right to intervene in the internal or external affairs of others."[67]

But for all the talk about disarmament and peace, the reality was that the United States, in an understandable reaction to the worsening international situation in general and the Japanese denunciation of the naval limitation treaty in particular, was beginning to rearm. On the very day that Roosevelt was speaking about peace in Buenos Aires, front-page stories in American newspapers, citing "high naval quarters," reported that before his departure, Roosevelt had instructed the Navy Department to proceed with plans to build two new large battleships, which Congress had authorized should any other power denounce the treaty. A formal White House statement confirmed the report early in the new year. It was, of course, still a battleship-minded navy. The same story quoted the opinion of Rear Admiral J. K. Taussig, assistant chief of naval operations, that airplanes could not sink American battleships, "for the principal reason that we will not let them get into a position to do so."[68]

13 The Battle about the Court
1937

ALTHOUGH THE SHADOW OF THE SUPREME COURT, sure to consider cases challenging the Wagner Act, the Social Security system, and many other reforms in its coming terms, was on Roosevelt's mind as he faced the challenges of his second term, it was not apparent in his annual message. Delivered in person before the new Congress and broadcast nationally at 2:00 p.m., it began with a brief review of the challenges met since "March 1933" and praise for the work he and the Congress had done to bring about "our recovery." He then insisted that "it is not enough that the wheels turn. They must carry us in the direction of a greater satisfaction in life for the average man. The deeper purpose of democratic government is to assist as many of its citizens as possible, especially those who need it most to improve their conditions of life, to retain all personal liberty which does not adversely affect their neighbors, and to pursue the happiness which comes with security and an opportunity for recreation and culture." Roosevelt acknowledged that "far-reaching problems" remained: poor housing, an "un-American type of tenant farming," the need to improve and broaden the new Social Security system, and unemployment, "the most far-reaching and the most inclusive problem of all."[1]

In striking language, he warned about "overproduction, underproduction and speculation," the "three evil sisters who distill the troubles of unsound deflation and disastrous inflation," indicating a new concern about more traditional economic evils. After a parting flick at the old order—"We know now that if early in 1931 Government" had acted decisively, the Depression would not have been as bad as it became—he broached the question of the Supreme Court by talking about the NRA. Insisting that the "broad objectives" of the NRA were sound but that "it tried to do too much," he noted, "The statute of N.R.A. has been outlawed," yet the problems of jobs, wages and hours, collective bargaining, child labor, and unfair trade and business practices remained and could not be addressed by "simultaneous action by forty-eight States." He then stipulated that "means must be found to adapt our legal forms and our judicial interpretation to the actual present national needs of the largest progressive democracy in the modern world."

At this point, many listeners must have expected a proposal for a constitutional amendment or perhaps a statutory change in the jurisdiction of the Court, but Roosevelt startlingly did neither. Instead, he proposed that the Court readjust itself! Claiming that "a growing belief" finds "little fault with the Constitution . . . as it stands today," he insisted that the vital need "is not an alteration of our fundamental law" but "an increasingly enlightened view with reference to it." After expressing his confidence that the "Legislative branch [will] continue to meet the demands of democracy" and noting that "the Executive branch must move forward . . . and provide better management," he suggested that the remaining branch pay attention to the election returns: "The Judicial branch also is asked by the people to do its part in making democracy successful. We do not ask the Courts to call non-existent powers into being, but we do have a right to expect that conceded powers or those legitimately implied shall be made effective instruments for the common good."[2]

His words misled both friends and foes. Senate majority leader Joseph T. Robinson, in a nationally broadcast speech that evening, repeated his previously expressed conviction that "the most practical way to deal with the subject, and the safest way, is through a constitutional amendment." Other congressional leaders, including Speaker Bankhead and Senate judiciary chair Henry Ashurst (D-AZ), spoke in favor of a constitutional amendment, with the latter assuring reporters that "I know the President has no intention of enlarging the court."[3] And Roosevelt himself, the very next day, sent a letter to fourteen governors and governors-elect, urging them to make ratification of the Child Labor Amendment, originally proposed in 1924, "one of the major items in the legislative program of your state," seemingly contradicting his rejection of the amendment process in the annual message.[4]

The annual budget message that followed was predicated on the false assumption that the "recovery" would continue and that the Depression was over. It projected increasing revenues, declining expenditures, and a "completely balanced budget" in fiscal 1939 after an actual deficit of $4.1 billion in fiscal 1936, a projected deficit of $2.2 billion in fiscal 1937, and a near balance in fiscal 1938.[5]

The assumptions on which the budget message rested had been championed by Treasury Secretary Morgenthau and budget director Daniel Bell. They were challenged within the administration chiefly by Federal Reserve Board chair Marriner Eccles, who insisted that any attempt to balance the budget would not only bring the economic recovery to a halt but also plunge the nation into another steep economic decline. While Eccles is properly credited as being the only person then in the upper echelons of power open to ideas that were what we now call Keynesian, it should be noted that in the early months of 1936 just after Keynes's *General Theory* was published, it appeared just twice on the *New York Times*' weekly lists of best sellers: both listings were provided by the five reporting stores in the nation's capital. Some of the sales surely were to young government economists who in later years would successfully champion the English economist's ideas.[6] In 1937 Morgenthau was cock-a-hoop that his and Bell's traditional ideas had seemingly won the day. They believed what classical economics taught: a long-term departure from balanced budgets would have disastrous consequences.[7] As his biographer regretfully reports, Morgenthau brought these beliefs with him to Washington in 1933 and held them until his dying day; in other words, as John Morton Blum is too polite to say, the nation's longest-serving secretary of the treasury was incapable of liberating himself from what passed for economic wisdom.[8] Franklin Roosevelt, as we have seen, shared those almost universally held prejudices, but, battered by experience, he would all but abandon them.

In March 1936, Roosevelt had informed Congress about a committee he had created to plan for the reorganization of the executive branch and that he would send up a proposal based on its recommendations at the start of the new Congress. The committee, composed of three distinguished academics, was led by Louis Brownlow and instructed to report after the election.[9] It gave its forty-seven-page report to Roosevelt after his return from South America. He accepted it and, before sending it to Congress, unveiled its results to seven of the top Democratic congressional leaders in a four-hour Sunday-afternoon meeting in the White House on January 10 while the committee and its staff watched silently. No transcript of the meeting exists. Louis Brownlow quotes Roosevelt as telling him after the leaders left, "This was quite a little package to give them this afternoon. Every time they recovered from a blow, I socked them under the jaw with another."

Although the discourse was polite, Roosevelt also took punches. According to Brownlow, Sam Rayburn[10] questioned the inclusion of some regulatory commissions.

RAYBURN: Is not the Interstate Commerce Commission, which is so popular and so successful, an exception?
ROOSEVELT: There will be no exceptions, not one.

There is general agreement that the leaders were stunned.[11]

The next day, the president held a separate several-hour press conference—he called it a "seminar"—to explain the reorganization plan to reporters, with the usual embargo until his message had gone to Congress. To emphasize further the extraordinary nature of the report and the proposal resulting from it, the entire cabinet along with the three committee members were present. The "seminar" was in fact an extended lecture in which Roosevelt showed his growing grasp of the details of governmental administration with relatively few questions from reporters. Except for Brownlow, the chairman, who made several brief explanatory comments, the other distinguished guests were window dressing.

A highlight of Roosevelt's bravura press conference was his use of what he called a "purple passage," when he read out the report's description of the six new presidential assistants who "should be possessed of high competence, great physical vigor, and a passion for anonymity." The mass reaction to the final characteristic was disbelief, with one correspondent insisting that "there ain't no such animal," to which Roosevelt replied, "Gentlemen, have you ever met Rudolph Forster, who is here in the room?" Forster, who had worked in the White House since 1897 and whose title was "executive clerk," had been, in effect, permanent secretary to eight successive presidents and the soul of discretion. Despite this example, Brownlow's high-flown language provoked ridicule. Roosevelt, who had laughed out loud when he first read it, should have suppressed it, but was proud that he had taken Brownlow's report as submitted.[12]

"Now that we are out of the trough of the depression," Roosevelt's confident message to Congress argued, "the time has come to set our house in order." He pointed out that despite the enormous growth in the size and scope of government, there had been no new departments since Labor and Commerce were divided in 1913 and no major administrative statute since 1921. Noting that the structure of government was "sadly out of date," he reminded Congress that four twentieth-century presidents—the first Roosevelt, Taft, Wilson, and Hoover—had called for administrative reform without significant success. The Brownlow report, he argued, was "a great document of permanent importance" whose broad goal was efficiency in government and whose chief target was "the practice of creating independent regulatory commissions." These, the report argued, were threatening to become "a fourth branch of the Government for which there is no sanction in the Constitution."

Roosevelt's summary focused on five "major recommendations":

1. Expand the White House staff.
2. Strengthen and develop governmental managerial agencies.
3. Extend and centralize the merit system.
4. Expand the number of Departments from ten to twelve by adding Departments of Social Welfare and Public Works and placing each of the 100 plus existing commissions, agencies, boards and other bodies as subordinate parts of one of the twelve Departments.
5. Create an office of Auditor General to restore to the Executive complete responsibility for accounts and current transactions which would provide "a genuine independent postaudit" of all spending.

In closing, Roosevelt denied what seemed self-evident: "I realize it will be said that I am recommending the increase of the powers of the Presidency. This is not true." Arguing that the Constitution "vested the entire Executive power of the national government" in the president, he insisted that "what I am placing before you is the request not for more power, but for the tools of management and the authority to distribute the work so that the President can effectively discharge those powers which the Constitution now places upon him. Unless we are prepared to abandon this important part of the Constitution, we must equip the President with authority commensurate with his responsibilities under the Constitution."[13]

Many lawmakers nonetheless saw the proposals as an attempt to grasp additional presidential power.[14] Actually, both Roosevelt and the skeptics, in and out of Congress, were correct. The Constitution did and does give great potential power to the president, but without adequate means to exercise that power modern presidents have often been hamstrung by a constantly expanding bureaucracy. Thus, tools that would improve the president's ability to control the bureaucracy, by placing it into executive departments directly in his control, were, in truth, an expansion of the chief executive's effective power without expanding any of the powers vested in his office by the Constitution.

Roosevelt had suggested during his seminar that the bill might go through in "May or June," but he probably knew that this was optimistic, to say the least. More than two years would pass before a truncated but nevertheless vitally important reorganization bill would pass Congress in April 1939. The topic is introduced here primarily to show what issues were on the table at the beginning of 1937. It is worth noting that there was a kind of consistency in Roosevelt's plans to reform simultaneously two of the three branches of government: his targets were a "horse-and-buggy" Court and a "sadly out of date" executive branch. But his method was different. As opposed to the careful preparation of the proposed reorganization of the executive branch, and its careful introduction to congressional leaders and then the press and public, the Court proposal would be thrown together in haste and sprung on an unprepared Congress and public. The president's claimed purpose in each instance was a return to the original intent of the Constitution. More than four years later, when he and Sam Rosenman put the finishing touches on the 1937 volume of his *Public Papers,* they titled it "The Constitution Prevails."[15]

Roosevelt's second inaugural—the first to occur on the now familiar January 20—took place in a daylong frigid downpour so severe that the Inaugural Committee considered moving everything indoors. Roosevelt, consulted about doing so that morning, asked if crowds were gathering. When told that they were, he replied, "If they can take it, I can." At ten the president, members of four generations of his family, his cabinet, and selected guests attended a brief ceremony in St. John's Episcopal Church, just across from the White House, celebrated by his Groton mentor, the Reverend Endicott Peabody, and three others. Just before noon, a convoy of limousines took the presidential party up Pennsylvania Avenue to the Capitol.[16]

If the day was dreary, the speech was sunlit. The second inaugural gave the nation a glimpse of the promised land that New Deal reforms might create. It did not, however, give its listeners, including the chief justice and the six of his brethren in attendance, any clues about how Roosevelt intended to overcome the barriers to that imagined future that their collective opinions presented. The Court was not even mentioned.

After taking the oath administered by Hughes with his left hand on the 1741 family Bible, cellophane wrapped for protection from the sleet and rain, Roosevelt began by reminding his "Fellow Countrymen"[17] that "four years ago . . . the Republic, single-minded in anxiety, stood in spirit here." He harked back to that time when "we of the Republic pledged ourselves to drive from the Temple of our ancient faith those who had profaned it [and we did] first things first."

He reviewed key first-term actions and noted that 1937 was the 150th anniversary of the Constitutional Convention that "found the way out of the chaos which followed the Revolutionary War [and] established the Federal Government . . . to promote the general welfare and secure the blessings of liberty to the American people." Here again he stressed that the "Constitution of 1787 did not make our democracy impotent."

As for the present, the nation's "progress out of the depression is obvious . . . we have come far from the days of stagnation and despair." But, he asked, "Have we met the goal of our vision of that fourth day of March, 1933? Have we found our happy valley?" The answer was a litany about the failings of American democracy, ending with its most remembered sentence, a sentence that Rosenman tells us Roosevelt wrote out himself: "I see one-third of a nation ill-housed, ill-clad, ill-nourished."

But for an understanding of what Roosevelt was about, we need to note the many sentences that preceded it. The first was positive: "I see a great nation, upon a great continent, with a great wealth of natural resources" at peace and prosperous. Then came the earlier negatives, each preceded by an "I see":

> tens of millions of its citizens—a substantial part of its population—who at this very moment are denied the greater part of what the very lowest standards of today call the necessities of life.
>
> millions of families trying to live on incomes so meager that the pall of family disaster hangs over then day by day.
>
> millions whose daily lives . . . continue under conditions labeled indecent.
>
> millions denied education, recreation, and the opportunity to better their lot.
>
> millions lacking the means to buy the products of farm and factory.

He assured his audience, which improved radio facilities and Roosevelt's increasing stature as a world leader made global, that his was not a message of despair but one of hope. "The test of our progress," he insisted, "is not whether we add more to the abundance of those who have much; it is whether we provide enough for those who have too little."

There followed thinly veiled challenges to the Court, in which he insisted that "our people" will demand effective government and argued that "government is competent when all who compose it work as trustees for the whole people." In closing, he assumed "the solemn obligation of leading the American people forward along the road which they have chosen to advance." As was his wont, the final words had a biblical cast, as he promised to do "my utmost" to do the people's will, "seeking Divine guidance to help us each and every one to give light to them that sit in darkness and to guide our feet into the way of peace."[18]

Twenty-first-century readers will be aware that the goals set forth in the second inaugural amounted to most of the domestic agenda for the next thirty years. Many will also note that there was no mention of what Swedish scholar Gunnar Myrdal would describe seven years later as "an American dilemma":[19] the unequal treatment imposed on one-tenth of a nation, black Americans. Apologists can argue that blacks were surely included in the one-third, but it is quite clear that although Roosevelt understood that they needed special protection, he was not then willing to make that case in public and would not do so until his hand was forced some three years later.

After the speech, Franklin and Eleanor were driven back to the White House in a slowly moving open car, despite the downpour, past crowds huddled under umbrellas. After the gala inaugural lunch, the president stood, often bareheaded, at the reviewing stand, a replica of Andrew Jackson's Hermitage, erected in front of the White House. At the last minute, Roosevelt directed workmen to remove the bulletproof glass that the Secret Service had installed to protect him. After an hour and a half, he went inside the White House to help greet three thousand guests at the reception. That evening, after a family dinner, only Eleanor attended the Inaugural Concert, which replaced the traditional Inaugural Ball. Farther up Pennsylvania Avenue, a mediation conference at the Labor Department failed to bridge the differences between the CIO and General Motors (GM), while on the other side of the Appalachians the waters of what became the greatest Ohio River flood continued to rise.

At his postinaugural press conference, Roosevelt affirmed that he did not even catch cold, though two silk top hats were ruined. He refused to comment on the strike impasse, and no reporter asked about the flood; the next day, he issued a proclamation appealing for public aid to the Red Cross's flood-relief efforts, and, as the flood became the first crisis of the new term, he created an ad hoc committee to direct flood relief. He soon installed Harry Hopkins in a White House office to coordinate flood-relief efforts and, after the flood reached the lower Ohio and streamed into the Mississippi, sent him to Memphis to coordinate actions from there.[20]

In the other ongoing crisis, the strike at General Motors in which his authority was dubious, he tried Fabian tactics, using his press conferences to issue what headlines called rebukes to both antagonists—indirectly in the case of John L.

Lewis when the union chief made statements invoking Roosevelt as an ally, directly in the case of Alfred P. Sloan, when the GM president refused even to meet with Labor Secretary Perkins. Lewis desisted, for a time, and Sloan soon met with Perkins. The serious business of getting the parties to talk was left to Perkins and Michigan governor Frank Murphy, who each received sub rosa directions from the White House.[21]

Only on February 5 did Roosevelt reveal what he had in mind for the Supreme Court's determined opposition to much of his legislative program. Five decision Mondays had come and gone in the new term without further anti–New Deal decisions, and nothing at all had come from the White House, though speculation and rumors abounded. At 10:55 a.m., the president opened his press conference by saying that he had "a somewhat important matter" to talk about and that no one must leave the room or reveal the text of the message they were about to get until it had been read in Congress. He had just unveiled his secret plan for the judiciary at a cabinet meeting with five Democratic congressional leaders present, but allowed no time for discussion.[22] In the press conference, Roosevelt went through his message describing the plan and the fifteen-hundred-word draft of a bill prepared in the Department of Justice that were to be read to Congress just after noon. The president's plan ignored constitutional questions and called for a reorganization and expansion of the federal judiciary on the ground that the work of the federal courts had greatly expanded.

An accompanying letter from Cummings argued that "delay in the administration of justice is the outstanding defect of our judicial system." It provided data showing that since 1913, the annual federal caseload in district courts had tripled, while the number of judges in those courts had increased by only about two-thirds. There was no data in Cummings's letter about the caseload of the Supreme Court, nor did it say anything about the age of its judges, but the draft bill provided that for every sitting federal judge who reached or had reached age seventy and had been on the bench for at least ten years, the president could appoint, with the advice and consent of the Senate, an additional judge to sit on that court and whose seat would represent a permanent increase in the size of that court. The appointment of new judges was subject to the following limitations: a maximum of "fifty judges" could be appointed under the bill's provisions, no judge could be appointed if that appointment would result in "more than fifteen members of the Supreme Court" or "more than two additional members" of other appellate and special courts, or "more than twice the number of judges now authorized" for any district court. That was the heart of what quickly became known as the Court-packing plan. The unstated bottom line was that if the bill became law, the president could appoint six Supreme Court judges, since Hughes, Brandeis, and the Four Horsemen were all over seventy. That he would also have been able to appoint forty-four lesser judges was never the issue. The bill's other provisions were genuine reforms, which, among other things, gave the chief justice an administrative role in overseeing the lesser federal courts; they were eventually enacted. The increase in judicial business can be seen in the following figures from Cummings's letter:

	1913	1936
Federal district judges	92	154
Criminal and civil cases	25,372	75,949
Cases per judge	276	484
Bankruptcy proceedings	20,788	60,624

Roosevelt's own summary of the bill minimized the enlargement of the Supreme Court.

This message has dealt with four present needs: [eliminating] congestion of calendars and [making] the judiciary . . . less static by the constant and systematic infusion of new blood; [making] the judiciary more elastic by providing for temporary transfers of judges [as needed]; [furnishing] the Supreme Court practical assistance in supervising [lower courts]; [eliminating] inequality, uncertainty, and delay [in determining] constitutional questions. . . . If these measures achieve their aim we may be relieved of the necessity of considering any fundamental changes in the powers of the courts or the constitution of our Government—changes which involve consequences so far-reaching as to cause uncertainty as to the wisdom of such course.[23]

That attempt to so focus the argument never got off the ground. From the beginning and throughout the more than five months of the Court fight, it was always about the simple question of whether the president would get to create new Supreme Court judges. That failure of that attempt epitomizes the utter ineptness of Roosevelt's strategy and tactics. Why this masterful politician was so uncharacteristically ineffective for so long remains a mystery that no biographer has adequately explained. The suggested explanations—overconfidence after a stunning victory, hubris, miscalculation, the absence of Louis Howe as a naysayer—are perhaps adequate to explain his initial errors, but not his continuing intransigence.

The fight itself took place on a changing battlefield. The initial impression was that Roosevelt, with his massive congressional majorities, would prevail on bills that needed only a bare majority. Herbert Hoover sprang into print immediately, denouncing the bill as an attempt to pack the Court, but the Republican Senate leadership sagely decided to let Democrats and progressives lead the fight against the bill. As Harold Ickes noted in his diary, the GOP senators were "as meek as skimmed milk." Soon iconic figures—many of them western progressives—came out in opposition. Many of those against the bill preferred some other method of curbing the Court. Nebraska's Norris saw "little merit" in the president's proposal and favored requiring a two-thirds majority to declare a statute unconstitutional, but eventually voted in favor of the president's bill. Democrat Burton K. Wheeler of Montana, who became the leader of the fight against the president's plan in the Senate, favored a constitutional amendment and eventually charged that Roosevelt aspired to "dictatorial powers." A third western progressive, Wisconsin's La Follette, spoke in favor of the president's plan in a coast-to-coast radio broadcast and called upon his colleagues to use their constitutional power to "unpack" the Supreme Court. He urged the people not to "submit to the chaos of judicial usurpation," which Congress could remedy.[24]

Roosevelt seemed to be winning during February, despite growing opposition. Perhaps in response to complaints about a lack of consultation, he held a number of conferences with legislators and continued to insist on the bill as he submitted it. He successfully fended off an attempt to split his bill in two, with needed procedural changes in one bill that would pass easily, leaving the controversial additional judges in a bill that would presumably be easier to defeat. He did agree to sign a bill being pushed by House judiciary chair Summers, which allowed Supreme Court justices to retire at full pay at age seventy if they had at least ten years on the Court. Hopes were expressed that, when enacted, two or three justices might retire.[25]

Scholars have been so concerned with the arguments and actions in Congress that eventually defeated the Court bill and the consequences of that defeat that they have largely ignored the president's secondary arguments in its favor. In early March, Roosevelt, who had been unnaturally silent for a month about the Court after his bombshell message, took his fight to the public in a double-barreled attack. On March 4, the anniversary of his first inauguration, he spoke at a fund-raising hundred-dollar-a-plate "Victory Dinner" in Washington's Mayflower Hotel. His remarks were broadcast to 1,268 similar dinners[26] around the nation attended by more than a half-million persons. Claiming that the nation was facing its greatest challenge since the Civil War, he described what was almost certainly an imaginary interview with "a distinguished member of Congress" who had come "to talk about national problems [and] the Judiciary in particular."

> I said to him: "John, I want to tell you something that is very personal to me—something that you have a right to hear from my own lips. I have a great ambition in life."
> My friend pricked up his ears.
> I went on: "I am by no means satisfied in having twice been elected President of the United States by very large majorities. I have an even larger ambition."
> By this time my friend was sitting on the edge of his chair.

I continued: "John, my ambition relates to January 20, 1941." I could feel just what horrid thoughts my friend was thinking. So in order to relieve his anxiety, I went on to say: "My great ambition on January 20, 1941, is to turn over this desk and chair in the White House to my successor, whoever he may be, with the assurance than I am . . . turning over . . . a Nation intact, . . . at peace . . . prosperous, a nation clear in its knowledge of what powers it has to serve its citizens. . . .

"I do not want to leave it . . . in the condition in which Buchanan left it to Lincoln."

Roosevelt went on to argue that the crisis over slavery had gone on for "at least forty years—two generations," but "economic freedom . . . will not wait . . . forty years [or even] four years. It will not wait at all." He pointed out that democracy had failed in many lands, but in the United States "democracy has not yet failed and need not fail." Then, using one of his favored rural metaphors, he compared the three branches of government to a three-horse plow team that could get heavy work done if all pulled together. But if "one horse lies down in the traces or plunges off in another direction, the field will not be plowed."

He challenged anyone to read the opinions with which the Court had invalidated various New Deal acts and then asked "what, if anything, we can do for the industrial worker" or "what we can do to control flood and drought" in the face of such decisions. In a closing litany, he tolled a list of problems that needed to be fixed, ranging from "one-third of a nation ill-nourished, ill-clad, ill-housed" to a "Dust Bowl beginning to blow again"—each followed by an emphatic "NOW" and capped with a final trope: "If we would keep faith with those who had faith in us, if we would make democracy succeed, I say we must act—NOW!"

Four days later, in the first Fireside Chat since the election, he offered, for the first time, his reasons for supporting legislation rather than a constitutional amendment. He divided the supporters of the amendment process into two groups: those who opposed modern social legislation—the same group that opposed "the mandate of the people" in the election—and those who honestly believed that the amendment process was best and "who would support a reasonable amendment if they could agree on one." He then gave his reasons for favoring his plan. "First, because I believe that it can be passed at this session of Congress. Second, because it will provide a reinvigorated, liberal-minded judiciary necessary to furnish quicker and cheaper justice from top to bottom. Third, because it will provide a series of Federal Courts willing to enforce the Constitution as written, and unwilling to assume legislative powers by writing into it their own political and economic policies." It was a more honest argument than the one he had made in his formal message, but most of his critics, then and later, have ignored it. No one can say whether things would have gone differently if Roosevelt had used this approach initially, but it surely would have improved his historical reputation. He himself clearly felt satisfied, and a week later he went off for his first Warm Springs vacation in more than a year.[27]

While Roosevelt was away, Chief Justice Hughes entered the political struggle with a two-pronged counterattack in defense of the Court as it was. On March 21, at a hearing of the Senate Judiciary Committee to consider the president's plan, Wheeler, the acknowledged leader of the fight against it, read a letter from the chief justice. Hughes claimed to have written it in response to "inquiries" from the Montanan and said it had the approval of Justices Van Devanter and Brandeis. The letter addressed only the claim that the Court was behind in its work—a claim that the president had never made—and refuted it with detailed statistics that neither the president nor his supporters attempted to rebut. Neither Hughes nor Wheeler revealed that they had met to plan their attack. Wheeler had first gone to see Brandeis, with whom he was friendly, and asked him to testify. Brandeis refused, but persuaded him to approach Hughes, who also refused to testify but agreed to write a letter. Had he testified, he would have been subjected to cross-examination.[28]

After reading Hughes's letter, Wheeler launched an all-out attack on the president's plan but did not yet directly attack Roosevelt, blaming instead the "young men" who Wheeler believed had given him bad advice. In fact, of course, the advice came from the attorney general, who was twelve years older than both the president and Wheeler.[29]

While the chief justice's letter was an important stroke against the Court-packing plan, the decision he read from the bench a week later was even more decisive. In the case of *West Coast Hotel v. Parrish,* which William Leuchtenburg has dubbed *"The Case of the Wenatchee Chambermaid,"* Hughes ruled that a minimum-wage law of the state of Washington was constitutional and that the litigant, Elsie Parrish, was entitled to the $216.19 she was due under the state law that her employer had violated.[30] This reversed not only the infamous *Adkins* decision of 1923, which had struck down a federal statute establishing minimum wages and hours for women and children workers in the District of Columbia,[31] but also the *Tipaldo* decision, striking down a quite similar New York state law that Justice Stone had criticized so vigorously in 1936. The personnel of the Court had not changed, but Roberts, who had silently supported Butler's opinion in *Tipaldo* in 1936, voted silently with Hughes in 1937.

This caused journalists and some historians to talk about Roberts's about-face as "the switch in time that saved nine." However, since the in camera voting on the "Chambermaid" case had taken place back in January, the suggestion that Roberts had acted in response to Roosevelt's February attack is unfounded. But surely his switch—and despite convoluted arguments to the contrary by some scholars, that is what it was—supports the old axiom that "the Supreme Court follows the election returns." For many years, some journalists and scholars have speculated that Hughes had somehow influenced Roberts to switch, but none could offer evidence to support it.

Only in 2005 was William Leuchtenburg, using remarks made by Frances Perkins in an oral history interview, able to show that Hughes's putative effort to change Roberts's mind *might* have occurred in the summer of 1936 as a preemptive strike against the onslaught he expected to come from Roosevelt after he won reelection. Perkins related, in remembered dialogue, what her "girlhood chum" Elizabeth Rogers, who had become Owen Roberts's wife in 1904, told her about an overnight visit Chief Justice and Mrs. Hughes had made to the Roberts farm:

> Says Mrs. Roberts to me, "All I know is that they walked up and down [our] terrace for hours. I said to myself, 'Owen is no walker. His feet will drop off. What in the world is the Chief Justice talking to him about so much? Why don't they stop this?' Twice I called them to come in and have tea, but they said, 'Just a minute,' and kept right on talking and talking, and walking up and down on that terrace, which is far enough from the house to be completely out of earshot, and yet it isn't actually down in the pasture where the cattle are."

Mrs. Roberts also told her about a long discussion in her husband's library and a similar one after breakfast the next day, complaining, "Much use we had of them. Much conversation we had out of those men. Mrs. Hughes and I talked to each other about the children, the servants, gardens, the weather, Washington gossip. We got to the end of our rope, but those two men still stayed in there."[32]

It may well be that Hughes, who was concerned for the country and the Court, influenced Roberts's crucial vote, and Hughes himself was not as consistent as either the liberal trio or the conservative quartet. Had Roberts voted against the chambermaid, it would have provided further ammunition for those supporting the president's plan.

Although it is now clear that Elsie Parrish's case was merely the first rock in the judicial avalanche historians call the Constitutional Revolution of 1937, Hughes and his brethren knew some of what was coming. They had already decided that the Wagner Act was constitutional, though it would not be announced until April 12. By early May, when the justices in effect put their imprimatur on the Social Security Act, two of the Horsemen had ridden over to the other side, leaving Butler and McReynolds to rail against a seven-man majority. The magnitude of the change was becoming apparent. Never again would the Court invoke laissez-faire doctrines to invalidate a regulatory statute.

But Roosevelt refused to accept victory. His refusal to do so has puzzled contemporaries and scholars. "Why," wondered the shrewd South Carolina senator James F. Byrnes, "run for a train after you've caught it?" It would have been easy for Roosevelt to claim his victory. Majority Leader Robinson sent word, even before Van Devanter resigned, that Roosevelt "ought to . . . say he's won."[33] All he had to do was announce that, since the Supreme Court had readjusted itself, as he had asked it to do in his annual message, no longer was there any need for that part of the Court reorganization bill that dealt with aging justices. Alternatively, he could have, as his congressional leaders pleaded with him to do, accepted one of several compromises floated by Democratic senators that would have given him the power to appoint two additional justices.[34]

What should have been the icing on his victory cake was provided on May 18 when Justice Van Devanter sent a letter to the White House announcing that he would retire at the end of the current term. It was clear that the Court was no longer a threat to the president's plans. In the face of Roosevelt's insistence that it was still necessary to change the rules, seven of the fourteen Democrats on the Senate Judiciary Committee joined with the three Republicans to send the Court bill to the Senate with an adverse recommendation, while the other seven Democrats and Norris voted for it. Even after this negative recommendation from the Judiciary Committee, the president continued to insist that his reforms must be enacted.[35]

Why did he insist on continuing the fight? Unlike his contemporary New York mayor Fiorello La Guardia, who readily admitted that "when I make a mistake, it's a beaut," Roosevelt was not given to public self-criticism. While willing to concede in the abstract that "presidents do make mistakes," his usual approach was to try to explain them away. He never admitted that continuing the Court fight had been a mistake, though years after the event he claimed the victory that his willful intransigence had turned into a defeat. The very elaborateness of his insistence in his *Public Papers* that he had really won the Court fight is prima facie evidence of the pain that the Court defeat inflicted on him. In an August 1939 signing statement for a statute establishing the Administrative Office of United States Courts, Roosevelt claimed that six of his seven proposals for court reform had been enacted and that "the seventh recommendation has been accomplished through the opinions of the Supreme Court itself."[36] Thus, Roosevelt was arguing that he lost the battle but won the war, an argument that has been put forth by some scholars. That argument would have had more force if he had made it in May or June 1937.

What Roosevelt could never bring himself to admit was that his stubborn refusal to accept the victory presented to him by the combination of the Court's 1937 decisions and Van Devanter's resignation not only was unnecessary but also contributed to the difficulties he had with the bipartisan congressional "conservative coalition" that impeded so many of his programs after his sweeping victory in 1936.[37] The president insisted that the majority leader, Robinson, continue the fight in the Senate, which went on as spring turned into summer. It was universally believed that Roosevelt had promised Robinson the first appointment to the Court, and his colleagues congratulated him publicly on the Senate floor when Van Devanter resigned.

Finally, in mid-June, realizing belatedly that his relations with Democratic legislators were deteriorating largely because of the Court fight, Roosevelt agreed to accept compromise legislation. He would gain authority to appoint two additional justices at the rate of one a year, if that many justices over age seventy-five remained on the Court. (Brandeis was eighty-one, while Hughes, McReynolds, and Sutherland, all born in 1862, were seventy-five.) Also, as a kind of peace offering, Roosevelt threw a three-day picnic at a private club on an island in the Chesapeake during the last week in June. All Democratic members of Congress were invited—in daily increments of 150—to come and socialize with the president, who dressed without coat or tie, his shirt open at the neck. The U.S. Navy and Coast Guard provided free transportation.[38]

Despite the fence mending, which was a social success, Robinson continued to have heavy going during a seemingly interminable Senate debate on the compromise bill. He apparently had enough votes for passage, but not enough to cut off a threatened filibuster. Still, he was confident he would eventually prevail. On the morning of July 14, the majority leader was found dead on the floor of his apartment. Any hope of a bill for extra justices died with him.[39]

As soon as senators returned from Robinson's funeral in Little Rock, a grudging agreement was reached with Roosevelt for a decent burial of the Court bill. Never voted upon, it was simply sent back to the Judiciary Committee by a vote of seventy to twenty. Robinson's death meant that a new majority leader had to be chosen. Roosevelt's apparent support for Kentucky's Alben W. Barkley (1877–1956), who had been in Congress since 1913 and was a loyal supporter of the New Deal, helped the Kentuckian prevail by a single vote over the more conservative Mississippian Pat Harrison, who had been in the Senate since 1919. While Roosevelt's intervention in what was supposed to be the Senate Democrats' business further alienated conservatives, it spared him from having a majority leader who opposed much of his program.[40]

Roosevelt has taken an almost universal and clearly justified pummeling from scholars over both his strategy and his tactics during the Court fight. But in the mythos that developed, its exponents contend that the New Deal was essentially over and it was the Court fight that killed it. An extreme version of this, in a major reference work, argues, under a heading "The New Deal's Demise and Its Legacy," that

the New Deal . . . began to fade by 1937, in part because of difficulties created by [Roosevelt's] vain effort . . . to "pack" the court [that] alienated many of the president's allies and reinvigorated his foes. Later in 1937, worried about deficit spending and assuming that the economy was rebounding, Roosevelt decided to cut back relief programs. The stock market promptly crashed and jobless rates again soared.

Other calamities ensued. . . . In 1938, conservatives on the House Committee on Un-American Activities mounted a damaging investigation into communist influence in New Deal agencies. These same conservatives ensured that the last great piece of New Deal legislation—the Fair Labor Standards Act of 1938—exempted agricultural workers and set minimum wages at a level that would not hurt low-waged southern industry. Increasingly under attack after 1938, administration liberals retreated from ambitious efforts to restructure the economy and contented themselves with pursuing economic growth policies.[41]

Such an analysis gives too much weight to the Court fight and ignores the fundamental difficulties Roosevelt faced in trying to modernize America with a party and a congressional base that gave disproportionate power to southern oligarchs intent on preserving a system based on segregation and inequality. The further notion that nothing much happened in the four and a half years between the end of the Court fight and Pearl Harbor is, as the subsequent chapters will demonstrate, a fundamental misunderstanding of the changes in Franklin Roosevelt and his America that took place in those fifty-four months.

In addition to attending to grand restructuring initiatives, Roosevelt took the occasion of his fifty-fifth birthday celebration to announce his support for a Georgia-based fund drive to establish a permanent $5 million endowment for Warm Springs.[42] The 1937 ball was the last promoted by Doherty. His team had raised large sums, but expenses were larger than net receipts and averaged twenty cents per participant, not a very efficient way to raise money.[43]

In his birthday radio message to the ball attendees and the nation, Roosevelt thanked listeners for "the finest birthday present" and repeated his call for donations to the Red Cross for flood victims. He promised that a "national effort" would diminish the probability of future floods. He went on to point out that "infantile paralysis" was not that kind of emergency but "an insidious and perfidious foe" that "lurks in unexpected places and its special prey is little children." The president then gave a one-paragraph history of the Warm Springs Foundation and reviewed the unchanged distribution formula for the Birthday Ball proceeds. He did not mention publicly that three weeks earlier, he had met with a small group in the White House to "discuss methods of combating infantile paralysis." Since the participants were not scientists but publicist Carl Byoir, the RFC's Jesse Jones, two other bankers (including the legendary Sidney Weinberg of Goldman, Sachs), and an advertising executive, the discussions were about fund-raising.[44]

More than seven months later, after meeting at Hyde Park with two key members of his Warm Springs Foundation, his former law partner Basil O'Connor and Keith Morgan, who had been associated with Roosevelt and Democratic fund-raising since at least 1928, Roosevelt issued a statement couched in the first person briefly reviewing the work in Georgia and announcing that "I firmly believe that the time has come when the whole attack on this plague should be led and directed, although not controlled, by one national body."

The new body, eventually named the National Foundation for Infantile Paralysis, would continue fund-raising and consciousness-raising efforts, but its new primary task would "be to lead, direct, and unify the fight on every phase of this sickness" and try to ensure "that every responsible research agency in the country is adequately financed" to investigate its causes and "the methods by which it may be prevented" as well as the problems of postpolio care. In the course of this statement, Roosevelt, who never as governor or president spoke about his own condition in public until one brief phrase shortly before his death, included a seemingly impersonal paragraph that surely describes some of his feelings about his own personal medical history. "Those who today are fortunate in being in full possession of their muscular power naturally do not understand what it means to a human being paralyzed by this disease to have that powerlessness lifted even to a small degree. It means the difference between a human being dependent on others, and an individual who can be wholly independent. The public has little conception of the patience and time and expense necessary to accomplish such results. But the results are of the utmost importance to the individual."

Although the trustees of the new foundation would not be named until late November, the president announced that he would not hold any position in it, though he would continue as president of the Warm Springs Foundation.[45] A little more than a month later, as the time to make arrangements for the 1938 birthday celebration approached, the White House released a letter from the president to O'Connor, transferring management of the responsibility for arrangements for the 1938 ball to his own Warm Springs Foundation. The new foundation would receive and distribute all of the net proceeds. This severed any connections with either Doherty or Byoir, neither of whom was mentioned.[46]

14 Roosevelt's Recession
1937–38

THE COURT FIGHT SO DOMINATED THE CONGRESSIONAL politics of 1937 that the New Deal seemed to have come to a halt. Of the five major innovative measures that Roosevelt requested, only one, the housing bill, was passed. The Wagner-Steagall Housing Act, passed as Congress was adjourning in mid-August, asserted the responsibility of the United States to "remedy the unsafe and insanitary housing conditions" that the urban and rural poor endured and created the United States Housing Authority.

It encouraged states and cities to create their own housing authorities, as most USHA activity involved loaning and granting money to state and city housing authorities for what was mostly slum clearance. Unlike the highly popular programs of the Federal Housing Administration and the Home Owners' Loan Corporation that financed or refinanced the homes of millions of middle-class Americans, public housing for the urban poor was strongly opposed by real estate interests, fiscal conservatives, and many rural legislators who supported other New Deal measures. Thus, the new housing program was not adequately funded.[1] Its sponsors envisaged a $1 billion program spread over four years; opponents whittled that down to $500 million, which was increased to $800 million in 1938.

Earlier New Deal housing had been under the aegis of Ickes's PWA, which in four years created some 21,000 dwelling units in forty-nine projects. About a third of them were occupied by African Americans, most but not all of them in segregated projects such as Atlanta's Techwood Homes. By the beginning of 1941, 118,000 USHA family units were under construction, with almost a third of them completed. Roosevelt, writing in 1941, called it "a beginning," but given its limited funding, public housing could not make even an appreciable dent in the ill-housed third of a nation highlighted in Roosevelt's vision.[2]

But after Congress had gone home and just before he left for Hyde Park, the president used the occasion of the 150th anniversary of the Constitutional Convention to make it clear that in his view, the process of reform and positive innovation should and would continue. In mid-September, speaking before sixty-five thousand people on the Mall near the Washington Monument, he argued:

In our generation, a new idea has come to dominate thought about government, the idea that the resources of the nation can be made to produce a far higher standard of living for the masses of the people if only government is intelligent and energetic in giving the right direction to economic life.

That idea . . . is wholly justified by the facts. [It] makes understandable the demands of labor for shorter hours and higher wages, the demands of farmers for a more stable income, the demands of the great majority of business men for relief from disruptive trade practices, the demands of all for the end of that kind of license often mistermed "Liberty," which permits a handful of the population to take far more than its tolerable share from the rest of the people. . . .

I am not a pessimist. I believe that democratic government in this country can do all the things which common-sense people, seeing that picture as a whole, have the right to expect. I believe that these things can be done under the Constitution. . . .

And I am determined that under the Constitution these things shall be done.[3]

Clearly, Roosevelt had not called a halt to New Deal measures, but he had been persuaded by continuing good economic news that he could do so without further deficit spending. Even though, after some hesitation, he eventually called Congress back for a special session that sat for more than a month (November 15–December 21), it failed to pass a single piece of major legislation. On the other hand, none of the president's other major bills was defeated, and all were still in process. Before the Congress expired in June 1938, he would get a wages and hours bill and the second AAA.

Congress passed without a dissenting vote the Revenue Act of 1937, which taxed personal holding companies at the same rates as the highest-income surtaxes; limited the deductions for yachts, country estates, and other luxuries; and made it more difficult to claim deductions on pro forma sales and exchanges of property. Although in many instances the chief economic results of the changes were to increase the income of lawyers and accountants specializing in tax avoidance, it was at least a minor success.[4]

Congress also enacted a number of measures that continued and modified existing New Deal programs. It appropriated additional funds for the WPA and other relief agencies, passed a version of the Guffey Coal bill previously declared unconstitutional that helped stabilize industrial relations in the soft-coal fields, and established a National Bituminous Coal Commission, which promulgated a code very similar to those issued by the NRA. In addition, the more comprehensive Wagner Act, which the Court had validated after Roberts's switch, helped to reduce the number of strikes that had dominated the headlines earlier in the year. Lesser successes included a reauthorization of the reciprocal trade agreements, an act establishing a loan program to reduce farm tenancy, and, in foreign affairs, the already noted changes to the Neutrality Act.[5]

A major disappointment for African American leaders was Roosevelt's continuing refusal to provide effective support of their efforts for antilynching legislation. It had been a major goal since the NAACP's James Weldon Johnson (1871–1938) had persuaded Missouri Republican L. C. Dyer in 1922 to introduce a federal antilynching bill, which had passed the House but was defeated by a Senate filibuster. During Roosevelt's first term, attempts to pass an antilynching bill failed in each Congress, despite the efforts of their major sponsor, New York's Senator Wagner, and the behind-the-scenes efforts of Eleanor Roosevelt.[6] In 1934 she not only spoke to Franklin about the bill but in May bypassed the Oval Office gatekeepers by setting up a Sunday meeting with the president for the NAACP's Walter White (1893–1955). Returning from a Potomac cruise in the afternoon, Franklin joined Eleanor and his mother, who were having tea with the NAACP leader on the south portico of the White House. As White recounted the event in his memoirs, after a discussion of the arguments, pro and con, for the antilynching bill, during which Franklin realized that Eleanor had briefed White thoroughly and that Sara supported the bill as well, the president finally told White, bluntly, in his best off-the-record style, how he perceived the current political realities. "I did not choose the tools with which I must work. . . . Had I been permitted to choose them I would have selected quite different ones. But I've got to get legislation passed to save America. The Southerners by reason of the seniority rule in Congress are chairmen or occupy strategic places on most of the Senate and House committees. If I come out for the anti-lynching bill now, they will block every bill I ask Congress to pass to keep America from collapsing. I just can't take that risk."[7] While White's reconstruction of Roosevelt's words is almost certainly not a verbatim account—and he managed to misdate the meeting by a year—they are compatible with the reasons Roosevelt regularly gave, off the record, for his failure to stand up for principles in which he believed.

A month later, Eleanor did pry from him permission to write White that "if the sponsors of the bill will go at once to Senator Robinson and say to him that, if, in a lull, the antilynching bill can be brought up for a vote, the President authorizes the sponsors to say that the President will be glad to see the bill pass and wishes it passed." Although this backhanded support came to nothing, as the president probably expected, it was more encouragement than he had previously given.[8]

At the beginning of the 1937 session, it seemed to some activists that the antilynching bill might become law: it was passed by the House, 227–118, after a bitter debate punctuated by news of the blowtorch lynching of two black men in Duck Hill, Mississippi. All but three of the negative votes were by Democrats; only one southerner, Maury Maverick of Texas, voted for the bill. But in the

Senate, the bill again failed to get a place on the calendar after Judiciary Committee approval. Late in the session, Wagner, through parliamentary devices and aided by the ineptitude of the new majority leader, Alben Barkley, managed to get the bill to the floor. But, faced with another filibuster, he agreed to drop it in return for an agreement that it would have a place on the calendar at the beginning of the 1938 session. Roosevelt had given the antilynching measure no public support but clearly would have signed a bill if it had been presented to him.[9]

These disappointing results over three years did not satisfy African American leaders and race liberals, or Roosevelt's wife and mother, or many later historians and other critics. What we need to understand about this episode is that it marks the beginning of a remarkable and unprecedented dialogue between Franklin Roosevelt and the unelected leaders of black America. Governor Roosevelt had seemed oblivious to the existence of black New Yorkers, and, if one looks only at his official statements, the same can be said about his first presidential term attitudes. But even before the 1936 election showed that northern black voters were a small but important part of the triumphant New Deal coalition, the dialogue had begun. Not until Lyndon Johnson reached the White House would a comparable dialogue recur. And although there would be no transforming presidential action in race relations until Roosevelt's third term, it can be argued that Roosevelt's little-noted appointment of William H. Hastie (1904–76), who had been an assistant solicitor in Ickes's Interior Department since 1933, as the nation's first African American federal judge just as he was sending the Court-packing bill to Congress was the first tiny fruit of his new awareness.[10]

Among the last significant acts of the session was the matter of replacing Justice Van Devanter. After meeting with Senator Hugo Black (1886–1971) on August 10, ostensibly about crop loans, Roosevelt sent the Alabaman's name to the Senate with the extreme secrecy he loved to employ. He filled out the nomination form in longhand and sealed it in an envelope and sent it to the Senate two days later. Even his staff had no prior knowledge.[11] When the president's messenger came to the Senate chamber, Vice President Garner in the chair opened the envelope and read out the nomination. Judiciary chair Ashurst, in on the secret, then tried to invoke the traditional courtesy that approved presidential appointments of members of the Senate without a committee vote. Such a procedure required unanimous consent, and two senators immediately objected. Black, an aggressive liberal first elected to the Senate in 1926, was best known for his advocacy of a thirty-hour workweek and had been one of twenty senators who had supported the Court-packing bill to the bitter end.

Most of the initial objections to Black were somewhat pettifogging, with some senators arguing that since Van Devanter had resigned rather than retired, no vacancy existed, while others claimed that Black and all other members of the present Congress were ineligible under the clause of the Constitution[12] that barred any federal legislator from holding "any civil office" created or whose "emoluments" had been increased during the legislator's tenure. A more serious charge—that Black had been or still was a member of the Ku Klux Klan—was alleged and discussed in the press and speculated about by a few senators, but neither the Senate nor the Department of Justice was interested in investigating the charge. Cummings said that it was not the business of his department to investigate a sitting senator. Black privately assured some senators with a lawyerly correct statement that he was not a member. After a brief hearing in which Black was not called, a subcommittee voted five to one in favor. Just five days after receiving Black's nomination, the Senate gave its consent, sixty-three to thirteen. Senatorial courtesy had prevailed.

Almost a month later, a series of stories in the *Pittsburgh Post-Gazette*, syndicated and discussed nationally, provided proof of what thousands of Alabamans knew: Hugo Black had been an open member of the Klan between 1923 and 1925 before his election to the Senate, which would have been highly unlikely without the Klan's support.[13] Black and his wife were vacationing in Europe, and he refused to be interviewed there. At his first press conference after the story broke, Roosevelt, anticipating the question, dictated the following statement: "I know only what I have read in the newspapers. I know that the stories are appearing serially and their publication is not complete. Mr. Justice Black is in Europe where, undoubtedly he cannot get the full text of these articles. Until such time as he returns, there is no further comment to be made." Asked whether he had received "any information from any source" about Black's Klan membership, the president answered, "No."[14]

Predictably, the Black affair came up again at the next conference. After again refusing to comment, Roosevelt gave his off-the-record views on the role of private life in public service.

THE PRESIDENT: A man's private life is supposed to be his private life. He may have certain marital troubles, which, if they came out, might be pretty disagreeable. It certainly is not incumbent on the Department of Justice or the President or anybody else to look into this as long as it does not come out and a fellow had led a perfectly good life.

MR. MCINTYRE: So long as it does not come out as a public scandal.

THE PRESIDENT: So long as it does not come out as a public scandal.[15]

Whether, at the time, Roosevelt was thinking of his own situation vis-à-vis Lucy Mercer, or the homosexuality of his foreign policy adviser, Sumner Welles, we shall never know.

Black, who had refused to talk to reporters in Europe, was jovial with those who queried him on his return to the United States on September 29, but he refused to answer questions. He got free airtime to address the nation two days later. He described the attacks on him as "a planned and concerted campaign . . . calculated to create racial and religious hatred" that threatened to resurrect the climate of the "Nineteen Twenties." To help avert "such a catastrophe," he admitted that he had joined the Klan "about fifteen years ago" and later resigned. Making no mention of the Klan's role in his election, he emphasized his own demonstrated liberalism as a senator and claimed that "among my friends [are] many members of the colored race." But he did not mention his role in successfully opposing antilynching legislation. He also claimed that "some of my best and most intimate friends are Catholics and Jews" and described "a trusted Jewish friend" who had been the executor of his will while he was in the army in 1918. His "discussion of the question is closed," he concluded. The reaction in the nation's press was overwhelmingly hostile and included many protests and calls for Black's resignation or removal.[16]

But three days later, at the Court's traditional first-Monday-in-October opening, Associate Justice Black filed in with his eight colleagues and took his place without ceremony at the far left of the chief justice in the seat assigned to the most junior justice. He had taken the unusual precaution of having himself sworn in before he left for Europe rather than by the chief justice on his initial appearance, as was the custom. Hughes formally announced his presence, noting that Black had taken the oath privately. Two attorneys filed protests challenging Black's right to sit, which Hughes took under advisement and the Court formally rejected a week later. The fact that during thirty-four years on the bench Black "grew into a passionate defender of the rights of minorities and political dissidents" does not expunge his unethical behavior in gaining confirmation.[17]

Although Roosevelt's legislative program had fallen short of his expectations and he was uncertain about his immediate tactics, many critics have overstated the impact of his 1937 setback. He understood that the real issue was majority rule and said so in a number of ways. While waiting for Congress to finish and adjourn, he went down to Virginia to participate in the 350th anniversary of the birth of Virginia Dare, the first English child born in North America, and used the occasion to celebrate majority rule. Quoting at length from some mid-nineteenth-century letters of "Lord Macaulay"[18] decrying majority rule and predicting disaster for the United States, Roosevelt delightedly remarked, "Almost, methinks, I am reading not from Macaulay but from . . . the United States Chamber of Commerce, the Liberty League . . . or the editorials written at the behest of some well-known newspaper proprietors in 1936 and 1937. . . . They do not believe in democracy—I do. My anchor is democracy—and more democracy."

He was convinced—and rightly so, if we are to believe contemporary Gallup polls—that "an overwhelming majority" of Americans supported his views. But he never argued, and perhaps never really understood, the degree to which the U.S. Constitution was designed to inhibit majority rule. In that very speech— and time and again—he iterated that "I seek no change in the form of American government" and followed it by insisting that "majority rule must be preserved as the safeguard of both liberty and civilization."[19] Neither he nor any of the other leading American political leaders who have succeeded him have proposed altering the major remaining constitutional barrier to true majority rule: a bicameral legislature that gives inordinate power to small, thinly populated states.

In his Labor Day message, the most prolabor president in American history assumed an air of seeming neutrality in the labor wars, arguing that "both sides have made mistakes" and ignoring the fact that murderous violence had been unleashed against peaceful picketers in late spring and early summer, most blatantly by police in Chicago's Memorial Day massacre; by Henry Ford's paramilitary forces in Dearborn, Michigan's "Battle of the Overpass" four days earlier; and by Tom Girdler's deputized strong-arm squads in Massillon, Ohio, on July 11.[20]

Previously, at the end of a June 29 press conference, in response to a reporter's question, Roosevelt used Shakespeare's phrase "A plague on both your houses" and authorized direct quotation, echoing the sentiments of much of the public. This was a reasonably accurate thumbnail analysis of public opinion, as Gallup polls suggested. But when, in response to a reporter's request, Roosevelt specifically allowed Shakespeare's phrase[21] to be quoted, and then repeated it, it was assumed that it represented his own views. Reaching for the center, he knew this would be the case.

John L. Lewis waited until he had a nationwide radio audience, more than two months later, to reply to the president. In a florid pre–Labor Day speech, the CIO chief threw Roosevelt's press conference quotation back in his face, without naming him or citing it: "Labor, like Israel, has many sorrows. Its women weep for their fallen and they lament for the future of the children of the race. It ill behooves one who has supped at labor's table and who has been sheltered in labor's house to curse with equal fervor both labor and its adversaries when they become locked in deadly embrace."[22]

Franklin Roosevelt, who won most rhetorical duels, clearly lost this one and attempted no direct reply. But when Lewis rashly challenged Roosevelt electorally in 1940, he not only lost that challenge but surrendered his role as leader of the CIO as well. The "captain of a mighty host" would soon lead only his loyal miners.

The president was not without support from organized labor. Many CIO leaders understood that Roosevelt was, in the final analysis, labor's best hope, and the AFL's William Green immediately denounced Lewis's attack on "the greatest friend of labor who has ever sat in the White House." Green argued that Roosevelt's "enemies" opposed him because of what he had done for labor. Frances Perkins, for her part, ignored Lewis's remarks and the growing split in the labor movement to concentrate on the demonstrable gains workers and farmers had made during the New Deal years. Even Lewis acknowledged such gains in a formal Labor Day statement and in a speech to a huge crowd in Pittsburgh. Without mentioning the president or the Wagner Act, he hailed the contract the CIO steelworkers had signed with U.S. Steel: "Last year they worked forty-eight hours a week and got 43 cents an hour. Today they work forty hours and get a $5 [daily] minimum."[23]

Despite the tensions between the president and Lewis and the bitter rift between the AFL and CIO that dominated Labor Day editorials in the nation's press, organized labor's gains after the Supreme Court's validation of the Wagner Act were remarkable. Unions claimed more than six million workers, topping for the first time the previous high-water mark of four million reached in 1920. Few observers assessing labor's gains since 1933 noted one salient fact accompanying labor's meteoric rise: not once in the turbulent years since he became president had Franklin Roosevelt called out federal troops to intervene in a strike. In addition, the president made it known that the failed wages and hours bill to impose conditions similar to those won at U.S. Steel on most industries would again be on his must list for 1938.[24]

Roosevelt soon left on a "nonpolitical" two-week train trip to the Pacific Northwest, accompanied by his wife and senior WPA official Colonel F. C. Harrington. In fact, this was very good presidential politics.

Some editors speculated foolishly that the president would take the opportunity to chastise western progressives and Democrats who had helped stymie his Court-packing plan on their home turf and that his popularity had declined in the West. Roosevelt, however, treated them most cordially; the closest Roosevelt came to a reprisal was failing to mention Montana's Wheeler during his time in that state while praising all four of Montana's other members of Congress. Most tour reporters found Roosevelt's popularity high. The *New York Times'* Warren Moscow found Roosevelt's hold on the public was not noticeably reduced and that the Court issue seemed of little importance for far western voters.

In his rear-platform talk at Boise, after a drive through the city, Roosevelt spoke about how much he enjoyed "going around the country" and likened himself to "an old mythological character by the name of Antaeus" whose strength redoubled every time his foot touched the ground. "I feel that I regain strength by just meeting the American people." His subtext was clear: I may have stumbled with Congress—something he never admitted directly—but I still have popular support. After a drive through fertile farmland from Boise to Ontario, Oregon, he congratulated locals for having given work to Dust Bowl "refugees."[25]

Returning to the just-completed Bonneville Dam on the Columbia River, Roosevelt spoke with understandable pride about one of the great physical accomplishments of the New Deal. That giant dam, along with the even larger Grand Coulee higher up the Columbia in eastern Washington, and the earthen Fort Peck Dam on the Missouri in Montana, constituted "the most far-reaching construction project ever undertaken by the federal government." The power and water they created and distributed helped to transform the urban areas around Seattle and Portland and the semiarid agriculture of the "inland empire." The president observed that if good conservation methods had been applied "twenty [or] forty years ago . . . in that great semi-arid strip in the center of the country . . . we could have prevented in great part the abandonment of thousands and thousands of farms . . . and the migration of thousands of destitute families" to the Pacific Coast states. He also reaffirmed support for additional regional planning and tied conservation to his definition of liberty: "My conception of liberty does not permit an individual citizen or group of citizens to commit acts of predation against nature in such a way as to harm their neighbors, and especially to harm the future generations of Americans." Later that day, high on Mount Hood, he dedicated Timberline Lodge, a National Forest facility built by WPA workers. After refurbishment it was described some seventy years later as "perhaps the most impressive national monument produced by the WPA."[26]

A day in Seattle was largely spent with his daughter, Anna, and her husband, John Boettiger, who were copublishers of the Hearst-owned *Seattle Post-Intelligencer*. The next morning, Anna's two children, aged ten and seven, accompanied their grandparents on a brief state visit to Canada aboard the destroyer *Phelps*. After a state luncheon and a three-question press conference at Victoria, the destroyer delivered the president at Port Angeles, Washington, at the tip of the Olympic Peninsula in the early evening and then took Eleanor and the grandchildren back to Seattle.[27]

At Port Angeles, the president was driven to the local high school, where three thousand schoolchildren were assembled beneath a banner pleading "Please, Mr. President, we children need your help. Give us an Olympic National Park." Roosevelt responded: "That sign on the school house is the appealingest appeal that I have seen in all my travels. I am inclined to think it counts more to have the children want that park than all the rest of us put together. So you boys and girls . . . can count on my help."[28]

Actually, the creation of what became Olympic National Park, a transforming expansion of the existing Olympic National Monument, was virtually a done deal. What was at issue was the size of the park, where its boundaries would be drawn, and whether, after it was created, the president would have the power to expand it. The struggle over the park divided both locals—conservationists versus timber interests—and federal agencies. Most of the Olympic Peninsula was already a national forest. The Forest Service, a part of the Department of Agriculture that viewed the timber industry as its most important constituent, had detailed plans for a relatively small park to be carved out of its holdings. The National Park Service, part of the Department of the Interior, which viewed potential visitors as its most important constituents, wanted a larger park that would include substantial stands of first-growth timber suitable for relatively easy harvesting. This clash between local units of the federal government was part of an ongoing struggle in what northwesterners call the "other Washington." Harold Ickes of Interior wanted to acquire the Forest Service as part of his never-realized plan of transforming Interior into a Department of Conservation, while Henry Wallace wanted to keep the federal timber crop in his agricultural domain. That conflict was mirrored in the reactions of local politicians. Washington state New Deal Democrats, including both Senators Homer T. Bone and Lewis B. Schwellenbach and Representative Monrad C. Wallgren, whose district included the park, favored the larger option, while conservative Democrats like Governor Clarence Martin and Representative Martin F. Smith of Hoquiam, more responsive to lumber and mining interests, supported the Forest Service view.

The Forest Service believed that it had control of the battlefield, and some thirty-five of its relatively high-level officials were deployed to show the president the merits of the smaller park they had planned. But before he left Hyde Park, Roosevelt got a two-page memo from Irving Brandt outlining the conservationist view of the park question, and on the evening of his arrival in the park his son-in-law brought two Park Service officials to his cabin to brief him. This was the kind of situation in which Roosevelt reveled: he loved to make individual decisions about projects whenever possible. In this instance, he opted for a larger park and later further expanded it by executive order.[29]

After spending most of the next day being driven through the length of the park, Roosevelt reboarded his train in Tacoma and proceeded northeast to the Grand Coulee, site of the largest of all the New Deal dams. The president described it as "the largest structure . . . that has ever been undertaken by man in one place" and well under way. When completed in 1942, it was 57 feet short of a mile in length and 550 feet high and was soon the nation's largest single producer of hydroelectric power. But Roosevelt never discussed its environmental impact publicly. Unlike Bonneville Dam, which had fish ladders to enable salmon to proceed upstream, Grand Coulee was impassable. It eliminated salmon and other species from about a thousand miles of the upper Columbia and destroyed ecosystems upon which several Native American tribes depended.[30]

At the final far western project of the tour, the massive Fort Peck Dam in Montana on the upper reaches of the Missouri River, Roosevelt stressed the value of "what we have been doing . . . [giving] useful work to millions; . . .

[bringing] water to dry places; [increasing and cheapening] the use of electricity; and we have completed literally thousands of projects of immediate usefulness in every county and every state in the Union." Then, as he often did when he spoke with a great project before him, he derided those who proposed budget balancing by ending work projects and placing relief recipients on the dole, which was less expensive. Yet in other venues, he himself would speak of the necessity of balancing the budget. Speaking from the train at Grand Forks, North Dakota, and St. Paul, Minnesota, he returned to domestic politics, but said little if anything new.[31]

In Chicago, on the last day of the tour, Roosevelt transformed what seemed to be a routine bridge dedication into an international sensation. Back in September, the State Department had suggested that a good way to counter growing isolationist sentiment would be to make "a speech of international cooperation . . . in a large city where isolation was entrenched." For such a purpose, no better venue could have been found than one located in plain sight of Colonel Robert R. McCormick's *Chicago Tribune* building, the major voice of those sentiments.[32]

In what quickly became known as the Quarantine Speech, Roosevelt deliberately risked going beyond what public opinion seemed ready to support. After commenting on the "happiness and security and peace" manifested during his tour of the West, he spoke of the "very different scenes being enacted in other parts of the world." He noted, without specifics, that the international situation was growing "progressively worse" and that "the present reign of terror and international lawlessness" had "now reached a stage where the very foundations of civilization are seriously threatened." He pointed to the "interdependence . . . of the modern world . . . which makes it impossible for any nation completely to isolate itself. . . . Therefore the sanctity of international treaties" is "a matter of vital interest . . . to the people of the United States." Using a well-known concept—the quarantine—in a new field, foreign affairs, he tried to make the strange familiar, as he had done successfully with "Good Neighbor." And, without his saying so, the use of the medical analogy implied that he was the doctor who could cure what was wrong. "It seems to be unfortunately true that the epidemic of world lawlessness is spreading. When an epidemic of physical disease starts to spread, the community approves and joins in a quarantine of the patients in order to protect the community."

At this point, the logic of the speech called for him to propose or even proclaim a quarantine of the unnamed aggressor nations, but he did not do so. Instead, he assured his listeners that "it is my determination to pursue a policy of peace . . . to adopt every practical measure to avoid involvement in war." In his closing emphasis, he chose to remind his audience of his Chautauqua address of the previous year: "America hates war. America hopes for peace. Therefore, America actively engages in the search for peace." It seems to me that in this speech, for all its tentativeness, Roosevelt for the first time as president showed his true colors as a Wilsonian advocate of collective security.[33]

The president's foes quickly emphasized Wilsonian parallels. McCormick's *Tribune,* transmuting "quarantine" into "boycott" and ignoring European aggressors, asked, "If the boycott is adopted [and] Japan's conquest continues, then what will Mr. Roosevelt do? The moment came when Mr. Wilson found himself with no alternative but war. Does not Mr. Roosevelt's policy invite the coming of the day when he, too, will have no alternative but resort to arms?"[34]

There are many references to Roosevelt's "proposal to quarantine the aggressors," and in the 1944 election campaign he himself said, "In 1937, I asked that aggressor Nations be quarantined. For this I was branded by isolationists in and out of public office as an 'alarmist' and a 'war-monger.'"[35] Actually, Roosevelt was more concerned about Europe than Asia. But much of the nation's press, including many Republican papers not normally friendly, praised the speech. And one Chicago publisher, Frank Knox of the *Daily News,* who had been Landon's running mate, called the speech "magnificent."[36] The historian of isolationism, among others, has argued that "the recession in late 1937" was a factor in Roosevelt's decision to make the Quarantine Speech.[37] Although it is true, as noted below, that later research has established that the recession actually began in September, it was the sharp market decline that began in mid-October, two weeks after the speech, that triggered contemporary awareness of serious economic decline.

In a Hyde Park posttour press conference, Roosevelt refused to comment on Black's speech or any aspect of the appointment. He did say that there would probably be a special session of Congress called for November, but he declined to explain what he meant by quarantine and did say, off the record, that "sanctions" and "conferences" were "out of the window."[38]

In the October 12 Fireside Chat, Roosevelt spoke of the evidences of prosperity he had seen on his trip and asked again for Congress to pass legislation for shortened hours and minimum wages: "Right now I am most greatly concerned in increasing the pay of the lowest paid . . . our most numerous consuming group . . . who today do not make enough to maintain a decent standard of living." He also wanted legislation for crop control, for governmental reorganization, for greater control of trusts, and to create regional land-use planning agencies. He reemphasized the search for peace, reminding listeners that he had personal experience of world events from 1913 to 1921 and that he had learned not only "what to do" but "much of what not to do." And without mentioning "quarantine," he repeated the closing sentences of his Chicago speech.[39]

A radio address on behalf of a national charity appeal on October 18, in which Roosevelt spoke of "returning prosperity," and a budget message the next day projecting a balanced budget for 1938 based on expected greatly reduced expenditures for WPA and other relief programs showed how poorly Roosevelt had been briefed about what was actually a deteriorating economic situation.[40] Although Treasury officials were aware that a recession was likely, as were a few other economists in the government, Morgenthau refused to believe them and did not pass on their views to the president.[41] Stock market turmoil on October 18–19 set off a wave of selling that resulted in some demands to shut down the stock exchange, which both Morgenthau and Roosevelt rejected. From Hyde Park, where he fielded panicky calls from Steve Early and Jimmy Roosevelt, the president told Morgenthau that he had been "quite rude to them."[42] On November 15, in a message to Congress opening the special session, the president for the first time recognized publicly that a recession was in progress. But his admission was cloaked in denial: "The present decline has not reached serious proportions."[43]

The classic brief econometric account of the severe 1937–38 economic downturn, often called the Roosevelt Recession, holds that "in severity the nine month decline from September, 1937, to June 1938, is without parallel in American economic history. Industrial production declined 33 percent. Durable-goods production declined by more than 50 percent, national income by 13 percent, profits by 78 percent, pay rolls by 35 percent, industrial stock averages by more than 50 per cent (with a 35 percent drop in five months), and manufacturing employment by 23 percent. At the same time, although raw-materials prices fell 21 per cent, prices and costs resisted the decline."[44]

Scholars draw very contrasting lessons from the Roosevelt Recession. Those with a Keynesian bent, to whom I am partial, use it as a horrible example of bad decision making, blaming it on Roosevelt's reduced spending in an effort to balance the budget.[45] Those with a free-market persuasion use it as evidence for their argument that the New Deal was a failure.[46]

Within the Roosevelt administration, the struggle between the budget balancers and those who believed that continued spending was vital to recovery continued for months and never really ended. The most senior spokesman for spending, Federal Reserve chairman Marriner Eccles, was supported by a small host of economists advocating more rather than less spending. The most forceful of these was Leon Henderson, who had called the turn back in the spring with a memorandum entitled "Boom and Bust" and whose views were supported by his boss, Harry Hopkins. Others in the spending camp included the legal team of Corcoran and Cohen, a previously unheralded economist named Lauchlin Currie, and Winfield Riefler, by then at the Institute for Advanced Study. The result of the struggle over spending, not fully ended until wartime necessity made it a nonissue, was in doubt well into 1938. Roosevelt, as will be shown, slowly reversed course to some effect, but not nearly to the degree that most spenders urged.

Keynes himself entered the argument with a trenchant analysis in a February 1, 1938, letter to Roosevelt. Noting that he had "access to few more sources than are generally available" but superbly confident—"those things that I see I see very clearly"—he argued that the New Deal recovery had come to a halt because "it requires for its continuance, not merely the maintenance of recovery, but always *further* recovery."

As for the steps Roosevelt had already taken, Keynes agreed that "the present policies will prevent the slump from proceeding to the disastrous degree as last time." But he insisted that they would not ensure prosperity "at a reasonable level" without further large-scale investment of government funds. Keynes had hoped that this would have been done "in time. It was obvious [that the sectors needing support] were . . . housing, public utilities, and transport." Openly disappointed in the results, he asked, "Can your administration escape criticism for the failure of these factors to mature?"

Keynes was also critical of Roosevelt's treatment of business and businessmen, as were many contemporaries and present-day free marketers. But, unlike most of those, Keynes did not have a high opinion of the business elite.

> Business men have a different set of delusions from politicians, and need, therefore, different handling. . . . You could do anything you liked with them, if you would treat them (even the big ones), not as wolves and tigers, but as domestic animals by nature, even though they have been badly brought up and not trained as you would wish. . . . [I]f you work them up into the surly, obstinate, terrified mood, of which domestic animals, wrongly handled are capable, the nation's burdens will not get carried to market; and public opinion will veer their way.

In conclusion, after giving Roosevelt a failing grade, he tried to take the curse off by asking forgiveness "for the candour of these remarks," identifying himself as "an enthusiastic well-wisher of you and your policies," and ticking off a number of things Roosevelt had done that he approved of. He went on to explain why he thought it necessary to intervene. "I am terrified lest progressive causes in all the democratic countries should suffer injury, because you have taken too lightly the risk to their prestige which would result from a failure measured in terms of immediate prosperity. There *need* be no failure. But the maintenance of prosperity in the modern world is extremely *difficult*; and it is so easy to lose precious time."[47]

Roosevelt sent the letter on to Morgenthau and signed the bland response his friend drafted.[48] If he ever reflected on the advice he ignored, we know nothing about it. A year and a half later, another European wise man also tried to save the new world with knowledge from the old with very different results. When Albert Einstein put his name to a letter describing the possibilities of atomic energy, Roosevelt took notice and eventually took decisive action. It is futile to fantasize about what kind of world we might have if Roosevelt had ignored Einstein's advice and acted on Keynes's. It should be remembered that

Einstein's wisdom had long been proverbial and that the word *Keynesian* had not yet appeared in popular discourse.[49]

* * *

The special session of Congress, which sat from mid-November until four days before Christmas, made progress on each of the bills Roosevelt stressed, but passed none. Roosevelt continued to call for a balanced budget, but he did provide a caveat: "If private enterprise does not respond, government must take up the slack." A week later, he told a press conference that "we have gradually come to an end or, rather a great diminution of the pump-priming." In addition, he tried, without success, to get Congress to reduce appropriations to the states for road building and argued that this was not an "isolated effort toward economy" but "merely one element in a general program of budget balancing." And his message on housing, rather than asking for the kind of additional stimulus that Keynesians were advocating, recommended only reducing interest rates and otherwise making terms easier for middle-class home owners.[50]

In late November, Roosevelt released the names of the some thirty-plus board members of his National Foundation for Infantile Paralysis. In addition to Basil O'Connor and Keith Morgan, who ran it, members were largely politicians and wealthy donors. Morgan, in announcing plans for the 1938 Birthday Balls, reported formation of a Publishers Council of more than a hundred to provide largely free publicity.[51]

The normal December routine of drafting budget documents and the annual message to Congress was interrupted on Sunday, December 12. News of a sudden air attack by Japanese aircraft that sank the USS *Panay*, a navy gunboat on China's Yangtze River, created grave concerns. In retrospect, the two navy seamen and the captain of a Standard Oil tanker who were killed and the seventy-four persons injured may be called the first American casualties of World War II.

Roosevelt's public reactions were restrained. He made no statement but instructed Secretary Hull to protest and demand an apology, and he spoke with advisers about possible economic action against Japan. When Tokyo promptly expressed regret and four months later paid an agreed-upon indemnity of $2.2 million, Roosevelt dropped, for a time, any notion of sanctions. But he did hint in later December press conferences that the navy's building program might be expanded. Most Americans who paid attention seemed more annoyed than outraged by Japan's actions and clearly desired peace. Extreme isolationists such as Senator Gerald P. Nye blamed Roosevelt for failing to apply the Neutrality Act to Japan's war in China, which he said would have taken American vessels out of harm's way. More significant reaction to the *Panay* attack gave life to the so-called Ludlow Amendment to the Constitution, which would have required a national referendum before a declaration of war. Its author, Louis L. Ludlow, an Indiana journalist first elected to Congress in 1928, had been trying to force a vote on his amendment since 1935; the current discharge petition had 205 signatures of the required 218 on the day of the *Panay* attack. Within two days, more than enough additional signatures were affixed, which meant that a full vote on the amendment would take place in the House early in 1938. Eight days later, the sterile second session adjourned.[52]

For a year that had begun with great expectations of what could be accomplished with large congressional majorities and the broad policy visions of the second inaugural, the accomplishments of 1937 seemed pale indeed. The president's agenda, while not defeated, was clearly stalled. But, in the longer view of things, the virtual removal of the threat that the Court might cancel the heart of the New Deal was an important positive. Reflecting on the year in the introduction to the 1937 volume of his *Public Papers*, Roosevelt wrote in June 1941:

> [The year 1937] was the year which was to determine whether the kind of government which the people . . . had voted for in 1932, 1934, and 1936, was to be permitted by the Supreme Court to function. If it had not been permitted to function as a democracy, it is my reasoned opinion that there would have been great danger that ultimately it might have been compelled to give way to some alien type of government—in the vain hope that the new form of government might be able to give the average men and women the protection and cooperative assistance which they had the right to expect.
>
> For that reason I regard the effort initiated by the message on the Federal Judiciary of February 5, 1937, and the immediate results of it, as among the most important domestic achievements of my first two terms in office.[53]

This is, of course, a self-serving, counterfactual analysis with which few if any scholars will agree and most do not seriously consider. But it ought to be set against the prevailing notion that, flush with success after a uniquely overwhelming electoral triumph, Franklin Roosevelt lost his way until rescued by World War II, which made him relevant again.

The very short period—thirteen days—between the close of one session of Congress and the opening of the next robbed the occasion of some of its impact. The nationally broadcast annual message began, for the first time, with a discussion of foreign affairs. Roosevelt noted that "present facts and future hazards" arising from "acts and policies" of other nations, in "a world where stable civilization is actually threatened," mean that "we must keep ourselves adequately strong in self-defense." While he named neither friend nor foe, he declared flatly that peace "is most greatly jeopardized in and by those nations where democracy has been discarded or has never developed." He iterated his faith that "in the long run," democracy would survive and prevail. Although the navy was not mentioned in the speech, congressional leaders informed reporters that an augmented naval appropriations bill would receive expedited handling.

The bulk of the president's message was devoted to economic matters, with a particular emphasis on the stalled wages and hours bill: "The people of this country, by an overwhelming vote, are in favor of having the Congress—this Congress—put a floor below which industrial wages shall not fall, and a ceiling beyond which the hours of industrial labor shall not rise." He also called again for farm legislation to provide a "balanced output" in agriculture and noted "gladly" that a measure doing that had progressed to the House and Senate conference-committee stage. He also spoke of two more measures to be passed: bills to make tax evasion more difficult and to break up monopolies and combat the growing concentration of economic power.

Speaking in a more sophisticated macroeconomic way than he had previously, Roosevelt explained that his programs had raised the "nation's income" from $38 billion in 1933 to some $68 billion in 1937. He now set a goal of a rise to $90 or $100 billion.[54] Admitting that the 1939 budget would not be in balance, he insisted that "I am as anxious as any . . . business man" to have the budget balanced, but only on certain conditions, the first of which was that "we continue the policy of not permitting any needy American who can and is willing to work to starve because the Federal Government does not provide the work." (As we know, there were several millions of unemployed whom the New Deal was never able to put to work in peacetime.)

Despite his conditions, he bowed to conventional wisdom and pledged again to cut spending whenever possible. He admitted that there was a recession but attempted no analysis of why it was occurring, invoking only the kind of bromide that politicians like to use: "All we need today is to look upon the fundamental, sound economic conditions to know that this business recession causes more perplexity than fear on the part of most people and to contrast our prevailing mental attitude with the terror and despair of five years ago."[55]

The budget message the next day called for cutting spending on relief from nearly $2.5 billion in 1937 to half that by 1939 and public works from $1.1 billion to $0.6 billion in the same period. In his specialized budget press conference, he indicated his belief that the recession had begun only in November.[56] It would take another three months of steep economic decline to impel him to take effective steps, the same kinds of steps that had been necessary in the winter of 1933–34.

Roosevelt got his views on the Ludlow Amendment on the record by answering a prearranged request for them from Speaker Bankhead. Acknowledging the sincerity of its advocates' belief that it would help keep the country out of war, he claimed that it would have "the opposite effect" and "cripple any President in his foreign relations." The House vote on the discharge petition failed, as 209 were against discharge, while 188 favored it; 55 members who signed the discharge petition failed to vote for it, evidence of the strong pressure from the administration. Even had all the signers voted for it and secured discharge, the total would have been well short of the two-thirds majority necessary to institute the ratification procedure. The great virtue of keeping the measure locked up in committee was that it prevented debate not only in the House but also in the Senate, where it would slow down other business. This vote was the clearest test of strength so far between the president and the isolationists, whose greatest congressional strength was in the trans-Mississippi Midwest. It was significant that 21 Republicans, about a quarter of their total, supported the president, as did many national party leaders, including Landon, Knox, and Stimson, while 13 of the Progressives and Farmer-Laborites in Congress opposed him.[57]

In a Jackson Day speech at a fund-raising $100-a-plate dinner for twelve hundred, Roosevelt placed himself in a presidential tradition that featured early Democrats Jefferson and Jackson, Republicans Lincoln and Theodore Roosevelt, and Woodrow Wilson. He had done this before, but he struck a new note in speaking about the need for change in the Democratic Party. Although he expressed "pride" that the contemporary Democratic Party was a "national party," he felt that "it is right that the Party should slough off any remains of sectionalism and class consciousness." At a time when the continuing resistance to some of his program from congressional Democrats, many of them southerners, was becoming more and more evident, he warned, "Party progress cannot stop just because some public officials . . . fail to move along with the times. Their places will be amply filled by the arriving generation."[58]

This marks, it seems to me, the first hint of what became the celebrated attempt to "purge" some sitting conservative Democrats in various 1938 primary elections. To be sure, Roosevelt continued to welcome the infrequent election of southern progressives. The early January victory by Alabama's New Deal congressman Lister Hill (1894–1984) in a special election to fill Hugo Black's Senate seat may have encouraged him. The win by Hill, one of the few southern House members to support the stalled wages and hours legislation, helped the president to persuade seven southeastern governors to announce support for that legislation. The reelection victory of another liberal, Florida senator Claude D. Pepper (1900–1989), in a May primary swamping four opponents seemed further evidence of a progressive trend in the South.[59]

On January 5, Justice Sutherland became the second Horseman to announce his retirement. In a letter to the president, he set January 18 as his last day on the Court. With the furor of the Black nomination a vivid memory, and with what would surely be a contentious congressional session just begun, the last thing Roosevelt needed was another bruising fight over a Court appointment. He made what was all but certain to be a noncontroversial choice by selecting his solicitor general, Stanley F. Reed (1884–1980). A skilled legal craftsman, the Kentucky-born Reed had come to Washington in the Hoover administration, serving as general counsel to the Federal Farm Board and then the RFC. His first New Deal assignment was as special counsel in the Justice Department. When Solicitor General J. C. Biggs, who had been less than a success, resigned, Reed got the job. His competence—he won eleven of thirteen cases he argued as solicitor general—made him an obvious choice. His nomination was approved without significant dissent.[60]

In Reed's place as solicitor general, Roosevelt chose a more dynamic figure, Assistant Attorney General Robert H. Jackson, an upstate New Yorker he had known for years. Because Jackson and Harold Ickes had been making aggressive speeches about monopolistic practices during the late fall and winter, providing a kind of "bad cop" image against which Roosevelt's milder prescriptions seemed "good cop," the press and Jackson himself expected some difficulties in confirmation. But as Jackson notes in his memoir, he was equitably treated, and only four senators voted against him.[61]

The only other major early 1938 personnel change involved the mercurial Joseph P. Kennedy, who wanted very much to be the ambassador in London. Roosevelt liked the idea of sending a Boston Irishman to be his personal representative to the king of Great Britain, but warned the extremely bowlegged Kennedy how ridiculous he would look in the knee breeches and silk stockings that were still the prescribed dress for the formal presentation at the Court of St. James. Kennedy managed to get advance permission to wear trousers. Later, when Kennedy became a supporter of appeasement while his government opposed Hitler, his appointment proved to have been an error.[62]

At the end of January, Roosevelt asked Congress for increased spending on armaments, primarily naval. He warned that "we cannot assume that our defense would be limited to one coast" and that the other ocean and its coast would be safe and noted the need to defend the "connecting link," the Panama Canal. Journalists and publicists quickly styled this a bill for a "Two Ocean Navy" and emphasized hemispheric defense. In his *Public Papers'* note to that message, written in mid-1941, Roosevelt admitted what he did not say in 1938: "The recommendations were but the beginning of a vast program of rearmament. . . . It was obviously impossible to do everything at once and these were but the first steps."[63]

Rearmament was the only major element of the president's 1938 program that was achieved without significant difficulties. By the time the bill reached the president's desk in mid-May, Congress had given him more than he had originally asked for. The cost, just over a billion dollars, was largely for accelerated naval construction, but only thirty million dollars was spent in the next fiscal year, so it had only a negligible effect as an economic stimulus. The largest item was for 35,000-ton battleships: two were already under construction, two others were authorized in the regular naval appropriations bill then pending in Congress, and the president's recommendations called for two more, for a total of six. Two 20,000-ton aircraft carriers, not in the January request, had been added.[64]

An innovation in the publicity for the 1938 Birthday Ball announced by Keith Morgan had immediate results. Entertainer Eddie Cantor (1892?-1964), star of one of the most popular radio shows, had coined the phrase "March of Dimes," playing off the name of the popular filmed news program *The March of Time*, and suggested that people be asked to send a dime to the president. Cantor argued that the appeal "will enable all persons, even the children, to show our President that they are with him in this battle against this disease." Basil O'Connor got Roosevelt's approval. Cantor not only plugged the drive on his show but also lined up a number of other radio stars, including comedian Jack Benny and the diva Lily Pons, to do likewise in the week before the birthday. After noting that all of the proceeds would go to the new national foundation, Roosevelt described the early results in his birthday broadcast: "Bags of mail have been coming, literally by the truckload. . . . Yesterday between forty and fifty thousand letters came. . . . Today an even greater number. . . . In all the envelopes are dimes and quarters and even dollar bills . . . mostly from children who want to help other children to get well."[65]

This was one of the first uses of mobilized star power organized for Roosevelt or a Roosevelt cause. To be sure, Mary Pickford and other stars of the silent screen had sold Liberty Bonds during World War I, but I believe that never before had there been such a focus on a president. A kind of natural progression began with Roosevelt's personal entry into millions of homes for Fireside Chats and on more formal occasions, to the initial mobilization by Cantor of radio stars for a charitable cause, to later celebrity enlistments for political purposes. Some of them became successful celebrity candidates. The first of these was Helen Gahagan Douglas (1900–1980), an opera, stage, and movie star who became Democratic national committeewoman for California in 1940 and won the first of three terms in the House of Representatives in 1944.[66]

In February some benefits from the seemingly sterile special session became apparent: the housing and agriculture bills, which had been largely completed before adjournment, were both enacted. The major thrust of the housing legislation was to expand federal loans for home improvements and the purchase of federal insurance. Once it was passed, Roosevelt ordered Jesse Jones's RFC (given the quasi-independent nature of the RFC, the precise language was "I wish") to create the Federal National Mortgage Association—which became known as Fannie Mae. It was to insure mortgages and home improvements at low interest rates with an initial capital of ten million dollars and a surplus of one million dollars. By the beginning of 1941, it had purchased some fifty thousand mortgages aggregating more than two hundred million dollars and was a major factor in the expansion of home ownership, one of the lasting achievements of the New Deal.[67]

The second Agricultural Adjustment Act was what Roosevelt and some later historians have called the third phase of New Deal agricultural policy. The first phase was the 1933 AAA, declared unconstitutional in the January 1936 *Butler* decision. The Soil Conservation Act of February 1936, which made payments to farmers based largely on maintenance of good conservation practices, began the second phase. Bumper crops in 1937 and the forecast of another good harvest in 1938 spurred adoption of the second AAA. While continuing soil conservation payments aimed at controlling output to achieve an "ever normal granary," the act also established a massive crop-loan program at 90 percent of parity for basic crops, combined with marketing agreements. What must be understood about the New Deal agricultural arrangements was that farm population was declining. Millions of poor farm families, white and black, were being forced off their land.

Between the 1930 and 1950 U.S. Censuses, the number of farms declined by nearly 15 percent, while total farm acreage grew at roughly the same rate. Although many farm families remained poor, the general economic status of the farm population was greatly improved. The verdict on Roosevelt's farm policy by agricultural historian Theodore Saloutos is judicious. "With all its limitations and frustrations, the New Deal, by making operational the ideas and plans that had been long on the minds of agricultural researchers and thinkers, constituted the greatest innovative epoch in the history of American agriculture."[68]

Ironically, the first group to desert the New Deal political coalition was American farmers outside of the South. In the 1938 elections, they began to return to their traditional political home in the Republican Party. Polls taken by the Department of Agriculture in 1938 showed that farmers particularly disliked relief in general, especially the WPA, though, like most Americans, they looked with favor on the CCC.[69]

Early in February, faced with unmistakable evidence of rising unemployment—"during the past three months approximately three million persons have lost their jobs"—and a general economic slowdown, Roosevelt sent a special message to Congress asking for an additional $250 million "to provide relief and work relief." The sum would add perhaps 500,000 persons to the WPA rolls. This followed a White House visit by a delegation of midwestern mayors who had asked the president for a $400 million appropriation and an increase of 3 million on the WPA rolls and subsequent consultation with advisers and congressional leaders. Roosevelt clearly hoped that the recession would soon be over and not require additional stimulus dollars, but some congressional leaders expected that additional extra funds would be necessary.[70]

Congress complied with relative speed: Aubrey Williams, WPA deputy administrator, testified before a House committee the next day that the appropriation would enable adding 500,000 persons to WPA rolls, but if it were not enacted, 450,000 persons would have to be cut from the rolls. He made similar statements before a Senate committee and added, in the face of calls by some

Senate liberals for a larger appropriation, that $250 million was sufficient, though he surely did not believe that. Five days later, the House passed the bill, 353–23, and the Senate, interrupting a filibuster on the antilynching bill, approved the measure, 67–1, and after a conference reconciled differences the bill was sent to the White House. In major urban centers, WPA hiring began on March 4, twenty-two days after the president has sent his request.[71]

While his request for WPA funds was still in Congress, the president tried to undo another aspect of his previous overconfidence in recovery. Early in 1937, he had authorized the RFC to "suspend the exercise of its lending authority," which virtually took the agency out of business. In mid-February, he tried to loosen credit markets by urging Jesse Jones to "make credit available too all deserving borrowers . . . especially loans that will maintain or increase employment." Although the ever-cautious Jones announced that he had $1.5 billion available, he also noted that he did not believe there would be "a demand for any considerable part of it." By mid-December, the RFC had authorized new loans totaling $837 million, almost half of it to bolster mortgage credit, and less than half of those funds had been disbursed by the agency.[72]

In a mid-February press conference, the president handed out a statement on prices and wages over the names of Morgenthau, Wallace, Perkins, and Eccles, designed to show an administration consensus on economic policy. Nothing was further from the truth: Morgenthau and Eccles—the Treasury and the Federal Reserve, respectively—had very different prescriptions for the economy. For the next two months, as the recession gathered momentum, the furious struggle over spending within the administration—sometimes described as antimonopolistic, as that was a more comfortable flag for many, like Robert Jackson, to fight under—saw Morgenthau's influence steadily diminish. Although the formal announcements that signaled the triumph of the spenders did not come until April 14, the crucial decision came almost two weeks earlier, during Roosevelt's ten-day break at Warm Springs.[73]

While the decision was still in flux, tensions stemming from the policy struggle, steadily deteriorating economic conditions, difficulties his major bills were encountering in Congress, and the growing crisis in Europe stemming from Hitler's annexation of Austria, the Anschluss of March 13, were surely reflected in the president's edgy behavior in a setting where he was usually relaxed. In his press conference of March 29, with the handful of pool reporters gathered around his car, he was questioned about his executive branch reorganization plan, which had survived in the Senate the preceding day by the narrowest of margins—a vote of forty-eight to forty-eight on a motion to recommit—before passing, forty-nine to forty-two. There had been an extensive organized campaign against it led by Father Coughlin and the National Committee to Uphold Constitutional Government, a right-wing pressure group first organized by newspaper publisher Frank E. Gannett (1876–1957) and the former progressive gadfly Amos R. E. Pinchot[74]

(1873–1944) in 1937 to fight the Supreme Court bill, which, among other things, generated seventy-five thousand telegrams to the Senate. Its propaganda insisted that Roosevelt was trying to make himself a dictator.[75]

Q: How about the Senate fight on the Reorganization Bill?

THE PRESIDENT: I would love to give you a direct quote on that.

Q: We would take it in a minute. (Laughter)

THE PRESIDENT: Mac [Secretary Marvin McIntyre] says, "No." Didn't he? (Laughter)

Q: I would love to get something on that bill.

THE PRESIDENT: Well, I will tell you, I will take a shot at it. It proves that the Senate cannot be purchased by organized telegrams based on direct misrepresentation.

MR. MCINTYRE: Do you want to use that word, "purchased"?

THE PRESIDENT: Yes it is all right.

Q: Can we put this in direct quotes?

THE PRESIDENT: Yes, it is all right.[76]

The use of the word *purchased*—if he had said *influenced,* there could have been no reasonable complaint—set off a brief tempest in the Senate, as his secretary had known it would. It was an act of foolish petulance, indicating his general frustration and the tensions inherent in the process of making a crucial decision about spending.

A key to that decision, and to many subsequent decisions, was the influence of Harry Hopkins. He had just gone through two personal crises. In October his second wife, Barbara, lost a two-year battle to breast cancer; two months later, Hopkins underwent surgery for stomach cancer at the Mayo Clinic and was away from Washington all winter. After his discharge from the hospital, he recuperated at Joseph P. Kennedy's compound at West Palm Beach and from there communicated with his allies. He joined Roosevelt at Warm Springs two days after the injudicious press conference—presumably to visit a nearby relief project with the president but actually to urge a basic shift in economic policy. He came armed with memoranda and supporting documents from Aubrey Williams, Leon Henderson, and Beardsley Ruml (1894–1960), an Eccles appointee as an outside director of the New York Federal Reserve Bank. The argument these men made was distinctly Keynesian, but, unlike Keynes's February letter, which none of the spending advocates seems to have been aware of, their efforts apparently contained nothing about adjusting the treatment of businessmen.[77]

The president had heard the message before. A man whose time was usually cut up into quarter- or half-hour increments, he had accepted a four-hour briefing the previous November from three economic technicians: Harry Hopkins's man, Leon Henderson; Isador Lubin (1896–1978), a student of Thorstein Veblen who was commissioner of labor statistics; and Lauchlin Currie (1902–93), a Canadian-born economist trained at the London School of Economics and Harvard (Ph.D., 1931) where he taught until, after becoming an American citizen in 1934, he was recruited by economist Jacob Viner (1892–1970) to join his "freshman brain trust" in the Treasury. By 1937 Currie was working for Marriner Eccles at the Federal Reserve. Although Roosevelt did not act then on the essentially Keynesian advice the three gave him, Currie must have impressed Roosevelt favorably. He later made him the first economist ever to serve on the White House staff.[78] But by April 1938, with perhaps four million added to the jobless rolls and the stock market in a steep nosedive along with all the economic indicators, Roosevelt found the spending argument irresistible.

Back in Washington on April 3, Roosevelt began preparation for the stimulus package he would present to Congress without recourse to his chief fiscal adviser or any of his deputies. Morgenthau, still on vacation at Sea Island, Georgia, first learned that something was afoot when Henry Wallace phoned on April 4 to tell him that Roosevelt, "rarin' to go," had tasked the agriculture secretary and Jesse Jones with framing proposals for housing, flood control, and rural rehabilitation. Morgenthau remained on vacation for six more days, but on his return Sunday evening, April 10, he went to the White House with a memorandum of his own to find the president in conference with Hopkins and Jimmy Roosevelt. He reported the next morning to his staff that the president told him they had been "travelling fast. . . . [Y]ou will have to hurry to catch up." Roosevelt then proceeded to spell out some of their plans and concluded by asking if Morgenthau agreed, though he surely knew that he did not.

Morgenthau replied that it "frightens me" and "will frighten the country" and asked how much it would cost. Roosevelt did not answer, and Morgenthau's request for an itemized list was not met, probably because one did not yet exist, although the president had sketched the broad outlines in a cabinet meeting earlier in the week, which Morgenthau's deputy had attended. Although Morgenthau had written a memorandum sketching an alternative, less sweeping proposal to be financed by bond issues, he did not present it but left after urging Roosevelt not to decide "until you sleep on it."

At a Monday-morning Treasury staff meeting, Morgenthau attacked the president and the spenders who had decided "the whole thing" without "a single person in the Treasury" being involved. "They have stampeded him like cattle." He then left that meeting to attend a White House briefing for congressional leaders in which Roosevelt sketched out his plans "to stimulate further recovery." As it was ending, Morgenthau broke in to note the fiscal implications of the plan: he predicted that revenue would be $900 million less than the January estimate and that the president's plan would increase the budget deficit to $3.5 billion. This, he later noted, gave everyone "quite a shock." He and Roosevelt then had their regular weekly lunch at which Roosevelt chastised him for his interjection during the congressional briefing. The next day, Morgenthau reported the following interchange with Jimmy Roosevelt:

MORGENTHAU: I wish you to take the following message to your father. "After giving the matter further consideration, I will let you know whether I can finance it."

JIMMY ROOSEVELT: Well, of course you can finance it.

MORGENTHAU: I don't know, Jimmy.

Morgenthau reports that after an anguished night, "he could see no choice but to resign." He telephoned Roosevelt and asked for a half-hour meeting for "his day in court" without stating his intention. At that meeting, on the day before Roosevelt's message was to go to Congress and he was scheduled to explain it in a Fireside Chat, Morgenthau did not quite resign, but he told the president, "If you insist on going through with this spending program I am seriously thinking of resigning."

After Roosevelt protested and complimented him on what a good job he had been doing, Morgenthau spelled out his grievances: "Nobody in the Treasury had been consulted. . . . You are asking your general, in charge of finances, to carry out a program when he had nothing to do with the planning." Roosevelt refused even to consider resignation. Morgenthau left, still contemplating resignation, and spent the next few hours in what he later described as a gloomy daze of indecision. But before he went to bed, he had decided not to resign.[79] It seems fairly clear that Roosevelt knew his man and never feared that his friend would resign. The episode shows the weakness—and the strength—of Roosevelt's sometimes bizarre administrative style. It was absurd to plan a massive spending program without involving the Treasury. But to have involved Morgenthau and his staff in the planning of a program of which they disapproved would have inevitably involved delay when time was of the essence. To replace Morgenthau with a spender—Eccles would have been a likely candidate—would have created confusion and engendered further controversy both within and without the administration at a time when unity was needed. In this instance, the seemingly foolish policy seems better than its alternatives. And Morgenthau continued to give good service throughout Roosevelt's presidency and beyond.

On April 14 at noon, a presidential message to Congress spelled out a two-part program "to stimulate further recovery." One part involved fiscal measures to loosen credit, which the administration could execute on its own authority; the other called for Congress to appropriate just over $2 billion to put people to work and to authorize nearly another $1 billion in loans for PWA projects and other large-scale construction. The total, $3.062 billion, was the largest single appropriation ever requested.[80]

That evening the president explained what he had done in a Fireside Chat. It was Maundy Thursday, and Roosevelt began by explaining that only the urgency of the matter had led him to act during Holy Week. He hoped that his message might give "greater peace of mind" and that "the hope of Easter may be more real at firesides everywhere."

He then briefly summarized the nation's economic history since 1933: four and a half years of recovery followed by a "visible setback" in the past seven months. He explained that the government had "waited patiently" for "the forces of business" to recover, but it was now clear that "government itself can no longer safely fail to take aggressive government steps to" combat the recession. He reassured his listeners that "recession has not returned us to the disasters and suffering of the beginning of 1933" and pointed out that "your money in the bank is safe," farmers are "no longer in deep distress," and "national income" was up by almost 50 percent over 1932. He went on, in a rare occurrence, to admit error. "Last autumn in a sincere effort to bring Government expenditures and Government income into closer balance, the Budget I worked out called for sharp decreases in Government spending. In the light of present conditions those estimates were far too low. This new program adds two billion and sixty-two million dollars to direct Treasury expenditures and another nine hundred and fifty million dollars to Government loans—and the latter sum, because they are loans, will come back to the Treasury in the future." He closed with a seafaring metaphor: "I believe we have been right in the course we have charted. To abandon our purpose of building a greater, a more stable and a more tolerant America, would be to miss the tide and perhaps to miss the port. I propose to sail ahead. . . . to reach a port, we must sail—sail, not tie at anchor—sail, not drift."[81]

The reaction from the nation's press was largely negative. For the vast majority of editorial writers, the notion of deficit spending as a way to recovery was counterintuitive. The *Cleveland Plain Dealer,* more moderate than most, held that the president's plan, except for relief, "is fruitage of unsound thinking." Wall Street was similarly critical, with bankers' comments focusing on the likelihood of inflation as the dollar dropped against other major currencies. While many congressional voices were raised against the whole idea of deficit spending—House Rules Committee chair John J. O'Connor's view that "priming the pump won't do any good if there's no water in the well" was held by many who were less articulate—the Democratic leadership was convinced, correctly as it turned out, that, in an election year with the economy deteriorating and growing distress visible, the president would get what he wanted. Doubt was expressed about whether the president would be given the freedom to disburse funds without the customary "earmarking" by Congress, as had been the case for earlier WPA and PWA appropriations.[82]

Final passage of the president's stimulus proposal came just over two months later, as Congress was adjourning on June 16. The total price tag had risen to

$3.7 billion, but that included $800 million in reappropriation of unused funds. Some broad earmarks were imposed on the president's use of WPA funds, which had been previously allocated at his discretion, but they were all but meaningless. The president had asked for $1.25 billion for the WPA: Congress eventually appropriated $1.425 billion, earmarked so that no more than $485.5 million could be used for roads, $655 million for construction, and $285 million for other projects, but Congress gave him discretion to increase the share of those categories by as much as 15 percent. Most other agencies included in Roosevelt's message got nonearmarked funds in at least the amounts that he asked for. All things considered, it was an administration triumph. Faced with obvious needs, Congress continued to support relief in the hope of further recovery. At the same time, as will be demonstrated in the next chapters, it was very difficult to get innovative reform legislation enacted, and those measures eventually passed were often seriously modified in passage.[83]

In the battle for Roosevelt's mind, the spenders had clearly won. Although he would continue to speak about eventually balancing the budget, he never again attempted to cut back total government spending. The results were, in the course of the coming months, gratifying. The economic decline was reversed, and, as noted, national income soon exceeded the level reached in mid-1937. But the New Deal never ended the Depression, and the weak recovery of the late 1930s was bolstered by greater spending on armaments. The 1938 session of Congress was the first to appropriate as much $1 billion for military purposes since the World War I era.

Most historians give Roosevelt failing grades for his performance as "economist in chief."[84] A sounder judgment, it seems to me, is that Roosevelt did err badly in taking his foot off the economic gas pedal after the 1936 election and was slow to realize that a serious recession was in progress. Once he realized it, he reacted far too mildly, remarking in late November 1937 that "we have gradually come to an end or, rather, a great diminution of pump-priming." But within a few months, he put together and sold to Congress a collection of measures that ended the decline and resumed the pattern of economic improvement that had begun in the hundred days. Compared with his initial understandings of the economy in 1933, his perception and understanding of the nation's economic processes had expanded enormously.

Roosevelt's failure publicly to embrace the Keynesian heresy is not surprising. The fact of the matter is that no American president either uttered or wrote the fearful words *Keynes* or *Keynesian* on a public occasion until 1981. Ronald Reagan, of course, was not praising Keynes but was celebrating the mistaken notion that Keynes's ideas had been buried.[85]

15   Economic Progress, Political Setback
1938–39

ROOSEVELT'S REFORM AGENDA FACED HEAVY legislative going during
the 1938 session of Congress. As noted, two of the four holdover measures from
the 1937 sessions, the AAA and housing bills, as well as new bills adding WPA
funds and expanding RFC loan authority, were passed early in the session.
But on April 8, as the stimulus package was being put together, the president's
sweeping executive reorganization plan was defeated in the House after barely
surviving in the Senate. A leading authority on the plan believes that the narrow defeat could have been a victory if the president's supporters had been
more adept; one might add that if the spending proposals had been presented
earlier, the entire dynamic of the legislative process might have been different.[1]

The filibuster against Robert Wagner's antilynching bill stalled most Senate
business. Wagner made two separate attempts to get cloture and cut off debate,
but neither motion even gained a majority; a two-thirds vote was required. On
February 21, he gave up the fight to allow debate to begin on the president's
request for $250 billion for the WPA. This concession ended the first real Senate
debate on civil rights during the New Deal.

While the major responsibility for cloture's failure clearly lay with northern
Democrats, all but one member of the party of Lincoln in the Senate refused
to vote to cut off debate. Most used the rationale that they were defending
what the minority leader, Charles McNary of Oregon, called "free speech . . .
the last barrier to tyranny," although in fact McNary had voted for cloture on
nine previous occasions. One of the prerequisites for the functioning of the
conservative congressional coalition was the increasing abandonment of once
traditional GOP support for at least pro forma civil rights. George Norris, never
a party to that coalition, excused his failure to support cloture by arguing that if
passed, the bill would provoke more violence. He further claimed that lynching
was "almost unknown," although there had been at least seven during 1937, and
five would occur in 1938. Roosevelt said that he thought the matter ought to be
pursued in other ways. He argued that Congress should investigate, or ask the
attorney general to investigate, all cases "where the taking of human life results
from mob violence of any kind." But he did not instruct the attorney general
to take any such action. Nor did the president ever confront the blatant racism

of Democratic officeholders, although he encouraged others, like Ickes and Hopkins, to do so.

Back in 1935, for example, when Georgia's governor, Eugene Talmadge (1884–1946), sent a letter to Roosevelt that criticized federal relief wage rates, the president forwarded it to Hopkins to draft an official reply. Hopkins wrote a blistering reply for Roosevelt, who had it returned to the relief administrator for him to sign instead.[2]

The final holdover measure, wages and hours legislation, may have been a beneficiary of the delay, as the crucial votes came after the introduction of the president's stimulus package, rather than before. Roosevelt's wages and hours goal was to restore the standards that had been swept away when the Supreme Court destroyed the NRA in the 1935 *Schechter* decision. The original 1937 bill applied a national forty-forty standard: a forty-hour week at a minimum pay of forty cents an hour, with "time and a half"—a 50 percent premium—for any hours worked in addition to eight in a day or forty in a week. While a number of legislators were against any such regulation, there were always enough votes in the House for a bill of some kind. The major opposition was in the Senate, where southern senators insisted that it would be disastrous for their section if their low-wage advantage were eliminated. They insisted on lower regional standards for the South. While Roosevelt never stipulated a specific standard, he was adamant that standards must be national.

In the House, the conservative chair of its Rules Committee, John J. O'Connor (D-NY), kept the bill bottled up. Roosevelt summoned him to the White House and urged him to bring the bill to a vote. On leaving O'Connor told reporters that they talked about "cherry blossoms." Roosevelt told his press conference what the subject really was and allowed them to say so. He then wrote a public letter to New Jersey's Mary T. Norton (1875–1959), chair of the Labor Committee, encouraging her to file a discharge petition; she did, and the required 218 signatures were affixed that day. Very different bills passed each house, though all versions barred the products of child labor from interstate commerce, as the NRA had done. Only the Senate version set lower standards for the South.[3]

The version that emerged from the conference committee and was enacted into law kept national standards but delayed the forty-forty formula. The 1938 Fair Labor Standards Act called for an initial maximum hour standard of a forty-four-hour week, dropping to forty hours in 1940. The initial minimum wage level was just twenty-five cents an hour for 1938, thirty cents for 1939, and rising to the original forty-cent level only after seven years. But even the twenty-five-cent level raised the wages of large numbers of workers, especially in the South, where, for example, it raised the wages of 44 percent of sawmill workers.[4]

Much more serious in the long run were the limitations placed on the occupations covered by the new law: those exempted from federal control included all agricultural employment, most service and intrastate retail establishments, and household help. These affected mostly African American and women workers and early school leavers of all kinds. When wartime full employment arrived, large-scale American agriculture outside of the South came to depend more and more on recruiting presumably temporary foreign labor, primarily from Mexico. (Florida was an exception: it came to depend on foreign labor from the Bahamas.) One of the consequences of the exemption of whole categories of occupations from federal wage and hour regulation was to mark them as jobs no American should want, as their pay and working conditions were below what became the American standard. However, the relative disdain with which many left-leaning historians have treated the act is often shortsighted and overstated.[5] The great fear of many in the labor movement that minimum wages would become veritable maxima has not been the case. In addition, the existence of federal legislation permitted and encouraged individual states to enact their own laws, almost always at a higher rate and covering occupations outside of federal jurisdiction.

Nothing better illustrates the three-ring-circus nature of Roosevelt's presidency than the fact that in mid-March 1938, while he was trying to decide about further intervention to reverse the recession, reacting to the Nazi takeover of Austria, and getting the wages and hours legislation passed, he found it necessary personally to conduct a hearing on a bitter dispute among the triumvirate in charge of the TVA. As early as 1935, TVA directors David Lilienthal and Harcourt Morgan began to outvote the chairman, Arthur E. Morgan, on a variety of issues, most crucially his willingness to make what they thought were unnecessary concessions to private power companies. Roosevelt probably should have settled the matter long before he did, but that was not his way. Whenever possible he avoided firing anyone, preferring to appoint them to other, usually less important, positions, as he had done with George Peek and many others.

As Roosevelt explained—on background—in his March 8 press conference, the TVA situation was "a long, long story" that he traced back to the chairman's September 1937 article in the *Atlantic Monthly* attacking his codirectors. The president went on to tell reporters that he would call the three to the White House that week, listen to their views, and then decide what to do.[6]

David Lilienthal's journal reports a different scenario. He came to see Roosevelt on March 3, five days before the press conference just described, and tells of being taken into Roosevelt's "bedroom, where he was stretched out in his underclothes [as his valet was dressing him]. He has that amazing assurance and nonchalance and complete lack of self-consciousness that made it seem entirely appropriate to be discussing matters of high policy with a gentleman in his B.V.D.s,[7] and particularly a man whose legs are shriveled up. . . . He sat up while his valet was strapping on his braces and said with a *terrific* scowl, 'What in hell are we going to do about Arthur Morgan? He's out again.'" Lilienthal says they discussed the problem of Morgan and that as the now dressed president was preparing to go to a state luncheon, Lilienthal offered to resign if he were in any way an embarrassment. Roosevelt responded, he reports: "Don't be silly. The only embarrassment is the embarrassment of having a befuddled old man on our hands."

Four days later, a letter from Chairman Morgan to Congressman Maury Maverick appeared in the papers, denouncing Lilienthal. During the day, Marvin McIntyre called, asking Lilienthal to come to the White House that afternoon. Upstairs in the Lincoln Study, Roosevelt explained what he called his "little plan," which was to do to Morgan what he had done to Jimmy Walker in 1932. After explaining the Walker affair, the president proposed calling all three directors to the White House and saying,

> "You, Chairman Morgan have made grave charges . . . against your colleagues; and you [Harcourt] and Lilienthal, have filed a statement with me saying that the chairman is obstructing the work of the board, etc. Now I want you to state the facts that support those charges, and I will ask the questions and I will be the judge." I will say to Morgan "Now I don't want any opinions and I don't want any speeches. I want cold facts." And if he starts going off into his usual harangues and personalities, I will just stop him and say, "I don't want that—I want the facts." And I will turn to you and [Harcourt] and say, "What is the answer to these charges, and again, I want the facts, not opinions." . . . What do you think of that?

Lilienthal thought that it was "a grand idea."[8]

Roosevelt's hopes that the process would result in a resignation, as in 1932, were not realized. Chairman Morgan, who at fifty-nine was fewer than four years older than Roosevelt, thwarted the president's plan and refused to answer most of Roosevelt's questions in three separate hearings, on March 11, 18, and 21. He insisted he would answer questions only to a congressional committee and denied the president's right to remove him. Lilienthal and H. A. Morgan, of course, answered Roosevelt's questions and made a case for the chairman's removal. The first session was a grueling six hours,[9] the other two much shorter. At the final session, Roosevelt gave the chairman forty-eight hours to respond more fully; he did not. On March 23, the president sent him a formal letter of dismissal, which Morgan refused to recognize. Eventually, in a case the Supreme Court refused to review, the president's right to remove Morgan and other federal officials was validated. Morgan and his lawyers had hoped that the Court would expand a 1937 decision that had restricted that right in a case involving a member of an independent commission.[10]

Whatever one may think of the ethics of Roosevelt's maneuvering, the result was a clear vindication of his position. Congress did not challenge it, despite partisan attacks on Morgan's dismissal by a few of Roosevelt's opponents. But surely the administrative disarray demonstrated by the internal struggle among the men the president had appointed contributed to the lack of confidence shown a few days later when the House narrowly rejected the 1938 reorganization plan.[11]

Although the president and Morgenthau had differed on the need for an economic stimulus, they were in general agreement about tax policy. Both had insisted that a tax on undistributed corporate profits be included in the 1936 Revenue Act over the objections of many conservatives. The existing law had exempted some four billion dollars in undistributed corporate profits from taxation, according to Treasury estimates. A compromise bill, despite the objections of Senate Finance Committee chair Pat Harrison, included a modest graduated tax on undistributed profits. Once the recession hit, Harrison renewed his attack on the undistributed-profits tax bill and other business taxes and had a lot of support, not only from economic conservatives like Joe Kennedy, Jesse Jones, and Baruch, who objected to such taxes on principle, but also from spenders like Hopkins and Eccles, who wanted to reduce taxes only as an antirecession measure. In a conference with Morgenthau and his tax expert, Roswell Magill (1895–1963), Roosevelt, according to Magill's notes, complained on other grounds, noting that a person with a capital gain of five thousand dollars would pay at the same 15 percent tax rate as one with a gain of a half-million dollars. Reluctant to sign the bill but unwilling to veto it because doing so would cause the government to lose other revenue it badly needed, the president allowed it to become law without his signature, the first time he had done so. He explained this to the nation in his broadcast commencement address for the thirteen graduating seniors at the high school in the New Deal–created community of Arthurdale, West Virginia, which was one of Eleanor Roosevelt's pet projects. What the students or their parents, few if any of whom had net incomes of twenty-five hundred dollars—the level that triggered income tax liability— thought of this high finance is not known, but "there could be no doubt" of their esteem for the president.[12]

Shortly after Congress adjourned, Roosevelt gave a Fireside Chat on June 24 that Rosenman labeled "on Party Primaries," although most of it was a summary of the just-concluded session. While Roosevelt had some complaints about Congress, particularly its failure to pass his reorganization plan, he praised its major accomplishments—including the farm bill and the "additional funds . . . to take care of what we hope is a temporary additional number of unemployed and to encourage production . . . by private enterprise," which he styled "our program for the national defense of our economic system." His highest praise was reserved for the Fair Labor Standards Act, which he hailed as second only to the Social Security Act as a "far-reaching, far-sighted program for the benefit of workers." Referring to the massive propaganda attack against it, he warned, "Do not let any calamity howling executive with an income of $1,000 a day who has been turning his employees over to the Government relief rolls in order to preserve his companies undistributed reserves, tell you—using his stockholders' money to pay the postage for his personal opinions—that a wage of $11 a week is going to have a disastrous effect on all American industry." Roosevelt immediately qualified this by saying that such an executive was a rarity. But he, and his more sophisticated opponents, understood that the vivid image of the greedy businessman would remain in the minds of most listeners.

Switching to the Court, Roosevelt briefly referred to his 1937 struggle as "a lost battle that won a war" and praised its recent decisions as "eloquent testimony of a willingness to collaborate with the two other branches of Government to make democracy work."

Praise for the Court was followed by an attack on unnamed opponents—"that small minority which . . . is always eager to resume its control over the Government of the United States." He likened them to "Copperheads"[13] and praised their rejection by both Congress and the American people. Using simple, commonsense language, he analyzed the economic situation: "It makes no difference whether you call it a recession or a depression. In 1932 . . . national income [was] thirty-eight billion dollars [it rose steadily by 1937] to seventy billion dollars. . . . This year, 1938 . . . we hope that [it] will not fall below sixty billion dollars."

After reminding his listeners that "banking and business and farming are not falling apart," as they had done in "the terrible winter of 1932–1933," he admitted that "last year mistakes were made by leaders of business, labor, and government." He detailed the errors of each group. Business leaders "pleaded for a curtailment of public spending," saying that "they would take up the slack." They increased "their inventories too fast" and set many prices "too high for their goods to sell." "Some labor leaders goaded by decades of oppression" went too far, "using methods which frightened many well-wishing people" and creating "jurisdictional disputes." But when it came to governmental errors, he admitted only "mistakes of optimism in assuming that industry and labor would . . . make no mistakes" and failures by Congress in "not passing" farm and wages and hours bills in 1937. The leader who could proclaim in general that "presidents err" could not bring himself to repeat the admission he had made in April that he had contributed to the economic downturn by insisting on cutting down on spending.[14] He ended his discussion of the economy by hoping that as a result of past "mistakes," capital and labor would "cooperate more intelligently together" and with government. He urged both to "resist wage cuts" and referred with pleasure to reduced steel prices that involved no wage cuts. More such decisions, he suggested, could replace "a great part of the Government spending which the failure of cooperation made necessary this year."

This pseudoanalysis might have attracted more attention had not the concluding minutes of the chat contained its real news: confirmation that the president, in his role as party leader, would intervene in the year's Democratic Party primaries, as had been rumored for months. After urging everyone to vote in the upcoming primaries, Roosevelt emphasized:

In the coming primaries . . . there will be many clashes between two schools of thought, generally classified as liberal and conservative. Roughly speaking the liberal school of thought recognizes that the new conditions throughout the world call for new remedies. . . . The opposing or conservative school of thought, as a general proposition, does not recognize the need for Government itself to step in and take action to meet these new problems. It believes that individual initiative and private philanthropy will solve them—that we ought to repeal many of the things we have done and go back, for instance, to the old gold standard. Or stop all this business of old age pensions and unemployment insurance, or repeal the Securities and Exchange Act, or let monopolies thrive unchecked—return, in effect, to the kind of Government we had in the twenties.

Assuming the mental capacity of all the candidates, the important question which it seems to me the primary voter must ask is this: "To which of these general schools of thought does the candidate belong?"

Roosevelt made a distinction that few presidents, or for that matter scholars, then made: the difference between his role "as President of the United States" and as "the head of the Democratic Party." He would not, as president, ask the voters to vote "for Democrats" in November, nor was he, "as President," taking part in Democratic primaries. But he insisted that as "head of the Democratic Party," he had "every right to speak" in the "few instances" where there was "a clear issue" involving basic "principles or involving a clear misuse of my own name."[15]

Thus began Roosevelt's overt involvement in what journalists and politicians had long been calling a "purge"[16] of Democratic candidates. Supposedly, it was managed by a perhaps mythical "elimination committee," whose chief members seemed to be Tom Corcoran and James Roosevelt. The president never used the word *purge* in that sense in his public discourse. The one use found in a computerized search was in his 1936 election-eve Madison Square Garden speech, accusing the Republicans of wanting "to purge the [relief] rolls by starvation."[17]

The earliest use of the word *purge* in this sense coupled with presidential politics that I have found came in Arthur Krock's *New York Times* column in mid-January 1938: he wrote of "the party purge which some New Dealers had been urging on" the president. In late May, Harry Hopkins, an Iowa native, endorsed an existing primary challenge to Iowa senator Guy M. Gillette (1879–1973) by House member Otha D. Wearin (1903–90), the youngest member of Congress. Both had been elected to the House in 1932, and each had supported most New Deal measures while voting against the NRA and the first AAA. In 1936 Gillette had been elected to fill a vacated Senate seat; he opposed the Court-packing plan and the wages and hours bill that Wearin supported. Asked about the contest in his press conference, Roosevelt adhered to his traditional "no comment," but, off the record, explained that if he said either "yes" or "no" it would be interpreted as an endorsement for one of the candidates, and in this particular case "I did not know a thing." When Gillette won, Roosevelt commented on June 7, "Perfectly good carrying out of a perfectly good system of party government," and noted that Gillette would call on him. Yet the mythic power of the purge is so attractive that a distinguished historian recently wrote that Roosevelt had "earned [Gillette's] unquenchable enmity" by campaigning against him in the 1938 primary.[18]

Just seventeen days later, as we have seen, Roosevelt formally announced a new policy of occasional negative intervention. What had happened in the interim? For one thing, Congress had adjourned. But even had Congress adjourned well before the Iowa primary, it is unlikely that the president would have intervened in it. Roosevelt's decision to intervene in party primaries was selective, purposeful, and secret. Although "informed sources" expected him to attempt purges of all nine of the senators who opposed his Court plan and were running for reelection, he intervened personally in only five contests. Three were aimed at well-established southern senators. All failed. The other two succeeded. One ensured the reelection of his Senate majority leader; the other removed the recalcitrant chair of the House Rules Committee, John J. O'Connor. Most scholars emphasize the losses and refer to the victories as if they were minor, but had those results been reversed the president's grip on Congress would probably have been even less secure.[19]

Roosevelt's overt tactical maneuvers masked his covert strategic objective: to change the American party system so that it resembled the ideal type he described in his Fireside Chat, one in which the parties were each ideologically consistent, the one thoroughly liberal, the other consistently conservative. He understood that the greatest barrier to making his party consistently liberal was the question of race, which explains his focus on southern senators. But Roosevelt never directly confronted white supremacy, a fundamental flaw in American democracy, and never initiated a frank conversation about race with the American people that might have hastened significantly the progress toward legal equality. It may have been more than a coincidence that just as he was drafting his Fireside Chat he signed a two-sentence note of greeting to the National Association for the Advancement of Colored People at its annual conference. In the note, he recognized that "no democracy can long survive which does not accept as fundamental to its very existence the recognition of the rights of its minorities."[20] No action accompanied or followed this gesture.

The first of Roosevelt's five personal primary interventions came on July 9, in Covington, Kentucky. The president praised both Majority Leader Barkley and his primary challenger, Governor A. B. (Happy) Chandler (1898–1991), who were both there, as "men of ability," and after insisting that "I am not interfering in any shape, manner or form in the primary campaign in Kentucky," he went on to express and explain his preference for Barkley. His justification was that "I have a clear right to tell you certain facts relating to the National Government." Among those facts was that Barkley was an important national figure and that Chandler, "who would make a good Senator from Kentucky," would, if elected, also be a very junior member of the Senate.[21] What he did not say was that if Barkley lost, his all but certain replacement would have been Mississippi's Pat Harrison, a popular reactionary whom Barkley had edged out by a single vote in 1937. This was not a "purge" but a preference for an important elected official. The president endorsed a number of others, none of them controversial, on his way to board the cruiser *Houston*.

The first speeches that could be called purge attempts came a month later, shortly after the *Houston* landed him at Pensacola, Florida. A three-week fishing cruise had taken him to the Galapagos Islands and back through the Panama Canal. Reporters were advised that in speeches in their states, the president would oppose the renominations of two southern Senate oligarchs, Georgia's Walter F. George (1878–1957) and South Carolina's Cotton Ed Smith. As the *New York Times*' White House correspondent wrote, Roosevelt had "no illusions as to the outcome of the Democratic primaries in either state, but [was] determined to take a clear stand in both contests 'just to keep the record straight.'"[22]

The next day, in Barnesville, Georgia, Roosevelt used the occasion of a political meeting with his target present to announce his opposition. Restating his conviction that the South was "the Nation's No. 1 economic problem," he indicated that one reason for that was poor political leadership.

As he had done in Kentucky, he complimented his target, "my old friend . . . Senator Walter George . . . a gentleman and a scholar," but explained that "on most public issues he and I do not speak the same language." He dismissed a second candidate, former Georgia governor Eugene Talmadge, who was not present, only noting that "his election would contribute very little to practical progress in government." The president endorsed Lawrence Camp, a former Georgia attorney general and currently the federal prosecutor in Atlanta, who was, along with George, seated on the platform, as a man "willing to fight" for economic and social progress.

As soon as the president finished, Senator George walked across the platform, shook his hand, and said, in words not heard by the audience, "Mr. President, I regret that you have taken this occasion to question my democracy and to attack my public record. I want you to know that I accept the challenge." This was a unique confrontation and the very opposite of Roosevelt's normal approach, which was not even to mention the names of his domestic opponents.[23]

That evening a very different kind of purge episode played out. When Roosevelt's train got to Greenville, South Carolina, Cotton Ed Smith and two challengers for his seat stepped aboard to be seen with the president on the rear platform. In his very brief whistle-stop talk, Roosevelt never mentioned Smith's name, but his last words—"I don't believe any family or man can live on fifty cents a day"—referenced a notorious Smith remark opposing the Fair Labor Standards Act, claiming that pittance was enough to keep a family head "in the lap of luxury."[24]

Washington insiders made it clear that the next purge targets would be Maryland's senator Millard E. Tydings and House Rules Committee chair John J. O'Connor. Tydings (1890–1961), a World War I hero, had been in the Senate since 1927, after two terms in the House. Initially a Roosevelt supporter, he soon turned against most of the New Deal. In his first full press conference since early July, Roosevelt read aloud a long editorial from the *New York Evening Post*, "Why the President 'Intervenes.'" It justified his actions and welcomed his reported choice of Tydings and O'Connor as targets. After declaring, "It's my statement now," he endorsed the two challengers.[25]

The contests were strikingly different. In Maryland it was a liberal against a conservative. Tydings's opponent, Congressman David J. Lewis (1869–1952), a former coal miner, had served in Congress for three terms in the Progressive Era and gave up his seat to run unsuccessfully for the Senate in 1916. He returned to Congress in 1931 and served four terms, during which he became a leading figure in the fight for Social Security. Roosevelt campaigned vigorously for Lewis in Maryland and praised him in a Labor Day talk carried on a nationwide radio network.[26]

In the Manhattan House race, both candidates were Irish American Catholic Tammany politicians. O'Connor, the brother of Roosevelt's longtime law partner, was a well-educated (Brown and Harvard Law) New Englander who migrated to New York and performed political chores for boss Murphy so well that he was successfully put up for a safe House seat in 1923. He became chair of its Rules Committee in 1935. His challenger, James H. Fay (1899–1948), was a more typical Tammanyite who, after military service in World War I, earned a degree from a noncollegiate law school, enjoyed city patronage jobs, and after narrowly failing to unseat O'Connor in the 1934 primary got a federal job as chief field deputy for the Internal Revenue Service. Once Fay got Roosevelt's endorsement, a desperate O'Connor entered the Republican primary as well. Roosevelt never campaigned for Fay in New York.[27]

By late September, the primaries were over, and, apart from Alben Barkley in Kentucky, only Fay of Roosevelt's controversial endorsements was still standing. In Georgia his candidate ran a poor third with just under a quarter of the votes, while George prevailed over Talmadge with 46 percent. In South Carolina and

Maryland, Smith and Tydings prevailed with majorities close to the 60 percent landslide threshold.[28]

The president's two victories came first in Kentucky, where Barkley prevailed with some 55 percent of the vote, and in New York City, where he had not campaigned at all.[29] Fay beat O'Connor in the Democratic primary, 8,532 to 7,799, but since O'Connor had won the Republican primary by defeating the future Central Intelligence Agency chief Allen W. Dulles by fewer than 100 votes of nearly 5,000 cast, the Fay-O'Connor contest was renewed in November, with Fay winning 24,500 to 22,037. But even if O'Connor had won in the general election, Roosevelt's objective—removal of an uncooperative Rules Committee chair—had been achieved in the primary.[30]

It has been traditional to treat the purge and the following general election as a major setback for Roosevelt. Few have questioned the conclusions of outstanding scholars, from James M. Burns in 1956, who approached those events with a subhead, "The Broken Spell," to David M. Kennedy in 1999, who, in a chapter entitled "The Ordeal of Franklin D. Roosevelt," speaks of the purge and the subsequent election as "a humiliating rebuke to the president . . . a knockout punch to the New Deal."[31] They and others have magnified the significance of the purge and underplayed the importance of other aspects of domestic politics in 1938. It is easy to gain the impression that Roosevelt, like Achilles, sulked in his tent after his failure to purge recalcitrant Democratic senators. Instead, he used the six-month respite from Congress as he usually did, to get out of Washington and fine-tune his administration.[32]

Once Congress adjourned, Roosevelt's chief concerns were seeing that the economy got back on track, continuing to advance his reform agenda, salvaging whatever was possible of his failed reorganization plan, and, of course, the November midterm elections. In early July, Roosevelt met with his three wise men of reorganization, Brownlow, Merriam, and Gulick, for a postmortem on the plan they had so confidently presented in the January 1937 press conference. Roosevelt made it clear to them that he intended to get a reorganization bill passed in 1939 but that in preparing to do so he would resort largely to congressional insiders, not administrative experts.

Meanwhile, events in Europe during 1938 were such that the question in the minds of most astute observers shifted in the course of the year from whether war would come to when war would come. And, last but not least, Roosevelt was increasingly concerned about who would be the Democratic candidate for president in 1940. On no question was Roosevelt more sphinxlike. I am persuaded that it was at least an open question in his own mind until sometime in the spring of 1940, when it seems clear that he had decided to run for a third term.

To a degree, the economic stimulus worked. The *New York Times* stock average, which had been at 135 in mid-August 1937, had slumped to 85 in mid-October and continued down, erratically, to 70 on April 14, when Roosevelt announced what he wanted Congress to do. It had climbed back to 95 in mid-September and was 103 in mid-December 1938. The precise measurement of unemployment is a continuing matter of debate among scholars, but it is reasonably clear that the nadir was reached in the winter of 1932–33 when, it has become traditional to say, perhaps 25 percent of the labor force was unemployed. Between then and the creation of the WPA in 1935, the unemployment rate crept downward to perhaps 20 percent and then dropped to perhaps as low as 12 percent, until the recession that began in the fall of 1937 saw it soar back above 20 percent by the time Roosevelt decided to act. From that point, it drifted downward slowly, spurred by increased defense expenditures and the peacetime draft beginning in the fall of 1940. Only toward the end of 1941 did the rate dip below 10 percent.[33]

Roosevelt did not talk much about unemployment in general and even less about unemployment statistics. In May 1938, while an experimental census of unemployment was being tabulated, he discussed the preliminary results briefly during a press conference in a manner that approached denial: "As the main breadwinner is thrown out of work, additional members of the family seek work which accentuates the number of unemployed in depression times. Likewise it proves the fact that to bring about recovery it is not necessary to provide jobs equal in number to the unemployed, because as breadwinners are restored to work, other potential workers vanish from the labor force."[34]

In a preelection radio address in 1938, he overemphasized progress by asserting that "the very fact that the business slump that began last fall and kept running into last summer did not become a major economic disaster, like the terrible slump that ran from 1929 all the way through to 1933, is the best kind of proof that fundamentally we have found the right track."[35] He spoke much more frequently about social progress, past and present. One concern, distinctly related to the purge, was the economic condition of the South, which he called "the nation's No. 1 economic problem" in a message opening a conference on the subject that he had the National Emergency Council organize. The resulting sixty-four-page document, *Report on the Economic Conditions of the South,* was available in time for the president's August speeches in Georgia. It covered fifteen topics, but race relations was not one of them.[36]

Just before his confrontation with Senator George, Roosevelt, speaking at the University of Georgia after receiving an honorary degree, related his own experience in the state in the 1920s. He recounted discovering that while Georgia law called for a full year's education for all children, many rural schools were open only four or five months due to lack of funds. He noted that "the Government in Washington" had helped by building schools and paying some of the salaries of many teachers, and would continue to do so, but it "should not and cannot rightly subsidize public education throughout the United States. That must remain wholly free, wholly independent. Education should be run by the states and not by the Federal government."[37] Thus, though the New Deal built thousands of schoolhouses and refurbished many thousands of others, the content of public education was largely left to the states, and of course segregated schools continued to enjoy a constitutionally protected status that Roosevelt's government never challenged. Millions of black American children lived in school districts without a high school they could attend.

In August Roosevelt celebrated the third anniversary of signing the Social Security Act with a radio address ticking off its accomplishments: some 27 million workers earning credits for unemployment insurance; 2.3 million "needy men, women, and children" receiving assistance; 1.7 million "old folks" not in poorhouses but "in surroundings they know"; and 600,000 dependent children "taken care of by their own families." Although retirees were not yet drawing benefits, grants to the states for various welfare payments were budgeted at $271 million for 1938 and $338 million for 1939.

But Roosevelt insisted that the government had not done enough. "To be truly national, a social security program must include all those who need its protection. Today many of our citizens are excluded from old-age insurance and unemployment compensation because of the nature of their employment. This must be set aright and it will be."[38]

In mid-July, Roosevelt, in a letter to Josephine A. Roche (1886–1976), who was chairing a national health conference, called for a "coordinated national health program." Roche, now largely forgotten, was an important midlevel figure in American reform from the Progressive Era into the Cold War years. She had been brought into the New Deal by Morgenthau as assistant secretary of the treasury with responsibility for health matters. (The Public Health Service was part of the Treasury Department until 1939.)[39] As such she served as Treasury's representative on the President's Committee on Economic Security, which planned the Social Security Act, and then, as chair of the interdepartmental Committee to Coordinate Health and Welfare Activities, she was Roosevelt's point person in the planning for a national health program. Roosevelt understood that "millions of citizens lack the individual means to pay for adequate medical care" and was aware that "we cannot do all at once everything that we should do," but he hoped that the conference would begin to draw up "a plan for continuing concerted action." This was the way that the Social Security Act had evolved.[40]

*   *   *

If the economic news was better and progress on the reform agenda maintained, the news from both Europe and Asia continued to be gloomy and frightening. Japan's undeclared war with China and the civil war in Spain went on with increasing barbarity. But it was Adolf Hitler's Germany that provided

Roosevelt with the most concern. He had made that concern quite clear in the Quarantine Speech in October 1937, and the successful push for increased military preparedness in early 1938 was his reaction to it. In the year and a half between the German annexation of Austria in mid-March 1938 and the start of what became World War II at the beginning of September 1939, Roosevelt was in essence an interested but impotent observer of events that he ached to help shape; Robert Dallek appropriately labels Roosevelt's futile attempts to influence the course of events in Europe "gestures."[41]

However, the Nazi takeover of Austria did cause Roosevelt finally to bestir himself on the refugee question: before that the word *refugee* does not occur in his *Public Papers*.[42] In a series of moves that startled the State Department, he ordered that the annual Austrian immigration quota (1,413) be added to the German quota (25,957) and "suggested" that State invite thirty-two European and American nations to cooperate in facilitating the emigration of "political refugees" from Austria and Germany. This was something the State Department had deliberately avoided from the beginning of the international refugee crisis shortly after Hitler came to power in January 1933. Positive responses eventually came from every nation asked except Italy. While the conference was pending, Roosevelt convoked a meeting of institutional and academic leaders, including representatives of the three major faiths, who met with him and a number of federal officials briefly in the White House and then reassembled in Secretary of Labor Frances Perkins's office. (The immigration service was then in Perkins's charge.) Most of the attendees became part of the president's Advisory Committee on Political Refugees, which met under the leadership of James G. McDonald (1886–1964), who had been the League of Nations' high commissioner for German refugees (1933–35). Roosevelt apparently never called upon it for advice, although McDonald became an important figure in the shaping of refugee policy.[43]

At the end of April, Roosevelt appointed a multimillionaire businessman and banker, Myron C. Taylor (1874–1959), as U.S. representative with rank of ambassador, to the international conference on refugees at Évian-les-Bains, France, which met at a resort hotel from July 6 to 15. As president of U.S. Steel, America's largest steel manufacturer, Taylor had created a sensation in March 1937 by breaking the united antiunion front of American steelmakers and signing an agreement with John L. Lewis and the Steel Workers Organizing Committee, later the United Steelworkers of America. Taylor, who was put in charge of the steel firm as a representative of the House of Morgan and viewed this as a sound money-saving venture, had been deeply involved with the NRA and supported other New Deal endeavors. Roosevelt had known him at least since his days as governor, when Taylor had served on volunteer relief committees.

Beyond focusing attention on the problem, the Évian meeting produced no significant change in the flow of refugees. It did set up, based on Taylor's initiative, an ongoing organization, the Intergovernmental Committee on Political Refugees Coming from Germany, directed by George Rublee (1868–1957), an American international lawyer who negotiated an agreement with lesser German officials signed shortly before Germany invaded Poland, which spoke of bringing four hundred thousand Jews out of Germany over a five-year period, which was not worth the paper it was written on. In the wake of the nationwide pogrom called Kristallnacht[44] on November 9–10, 1938, Roosevelt ordered that refugees in the United States on six-month visitor visas could renew them indefinitely.[45] He also performed a number of minor actions that showed where his sympathies lay. From Warm Springs at Thanksgiving, he issued a curious two-sentence statement expressing his "hope" that a report that the number of refugees admitted to Palestine would be "materially increased" was "true." Resulting press inquiries in London failed to find any basis for the alleged report, and British policy did not change. In mid-December, he sent a note to the Harvard Committee to Aid German Student Refugees, praising its work as "in the best traditions of the University." He knew well that Harvard, like most elite American universities, had a very different tradition in the 1920s when it imposed quotas to restrict the numbers of Jewish students admitted, which, as a member of Harvard's Board of Overseers, Roosevelt helped shape.[46]

But when it came to policy changes with political implications, he could suppress his humanitarian principles. In 1939 Senator Wagner and Massachusetts Republican Edith Nourse Rogers (1881–1960), who had entered the House in 1925, cosponsored a bill to admit twenty thousand refugee children. It had broad support among the elite—including Herbert Hoover—but little popular support according to the polls and very little prospect of passing. Roosevelt was willing to let administration officials testify favorably, and both Frances Perkins and Children's Bureau head Katherine Lenroot did, while Eleanor Roosevelt gave public support. She also sent word to her husband, cruising in the Caribbean in February, asking, "Are you willing I should talk to Sumner Welles saying that we approve passage of the child's refugee bill." "It is all right for you to support the refugee bill," he responded, "but it is best for me to say nothing now." Now became never. In June, when the Roosevelts' close friend New York representative Caroline O'Day asked, through military aide Pa Watson, if the president would give his views, Roosevelt annotated the memo, "File, No Action, FDR." The bill died in committee.[47]

In a very long first-person note in his *Public Papers,* written in mid-1941 to magnify the significance of the Évian Conference and his other prorefugee activities in 1938, Roosevelt used words he never spoke to the American people. They seem to be evidence of a guilty conscience. "For centuries this country has always been the traditional haven of refuge for countless victims of religious and political persecution in other lands. These immigrants have made outstanding contributions to American music, art, literature, business, finance, philanthropy, and many other phases of our cultural, political, industrial, and commercial life."[48]

As inadequate as Roosevelt's responses to the refugee crisis were, it must be noted that the United States took in by 1945 perhaps something less than two hundred thousand Jewish refugees, more than the rest of what came to be called the free world combined. Britain took in fifty-five thousand, which was more than any of the other nations. While it is clearly ahistoric to view the actions of Roosevelt and other Western leaders through the prism of the Holocaust, which they could not even imagine, this does not exempt them from historical accountability. I find it difficult to improve upon the summary judgment of Walter F. Mondale in 1979; speaking as vice president, he declared that the United States and other nations of asylum had "failed the test of civilization."[49]

Roosevelt did continue the warnings about the possibility of war that had begun at Chautauqua in 1936 and highlighted in Chicago in 1937. In early 1938, he spoke of "a world of high tension and disorder . . . where stable civilization is actually threatened," and he repeatedly referred to threats to freedom. Speaking to an organization of the nation's teachers at the end of June, he noted that "when the clock of civilization can be turned back by burning libraries, by exiling scientists, artists, musicians, writers, and teachers . . . freedom and civil liberties must be strengthened here." In San Francisco, speaking at the future site of the 1939 World's Fair and in full view of sixty-three American naval vessels massed for his review, Roosevelt hailed "the Fleet . . . a potent ever ready fact in the national defense of the United States." But he noted that "every right-thinking" person "wishes that it were possible to spend less" on "armaments," and he hoped "for the day when the other leading nations of the world will realize that their present course must inevitably lead to disaster." He declared that the United States was ready to cooperate in "a definite reduction in world armament." The next month, in Canada to dedicate an international bridge and receive an honorary degree, he electrified the crowd in the Queen's University stadium when, after noting that "we in the Americas are no longer a far away continent," he pledged that "the people of the United States will not stand idly by if domination of Canadian soil is threatened by any other power." This extension of the Monroe Doctrine northward—with Prime Minister Mackenzie King applauding on the platform behind him—presaged a series of cooperative military agreements between the two nations.[50]

The Munich crisis at the end of September, from which Britain's Neville Chamberlain returned voicing the delusion that he had achieved "peace in our time" by agreeing to the dismemberment of Czechoslovakia, impelled Roosevelt to make the most dramatic of his futile gestures. He sent a formal appeal to the four governments directly involved, the Czechs, Germans, British, and French, to avoid the war that would become a "world catastrophe." This was followed by an ineffectual exchange with Hitler. The episode was of so little import that

Gerhard Weinberg sees no need to mention it while discussing Munich in his massive history of World War II.[51]

In his first foreign policy speech after Munich, a radio address from the White House to the annual *Herald-Tribune* forum in New York, Roosevelt began by noting that "no one who lived through the grave hours of last month" could doubt the near-universal longing for peace. Then, in a series of sentences beginning "There can be no peace if . . .," he outlined the difficulties of maintaining peace in a world where "national policy adopts as a deliberate instrument the dispersion all over the world of millions of helpless wanderers with no place to lay their heads." He called for disarmament but insisted that "if there is not general disarmament, we ourselves must continue to arm."

In striking contrast, former president Herbert Hoover, speaking in person to the same audience, also supported peace and believed that "there is more realistic hope of military peace for the next few years than there has been for some time." But, he added, "if European war should take place between liberal and totalitarian countries the only hope for democracy is for us to stay out of it and keep the lamp of liberty alight in the world." The one positive action urged by Hoover was the resumption of world economic conferences, "which were ended by our country in 1933."[52]

As election day approached, there was much speculation about whether the president would campaign further, but his efforts against Tydings in the Maryland primary were his final appearances. Instead, he made a relatively long radio appeal on the Friday evening before the election, emphasizing the importance of liberal continuity. He pointed to the lack of progress that occurred when Taft followed Theodore Roosevelt and Harding replaced Wilson, contrasting this with New York State's "magnificent liberal program" over the past sixteen years. Although that period began with six years of Al Smith's tenure, his name was not mentioned; the point was to stress the achievements of Herbert Lehman, who faced a strong challenge from Thomas E. Dewey (1902–71), who gained fame as a successful prosecutor of gangland figures, after Lehman had appointed him a special prosecutor in 1935, despite the fact that he was a Republican. His election as Manhattan district attorney in 1937 on a Fusion ticket headed by Fiorello La Guardia was followed by his gubernatorial candidacy. Roosevelt, while praising Lehman as an experienced fighter for social justice, attacked Dewey, without mentioning his name, as inexperienced and unqualified and for abandoning his elective office. In addition to Lehman, the president supported the senatorial candidacies of Robert Wagner and James M. Mead (1885–1964) and urged voters "to look over the rest of the names on the ballot" and choose experienced candidates "known for their liberalism."[53]

Although Lehman and the top of the Democratic ticket in New York achieved a modest victory in the off-year election, nationally the result was a not surprising setback for the Democrats and for liberals within the party. Yet given the fact that off-year elections almost always result in losses for the party in power, and the fact that the economy had suffered a severe setback that could not be blamed on Herbert Hoover or his party, the results could have been a lot worse. Republicans picked up 8 Senate seats and lost none, but the Democrats filled 69 seats in what was still a 96-seat body. The most important Republican Senate winner was Ohio's Robert A. Taft (1889–1953), the son of the former president, who unseated Robert Bulkley, a New Deal supporter endorsed by Roosevelt. He and New York's Dewey, who received almost 49 percent of the gubernatorial vote in New York, each became someone to be reckoned with in Republican ranks. In the House, the Republicans picked up 80 seats, but the Democrats retained a 261–164 control. In the states, Republicans had a net gain of eleven governors, defeating most notably Frank Murphy in Michigan, whom Roosevelt had endorsed; conversely, Democrats won the California governorship for the first time in the twentieth century, instituting a state New Deal as the national momentum waned.[54]

In a Hyde Park press conference three days after the election, Roosevelt said it had come out about as he had expected: he had been right about New York and had expected to lose 7 Senate seats rather than 8 and to lose only 65 seats in the House. But when asked about what it all meant, he claimed not to be concerned.

> Q: Do you believe, Mr. President, or will you comment on the election returns in regard to your radio "Fireside Chat" last Friday night? Do you think they indicate a defection from liberal government as you outlined it?
>
> THE PRESIDENT: No, certainly not.
>
> Q: How will it affect your program in Congress?
>
> THE PRESIDENT: Just exactly what I have had before—only state it right!
>
> Q: Will you not encounter coalition opposition?
>
> THE PRESIDENT: No, I don't think so.[55]

If Roosevelt believed this, he was deluding himself. The de facto conservative coalition, which had been in play since the Court fight in 1937, would loom even larger in the coming Congress. In addition, there would be increasing speculation about a third term and who might be the Democratic candidate in 1940 if Roosevelt chose to follow tradition and retire.

The president's two weeks at Warm Springs were relaxing and uneventful. He made a brief radio address just before the traditional Thanksgiving dinner for the patients there: the highlight of the five-minute talk was a two-sentence greeting from Eddie Cantor, which Roosevelt read over the air: "May you and yours have a happy Thanksgiving. I am thankful that I live in a country where our leaders sit down on Thanksgiving Day to carve up a turkey instead of a Nation."[56]

Real news did emanate from Warm Springs during the Thanksgiving break, but the reporters there were not aware of it. Back in June, two southern radicals, Lucy Randolph Mason (1882–1959) and Joseph S. Gelders (1898–1950), had an unpublicized meeting at Hyde Park with both Roosevelts that Eleanor had arranged about a project to establish a broad interracial organization of southern liberals that became the Southern Conference of Human Welfare (SCHW).[57] Roosevelt agreed to give it public support, and Eleanor suggested that its initial Birmingham meeting be scheduled for Thanksgiving week so she could conveniently come over from Warm Springs.

Much of the advance publicity about the meeting focused on its honoree, Justice Hugo Black, who would make his first formal engagement since taking his seat on the Court. But the best-known event of the meeting became Eleanor Roosevelt's largely mythic confrontation with segregation. On the meeting's first day in Birmingham's municipal auditorium, there was no formal segregation, even though a city ordinance forbade racially mixed seating. During the second day, however, the now notorious Eugene (Bull) Connor, Birmingham's commissioner of public safety, appeared and announced that "I ain't gonna let no darkies and white folks segregate together in this town." From that point, the attending African Americans, perhaps a quarter of some twelve hundred attendees, were restricted to one side of the auditorium. As Eleanor Roosevelt remembered eleven years later, she was told by police that "I could not sit on the colored side. Rather than give in I asked that chairs be placed for us facing the whole group." Many versions of this event have her placing a chair for herself in the center aisle, sometimes drawing a chalk line or box.[58]

What ought to be stressed is that Roosevelt promoted this organization to encourage social and economic change in the South and that it is part and parcel of his other southern initiatives in 1938, the *Report on the Economic Conditions of the South* and the much-misunderstood purge. In his two-paragraph letter of greeting and endorsement that was read at the meeting, he spoke of the "long struggle by liberal leaders of the South for human welfare" and showed his understanding of how difficult the struggle would be: "If you steer a true course, and keep everlastingly at it, the South will long be thankful for this day."[59]

On his way back to Washington from Warm Springs in early December, Roosevelt arranged to pick up an honorary degree at the University of North Carolina, the intellectual center of southern liberalism, whose president, Frank P. Graham (1886–1972), chaired the SCHW. Roosevelt was unusually secretive about what he would talk about, but the press assumed that it would be foreign affairs—and important, because arrangements had been made to have it broadcast nationally and internationally.[60]

It was a confident, sunny speech offering his first real response to the month-old election results. After directly addressing the undergraduates and assuring them that he was not "the ogre" they had read about and did not "breakfast . . .

on grilled millionaire," he noted, "You have read that as a result of the balloting last November, the liberal forces in the United States are on their way to the cemetery—yet I ask you to remember that liberal forces in the United States have often been killed and buried, with the inevitable result that in short order they have come to life again with more strength than they had before." He went on to underline the importance of a liberal America:

> The future, however, rests not on chance alone, not on mere conservatism, mere smugness, mere fatalism, but on the affirmative action which we take in America. What America does or fails to do in the next few years has a far greater bearing and influence on the history of the whole human race for centuries to come than most of us who are here today can ever conceive.
>
> We are not only the largest and most powerful democracy in the whole world, but many other democracies look to us for leadership in order that world democracy may survive.
>
> I am speaking not of the external policies of the United States Government. They are exerted on the side of peace and they are exerted more strongly than ever before toward the self-preservation of democracies through the assurance of peace.
>
> What I would emphasize is the maintenance of successful democracy at home. Necessarily democratic methods within a nation's life entail change the kind of change to meet new social and economic needs through recognized processes of Government.[61]

Historians have not paid much attention to the North Carolina speech: of his major biographers, Freidel does not mention it, and Burns notes only the "grilled millionaire" quip. The general notion that by the end of 1938, the New Deal had "been reduced to a movement with no program, with no effective political organization, with no vast popular party strength behind it, and with no candidate" has been iterated and reiterated for more than seven decades.[62] It is true that Roosevelt would never again, in peace or war, have the same control of Congress that he had once exercised, but there would be future New Deal victories, not so much in new programs, but in the refinement and expansion of existing ones. And, of course, there would be a most successful candidate.

Back in Washington, most of the president's energies for the rest of the year were, as usual, directed toward budget and annual message preparation and strategy for the coming session. He made it clear in his regular press conferences that the most important legislative goal for 1939 was to pass a reorganization bill; he pointedly noted that there would be conferences with Speaker Bankhead, Vice President Garner, and other important congressional figures.[63]

On Thursday, December 10, not a press conference day, correspondents were summoned to the president's study late in the afternoon for one of his beloved surprises: the first public announcement of what became the Franklin D. Roosevelt Library (FDRL) at Hyde Park. It would spawn the system of presidential libraries that have been created by and for each of his successors and his immediate predecessor. He had been advised by an elite group of historians, the archivist of the United States, librarians, and others and had just come from a luncheon and meeting with them. He was deeding his home and some one hundred acres to the United States and was creating a committee, headed by Frank Walker, to raise funds to build the library adjacent to his home. It was initially to house his public and private papers, books, pamphlets, and collection of marine prints and naval papers, and he expected that many persons associated with him would also donate their papers.

He had one of the historians with him, Harvard's Samuel Eliot Morison (1887–1976), who spoke to reporters about the past practices of presidents with their papers. Those of both Adamses, he noted, "are shut in a vault in Boston where nobody can get at them."

THE PRESIDENT: Really? I didn't know that.

PROFESSOR MORISON: Nobody allowed in except the family. Others have generally gone back to the President's old home where they have been subjected to a great deal of dilapidation. The Presidents have sometimes spent their declining years in trying to rearrange them, with unfortunate results because the order of the documents has been entirely spoiled. . . . A great deal of the important evidence has been destroyed, some purposely, others by neglect and accident.

Thus President Roosevelt has proposed, for the first time, to keep all of his files intact. Of his predecessors I believe President Hoover was the first one who did not destroy a considerable part of the White House files before he left. President Roosevelt proposes not only to keep his files intact, but to place them immediately under the administration of the National Archivist so that from the time they leave the White House they will be under public control and will not be subject to dilapidation or destruction or anything else. The whole thing will come down in its entirety to the historians of the future.[64]

The end of one year and the beginning of the next saw significant changes in personnel around the president. The retirement of Molly Dewson as a member of the Social Security Board marked an end to a career in reform that had begun after her graduation from Wellesley College in 1897, when she went to work for Boston's Women's Educational and Industrial Union. After serving in France with the American Red Cross during World War I, she became research secretary for the National Consumers League and was so astute that she wrote the factual parts of Felix Frankfurter's Brandeis-type brief in the unsuccessful attempt to establish minimum wages for women—stifled in 1923 by the Supreme

Court in *Adkins v. Children's Hospital.* In those years, she met Eleanor Roosevelt, who recruited her to join the 1928 Al Smith campaign, which became a Roosevelt campaign as well. In resigning she wrote Roosevelt of her "ten years of working for a more worthwhile world under your great and understanding leadership." After the 1932 election, Dewson used her friendships with both Roosevelts to "lobby successfully for the appointment of unprecedented numbers of women to high-level positions within the New Deal," beginning with Frances Perkins as secretary of labor. Of her work in helping to create the Social Security Act, she wrote in 1935 to Arthur Altmeyer, who would become her colleague on the Social Security Board, that she could not "believe that I have lived to see this day . . . the culmination of what us girls and some of you boys have been working for so long it's just dazzling."

In accepting her resignation, the president wrote of Dewson's "great assistance in administering [the Social Security Act] which, as the years go by, will be increasingly recognized as a great step forward in the development of American civilization." Quite appropriately, the president replaced her with Ellen S. Woodward, a woman whose career Dewson had helped promote. Woodward had risen to become an assistant administrator of the WPA, heading its Women's and Professional Projects Division, which, at its height, employed 450,000 women. In his press conference comments on Dewson's retirement and replacement, Roosevelt, who delighted in telling reporters how to do their jobs, fantasized, "If I were a lady writer, I would say, perhaps, 'This is creating a precedent for all time—one woman on the [three-person] Social Security Board. Now that does not come from me, it comes from you.'"[65]

Two days later, a long-expected promotion named Harry Hopkins secretary of commerce, replacing Dan Roper, whose resignation had been announced earlier. Hopkins's promotion meant that a new WPA administrator had to be appointed. As there was bound to be a great deal of controversy over the WPA in the coming session of Congress, Roosevelt passed over the obvious choice, Aubrey Williams, whose radical statements had antagonized many in Congress, and appointed a serving army officer, Colonel F. C. Harrington (1887–1940), a West Pointer who had been on loan to the WPA since its inception and boasted that he had never voted. That Roosevelt told the disappointed Williams in advance what he was going to do was a mark of his regard for him, because the president did not like such interviews and usually managed to avoid them. He successfully urged Williams to continue as head of the National Youth Administration, whose program would be expanded. At a well-attended White House ceremony in which Hopkins was sworn in and Harrington and Williams were given new commissions, the president praised the NYA leader as "a loyal and efficient worker for government and society."

Hopkins's appointment immediately fueled political speculations. One Democratic loyalist, Illinois's J. Hamilton Lewis (1863–1939), who had been in the

Senate since 1913, observed, "The President can't be blind to the fact that Hoover got the presidency first by being Secretary of Commerce. Shortly I shall go to the big boss and make bold to ask whether he wishes by this appointment to direct me to abandon Roosevelt for a third term and accept Hopkins for a first term."[66]

It is clear that Roosevelt encouraged Hopkins in his presidential ambitions. Whether he was using Hopkins as a stalking horse while he made up his mind about a third term is something that we shall never know. Hopkins had many negatives, including his divorce and the fact that he was a polarizing figure. A Gallup poll published just as his long-discussed promotion was being announced asked if the respondents thought that Hopkins had done a "good job" or a "poor job" as WPA director and whether they would approve his appointment as secretary of commerce. A slight majority of those having opinions, 53 percent to 47 percent, opted for "poor" as opposed to "good" job on the WPA, and a larger majority, 66 percent to 34 percent, opposed his getting the cabinet job. Gallup cautioned that very large percentages of the respondents—25 percent on the first question and 40 percent on the second—expressed no opinion and that most of them were in the lower socioeconomic strata. He also reported, without giving the other names or figures, that Hopkins stood ninth in a list of ten Democratic presidential possibilities.[67] I find it difficult to believe that Roosevelt seriously thought that Hopkins, even if he managed to get the Democratic nomination, could be elected president.

The day before Christmas, the administration's Good Neighbor policy paid another dividend, as Secretary Hull, despite traditional resistance led by Argentina, won unanimous agreement to the Declaration of Lima. The republics agreed, while reasserting individual sovereignty, to a joint defense "against all foreign intervention and activity that may threaten them." The State Department and Roosevelt had overwrought fears about Nazi and Japanese intervention and influence in Latin America, but the cooperation of most Latin American nations during World War II, particularly in regard to bases, would be of real importance.[68]

Roosevelt in his annual Christmas message praised the Lima agreement and ended with a pledge to "do whatever lies within my own power to hasten the day foretold by Isaiah when men 'shall beat their swords into plowshares and their spears into pruning hooks; nation shall not lift up sword against nation, neither shall they learn war anymore.'"[69] Yet all that month, he continued to plan for the accelerated national defense expenses occasioned by the European war, which he and most experienced observers expected to come in 1939.

Nothing Roosevelt ever said or wrote, then or later, can be cited to demonstrate that, in 1938–39, he believed that the impending European war would necessarily involve the United States. The mind-boggling chain of events in the twenty-two months between the Nazi-Soviet pact of August 1939 and the collapse of France in 1940 transformed the Western world and soon reshaped the entire globe. We can now see that in the process, the whole thrust of Roosevelt's presidency shifted. Before that, although he had achieved enormous prestige throughout the world, his primary concerns were the restoration of domestic prosperity, the expansion of its benefits beyond the middle class, and the reforms that would enable that expansion to occur.

After the fall of France, even during the seventeen remaining months when the United States remained officially at peace, Roosevelt would function as the undisputed leader of an ill-matched coalition of nations that he would lead to the brink of final victories he did not live to see. His war presidency would feature an "Arsenal of Democracy" that achieved what can be called full employment, something his New Deal presidency never accomplished.

Notes

Chapter 1. Beginnings

1. James MacGregor Burns and Susan Dunn, *The Three Roosevelts: Patrician Leaders Who Transformed America.* See Rexford G. Tugwell, "The Two Great Roosevelts"; and Stephen Hess, "The Roosevelt Dynasty."

2. Frank Freidel, "The Dutchness of the Roosevelts," is an engaging account.

3. *NYT,* July 18, 1871, 1.

4. FDR perhaps overstated this in a 1928 interview. "Nearly all [Roosevelts] used to be Democrats, all except T.R.'s father." S. J. Woolf, "The Roosevelt Who Is a Firm Democrat: Governor Smith's Nominator Explains Why He Is Not of the Republican Faith—a Long Fight Won with Honor."

5. The fire destroyed most of the family papers and records so that much of the previous history of the Hyde Park branch of the Roosevelt family remains obscure.

6. William H. Harbaugh, *The Life and Times of Theodore Roosevelt,* 25. This is the revised version of his *Power and Responsibility* (1961) and, hands down, the best biography.

7. James I. Roosevelt (1795–1815), a lawyer, served one term in Congress (1841–43) and was a New York state judge and U.S. attorney for the southern district of New York. His nephew Robert Barnwell Roosevelt (1829–1906), Theodore Roosevelt's uncle, was a political reformer, writer, and pioneer in conservation, who served in Congress (1871–73) and was minister to the Netherlands (1888–90). Other prominent early Roosevelts include Nicholas J. Roosevelt (1767–1854), engineer and inventor (*Dictionary of American Biography* and *ANB*), and Hilborne Lewis Roosevelt (1849–86), organ builder and inventor, Theodore's first cousin (*Dictionary of American Biography*).

8. Jake Riis, as he called him, was important to Theodore's career as a source of effective publicity. His *Theodore Roosevelt: The Citizen* is a panegyric.

9. *New York Journal,* February 17, 1898, facsimile in Richard Hofstadter, William Miller, and Daniel Aaron, *The United States: The History of a Republic,* 560; *NYT,* February 17, 1898, 2.

10. TR, *An Autobiography,* 214; George Dewey, *Autobiography of George Dewey, Admiral of the Navy,* 167–68.

11. It was *not* San Juan Hill: the Americans got the name wrong but the battle right.

12. Harold F. Gosnell, *Boss Platt and His New York Machine: A Study of the Political Leadership of Thomas C. Platt, Theodore Roosevelt, and Others,* 143.

13. TR, *An Autobiography,* 263–309.

14. Elting E. Morison, ed., *The Letters of Theodore Roosevelt,* 2:1338n.

15. Neither this language nor the frequently cited "that madman" can be definitively attributed to Hanna.

16. In 1896 McKinley won the popular vote by 51.02 percent to Bryan's 46.70 percent; the 1900 figures were 51.61 percent and 45.53 percent. The 1896 electoral vote was 271 to 176; in 1900 it was 292 to 155.

17. I was assured, many years ago, by several West Texas politicians who knew him, that Garner had in fact named another bodily fluid more appropriately measured in buckets. He is said to have given this evaluation in early 1960 to Lyndon Johnson when asked for his advice about accepting the vice presidential nomination.

18. Letter to Leonard Wood, March 27, 1901, in E. Morison, *Letters of Theodore Roosevelt*, 3:30–31.

19. For a fascinating account and analysis of the assassination and some of its consequences, see Eric Rauchway, *Murdering McKinley: The Making of Theodore Roosevelt's America*.

20. Letter to Henry Cabot Lodge, September 23, 1901, in E. Morison, *Letters of Theodore Roosevelt*, 3:150.

21. The strongest case for McKinley is in H. Wayne Morgan, *William McKinley and His America*.

22. ER, *This Is My Story*, 237. Logic suggests that Adams said "that white house," but it is capitalized in Eleanor's memoir.

23. Rita Halle Kleeman, *Gracious Lady: The Life of Sara Delano Roosevelt*, 125.

24. The most accessible account of Delano family history is in Geoffrey C. Ward, *Before the Trumpet: Young Franklin Roosevelt, 1882–1905*. There is a direct-line genealogical chart on the FDRL website.

25. Wharton (1862–1937) was twenty years older than Franklin and eight years younger than his mother, who knew her when the writer was a fifteen-year-old. Kleeman, *Gracious Lady*, 133.

26. Ward, *Before the Trumpet*, 105–6, describes the wedding and the journey.

27. Kleeman, *Gracious Lady*, 138–39; Blanche Wiesen Cook, *Eleanor Roosevelt*, 1:25.

28. William Penca, "Amasa Delano," *ANB*. Amasa Delano was the son of Samuel Delano, who was a brother of Ephraim Delano (1733–1815), Franklin Delano Roosevelt's great-great-grandfather. Daniel W. Delano Jr., *Franklin Roosevelt and the Delano Influence*, 55.

29. Hsin-pao Chang, *Commissioner Lin and the Opium War*, tells of China's vain struggle against the British insistence that it accept opium. Warren Delano knew Lin. Jacques M. Downs, *The Golden Ghetto: The American Commercial Community at Canton and the Shaping of American China Policy, 1784–1844*, is the best account of that era and contains some of Warren Delano's business correspondence about China in an appendix.

30. Robert J. C. Butow, in a brilliant article, documents specific significant instances on which Franklin, after his election as president, used that mythical relationship to "settle" arguments with his advisers ("A Notable Passage to China: Myth and Memory in FDR's Family History"). In late 1935, Franklin learned of some family papers in a collection at the Library of Congress. His uncle Frederick A. Delano investigated and informed him that they demonstrated the "importance of the opium trade" to Delano's firm. Fewer than six months before Franklin's death, Westbrook Pegler (1894–1969) wrote a column about Warren Delano and the opium trade and accused both Franklin

and Eleanor of hypocrisy in concealing it. Neither FDR nor his spokesmen responded. "Fair Enough," *Washington Times Herald,* October 23, 1944.

31. Catherine Robbins Lyman Delano (1825–96) gave birth to seven daughters and four sons between 1844 and 1864. One daughter and one son died as infants, and only four daughters and two sons survived their parents' deaths in 1896 and 1898. Four of these, three daughters and a son, lived into Franklin's presidency.

32. Frank Freidel, *Franklin D. Roosevelt: A Rendezvous with Destiny,* 3. The acerbic critic was John T. Flynn, *Country Squire in the White House.*

33. Sara Delano Roosevelt, *My Boy Franklin, as Told by Mrs. James Roosevelt to Isabel Leighton and Gabrielle Forbush,* 33. Two foreign-language editions were published during World War II. A French edition was published in New York in 1942, and a Spanish-language edition appeared in Barcelona in 1943.

34. Her biographer and friend Rita Halle Kleeman was the first to utilize this important source. Her *Gracious Lady* deals almost exclusively with what William Dean Howells called "the smiling aspects of life."

35. Letter to Edmond R. Rogers, n.d. but postmarked from Ireland, May 13, 1891, in Elliott Roosevelt, ed., *F.D.R.: His Personal Letters,* 1:19, hereafter cited as *FDR Letters.* Rogers was a boyhood playmate whose father, a Standard Oil executive, was a Hyde Park neighbor. The vessel was the White Star line RMS *Teutonic.*

36. In 1946 his stamp collection was sold in lots at auction for three hundred thousand dollars, far above the price it would have fetched as stamps because of its associational value. A few special presentation albums from foreign governments were retained for the FDRL. "F. D. Roosevelt: The World's Best Known Stamp Collector," 10–11.

37. William F. Halsey and J. Bryan III, *Admiral Halsey's Story,* 18; Robert F. Cross, *Sailor in the White House: The Seafaring Life of FDR,* is a detailed account of the maritime aspects of Franklin's life.

38. Peabody became a legendary figure. He and his wife shook hands with every boy before bedtime every night, and, though he barred "fagging"—the forced virtual indenture of younger boys to older ones—he did allow, and probably established, a system whereby the senior boys terrorized those who, somehow, had let down the school and could today result in a criminal indictment. Frank D. Ashburn, *Peabody of Groton: A Portrait,* verges on hagiography. The *ANB* sketch by John W. Tyler is more restrained.

39. *FDR Letters,* 1:39. Taddy was properly James Roosevelt Roosevelt Jr. (1879–1958).

40. *FDR Letters,* 1:110.

41. *FDR Letters,* vol. 1: Peabody's final assessment at 413; grade summary compiled from letters listed in the index, "Reports at Groton," 541. In December 1932, Peabody wrote a Groton alumnus: "There has been a good deal written about Franklin Roosevelt when he was a boy at Groton, more than I should have thought justified by the impression that he left at the school. He was a quiet, satisfactory boy of more than ordinary intelligence, taking a good position in his form, but not brilliant" (Ashburn, *Peabody of Groton,* 341).

42. See, for example, Freidel, *Rendezvous with Destiny,* 9–10.

43. Irving Brandt, *Adventures in Conservation with Franklin D. Roosevelt,* 89.

44. ER, *This Is My Story*, 149–50.

45. Frank Freidel, *Rendezvous with Destiny*, 8, makes this point. See also Freidel, *Franklin D. Roosevelt: The Apprenticeship*, 39. Many other writers, seeing the few illustrious Grotonian names in addition to Roosevelt's—Senator Bronson Cutting and five men associated with Roosevelt's administration, Dean Acheson, Francis Biddle, Joseph Grew, Averell Harriman, and Sumner Welles—have accepted Peabody's claim. For a defense of that claim, see Ashburn, *Peabody of Groton*, 315–23.

46. *NYT,* June 3, 1934, 5. The headline was "Roosevelt Relives His Boyhood Days," and an imaginative subhead read "Executive Spends a Carefree Day with Old Chums." As Geoffrey Ward points out, some of his old "chums" were on the verge of making a protest at his presence (*Before the Trumpet*, 210).

47. Ashburn, *Peabody of Groton*, 342–43, no data beyond 1935 given.

48. He remained for an extra year and thought of himself as "Harvard, 04," listing that date in his "Who's Who" entry (Albert N. Marquis, ed., *Who's Who in America, 1934-35*, 2042).

49. Franklin did list himself as Phi Beta Kappa, but that was an honorary appointment.

50. Freidel, *Apprenticeship*, 52.

51. Kenneth S. Davis, *FDR: The Beckoning of Destiny*, 140.

52. Freidel, *Apprenticeship*, 57, does not name her and calls it "an unfortunate marriage." K. Davis, *Beckoning of Destiny*, identifies her as "Sadie Messinger . . . a frequenter of the Haymarket Dance Hall . . . where she was known to all as "Dutch Sadie." Ward, *Before the Trumpet*, 217–22, describes her as "a Hungarian-born prostitute" and provides much detail but no evidence for the characterization.

53. Ward, *Before the Trumpet*, 218. The letter to "My Darling Mama and Papa," dated October 23, 1900, in *FDR Letters*, 1:429–30, has an acknowledged deletion of these sentences followed by a vague account of the affair.

54. Ward, *Before the Trumpet*, 222.

55. Freidel, *Apprenticeship*, 57.

56. Samuel I. Rosenman, ed., *Public Papers and Addresses of Franklin D. Roosevelt*, 1938 volume, 38, hereafter cited as *PPA* plus date and page.

57. S. Roosevelt, *My Boy Franklin*, 55–56.

58. Cook, *Eleanor Roosevelt*, 1:132.

59. On her mother's side, Eleanor could trace her ancestry to Robert R. Livingston, chancellor of New York State and a member of the five-man committee that drafted the Declaration of Independence and negotiated the Louisiana Purchase. He was wealthier and more politically significant than anyone else in the Roosevelt or Delano pedigrees.

60. Elliott Roosevelt's decline and death, which involved drugs, adultery, and public scandal, are well described from separate points of view in Edmund Morris, *The Rise of Theodore Roosevelt*, chap. 17; and, Cook, *Eleanor Roosevelt*, vol. 1. Theodore's reactions to his brother's transgressions can only be described as hysterical.

61. Cook, *Eleanor Roosevelt*, 1:21; ER, *This Is My Story*, 1.

62. To Eleanor she was Aunt Bye.

63. ER, *This Is My Story*, 53–97; letters and a cable quoted in Cook, *Eleanor Roosevelt*, 1:120–24.

64. This feeling of responsibility lasted until his death in 1941. Like his father, he became an alcoholic. Eleanor's other sibling was Elliott Hall Roosevelt (1889–93).

65. Freidel, *Rendezvous with Destiny*, 25–26.

66. Jonathan Daniels, *The Time between the Wars: Armistice to Pearl Harbor*, 208–9, 211, 279, and *Washington Quadrille: The Dance beside the Documents*. Frank Freidel had long known about this but did not write about it until Daniels broke the story. Freidel's account in *Rendezvous with Destiny*, 33–36, is as close as we are ever likely to get to the "truth" of that affair. In Freidel's *Apprenticeship*, Mercer's name is not mentioned. The fullest account is Joseph E. Persico, *Franklin and Lucy*, but his notion of evidence is curious.

67. Kleeman, *Gracious Lady*, 233.

68. Both this letter and the next are in *FDR Letters*, 1:517–18. His was written from Cambridge on Friday, December 4, 1903, and Eleanor's of December 2, 1903, from the home of her Ludlow cousins Susan and Henry Parish, at 8 East Seventy-Sixth Street in Manhattan. She and Franklin would be married in this and the adjoining town house, owned by Susan's mother, some fifteen months later.

69. "President Roosevelt Gives the Bride Away. His Niece Weds His Cousin, Franklin Delano Roosevelt," *NYT*, March 18, 1906, 2. A sidebar on the same page identified the groom as "Frank D. Roosevelt."

70. A myth persists that Theodore marched in the Saint Patrick's Day parade. He did not, but his carriage passed through some of the parade crowds.

71. Joseph P. Lash, *Eleanor and Franklin: The Story of Their Relationship, Based on Eleanor Roosevelt's Private Papers*, 138–41.

Chapter 2. Roosevelt Enters Politics

1. *FDR Letters*, 2:10.

2. ER's account is in *This Is My Story*, 127–38.

3. Freidel, *Apprenticeship*, 74–77.

4. ER, *This Is My Story*, 152, 162.

5. Joseph P. Lash, *Love, Eleanor: Eleanor Roosevelt and Her Friends*, 56. Freidel, *Rendezvous with Destiny*, 612n16, says that Eleanor continued to hold such views in an interview he conducted in 1948.

6. U.S. Department of Commerce, *Historical Statistics of the United States: Colonial Times to 1957*, 91, Series D, 603–17.

7. ER, *This I Remember*, 14–15; Freidel, *Apprenticeship*, 80.

8. The six were Anna Eleanor Roosevelt (1906–75); James Roosevelt (1907–91), named for FDR's father; Franklin Delano Roosevelt Jr. (1909–9); Elliott Roosevelt (1910–90), named for ER's father; Franklin D. Roosevelt Jr. (1914–88); and John Aspinwall Roosevelt (1916–81), named for an FDR uncle.

9. *FDR Letters*, 2:136; Freidel, *Apprenticeship*, 82–84; Freidel, *Rendezvous with Destiny*, 15. For a succinct summary of Franklin's law firm associations, see *FDR Letters*, 2:168.

10. *Harvard Alumni Bulletin* 47 (April 28, 1945): 451–52. That issue was largely devoted to the fallen president. See Gerald T. Dunne, *Grenville Clark: Public Citizen.*

11. For a good example of a "second generation" progressive history, see George E. Mowry, *Theodore Roosevelt and the Progressive Movement.* For a more recent perspective, see Alan Dawley, *Changing the World: American Progressives in War and Revolution.*

12. TR, *Letters from Theodore Roosevelt to Anna Roosevelt Cowles, 1870–1918*, 289, letter dated August 10, 1910. Franklin's name is not in the index. See also Freidel, *Apprenticeship*, 88.

13. *Biographical Directory of the United States Congress, 1774–Present.*

14. *FDR Letters*, 2:193.

15. *NYT*, November 9, 1910.

16. *NYT*, January 1, 1911, 1; W. A. Warn, "Senator F. D. Roosevelt, Chief Insurgent at Albany."

17. That partnership endured until 1920 when it was replaced by the firm of Emmet, Marvin, and Roosevelt.

18. Christopher M. Finan, *Alfred E. Smith: The Happy Warrior*, is good on accommodations for "ordinary" legislators.

19. Warn, "Senator F. D. Roosevelt." Roosevelt also modestly denied that he was a leader, but his actions and the fact of the interview belied his denial.

20. *NYT*, January 17, 1911, 1, lists the twenty-two.

21. For O'Gorman, see *Biographical Directory of the United States Congress.*

22. Nancy J. Weiss, *Charles Francis Murphy, 1858–1924: Respectability and Responsibility in Tammany Politics*, 48–49.

23. Freidel, *Apprenticeship*, 115–16.

24. Alfred B. Rollins Jr., *Roosevelt and Howe*, 63–83. Lela Stiles, *The Man behind Roosevelt: The Story of Louis McHenry Howe*, is useful for Howe's career after 1928 when she went to work for him.

25. ER, *This Is My Story*, 187–89.

26. Ibid., 192–193; ER, *This I Remember*, 65–66; Elliott Roosevelt, "The Most Unforgettable Character I've Ever Met," 27; Rollins, *Roosevelt and Howe*, 185.

27. *FDR Letters*, 2:192.

28. Theodore Roosevelt got 27.4 percent, Taft 23.2, and Socialist Eugene Debs 6 percent. A Prohibitionist got 1.4 percent and a Socialist Labor candidate 0.2 percent.

29. A facsimile of the undated letter appears in Stiles, *Man behind Roosevelt*, facing page 25, but by its reference to Franklin's presence in Baltimore it can be roughly dated. In a rare slip Freidel, *Apprenticeship*, 149, dated it "autumn of 1912," that is, during or after Howe managed his 1912 campaign, but Rollins, *Roosevelt and Howe*, 53, dates it "[July 1912]." Freidel, *Rendezvous with Destiny*, 23, says "during the 1912 campaign" but mentions it after discussing Franklin's reelection campaign. Based on the contents of the letter, I would date it June 1912, before the convention began. Both that and Rollins's slightly later dating show Howe, facing unemployment, "advertising" his interest rather than an employee flattering his boss. Franklin could also be "cute" in salutation; later, he addressed Howe as "Ludwig." Josephus Daniels wrote in his memoirs that "even in 1913 [Howe] expected to see Franklin occupy the White House" (*The Wilson Era: Years of Peace, 1910–1917*, 128).

30. ER, *This Is My Story*, 193.

31. John J. Broesamle, *William Gibbs McAdoo: A Passion for Change, 1863–1917,* 86.

32. Josephus Daniels, *Years of Peace,* 69.

33. E. David Cronon, ed., *The Cabinet Diaries of Josephus Daniels, 1913–1921,* 10.

34. Freidel, *Apprenticeship,* 157; Ward, *Temperament,* 201.

35. Rollins, *Roosevelt and Howe,* 89.

36. ER, *This Is My Story,* 196–99.

37. Although in this passage ER named "two old colored servants, Millie and Francis," inherited from the Cowells, the social secretary remained anonymous. She was Lucy Mercer.

38. Cronon, *Cabinet Diaries of Daniels,* 543–44, entry for Friday, August 6, 1920. See also the index entry under Franklin's name, subheading "relations with J.D.," and the editor's notes at 212n44 and 490n3.

39. See the comments on Daniels's role in and satisfaction about the disfranchisement of North Carolina's African Americans in C. Vann Woodward's *Origins of the New South, 1877–1913,* 334, 339. Daniels continued to support segregation throughout his life.

40. Joseph L. Morrison's two volumes *Josephus Daniels Says . . . : An Editor's Political Odyssey from Bryan to Wilson and F.D.R., 1894–1913* and *Josephus Daniels: The Small-d Democrat* are the best biography.

41. Ronald H. Spector, "Josephus Daniels, Franklin Roosevelt, and the Reinvention of the Naval Enlisted Man."

42. Frederick S. Harrod, *Manning the New Navy: Development of a Modern Naval Enlisted Force, 1899–1940,* 59.

43. Letter to Major General William C. Gorgas, August 7, 1917, as cited in Freidel, *Apprenticeship,* 334.

44. Freidel, *Apprenticeship,* 163–64.

45. Josephus Daniels, *The Wilson Era: Years of War and After, 1917–1923,* quotes this phrase at the beginning of his chapter "Franklin Roosevelt, Navy Statesman" (253–74).

46. *NYT,* August 13, 1914, 12. Freidel, *Apprenticeship,* 184–88, is the best account of the episode.

47. *NYT,* September 9, 1914, 9. Broesamle, *William Gibbs McAdoo,* 88–90, gives an account of the independent Democrat's strength and possibilities. Gerard owed his post in Berlin to his large contributions to Wilson's campaign.

48. See *NYT,* September 29, 1914, 1, and November 3, 1914, 1; and Harold F. Gosnell, *Champion Campaigner: Franklin D. Roosevelt,* 52–59, for discussions of primary and general election results. The senatorial victor, James W. Wadsworth Jr. (1877–1952), served two terms and was defeated in 1926 by Tammany Democrat Robert F. Wagner, who had served in the state senate with Franklin and became one of the truly great senators; Wadsworth returned to politics in 1932 and won a seat in the House of Representatives, which he held until he retired in 1950. His greatest achievement was the bipartisan Burke-Wadsworth Act establishing the peacetime draft in 1940.

49. *FDR Letters,* 2:232–33.

50. Robert E. Quirk, *An Affair of Honor: Woodrow Wilson and the Occupation of Veracruz.*

51. Freidel, *Apprenticeship*, 270.

52. David Healy, *Gunboat Diplomacy in the Wilson Era: The U.S. Navy in Haiti, 1915–1916*, contains only one minor reference to Franklin at 149.

53. Hans Schmidt, *The United States Occupation of Haiti, 1915–1934*, 111. The author of the comment, John A. McIlhenny, scion of a Louisiana plantation-owning family and chair of the federal Civil Service Commission, was later made the chief civilian official in Haiti. He had been one of Theodore's Rough Riders and was a favorite golf partner of Franklin's.

54. Ibid., 112.

55. See, for example, Freidel, *Apprenticeship*, 285. However, in his capstone volume, Freidel wrote that by 1927, "the occupations [of] the Wilson administration now seemed to [FDR] unwise, and he moved toward what he was later to call the Good Neighbor policy" (*Rendezvous with Destiny*, 51).

56. Freidel, *Franklin D. Roosevelt: The Ordeal*, 135.

57. Freidel, *Apprenticeship*, 280.

58. See, for example, Anne Wintermute Lane and Louise Herrick Wall, eds., *The Letters of Franklin K. Lane, Personal and Political*, 239–40.

59. PPA, 1939, "Extemporaneous, Informal Remarks at a Dinner of the Trustees of the Franklin D. Roosevelt Library, Inc., Washington, DC—Feb. 4, 1939," 117–18. See the comments in Freidel, *Apprenticeship*, 288–89.

60. Cronon, *Cabinet Diaries of Daniels*, 118.

61. ER, *This Is My Story*, 245.

62. Ibid., 246.

63. Frederic A. Delano (1863–1958) was Sara's younger brother and in 1917 a member of the Federal Reserve Board.

64. *NYT*, July 17, 1917, 3. The story has no byline. An account of it, including the letters quoted, is in *FDR Letters*, 2:349–50.

65. Cronon, *Cabinet Diaries of Daniels*, 318–19. See also Carroll Kilpatrick, ed., *Roosevelt and Daniels: A Friendship in Politics*, 34, 51–52, 72–74. The two later references are to FDR's 1918 and 1921 reconstructions of the genesis of the project.

66. Harris told a Roosevelt biographer in 1931, "If Roosevelt had not been there the North Sea Barrage would never have been laid down. . . . Certainly my own interest in it was due to his enthusiasm and encouragement" (Ernest K. Lindley, *Franklin D. Roosevelt: A Career in Progressive Democracy*, 160–61).

67. Winston S. Churchill, *The World Crisis, 1916–1918*, 84.

68. PPA, 1936, 289.

69. *FDR Letters*, 2:422. An edited version of the diary plus letters from the trip are printed at 375–440. Several letters to Daniels from Europe are printed in Kilpatrick, *Roosevelt and Daniels*, 45–50.

70. For the Washington meeting, see *FDR Letters*, 2:354–55. For London, see Freidel, *Apprenticeship*, 354.

71. Alfred W. Crosby, *America's Forgotten Pandemic: The Influenza of 1918*.

72. Freidel, *Apprenticeship*, 321. For Camp, see Ronald A. Smith's *ANB* sketch, which does not mention Franklin.

73. Kilpatrick, *Roosevelt and Daniels*, 36; Josephus Daniels, *Years of War*, 193–95.

74. Stacy A. Cordery, *Alice: Alice Roosevelt Longworth, from White House Princess to Washington Power Broker*.

75. Freidel, *Apprenticeship*, 370, citing a letter from Roosevelt to Daniels written in 1941. It is printed in Kilpatrick, *Roosevelt and Daniels*, 199–200.

76. ER, *This Is My Story*, 272; *FDR Letters*, 2:444; Freidel, *Ordeal*, 6. All accept this rationale for ER's presence, which seems to me special pleading. Assistant Attorney General Spellacy's wife went along too, and he was not ill.

77. FDR to Josephus Daniels, January 9, 1919, as cited in Joseph W. Coady, "Franklin D. Roosevelt's Early Washington Years (1913–1920)," 206.

78. Freidel, *Ordeal*, 276nn15, 19, citing a 1948 interview with Hancock.

79. The trip is documented in *FDR Letters*, 2:442–71. See also ER, *This Is My Story*, 273–93.

80. Freidel, *Ordeal*, 6, 14.

81. ER, *This Is My Story*, 239. She wrote that she had copied the phrase into her diary. The luncheon is documented in the sixty-nine-volume *Papers of Woodrow Wilson* (55:224); the stateroom meeting is not.

82. *NYT*, February 25, 1919, 1 (Wilson), 10 (FDR); *FDR Letters*, 2:470; ER, *This Is My Story*, 292–93.

83. *NYT*, July 5, 1917, 4.

84. Cronon, *Cabinet Diaries of Daniels*, 313, entry of June 18, 1918.

85. FDR to Wilson, July 18, 1918, as quoted in Freidel, *Apprenticeship*, 342–43.

86. Freidel, *Apprenticeship*, 339–43. For an exchange of letters between FDR and Smith about the endorsement, see Coady, "Roosevelt's Early Washington Years," 182–83.

87. Smith won the governor's race in 1918, lost it in 1920, and won it again in 1922, 1924, and 1926, and he lost the 1928 presidential election. In 1932 they would be rivals for the Democratic presidential nomination, but even then Smith's postconvention support was useful to FDR.

88. *NYT*, February 2, 1920, 7 (the larger story on the Brooklyn speech at the top of the page) and 6 (the smaller story on the debate at the bottom of the page). No account I have seen mentions the debate. Mills specifically charged that the administration was unprepared, but Franklin, who left early and had a political ally stay to answer questions, may not have heard the charge. For the 1919 Boston speech, see Freidel, *Apprenticeship*, 294. There seems to be no copy of the Brooklyn speech, which may have been ad-libbed.

89. "Explains Brooklyn Talk," *NYT*, February 3, 1920, 9.

90. See, for example, Cronon, *Cabinet Diaries of Daniels*, entry of February 21, 1920, 497; and Morrison, *Small-d Democrat*, 135.

91. Stanley Coben, *A. Mitchell Palmer: Politician*, is the standard work. See also Robert K. Murray, *Red Scare: A Study in National Hysteria, 1919–1920*.

92. Freidel, *Ordeal*, 53.

93. *NYT*, May 30, 1913, 3. Unlike the *Tribune*, the *Times* made no comparison and gave Palmer precedence in the story and a little more space than it gave Franklin.

94. Nixon was elected in 1968, but when he ran as an incumbent vice president in 1960, he lost, as did Gore in 2000.

95. *NYT*, June 27, 1920, 1; June 19, 1920, 1; Wesley M. Bagby, *The Road to Normalcy: The Presidential Campaign and Election of 1920*, 120; Freidel, *Ordeal*, 63.

96. *NYT,* June 30, 1920, 1.

97. *Official Report of the Proceedings of the Democratic National Convention . . . 1920,* 140–41; Cockran's speech is on 135–40. Roosevelt's speech is in *NYT,* July 1, 1920, 2, as well.

98. *NYT,* July 2, 1920, 1.

99. *Democratic National Convention, 1920,* 419–20. On the previous ballot, the forty-third and the last completed, with 726 votes necessary to nominate, the final tally was Cox, 568; McAdoo, 412; with 109 votes divided among seven candidates. The details of each ballot are given on 267–420.

100. *NYT,* July 3, 1920, 4.

101. Quoted in Freidel, *Ordeal,* 66 citing James M. Cox, *Journey through My Years,* 40.

102. Cox, *Journey through My Years,* 232. See also James M. Cebula, *James M. Cox: Journalist and Politician.*

103. *NYT,* July 7, 1920, 4.

104. ER, *This Is My Story,* 310–11.

105. *FDR Letters,* 2:495–97.

106. Roosevelt told this story, sometime after 1939, to Claude G. Bowers, then his minister to Chile, for transmission to Cox, who was writing his memoirs. In his memoirs, Cox prints the letter without giving its date, which Bowers wrote him subsequently from Santiago. Cox, *Journey through My Years,* 241.

107. "Poughkeepsie Hails F. D. Roosevelt," *NYT,* July 14, 1920, 2. In her first memoir, Eleanor conflated this informal meeting on July 13 and the formal notification of August 9 (*This Is My Story,* 311–13).

108. Cronon, *Cabinet Diaries of Daniels,* 544; Rollins, *Roosevelt and Howe,* 158.

109. The advance text is printed in *NYT,* August 10, 1920, 4, and in *FDR Letters,* 2:500–508. The interpolations "some little people" and the phrase about "normalcy" are noted in the *Times'* front-page story about the event. For the buildup to the acceptance speech, see *NYT,* August 9, 1920, 3.

110. The others were Howe; Renah F. Camalier, from his Navy Department staff; James Sullivan, a secretary; Tom Lynch, an old friend from Poughkeepsie who was disbursing officer; and Stanley Prenosil, the AP correspondent who was the only reporter permanently assigned to the campaign train. *FDR Letters,* 2:515.

111. ER, *This Is My Story,* treats the campaign on 313–21, quote on 315.

112. James R. Kearney, *Anna Eleanor Roosevelt: The Evolution of a Reformer,* 100.

113. "Says America Has Twelve League Votes," *NYT,* August 19, 1920, 11.

114. Freidel, *Ordeal,* 80–83, gives a convincing analysis.

115. Ibid., 84.

116. ER, *This Is My Story,* 320.

117. Freidel, *Ordeal,* 91.

Chapter 3. Roosevelt and the Old Order

1. *NYT,* January 8, 1921; Rollins, *Roosevelt and Howe,* 173–75, 177, 193–96; Freidel, *Rendezvous with Destiny,* 40.

2. FDR to Van-Lear Black, September 19, 1924, as cited in Freidel, *Ordeal,* 143.

3. *FDR Letters,* 1:168, quoting Marvin Langdon.

4. Letter to Henry Morgenthau Jr., December 4, 1928, as cited in Freidel, *Ordeal,* 151.

5. *NYT,* July 11, 1921, 9; Freidel, *Ordeal,* 94; Marguerite Green, *The National Civic Federation and the American Labor Movement.*

6. *NYT,* June 4, 1922, 91; June 21, 1922, 34; Freidel, *Ordeal,* 151–58; Rollins, *Roosevelt and Howe,* 199–201.

7. J. Flynn, *Country Squire in the White House,* 25–46; Richard Hofstadter, *The American Political Tradition and the Men Who Made It,* 324–26. The key characterization in the latter was "superficial and complacent."

8. *NYT,* December 5, 1920, 105; January 13, 1921, 13; July 4, 1922, 12; July 21, 1921, 5; May 14, 1921, 1, 2; January 22, 1921, 19; Scott M. Cutlip, *Fund Raising in the United States: Its Role in American Philanthropy,* 273–76.

9. *NYT,* May 1, 1921, 22; December 12, 1920, X2; April 24, 1921, 16.

10. Cook, *Eleanor Roosevelt,* 1:288.

11. Letter, Wilson to Roosevelt, September 16, 1921 in Arthur S. Link et al., ed., *The Papers of Woodrow Wilson,* 67:392. Presumably, Wilson saw the front-page story in the *New York Times.*

12. Link et al., *Wilson Papers,* 68:36, 68, 245–46, 280, 511, 513.

13. *NYT,* April 30, 1924, 18; Freidel, *Ordeal,* 126–27.

14. David J. Pivar, *Purity and Hygiene: Women, Prostitution, and the "American Plan," 1900–1930,* 201–38, does not examine military efforts.

15. Rathom (1868–1923), an Australian-born former war correspondent, was a director of the Associated Press. *NYT,* December 12, 1923, 20, 21. For the role of naval officers, see Freidel, *Ordeal,* 46–47. Josephus Daniels, *Years of War,* 199–200, has four paragraphs under the heading "Newport Needed Bitter Medicine," which ignore the scandal.

16. The *Times* headlines tell the story nicely: "Rathom Sees 'Plot' in Navy Vice Inquiry; Tells Judge Advocate That Daniels and Franklin Roosevelt Seek to Injure Him; Court Strikes Out Answer; Witness Admits He Has No Proof That Heads of Navy Knew of Methods of Vice Squad," *NYT,* May 28, 1920, 9.

17. *NYT,* October 25, 1920, 16; October 26, 1920, 16, 19; October 28, 1920, 10 (two stories); October 29, 1920, 16.

18. Geoffrey C. Ward, *A First Class Temperament: The Emergence of Franklin Roosevelt,* 570; Rollins, *Roosevelt and Howe,* 178.

19. "Lay Navy Scandal to F. D. Roosevelt," *NYT,* July 20, 1921, 4.

20. "Minority Report Dissents," *NYT,* July 20, 1921, 4.

21. Ward, *First Class Temperament,* 574, letter dated July 21, 1921.

22. *FDR Letters,* 1:516–18, letter to ER, July 21, 1921.

23. The photo, unattributed, is between pages 98 and 99 in Freidel, *Ordeal.*

24. Lindley, *Franklin D. Roosevelt;* Earle Looker, *This Man Roosevelt.*

25. The letters, dated August 14, 18, and 25, are in *FDR Letters,* 1:523–26. See also ER, *This Is My Story,* 328–40. Many of the details in the latter are unreliable, some of them almost certainly deliberately so.

26. Lovett (1859–1924) was the author of *The Treatment of Infantile Paralysis* (1917). Rollins, *Roosevelt and Howe,* 180–81.

27. The letter is printed in *FDR Letters*, 1:527. Sara Roosevelt's sister Katherine Robbins Delano Collier (1860–1953), known as Aunt Kassie, also met her.

28. Sara Delano Roosevelt to Frederick A. Delano, September 2, 1921, as quoted in Freidel, *Ordeal*, 100.

29. Hugh G. Gallagher, *FDR's Splendid Deception*.

30. *NYT*, August 27, 1921, 7. Appended was a two-sentence biography.

31. Freidel, *Ordeal*, 101–2; *NYT*, September 15, 1921, 11.

32. *NYT*, September 16, 1921, 1.

33. Draper, Harvard '03, came from a distinguished medical family and did important work on the relationship between the physical characteristics and personality of patients and their susceptibility to certain diseases. His *NYT* obituary, July 2, 1959, 25, made no mention of his most famous patient.

34. Lovett to Draper, September 12, 1921, and Draper to Lovett, September 24, 1921, printed in John Gunther, *Roosevelt in Retrospect: A Profile in History*, 243–45. This perceptive account by a journalist best known for books summarizing countries and continents should be read by any serious student of Roosevelt. Many biographers have ignored it to the detriment of their work.

35. Draper to Lovett, October 24, 1921, as printed in ibid., 244. Although Draper lived to almost the end of the Eisenhower administration, no one seems to have interviewed him about his most famous patient.

36. PPA, "Address to Congress on the Yalta Conference," March 1, 1945.

37. Naomi Rogers, *Dirt and Disease: Polio before FDR*. See especially her "Epilogue: Polio since FDR."

38. *NYT*, September 18, 1921, 17. The data from 1916 are from Rogers, *Dirt and Disease*, 10–11.

39. Cook, *Eleanor Roosevelt*, 1:302.

40. Ibid., 323–28. ER and her friends Nancy Cook and Marian Dickerman put up twelve thousand dollars, and FDR drafted a lease giving them a life interest. See the National Park Service Val-Kill website: http://www.nps.gov/elro/index.htm.

41. *NYT*, July 21, 1921, 8; August 6, 1921, 7; August 21, 1921, 61. The other concerned the Netherland-America Foundation. I say "at least" because the search engine for the digital *Times* is imperfect. If *Roosevelt* fell at the end of a line and had to be hyphenated, it would not be reported.

42. Letter to Dr. Lovett, March 25, 1922, as quoted in Richard Thayer Goldberg, *The Making of Franklin D. Roosevelt: Triumph over Disability*, 48.

43. The letter is printed in *NYT*, August 13, 1922, 13. "Smith Urged to Act by F. D. Roosevelt; Tells Him He Can Be Re-elected Governor If He Declares Himself." Smith's positive reply is in *NYT*, August 16, 1933, 1.

44. *NYT*, August 17, 1922, 1.

45. *NYT*, September 27, 1922, 3; September 30, 1922, 2; Howe to Roosevelt, September 29, 1922, as cited in Rollins, *Roosevelt and Howe*, 209.

46. Smith to FDR, October 9, 1922, as cited in Freidel, *Ordeal*, 118.

47. John Higham, *Strangers in the Land: Patterns of American Nativism, 1860–1924*, 265–99. John D. Buenker speaks of an "American Kulturkampf" in his *Urban Liberalism and Progressive Reform*, 163–97.

48. See Freidel, *Ordeal*, 22–23; and Rollins, *Roosevelt and Howe*, 210–12. The best single work on postamendment Prohibition politics is David E. Kyvig, *Repealing National Prohibition*.

49. "Democratic Women to Help on Platform," *NYT*, March 31, 1924, 2.

50. "Democratic Women Win: Party Leaders Concede Their Right to Name Their Delegation," *NYT*, April 16, 1924, 2. In 1922 the women, including ER, had lost a similar fight but supported Smith anyway.

51. "All Plans Now Laid to Win Nomination for Governor Smith," *NYT*, May 1, 1924, 1, 2.

52. "Governor Smith's Friends," *NYT*, May, 2, 1924, 18.

53. See Oscar Handlin's snide remark: "[Roosevelt] had made a dramatic appearance in Madison Square Garden after he had been told what to say" (*Al Smith and His America*, 140).

54. Joseph M. Proskauer, *A Segment of My Times*, 50–51.

55. Elmer Davis, "Outburst Beats McAdoo's," *NYT*, June 27, 1924, 1.

56. James Roosevelt and Sidney Shalett, *Affectionately, F.D.R.: A Son's Story of a Lonely Man*, 205.

57. Freidel, *Ordeal*, 180.

58. Robert K. Murray, *The 103rd Ballot: Democrats and the Disaster in Madison Square Garden*.

59. Cook, *Eleanor Roosevelt*, 1:352.

60. "G. F. Peabody Dead; Philanthropist, 85," *NYT*, March 5, 1938, 17.

61. *FDR Letters*, vol. 2, to Sara Roosevelt, early October 1924.

62. AP, "F. D. Roosevelt Buys Spa," *NYT*, April 27, 1926, 3.

63. Cleburne F. Gregory, "Franklin D. Roosevelt Will Swim to Health."

64. PPA, 1938, "Message to the Conference on Economic Conditions of the South," July 4.

65. Alden Whitman, "Basil O'Connor, Polio Crusader, Dies," *NYT*, March 10, 1972, 40.

66. "Smith Sticks to Retirement Plan," *NYT*, January 26, 1926, 1.

67. "Odds Quoted in Wall Street on Next New York Governor," *NYT*, February 17, 1926, 1.

68. "Democrats Map Out Congress Plan for Next Election," *NYT*, February 1, 1926, 1.

69. "Leaders Seek Anew to Make Smith Run for Another Term," *NYT*, June 28, 1926, 1.

70. "F. D. Roosevelt Is Democratic Keynoter; Mills, Republican, to Precede Him on Radio," *NYT*, August 30, 1926, 17.

71. The *NYT* summary is accurate: "Predicting victory for the complete Democratic ticket at the November election, Franklin D. Roosevelt, former Assistant Secretary of the Navy, as Temporary Chairman of the Democratic State Convention, criticized the Administration of President Coolidge, attacked the influence of Secretary of the Treasury Andrew Mellon and ridiculed the New York Republican leadership of United States Senator James W. Wadsworth Jr. in his keynote speech in the Arena here tonight" (September 28, 1926, 1; FDR's text is on 14).

72. See, for example, *NYT,* September 28, 1926, 13; October 3, 1926, 3; and October 16, 1926, 3.

73. See *NYT* front-page stories on January 12, 30, 1927.

74. *NYT,* February 27, 1927, 1.

75. Roosevelt to Josephus Daniels, June 23, 1927, as cited in Freidel, *Ordeal,* 233.

76. FDR, "Shall We Trust Japan?" For an analysis of his prepresidential views on Japan, see William L. Neumann, "Franklin D. Roosevelt and Japan, 1913–1933."

77. FDR, "Our Foreign Policy: A Democratic View," 583–85; *NYT,* June 11, 1928, 23.

78. Hofstadter, *American Political Tradition,* 324.

79. FDR, *Whither Bound?* See also Thomas H. Greer, *What Roosevelt Thought: The Social and Political Ideas of Franklin D. Roosevelt.*

80. "Roosevelt Sr. Urged Catholic President," *NYT,* January 25, 1928, 4.

81. *NYT,* February 5, 1928, 3. ER's friend Caroline O'Day, a party official, was chosen, and later Elinor Morgenthau was added.

82. ER, "Women Must Learn to Play the Game as Men Do"; *NYT,* March 10, 1928, 3. "Mrs. F. D. Roosevelt for Women Bosses," *NYT,* March 10, 1928, 3.

83. S. J. Woolf, "A Woman Speaks Her Mind: Mrs. Franklin D. Roosevelt Points Out That in Spite of Equal Suffrage the Men Still Run the Parties."

84. *NYT,* April 18, 1928, 1; May 31, 1928, 10.

85. *NYT,* April 23, 1928, 10, 12; April 30, 1928, 6.

86. Richard Oulahan, "Big Smith Demonstration," *NYT,* June 28, 1928, 1.

87. "A High-Bred Speech," *NYT,* June 28, 1928, 24.

88. *FDR Letters,* 2:637, 645, to "Dearest Mamma," April 1, September 30, 1928.

89. Edward J. Flynn, *You're the Boss,* 67–70.

90. My account follows that first put forth in Lindley, *Franklin D. Roosevelt,* 15–20, which has been used by Freidel and many others. None of the principals ever challenged it. For Flynn's role, see Arthur M. Schlesinger Jr., *The Crisis of the Old Order, 1919–1933,* 381.

Chapter 4. Running the Empire State

1. "Choice of Roosevelt Elates Smith," *NYT,* October 3, 1928, 1.

2. "The Press on the Ticket," *NYT,* October 4, 1928, 13; *New York World* as cited in Lindley, *Franklin D. Roosevelt,* 21.

3. "Roosevelt Denies That Smith 'Dragooned' Him into Running," *NYT,* October 5, 1928, 1.

4. "F. D. Roosevelt Hits Bigotry 'Flare Up,'" *NYT,* October 5, 1928, 2.

5. "Bigotry Is Receding Says F. D. Roosevelt," *NYT,* October 7, 1928, 24.

6. The acceptance speech is in PPA, 1928–32, 13–16; "Roosevelt Demands State Keep Power," *NYT,* October 17, 1928, 1, 18.

7. See Samuel B. Hand, *Counsel and Advise: A Political Biography of Samuel I. Rosenman.*

8. Freidel, *Ordeal,* 262.

9. Samuel I. Rosenman, *Working with Roosevelt,* 14–20. Much of the Buffalo speech is in PPA, 1928–32, 30–38.

10. Interestingly, in 1928 Roosevelt made no mention of federal responsibility.

11. PPA, 1928–32, 41.

12. "Roosevelt to End Campaign in Spurt," *NYT*, November 5, 1928, 3.

13. Freidel, *Ordeal*, 41.

14. Presidential results from Edgar E. Robinson, *The Presidential Vote, 1896–1932*. Other results from James Malcolm, ed., *The New York Red Book*.

15. Frances Perkins, *The Roosevelt I Knew*, 46.

16. Samuel Lubell, *The Future of American Politics*, 49; Ruth C. Silva, *Rum, Religion, and Votes: 1928 Reconsidered*.

17. For Moskowitz, see Elisabeth Israels Perry, *Belle Moskowitz: Feminine Politics and the Exercise of Power in the Age of Alfred E. Smith*.

18. Rosenman, *Working with Roosevelt*, 30–31; Hand, *Rosenman*, 24–25; *NYT*, December 29, 1922.

19. E. Flynn, *You're the Boss*, 73–126.

20. Frances Perkins, interview, Columbia Oral History Collection, Columbia University, New York, 3:32.

21. "Smith Quits Albany as Private Citizen," *NYT*, January 2, 1929, 1.

22. Finan, *Alfred E. Smith*, 242. For a nuanced account of the transfer of power, see Perry, *Belle Moskowitz*, esp. 206–7.

23. "Mrs. Roosevelt to Keep on Filling Many Jobs Besides Being the 'First Lady' at Albany," *NYT*, November 10, 1928, 1. See also Diana Rice, "Mrs. Roosevelt Takes on Another Task," 5, 22. For details of her Albany years, see Cook, *Eleanor Roosevelt*, 2:381–96. Curiously, Cook begins the chapter describing ER as a woman whose "children were grown." For an account of those networks, see Susan Ware, *Beyond Suffrage: Women in the New Deal*.

24. "Roosevelt Inaugurated as Governor . . .," *NYT*, January 2, 1929, 1.

25. PPA, 1928–32, 75–80.

26. This message is excerpted in PPA, 1928–32, 80–86.

27. Article III, Section 3, as printed in Malcolm, *New York Red Book*, 604–6. Two sparsely populated Adirondack counties were treated as one. Apportionment at 346; population at 539. Warren Moscow, *Politics in the Empire State*, 166–85, provides a caustic portrait of the legislature. Such arrangements were outlawed by the Supreme Court in *Baker v. Carr*, 369 U.S. 186 (1962).

28. Arthur M. Schlesinger Jr., *The Politics of Upheaval*, 56.

29. There are detailed accounts in Bernard Bellush, *Franklin D. Roosevelt as Governor of New York*, 37–57; and Frank Freidel, *Franklin D. Roosevelt: The Triumph*, 47–95, passim. The case is *People v. Tremaine*, 252 N.Y. 27 (1929).

30. PPA, 1928–32, 78.

31. Bellush, *Roosevelt as Governor*, 208–42; and Freidel, *Triumph*, 100–119, treat the issue at some length.

32. Bonbright eventually became a trustee and then chair of the New York State Power Authority. He was an adviser to Roosevelt during the 1932 campaign and from time to time throughout his presidency.

33. Rosenman, *Working with Roosevelt*, 31. Toward the end of 1929, the governor published a cogent argument for public power: FDR, "The Real Meaning of the Power Problem."

34. The other two were Frank P. Walsh (1864–1838) and Morris Llewellyn Cooke (1872–1960). All three have entries in *ANB*.

35. "Roosevelt Fosters Health Projects," *NYT*, June 5, 1929, 12. Other committee members included O'Connor, John J. Raskob, and Jeremiah Milbank. Dollar amount from David L. Sills, *The Volunteers, Means and Ends in a National Organization: A Report*, 42.

36. "Roosevelt Hailed at Fair in Atlanta," *NYT*, October 11, 1929, 4; the editorial is in *NYT*, October 14, 1929, 20.

37. Herbert C. Hoover, "Statement on the National Business and Economic Situation," October 25, 1929, in *Public Papers of the Presidents of the United States*, hereafter cited as HHPP.

38. "News Conference," November 5, 1929, in ibid.

39. "Roosevelt Criticizes 'Fever of Speculation,'" *NYT*, October 26, 1929, 3.

40. "Gov. Roosevelt Gives Hoover Assurance," *NYT*, November 25, 1929, 5.

41. Perkins, *The Roosevelt I Knew*, 94–96. Despite the naïveté suggested in her account, Perkins was adept at personal publicity. In the first year of Roosevelt's governorship, her name was in the *New York Times* about every three days.

42. The controversy may be followed in the *NYT*: "Employment Turns Upward, Hoover Reports; Changes for First Time since Stock Slump," January 22, 1930, 1; "Disputes Hoover on Employment," January 23, 1930, 11; and "Reports Business Back Near Normal," January 24, 1930, 38. The president's initial statement is in "The President's News Conference of January 21, 1930," HHPP. There is a minor factual error in Perkins's account. Her train ride was on January 22, not January 21, as she reported, and subsequent events are described as happening one day early. For the Depression's course, see Albert U. Romasco, *The Poverty of Abundance: Hoover, the Nation, the Depression*.

43. "Reds Battle Police in Union Square; Scores Injured, Leaders Are Seized; Two Dead, Many Hurt in Clashes Abroad" was the three-line front-page banner, *NYT*, March 7, 1930.

44. Daniel J. Leab, "United We Eat: The Creation and Organization of Unemployed Councils in 1930."

45. "City Asked to Rush Building Projects to Aid Unemployed," *NYT*, March 7, 1930, 1.

46. "Hearings Are Ordered on Unemployment Bills," *NYT*, March 7, 1930, 1; J. Joseph Huthmacher, *Senator Robert F. Wagner and the Rise of Urban Liberalism*, 59–63, shows that Wagner challenged the Hoover administration's figures on unemployment as early as March 1928.

47. FDR, *Public Papers of Franklin D. Roosevelt, Forty-Eighth Governor of New York*, 1930, 505–8 (hereafter cited as GPA); W. A. Warn, "Board on Unemployment Appointed by Roosevelt to Draft State Aid Plan," *NYT*, March 31, 1930, 1; Udo Sautter, *Three Cheers for the Unemployed: Government and Unemployment before the New Deal*, 231. Bruère had published a brief essay on unemployment during the short depression that followed the onset of World War I.

48. Henry Bruère, *America's Unemployment Problem*; Stuart D. Brandes, *American Welfare Capitalism, 1880–1940*. The two reports of Bruère's committee are in GPA, 1930, 508–17, 589–670.

49. GPA, March 29, 1930, 506.

50. New York [State] Governor's Commission on Unemployment, *Problems: Preventing Unemployment; Preliminary Report . . . ; NYT,* April 21, 1930, 1. The report contained little that was not in Bruère's 1915 pamphlet, *America's Unemployment Problem.* The New York [State] Governor's Commission on Unemployment's final report in November, *Less Unemployment through Stabilization of Operations,* was more of the same.

51. "Address to the Gridiron Club," April 26, 1930, HHPP.

52. GPA, "Address," Albany, April 12, 1930, and radio addresses, Albany, April 16, 23, 1930, 728–39.

53. New York State, *Old Age Security: Report of the New York State Commission;* GPA, "Statement by the Governor . . . Old Age Security," 533–34; "Gov. Roosevelt Signs Old Age Pension Bill; Praises Move, but Calls for Further Steps," *NYT,* April 10, 1930, 3.

54. GPA, "Radio Address to Thirty Luncheons in Honor of Thomas Jefferson, April 12, 1930," 726–28.

55. *Commonweal* quoted in "Views Roosevelt as 1932 Nominee," *NYT,* April 13, 1930, 20.

56. PPA, 1928–1932, 75–80.

57. "Roosevelt Can Win Presidency in 1932 Wheeler Says Here," *NYT,* April 27, 1930, 1. In his memoirs, Wheeler says that at the dinner Ambassador Gerard asked him if it was true that he was going to propose Roosevelt for president. Wheeler said yes and presumed that Gerard tipped Roosevelt off. Burton K. Wheeler, with Paul F. Healy, *Yankee from the West,* 294–95.

58. "Roosevelt Doubts Labor Gain in May," *NYT,* May 4, 1930, contains the text of Roosevelt's telegram to Lamont, April 30, 1930. The headline is a poor summary of the text.

59. Bellush, *Roosevelt and Governor,* 183. Perkins describes his preparation in *The Roosevelt I Knew,* 104–8.

60. "Address to the Governors' Conference," June 30, 1930, HHPP.

61. Even more extreme is Bellush's claim that "the seeds of the New Deal were first planted by . . . Alfred E. Smith" (*Roosevelt as Governor,* 282). Smith never conceived of a national program of reform.

62. Letter to John A. Kingsbury, May 12, 1930, *FDR Letters,* 3:30.

63. Chapter 3 of Rosenman's major opus is titled "The Genesis of the New Deal: The First Term as Governor, 1929–1930," in *Working with Roosevelt,* 28–47. This is an elaboration of the notion put forth, with Roosevelt's participation, in 1938 by titling the first volume of his presidential papers "The Genesis of the New Deal, 1928–1932," *NYT,* July 6, 1930, 25. The earlier stories by Warn were June 27, 9; June 28, 2; June 29, 7; June 30, 2; July 1, 1; July 2, 17; July 3, 2; July 4, 11; and July 6, 25.

64. GPA, 1930, veto message "Creating a Temporary State Commission . . .," 171–72.

65. PPA, 1928–32, 319–23; "Roosevelt for Dry Repeal . . .," *NYT,* September 11, 1930, 1.

66. "Roosevelt Nominated by Acclamation," *NYT,* October 1, 1930, 1.

67. "J. A. Farley Heads State Committee," *NYT,* October 1, 1930, 1. Compare Farley's two memoirs, *Behind the Ballots: The Personal History of a Politician* and *Jim Farley's Story: The Roosevelt Years.*

68. GPA, 1930, "Before National Democratic Club, New York City, Oct. 3, 1930, Acceptance Address of the Governor," 759–62.

69. GPA, 1930, "Movietone Talk by Governor, Albany, Sept. 25, 1930, Daily Duties of the Governor," 758–59; radio addresses in Albany: "Businesslike Administration under Democratic Rule," October 9, 1930; "Unemployment, Water Power, Milk Racketeering," October 13, 1930; and "What the State Is Doing for the People in Education, Conservation and Public Works," October 16, 1930, 763–73. For the political impact of newsreels, see Raymond Fielding, *The American Newsreel, 1911–1967.*

70. Roosevelt's request and the court's response are in GPA, 1930, 370–72. See also "Cash Says He Paid Healy $2,000 for Marshal's Job," *NYT,* August 26, 1930, 1.

71. "Text of Gov. Roosevelt's Speech," *NYT,* November 4, 1930, 20.

Chapter 5. Winning the White House

1. "The President's News Conference of November 7, 1930," HHPP.

2. "Roosevelt Hailed by Albany Crowds," *NYT,* November 6, 1930, 1; "Roosevelt Denies Seeking Presidency," *NYT,* November 8, 1930, 1; Farley, *Behind the Ballots,* 62.

3. "Mr. Rogers Views the Debris and Seems to Be Cheerful," *NYT,* November 6, 1930, 27.

4. E. Flynn, *You're the Boss,* 64–65; Stiles, *Man behind Roosevelt,* 117ff.

5. GPA, 1930, 670–72; "Governor Plans Loan Funds for Isle through His Board," *NYT,* November 17, 1930, 1. The Bruère report is in GPA, 1930, 589–670.

6. "Roosevelt Offers Armories for the Homeless, Asks Mayors to Report on Needs of Unemployed," *NYT,* November 18, 1930, 4.

7. "Roosevelt Will Invite Six Governors to Confer on the Jobless Problem," *NYT,* November 18, 1930, 1.

8. "Roosevelt Predicts Farm Recovery," *NYT,* November 15. 1930, 15. Rosenman did not include this speech text in GPA, 1930. At the same meeting, Hoover's secretary of agriculture, Arthur M. Hyde, more realistically spoke of the problem of agricultural surpluses.

9. "Wider Aged Relief Urged to Aid Idle," *NYT,* November 23, 1930, 33. His January 1931 annual message contains a cogent statement of his goals for "Old Age Security," GPA, 1931, 39. For Epstein, see Louis Leotta, "Abraham Epstein and the Movement for Old Age Security."

10. GPA, 1931, 11–15, quote on 13. Also in *NYT,* January 2, 1931, 5. The *Times'* page 1 headline was "Roosevelt, in Inaugural, Lays Breakdown in Local Government to Voters."

11. Vincent P. Carosso with the assistance of Rose C. Carosso, *The Morgans: Private Investment Bankers, 1854–1913.*

12. "3 in Bank of U.S. Guilty . . .," *NYT,* June 20, 1931, 1; "Carl J. Austrian, Lawyer, Dies; Aided Depositors in Depression," *NYT,* June 26, 1970, 41.

13. GPA, 1931, 37–46; "Text of the Governor's Message," *NYT,* January 8, 1931, 2.

14. The proceedings may be found in GPA, 1931, 530–82. All four experts figure significantly in Sautter, *Three Cheers for the Unemployed.* Governors came from Massachusetts, Rhode Island, Connecticut, New Jersey, and Ohio, while Pennsylvania's Pinchot sent a representative.

15. W. A. Warn, "Unemployed Make Pleas to Governors," *NYT*, January 25, 1931, 1. The appearance of the protesters is ignored in the printed proceedings. Other stories on the conference were front-page news on January 23 and 24.

16. GPA, 1931, 129–30; "Asks 2 State Bodies to Aid the Jobless," *NYT*, March 26, 1931, 20. See also Freidel, *Triumph*, 194–95.

17. GPA, 1931, "Accomplishments and Failures of Legislative Session of 1931," April 24, 1931, 722–27.

18. GPA, 1931, "The Three Aims of the Founders of New York University," 727–28.

19. Charles G. Dawes, *Journal as Ambassador to Great Britain*, 346–47. For Elliott, see James Roosevelt, with Bill Libby, *My Parents: A Differing View*, 227. See also "'A Fine Gentleman,' Says Dawes, of His Shipmate, Roosevelt," *NYT*, May 28, 1931, 1.

20. GPA, 1931, "Acres Fit and Useful," 732–38. For descriptions of the conference and its political impact, see W. A. Warn, "Roosevelt Meets Acclaim in Indiana," *NYT*, June 1, 1931, 1; and "Pinchot Stirs Assembly," *NYT*, June 3, 1931, 1.

21. "Action by Governor Due in 48 Hours," *NYT*, August 15, 1931, 1; "Legislature Meets August 25 to Widen Immunity Power . . . ," *NYT*, August 16, 1931, 25; GPA, 1931, "Convening the Legislature in Extraordinary Session," *NYT*, August 14, 1931, 27; "Cuvillier Says Special Session Will Put Governor 'in the Hole,'" *NYT*, August 16, 1931, 1.

22. For an analysis, see Lyle W. Dorsett, *Franklin D. Roosevelt and the City Bosses*.

23. The proclamation "Convening the Legislature in Extraordinary Session" was issued on August 14, 1931, calling for the session to begin at noon on August 25 (GPA, 1931, 27).

24. Rosenman, *Working with Roosevelt*, 50.

25. The two messages are in GPA, 1931, 167–72.

26. The TERA message is in GPA, 1931, 172–80, and in *NYT*, August 29, 1931, 2; the text of the bill he sent the legislature is on the next page and two front-page stories.

27. "Republicans Back Roosevelt's Plan," *NYT*, August 30, 1931, 1; "Roosevelt Credit Irks Republicans," *NYT*, August 31, 1931, 1; "State Socialists Urge General 5-Day Week," *NYT*, August 31, 1931, 2. Roosevelt's bill called for a five-day week on all work contracted by the state.

28. The process can be conveniently traced in *NYT* stories between September 1 and September 20, 1931. The New York City social work establishment, mistrusting Roosevelt, wanted the money to be controlled by the existing bureaucracy. See William W. Bremer, *Depression Winters: New York Social Workers and the New Deal*, 79–81.

29. "To Aid 'White Collar' Workers," *NYT*, September 23, 1931, 16.

30. "Straus Known as Organizer," *NYT*, September 30, 1931, 3. For Straus, see Reginald W. Kauffman, *Jesse Isidor Straus: A Biographical Portrait*.

31. Freidel, *Triumph*, 222.

32. "Mayor Speeds Plan for City Aid to Idle . . . Hopkins Is Straus Aide . . . ," *NYT*, October 8, 1931, 4. Hopkins's promotion was a two-stage affair. When Straus resigned in March, Wickser became chair and Hopkins moved into his position; when Wickser resigned in April, Hopkins took over. Most accounts are inaccurate about this.

33. There is no full history of TERA, in part because its files cannot be located. The agency was headquartered in New York City, outside of the easy grasp of the state archivist. It is possible that the records were donated to a wartime scrap-paper drive. The fullest account is Alexander L. Radomski, *Work Relief in New York State, 1931–1935*,

which is based on printed TERA documents. A most perceptive brief analysis is William R. Brock, *Welfare, Democracy and the New Deal,* 94–102.

34. Farley, *Beyond the Ballots,* 81–87.

35. "'Vindication' Rally by Tammany Gives Smith Ovation," *NYT,* October 15, 1931, 1.

36. "Gov. Roosevelt Enters Race," *NYT,* January 24, 1932, 1; text of letters on 2. Roosevelt's letter is also in PPA, 1928–32, 623–24.

37. "Text of Ex-Governor Smith's Announcement of His Willingness to Be Democratic Candidate," *NYT,* February 8, 1932, 1.

38. Allan Nevins, *Herbert H. Lehman and His Era,* 120.

39. For Dewson, see Susan Ware, *Partner and I: Molly Dewson, Feminism, and New Deal Politics.* For her impact, see Farley, *Behind the Ballots,* 121, 160, 354.

40. Walter Lippmann, "Governor Roosevelt's Candidacy." Within days of Roosevelt's assumption of the presidency, Lippmann was full of praise; see his March 11, 1933, column, "First Roosevelt Policies," 27.

41. GPA, 1932, "Annual Message," 29. See also William E. Leuchtenburg, "The New Deal and the Analogue of War."

42. "678 for Roosevelt Figured by Friends," *NYT,* January 24, 1932, 2.

43. Jordan A. Schwarz, "John Nance Garner and the Sales Tax Rebellion of 1932."

44. GPA, "Problem of Adequate Markets for American Industry and Agriculture," February 2, 1932, 550–52. As Freidel points out, the passages about the league are not included in the excerpts from that speech published in PPA, 1928–32, 155–57 (*Triumph,* 401n26). An obviously inspired story reported that Roosevelt's stand got widespread approval ("Praise Roosevelt for League Stand," *NYT,* February 4, 1932, 2).

45. Robert A. Divine, *Roosevelt and World War II.*

46. Rosenman, *Working with Roosevelt,* has a chapter titled "The Brain Trust," 56–66, quote on 56–57. The earliest user in print of the term *brains trust* seems to be James Kieran (1892–1981). His *NYT* feature story "The 'Cabinet' Roosevelt Already Has," November 20, 1932, XX2, is the first extended discussion. Kieran's precise "brains trust" often became "brain trust."

47. PPA, 1928–32, "The 'Forgotten Man' Speech. Radio Address. Albany, N.Y., Apr. 7, 1932," 624–27.

48. "Aggressive Speech of Ex-Governor Smith," *NYT,* April 14, 1932, 6. A bylined story on the speech by Arthur Krock was on page 1.

49. The foregoing is drawn from GPA, 1932, "Removal Proceedings and Investigations," 247–87.

50. "Farley Is Removed," *NYT,* February 25, 1932, 1.

51. The best account of Walker's mayoralty is in Thomas Kessner, *Fiorello H. La Guardia and the Making of Modern New York.*

52. Except when otherwise noted, the account of the convention generally follows those in Freidel, *Triumph,* 275–311; Farley, *Behind the Ballot,* 92–154; and Herbert Mitgang, *The Man Who Rode the Tiger: The Life and Times of Judge Samuel Seabury,* 259–310. The last, while based on Seabury's papers, is undocumented.

53. James M. Kieran Jr., "Message Written on Way," *NYT,* July 3, 1932, 9. A *NYT* photo shows him standing beside the plane in Albany, holding a crutch in one hand (July 3, 1932, 9).

54. The text of the acceptance speech is in PPA, 1928–32, 647–59. The *Times* used the phrase in a subhead of a front-page story on the nomination, but of the twenty-four newspapers cited in its roundup of national reactions to the speech, only the *Des Moines (Iowa) Register* used the term (July 3, 1932, 1, 11).

55. "Democrats Name Farley Chairman," *NYT*, July 3, 1932, 1; "Ex-Governor Avoids Meeting Roosevelt," *NYT*, July 3, 1932, 10.

56. The charges against Walker are laid out extensively in GPA, 1932, 297–415. The day-by-day proceedings may be followed in the *New York Times*. The most detailed secondary account is in Mitgang, *Man Who Rode the Tiger*, 159–310.

57. "Walker's Statement Explaining His Decision to Resign as Mayor" and "Walker Resigns, Denouncing the Governor," *NYT*, September 2, 1932, 1. For Tammany, see James A. Haggerty, "Roosevelt Chances Hurt," *NYT*, September 3, 1; and Rosenman, *Working with Roosevelt*, 83.

58. Walker returned to New York in the mid-1930s, and in 1940 Fiorello La Guardia appointed him as impartial arbiter for the New York women's clothing industry.

59. See summaries of press opinion in "Nation's Press Comment Is Hostile to Ex-Mayor Walker," *NYT*, September 3, 1931, 2. An exception was the dyed-in-the-wool Republican *Los Angeles Times*, which saw it all as a plot to boost Roosevelt's standing among independent voters outside New York.

60. "Seabury . . . Praises Governor," *NYT*, September 3, 1932, 2.

61. Rosenman, *Working with Roosevelt*, 83–84; "Governor's Man Ignored: Rosenman Turned Down as Tammany Joins with Republicans," *NYT*, September 30, 1932, 1. A second Roosevelt nominee was also denied nomination.

62. "Lehman Comes Out for Governorship," *NYT*, August 5, 1932, 1. The best account of the attempted coup against Lehman's candidacy comes in two *NYT* stories by Warren Moscow: "Smith Urges Curry to Support Lehman," October 5, 1932, 1; and "Curry Defeat Complete," October 5, 1932, 1.

63. Farley, *Behind the Ballots*, 170–78. This is an eyewitness account. In the photo illustrating Moscow's October 5 story cited in note 62, Farley can be seen standing behind the Smith-Roosevelt handshake. He says that the reported and oft-repeated Smith greeting to Roosevelt, "Hello, you old potato," was a journalist's invention.

64. The perceptive account of the twilight of Smith's career by Jordan A. Schwarz, "Al Smith in the 1930s," does not discuss the fight over Lehman's nomination.

65. Rexford G. Tugwell, *The Brains Trust*, 358–59. See also Roger Daniels, *The Bonus March: An Episode of the Great Depression*. A variant of the anecdote appears in Tugwell's essay "Roosevelt and the Bonus Marchers of 1932," in his *In Search of Roosevelt*, 181–94.

66. Rosenman, *Working with Roosevelt*, 86–87.

67. PPA, 1928–32, 811–12.

68. "Governors Elected," *NYT*, November 9, 1932, 9.

69. "Roosevelt Buoyant, Gets Returns Here," *NYT*, November 9, 1932, 9.

70. ER, *This I Remember*, 74–75.

71. "Women's Aid Asked by Mrs. Roosevelt," *NYT*, November 16, 1932, 9.

72. "Roosevelt Is in Bed with a Slight Cold," *NYT*, November 12, 1932, 1; Frank Freidel, *Franklin D. Roosevelt: Launching the New Deal*, 16.

73. "Roosevelt Started Fighting Tammany," *NYT,* November 9, 1932, 9.

74. W. A. Warn, "Roosevelt's Approach to the Great Task," *NYT,* November 13, 1032, XX1. Even hostile papers tended to follow suit. The *Chicago Tribune,* for example, wrote: "Infantile paralysis struck at Mr. Roosevelt in 1921. He immediately began his successful fight to gain control of his lower limbs" (November 9, 1932, 3).

Chapter 6. The Interregnum

1. "Telegram to President-Elect Franklin D. Roosevelt about Intergovernmental Debts," November 12, 1932, HHPP. It and Roosevelt's response are also in PPA, 1928–32, "An Exchange of Letters [*sic*] between President Hoover and President-elect Roosevelt, Nov. 12, 1932, and Nov. 14, 1932," 873–76. Just preceding those documents, Roosevelt, himself, in a brief first-person account of his activities during the interregnum, adds that he telephoned Hoover on November 17 and arranged for the November 22 meeting. "Between Election and Inauguration—November, 1932, to March 4, 1933," PPA, 1928–32, 867–71. Frank Freidel has commented on the two presidents' relations during the interregnum most extensively in "Herbert Hoover and Franklin Roosevelt: Reminiscent Reflections" and *Launching the New Deal,* 19–30 and passim.

2. *FDR Letters,* 3:98–99. The Roosevelt-Stimson talks will be discussed in chapter 12.

3. "Roosevelt to Meet Hoover on Tuesday," *NYT,* November 16, 1932, 3.

4. United Press White House correspondent Henry F. Misselwitz to Raymond Clapper [n.d. but December 1932], Clapper Mss., as cited in Freidel, *Launching the New Deal,* 43.

5. GPA, 1932, 24; "Prayer Invoking Help for the 'Forgotten Man' Used by Roosevelt to Proclaim Thanksgiving," *NYT,* November 19, 1932, 1. President Hoover's proclamation had ignored the Depression. Proclamation 2015, "Thanksgiving Day, 1932," November 3, 1932, HHPP.

6. "Roosevelt Confers with Lehman," *NYT,* November 22, 1932, 2.

7. McGeorge Bundy's claim that "President Hoover asked for Mr. Roosevelt's help in developing a policy" is erroneous. Hoover wanted Roosevelt to endorse his already established policies. See Henry L. Stimson and McGeorge Bundy, *On Active Service in Peace and War,* 289.

8. "White House Statement about a Meeting with President-Elect Roosevelt," November 22, 1932, HHPP.

9. "Roosevelt Outlines 4-Fold Program . . . Has Many Visitors in Day," *NYT,* November 24, 1932, 1. (Much of the speculation in the story was inaccurate; it predicted no special session of Congress in March.) "Roosevelt Finds Time in Busy Day to Cheer Girl Paralysis Victim," *NYT,* November 24, 1932, 3.

10. "Farley Appeals against Job Fight," *NYT,* January 3, 1933, 14; "Farley and Howe to Rule Patronage," *NYT,* January 11, 1933, 3.

11. FDR, "The New Deal: An Interpretation"; "Roosevelt Defines Plan for 'New Deal,'" *NYT,* November 30, 1932, 12.

12. "Lehman Assumes Office," *NYT,* January 3, 1933, 1, 12. As January 1 was a Sunday, the inaugural was on Monday.

13. "The British Government has asked for a discussion of the debts. The incoming administration will be glad to receive their [*sic*] representative early in March for this purpose. It is, of course, necessary to discuss at the same time the world economic problems in which the United States and Great Britain are mutually interested, and therefore that representatives should also be sent to discuss ways and means for improving the world situation." "White House Statement about a Meeting with President-Elect Roosevelt," January 20, 1933, HHPP.

14. PPA, 1933, 739–40, 886–89; James A. Hagerty, "Government Operation of Muscle Shoals Plant Pledged by Roosevelt," *NYT*, January 22, 1933, 1; "Senators Confer with Roosevelt on Federal Relief," January 23, 1933, 1; Richard Lowitt, *George W. Norris: The Persistence of a Progressive, 1913–1933*, 197–98, 557–58, 567–68.

15. "Roosevelt, at 51, Celebrates His Birthday; Cuts 80-Pound Cake for Georgia Children," *NYT*, January 31, 1933, 1.

16. "Roosevelt Hailed at End of Cruise," *NYT*, February 16, 1933, 3; PPA, 1928–32, "Informal Extemporaneous Remarks at Miami, Fla., Immediately Preceding Attempted Assassination of the President Elect, Feb. 15, 1933," 889–90.

17. "Roosevelt Thanks Heroine in Miami," *NYT*, February 20, 1933, 3.

18. "How Roosevelt Saw It," *NYT*, February 17, 1933, 1. There are numerous minor differences in the contemporary accounts of the event. In Jim Hagerty's on-the-scene account, there are a number of details that vary from Roosevelt's account. Hagerty, for example, says that Roosevelt immediately assured the crowd that "I am alright," a detail absent from the target's report. I use Roosevelt's account in the text, not because I believe that it is accurate in all details, but because it throws more light on him. There are clear errors in the *Times*' immediate reports: for example, they consistently called Zangara "Zingara." James M. Hagerty, "Assassin Fires into Roosevelt Party at Miami," *NYT*, February 16, 1933, and eight other stories that day.

19. "Mrs. Roosevelt Takes News Calmly," *NYT*, February 16, 1933, 1.

20. "Woman Diverted Aim of Assassin," *NYT*, February 16, 1933, 1. Mrs. Cross told reporters that she weighed one hundred pounds and was five feet, four inches tall.

21. "Zangara Receives 80-Year Sentence," *NYT*, February 21, 1933, 1.

22. "Cermak Succumbs to Assassin's Shot," *NYT*, March 7, 1933, 1; "Zangara Defiant in Plea of Guilty," *NYT*, March 10, 1933, 16; "Zangara Defiant at Death Verdict," *NYT*, March 11, 1933, 28; "Zangara Executed for Killing Cermak," *NYT*, March 23, 1933, 36.

23. James M. Hagerty, "War Post Still Open," *NYT*, February 18, 1933, 1; "Drawn Guns Protect Him," *NYT*, February 18, 1933; "Mrs. Roosevelt Left Unguarded All Day," *NYT*, February 18, 1933, 3.

24. Freidel, *Rendezvous with Destiny*, 88–89. A text of the letter, written February 17, 1933, and delivered the next day, is in William S. Myers and Walter H. Newton, *The Hoover Administration: A Documented Narrative*, 338–40. It does not appear in HHPP, which does contain a February 17 "Message to President-Elect Roosevelt about His Escape from Assassination."

25. Myers and Newton, *Hoover Administration*, 341.

26. The standard account of the banking crisis is Susan E. Kennedy, *The Banking Crisis of 1933*.

27. "Glass Declines Post in Cabinet," *NYT*, February 21, 1933, 1.

28. For a good account of Virginia politics in the New Deal era, see Ronald L. Heinemann, *Depression and New Deal in Virginia.*

29. Irwin F. Gellman, *Secret Affairs: Franklin Roosevelt, Cordell Hull, and Sumner Welles.*

30. "Walsh Found Dead by Bride of 5 Days on Way to Capital" and "Cummings Picked to Succeed Walsh," *NYT,* March 3, 1933, 1.

31. See Daniel C. Roper with the collaboration of Frank H. Lovette, *Fifty Years of Public Life* (Durham, NC, 1941).

32. Harold L. Ickes, *The Autobiography of a Curmudgeon.*

33. "Economists Advise Credit Expansion," *NYT,* January 16, 1932, 30; "Economist Links Tariffs and Wars," *NYT,* December 31, 1932, 7.

34. Russell Lord, *The Wallaces of Iowa* (Boston, 1947).

35. "Approve and Oppose Her," *NYT,* March 2, 1933, 3.

36. "Miss Perkins Cool under Green's Fire," *NYT,* March 3, 1933, 2; Perkins, *The Roosevelt I Knew,* 151–54; George Martin, *Madam Secretary: Frances Perkins,* 3–4.

37. Robert Paul Browder and Thomas G. Smith, *Independent: A Biography of Lewis W. Douglas.*

38. Tugwell diary, December 23, 1932, as cited in Freidel, *Launching the New Deal,* 40.

39. Freidel, *Launching the New Deal,* 188–89.

40. "Status of Banking Restrictions by States," *NYT,* March 3, 1933, 9.

41. "Two-Day Holiday for Banks Here, Lehman's Order," *NYT,* March 4, 1933.

42. There is no biography of Pecora. For the investigations, see Ferdinand Pecora, *Wall Street under Oath: The Story of Our Modern Money Changers;* and "Mitchell Avoided Income Tax in 1929 by $2,400,000," *NYT,* February 22, 1933, 1.

43. Irwin H. Hoover, *Forty-Two Years in the White House,* 227; Grace G. Tully, *FDR, My Boss,* 64. His son's account is a variant version written much later. J. Roosevelt and Shalett, *Affectionately, F.D.R.,* 250–52.

44. "Roosevelt Confers with the President," *NYT,* March 4, 1933, 3.

45. PPA, 1928–32, "Between Election and Inauguration—November 1932 to March 4, 1933," 867–71. This gives a truncated account of his meetings with Hoover, with no mention of any unpleasantness.

46. PPA, March 4, 1933. Incredibly, the text as printed in the Roosevelt Papers does not have that sentence, and many versions of the speech have been printed and placed on the Internet without it.

47. Leuchtenburg, "New Deal and the Analogue of War."

48. This last phrase was a bow to Justice Louis D. Brandeis's famous book, *Other People's Money and How the Bankers Use It.* Arthur M. Schlesinger used the "old order" phrase in the title of his brilliant, partisan *Crisis of the Old Order.*

Chapter 7. Improvising the New Deal

1. John Maynard Keynes, "Economic Possibilities for Our Grandchildren," in his *Essays in Persuasion.*

2. That period, March 9–June 16, constitutes the famous "hundred days," and most new administrations since then are judged by the press after that period. But the press, like John Kennedy who spoke in his inaugural "of the first one hundred days," uses the first hundred days after the inauguration as the measuring rod.

3. FDR, *The Complete Presidential Press Conferences of Franklin D. Roosevelt,* #4 (March 17, 1933), 1:52–53, hereafter cited as *Press Conf.*

4. PPA, "The President Proclaims a Bank Holiday: Gold and Silver Exports and Foreign Exchange Transactions Prohibited," March 6, 1933, Proclamation no. 2039. The 1917 statute was Section 5(b) of the act of October 6, 1917 (40 *Stat.* 411), as amended.

5. PPA, "The Support Is Given: Resolution Passed at the Governors Conference," March 6, 1933. Twenty-five governors attended, and twelve others sent representatives.

6. Edmund W. Starling, *Starling of the White House,* 306–7.

7. The morning papers were the *New York Times* and *Herald-Tribune,* the *Washington Post* and *Times-Herald,* the *Baltimore Sun,* and the *Chicago Tribune;* the afternoon papers were the *New York World-Telegram, Journal American,* and *Sun,* plus the *Washington Evening Star* and *Daily News.* He was also provided with clippings by the White House service established in the Wilson administration.

8. McIntire, a U.S. Navy physician, and Watson were both recommended by Admiral Cary Grayson, who had been President Wilson's physician.

9. The routine is spelled out in Tully, *FDR, My Boss,* 76–85.

10. "President Enjoys First Conference with Correspondents," *NYT,* March 9, 1933, 3. See Jonathan Daniels's introduction to *The Complete Presidential Press Conferences of Franklin D. Roosevelt.* Eleanor Roosevelt soon established her own press conferences that only women reporters attended. See Maurine H. Beasley, *Eleanor Roosevelt and the Media: A Public Quest for Self-fulfillment* and her edition of *The White House Press Conferences of Eleanor Roosevelt.*

11. PPA, 1933, 38.

12. Felix Frankfurter, *Felix Frankfurter Reminisces: Recorded in Talks with Dr. Harlan B. Phillips,* 241–43, 247.

13. PPA, "Recommendation to the Congress for Legislation to Control Resumption of Banking," March 9, 1933. For details of banking legislation, I rely on S. Kennedy, *Banking Crisis of 1933.*

14. "Hoover Upholds Roosevelt Program," *NYT,* March 10, 1933, 6.

15. PPA, "The President Proclaims an Extension of the Bank Holiday: The Gold and Silver Embargo and the Prohibition on Foreign Exchange. Proclamation No. 2040," March 9, 1933.

16. PPA, "EO 6073 Relative to the Reopening of Banks: Embargo on Gold Payments and Exports, and Limitation of Foreign Exchange Transactions Continued," March 10, 1933.

17. PPA, "Statement by the President on Reopening Banks—Announcement of the First Radio 'Fireside Chat,'" March 11, 1933. For uses by other presidents, see William E. Leuchtenburg, *In the Shadow of FDR: From Harry Truman to Barack Obama.* For technical details on their number, see the useful "A Note on the Fireside Chats," in Lawrence

Levine and Cornelia Levine, *The President and the People: America's Conversation with FDR*, 571–72.

18. PPA, "The First 'Fireside Chat,'" March 12, 1933.

19. The classic New Left statement is Barton J. Bernstein, "The New Deal: Conservative Achievements of Liberal Reform."

20. The Economy Act—officially "An Act to Maintain the Credit of the United States Government"—was signed on March 20, 1933, becoming 48 *Stat.* 8.

21. See the discussion in Cook, *Eleanor Roosevelt*, 2:70–74.

22. For a more detailed analysis of the final cuts, see R. Daniels, *Bonus March*, 211–17. The restorations were effected by EOs 6156–59. Further liberalization was provided by Congress in riders attached to the Independent Offices Appropriation Act, signed June 16, 1933. For a summary, see PPA, "White House Statement on Ameliorations of Cuts in Veterans' Allowances," June 6, 1933, and appended note.

23. "Senate Votes 51–39: Adopts New Increases for Veterans Despite Leaders' Pleas," *NYT,* June 15, 1933, 1.

24. *Press Conf* #26 (June 2, 1933), 339. Total federal employment on June 30, 1932, was 605,496; on June 30, 1933, it was 603,587; and on June 30, 1934, it was 698,649. U.S. Department of Commerce, *Historical Statistics of the United States: Colonial Times to 1957*, Series Y, 241–50 at 710.

25. PPA, 1933, "Note," 51–54.

26. Roosevelt's comment is in Freidel, *Launching the New Deal*, 246; PPA, "The First Step toward the Repeal of the Volstead Act," March 13, 1933; "President Signs Bill for Legal Beer," *NYT*, March 23, 1933, 1; Arthur Krock. "Capital Studies Repeal; President Remains Mum," *NYT*, April 9, 1933, E1.

27. *Press Conf* #3 (March 15, 1933), 1:32–33; "Farm and Job Bills to Go to Congress," *NYT*, March 16, 1933, 1.

28. My account of agricultural policy relies heavily on Theodore Saloutos, *The American Farmer and the New Deal*, 34–49, quote on 43. Two short essays by Richard S. Kirkendall, "Agricultural Adjustment Act" and "Agriculture," in *Franklin D. Roosevelt: His Life and Times; An Encyclopedic View*, edited by Otis L. Graham Jr. and Meghan R. Wander, 1–5, constitute an ideal summary of Roosevelt-era agricultural policy. The Topeka speech is in PPA, 1932, 693–711.

29. PPA, "New Means to Rescue Agriculture," March 16, 1933.

30. For earlier speeches spelling out his notions on this subject, see the two 1931 speeches printed in PPA, 1928–32, 501–14.

31. As quoted in Arthur M. Schlesinger Jr., *The Coming of the New Deal*, 40.

32. PPA, "A Request to Congress for Authority to Effect Drastic Economies in Government," March 10, 1933. The single example would have been Germany's Weimar Republic, whose problems were exacerbated by conditions created by defeat in World War I and the Treaty of Versailles.

33. Browder and Smith, *Independent,* 92; for Morgan, see "Morgan Praises Gold Embargo as the 'Best Possible Course,'" *NYT*, April 20, 1933, 1.

34. *Press Conf* #13 (April 19, 1933), 1:153–55. He made the same argument in the same way two days later: see *Press Conf* #14 (April 21, 1933), 1:165–66.

35. See James W. Ely Jr., "Gold Clause Cases," in *The Oxford Guide to Supreme Court Decisions,* edited by Kermit L. Hall, 107.

36. The Le Mars incident is well known. See, for example, an insightful *NYT* feature story by Harlan Miller, "Watchfully the Farmer Awaits Events," May 7, 1933, XX1. The best account of the Farmers' Holiday movement is John L. Shover, *Cornbelt Rebellion: The Farmer's Holiday Association*.

37. John M. Blum, *From the Morgenthau Diaries: Years of Crisis, 1928–1938*, 1:45.

38. The entire act is 48 *Stat.* 31. Its text, and that of every subsequent major farm bill, may be consulted at http://www.nationalaglawcenter.org/assets/farmbills.

39. Mark H. Leff, *The Limits of Symbolic Reform: The New Deal and Taxation, 1933–1939*.

40. PPA, EO 6084, March 27, 1933; Blum, *Years of Crisis*, 1:42–50. The average value of farmland had plummeted from about forty-nine dollars an acre in 1929 to about thirty dollars an acre in 1933.

41. PPA, "Establishment of the Rio Grande Wild Life Refuge, EO 6086," March 28, 1933, and appended note.

42. *Press Conf #3* (March 15, 1933), 1:33–40; PPA, "Three Essentials for Unemployment Relief (C.C.C., F.E.R.A., P.W.A.), March 21, 1933." The parenthetical alphabet soup was intended to give the impression that these future agencies were already planned in mid-March.

43. Perkins, *The Roosevelt I Knew*, 181.

44. For text of the initial bill, see "Text of the Work Relief Bill," *NYT*, March 22, 1933, 2.

45. Connery (1887–1937) became a New Deal paladin. Like many supporters of labor, he had to be convinced that Roosevelt was labor's friend. In an obituary tribute, Roosevelt hailed him as "a champion of the rights of the underprivileged" ("Tribute to Connery Paid by Roosevelt," *NYT*, June 17, 1937, 23).

46. *Press Conf #5* (March 22, 1933), 1:64–67.

47. "Quick Job Action Sought," *NYT*, March 22, 1933, 1; "Miss Perkins Firm in Job Bill Defense," *NYT*, March 24, 1933, 10; "Job Bill 'Fascism' Alleged by Green," *NYT*, March 25, 1933, 4.

48. "An act for the relief of unemployment through the performance of useful public work, and for other purposes [48 *Stat.* 22]" is in Edgar B. Nixon's wonderful compilation *Franklin D. Roosevelt and Conservation, 1911–1945*, 1:146–49.

49. The chart is reproduced in ibid., 150. The bureaucrats were from the National Park Service, the Forest Service, and the War and Labor Departments, along with a New York State forester.

50. Franklin had long used his initials in family correspondence and designated other family members by initials. In did not catch on with the press until later in the New Deal. For a time, some papers used "FD," but FDR eventually became universal.

51. See Rollins, *Roosevelt and Howe*, 384ff.

52. PPA, "The Civilian Conservation Corps Is Started, EO 6101," April 5, 1933; "Roosevelt Issues Forest Job Order," *NYT*, April 6, 1933, 6; "Start Recruiting for Forestry Jobs," *NYT*, April 7, 1933, 3.

53. Leuchtenburg, *Franklin D. Roosevelt and the New Deal*, 11.

54. PPA, "The Governor Accepts the Nomination for the Presidency, Chicago, Ill.," July 2, 1932.

55. A list of those at the meeting is in Nixon, *Roosevelt and Conservation,* 1:150–51. For Persons, see "W. F. Persons, 78, U.S. Ex-Aide, Dies," *NYT,* May 29, 1955, 45.

56. There is no biography of Fechner. See *Time,* February 6, 1939 (Fechner was on the cover); and "Robert Fechner, CCC Head, Dies," *NYT,* January 1, 1940, 29. Conrad L. Wirth, *Parks, Politics, and the People,* has a great deal of information about the early days of the CCC. Wirth was the National Park Service's day-to-day representative on the board that oversaw it. Rollins, *Roosevelt and Howe,* 403–6.

57. The accolade is in Freidel, *Launching the New Deal,* 263.

58. Martin, *Madam Secretary.* In her memoir, Perkins devotes a brief chapter to the CCC (177–81), mentioning both Fechner and Persons but not the controversy. There is no mention of blacks or race relations in her book.

59. Harold L. Ickes to Robert Fechner, September 20, 1935, "CCC Negro Foremen" file, Box 700, General Correspondence of the Director, Record Group 35, National Archives, College Park, Maryland, as cited on the New Deal Network website. See also its collection "African Americans in the Civilian Conservation Corps."

60. John A. Salmond, *The Civilian Conservation Corps, 1933–1942: A New Deal Case Study,* is the standard study. His chapter "The Selection of Negroes, 1933–1937," 88–101, is the source of quotations.

61. Ralph J. Bunche, *The Political Status of the Negro in the Age of FDR,* 615. For the Black Cabinet, see Nancy J. Weiss, *Farewell to the Party of Lincoln,* 136–56.

62. Memo, Roosevelt to Marvin H. McIntyre, August 3, 1933, as cited in Nixon, *Roosevelt and Conservation,* 1:197. For the trip, see "President Inspects Five Forest Camps," *NYT,* August 13, 1933, 3.

63. Roosevelt to George W. Norris, March 13, 1933, as cited in Richard Lowitt, *George W. Norris: The Triumph of a Progressive, 1933–1944,* 16.

64. Harold L. Ickes, *The Secret Diary of Harold L. Ickes,* 1:15.

65. Lowitt, *Triumph of a Progressive,* 16.

66. PPA, "A Suggestion for Legislation to Create the Tennessee Valley Authority," April 10, 1933. The second quoted segment preceded the first in the message.

67. Lowitt, *Triumph of a Progressive,* 19–22; Nixon, *Roosevelt and Conservation,* 1:152.

68. *Press Conf #26* (June 2, 1933), 1:345; Lowitt, *Triumph of a Progressive,* 23. Norris submitted a list of candidates for the other two directorships to Arthur Morgan, but none of them was appointed. Morgan tells his side of the story in his *The Making of the TVA.* See also Roy Talbert, *FDR's Utopian: Arthur Morgan of the TVA.*

69. A. Schlesinger, *Coming of the New Deal,* 333.

70. For the fight, see Thomas K. McGraw, *Morgan vs. Lilienthal: The Feud within the TVA*; and Erwin C. Hargrove, "The Task of Leadership: The Board Chairman." Lilienthal's popular account *TVA: Democracy on the March* gives his side. The first of his seven volumes of published diaries, *The Journals of David E. Lilienthal: The TVA Years, 1939–1945,* contains interesting comments about FDR.

71. C. Herman Pritchett, *The Tennessee Valley Authority: A Study in Public Administration.*

72. Richard H. Rovere, *The Goldwater Caper,* 39.

73. *Press Conf #22* (May 19, 1933), 1:282–83; "Roosevelt Greets Group of Veterans," *NYT,* May 20, 1933, 11. See also R. Daniels, *Bonus March,* 209–32. In her press confer-

ence, Eleanor Roosevelt reported, "It was as comfortable as a camp can be, remarkably clean and orderly, grand-looking boys, a fine spirit. There was no kind of disturbance, nothing but the most courteous behavior" (#9, May 16, 1933).

74. PPA, "The Second 'Fireside Chat,'" May 7, 1933.

75. Blum, *Years of Crisis,* 1:31.

76. Hodson, like Hopkins, a midwesterner, became New York City's commissioner of public welfare in 1934 and took over Hopkins's old job at TERA in 1937. In 1943, on the way to a wartime relief assignment in North Africa, he was killed in a plane crash. "Hodson Killed in Plane Accident," *NYT,* January 21, 1943, 1.

77. The Senate had acted on March 30. Roosevelt made no effort to expedite the House's action.

78. This story has been told many times. The basic source is Perkins, *The Roosevelt I Knew,* 13–85. See also A. Schlesinger, *Coming of the New Deal,* 263–77; Martin, *Madam Secretary,* 247–48, 257–58; and George McJimsey, *Harry Hopkins: Ally of the Poor and Defender of Democracy,* 45–52.

79. The text of the act may be found at http://tucnak.fsv.cuni.cz/~calda/Documents/1930s/EmergRelief_1933.html.

80. PPA, "The President Signs Farm Relief Bill Including Agricultural Adjustment and Urges Delays in Foreclosures," May 12, 1933; "The President Signs the Unemployment Relief Bill and Stresses State, Local and Individual Responsibility," May 12, 1933.

81. PPA, 1933, "Note," 184.

82. *Press Conf* #4 (March 17 1933), 1:55; #22 (May 19, 1933), 1:290.

83. Telegram, Roosevelt to Lehman, May 19, 1933, as cited in June Hopkins, *Harry Hopkins: Sudden Hero, Brash Reformer,* 162.

84. His office was in the Walker-Johnson Building, at 1734 New York Avenue NW, because it housed the unemployment division of the RFC, soon to be disbanded.

85. PPA, "Informal and Extemporaneous Remarks to Relief Administrators," June 14, 1933. In this statement, he also explained the Hopkins appointment: "As you probably know, I go back quite a long way in this relief work. It was three years ago, very nearly, when I was Governor of New York, that we passed a perfectly unheard of relief bill—twenty-five million dollars for one year's expenditures—and Harry Hopkins took charge of it. We did a great deal and I learned a lot about relief from him in his work. That is the reason I brought him down here to Washington when we started this work." Actually, Roosevelt and Hopkins had very little personal contact before May 1933. See also "Roosevelt Warns States on Relief," *NYT,* June 15, 1933, 8.

86. PPA, "The Securities Bill Is Signed," May 27, 1933; "Roosevelt Signs the Securities Bill," *NYT,* May 28, 1933, 2. The text of the act may be found at http://www.sec.gov/divisions/corpfin/33act/index1933.shtml. Michael E. Parrish, *Securities Regulation and the New Deal,* is the best account. For a comparison of the 1933 and 1934 statutes, see 142–44.

87. PPA, "A Message Asking for Legislation to Save Small Home Mortgages from Disclosure," April 13, 1933. For an assessment of New Deal housing policy generally, see Gail Radford, *Modern Housing for America: Policy Struggles in the New Deal Era.*

88. PPA, "The Home Owners Loan Act Is Signed—The President Urges Delay in Foreclosures," June 13, 1933. See also C. Lowell Harriss, *History and Policies of the Home Owners' Loan Corporation.*

89. *Press Conf #78* (December 15, 1933), 2:550–51. Glass, of course, was Carter Glass (D-VA); Henry B. Steagall, chair of the House Banking Committee, was an Alabama Democrat who served from 1915 until his death in 1943. The mandatory separation of commercial and investment banking endured until 1999.

90. PPA, 1933, 439n; "13,423 Banks Begin Deposit Insurance," *NYT,* January 2, 1934, 12.

91. Ellis W. Hawley, "National Recovery Administration," in *Franklin D. Roosevelt,* edited by Graham and Wander, 275–77. His *The New Deal and the Problem of Monopoly* remains the outstanding treatment of his subject.

92. Frances Perkins, however, testified in favor of it, an example of the latitude that Roosevelt allowed his subordinates. See Louis Stark, "Miss Perkins Firm for 30-Hour Bill," *NYT,* April 26, 1933, 5.

93. PPA, "A Recommendation to the Congress to Enact the National Industrial Recovery Act to Put People to Work," May 17, 1933.

94. The parliamentary situation was complex, and no analysis of a single vote tells the whole story. A detailed analysis is in Bernard Bellush, *The Failure of the NRA,* 22–25.

95. PPA, "The Goal of the National Industrial Recovery Act: A Statement by the President on Signing It," June 16, 1933.

96. John K. Ohl, *Hugh S. Johnson and the New Deal.*

97. A. Schlesinger, *Coming of the New Deal,* 102–5, citing Hugh S. Johnson's memoir, *The Blue Eagle from Egg to Earth,* 197, 200, 206–11; Perkins, *The Roosevelt I Knew,* 201–3; Alexander Sachs to FDR, September 14, 1936, Roosevelt Papers, FDRL; Ickes, *Secret Diary,* 1:52–55. Much of Perkins's narrative must be modified by the account in Martin, *Madame Secretary,* 270–75, based on materials not available to Schlesinger in 1957.

98. PPA, "Organization of Public Works Administration Is Established; Naval Construction," EO 6174, June 16, 1933.

99. PPA, "Appointment of Harold L. Ickes as Administrator of Public Works," EO 6198, July 8, 1933.

100. Warren F. Kimball, *The Juggler: Franklin Roosevelt as Wartime Statesman;* William Smith White, *Majesty & Mischief: A Mixed Tribute to F.D.R.*

Chapter 8. Getting the New Deal Moving

1. Through 1939 Congress adjourned in either June or August, though in 1937 Roosevelt did call it back in mid-November to meet for a little more than a month. But shortly after the war began on September 1, 1939, Congress was called back into session, and during the rest of Roosevelt's presidency it would be in almost perpetual session with relatively brief recesses.

2. Lester G. Seligman and Elmer G. Cornwell, eds., *New Deal Mosaic: Roosevelt Confers with His National Emergency Council,* which provides transcripts of its thirty-one meetings. The quoted passage is from its first meeting on December 19, 1933, 3.

3. Coldbeth's presence in 1933 was not noted in the press coverage until 1936. "Roosevelt's Sons Sail On," *NYT,* July 9, 1936, 23.

4. "Congressmen [*sic*] Quit Capital for Homes," *NYT*, June 17, 1933, 3; "Roosevelt Takes Special Train for Boston to Embark on Vacation Voyage 'Down East,'" *NYT*, June 17, 1933, 1; "Roosevelt Boards Yacht for Cruise; Hailed by Crowds," *NYT*, June 18, 1933, 1.

5. Charles W. Hurd, "Arms Parlay Gains Told to Roosevelt," *NYT*, June 29, 1933, 1.

6. Charles W. Hurd, *When the New Deal Was Young and Gay*, 166. The entire trip is treated on 145–71.

7. It was during this trip that crucial decisions about the London Economic Conference were made, to be discussed in chapter 12.

8. There was at least one story a day in the *Times* on the president's trip, usually on the front page. Among the more important were "President Calls Davis for Talks," June 26, 1933, 1; "Arms Parlay Gains Told to Roosevelt," June 29, 1933, 1; "Roosevelt Greeted Royally at Campobello Isle," June 30, 1933, 1; "President Gets Rest Despite Problems," July 1, 1933, 2; and "Sees Cabinet on Cruiser," July 3, 1933, 1. See also Ickes, *Secret Diary*, 1:58–59.

9. ". . . President Takes Control upon Return at Night to White House," *NYT*, July 5, 1933, 1; "First Lady Flies Home," *NYT*, July 3, 1933, 5. See also Cook, *Eleanor Roosevelt*, 2:104–14; and "President Faces Busy Return," *NYT*, July 4, 1933, 3.

10. E. Pendleton Herring, "Second Session of the Seventy-Third Congress, January 3, 1934, to June 18, 1934," 864.

11. Chester M. Morgan, *Redneck Liberal: Theodore Bilbo and the New Deal*, 63–64. For Harrison, see Martha H. Swain, *Pat Harrison: The New Deal Years*.

12. The fullest account of this oft-told tale is in Bernard Sternsher, *Rexford Tugwell and the New Deal*, 252–58. Roosevelt's "murderer" was a typical embellishment; the appointee had been convicted of manslaughter. Tugwell, who claimed years later not to know the details, remembered that the president had told him about a trade for "two murderers."

13. Andrew Buni, *Robert L. Vann and the "Pittsburgh Courier": Politics and Black Journalism*. The Guffey-Roosevelt dialogue is from N. Weiss, *Farewell to the Party of Lincoln*, 43, citing Joseph Alsop and Robert Kintner, "The Guffey: Biography of a Boss, New Style," *Saturday Evening Post*, March 28, 1938, 6. See also "Robert L. Vann," *NYT*, October 25, 1940, 26.

14. See, for example, Gertrude F. Zimand, "Will the Codes Abolish Child Labor?," 290.

15. Section 7(a), using language borrowed from the Railway Labor Act of 1926, guaranteed workers the right to bargain collectively through representatives of their own choosing.

16. PPA, "The Third 'Fireside Chat,'" July 24, 1933.

17. Issues of January 1 and September 10, 1934.

18. For Humphrey (1862–1934), whose insistence that his removal was improper received posthumous vindication by the Supreme Court, see William E. Leuchtenburg, "The Case of the Contentious Commissioner," in his *The Supreme Court Reborn: The Constitutional Revolution in the Age of Roosevelt*, 52–81, 266–73.

19. PPA, "N.I.R.A. Administration over Certain Farm Products Transferred to the Department of Agriculture, EO 6182, June 26, 1933"; EO 6345, October 20, 1933; and EO 6551, January 9, 1934.

20. PPA, "The Executive Council Is Set Up, EO 6202A, July 11, 1933" and "The Creation of the National Emergency Council, EO No. 6433A, November 1933." Frank C. Walker ran both bodies.

21. Broadus Mitchell, *Depression Decade: From New Era through New Deal*, 241–42.

22. A. Schlesinger, *Coming of the New Deal*, 115.

23. PPA, "The President's Reemployment Agreement, July 27, 1933."

24. "Johnson Hails Rising of Nation," *NYT*, July 25, 1933, 4; "Sees Six Million More Jobs," *NYT*, July 25, 1933, 5; "Seeks Five Million Pledges," *NYT*, July 26, 1933, 1.

25. "Johnson Stirred by Huge Parade," *NYT*, September 14. 1933, 2.

26. Irving Bernstein, *The New Deal Collective Bargaining Policy*, is a good guide.

27. Thomas E. Vadney, *The Wayward Liberal: A Political Biography of Donald Richberg*, 115; Louis Stark, "Labor in Big Drive 'Signs' Thousands," *NYT*, July 16, 1933, 16; Mitchell, *Depression Decade*, 273–74; Green and Lewis quotations from Huthmacher, *Senator Robert F. Wagner*, 152; Max Freedman, ed., *Roosevelt and Frankfurter: Their Correspondence, 1928–1945*, 151–54. See also "Roosevelt Directs Steps," *NYT*, September 7, 1933, 1–2.

28. Louis Stark, "Roosevelt to Act to Prevent Strike of Steelworkers . . . Call NRA 'National Run Around,'" *NYT*, June 6, 1934, 1.

29. "Chamber to Work for NRA Reforms: Codes Are Unenforceable and Lead to Chiseling," *NYT*, November 20, 1933, 1; "A Warrior Economist," *NYT*, November 27, 1933, 16.

30. Ohl, *Johnson and the New Deal*, 197. Green and Lewis phrases from Huthmacher, *Senator Robert F. Wagner*, 152.

31. For a detailed analysis of this phenomenon, see Otis L. Graham, *An Encore for Reform: Old Progressives and the New Deal*.

32. PPA, "The First National Labor Board Is Appointed," August 5, 1933. The other six original appointees were William Green; John L. Lewis; Leo Wolman, a labor economist who had been director of research for the Amalgamated Clothing Workers; Walter C. Teagle of Standard Oil; Gerard Swope; and Louis E. Kirstein. Wagner's biographer notes that their appointment letters were not sent until October. Huthmacher, *Senator Robert F. Wagner*, 160.

33. Irving Bernstein, *Turbulent Years: A History of the American Worker, 1933–1941*.

34. Louis Stark, "Labor Clash Nears on Code Provisions: Steel's 'Company Union' Will Never Be Accepted, A.F. of L. Leaders Accept," *NYT*, July 18, 1933, 11. Stark was the first labor specialist on an American general newspaper from 1924 until his death. "Louis Stark, 66, Times Newsman," *NYT*, May 18, 1954, 29.

35. Vadney, *Wayward Liberal*, 130, quoting NRA documents.

36. Louis Stark, "Labor Fears Curbs on Its NRA Rights," *NYT*, August 23, 1933, 3; "Labor's Critical Labor Day," *NYT*, September 3, XX3.

37. PPA, "Address at the Dedication of the Samuel Gompers Memorial Monument, Washington, D.C., Oct. 7, 1933"; Louis Stark, "Roosevelt Warns Capital and Labor," *NYT*, October 8, 1933, 1.

38. For details, see PPA, "The Powers of the National Labor Board Are Increased, EO 6511, Dec. 16, 1933"; and Huthmacher, *Senator Robert F. Wagner*, 160–64.

39. The reports were written by economist Winfield W. Riefler (1897–1974), a longtime staff member of the Federal Reserve who became the coordinating statistician

of the Central Statistical Board, which Roosevelt created by EO 6225, July 27, 1933. Some are cited in Irving Bernstein, *A Caring Society: The New Deal, the Worker and the Great Depression,* 36; and Marriner S. Eccles, *Beckoning Frontiers: Public and Personal Recollections,* 127. Roosevelt, when he quoted Riefler's reports in his press conferences, called him the "Interpreting Economist" (*Press Conf* #65 [November 1, 1933], 2:393–97). See also Frank C. Walker, *FDR's Quiet Confidant: The Autobiography of Frank C. Walker,* 87–88.

40. Harry L. Hopkins, *Spending to Save: The Complete Story of Relief,* 417. In addition to the $400 million in PWA funds, $88,960,000 came from FERA funds and $345 million from a February 1934 congressional appropriation. Accounts of the origins of CWA, with minor differences, appear in all of the biographies of Hopkins, beginning with Sherwood's *Roosevelt and Hopkins* (1948). Important details are in John A. Salmond, *A Southern Rebel: The Life and Times of Aubrey Willis Williams, 1890–1965,* 54–55; I. Bernstein, *Caring Society,* 36–37; and Bonnie Fox Schwartz, *The Civil Works Administration, 1933–1934: The Business of Emergency Employment in the New Deal,* 39–40. The best account of its origins by a participant is Louis Brownlow, *A Passion for Anonymity,* 286–91.

41. The major outsiders were Frank Bane (1893–1983) and Louis Brownlow (1879–1963).

42. Ickes, *Secret Diary,* 1:316.

43. PPA, "Extemporaneous Speech to C.W.A. Conference in Washington, Nov. 15, 1933."

44. The best account is the chapter "Civil Works for the 'Forgotten Woman,'" in *Civil Works Administration,* by Schwartz, 156–80. See also Martha H. Swain, *Ellen S. Woodward: New Deal Advocate for Women;* "Civil Works Help Pledged to Women," *NYT,* November 21, 1933, 1; and "100,000 Women Get Civil Works Jobs," *NYT,* December 20, 1933, 17. The pathbreaking work on women activists in the New Deal is S. Ware, *Beyond Suffrage.*

45. Walker quoted in Robert E. Sherwood, *Roosevelt and Hopkins: An Intimate History,* 54–55.

46. "Professional Giver," *Time,* February 19, 1934.

47. Bane, a major figure in the history of American social work, moved between private and public agencies. He was the first executive director of the Social Security Board (1935–38) and held a similar position with the Council of State Governments (1938–58), interspersed with various federal positions. His papers are in the library of the University of Virginia, and there is an interview in the Columbia Oral History Collection, Columbia University, New York. See the Social Security History website, http://www.ssa.gov/history/fbane.html.

48. Salmond, *Southern Rebel,* 1–62; Richard A. Reiman, "The New Deal for Youth: A Cincinnati Connection."

49. For front-page headlines at a time when Roosevelt still denied policy differences, see "Roosevelt Curbs AAA Codes as Peek Revolts," *NYT,* December 7, 1933. For Peek, see George N. Peek, with Samuel Crowther, *Why Quit Our Own.*

50. PPA, "A Letter on the Improvement of Agriculture, Dec. 8th, 1933"; "Roosevelt Hails Farm Recovery," *NYT,* December 12, 1933, 1.

51. "1933 Crop Values Rose 42 Per Cent," *NYT*, December 20, 1933, 33. Detailed data may be found in the annual USDA *Yearbook of Agriculture*. See also Saloutos, *American Farmer*, 127.

52. "Peek Ready to Go as Chief of AAA: President Refuses to Support Him in Differences with Tugwell and Frank," *NYT*, December 8, 1933, 1; Arthur Krock, "Tugwell Defeats Peek in Duel over AAA Policy," *NYT*, December 10, 1933, E1.

53. For Frank, see Robert J. Glennon, *The Iconoclast as Reformer*; and "'Old Dealers' Held the Real Radicals," *NYT*, December 30, 1933, 15.

54. PPA, "Proclamation and Statement Ratifying the London Agreement on Silver, Dec. 21, 1933," and appended note; "2½ c above Today's Market," *NYT*, December 22, 1933, 1.

55. *Press Conf* #69 (November 15, 1933), 2:453–55.

56. Quotation from Robert A. Divine, "Dean Gooderham Acheson," *ANB*; Arthur Krock, "Sprague Revolt Draws Battle Line," *NYT*, November 22, 1933, 2. See also A. Schlesinger, *Coming of the New Deal*, 242–43; at 291 he quotes Roosevelt as saying, some months later, "After I fired Dean Acheson," 291.

57. "Woodin Quits Post; Morgenthau Made Head of Treasury," *NYT*, January 2, 1934, 1; PPA, "Secretary of the Treasury Woodin Resigns," January 1, 1934. The lack of a Woodin biography is a major gap in the history of the early New Deal. See Gerald D. Nash, "William Hartman Woodin, " *ANB*. The quote is from Rexford G. Tugwell, *The Democratic Roosevelt*, 378.

58. Initially, the key figure on Morgenthau's staff was legal scholar Herman Oliphant (1884–1939), who had been his general counsel at the FCA and whom he brought to the Treasury in the same capacity. "Herman Oliphant of Treasury Dies," *NYT*, January 12, 1939, 25.

59. The first was German immigrant Oscar S. Straus (1859–1926), Theodore Roosevelt's secretary of commerce and labor (1906–9).

60. "Jews and Jobs," *Time*, May 31, 1934, citing Arthur T. Weil, "Exploding the Myth of a 'Jewish Hierarchy.'" The "young Hebrews" *Time* found significant were Jerome Frank, Mordecai Ezekiel, Nathan R. Margold, Robert D. Kohn, Isidor Lubin, Charles E. Wyzanski, Herbert Feis, Sol Arian Rosenblatt, Alexander Sachs, Leo Wolman, Rose Schneiderman, Benjamin Victor Cohen, Jacob Viner, Norman Meyers, Abe Fortas, and Lee Pressman. All but the last five were mentioned in Weil's article.

61. PPA, "A Letter on the Religion of the President's Ancestors, Mar. 7, 1935"; "Roosevelt Unworried over His Ancestors, He Writes Jewish Editor Who Asked of Faith," *NYT*, March 15, 1935, 1.

62. "Service for Negro Farmers," *NYT*, November 8, 1933, 19.

63. John Morton Blum, *Roosevelt and Morgenthau*, xiii; "Morgenthau Made Farm Aid Record," *NYT*, January 2, 1934, 9.

64. Arthur Krock, "In Washington: Morgenthau Earns Degree of 'Straight Shooter,'" *NYT*, January 31, 1934, 16. See also "Roosevelt Urged to Bar Censorship: Writers Wire Protest on Morgenthau's Restrictions on Treasury Data," *NYT*, November 22, 1933, 1.

65. F. Raymond Daniel, "Roosevelt Is Asked to Intervene to Protect Scottsboro Negroes," *NYT*, November 20, 1933, 1; "Roosevelt Declines to Act," *NYT*, November 1, 1933, 14; Dan T. Carter, *Scottsboro: A Tragedy of the American South*.

66. "Rebuke to Rolph Seen" and "Roosevelt Address to Church Group," *NYT*, December 7, 1933, 1, 2. Rolph had said, "This is the best lesson that California has ever given the country. We show the country that the State is not going to tolerate kidnapping" ("'A Lesson' Says Gov. Rolph," *NYT*, November 27, 1933). See also *Press Conf* #73–75 (November 29, December 2, 6, 1933), 2:490–91, 506, 509, 513, 517.

67. PPA, "The President Proclaims the Repeal of the Eighteenth Amendment. Proclamation No. 2065, Dec. 5, 1933" and "The Establishment of the Federal Alcohol Control Administration, EO 6474," December 4, 1933. For an account of the Twenty-First Amendment, see David E. Kyvig, *Explicit and Authentic Acts: Amending the U.S. Constitution, 1776–1995*, 289–314.

68. "Roosevelt Address to Church Group," *NYT*, December 7, 1933, 2.

69. "Roosevelts Ready to Hail Christmas," *NYT*, December 24, 1933, 3; PPA, "The Christmas Amnesty Proclamation" and "Proclamation No. 2068," December 23, 1933, and "A Christmas Greeting to the Nation," December 24, 1933.

70. ". . . President Plays Santa," *NYT*, December 25, 1933, 1. In addition, every member of the White House clerical staff received a book signed by the president.

71. "Gifts to President Flood White House; Special Staffs Sort Presents and Mail," *NYT*, December 23, 1933, 1.

72. Richard Lowitt and Maurine Beasley, eds., *One Third of a Nation: Lorena Hickok Reports on the Great Depression*, 215. The broadest study of Roosevelt's mail is Levine and Levine, *People and the President*. See also Louis McHenry Howe, "The President's Mailbag"; Ira Robert Taylor Smith, *"Dear Mr. President . . .": Fifty Years in the White House Mail Room*; and Frances M. Seeber, "I Want You to Write to Me: The Papers of Anna Eleanor Roosevelt."

73. Jefferson never appeared before Congress, and every president but Wilson and Harding followed suit until 1934; since 1934 all have spoken there.

74. PPA, "Annual Message to the Congress, Jan. 3, 1934"; "'New Deal' Is Here to Stay, the President Tells Congress," *NYT*, January 4, 1934, 1; E. Herring, "Second Session of the Seventy-Third Congress," is a useful guide.

75. Throughout the Roosevelt era, the fiscal year ended on June 30.

76. PPA, "The Annual Budget Message, Jan. 1, 1934."

77. "Size of the Budget Staggers Wall St.," *NYT*, January 5, 1934, 1; "Democrats Fear Issue in Elections: Party Leaders See Recovery Cost as a Basis of Attack in Fall Campaign," *NYT*, January 5, 1934, 1.

78. "Keynes to Roosevelt: Our Recovery Plan Assayed," *NYT*, December 31, 1933, XX2. It was distributed by the North American Newspaper Alliance. Frankfurter's letter was dated December 16, 1933, and Roosevelt's reply December 22, 1933. Freidel, *Rendezvous with Destiny*, 133, cites from the printed letter only Keynes's wisecrack about Roosevelt's monetary manipulation, "a gold standard on booze," rather than "the ideal managed currency of my dreams." Frankfurter and Keynes had met during the Versailles Conference, and the American had helped Keynes find an American publisher for *The Economic Consequences of the Peace* (1920). See also Robert Skidelsky, *John Maynard Keynes*. The *Times* itself, in an editorial the same day, made it clear that "it entertains small sympathy for [Keynes's] particular monetary theories," but used his wisecrack about a "gold standard on booze" to support its own views of the

monetary situation while ignoring the major thrust of his remarks ("Views of Dollar Manipulation," December 31, 1933, E4).

79. "Delays New Check on Recovery Funds," *NYT,* January 5, 1934, 7; "Delays New Check on Recovery Funds," *NYT,* January 8, 1934, 7; "President Annuls Curb on Aid Costs: Order Giving Douglas Power on Recovery Expenditures Is Revoked in Three Days," *NYT,* January 9, 1934, 5; Arthur Krock, "A Wise Check on Spending Is Lifted by the President," *NYT,* January 9, 1934, 20; Ickes, *Secret Diary,* 1:134–36. The EOs in question were 6548 and 6550, dated January 3 and 6, 1934.

80. PPA, "Request for Legislation to Organize a Sound and Adequate Currency System, Jan. 15, 1934"; "White House Statement on Presidential Proclamation (No. 2072) Fixing the Weight of the Gold Dollar, Jan. 31, 1934"; and "Presidential Proclamation (No. 2072) Fixing the Weight of the Gold Dollar, Jan. 31, 1934," and appended notes.

81. PPA, "White House Statement on Executive Order Fixing Reduction in Pay of Federal Employees, Jan. 9, 1934" and "A Recommendation for Legislation to Guarantee Principal of Farm Mortgage Bonds, Jan. 10, 1934." The resultant Federal Farm Mortgage Corporation Act of January 31 did that. By late 1937, the federal government had refinanced or financed 3.7 million farm loans totaling $5.3 billion. PPA, "Request for Legislation to Organize a Sound and Adequate Currency System," January 15, 1934.

82. PPA, "Message to the Senate Requesting Ratification of the St. Lawrence Treaty with Canada, Jan. 10, 1934"; "Treaty Foes Win Easily," *NYT,* March 15, 1934, 1, 4; Arthur Krock, "Senate Vote on Seaway Is Not a Formal Revolt," *NYT,* March 15, 1934, 22. Twenty-two of the no votes came from Democrats. In addition, on the Canadian side, Quebecois generally opposed, and there was doubt that the Dominion could afford its share of construction costs. For Roosevelt's confidence about the eventual result, see *Press Conf* #105 (March 1, 1934), 3:232–35. The delay in ratification was due to details that had to be worked out. Roosevelt wisely did not try to force the issue. Only in 1954 was such a treaty ratified.

83. "Recalls President's Birthday," *NYT,* November 24, 1933, 8; "Roosevelt Fetes to Benefit Springs," *NYT,* December 14, 1933, 26; "Henry L. Doherty, Oil Man, Dies at 69," *NYT,* December 27, 1939, 1; "Carl Byoir Dead; Publicist Was 68," *NYT,* February 4, 1957, 18; Cutlip, *Fund Raising in the United States,* 359–93. See also David Oshinsky, *Polio: An American Story,* 48–50. Turnley Walker, *Roosevelt and the Warm Springs Story,* 176–86, is a pioneering journalistic account filled with direct discourse and no footnotes.

84. "Nation Honors President at 6,000 Birthday Dinners," *NYT,* January 31, 1934, 1, 5; PPA, "Radio Address on the President's First Birthday Ball for Crippled Children, Jan. 30, 1934" and "Remarks on Reception of Monies Raised in Behalf of Crippled Children, May 9, 1934." One hundred thousand dollars was earmarked to fund medical research, the rest to support Warm Springs and the foundation. None went to redeem funds advanced by previous benefactions.

85. See PPA, "Letter on Federal Supervision of Securities Sales," March 26, 1934; "Message to Congress on Legislation for the Sugar Industry," February 8, 1934; "Letter to Marvin Jones Urging Crop Control of Cotton," February 16, 1934; "Message to Congress Recommending Legislation to Guarantee Principal on Home Owners Loan

Bonds," March 1, 1934; "Message to Congress Recommending Creation of the Federal Communications Commission," February 26, 1934; "Message to Congress Recommending Legislation to Guarantee Principal on Home Owners Loan Bonds," March 1, 1934; "Message to Congress Requesting Authority Regarding Foreign Trade," March 2, 1934; "Letter to Senator Henry P. Fletcher Requesting Legislation for Credit for Small Industries," March 19, 1934; "Message to Congress Regarding Independence for the Philippine Islands," March 2, 1934; and "Letter to Congressman Robert L. Doughton on Unemployment Insurance," March 23, 1934.

86. PPA, "The President Vetoes the Appropriation Bill," March 29, 1934. Such a pension had been established for Civil War veterans; the pension legislation of the Wilson administration had sought to prevent a recurrence. See R. Daniels, *Bonus March*, chap. 1.

87. Although it is widely reported that Roosevelt vetoed no bills in 1933, he effected one pocket veto of an amendment to the Federal Farm Loan Act (*Congressional Record*, 77:6197).

88. "House, 310 to 72, Overrides Roosevelt's Veteran Veto," *NYT*, March 28, 1934, 1; "Senate Overrides Veterans Veto Crippling Whole Economy Program; 29 Democrats Desert the President," *NYT*, March 29, 1934, 1; "Victory of Legion Called 'Greatest,'" *NYT*, April 1, 1934, 26; Arthur Krock, "Progressives Defection on Veto a Striking Move," *NYT*, March 30, 1934, 20.

89. "Roosevelt Sails in Open Atlantic," *NYT*, March 29, 1934, 1; "Roosevelt Pauses for Call at Nassau," *NYT*, March 31, 1934, 1; "Roosevelt Leads Easter Service on Yacht," *NYT*, April 2, 1934, 2; "50,000 Roll Eggs at White House," *NYT*, April 3, 1934, 23; "Roosevelt Signs Two Major Bills," *NYT*, April 8, 1934, 30; "Roosevelt Orders Veterans Change," *NYT*, April 9, 1934, 3. *Press Conf* #110–11 (April 9 and 12, 1934), 3:267–72, were held aboard the *Nourmahal* and the train returning to Washington. The party consisted of McIntyre, stenographer H. M. Kanee, nine reporters, five newsreel and still photographers, two telegraphers, and a railroad representative, along with the wives of three reporters. They represented four wire services, four newsreel companies, two telegraph companies, and five newspapers: the *New York Times, Herald-Tribune,* and *Daily News;* the *Washington Post;* and, curiously, the *National Methodist Press.* The government was reimbursed by their employers.

90. PPA, "'I Am a Tough Guy': Informal Remarks to a Congressional Delegation," April 13, 1934; "Washington Plans Stirring Welcome," *NYT*, April 13, 1934, 3; "Big Crowd Meets Train," *NYT*, April 14, 1934, 1. The "bystander" remark is from the second story; Roosevelt's comment about an "allegory" is from *Press Conf* #112 (April 13, 1934), 3:273.

91. "President Charts Congress Program to Speed Closing," *NYT*, April 15, 1934, 1; "President to Ask Congress to Vote $1,500,000,000 Relief," *NYT*, April 16, 1934, 1.

92. PPA, "A Second Message to Congress on the 1935 Budget," May 15, 1934.

93. John Kenneth Galbraith, *The Great Crash*, 141–51.

94. Parrish, *Securities Regulation*, remains the standard work. "Roosevelt Signs Exchange Curb Bill," *NYT*, June 7, 1934, 7; PPA, "Recommendation for the Securities Exchange Commission, Feb. 9, 1934," and appended note. *Press Conf* #122 (May 16, 1934), 3:348–49; Whitney quotation from A. Schlesinger, *Coming of the New Deal*, 461.

95. PPA, "A Recommendation for the Creation of the Federal Communications Commission, Feb. 26, 1934," and appended note.

96. *Press Conf* #89 (January 17, 1934), 3:81–82; "$950,000,000 More for Relief Is Asked of House by Roosevelt," *NYT*, January 28, 1934, 1; PPA, "White House Statement on a Plan for Relief," February 28, 1934, and appended note; PPA, "EO 6420B ... Nov. 9, 1933," and appended note.

97. Aubrey Williams, "The New Relief Program: Three Great Aims," *NYT*, April 1, 1934, XX1. A specialist in semiotics might note that in using two forms of the very negative word *abandon* in one sentence, Williams was revealing his true feelings.

98. Quotations from Salmond, *Southern Rebel,* 63. Salmond quotes from Williams's *NYT* apologia, but not the initial paragraph quoted in the text. For a devastating account of the CWA's demolition, see Schwartz, *Civil Works Administration,* 213–76. She, like many who wrote about poverty after the collapse of Johnson's Great Society programs, was influenced by so-called New Left approaches such as Frances Fox Piven and Richard Cloward, *Regulating the Poor: The Functions of Public Welfare.*

99. PPA, "A Recommendation for 'Sound, Stable and Permanent Air Mail' Legislation," March 7, 1934, and "The Army Stops Flying the Mail," March 10, 1934, and appended note; Henry Harley Arnold, *Global Mission,* 109–11. The only documented study is Paul Tillett, *The Army Flies the Mails.*

100. "Consumer Board Asked to Resign," *NYT,* December 23, 1933, 24; "Holds Consumers Suffer under NRA," *NYT,* February 25, 1934, N15; PPA, "The National Recovery Review Board Is Created, EO 6632, Mar. 7, 1934"; Barbara Blumberg, "Leon Henderson," *ANB.*

101. PPA, "The National Recovery Review Board Is Created, EO 6632," March 7, 1934, and appended note. The quotation from Johnson is from his cover letter to the president, May 15, in *NYT,* May 21, 1934, 1. The *Times* ran ten other stories and documents on the report that day, the most comprehensive of which was "Darrow Board Finds NRA Tends toward Monopoly," 1. See also H. Johnson, *Blue Eagle,* 272; and Andrew E. Kersten, *Clarence Darrow: American Iconoclast,* 234–37.

102. Joseph B. Kincer, Chief Meteorologist, U.S. Weather Bureau, "Present Drought Worst on Record," *NYT,* June 24, 1934, E7; "Huge Dust Cloud, Blown 1,500 Miles, Dims City 5 Hours," *NYT,* May 12, 1934, 1; "More Dust Clouds from West Likely," *NYT,* May 20, 1934, XX2; PPA, "White House Statement Following a Conference on Drought Relief, May 14, 1934"; *Press Conf* #128 (June 6, 1934), 3:386–89; PPA, "The President Asks Congress for Additional Funds to Carry on Drought Relief, June 9, 1934." Quotation and data are from the "Notes" to the last two items. Two contemporary essays by Lawrence Westbrook (1889–1964), an FERA official and director of drought relief and a participant in the May 14 conference, provide detail: "Rehabilitation of Stranded Families" and "The Program of Rural Rehabilitation of the FERA." For generalizations about the problems of the region, see Saloutos, *American Farmer,* 192–207. The most detailed historical work on the shelterbelt project is Wilmon H. Droze, *Trees, Prairies, and People: A History of Tree Planting in the Plains States.* To trace Roosevelt's continuing interest, see "Shelterbelt" in the index of Nixon, *Roosevelt and Conservation.*

103. Perkins, *The Roosevelt I Knew,* 225–26. Her gloss on the failed interview was: "[Keynes] pointed out [to her] that a dollar spent on relief by the government was a

dollar given to the grocer, by the grocer to the wholesaler, and by the wholesaler to the farmer, in payment of supplies. With one dollar paid out for relief or public works or anything else, you have created four dollars worth of national income. I wish he had been as concrete when he talked to Roosevelt, instead of treating him as though he belonged to the higher echelons of economic knowledge." Perkins's biographer makes no mention of either Keynes or Keynesian economics.

104. John Maynard Keynes, "Sees Need for $400,000,000 Monthly to Speed Recovery," *NYT*, June 10, 1934, E1. In a letter to the editor from London dated June 23, 1934, Keynes amplified some of the statistics used in the article and continued his analysis. "Keynes on Recovery," *NYT*, July 7, 1934, 12.

105. John Kenneth Galbraith, "How Keynes Came to America," which originally appeared in the *New York Times Book Review*, May 16, 1965. See also Veritas Foundation, *Keynes at Harvard: Economic Deception as a Political Credo*.

106. Tugwell, *The Democratic Roosevelt*, 371–75, quote on 375. Arthur Schlesinger popularized this interpretation, but the first use I can discover was by publicist Stanley High in 1937.

107. Turner Catledge, "Congress Adjourns Sine Die after Voting Housing Bill," *NYT*, June 19, 1934, 1.

108. "Important Bills Failed of Passage," *NYT*, June 20, 1934, 2. A similar thirty-hour bill sponsored by Senator Hugo Black (D-AL) had developed strong support in 1933; Patman's bill passed the House but did not come to a vote in the Senate.

109. Radford, *Modern Housing for America*, 179–80; PPA, "Recommendation for Legislation to Provide Assistance for Repairing and Constructing of Homes," May 14, 1934. For redlining, see Kenneth T. Jackson, "Race, Ethnicity, and Real Estate Appraisal: The Home Owners Loan Corporation and the Federal Housing Administration."

110. *Press Conf* #117 (May 2, 1934), 3:311–12. For Roosevelt's evaluation of and support for the new Indian policies, see PPA, "Presidential Statement Endorsing the Wheeler-Howard Bill, Apr. 28, 1934," and appended note; Lawrence C. Kelly, *The Assault on Assimilation: John Collier and the Origins of Indian Policy Reform*; and Graham D. Taylor, *The New Deal and American Indian Tribalism: The Administration of the Indian Reorganization Act*.

111. PPA, "Statement on Signing Bill for Federal Regulation of Grazing on Public Lands," June 28, 1934" and "A Typical EO (6910) on Withdrawal of Public Lands, Nov. 26, 1934," and appended note. Nixon, *Roosevelt and Conservation*, 1:305–13, provides the memos on the Taylor Act from both Ickes and Wallace. For a scholarly view stretching beyond the New Deal years, see Wesley C. Calef, *Private Grazing and Public Lands: Studies of the Local Management of the Taylor Grazing Act*.

112. For a breakdown of the spending, see PPA, "A Second Message to Congress on the 1935 Budget," May 15, 1934.

113. PPA, "Statement on Signing Bill to Help the Federal Government Wage War on Crime and Gangsters," May 18, 1934, and appended note.

114. PPA, "Request for Authority to Consummate Reciprocal Trade Agreement for the Revival of Foreign Trade," March 2, 1934, and appended note.

115. PPA, "Presidential Statement upon Signing the Vinson Navy Bill," March 27, 1934, and appended note; *Press Conf* #108 (May 27, 1934), 3:260–61.

116. His lukewarm signing statement began by noting "many arguments pro and con" and closed by admitting that it "was in some respects loosely worded and will require amendment at the next session of Congress." Before that could occur, the Supreme Court struck it down, unanimously, as a violation of the due-process clause of the Fifth Amendment. An amended version was then enacted that received the Court's approval in 1937. PPA, "Statement by the President Approving Amendments to the Bankruptcy Law," June 30, 1934, and appended note.

117. PPA, "The First 'Fireside Chat' of 1934, Jun. 28, 1934." See also PPA, "Message to the Congress Reviewing the Broad Objectives of the Administration, June 8, 1934."

Chapter 9. Advancing Reform

1. Useful friendly works include Richard J. Whalen, *The Founding Father: The Story of Joseph P. Kennedy*; and Doris Kearns Goodwin, *The Fitzgeralds and the Kennedys*.

2. Parrish, *Securities Regulation*, has a good account of its New Deal years; quote on 179. See also PPA, "Another Step to Protect Investors—Recommendation for the Securities Exchange Commission," February 9, 1934, and appended note; and "Exchange, Labor Boards Named," *NYT*, July 1, 1934, 1.

3. PPA, "A Recommendation for the Creation of the Federal Communications Commission, Feb. 26, 1934," and appended note. See the second volume of Eric Barnouw's indispensable *The Golden Web: A History of Broadcasting in the United States, 1933 to 1953*.

4. I. Bernstein, *Turbulent Years*, 217–317.

5. PPA, "The President Seeks to Adjust a Labor Dispute in the Steel Industry, June 19, 1934" and "The National Steel Labor Board Is Established, Presidential Statement, June 28, 1934," and appended notes.

6. PPA, "Creation of the First National Labor Relations Board, EO 6763, June 29, 1934" and "Statement by the President Accompanying the Foregoing EO, June 30, 1934"; "Roosevelt Sets Up a New Labor Board," *NYT*, July 1, 1934, 20. Garrison, great-grandson of the abolitionist, had a long career as a social and political activist. "Lloyd K. Garrison, Lawyer, Dies," *NYT*, October 3, 1991, D20. The other members were Harry A. Millis (1873–1948), a University of Chicago labor economist, and Edwin S. Smith (b. 1891), a former Massachusetts official who served until 1941 and took the Fifth Amendment in 1953 when asked if he was or had been a member of the Communist Party. "Mr. Smith Went to Washington," *Time*, June 1, 1953.

7. As cited in I. Bernstein, *Turbulent Years*, 320. See also Lloyd K. Garrison, "The National Labor Boards."

8. Minorities here meant workers who had opted for another union or no union at all. Its current usage to refer to persons of color was all but unknown in the 1930s.

9. *Press Conf* #130 (June 15, 1934), 3:418–19.

10. PPA, "The Initiation of Studies to Achieve a Program of National Social and Economic Security, EO 6757, June 29, 1934," and appended note; "Roosevelt Cabinet Group to Gather National Data for Wide Social Program," *NYT*, June 30, 1934, 1.

11. See Eliot's memoir, *Recollections of the New Deal: When the People Mattered*, 88ff.

12. John Kenneth Galbraith, *Name Dropping: From F.D.R. On*, 13. There is a similar passage in his autobiography, *A Life in Our Times*, 35–39.

13. For an overview of the session's accomplishments, see "Record of the Achievements of the History-Making Seventy-Third Congress," *NYT*, June 17, 1934, 24; "Roosevelt Signs 124 Bills, Bars 31," *NYT*, June 28, 1934, 3; "Roosevelt Sets Record for Office," *NYT*, July 2, 1934, 8; PPA, "A Typical Veto of a Private Bill" and "Another Typical Veto of a Private Bill," both May 9, 1934, and "White House Statement on Presidential Practice in Explaining All Vetoes of Bills," June 26, 1934. For a detailed analysis of Roosevelt's vetoes, see Carlton Jackson, *Presidential Vetoes, 1792–1945*, 205–24.

14. "Roosevelt Orders Vacations for Aides," *NYT*, July 1, 1934, 22.

15. "Cruiser Houston Off to Await Roosevelt," *NYT*, June 26, 1934, 3; "Roosevelt to Find Rare Sea Comforts," *NYT*, July 1, 1934, N2; "President Steams Away on Houston for Month's Cruise," *NYT*, July 2, 1934, 1; "President Hooks Large Barracuda," *NYT*, July 5, 1934, 3; "Roosevelt Bathes in Caribbean Sun," *NYT*, July 10, 1934, 3. The story on sea comforts, not bylined, was probably written by Mildred Adams, who also published a magazine piece, "The President Takes to the Sea Lanes," July 1, 1934, SM7. The *Houston* was already fitted out as a flagship cruiser with a large suite for an admiral consisting of a sitting room, a smaller bedroom, a bath, and an adjoining kitchen. In a three-week refitting at the Brooklyn Navy Yard, a bulkhead was cut through to the captain's sitting room to provide a place for the president to receive visitors and to provide cross-ventilation. If any alterations were made to accommodate Roosevelt's disability, they were not mentioned. Forty new movies were brought aboard. At Annapolis, where Roosevelt would go aboard, a favorite bed was brought from the *Sequoia,* a Commerce Department yacht that the president often used, as were its Filipino mess attendants.

16. Charles P. Taft, a son of the former president, was a Roosevelt-appointed mediator in Toledo.

17. *Press Conf* #125 (May 25, 1934), 3:373–74. For the Toledo strike, see I. Bernstein, *Turbulent Years*, 218–29.

18. "Roosevelt in Haiti Renews His Pledge to Recall Marines," *NYT*, July 6, 1934, 1; PPA, "Joint Statement on Conversations in Haiti between the President and President Vincent, July 5, 1934" and "Extemporaneous Remarks at Cape Haitien, Haiti, July 6, 1934." In a note appended to the joint statement, Roosevelt in 1937 wrote a brief narrative of the trip (*FDR Letters*, 3:127).

19. Cook, *Eleanor Roosevelt*, 2:167–75; "President Motors over Puerto Rico," *NYT*, July 7, 1934, 1; "St. Thomas Crowds Hail Roosevelt," *NYT*, July 8, 1934, 1; "Roosevelt Off for Cartagena, Colombia," *NYT*, July 8, 1934; *FDR Letters*, 3:128–29. PPA contains three brief "Extemporaneous Remarks" delivered in San Juan, St. Thomas, and St. Croix on July 7, 8, 1934.

20. *FDR Letters*, 3:129; PPA, "Extemporaneous Remarks in Cartagena, Colombia, July 10, 1934"; "President Hailed in Colombia," *NYT*, July 11, 1934, 1.

21. *FDR Letters*, 3:130; "Enters the Canal Today," *NYT*, July 11, 1934, 3; "Roosevelt Cruiser Traverses Canal," *NYT*, July 12, 1934, 1; "President Leaves Canal for Hawaii," *NYT*, July 13, 1934, 1; AP, "Houston Crew Found Roosevelt Sociable; Merely Treated Him as 'One of the Bunch,'" *NYT*, August 10, 1934, 3.

22. My account of what became the San Francisco general strike owes much to I. Bernstein, *Turbulent Years,* 252–98, and to conversations with participants in 1948–49.

23. PPA, "White House Statement on President's Efforts to Settle by Negotiation Impending Pacific Coast Longshoremen's Strike, Mar. 22, 1934."

24. The board was created by EO 6748, June 26, 1934. "Roosevelt Sets Up Board in Longshoremen Strike," *NYT,* June 27, 1934, 1; "Edward M'Grady, Ex–U.S. Aide, Dies," *NYT,* July 18, 1950, 27.

25. "Archbishop Edward J. Hanna's July 13, 1934, General Strike address as broadcast by KGO, KPO and KFRC," from the online Virtual Museum of the City of San Francisco, which contains many documents about the general strike.

26. Unnamed businessman cited in Paul S. Taylor and Norman Leon Gold, "San Francisco and the General Strike." This essay contains a useful chronology of the strike.

27. *FDR Letters,* radiogram to Frances Perkins, 3:130. The editors have dated it only "[July 1934]," but it was almost certainly written on Sunday, July 15. Perkins sent her message a few minutes after midnight Sunday.

28. *Press Conf* #141 (September 5, 1934), 4:45–46.

29. See sources cited in notes 21, 24, and 25 above.

30. FDR to Chief of [Naval] Operations, August 10, 1934, as cited in Gary Y. Okihiro, *Cane Fires: The Anti-Japanese Movement in Hawaii, 1865–1945,* 173–74.

31. PPA, "Extemporaneous Remarks in Hawaii, Jul. 28, 1934"; "Roosevelt Leaving Hawaii Pledges America to Peace," *NYT,* July 29, 1934, 1. Tsukiyama, a graduate of the University of Chicago Law School, would be appointed the state's first chief justice in 1959. "Justice Tsukiyama Dies at Age 68," *Honolulu Star-Bulletin,* January 6, 1966, 1.

32. Ernest Gruening, *Many Battles: The Autobiography of Ernest Gruening,* 230. Mr. Moto was a Japanese detective/secret agent in a series of works by John P. Marquand and was portrayed in films by the Hungarian-born actor Peter Lorre.

33. "Northwest Eager to See Roosevelt," *NYT,* August 1, 1934, 5; "Roosevelt Arrives Off Pacific Coast," *NYT,* August 3, 1934, 1; "Portland Hails Roosevelt," *NYT,* August 4, 1934, 3; "Roosevelt Pledges Control of Power for Whole People," *NYT,* August 4, 1934, 1; PPA, "Extemporaneous Remarks at the Site of the Bonneville Dam, Oregon, Aug. 3, 1934."

34. "Roosevelt Visions Trek to Northwest with Cheap Power," *NYT,* August 5, 1934, 1; PPA, "Extemporaneous Remarks at . . . the Grand Coulee Dam, Washington, August 4, 1934."

35. Ickes, *Secret Diary,* 1:184.

36. PPA, "Radio Address Delivered at Two Medicine Chalet, Glacier National Park, Aug. 5, 1934"; "Roosevelt Tells of Fight to Save Resources," *NYT,* August 6, 1934, 1.

37. PPA, "Extemporaneous Rear Platform Remarks at Havre, Montana, Aug. 6, 1934" and "Extemporaneous Remarks at Fort Peck Dam, Montana, August 6, 1934"; "Drought Damage Now $5,000,000,000, Roosevelt Is Told," *NYT,* August 7, 1934, 1. The Subsistence Homesteads Division had been created with a $25 million appropriation in the 1933 NRA legislation. It was idealistic, underfunded, and largely unsuccessful. There were thirty-four such communities, involving as few as 20 families and as many

as 287 per unit. See Paul Conkin, *Tomorrow a New World: The New Deal Community Program.*

38. In the event, no dam was built. The lake continued to dry up for six more years, but since 1940 climatic change has caused the water level to rise so high that the lake has flooded sections of northern North Dakota and parts of adjoining Manitoba. Sherilyn C. Fritz, "Twentieth-Century Salinity and Water-Level Fluctuations in Devils Lake, North Dakota: Test of a Diatom-Based Transfer Function."

39. "Roosevelt Visibly Moved in Tour of Drought Area," *NYT,* August 8, 1934, 1; "Roosevelt Urged to Aid Minneapolis," *NYT,* August 9, 1934, 2; I. Bernstein, *Turbulent Years,* 248–52.

40. PPA, "A Tribute to the Mayo Brothers: An Address Delivered at Rochester, Minnesota, Aug. 8, 1934"; "Roosevelt Scans Big River Works; Pays Mayos Honor," *NYT,* August 9, 1934, 1.

41. PPA, "Address Delivered at Green Bay, Wisconsin, Aug. 9, 1934"; "Speech Hails Confidence," *NYT,* August 10, 1934, 1; "La Follette Is Ready to Uphold Roosevelt," *NYT,* August 13, 1934, 4.

42. "50,000 Cheer at Milwaukee," "Chicago Crowds Cheer Roosevelt," and "Triumphal Progress," *NYT,* August 10, 1934, 3; "Roosevelt Back, Immersed in Work," *NYT,* August 11, 1934, 1.

43. Meeting of August 21, 1934, in *New Deal Mosaic,* edited by Seligman and Cornwell, 282.

44. "League Is Formed to Scan New Deal, 'Protect Rights,'" *NYT,* August 23, 1934, 1. For the salon, see Eliot, *Recollections of the New Deal,* 22–23.

45. *Press Conf* #137 (August 24, 1934) 4:18–20; "Topics in Wall Street," *NYT,* August 24, 1934, 23; "Roosevelt Twits League as Lover of Property," *NYT,* August 25, 1934, 1. For a full-length treatment of the league, see George Wolfskill, *The Revolt of the Conservatives.*

46. Greg Mitchell, *The Campaign of the Century: Upton Sinclair's Race for Governor of California and the Birth of Media Politics,* is a thorough if somewhat overheated account. For the Sinclair campaign's long-term effect, see Robert E. Burke, *Olson's New Deal for California,* 1–5; and George Creel, *Rebel at Large: Recollections of Fifty Crowded Years,* 285–86.

47. *Los Angeles Times,* August 30, 1934, as printed in "California Press Attacks Sinclair," *NYT,* August 31, 1934, 3.

48. "Sinclair Arrives to See Roosevelt," *NYT,* September 4, 1934, 16; "Sinclair Is Elated by Roosevelt Talk," *NYT,* September 5, 1934, 1; *Press Conf* #141 (September 5, 1934), 4:38–39.

49. The Republican Merriam got 1,138,620, Sinclair 879,537, while a progressive Republican, Haight, garnered 302,519. A regular Democrat might well have won a two-man race.

50. "Douglas to Resign from Budget Post, the Capital Hears; Opposed PWA Spending," *NYT,* September 1, 1934, 1; "Douglas Replaced by Daniel W. Bell as Head of Budget," *NYT,* September 2, 1934, 1; "Bell a Federal Veteran," *NYT,* September 2, 1934, 2; "Says He Has No Politics," *NYT,* September 2, 1934, 2; "Bell, 80, Retired Banker," *NYT,* October 4, 1971, 44; Browder and Smith, *Independent.*

51. *FDR Letters,* 4:131–32; "Johnson Quits NRA Post" and "Johnson's Letter of Resignation and Roosevelt's Note Accepting It," *NYT,* September 26, 1934, 1, 12; PPA, "N.R.A. Is Reorganized—the National Industrial Recovery Board Is Established, EO 6859, Sept. 27, 1934," and appended note. Its companion, EO 6860, same date, is not in PPA but is in "President's Order on NRA," which included both orders; see also "Roosevelt Picks 2 Boards to Direct Reorganized NRA," both *NYT,* September 28, 1934, 4, 1; and Ohl, *Johnson and the New Deal.*

52. PPA, "Second 'Fireside Chat' of 1934, Sept. 30, 1934"; "Will Call a Conference: 'Specific Peace Period' Must Result, Roosevelt Asserts on Radio," *NYT,* October 1, 1934, 1 (the use of "Conference" was inaccurate; the president called a series of small meetings at which he would try to get the parties closer together); "Green Praises Call for Truce in Industry," *NYT,* October 1, 1934, 2; Louis Stark, "Industrial Truce at Vanishing Point; Labor Sees Strife," *NYT,* November 1, 1934, 1.

53. PPA, "Address at Constitution Hall, Washington, D.C., Oct. 24, 1934"; "Bankers Greet Roosevelt with Ovation as He Offers Cooperation," *NYT,* October 25, 1934, 1. The *Times* story noted that "considerable interest" was given to the president's one departure from his written text. "This is what we call a profit system" was altered to "This is what we call and accept as a profit system" and that auditors believed that he "emphasized strongly" the words "accept as." The text in PPA does not contain the change.

54. Cook, *Eleanor Roosevelt,* 2:221ff; "Notables on List for O'Day Dinner," *NYT,* October 24, 1934, 8.

55. "Roosevelt Ready to Give His Backing to Lehman Drive," *NYT,* October 17, 1934, 1; "President Retires Early," *NYT,* November 7, 1934, 5.

56. "Both Parties Hold New Deal at Stake," *NYT,* November 4, 1934, N4. The Republican chairman, Harry P. Fletcher, predicted that his party would hold all its Senate seats and gain sixty to seventy in the House. Most leading Republicans had a better grip on reality, and Fletcher may well have known better.

57. Oswald Garrison Villard, "The Plight of the Negro Voter."

58. The characterization of Mitchell's victory is in N. Weiss, *Farewell to the Party of Lincoln,* 88. Revels Cayton is quoted from Quintard Taylor, *The Forging of a Black Community: Seattle's Central District, from 1870 through the Civil Rights Era,* 104.

59. *Corrido de Relief* by Emilio Martinez, as printed in Gilbert G. González, *Labor and Community,* 73–74.

60. Seligman and Cornwell, *New Deal Mosaic,* 366–68, December 11, 1934. The president had given a similar but somewhat less focused disquisition "off the record" in a press conference (*Press Conf* #161 [November 28, 1934], 4:238–48). See also "President to Push Housing for the Poor," *NYT,* November 29, 1934, 23.

61. PPA, "The Second Inaugural Address, Jan. 20, 1937."

62. Nathan Straus, *Two-Thirds of a Nation: A Housing Program.*

63. ". . . M. S. Eccles, Favoring Broad Program of Socialization, Says Congress Has Not Done Much," *NYT,* February 25, 1933, 23; "Morgenthau Aide Picked," *NYT,* January 12, 1934, 2; Radford, *Modern Housing for America,* 179; "M. S. Eccles Heads Federal Reserve," *NYT,* November 11, 1934, 1; Sidney Hyman, *Marriner S. Eccles: Private Entrepreneur and Public Servant;* Eccles, *Beckoning Frontiers;* Sternsher, *Tugwell and*

the New Deal, 75. For Morgenthau, see Blum, *Roosevelt and Morgenthau*, 143–44. See also "Marriner S. Eccles Is Dead at 87," *NYT*, December 20, 1977, 38.

64. "President to Begin Trip South Today," *NYT*, November 14, 1934, 1; "Roosevelt Hails TVA Development as New Kind of War," *NYT*, November 17, 1934, 1; "Tennessee Cheers Roosevelt on Tour," *NYT*, November 18, 1934; PPA, "Extemporaneous Remarks at Clinch River below Norris Dam, Nov. 16, 1934." The crowd estimate at Fisk is from N. Weiss, *Farewell to the Party of Lincoln*, 41.

65. Press release, Warm Springs Foundation, November 21, 1934, and Roosevelt to Col. Henry L. Doherty, November 20, 1934, both printed in *Press Conf* #159 (November 21, 1934), 4:196–97; "Roosevelt Ball Aims at Wide Aid," *NYT*, December 17, 1934, 22.

Chapter 10. *The Triumph of Reform*

1. For cogent early reviews of the historiography of this concept, see William H. Wilson, "The Two New Deals: A Valid Concept?"; and Jerold S. Auerbach, "New Deal, Old Deal, or Raw Deal: Some Thoughts on New Left Historiography."

2. "Views of Press on President's Message," *NYT*, January 5, 1935, 3. The *Baltimore Sun*, with greater comprehension, argued that it would be less expensive to continue the dole.

3. Throughout 1934 and 1935, official unemployment figures, which understated the problem, averaged between ten and eleven million persons, more than one-fifth of the labor force. U.S. Department of Commerce, *Historical Statistics of the United States*, Series D, 46–47, 73.

4. PPA, "Annual Message to the Congress, Jan. 4, 1935." See also "Roosevelt to Make Jobs for 3,500,000 Now on Relief," *NYT*, January 5, 1935, 1.

5. "Budget Totals $8,520,413,609; $4,000,000,000 for New Jobs; NIRA Oil Control Illegal," *NYT*, January 8, 1935, 1.

6. PPA, "The Annual Budget Message, Jan. 3, 1935."

7. The actual 1936 deficit was marginally smaller than predicted: $4.424 billion as opposed to $4.528 in the budget message. U.S. Department of Commerce, *Historical Statistics of the United States*, Series Y, 256, 711.

8. *Press Conf* #172 (January 5, 1935), 5:23, 32–33.

9. *Panama Refining Co. v. Ryan*, 293 U.S. 388 (1935).

10. Bernard Kilgore, "New Deal in Court," *Wall Street Journal*, January 9, 1935, 3.

11. *Press Conf* #173 (January 9, 1935), 5:42–45.

12. "Federal 'Hot Oil' Ban Voted in Both Houses," *NYT*, February 23, 1935, 6; PPA, "The Secretary of the Interior Is Designated to Carry Out the Oil Regulation Prescribed by the Congress, EO 6979, Feb. 28, 1935," and appended note.

13. "Gravity of Issue in Gold Decision Urged on Court," *NYT*, January 12, 1935, 1.

14. Ickes, *Secret Diary*, 1:273, entry of January 11, 1935.

15. Readers should not automatically accept Morgenthau's assumption that he and Roosevelt were equally ignorant. Roosevelt's technique of asking obvious questions was an essential part of his method of gaining information.

16. Blum, *Years of Crisis*, 1:130–31.

17. *Gold Clause Cases*, 294 U.S. 240 (1935), et seq.

18. "Constitution Gone, Says M'Reynolds," *NYT,* February 19, 1935, 1; "Gratified Is Only White House Comment," *NYT,* February 19, 1935; "Financial Markets: Stocks, Bonds and Commodities Advance Sharply on News of Decision in Gold Cases," *NYT,* February 19, 1935, 33.

19. "Memorandum for J.P.K. from F.D.R.," in *FDR Letters,* February 19, 1935, 3:144. The Shakespearean tag may well have been in the undelivered and apparently unsaved speech.

20. *Jackson (Miss.) Daily News,* June 20, 1935, as cited in Leuchtenburg, *Roosevelt and the New Deal,* 131. I suspect that the capitalization of *Negroes* was done by a New York proofreader.

21. PPA, "A Message to Congress on Social Security, Jan. 17, 1935." In its appended letter, his committee wrote, "The medical advisory board, the dental advisory committee, and the hospital advisory committee are still continuing their consideration of health insurance, but have joined with the public health advisory committee in endorsement of the program for extended public health services which we recommend."

22. Perkins, *The Roosevelt I Knew,* 278–301, esp. 282–84.

23. Luther Gulick, "Memorandum on Conference with FDR Concerning Social Security Taxation, Summer 1941," FDRL, as reproduced in Larry DeWitt, "Luther Gulick Memorandum Re: Famous FDR Quote," Research Note #23, Social Security Online History, July 21, 2005, http://www.socialsecurity.gov. The quotation's fame came from a slightly corrupt version in A. Schlesinger, *Coming of the New Deal,* 308–9.

24. "Summary of the Principal Acts of Congress . . .," *NYT,* August 27, 1935, 10–11.

25. PPA, "The National Resources Board Is Established, EO 6777, June 30, 1934" and "White House Statement on the Establishment of the National Resources Board, July 3, 1934"; "Resources Board to Study Drought," *NYT,* July 3, 1934, 11.

26. PPA, "A Message to Congress on the Use of Our National Resources," January 24, 1935.

27. The organizational genealogy is complex. Originally a committee of Ickes's PWA early in 1933, it developed into an independent agency, over Ickes's strong objection, in July 1934 as the National Resources Board (1934–35), the National Resources Committee (1935–39), and, finally, the National Resources Planning Board (1939–43).

28. See his diary entry for June 24, 1934. The board had originally been in his department. Ickes, *Secret Diary,* 1:171.

29. For the NRPB, see Marion Clawson, *New Deal Planning: The National Resources Planning Board;* and Alan Brinkley, "The National Resources Planning Board and the Reconstruction of Planning."

30. PPA, "The President Enumerates the Gains under N.R.A. and Recommends Its Extension for Two Years, Feb. 20, 1935."

31. Turner Catledge, "New Deal Push Will Start Today in Both Houses," *NYT,* May 27, 1935, 1; *Schechter v. U.S.,* 295 U.S. 495 (1935); Arthur Krock, "Court Is Unanimous," *NYT,* May 28, 1935, 1.

32. PPA, "A Message to the Congress on the United States Merchant Marine, Mar. 4, 1945," "A Recommendation on the Regulation of Public Utility Holding Companies, Mar. 12, 1935," "A Message to Congress on Pure Food and Drugs, Mar. 22, 1935," and "A Letter on a Proposed Amendment to the Public Utility Holding Bill, Aug. 21, 1935."

33. AP, "Roosevelt Plans to Go South for Fishing Despite the Critical Situation in Congress," *NYT*, March 13, 1985, 1.

34. Charles W. Hurd, "Roosevelt Signs Work Relief Bill; Begins Allocating," *NYT*, April 9, 1935, 1; *Press Conf* #194 (April 1, 1935), 5:189–92.

35. "Warren D. Robbins Dies of Pneumonia," *NYT*, April 8, 1935, 19; "President Coming to Robbins Service," *NYT*, April 9, 1935, 19; "President Makes Short Visit Here" and "President at Bier of W. D. Robbins," *NYT*, April 10, 1935, 5, 21.

36. "President Goes to Howe," *NYT*, April 19, 1935, 5; Rollins, *Roosevelt and Howe*, 428–38.

37. "Parley at White House Decides on a Program to Speed Up Congress," *NYT*, April 10, 1935, 1.

38. PPA, "The Resettlement Administration Is Established, EO 7027, May 1, 1935," and appended note; and "Transfer of Land Program of F.E.R.A. to the Resettlement Administration, EO, 7028, May 1, 1935."

39. PPA, "The Establishment of the Rural Electrification Administration, EO 7037, May 31, 1935," and appended note; D. Clayton Brown, *Electricity for Rural America: The Fight for REA*.

40. PPA, "Three White House Statements Outlining the Machinery for Handling the Four-Billion Dollar Works Relief Appropriation, Apr. 23, 25, 26, 1935" and "The Creation of Machinery for the Works Progress Administration, EO 7034, May 6, 1935."

41. For Baker, see the interview conducted by Harlan Philips in the Smithsonian Archives of American Art. For Gill, see Howard B. Myers, "Corrington Calhoun Gill, 1898–1945," 393–94. For Woodward, see Swain, *Ellen S. Woodward*.

42. PPA, "The First 'Fireside Chat' of 1935," April 28, 1935.

43. American Legion, *Proceedings of the Sixteenth National Convention of the American Legion, Miami, Florida, October 22–25, 1934*, 72–73.

44. PPA, "The President Vetoes the Bonus Bill, May 22, 1935"; "House Overrides Bonus Veto, 322–398," *NYT*, May 23, 1935, 1; "Senate Kills Cash Bonus Sustaining Veto by 8 Votes, but Campaign Begins Anew," *NYT*, May 24, 1935, 1; Rosenman, *Working with Roosevelt*, 94; *Press Conf* #209 (May 24, 1935), 5:299. An analysis of Roosevelt and the bonus is in R. Daniels, *Bonus March*, 211–41.

45. Arthur Krock, "Court Is Unanimous," *NYT*, May 28, 1935, 1; *Schechter v. U.S.*

46. William E. Leuchtenburg, "Mr. Justice Roberts and the Railroaders," in his *Supreme Court Reborn*, 26–51, quotes on 51, 50. For the settlement of the railroad retirement question, see PPA, "An Exchange of Letters Relative to Railroad Retirement Legislation, June 6, 1935," and appended note.

47. *Press Conf* #203 (May 10, 1935), 5:280.

48. *Press Conf* #208 (May 29, 1935), 5:305.

49. *Schechter v. U.S.* at 543–44; *Press Conf* #209 (May 31, 1935), 5:313. That Justice Brandeis sat in silent agreement to this passage, which ignored his concept of "a stream of commerce" that has come to prevail, is evidence of the passions that New Deal regulation of the economy engendered.

50. Rosenman, *Working with Roosevelt*, 111.

51. *Press Conf* #209 (May 31, 1935), 5:310–37; Charles W. Hurd, "President Says End of NRA Puts Control Up to People," *NYT*, June 1, 1935, 1.

52. For Roosevelt's later extended summary of the cases of 1935–36, see his introduction to the 1935 volume of his *Public Papers,* which is dated December 6, 1937.

53. PPA, "White House Statement on Conference with Legislative Leaders after Supreme Court Decision on N.R.A., Jun. 4, 1935"; *Press Conf* #210 (June 4, 1935), 5:338–51; "Roosevelt Will Keep NRA, Stripped of Basic Powers," *NYT,* July 5, 1935, 1. Eight other documents in PPA during the next two weeks spell out further adjustments stemming from the *Schechter* decision.

54. PPA, "Informal Extemporaneous Remarks to State Works Progress Administrators, June 17, 1935." The speech was also published in *NYT,* June 18, 1935, 2.

55. EO 7046, May 20, 1935. This order is *not* printed in PPA. A "Schedule of Monthly Earnings" from that order is printed in Lewis Meriam, *Relief and Social Security,* 386. That work and Donald S. Howard, *The WPA and Federal Relief Policy,* are indispensable for an understanding of federal relief.

56. PPA, "White House Release of Presidential Statement Fixing Respective Jurisdictions of P.W.A. and W.P.A., July 3, 1935"; *Press Conf* #217 (June 3, 1935), 6:7; "President Replies to Critics, Citing Works Projects," *NYT,* July 4, 1935, 1. The *New York Times* also printed the material cited above from PPA.

57. PPA, "The National Youth Administrative Is Established, EO 7086, June 26, 1935," and appended note; Salmond, *Southern Rebel;* Richard A. Reiman, *The New Deal and American Youth: Ideas and Ideals in a Depression Decade.* For youth, generally, see Kriste Lindenmeyer, *The Greatest Generation Grows Up: American Childhood in the 1930s.*

58. I owe the data on race and gender to Professor Kevin P. Bower from his analysis of official reports by and about the NYA. He points out that in the war years, as more young white men found jobs and men of military age entered the armed forces, the percentages of women and African Americans rose sharply, except that the participation of African Americans in the college program remained steady.

59. PPA, "A Message to the Congress on Tax Revision, June 19, 1935"; "Roosevelt Asks Inheritance Taxes and Other Levies on Great Fortunes," *NYT,* June 20, 1935, 1. For a good overall appraisal, see Leff, *Limits of Symbolic Reform.*

60. *Press Conf* #225 (July 31, 1935), 6:66–70.

61. PPA, "Address at University of North Carolina, Chapel Hill, North Carolina, Dec. 5, 1938."

62. T. Harry Williams, *Huey Long;* Abraham Holtzman, *The Townsend Movement: A Study of Old Age Pressure Politics.* For Townsend's socialist background, see J. D. Gaydowski, "Eight Letters to the Editor: The Genesis of the Townsend Plan"; and Alan Brinkley, *Voices of Protest: Huey Long, Father Coughlin, and the Great Depression.*

63. "Roosevelt Maps His Tax Bill Drive with House Chiefs," *NYT,* July 5, 1935, 1.

64. "Texan's Oil Code Story Makes Hughes Smile" and "Oil and Auto Codes in Supreme Court," *NYT,* December 11, 1934, 4; "Code Records Hit by Supreme Court," *NYT,* December 12 1934, 27.

65. Public Law 74-220, July 26, 1935. An excellent pocket history issued on its seventieth anniversary is "A Brief History Commemorating the 70th Anniversary of the Publication of the First Issue of the Federal Register, March 14, 1936," http://www.archives.gov/federal-register/the-federal-register/history.pdf; Erwin W. Griswold,

"Government in Ignorance of the Law: A Plea for Better Publication of Executive Legislation," 198. For contemporary comment, see "President Seeks Way to Publicize Orders," *NYT*, December 13, 1934, 3; "Tracing Executive Orders," *NYT*, December 15, 1934, 12; "A Mighty Maze," *NYT*, December 17, 1934, 18; and "Guidebook to List Federal Decrees," *NYT*, August 25, 1935, E7.

66. PPA, "Presidential Statement upon Signing the Social Security Act, Aug. 14, 1935," and appended note.

67. Also known as the Guffey Coal Act. The act primarily regulated wages and prices and would be declared unconstitutional in 1936. For contemporary speculation about its constitutionality, see PPA, "A Frequently Misquoted Letter, Jul. 6, 1935," and attached note.

68. PPA, "A Letter on a Proposed Amendment to the Public Utility Holding Company Bill, Aug. 21, 1935," and appended note. The letter was to Sam Rayburn okaying the compromise. "Utilities Measure Sent to President," *NYT*, August 25, 1935, 1; "Utility Bill Made Law," *NYT*, August 27, 1935, 1; Freidel, *Rendezvous with Destiny*, 169.

69. "Senate Revolt Settled; Hint of Power by Roosevelt to Adjourn Session Turns Tide," *NYT*, August 27, 1935, 1.

70. The other was Douglas MacArthur. Freidel, *Launching the New Deal*, 128. His source was Rex Tugwell. Roosevelt never made a public criticism of Long.

71. PPA, "Presidential Statement on the Murder of Senator Huey P. Long of Louisiana, Sept. 9, 1935." This mistitled item was a terse statement of regret issued from Hyde Park while Long was still alive. The shooting occurred on Sunday night, September 8, after Roosevelt had gone to bed. The statement was issued early Monday morning. Long did not die until early Tuesday morning. Franklin and Eleanor each sent a private note to the widow. "President Is Grieving," *NYT*, September 10, 1935, 1.

72. The letter is printed in "Text of Roosevelt Plea to Retrieve NRA," *NYT*, August 25, 1935, 25. The headline overstates what the president said. PPA, "The National Recovery Administration Is Terminated, EO 7252, Dec. 21, 1935."

73. PPA, "A Radio Address to the Young Democratic Clubs of America, Aug. 24, 1935."

74. *Press Conf* #237 (September 11, 1935), 6:155.

75. Blum, *Years of Crisis*, 1:269.

76. See *Press Conf* #244 (October 30, 1935), 6:230–32, and #259 (December 23, 1935), 354–55. In the first, the president showed a sophisticated awareness of some of the difficulties in defining unemployment, while in the second he tried to defend the false notion that the 3.5 million unemployed that the WPA was trying to put to work were the totality of the unemployed. One correspondent suggested he was doing what Frances Perkins had accused Hoover of doing. For a good brief analysis of the ways that the New Deal transformed government statistics, see Margo Anderson, *The American Census: A Social History*, 159–90.

77. "President Starts Far West Journey; To Speak Four Times," *NYT*, September 27, 1935, 1.

78. Ickes, *Secret Diary*, 1:444, entry for September 30, 1935.

79. Charles W. Hurd, "Roosevelt Defends AAA to Farmers in Nebraska as Based on Constitution," *NYT*, September 29, 1935, 1; "AAA Not an Issue, Capper Declares,"

NYT, September 29, 1935, 27; PPA, "An Address on the Accomplishments and Future Aims for Agriculture, Fremont, Nebraska, Sept. 28, 1935."

80. The authorizing legislation had been signed by President Coolidge in 1928. It was first called Boulder Dam, for Boulder Canyon, the original site. But during the early planning, it was decided that Black Canyon was a preferable site, and the dam was placed there. In 1931 Hoover's interior secretary renamed it Hoover Dam. In 1933 Ickes restored the original name. It remained Boulder Dam until 1947, when a Republican Congress restored the name Hoover Dam.

81. Beverley B. Moeller, *Phil Swing and Boulder Dam,* is a fine account of the politics of dam building.

82. PPA, "Address at the Dedication of Boulder Dam, Sept. 30, 1935"; Charles W. Hurd, "President Asks Industry to Take the Responsibility for Speeding Employment; Speaks at Boulder Dam," *NYT,* October 1, 1935, 1.

83. Charles W. Hurd, "Roosevelt Urges Liberals to Fight on United Front," *NYT,* October 2, 1935, 1; PPA, "Address at Los Angeles, California, 'Democracy Is Not a Static Thing; It Is an Everlasting March,' Oct. 1, 1935." For the complex political situation in California, see Burke, *Olson's New Deal,* 1–10.

84. A misquotation of *Macbeth,* act 3, scene 2: "malice domestic, foreign levy."

85. Charles W. Hurd, "President Warns Nation: Foreign War a Potent Peril," *NYT,* October 3, 1935, 1; PPA, "Address at San Diego Exposition, San Diego, California, Oct. 2, 1935."

86. "Roosevelt as 'Foe' Sees Navy Fight," *NYT,* October 3, 1935, 14; "Roosevelt Fishing Off Mexican Coast," *NYT,* October 4, 1935, 1.

87. PPA, "The President Prohibits Export of Arms, Ammunition and the Implements of War to Ethiopia and Italy. Proclamation No. 2141"; "The President Warns American Citizens against Travel on Vessels of Belligerent Nations during Italian-Ethiopian War, Proclamation No. 2142"; "Presidential Statement on the Foregoing Proclamations, Oct 5, 1935."

88. "Roosevelt's Train Is Halted for Sailfish; Pacific Trophy Put Aboard for Smithsonian," *NYT,* October 23, 1935, 15.

89. Ickes, *Secret Diary,* 1:449–50, entry of October 27, 1935.

90. *Press Conf* #242 (October 22, 1935), 6:208–13; Charles W. Hurd, "President Renews Pledge of No War," *NYT,* October 24, 1935, 1; PPA, "Informal Extemporaneous Remarks at the Citadel, Charleston, South Carolina, Oct. 23, 1935."

91. "President Returns to the White House," *NYT,* October 25, 1935, 1; Rollins, *Roosevelt and Howe,* 445–46.

92. PPA, "Radio Address on Behalf of the 1935 Mobilization for Human Needs, Oct. 24, 1935"; "The End of the Dole by Dec. 1 Seen by Roosevelt," *NYT,* October 25, 1935, 1. The "end of the dole" remark was taken from a Harry Hopkins press conference cited in the same story and was not a statement by Roosevelt.

93. "Calls for Big Farm Vote," *NYT,* October 26, 1935, 2; "AAA to Increase 1936 Pork Output: Control Wins 6–1," *NYT,* October 26, 1935, 1; "Farm Holiday Group Attacks Wallace," *NYT,* October 24, 1935, 6; "'Half-Baked' Ideas Laid to Roosevelt," *NYT,* October 28, 1935, 2; "Quick Ruling Asked by AAA on Tax Suit," *NYT,* October 24, 1935, 2.

94. PPA, "Presidential Statement on the Transition from an Emergency to a More Permanent Plan for American Agriculture, Oct. 25, 1935"; "Roosevelt's Discussion of Farm Problem," *NYT*, October 26, 1935, 2. I had the enduring nature of New Deal farm programs brought home to me vividly in 1962 when, at my first teaching post in southwestern Wisconsin, a local farmer showing me his small spread explained that he had a three-field operation: "This one is in corn, that one in soy beans, and that one in government." He explained that he used half the government money to buy extra fertilizer for the growing fields and spent the rest on a winter trip to Florida.

95. U.S. Department of Commerce, *Historical Statistics of the United States,* Series K, 1–7, 278.

96. *Press Conf* #191 (February 6, 1935), 5:98.

97. *Press Conf* #244 (October 30, 1935), 6:223. Later Eleanor gave the women who attended her press conferences a tour of the new kitchen facilities in the White House basement. "First Lady Shows Her New Kitchen," *NYT,* December 17, 1935, 25.

98. *New York Times* readers could not learn of this visit. Charles Hurd's story spoke of three events, but only two were in the story. Roosevelt mentioned both projects but not their segregated nature. The crowd size is from N. Weiss, *Farewell to the Party of Lincoln,* 41–42.

99. "Roosevelt Starts for Warm Springs," *NYT,* November 21, 1935, 9; Charles W. Hurd, "Roosevelt Takes Role of 'Kibitzer,'" *NYT,* November 24, 1935, 4; Hurd, "Children Prepare Roosevelt Tribute," *NYT,* November 28, 1935, 2; Hurd, "Roosevelt Carves for Child Patients," *NYT,* November 28, 1935, 15; Hurd, "Spending Peak Is Passed, Our Credit Best in World, Roosevelt Assures Nation," *NYT,* November 29, 1935, 1; PPA, "'Address at Atlanta, Georgia, Nov. 29, 1935." For the PWA projects, see Radford, *Modern Housing for America,* 100.

100. Roosevelt to George N. Peek, November 22, 1935, and note; *FDR Letters,* 159–60; "Peek Resigns Trade Post over Pact with Canada; Long AAA Storm Center," *NYT,* December 1, 1935, 1.

101. Charles W. Hurd, "Roosevelt Talks to Farmers Today," *NYT,* December 9, 1935, 1; "Roosevelt Defends AAA before 14,000 in Chicago," *NYT,* December 10, 1935, 1; PPA, "Address [at] Chicago, Illinois, Dec. 9, 1935."

102. See Dorsett, *Roosevelt and the City Bosses.* Kelly, who had been appointed to fill the remainder of the assassinated Cermak's term, had just been overwhelmingly elected in November. Horner had clashed with Hopkins over control of the WPA in the state in addition to the traditional hostility between Springfield and Chicago. See Roger Biles, *Big City Boss in Depression and War: Mayor Edward J. Kelly of Chicago;* and Charles J. Masters, *Governor Henry Horner, Chicago Politics and the Great Depression.*

103. NIXON *FDR & FA,* in a note to an excerpt from the president's speech, analyzes the significance of Mundelein's welcome (3:118n1).

104. "Notre Dame Hails Roosevelt's Aims," *NYT,* December 10, 1935, 13. See Edward R. Kantowicz, *Corporation Sole: Cardinal Mundelein and Chicago Catholicism.* See also his "Cardinal Mundelein of Chicago and the Shaping of Twentieth-Century American Catholicism," 67.

105. "Speaks to a Toledo Crowd," *NYT,* December 10, 1935, 13; Louis Stark, "Business Fights New Deal," *NYT,* December 5, 1935, E7.

106. PPA, "Presidential Statement on New Agricultural Building at Tuskegee Institute, Dec. 14, 1935" and "A Letter on the Progress Made by the Negro Race since the Emancipation Proclamation, Dec. 26, 1935"; "Roosevelt . . . Emancipation Day Message Read at Celebration at St. Mark's Church," *NYT,* January 2, 1936, 18. For an example of the struggle of black Democrats in New York's Harlem to get recognition, see "Lawyer Slugged in Tammany Row," *NYT,* October 14, 1935, 1. Interestingly, one of the lawyers representing a black Democrat was Jerome Frank, who was neither the slugger nor the slugee.

107. "Roosevelt Family Marks Day Simply," *NYT,* December 26, 1935, 13.

108. PPA, "The National Recovery Administration Is Terminated, EO 7252, Dec. 21, 1935." The appended note traces the liquidation process.

109. PPA, "Informal Extemporaneous Remarks to State Superintendents of Education at the White House," December 11, 1935; James MacGregor Burns, *Roosevelt: The Lion and the Fox,* 266.

Chapter 11. Landslide

1. The quoted words are from the 1933 inaugural. For Roosevelt's discussion of his strategy, see his introduction to the 1936 volume of his papers, dated January 17, 1938.

2. PPA, "Annual Message to the Congress, Jan. 3, 1936"; Turner Catledge, "Roosevelt in Message Dares Critics to Seek Repeal of New Deal Laws," *NYT,* January 4, 1936, 1.

3. PPA, "The Annual Budget Message, Jan. 3, 1936"; Turner Catledge, "Roosevelt Budget Asks $6,752,000,000," *NYT,* January 7, 1936, 1.

4. On January 13, 1936, a unanimous Supreme Court had ruled that two hundred million dollars in impounded processing taxes, mostly on New England textile producers who had sued, claiming that they were unconstitutional, should be refunded. As most of the taxes had already been passed on to consumers, the administration and a majority of Congress felt that this would be an unjustified windfall; a provision recouping such windfalls with a special tax was enacted in the 1936 tax law bill. For details, see Leff, *Limits of Symbolic Reform,* 49ff.

5. *U.S. v. Butler,* 297 U.S. 1 (1936); Arthur Krock, "Farm Act Is Swept Away," "Decision Astounds Congress Members," and "Roosevelt Receives Decision with a Smile," *NYT,* January 7, 1936, 1.

6. *Press Conf* #263 (January 7, 1936), 7:56–60.

7. "Farmers Called to Capital to Draft New Aid Program," *NYT,* January 8, 1936, 1, and several related stories on page 4. Roosevelt discussed the soil conservation approach extensively in *Press Conf* #265 and #267 (January 10, 17, 1936), 7:61–70, 78–85; and in the detailed signing statement and attached note in PPA, "Presidential Statement . . . Mar. 1, 1936." See also "The AAA: 1936–1928," in Saloutos, *American Farmer,* 236–53.

8. PPA, "Address at the Jackson Day Dinner, Washington, D.C., Jan 8, 1936."

9. PPA, "The President Vetoes for a Second Time the Soldiers' Bonus . . . Jan. 24, 1936"; R. Daniels, *Bonus March,* 240–41.

10. Douglas North was one of the first to analyze the impact of the bonus payments. *Growth and Welfare in the American Past,* 175.

11. Cf. Freidel, *Rendezvous with Destiny,* 192–93.

12. PPA, ". . . Address to the Young Democratic Club, Baltimore, Md., Apr. 13, 1936."

13. PPA, "Supplemental Message to the Congress, Mar. 3, 1936"; Turner Catledge, "Roosevelt Asks $620,000,000 in Undivided Profits Tax" and "Bankers See Peril in Tax on Surplus," *NYT,* March 4, 1936, 1, 2.

14. PPA, "White House Statement on the Appointment of a Committee to Formulate a Plan for the Reorganization of the Executive Branch of the Government, Mar. 22, 1939."

15. PPA, "Radio Address on the Occasion of the President's Third Birthday Ball, Jan. 30, 1936." Milbank had organized the International Committee for the Study of Infantile Paralysis in 1928. For de Kruif, see Charles Rosenberg, "Martin Arrowsmith: The Scientist as Hero."

16. *Aswander v. Tennessee Valley Authority,* 207 U.S. 288 (1936); Arthur Krock, "Supreme Court, 8–1, Backs TVA," *NYT,* February 18, 1936, 1; *Press Conf #276–77* (February 18, 21, 1936), 7:143, 146–48. See also PPA, "The President Reaffirms the Administration's Program for the Development of the Great Lakes–St. Lawrence Seaway and Power Project, March 11, 1936," and appended note.

17. All page 1 headlines, *NYT,* March 19, 1936; *Press Conf #284* (March 19, 1936), 7:197–99; PPA, "White House Statement on Allocation of Funds for Repairs and Replacement of Public Property Damaged by Floods, Mar. 21, 1936"; "Raging Waters," *NYT,* March 22, 1936, E1.

18. The statutes are described in *NYT,* June 22, 1936, 14.

19. PPA, "Letters on the Continuation of the CCC Program, Mar. 23, 1936"; Salmond, *Civilian Conservation Corps,* 65–69. For Roosevelt's praise of the CCC, see PPA, "Radio Address on the Third Anniversary of the CCC, Apr. 17, 1936," and appended note; "Roosevelt Widens Flood Control Aim," *NYT,* April 28, 1936, 13. See also PPA, "A Résumé of the Participation of Federal Groups in Rescue Work in Flood Areas, May 7, 1936."

20. Charles W. Hurd, "Roosevelt Departs for Florida . . .," *NYT,* March 23, 1936, 1; PPA, "Telegram to Admiral Cary T. Grayson, Chairman of the American Red Cross, on Flood Relief, Apr. 7, 1936"; *Press Conf #286* (March 31, 1936), 7:202–6; PPA, "A Résumé of the Participation of Federal Groups in Rescue Work in Flood Areas, May 7, 1936."

21. Charles W. Hurd, "Roosevelt Lands and Starts North to Meet Problems," *NYT,* April 9, 1936, 1; "Roosevelt Lauds Gainesville Spirit in Storm Problem," *NYT,* April 10, 1936, 1; "Roosevelt Back at Desk in Capital," *NYT,* April 11, 1936, 3; *Press Conf #287* (April 8, 1936), 7:207–10.

22. "Memorandum for the Postmaster General," in *FDR Letters,* March 26, 1936, 3:175. Michelson (1869?–1948) was publicity director of the DNC; Edwin A. Halsey (1881–1945), secretary of the Senate, was the party liaison with Democratic members of Congress; and Forbes Morgan (1879–1937), an investment banker and Eleanor Roosevelt's uncle, was DNC treasurer. Stanley H. High (1895–1961) was briefly a key member of the Roosevelt entourage during 1936–37. Later a speechwriter for Tom Dewey in 1940 and 1944 and Dwight Eisenhower in 1952 and a theologically trained Protestant religious publicist, he had been a Republican before the New Deal. From

1940 until his death, he was an editor of the *Reader's Digest*. "Stanley High, Writer-Editor," *Washington Post*, February 4, 1961, C3.

23. "Democrats Shape an Outdoor Climax," *NYT*, April 26, 1936, 33; PPA, "Address to the Young Democratic Club, Baltimore, Md., Apr. 13, 1936"; Charles W. Hurd, "President at Baltimore," *NYT*, April 14, 1936, 1; PPA, "Address at the Thomas Jefferson Dinner, New York City, Apr. 25, 1936"; "Roosevelt, Here, Defends Cost of Rebuilding the Nation," *NYT*, April 26, 1936, 1.

24. "Louis M'H. Howe, Roosevelt Friend, Dies at Capital," *NYT*, April 18, 1936, 1; "President Mourns Death of Howe," *NYT*, April 20, 1936, 19; "Roosevelt Will Go to Burial of Howe," *NYT*, April 21, 1936, 23; "President Attends Services for Howe," *NYT*, April 22, 1936, 23; "Last Howe Tribute Paid by Roosevelt," *NYT*, April 23, 1936, 24; Charles W. Hurd, "President Feels Loss of Advisor," *NYT*, April 26, 1936, E6. Rollins, *Roosevelt and Howe*, 433–49, chronicles Howe's last days.

25. *Press Conf* #292 (May 5, 1936), 7:233–37; "Roosevelt Agrees on Housing Plans," *NYT*, May 6, 1936, 4.

26. *Carter v. Carter Coal Company*, 298 U.S. 238 (1936).

27. *Press Conf* #296 (May 19, 1936), 7:26–31.

28. *Ashton v. Cameron County Water District No. 1*, 298 U.S. 513 (1936); "Law to Help Cities in Distress Is Void," *NYT*, May 26, 1936, 1. Cardozo noted that in January 1934, 2,019 governmental bodies were in default and that in January 1933, of $14 billion in securities issued by units less than a state, $1 billion was in default.

29. *Morehead v. New York ex rel. Tipaldo*, 298 U.S. 387 (1936). There was also a bitter dissent from Stone, joined by Brandeis and Cardozo, which concluded: "We should follow our decision in the Nebbia case" and leave socioeconomic solutions to Congress where "the Constitution has left them." "Supreme Court, 5–4, Voids State Minimum Wage Law," *NYT*, June 2, 1936, 1. Roberts quotation from *Nebbia* at 291 U.S. 537 (1934).

30. *Press Conf* #300 (June 2, 1936), 7:280–81.

31. "Hoover Advocates Women's Wage Law," *NYT*, June 7, 1936. The GOP plank read: "Support the adoption of state laws and interstate compacts to abolish sweatshops and child labor, and to protect women and children with respect to maximum hours, minimum wages and working conditions. We believe that this can be done within the Constitution as it now stands."

32. Ibid. The full passage reads: "If these problems cannot be effectively solved by legislation within the Constitution, we shall seek such clarifying amendment as will assure to the legislatures of the several States and to the Congress of the United States, each within its proper jurisdiction, the power to enact those laws which the State and Federal legislatures, within their respective spheres, shall find necessary, in order adequately to regulate commerce, protect public health and safety and safeguard economic security. Thus we propose to maintain the letter and spirit of the Constitution." Leuchtenburg calls this passage, drafted by Don Richberg, "opaque" (*Supreme Court Reborn*, 107). I find it clear if convoluted.

33. Turner Catledge, "Byrns's Death Bars Adjournment," *NYT*, June 4, 1936, 1; PPA, "A Tribute to Speaker Joseph W. Byrns on the Occasion of His Death, June 4, 1936"; "Nashville Pays Honor to Byrns," *NYT*, June 7, 1936, 2; "Roosevelt Drafts Speeches on Train," *NYT*, June 7, 1936, 2; "Roosevelt Starts Long Trip Tonight," *NYT*, June 7, 1936,

1; "Roosevelt Meets Congress Leaders on Tax Compromise" and "Roosevelt Starts Journey to Texas," *NYT*, June 9, 1936, 1, 10.

34. Charles W. Hurd, "Roosevelt Greets Knoxville Crowd on His Way South," *NYT*, June 10, 1936, 1; Hurd, "Roosevelt Calls for Broader View of the Constitution" and "Arkansas Crowds Cheer Roosevelt," *NYT*, June 11, 1936, 1, 9; PPA, "Informal Extemporaneous Remarks at a Religious Service in Rockport, Arkansas," June 10, 1936, and "Address at Little Rock, Arkansas, June 10, 1936."

35. PPA, "'Address at San Jacinto Battleground, Texas, Jun. 11, 1936," "Address at the Alamo, San Antonio, Texas, June 11, 1936," and "Address at the Texas Centennial Exposition, Dallas, Texas, Jun. 12, 1936"; Charles W. Hurd, "Roosevelt Assails Monopoly as Foe of Real Freedom," *NYT*, June 13, 1936, 1; PPA, "Informal Extemporaneous Remarks at a Luncheon in Dallas, Texas, Jun. 12, 1936"; "Roosevelt Heads for Indiana Fete," *NYT*, June 14, 1936, 1; PPA, "Address at George Rogers Clark Memorial, Vincennes, Indiana, June 14, 1936"; "On Visiting the Birthplace of Abraham Lincoln, June 14, 1936"; Charles W. Hurd, "Roosevelt Urges That Our Land Be 'Saved,'" *NYT*, June 15, 1936, 1; *Press Conf* #301 (June 16, 1936), 7:284–87; PPA, "Informal Extemporaneous Remarks at a Luncheon in Dallas, Texas, Jun. 12, 1936."

36. Rosenman, *Working with Roosevelt*, 104–5.

37. "Congressmen Quit Capital for Homes," *NYT*, June 22, 1936; 1; "'$20-Billion-Dollar Congress' Set a New Spending Record for Nation," *NYT*, June 21, 1936, 1. (The arithmetic was from Carter Glass and included both amounts not yet appropriated and funds that would not be spent for several years.) See Leff, *Limits of Symbolic Reform*.

38. Hal H. Smith, "Review of Important Legislation by 74th Congress, in Second Session," *NYT*, June 22, 1936, 14; "Roosevelt Signs Ship Subsidy Bill," *NYT*, June 30, 1936, 19.

39. Anne O'Hare McCormick, "'Still a Little Left of Center,'" *NYT*, June 21, 1936, SM1. The variance between the quotation in the text and the title exists in the original.

40. "Roosevelt . . . Talks with Lewis," *NYT*, June 23, 1936, 12; Forbes Morgan obituary, *NYT*, April 21, 1937, 23; A. Schlesinger, *The Politics of Upheaval*, 594–95; "Forms Labor Body to Back Roosevelt," *NYT*, April 1, 1936, 9.

41. "Defend Two-Thirds Rule: Southerners Oppose Abrogation, but Farley Again Predicts It," *NYT*, June 22, 1936, 5; Charles R. Michael, "South Bows to Change . . . Accepts End of Two-Thirds Rule," *NYT*, June 26, 1936, 1.

42. "Senator Smith Quits over Negro's Prayer; Convention Colleagues Let Him Go Alone," *NYT*, June 25, 1936, 12. The *Times* headline, but not the AP story beneath it, is in error about Smith being "alone." For the event's significance, see A. Schlesinger, *The Politics of Upheaval*, 598–99. For the "melted midnight" phrase and other comments from the Charleston press, see Nadine Cohodas, *Strom Thurmond and the Politics of Southern Change*, 47.

43. "Ickes Tells Negroes of New Deal's Help," *NYT*, June 30, 1936, 10.

44. James A. Hagerty, "Day of Oratory Starts Early," *NYT*, June 27, 1936; Turner Catledge, "Drama in Night Session," *NYT*, June 27, 1936, 1; Arthur Krock, "Campaign Issue Defined," *NYT*, June 28, 1936, 1; "Garner's Acceptance Speech," *NYT*, June 28, 1936, 25.

45. Arthur Krock, "Campaign Issue Defined. The President Avoids All Personalities in His Philadelphia Speech," *NYT*, June 28, 1936, 1. Garner had been notified and pledged that "I shall stand with him . . . as I have stood . . . since March 4, 1933."

46. The words, spoken back on the presidential train, were reported by Grace Tully in *FDR, My Boss,* 202. The "maddest white man" is as close as President Roosevelt ever came to the casual racism of contemporary American speech. He used the phrase again a few days later in a press conference (#308, 8:24). The same cannot be said for Eleanor, whose early correspondence contains derogatory references to "negroes" and "Jews."

47. Rosenman says that the term was coined by Stanley High (*Working with Roosevelt,* 106).

48. PPA, "Acceptance of the Renomination for the Presidency, Philadelphia, Pa., June 27, 1936." Rosenman says that "rendezvous with destiny" came from Tom Corcoran.

49. A private letter to Lehman is in *FDR Letters,* 3:180–81; the public one is PPA, "A Letter Urging Governor Herbert H. Lehman, of New York, to Become a Candidate for Reelection, June 29, 1936." The letter to Morgenthau, March 19, 1936, is in *FDR Letters,* 3:174. Nevins, *Lehman and His Era,* 187, writes that Lehman had told Roosevelt of his decision in January. See also Freidel, *Rendezvous with Destiny,* 204. Lehman's original public statement is in "The Governor's Statement," *NYT,* May 21, 1936, 1. In the event, both carried New York handily, but for once Roosevelt outpolled Lehman. Lehman ran and won again in 1938 for the first four-year gubernatorial term, served as an overseas relief administrator during World War II, and succeeded Robert F. Wagner in the Senate, serving from 1949 to 1957. After Lehman only Averill Harriman's term (1955–58) interrupted Republican hegemony in Albany between 1942 and 1975.

50. "Memorandum for J.A.F.," May 22, 1936, as cited in Rosenman, *Working with Roosevelt,* 129.

51. "Roosevelt Clears Desk by Vetoing the Last Four Bills from Congress," *NYT,* July 2, 1936, 1; *Press Conf* #305 (June 30, 1936), 7:306–8.

52. "Plans Remodeling of the White House," *NYT,* July 3, 1936. 5. For a perceptive account, see Kathleen McLaughlin, "Mrs. Roosevelt Goes Her Way," *NYT Magazine,* July 5, 1936, 7. Remodelers discovered that much of the electric wiring dating from TR's time had to be replaced.

53. PPA, "Address at Shenandoah National Park, July 3, 1936"; Charles W. Hurd, "Roosevelt Urges New Park Areas to Correct 'Tragedy of Waste,'" *NYT,* July 4, 1936, 1; PPA, "Address at Monticello, Virginia, July 4, 1936"; Charles W. Hurd, "President Points to 'Spirit of Youth' as Aid to Freedom," *NYT,* July 5, 1936, 1; Hurd, "Roosevelt Visits Historic Church," *NYT,* July 6, 1936, 3; "President Boards Yacht for Cruise," *NYT,* July 5, 1936, 3.

54. Frank N. Kluckhohn, "President Takes Control of Drought Relief Plans," *NYT,* July 7, 1936, 1; *Press Conf* #306 (July 7, 1336), 8:1–13; "Relief for 134,000 Families Planned for Drought Area," *NYT,* July 8, 1936, 1.

55. "Roosevelt Closes Office for Holiday," *NYT,* July 11, 1936, 4; "Cheering Crowds Greet Roosevelt," *NYT,* July 12, 1936, 22; Ickes, *Secret Diary,* 1:466–67, 636–37; Robert A. Caro, *The Power Broker: Robert Moses and the Fall of New York;* PPA, "'Address at the Dedication of the Triborough Bridge, New York City, July 11, 1936."

56. Charles W. Hurd, "Roosevelt Rests in Hyde Park Home," *NYT,* July 13, 1936, 3; "President Pledges Flood Control Aid," *NYT,* July 14, 1936, 1.

57. "President Charters Boat," *NYT*, March 20, 1936, 27; "Roosevelt Plans Sea Trip with Three Sons in July," *NYT*, June 17, 1936, 3; "Roosevelt to Cruise in 56-Foot Schooner," *NYT*, July 6, 1936; "Roosevelt's Sons Sail On," *NYT*, July 9, 1936, 23; "Sewanna on Maine Coast," *NYT*, July 10, 1936; Charles W. Hurd, "Roosevelt Nears Campobello Goal," *NYT*, July 26, 1936, N1.

58. For a good account of the Landon campaign, see Donald R. McCoy, *Landon of Kansas*, 262–339. For the movements that created the Union Party, see Brinkley, *Voices of Protest*. For Lemke, see Edward C. Blackorby, *Prairie Rebel: The Public Life of William Lemke*; "Landon Pledges Strict Economy but Full Relief to Those in Need," *NYT*, July 24, 1936, 1; and F. Raymond Daniell, "Coughlin Wins Townsend and Long Group to Lemke as He Sways Convention," *NYT*, July 17, 1936, 1. Ickes, *Secret Diary*, 1:638–47 (July 18–23), is a long rant. Eleanor's memo, July 16, 1936, is in Cook, *Eleanor Roosevelt*, 2:378–79.

59. Charles W. Hurd, "Roosevelt Sails through Fog Bank," *NYT*, July 19, 1936, 1.

60. Charles W. Hurd, "Roosevelt Lands at Summer Home," *NYT*, July 29, 1936, 5; "Roosevelt Will Confer on Long-Time Power Plan with Officials in Canada," *NYT*, July 30, 1936, 1; "Cruise a Treat for President," *NYT*, August 2, 1936, E10, which is a concise summary; *Press Conf* #309 (July 29, 1936), 8:30–35.

61. Charles W. Hurd, "Roosevelt Leaves for Quebec Parlay after Quoddy Visit," *NYT*, July 31, 1936, 1; "Roosevelt Lauds Ties with Canada," *NYT*, August 1, 1936, 1; PPA, "Address on the Occasion of a Visit to Quebec, Canada, July 31, 1936," and appended note. The president's remarks were shaped, in part, by drafts from the State Department and the American minister in Ottawa, Norman Armour. See Norman Armour to Marvin H. McIntyre, July 28, 1936, printed with annotations in NIXON *FDR & FA*, 3:357–58.

62. Charles W. Hurd, "President Studies Flood Area Needs," *NYT*, August 2, 1936, 1; *Press Conf* #310–11 (August 1, 1936), 8:36–45. William E. Leuchtenburg, *Flood Control Politics: The Connecticut River Valley Problem, 1927–1950*, is the key work.

63. "Roosevelt to Stay Long at Hyde Park," *NYT*, August 3, 1936, 13; Charles W. Hurd, "Roosevelt Calls All Party Chiefs to Map Campaign," *NYT*, August 3, 1936, 1. Other attendees were W. Forbes Morgan, Frank Walker, Steve Early, Molly Dewson, L. N. (Chip) Robert, and Stanley High.

64. "Form Labor Body to Back Roosevelt," *NYT*, April 1, 1936, 9; PPA, "A Greeting to Labor's Non-Partisan League, Aug. 3, 1936"; Louis Stark, "Roosevelt's Allies in Labor Propose 1940 Liberal Party," *NYT*, August 11, 1936, 1. Both Tobin and Berry had actively campaigned for Roosevelt in 1932, and each had hoped to be named secretary of labor. Tobin had been offered a minor post but turned it down. For an astute contemporary analysis, see Louis Stark, "Roosevelt Avoids Any Intervention in Labor Union Row," *NYT*, July 12, 1936, 1. For labor's hopes, see Stark, "Labor Takes First Step toward Political Party," *NYT*, August 16, 1936, E7; "President Favored Labor Says AFL," *NYT*, October 17, 1936, 31; "Labor Backs Roosevelt," *NYT*, September 30, 1936; "Louis Stark, 66, Times Newsman," *NYT*, May 18, 1954, 29; and Charles W. Hurd, "[Green] Says 90% of Labor Is for Roosevelt," *NYT*, October 6, 1936, 1.

65. Rollins, *Roosevelt and Howe*, 428–29; "Roosevelt Drafts Stanley High," *NYT*, February 18, 1936, 11; "'Good Neighbors' Call on Roosevelt," *NYT*, April 26, 1936, 3;

"New Deal Starts Negro Vote Drive," *NYT*, September 3, 1936, 10; "26 Negro Rallies Back Roosevelt," *NYT*, September 22, 1936, 4; PPA, "A Greeting on the Seventy-Fourth Anniversary of the Proclamation of Emancipation, Sept. 16, 1936"; *Afro-American* (Baltimore), October 17, 1936; N. Weiss, *Farewell to the Party of Lincoln*, 180–208; Thomas T. Spencer, "Democratic Auxiliary and Non-party Groups in the Election of 1936" and "The Good Neighbor League Colored Committee and the 1936 Democratic Presidential Campaign." See also Donald R. McCoy, "The Good Neighbor League and the Presidential Campaign of 1936."

66. Roosevelt's predecessor and successor each made a single formal visit to Howard. Those visits also occurred in presidential election years on June 6, 1932, and June 13, 1952.

67. PPA, "Address at the Dedication of the New Chemistry Building, Howard University Washington, D.C., Oct. 26, 1936"; "Roosevelt at Howard," *NYT*, October 27, 1936, 1; "Roosevelt Wins Howard Poll," *NYT*, November 3, 1936, 8.

68. The actual New York State vote for president by line in 1936 was:

Democratic	3,018,298	53.4 percent
Republican	2,180,670	39 percent
Other	397,480	7.1 percent

Most of the "other" vote—274,924 ballots—was on the ALP line for Roosevelt, and 78.6 percent of the other vote was in New York City. Edgar E. Robinson, *They Voted for Roosevelt*, 130–31, 199; "Olson, from Bed, Backs Roosevelt," *NYT*, August 19, 1935, 14.

69. I have found most useful William E. Leuchtenburg's "The Election of 1936," in his *The FDR Years: On Roosevelt and His Legacy*, 100–158; and "Mayor Joins Drive of Progressives to Aid Roosevelt," *NYT*, September 2, 1936, 1.

70. Charles W. Hurd, "Roosevelt Visits Johnstown to Map Flood Control Aid," *NYT*, August 14, 1936, 1; "Great Crowds Acclaim Roosevelt on Inspection Tour," *NYT*, August 16, 1936, 1; PPA, "Informal Extemporaneous Remarks at the C.C.C. Camp Near Johnstown, PA, Aug. 13, 1936"; *Press Conf* #316 (August 18, 1936), 8:83–84.

71. There had been and continued to be complaints about materials produced by Rex Tugwell's Farm Security Administration, particularly Pare Lorentz's now classic film *The Plow That Broke the Plains* and a notorious series of photos by FSA photographer Arthur Rothstein, decorated by a bleached cattle skull that he had found and used as a movable prop. One of his "fake" photos was on the front page of a Fargo, North Dakota, paper the day Roosevelt arrived.

72. Charles W. Hurd, "Western Crowds Hail Roosevelt as He Speeds West," *NYT*, August 27, 1936, 1; "President Warned of 'Desert Trend' in Drought Region," *NYT*, August 28, 1936, 1; PPA, "Informal Extemporaneous Remarks at Bismarck, N.D., Aug. 27, 1936"; "Summary of the Great Plains Drought Area Committee's Preliminary Report and Conclusions, Aug. 27, 1936." For Lorentz, see Robert L. Snyder, *Pare Lorentz and the Documentary Film*. The film's script is in Pare Lorentz, *FDR's Moviemaker: Memoirs and Scripts*. For FSA photography, see James C. Curtis, *Mind's Eye, Mind's Truth: FSA Photography Reconsidered*.

73. Charles W. Hurd, "Roosevelt Finds WPA Aid Cheering Drought Regions," *NYT*, August 29, 1936, 1; PPA, "Rear Platform Extemporaneous Remarks at Jamestown, N.D.,

Aug. 28, 1936" and "Rear Platform Extemporaneous Remarks at Aberdeen, S.D., Aug. 28, 1936"; Charles W. Hurd, "Roosevelt Pledges Soil Plan to Curb Great 'Human Loss,'" *NYT*, August 30, 1936, 1; "President Praises Sculpture in Hills," *NYT*, August 31, 1936, 5; "President Attends Services for Dern," *NYT*, September 2, 1936, 12; Keith McFarland, *Harry H. Woodring: A Political Biography of FDR's Controversial Secretary of War*.

74. Charles W. Hurd, "Roosevelt Speeds to Drought Parlay Set in Des Moines," *NYT*, September 3, 1936, 1; "Rivals Meet with Smiles," *NYT*, September 4, 1936, 1.

75. PPA, "Informal Extemporaneous Remarks at Luncheon at Indianapolis, Sept. 5, 1936"; Charles W. Hurd, "Roosevelt Studies Last Drought Area," *NYT*, September 5, 1936, 1.

76. PPA, "The First 'Fireside Chat' of 1936," September 6, 1936.

77. William L. Laurence, "Pledge to Fight for Truth Ends Harvard Tercentenary," *NYT*, September 19, 1936, 1; PPA, "Address Delivered at the Harvard University, Sept. 19, 1936"; "Harvard '05, for Landon," *NYT*, October 22, 1936, 20; "President Hits Tax Foes," *NYT*, October 22, 1936, 1.

78. The Landon campaign is well described in McCoy, *Landon of Kansas*, 262–349. For Lippmann, see *Time*, September 21, 1936; and *Press Conf* #318 (September 8, 1936), 8:105.

79. PPA, "Informal Extemporaneous Remarks at the Dedication of the Medical College, Syracuse University, Sept. 29, 1936"; "President Lays Cornerstone for Medical Building at Syracuse University," *NYT*, September 30, 1936, 17; PPA, "Address Delivered at Democratic State Convention, Syracuse, N.Y., Sept. 29, 1936"; Charles W. Hurd, "The President Opens Fire," *NYT*, September 30, 1936, 1; "President Leaves Car to Sing with Legion," *NYT*, September 30, 1936, 17; "Hamilton Warns of Reds," *NYT*, September 30, 1936, 19.

80. *Press Conf* #320 (September 15, 1936), 8:113.

81. PPA, "Note," September 29, 1936; Rosenman, *Working with Roosevelt*, 11–12. For a recent survey of presidential ghostwriting, see Robert Schlesinger, *White House Ghosts: Presidents and Their Speechwriters*.

82. Charles W. Hurd, "President Starts on Another Swing," *NYT*, October 1, 1936, 1; "President Defends Costs," *NYT*, October 2, 1936, 1; PPA, "Rear-Platform Extemporaneous Remarks at Grafton, W. VA., Oct. 1, 1936" and "Campaign Address at Forbes Field, Pittsburgh, Pa., Oct. 1, 1936."

83. Arthur J. Daley, "Roosevelt Smiles at Rout of Smith," *NYT*, October 3, 1936, 11.

84. Charles W. Hurd, "President Is Home, Tired but Cheery," *NYT*, October 3, 1936, 3; "President Plans for Denver Trip," *NYT*, October 4, 1936, 41; "President Goes to Country as Candidate," *NYT*, October 4, 1936, E3; "Roosevelt Works on Stumping Plans," *NYT*, October 5, 1936, 3; "[Green] Says 90% of Labor Is for Roosevelt," *NYT*, October 6, 1926, 1; "Roosevelt Starts Swing to Rockies on 13-State Tour," *NYT*, October 9, 1936, 1; Rosenman, *Working with Roosevelt*, 118–39.

85. PPA, "Campaign Address at St. Paul, Minn., Oct. 9, 1936" and "Campaign Address at Omaha, Oct. 10, 1936"; Charles W. Hurd, "President Praises Pacts," *NYT*, October 10, 1936, 1; "New 4-Point Farm Plan Is Outlined by Roosevelt," *NYT*, October 11, 1926, 1; PPA, "Campaign Address at Denver, Colo., Oct. 12, 1936"; Charles W. Hurd, "Two-Faced Pledge Laid by Roosevelt to Rival Leaders," *NYT*, October 13, 1936, 1.

86. PPA, "Campaign Address at Wichita, Kansas, Oct. 13, 1936"; "Rear Platform Extemporaneous Remarks at Emporia, Kansas, Oct. 10, 1936"; Charles W. Hurd, "President Offers Kansans Security as New Deal Fact," *NYT*, October 14, 1936. For some of the White-Roosevelt correspondence, see Walter Johnson, ed., *Selected Letters of William Allen White*.

87. PPA, "Campaign Address at Kansas City, MO., Oct.13, 1936"; "Campaign Address at Chicago, IL., Oct. 14, 1936"; Charles W. Hurd, "Chicago Hails President," *NYT*, October 15, 1936, 1.

88. PPA, "Campaign Address at Detroit, Mich., Oct. 15, 1936"; Charles W. Hurd, "Roosevelt Holds Rise in Year Wage Must Be Planned," *NYT*, October 16, 1936, 1.

89. The magazine, founded in 1890, had correctly predicted the results of every presidential election from 1916 to 1932. Only the first of those was close. Its final 1936 poll, released on October 31, gave Landon 57 percent of the popular vote; publication ceased shortly thereafter.

90. PPA, "Campaign Address in Cleveland, Ohio, Oct. 16, 1936"; Charles W. Hurd, "Roosevelt Hailed in Ohio," *NYT*, October 17, 1936, 1; "Roosevelt Ends 5,000 Mile Tour," *NYT*, October 18, 1936, 1; "Roosevelt Maps New England Trip; At Capital Today," *NYT*, October 19, 1936, 1. Roosevelt attacked the trickle-down theory in at least three other 1936 campaign speeches: Denver, Chicago, and the October 23 radio address.

91. Rosenman, *Working with Roosevelt*, 131–32.

92. PPA, "Informal Extemporaneous Remarks at Dedication of Brooklyn College, Brooklyn, N.Y., Oct. 28, 1936," "Address on the Occasion of the Fiftieth Anniversary of the Statue of Liberty, Oct. 28, 1336," and "Address at Roosevelt Park, New York City, Oct. 28, 1936"; "President on Visit to City Today," *NYT*, October 28, 1936, 18; "City Throngs Hail Roosevelt and Landon," *NYT*, October 29, 1936, 1; "President Hails Brooklyn College," *NYT*, October 29, 1936, 20; "Roosevelt Urges Guarding of Peace," *NYT*, October 29, 1936, 21.

93. "Experts Predict Roosevelt Victory with Probably 406 Electoral Votes," *NYT*, November 1, 1936, 1; "Walker Denounces Smith Walk-Out," *NYT*, October 30, 1936, 11; Raymond Daniell, "Smith Links Reds with Roosevelt," *NYT*, November 1, 1936, 1.

94. PPA, "Campaign Address at Brooklyn, Oct. 30, 1936," "Informal Extemporaneous Remarks at a Gathering of Workers at National Campaign Headquarters, New York City, Oct. 31, 1936," and "Campaign Address at Madison Square Garden, Oct. 31, 1936"; Russell B. Porter, "Partial Reply to Landon," *NYT*, October 31, 1936, 1; "President Thanks Aides Here," *NYT*, November 1, 1936, 36; "President Ends Campaign," *NYT*, November 1, 1936, 1.

95. Rosenman, *Working with Roosevelt*, 135–36.

96. PPA, "Informal Extemporaneous Remarks at Poughkeepsie, N.Y., Nov. 2, 1936"; "Final Campaign Radio Speech, Nov. 2, 1936"; Charles W. Hurd, "Roosevelt Plans Five Speeches Today," *NYT*, November 2, 1936, 1; "President in Wind-Up," *NYT*, November 3, 1936, 1; "Roosevelt Speaks in Neighbor Towns," *NYT*, November 3, 1936, 4.

97. Rosenman, *Working with Roosevelt*, 137–38, the only eyewitness account, mentions only sandwiches.

98. Some sources give 60.2, but that is without the 275,000 votes cast in New York on the American Labor Party line.

99. *Press Conf* #325 (November 6, 1936), 8:143–48; "Roosevelt 162 Short on Electoral Guess," *NYT*, November 7, 1936, 3.

100. The *New York Times* published a disgraceful editorial calling Tugwell "a visible and personal link, as it were, between the Comintern in Moscow and the aspiring young reformers in Washington" ("Mr. Tugwell Retires," *NYT*, November 19, 1936, 24).

101. Sternsher, *Tugwell and the New Deal*, 321–22; "Tugwell Quits Post," *NYT*, November 18, 1936, 1; "M. L. Wilson Moved to Tugwell's Post," *NYT*, January 1, 1937, 18; "Wallace Opposes Big Tenancy Grant," *NYT*, December 17, 1936, 9. For Alexander, see Wilma Dykeman, *Seeds of Southern Change: The Life of Will Alexander*.

102. PPA, "A Christmas Greeting to the Nation, Dec. 24, 1936"; "Roosevelt Calls Nation to Peace," *NYT*, December 25, 1936, 1.

103. PPA, "An Exchange of Letters with Andrew W. Mellon on the Gift of an Art Gallery to the United States (Excerpts), Dec. 22, 1936–Jan. 1, 1937"; "Mellon Gives Art to U.S." and three other stories, *NYT*, January 3, 1937, 1. The details of the White House meeting come from David Cannadine, *Mellon: An American Life*, xi–xii, 558–65. Mellon's visit to the White House, which would have been a good story, was missed by the press. "President Stays in on New Year's Eve," *NYT*, January 1, 1937, 1. For Morgenthau's role, see Blum, *Roosevelt and Morgenthau*, 162–65.

104. *Press Conf* #330–33 (December 18, 22, 29, 1936), 8:177–212.

Chapter 12. Foreign Affairs

1. Remarkably, Robert Dallek, *Franklin D. Roosevelt and American Foreign Policy, 1932–1945* (1979), remains the best single account; the 1995 edition contains a retrospective brief afterword. Hereafter cited as DALLEK.

2. Freidel, *Rendezvous with Destiny*, 69; his treatment here is less censorious than earlier comments about Roosevelt's "humiliation" by Hearst in *Triumph*, 254.

3. For Stimson's views, see Stimson and Bundy, *On Active Service*, 288–96. The heading for the section on the meetings is "Middleman after Election." The January 9 Hyde Park meeting was followed by one in Washington, January 19. They also spoke by telephone. Stimson and Cordell Hull met after the latter's appointment was revealed in late February. There was no formal transition; that process was invented by President Truman and his aides after Eisenhower's election in 1952.

4. "Roosevelt Reveals Policy in the Far East Will Be Continued," "Washington Is Gratified," and "Japanese Regret Roosevelt Stand," *NYT*, January 18, 1933, 1, 18, 11. See also U.S. Department of State, vol. 1 of *Japan, 1931–1941*, in *Foreign Relations of the United States, 1933–1945*.

5. "Johnson Loan Bill Passed," *NYT*, April 5, 1934, 5. There was much confusion about what the law permitted; see the two press conference excerpts in NIXON *FDR & FA*, 2:91, 97. See also "War Debt Ruling Divides Congress," *NYT*, May 7, 1934, 11; "Payment of Debt Tokens Will Not Avert Default," *NYT*, May 11, 1934, 1.

6. He was also Franklin's personal friend, married one of the president's second cousins, and was one of the many Republicans who supported Roosevelt in 1932.

7. For Dodd, see Robert Dallek, *Democrat and Diplomat: The Life of William E. Dodd*.

8. E. David Cronon, *Josephus Daniels in Mexico*, 1–29. For Daniels's account of his mission, see *Shirt-Sleeve Diplomat*.

9. PPA, "The President Begins to Carry Out the Good Neighbor Policy, Apr. 12, 1933," and appended note.

10. *Naboth's Vineyard, 1844–1924* (1924). In the Old Testament (1 Kings 21), Jezebel arranges for the murder of Naboth so her husband, King Ahab, can acquire his choice vineyard.

11. PPA, "Presidential Message to Delegates of Opposing Factions in Cuba, July 1, 1933," and appended note; "Joint Statement by the President and Ambassador Cintas on the Cuban Situation, Aug. 9, 1933," and appended note; "The Good Neighbor Policy Begins to Work in Cuba, Aug. 13, 1933," and appended note; ". . . Welles Will Assist Hull," *NYT*, April 4, 1933, 4; "Latin Affairs Post for Welles," *NYT*, April 11, 1933, 2; "Welles Is Named Envoy in Havana," *NYT*, April 22, 1933, 6; "Welles Denies Aim Is to Oust Machado," *NYT*, April 25, 1933, 6; Freidel, *Rendezvous with Destiny*, 212–13. Gellman, *Good Neighbor Diplomacy*, is a good account.

12. PPA, "Presidential Statement of Non-Intervention in Cuba, Nov. 23, 1933," and appended note.

13. The United States exercised the right of reoccupation in 1906 and 1912. The United States also received a ninety-nine-year lease on Guantánamo, which it continues to occupy after the lease expired.

14. PPA, "Request for Authority to Consummate Reciprocal Trade Agreements, Mar. 2, 1934," and appended note; "Request for Approval of a New Treaty with Cuba, May 29, 1934," and appended note. The notes to these documents plus the similar notes in the preceding two endnotes, if read in chronological order, provide a presidential narrative that can be instructively compared with that provided in U.S. Department of State, *Foreign Relations of the United States.*

15. For an example of the continuing favorable historical consensus about the policy as late as the mid-1980s, see John E. Wilz's essay "Good Neighbor Policy," in *Franklin D. Roosevelt,* edited by Graham and Wander, 136–39.

16. PPA, "The President and Prime Minister MacDonald Issue a Joint Statement about Their Conference, Apr. 22, 1933," and additional statements on each of the next four days.

17. PPA, "An Appeal to the Nations of the World for Peace by Disarmament and for the End of Economic Chaos, May 16, 1933"; "The Congress Is Informed of the President's Appeal, May 16, 1933"; "The Nation's Answer, May 17, 1933"; [Paul] Claudel to Paul-Boncour, April 5, 1933, *Documents Diplomatiques Français,* ser. 1, 3:148–49, as cited in Freidel, *Rendezvous with Destiny,* 113.

18. Actually, the conference was failing even before Roosevelt's message was released. The Paris Sunday newspapers of July 2—before the president's message was written—were full of inspired stories saying that the conference was as good as over. "Paris Press Urges Parley to Adjourn," *NYT*, July 2, 1933, 2.

19. PPA, "Statement by Secretary of the Treasury Denying London Rumors of Currency Stabilization, June 15, 1933"; "Woodin Denies Stabilization by Our Delegates to London," *NYT*, June 16, 1933, 1. An obviously inspired story, "Washington Cool to Stabilization," *NYT*, June 16, 1933, 2, laid out the reasons. The so-called bombshell

is PPA, "A Wireless to the London Conference, July 3, 1933." Despite the date, the bombshell was actually sent from the *Indianapolis* at 6:00 p.m., July 2, to Phillips in Washington with the instruction "Please send the following to Hull as soon as possible." The message included an instruction not published in PPA: "Herewith is a statement which I think you can use Monday [July 3] morning as a message from me to you. If you think it best not to give it out in London let me know at once and in that event I will release it here as a White House statement" (NIXON *FDR & FA*, 1:268–69). See also Louis Howe's account broadcast on July 9 in ibid., 295–97. For some of the melodrama involved in the conference, see the memoir by Herbert Feis, *1933: Characters in Crisis*, 169–258. Pertinax (André Géraud [1882–1974]), the most celebrated French journalist of his era, wrote on the eve of the bombshell: "The continuation of the London Conference is no longer justifiable. It would only be if the countries still on the gold standard also decided to adopt inflationist methods. The American delegates are indeed unlucky. George Harrison was called home a fortnight ago. Now it is poor Professor Moley's turn. Will Bernard Baruch take his place to prolong this interminable comedy?" ("Paris Press Urges Parley to Adjourn," *NYT*, July 2, 1933, 2).

20. NIXON *FDR & FA* documents details of the conference in 1:560, 573, 314, 330, 439–40, 459–60, 467–68, 552, 560, 573, and passim.

21. For a somewhat overheated account of Hull's problems, see Gellman, *Secret Affairs*.

22. Blum, *Years of Crisis*, 1:54–57, contains an account of these meetings. See also Bullitt to Roosevelt, July 8, 1933, in NIXON *FDR & FA*, 1:289–94; and PPA, "An Exchange of Letters with Mikhail Kalinin, Oct. 10 and 17, 1933."

23. DALLEK, 39, 78–81.

24. PPA, "Exchange of Communications between the President of the United States and Maxim Litvinoff of the Union of Soviet Socialist Republics, Nov. 16, 1933" and "Another Exchange of Letters between the President and Mr. Litvinoff, Nov. 22, 1933" were brief, warm notes marking Litvinov's departure.

25. PPA, "Address Delivered at Savannah, Georgia, Nov. 18, 1933."

26. For the definitive account in English of the still-little-known Japanese-Soviet War, see Alvin D. Coox, *Nomonhan: Japan against Russia, 1939*.

27. PPA, "A Promise Fulfilled, Mar. 2, 1934," and appended note; "Statement by the President on Certification of the Proposed Constitution of the Philippine Islands, Mar. 23, 1935"; "A Message to the Congress on the Proposed Constitution of the Philippine Islands, Mar. 23, 1935," and appended note; "Address at Notre Dame University upon Receiving an Honorary Degree, Dec. 9, 1935." For a detailed account of the struggle for independence, see Theodore Friend, *Between Two Empires: Philippine Ordeal and Development from the Great Depression through the Pacific War, 1929–1946*.

28. PPA, "Organization of Public Works Administration Is Established, EO 6174, June 16, 1933," and appended note.

29. Charles F. Howlett, ed., *History of the American Peace Movement, 1890–2000: The Emergence of a New Scholarly Tradition*, is a good introduction. For Detzer, see Rhodri Jeffreys-Jones's *ANB* sketch.

30. Officially, the committee was the Senate Munitions Inquiry, but the term *Nye Committee* was all but universally used.

31. "Roosevelt to the Senate, May 18, 1934" and "Roosevelt to Senator Gerald P. Nye," in NIXON *FDR & FA*, 2:111–12, 159, 475. The phrase "merchants of death" came from the current best seller and Book of the Month Club choice, H. C. Engelbracht and F. C. Hanighen, *Merchants of Death: A Study of the International Armament Industry* (1934). In a March 1934 *Fortune* article widely circulated in pamphlet form, the charge appeared that a group of named European armament makers and brokers "are conspirators because they have no loyalties; because theirs is the sword that knows no brother. The rise of Hitler to power in Nazi Germany provides a neat example of this and into the bargain shows what a double-edged sword it is that the armament makers wield" (53–57, 113–26). See also Walter Millis, *Arms and Men: A Study in Military History*. The phrase became associated with the Nye Committee's hearings, often called the "merchants of death" investigation.

32. *Press Conf* #164 (December 12, 1934), 4:270–74.

33. Myers and Newton, *Hoover Administration*, 444, 491.

34. "Roosevelt Will Ask Laws to Take Profit Out of War," *NYT*, December 13, 1934, 1.

35. Wayne S. Cole, *Roosevelt and the Isolationists, 1932–1945*, 162. Cole, the premier historian of isolationism, tends to treat many, like Detzer, who supported peace and internationalism as if they were isolationists.

36. For the committee and its reputation, see John E. Wiltz, *In Search of Peace: The Senate Munitions Inquiry, 1934–1936*, esp. 221–32; "Cordell Hull, Secretary of State, to Roosevelt, Apr. 15, 1935" [Memorandum: Cooperation with the Nye Committee], in NIXON *FDR & FA*, 2:470–76; and Harry S. Truman, *Memoirs*, 1:190.

37. PPA, "Annual Message to the Congress, Jan. 4, 1935."

38. Properly the Permanent Court of International Justice. It should not be confused with the Permanent Court of Arbitration of which the United States was a founding member in 1899. Both sit in The Hague.

39. Roosevelt to Robinson, January 30, 1933. The struck-through words are indicated in NIXON *FDR & FA*, 2:381, but not in the version published in *FDR Letters*, 3:449–50.

40. "Roosevelt to Senator Joseph T. Robinson," January 8, 1934, in NIXON *FDR & FA*, 1:581–82; "Roosevelt to Cordell Hull," in NIXON *FDR & FA*, January 3, 1935, 1:333–34; PPA, "A Recommendation for Adherence to the World Court, Jan. 16, 1935"; "World Court Vote Is Due This Week; Adherence Seen," *NYT*, January 28, 1935, 1; "Senate Beats World Court, 52–36; Seven Less than 2/3 Vote," *NYT*, January 30, 1935, 1; letter to Elihu Root, February 9, 1935, *FDR Letters*, 3:451–52.

41. George W. Baer, *The Coming of the Italian-Ethiopian War*, is standard. Two more recent works, William R. Scott, *The Sons of Sheba's Race: African-Americans and the Italo-Ethiopian War, 1935–1941*, and Joseph E. Harris, *African-American Reactions to War in Ethiopia, 1936–1941*, examine a topic that was of no discernible concern to the Roosevelt administration.

42. Walter Millis, *The Road to War: America, 1914–1917*.

43. Senate Joint Resolution 173 (49 Stat. 1081). It also set up a system of supervision and control of the manufacture and traffic in arms and ammunition and established a National Munitions Control Board in the State Department. PPA, "Presidential Statement on Approval of Neutrality Legislation, Aug. 31, 1935."

44. PPA, "The President Prohibits the Export of Arms . . . to Ethiopia and Italy, Proclamation No. 2141, Oct. 5, 1935," plus appended note and two subsequent state-

ments, same date; "Stephen T. Early to [Reporters]," October 4, 1933, in NIXON *FDR & FA*, 3:14–15; AP, "Roosevelt in Touch with African Crisis," *NYT*, October 5, 1935, 6. See also PPA, "Presidential Statement against American Profiteering in Italian-Ethiopian War, Oct. 5, 1935."

45. PPA, "Annual Message to the Congress, Jan. 3, 1936."

46. NIXON *FDR & FA*, 3:150n1, gives a good legislative history of the 1936 act. See also PPA, "A Presidential Statement Renewing His Appeal against Profiteering in the War between Italy and Ethiopia, Feb. 29, 1936," and appended note.

47. DALLEK, 127; *Press Conf* #309 (July 29, 1936), 8:30; "Washington Is Uninformed," *NYT*, July 29, 1936, 2.

48. PPA, "Address at Chautauqua, N.Y., Aug. 14, 1936." Later in the speech, he spoke of defense, noting, "Our closest neighbors are good neighbors. If there are remoter Nations that wish us not good but ill, they know that we are strong; they know that we can and will defend ourselves and defend our neighborhood." The State Department's Phillips annotated this paragraph: "There is something threatening about this. Coming at the end it seems to change the tone of the speech." Roosevelt crossed out the comment. NIXON *FDR & FA*, 3:384n15.

49. PPA, "The Annual Message to the Congress, Jan. 6, 1937"; DALLEK, 135–36. Technically, however, the bill could not be enacted that day because the Senate had adjourned and the bill could not be sent to the White House until the next day—allowing a ship to sail carrying six aircraft sold to the Spanish government. The single negative vote came from a newly elected one-term representative from Minnesota's Mesabi Range, Farmer-Laborite John Toussaint Bernard, on his first day in Congress. His objection was not to the bill, but to the rushed procedure. "Rush by Congress Fails to Stop Ship with Arms Cargo" and "Minnesotan Defends Delaying Neutrality," *NYT*, January 7, 1937, 1, 11.

50. NIXON *FDR & FA*, 3:593. The January 25, 1937, letter was drafted in the State Department.

51. NIXON *FDR & FA*, 2:357, 490–91, 537, 548, 556, 618; 3:62–63, 80–81, 536, which traces the dispute; PPA, "A Letter on the Administration's Policy toward Religious Activities in Mexico, Nov. 13, 1935." See also Cronon, *Josephus Daniels in Mexico,* 82–111.

52. PPA, "Letter to Argentine President Agustín P. Justo Suggesting the Conference, Jan. 30. 1936"; *Press Conf* #320 (September 15, 1936), 8:115, and #325 (November 6, 1936), 144–46.

53. Charles W. Hurd, "Roosevelt Sails on Peace Mission," *NYT*, November 19, 1936, 1.

54. This meeting must have occurred between 1889 and 1891 when Roosevelt was between seven and nine years of age.

55. PPA, "[Formal Address, Rio de Janeiro], Nov. 27, 1936" and "Informal Address at Banquet, Nov. 27, 1936"; "Roosevelt Pledges Peace but Warns 'Aggressors'" and "Roosevelt's Democracy and Smile Please Brazil," *NYT*, November 28, 1936, 1; *FDR Letters,* to ER, November 30, 1936, 3:196.

56. Harold B. Hinton, "Ovation Is City's Biggest," *NYT*, December 1, 1936, 1.

57. *FDR Letters,* to ER, December 2, 1936; "President's Guard Dies in Restaurant," *NYT*, December 22, 1936, 22.

58. "Roosevelt Gives Views at Press Conference with Newspapermen of Buenos Aires" and "Throng Hails President," *NYT,* December 2, 1936, 1.

59. With his knowledge of history, Roosevelt may have been playing off British foreign minister George Canning's 1826 boast that "I called the New World into existence to redress the balance in the old."

60. "Roosevelt Calls on the New World to Unite to Help the Old Avert War," *NYT,* December 2, 1936, 1; PPA, "Address, Buenos Aires, Argentina, Dec. 1, 1936." The authority for the insertion of the religious statement is from the diary of Beatrice Bishop Berle, who attended with her husband and, as a ghostwriter's wife, carefully monitored the reactions to her husband's words. (A. A. Berle and Sumner Welles were the draft's authors.) Adolf A. Berle, *Navigating the Rapids, 1918–1971: From the Papers of Adolf A. Berle,* 120. See also NIXON *FDR & FA,* 3:521n1.

61. "President Justo's Son Seized as Heckler of Roosevelt," *NYT,* December 2, 1936, 23.

62. Berle, *Navigating the Rapids,* 120. NIXON *FDR & FA,* 3:522–23, prints Roosevelt's toast.

63. John W. White, "Argentines Cheer Roosevelt in Rain as He Starts Home," *NYT,* December 3, 1936, 1.

64. Harold B. Hinton, "Roosevelt Hailed in Uruguay at End of His Peace Trip," *NYT,* December 4, 1936, 1; "200,000 Bid Him Farewell," *NYT,* December 4, 1936, 16; PPA, "Address in Montevideo, Uruguay, Dec. 3, 1936."

65. "Text of Saavedra Lamas' Speech," *NYT,* December 5, 1935, 9; John W. White, "Roosevelt's Visit Proved a Godsend, Asserts Saavedra," *NYT,* December 5, 1935, 1.

66. Cordell Hull, *The Memoirs of Cordell Hull,* vol. 1, chap. 35.

67. PPA, "Statement by the President on His Return from the Inter-American Conference, Dec. 16, 1936," and the appended note written some two years later from which the quotation in the text is taken.

68. "President to Give Orders to Build Two Great Warships," *NYT,* December 1, 1936, 1; PPA, "Presidential Statement on Construction of Replacement Capital Ships, Jan. 8, 1937."

Chapter 13. The Battle about the Court

1. Between 1933 and 1937, unemployment declined from perhaps 25 percent of the labor force to about 14 percent. Present-day readers will wonder how a situation in which every seventh worker was unemployed could be called recovery, but that is how it seemed to most contemporaries.

2. PPA, Annual Message . . . Jan. 6, 1937."

3. Turner Catledge, "Roosevelt Calls on Courts to Help Adapt Constitution to Our Needs," *NYT,* January 7, 1937, 1; "Basic Law Change Gains in Congress," *NYT,* January 8, 1937, 1.

4. PPA, "The President Urges Ratification of the Child Labor Amendment, Jan. 7, 1937, 5"; "Roosevelt Pleads on Child Labor Act," *NYT,* January 9, 1937. At the time of the message, twenty-four of the required thirty-six states had ratified. Only three states

responded positively, but the "constitutional revolution" of 1937 made the amendment unnecessary.

5. PPA, "The Annual Budget Message to the Congress, Jan. 7, 1937"; Turner Catledge, "Balanced Budget Next Year Is Promised by Roosevelt," *NYT,* January 9, 1937, 1.

6. "Best Sellers of the Week, Here and Elsewhere," *NYT,* April 20, 1936, 13, and May 18, 1936, 15.

7. Blum, *Years of Crisis,* 1:276–81.

8. Blum, *Roosevelt and Morgenthau,* xii–xiii.

9. Louis Brownlow (1879–1963), of Chicago, was director of the Public Administration Clearing House; his two colleagues were Luther Gulick of New York, director of the Institute of Public Administration, and Charles E. Merriam, who headed the University of Chicago's Department of Political Science. Joseph P. Harris of the Social Science Research Council directed the committee's research staff.

10. In addition to Rayburn, Vice President Garner, Speaker Bankhead, Senators Robinson and Harrison, and Representatives Robert Lee Doughton and James Paul Buchanan attended. All were southerners.

11. PPA, "White House Statement on the Appointment of a Committee to Formulate a Plan for the Reorganization of the Executive Branch of the Government, Mar. 22, 1936"; "Summary of the Report of the Committee on Administrative Management, Jan. 12, 1937," in *Administrative Management in the Government of the United States,* by Louis Brownlow [United States, President's Committee on Administrative Management]; Brownlow, *A Passion for Anonymity,* 383–99. Richard Polenberg, *Reorganizing Roosevelt's Government,* is the standard account.

12. *Press Conf* #336 (January 11, 1937), 9:44–95. A reading of these annual sessions shows an increasingly technically literate Roosevelt.

13. PPA, "A Recommendation for Legislation to Reorganize the Executive Branch of the Government, Jan. 12, 1937." See also "A Summary of the Report of the Committee on Administrative Management Transmitted with the Preceding Message, Jan. 12, 1937."

14. Turner Catledge, "Capital Startled," *NYT,* January 12, 1937, 1. Catledge's analysis found that "the program would involve twelve major changes." See also the AP summary, which had five points, somewhat different from those of the committee: "Roosevelt Plan in Brief," *NYT,* January 12, 1937, 1.

15. Roosevelt's introduction is dated June 3, 1941.

16. Charles W. Hurd, "Downpour Fails to Depress Chief Executive's Spirits or Mar His Big Day," *NYT,* January 21, 1937, 14; "Roosevelt and Family at Special Service Hear Ministers Pray for His Guidance," *NYT,* January 21, 1937, 15.

17. The text in PPA omits the salutation "My Fellow Countrymen." See the Associated Press version in "The Inaugural Address," *NYT,* January 21, 1937, 1.

18. PPA, "The Second Inaugural Address, Jan. 20, 1937"; Arthur Krock, "President Speaks," *NYT,* January 21, 1937, 1; Turner Catledge, "Address Is Praised," *NYT,* January 21, 1937, 1; "Short Waves Carry the President's Speech," *NYT,* January 21, 1937, 16; Rosenman, *Working with Roosevelt,* 143.

19. Gunnar Myrdal, *An American Dilemma: The Negro Problem and Modern Democracy.*

20. "Roosevelts Hosts Thrice in the Day" and "Concert Replaces Inaugural Ball," *NYT,* January 21, 1937, 16; "New Auto Parlay in Capital Fails," *NYT,* January 21, 1937, 1; *Press Conf* #338 (January 22, 1937), 9:99–103; PPA, "An Appeal for Public Aid for American Red Cross Relief Efforts for Flood Sufferers, Proclamation No. 2222, Jan. 23, 1937." The appended note gives a capsule history of flood relief and subsequent actions. "President Mobilizes Army, Navy, Coast Guard, WPA and CCC for Flood Work," *NYT,* January 25, 1937, 1; "President Meets Flood Committee," *NYT,* January 31, 1937, 32.

21. *Press Conf* #338–39 (January 22, 26, 1937), 9:100, 106–7; "President Is Sharp . . . Lewis Is Rebuked," *NYT,* January 23, 1937, 1; Felix Belair Jr., "Roosevelt Rebukes Sloan," *NYT,* January 27, 1937, 1.

22. Apparently, Attorney General Homer Cummings, who had largely devised the plan, was the only other person in the room who had known what was coming. The five were Speaker Bankhead, Senate Majority Leader Robinson, House Majority Leader Rayburn, and the two Judiciary Committee chairs, Senator Henry F. Ashurst (AZ) and Representative Hatton W. Sumners (TX).

23. *Press Conf* #342 (February 4, 1937), 9:130–47; PPA, "The President Presents a Plan for the Reorganization of the Judicial Branch of the Government, Feb. 5, 1937."

24. Turner Catledge, "Roosevelt Asks Power to Reform Courts, Increasing the Supreme Bench to 15 Justices; Congress Startled but Expected to Approve" and "Aim to Pack Court, Declares Hoover," *NYT,* February 6, 1937, 1; Ickes, *Secret Diary,* 2:93; Lowitt, *Persistence of a Progressive,* 1:178–91; Turner Catledge, "Glass, Wheeler Denounce Court Plan, as La Follette Broadcasts in Its Defense," *NYT,* February 14, 1937, 1.

25. Turner Catledge, "Roosevelt Is Firm," *NYT,* February 11, 1937, 1.

26. The other dinners ranged in cost from $1.25 to $50. A dinner for fourteen hundred Young Democrats at the Willard Hotel was only $10 and included a visit from Eleanor, who came over from the Mayflower. "Hail 'Happy Days' at Victory Dinner," *NYT,* March 5, 1937, 15.

27. Turner Catledge, "President Puts Court Plan on Basis of Party Loyalty," *NYT,* March 5, 1937, 1; "Roosevelt Asks That Nation Trust Him in Court Move," *NYT,* March 10, 1937, 1; PPA, "Address at the Democratic Victory Dinner, Washington, D.C., Mar. 4, 1937" and "A Fireside Chat, Washington, D.C., Mar. 9, 1937." The president left Washington on March 12 and returned on the 27th.

28. The best explication of the details of the Court fight is in Marian McKenna, *Franklin Roosevelt and the Great Constitutional War: The Court-Packing Crisis of 1937.* For the Wheeler-Hughes episode, see 367–78, 388, 406–7, 440.

29. Turner Catledge, "Hughes against Court Plan; Wheeler Says It Originated with 'Young Men' Last Year," *NYT,* March 23, 1937, 1. Hughes's letter was also printed there.

30. *West Coast Hotel v. Parrish,* 300 U.S. 379 (1937).

31. *Adkins* was a landmark case supporting extreme laissez-faire views, from which even conservative chief justice Taft had dissented. *Adkins v. Children's Hospital,* 261 U.S. 525 (1923).

32. William E. Leuchtenburg, "Charles Evans Hughes: The Center Holds."

33. Freidel, *Rendezvous with Destiny,* 235.

34. Turner Catledge, "Foes of Court Bill Insist That Roosevelt Aids Their Cause," *NYT,* May 16, 1937, 1; "Court Bill Pilots Seek Compromise on 2 New Justices," *NYT,* May 21, 1937, 1.

35. Turner Catledge, "A New Deal Foe: Conservative Writes to President He Will Quit," *NYT,* May 19, 1937, 1. The exchange of letters between Van Devanter and the president is on the same page. See, for example, Roosevelt's remarks after the Court recessed for the summer in *Press Conf* #371 (June 4, 1937), 9:408–13.

36. The crucial note on the Court fight is in the 1939 volume of Roosevelt's *Public Papers* published after his third-term reelection: "(For an account of the Supreme Court fight of 1937, see introductions to 1935 and 1937 volumes, items 2 (page 9), 11, 17 (pages 74–77), 30, 31, 40 (pages 153–56), 54 (pages 204–5), 58 (pages 220–21), 71 (pages 263–64), 89, 91 (pages 310–12) 1937 volume; and Item 105, this volume)." Item 105 is "President's Statement on Attaining the Objectives of the Court Fight of 1937, Aug. 7, 1937." The preface to the 1939 volume is dated July 10, 1941.

37. James T. Patterson, *Congressional Conservatism and the New Deal: The Growth of the Congressional Coalition in Congress, 1933–1939.*

38. "Island 'Harmony' Lures Democrats," *NYT,* June 25, 1937, 1; "Roosevelt Is Coatless as He Greets His Guests," *NYT,* June 27, 1937, 20. The *Times* ran at least fourteen other stories about the affair in the next four days.

39. Many accounts of Robinson's death stress the oppressive Washington summer heat. The Senate and House chambers were air-conditioned by 1929, the rest of the Capitol by 1935. William C. Allen, *History of the United States Capitol,* 401–3. Some historians make much of the fact that Roosevelt did not go the Arkansas funeral without noting that the president and the entire cabinet attended an earlier funeral in the Senate chamber.

40. Polly Davis, *Alben Barkley: Senate Majority Leader and Vice President;* Swain, *Pat Harrison.*

41. Joseph A. McCartin, "The New Deal Era," in *The Oxford Companion to United States History,* edited by Paul Boyer. Perhaps the most nuanced exposition of this general point of view is Alan Brinkley, *The End of Reform: New Deal Liberalism in Recession and War.*

42. For the first four years, net receipts from the balls were as follows: 1934, $1,003,173; 1935, $750,856; 1936, $572,756; and 1937, $952,293. "Publishers United to Fight Paralysis," *NYT,* November 15, 1937, 24.

43. "Nation Will Honor Roosevelt Jan. 30," *NYT,* December 23, 1936, N2; "President Thanks Millions for Gifts," *NYT,* January 31, 1937, 39; "Birthday Ball Total $1,090,779," *NYT,* September 15, 1937, 25; "$1,000,000 Advertising Promoted Birthday Ball," *NYT,* February 12, 1936, 2; "Endowment Sought for Warm Springs," *NYT,* December 17, 1936, 12.

44. PPA, "Radio Address on the Occasion of the President's Fourth Birthday Ball, Jan. 30, 1937"; "Confer on Paralysis; Roosevelt and Group Discuss Methods to Combat Disease," *NYT,* January 9, 1937, 15.

45. PPA, "Presidential Statement on the New National Foundation for Infantile Paralysis, Sept. 23, 1937"; "Roosevelt Starts Drive on Paralysis," *NYT,* September 23, 1937, 3. For the meeting with O'Connor and Morgan, see *Press Conf* #399 (September

21, 1937), 10:215–18. The name was first used in a statement released on November 24. "To Lead Paralysis Drive," *NYT*, November 25, 1937, 5.

46. "Birthday Fetes Set for President," *NYT*, November 8, 1937, 8, contains a letter, not in PPA, that seems not to have been used by previous scholars. See Oshinsky, *Polio: An American Story*, 52–53. Roosevelt's letter approved suggestions made in a letter to him from O'Connor, naming the ad hoc group "the Committee for the Celebration of the President's Birthday for Fighting Infantile Paralysis," with Keith Morgan as chair and W. Averell Harriman, George E. Allen, Marshall Field, and Edsel Ford among the members.

Chapter 14. Roosevelt's Recession

1. It must be remembered that in the 1930s, public housing was largely for poor white people who had to have enough income to pay the subsidized rents.

2. PPA, "Federal Housing Projects Are Transferred to the United States Housing Authority, EO 7732, Oct. 27, 1937," and appended note; "Billion in Low-Rent Housing Work over 4 Years Projected for Nation," *NYT*, February 25, 1937, 1; Huthmacher, *Senator Robert F. Wagner*, 224–30; Richard Sterner, *The Negro's Share: A Study of Income, Consumption, Housing, and Public Assistance*, 310–23. For a comprehensive survey, see Radford, *Modern Housing for America*.

3. PPA, "Address on Constitution Day, Washington, D.C., Sept. 17, 1937"; Robert P. Post, "Roosevelt Renews Fight," *NYT*, September 18, 1937, 1.

4. PPA, "The President Urges Legislation to Prevent Tax Evasion, June 1, 1937"; Blum, *Roosevelt and Morgenthau*, 171.

5. The original 1935 coal act had been struck down in May 1936 in *Carter v. Carter*, 298 U.S. 239 (1936). For the commission, see PPA, "The Bituminous Coal Code Is Promulgated, EO 7040, June 21, 1937," and the appended note.

6. The pioneering scholarly account is Robert Zangrando, *The NAACP Crusade against Lynching, 1909–1950*. Huthmacher, *Senator Robert F. Wagner*, 171–74, 238–43, adds details of the congressional struggle. The chapter on lynching in N. Weiss, *Farewell to the Party of Lincoln*, 96–119, is a convenient and astute summary. See also the several discussions of antilynching in volume 2 of Cook, *Eleanor Roosevelt*.

7. Walter White, *A Man Called White: The Autobiography of Walter White*, 166–73.

8. Huthmacher, *Senator Robert F. Wagner*, 173. Their bills were favorably reported out of the Judiciary Committee, which had few southern members.

9. "Lynchers Torture, Burn Two Negroes," *NYT*, April 14, 1937, 52; "Anti-lynching Bill Passed by House after Bitter Talk," *NYT*, April 16, 1937, 1.

10. "Negro for Federal Judge," *NYT*, February 6, 1936, 9. Hastie had been appointed an assistant solicitor of the Interior Department by Harold Ickes, who worked to secure confirmation of his judgeship. It was in the Virgin Islands and was for a four-year term rather than lifetime tenure. See also Gilbert Ware, *William Hastie: Grace under Pressure*.

11. For his own account, see *Press Conf* #391 (August 13, 1937), 10:156–57.

12. Article I, Section 6.

13. Russell B. Porter, "Alabama Aware of Black's Ties," *NYT*, September 13, 1937, 3; "Black Ouster Now Is Held Impossible," *NYT*, September 14, 1937, 18. The *Pittsburgh*

Post-Gazette stories won a Pulitzer Prize for its author Raymond Sprigle in 1938. It provided clear proof of Black's membership from 1923 to 1925. But Sprigle made a meal of the evidence he had. His lead paragraph read: "Hugo L. Black, Associate Justice of the Supreme Court, is a member of the hooded brotherhood that for 10 long, blood-drenched years ruled the Southland with lash and noose and torch, the Invisible Empire, Knights of the Ku Klux Klan. He holds his membership in the masked and oath-bound legion as he holds his office on the nation's supreme tribunal—for life." After he had resigned from the Klan before his 1926 election campaign, Black was given a "grand passport" at a meeting celebrating his primary victory. It said nothing about life membership but had no expiration date. There was no evidence produced to show any membership or other Klan association after his election. Many of his public actions, including support for the Catholic Al Smith in the 1928 presidential election, were counter to Klan policies. The Sprigle text is from Black's *NYT* obituary, September 25, 1971, 1.

14. David M. O'Brien writes confidently that "Roosevelt must have known" that Black was a former Klansman but cites as evidence only a statement written by Black in 1968, which tells of a lunch the Alabaman had with the president at which Roosevelt joshed about and downplayed the significance of Klan membership. What O'Brien does not reveal is that the lunch, during which the president presented him with his engrossed commission, was on August 19, 1937, by which time allegations about Black's membership were common currency. "The Nation . . . Mr. Justice Black," *NYT*, August 22, 1937, E1. See also O'Brien, *Storm Center: The Supreme Court in American Politics,* 70; and Roger K. Newman, *Hugo Black: A Biography,* 243–44. The latter contains the most detailed account of the controversy over Black's appointment.

15. *Press Conf* #399 (September 21, 1937), 10:219–23. Most unusually, the following comment is included in the midst of the discussion of the Black affair: "(By instructions, no notes were taken of about five minutes of discussion off the record.)" (221).

16. Russell B. Porter, "Jovial at Norfolk," *NYT*, September 30, 1937, 1; "Black Admits He Joined the Klan," "Bar Asks Inquiries of Future Judges," and "Justice Black's Speech," *NYT*, October 2, 1937, 1; "Nation's Press Almost United in Denouncing Black's Speech," *NYT*, October 3, 1937, 2.

17. "Justice Black on Bench as High Court Receives Protests on Seating Him," *NYT*, October 5, 1937, 1; "Black Suit Barred by Supreme Court," *NYT*, October 12, 1937, 1. The quotation is from his *ANB* biography by Norman Dorsen and Sarah Barringer Gordon.

18. Thomas Babbington Macaulay, English historian (1800–1859).

19. PPA, "Address at Roanoke Island, N.C., Aug. 18, 1937"; Robert P. Post, "Program Upheld," *NYT*, August 19, 1937, 1. The *New York Times* noted a rare grammatical error in the speech, and, when the speech was printed in PPA, Rosenman and Roosevelt silently made the correction. "The Nation . . . Democracy Defended," *NYT*, August 22, 1937, E1.

20. PPA, "Labor Day Statement by the President, Sept. 5, 1937"; Robert P. Post, "Both Sides Erred in Recent Strikes, Roosevelt Says," *NYT*, September 5, 1937, 1.

21. *Romeo and Juliet,* act 3, scene 1: Mercutio, dying.

22. "Text of John L. Lewis's Radio Talk," *NYT*, September 4, 1937, 6; "Lewis Warns the President to Back C.I.O. or Face Bolt," *NYT*, September 4, 1936, 1. In Chicago's

Memorial Day massacre, ten were shot dead and perhaps fifty wounded; in Massillon, Ohio, two were shot dead, fifteen wounded; Ford's "servicemen" administered severe beatings as Dearborn police watched, but killed no one. Among those bloodied was Walter Reuther (1907–70). An outraged contemporary account is Paul Y. Anderson, "Armed Rebellion on the Right." See also Jerold S. Auerbach, *Labor and Liberty: The La Follette Committee and the New Deal.*

23. "Green Defends President" and "Miss Perkins Sees Nation Advanced by Labor's Gains," *NYT,* September 6, 1937, 14, 1; "Lewis Urges Labor to Help Rule Plants," *NYT,* September 7, 1937, 3.

24. Two think pieces by Louis Stark, "Labor Listing Its Gains, Ponders Its Future" and "Two Labor Strategies Now Clearly Defined," *NYT,* September 5, 1937, 3, 6, are useful. I. Bernstein, *Turbulent Years,* remains the best scholarly account.

25. Robert P. Post, "Roosevelt Starts Tour to Northwest," *NYT,* September 23, 2937, 1; Delbert Clark, "Roosevelt on His Trip Starts No Reprisals," *NYT,* September 26, 1937, 65; Robert P. Post, "President Tells of His 'Planning' for a Better Nation," *NYT,* September 28, 1937, 1; "Roosevelt Omits Wheeler's Name in Montana Talks," *NYT,* October 4, 1937, 1; PPA, "Informal Extemporaneous Remarks at Boise, Idaho, Sept. 27, 1937"; "Dust Bowl Refugees Hired," *NYT,* September 28, 1937, 2; Robert P. Post, "Roosevelt Omits Wheeler's Name in Montana Talks," *NYT,* October 4. 1937, 1. See Moscow's bylined stories on September 23, 25, 26, 28, 29, and October 4.

26. Richard Neuberger, "Roosevelt Goes to See," *NYT Magazine,* September 26, 1937, 17–20; PPA, "Address at Bonneville Dam, Oregon, Sept. 28, 1937," 1; Robert P. Post, "Roosevelt Says Budget Will Be Balanced in 1939," *NYT,* September 29, 1937, 1; Warren Moscow, "Roosevelt Speech Hits Popular Key," *NYT,* September 229, 1937, 17; "The WPA Story: FDR, Its Workers and Its Great Northwest Projects," *Seattle Times,* March 18, 2008, D1.

27. Robert P. Post, "Roosevelt Gives Day to His Family," *NYT,* September 30, 1937, 4; "Victoria Throngs Greet Roosevelt," *NYT,* October 1, 1937, 1; Frank Freidel, "Franklin D. Roosevelt in the Northwest: Informal Glimpses," 127; *Press Conf #399-A* (September 30, 1937), 10:231, and #400 (October 6, 1937), 233.

28. "Mrs. Roosevelt Flies East," *NYT,* October 1, 1937, 12. Long quotation of John Boettiger is printed in Freidel, "Roosevelt in the Northwest," 126–28.

29. Nixon, *Roosevelt and Conservation,* 2:130–31; Brandt, *Adventures in Conservation;* Freidel, "Roosevelt in the Northwest," 127–29.

30. PPA, "Informal Extraneous Remarks at Grand Coulee Dam, Oct. 2, 1937"; Robert P. Post, "Roosevelt Hails a 'Promised Land,'" *NYT,* October 3, 1937, 1. The availability of Columbia River power made Hanford, Washington, an atomic factory in the same way that TVA power made possible the facility at Oak Ridge, Tennessee. Hanford became—and remains for the foreseeable future—the most dangerous contaminated radioactive site in the United States. In a project running from 1966 to 1974, initiated in the Johnson administration, Grand Coulee was significantly enlarged and is now more than a mile in length.

31. PPA, "Informal Extemporaneous Remarks at Fort Peck, Montana, Oct. 3, 1937," "Address at Grand Forks, North Dakota, Oct. 4, 1937," and "Address at St. Paul, Minnesota, Oct. 4, 1937."

32. DALLEK, 147–48; Dorothy Borg, "Notes on Roosevelt's Quarantine Speech."

33. PPA, "Address at Chicago, Oct. 5, 1937."

34. "Nationwide Press Comment on President's Address," *NYT*, October 6, 1937, 17.

35. PPA, "Radio Address at Dinner of Foreign Policy Association, New York, N.Y., Oct. 21, 1944."

36. "Knox Praises Speech," *NYT*, October 6, 1937, 19.

37. W. Cole, *Roosevelt and the Isolationists,* 243.

38. *Press Conf* #400 (October 6. 1937), 10:232–52.

39. PPA, "A 'Fireside Chat,' Oct. 12, 1937"; "No Leap into War," *NYT*, October 13, 1937, 1. For Roosevelt's comment about "little TVAs," see *Press Conf* #400 (October 6, 1937), 10:237–39. For the never-realized plan, see Leuchtenburg. "Roosevelt, Norris, and the 'Seven Little TVAs,'" in *FDR Years,* 159–95.

40. PPA, "A 'Fireside Chat' Discussing Legislation to Be Recommended to the Extraordinary Session of the Congress, Oct. 12, 1937."

41. Blum's chapter "Recession, 1937–1938" is a good account of Morgenthau's role during the recession (*Roosevelt and Morgenthau,* 172–209).

42. "Stocks Off 2 to 15 in Heavy Selling," *NYT*, October 19, 1937, 1; "Stock Prices Up Sharply after Drop to New Lows," *NYT*, October 20, 1937, 1; Blum, *Years of Crisis,* 1:386.

43. PPA, "The Message to the Extraordinary Session of the Congress Recommending Certain Legislation, Nov. 15, 1937." Roosevelt, claiming that he had called attention to some of the problems, cited an economist who argued that recovery depended more on business than on government.

44. Kenneth D. Roose, "The Depression of 1937–38," 240. Many historians, citing Roose's account, assume that Roosevelt and others were aware of the recession as soon as it began, but that was not the case.

45. Robert Lekachman, *The Age of Keynes,* is a classic account. For presidential economics, see Herbert Stein, *Presidential Economics: The Making of Economic Policy from Roosevelt to Clinton.* For more recent presidents, see the journalism and scholarship of Paul Krugman.

46. Gene Smiley, *Rethinking the Great Depression,* is a good scholarly example. Amity Shlaes, *The Forgotten Man: A New History of the Great Depression,* is meretricious.

47. Keynes, letter to Roosevelt, February 1, 1938, FDRL, cited in Howard Zinn, ed., *New Deal Thought,* 404–9.

48. "It was very pleasant and encouraging to know that you are in agreement with so much of the Administration's economic program. This confirmation coming from so eminent an economist is indeed welcome. Your analysis . . . is very interesting. The emphasis you put upon . . . housing . . . is well placed" (Blum, *Roosevelt and Morgenthau,* 187).

49. The *Oxford English Dictionary* gives the first such citation as 1942 in *Fortune.*

50. PPA, "The Message to the Extraordinary Session of the Congress Recommending Certain Legislation, Nov. 15, 1937"; *Press Conf* #411 (November 23, 1937), 10:364–65; PPA, "A Message to Congress on Highways and Roads, Nov. 27, 1937," and appended note, and "A Recommendation for Legislation to Encourage Private Construction of Housing, Nov. 27, 1937."

51. "Drive Is Extended for Paralysis Aid," *NYT*, November 29, 1937, 24; "To Lead Paralysis Drive," *NYT*, November 25, 1937, 5. Political figures included James V. Forrestal and George E. Allen, while philanthropists included Marshall Field, Edsel Ford, Jeremiah Milbank, and Robert Woodruff of Coca-Cola; W. Averill Harriman fits either. "Publishers Unite to Fight Paralysis," *NYT*, November 15, 1937, 24.

52. PPA, "Memorandum to the Secretary of State on the Bombing of the *S.S. Panay*, Dec. 13, 1937," and attached note; *Press Conf* #416–18, #420 (December 14, 21, 31, 1937), 10:409–10, 416, 425–26, 440–41; DALLEK, 153–57; "Nye Blames Roosevelt for Loss of Our Gunboat," *NYT*, December 14, 1937, 23; "Congress Closes," *NYT*, December 22, 1937, 1.

53. PPA, 1937, xlvii.

54. The final national income figures in billions are 1932, $42.5; 1937, $73.6. For 1941 it would be $104.7 and had been $87.8 in 1929. U.S. Department of Commerce, *Historical Statistics of the United States*, Series F7.

55. PPA, "Annual Message to Congress, Jan. 3, 1938"; "Roosevelt Asks Capital and Labor to Cooperate in National Recovery" and "Big Navy Speeded," *NYT*, January 4, 1938, 1.

56. PPA, "The Annual Budget Message, Jan. 3, 1938"; *Press Conf* #421 (January 4, 1938), 11:12–13.

57. PPA, "The President States His Views on the Proposed Referendum to Declare War, Jan. 6, 1938"; Bertram D. Hulen, "Ludlow War Referendum Is Defeated in the House as Roosevelt Scores It," *NYT*, January 11, 1938, 1; W. Cole, *Roosevelt and the Isolationists*, 253–62.

58. PPA, "Address at the Jackson Day Dinner, Washington, D.C., Jan. 8, 1938."

59. "Hill, New Dealer [Wins] Seat Vacated by Black," *NYT*, January 5, 1938, 1; Felix Belair Jr., "7 Governors Act," *NYT*, January 8, 1938, 1. Hill actually succeeded Dixie Bibb Graves, the wife of Alabama's governor, who had been appointed as a placeholder until a special election could be held.

60. "Sutherland Quits Supreme Court," *NYT*, January 6, 1938, 1; "Both Parties Join in Praise of Reed," *NYT*, January 16, 1938, 36. For a general evaluation of court appointments, see C. Herman Pritchett, *The Roosevelt Court: A Study in Judicial Politics and Values, 1937–1947*.

61. "Jackson to Become Solicitor General as Reed Quits Post," *NYT*, January 22, 1938, 1; "Jackson Is Named Solicitor General," *NYT*, January 28, 1938, 1; "People Rule Court Jackson Asserts," *NYT*, February 11, 1938, 6; Robert H. Jackson, *That Man: An Insider's Portrait of Franklin D. Roosevelt*, 151–52.

62. There are various versions of the "breeches" story. One of the most elaborate is in Michael R. Beschloss, *Kennedy and Roosevelt: The Uneasy Alliance*, 152–57.

63. PPA, "The President Recommends Increased Armaments for Defense, Jan. 28, 1938," and appended note.

64. Bertram D. Hulen, "Vinson Offers Bill," *NYT*, January 29, 1938, 1; "Text of Vinson Bill to Enlarge Navy," *NYT*, January 29, 1938, 4; "New Navy Bill Is Signed," *NYT*, May 18, 1938, 8.

65. "Dimes Are Sought in Paralysis Drive," *NYT*, January 24, 1938, 23; PPA, "Radio Address on the Occasion of the President's Fifth Birthday Ball for the Benefit of Crippled Children, Jan. 29, 1938." See also Oshinsky, *Polio: An American Story*, 53–54.

66. Ingrid Winther Scobie, *Center Stage: Helen Gahagan Douglas, a Life.*

67. "Housing Bill Wins by Only Two Votes," *NYT*, February 6, 1938, 6; PPA, "A Recommendation Extending Financial Assistance for Home Builders, Feb. 7, 1938," and appended note; James S. Olson, *Saving Capitalism: The Reconstruction Finance Corporation and the New Deal, 1933–1940*, 196. Olson fails to connect Fannie Mae to the Housing Act proposed early in 1937 and thus assumes that it was created as part of a recession-fighting project. When the housing bubble burst in 2008 and "Fannie Mae," along with "Freddie Mac," a similar federal creation of 1970, became "insolvent government enterprises," the two owned or guaranteed about half of the U.S. mortgage market, then valued at $12 trillion.

68. "Market Controls Set in Farm Bill," *NYT*, February 15, 1938, 6; PPA, "Presidential Statement on Signing the Agricultural Adjustment Act of 1938, Feb. 16, 1938," and appended note; "Farm Bill Signed," *NYT*, February 17, 1938, 1; Saloutos, *American Farmer*, 236–53, quote on 270.

69. "Farmer Opinions on the Best and Worst Parts of the New Deal," July 12, 1938, as cited in Saloutos, *American Farmer*, 245–46.

70. PPA, "A Request for Supplemental Appropriations for Unemployment Relief, Feb. 12, 1938"; Felix Belair Jr., "President to Ask More Relief Funds before Week Ends," *NYT*, February 9, 1938, 1; Belair, "250,000,000 More Is Set for Relief," *NYT*, February 11, 1938, 1; "$250,000,000 Asked for Added Relief," *NYT*, February 11, 1938, 1.

71. Williams was acting for the seriously ill Hopkins. "WPA Chief Pleads for $250,000,000 to Care for 950,000," *NYT*, February 12, 1938, 1; "Votes $250 Million to Augment Relief," *NYT*, February 17, 1938, 10; "$250,000,000 Is Held Ample Now by WPA," *NYT*, February 18, 1938, 11; "$250,000,000 Relief Is Voted by Senate," *NYT*, February 24, 1938, 4; "WPA Begins Hiring," *NYT*, March 5, 1937, 21. For a franker statement of Williams's view, see his "Twelve Million Unemployed: What Can Be Done?," *NYT Magazine*, March 27, 1938, 3, 13. Curiously, most historical narratives dealing with the 1937–38 recession fail to mention this episode, leaving the impression that Roosevelt took no significant action about the recession until his mid-April actions discussed below. See also Leuchtenburg, *Roosevelt and the New Deal*, 244–46, 248–50, 256.

72. PPA, "Recommending Credit for Borrowers to Help Employment, Feb. 18, 1938," and appended note; Rodney Bean, "Jones Opens Funds," *NYT*, February 19, 1938, 1; Olson, *Saving Capitalism*, 187–215, dollar amounts on 204–5.

73. Felix Belair Jr., "Roosevelt Leaves for Warm Springs Visit," *NYT*, March 23, 1938, 1.

74. Pinchot had once been polished off by Theodore Roosevelt, who wrote him that "when I spoke of the Progressive Party having a lunatic fringe, I had you, specifically, in mind."

75. Lauren D. Lyman, "Senate Acts Today on Reorganization; Protests Pour In," *NYT*, March 28, 1938, 1; "Wide Power Given," *NYT*, March 29, 1938, 1; Polenberg, *Reorganizing Roosevelt's Government*, devotes a chapter to Gannett's committee.

76. *Press Conf* #446 (March 29, 1938), 11:260.

77. Hopkins memoranda in Dean L. May, *From the New Deal to the New Economics*, 129–34.

78. Briefing described in Robert J. Sandilands, *The Life and Political Economy of Lauchlin Currie*, 91–92.

79. Morgenthau's diaries are the source for the quotations. Blum has provided two similar versions: *Roosevelt and Morgenthau,* 194–209; and *Years of Crisis,* 1:417–26.

80. PPA, "Recommendations to the Congress Designed to Stimulate Further Recovery," Apr. 14, 1936," and appended note and tables.

81. PPA, "Fireside Chat on Present Economic Conditions," April 14, 1938.

82. "Press Is Critical of President Roosevelt's Spending Proposal," *NYT,* April 15, 1938, 13; "Bankers Question Expansion Wisdom," "Congress Divided," and Turner Catledge, "War on Recession," *NYT,* April 15, 1938, 1.

83. Turner Catledge, "Congress Adjourns Sine Die," *NYT,* June 17, 1938, 1.

84. The tone was set by the eight-page segment "Roosevelt as an Economist," in which James MacGregor Burns gives the president's performance during the 1937–38 recession an "F," likening him to "a child in a playroom running from toy to toy" (*Lion and the Fox,* 328–36).

85. This is based on an electronic search of presidential documents. A Kennedy commencement address at Yale showed the influence of his Keynesian economic adviser, Walter Heller, but the dreaded word was not used. The fact is, of course, that every president after Calvin Coolidge has practiced deficit spending. "Commencement Address at Yale University, Jun. 11, 1962," in *Kennedy Public Papers.*

Chapter 15. Economic Progress, Political Setback

1. See Polenberg, *Reorganizing Roosevelt's Government,* 125–80, for a detailed analysis of the fate of the 1938 bill. A fuller treatment will be found in the next chapter.

2. Huthmacher, *Senator Robert F. Wagner,* 238–43; Lowitt, *Triumph of a Progressive,* 226; *Press Conf* #444 (March 22, 1938), 11:245–46; "President Wants Lynching Inquiries," *NYT,* March 23, 1938, 4. For the Talmadge correspondence, see the original letter of Talmadge to Roosevelt, February 13, 1935, and associated documents, Hopkins Papers, FDRL. See also A. Schlesinger, *Coming of the New Deal,* 274, 612n7.

3. "New Wages Bill Will Go to House," *NYT,* January 12, 1938, 1; *Press Conf* #434 (April 26, 1938), 11:392; "President Pushes Wage Bill Passage," *NYT,* April 27, 1938, 1; PPA, "Urging That the Congress Be Permitted to Vote on the Wages and Hours Bill, Apr. 30, 1938"; "218 Sign in a Rush," *NYT,* May 7, 1938; Louis Stark, "Conferees Reach Unanimous Truce on Pay-Hour Bill," *NYT,* June 12, 1938, 1; Freidel, *Rendezvous with Destiny,* 281.

4. PPA, "The President Recommends Legislation Establishing Minimum Wages and Maximum Hours, May 24, 1937." The long note to this message is a history of wages and hours legislation going back to 1918. Freidel, *Rendezvous with Destiny,* 281.

5. Huthmacher, for example, writes that "in its final form disappointed many of its keenest proponents" and minimizes its impact (*Senator Robert F. Wagner,* 246–47).

6. *Press Conf* #440 (March 8, 1937), 11:216–19.

7. What we now call boxer shorts.

8. Lilienthal, *Journals of Lilienthal,* 69–75, quotes from entries dated March 3, 7, 1938.

9. On leaving the White House, Lilienthal met Secretary Hull, who told him, "Well, I have had quite a day too; Germany has just taken over Austria" (ibid., entry of March 11, 1938, 1:74).

10. PPA, "The President Transmits to the Congress the Record of the Removal of the Chairman of the Tennessee Valley Authority, Mar. 23, 1938," and appended note. The president's right to make such a removal was upheld in *Morgan v. Tennessee Valley Authority* (28 *Fed Supp.* 732) (August 11, 1938), upheld by the Sixth Circuit (115 *Fed* [2d] 990) (December 6, 1940); the Supreme Court denied certiorari on March 17, 1941. For the 1937 case, see "The Case of the Contentious Commissioner," in Leuchtenburg, *Supreme Court Reborn,* 52–81.

11. For an analysis of Roosevelt's popularity that spring, see Polenberg, *Reorganizing Roosevelt's Government,* 146–61.

12. Blum, *Roosevelt and Morgenthau,* 158–61; PPA, "Address at Arthurdale, West Virginia, May 27, 1938"; Felix Belair Jr., "Roosevelt Scores Tax Bill," *NYT,* May 28, 1938, 1. For Arthurdale and the community program, see Conkin, *Tomorrow a New World.*

13. The copperhead is a venomous snake (*Agkistrodon contortrix*) common in the United States. Beginning in 1862, the term was applied to Northern supporters of the Confederacy.

14. He also admitted error in the introduction to the 1938 volume of his *Public Papers:* PPA, 1938, *The Continuing Struggle for Liberalism,* xxiii.

15. PPA, "Fireside Chat, June 24, 1938." Clinton Rossiter, *The American Presidency,* the classic formulation of the multirole presidency, used Franklin Roosevelt as the chief exemplar and identified ten roles.

16. Purges by both Hitler and Stalin in the mid-1930s that usually meant death for the victims brought the word into relatively wide general use.

17. Arthur Krock, "The Political Problem of the South," *NYT,* January 14, 1938, 22; PPA, "Address at Madison Square Garden, Oct. 31, 1936."

18. Roland M. Jones, "Real Senate Race in Iowa Started by Hopkins," *NYT,* May 28, 1938, 44; *Press Conf* #462 (May 31, 1938), 11:439, and #464 (June 7, 1938), 451. Comparative voting records from Jerry Harrington, "Senator Guy Gillette Foils the Execution Committee," an essay without notes. David M. Kennedy names Gillette as a Roosevelt purge target (*Freedom from Fear: The American People in Depression and War,* 422).

19. *Press Conf* #472 (July 5, 1938), 12:10. For example, see Charles R. Michael, "Garner Won't Run for a Third Term; Senators See a Hint to Roosevelt," *NYT,* July 5, 1938, 1.

20. PPA, "A Greeting to the National Association for the Advancement of Colored People, June 25, 1938." This was the first such greeting by Roosevelt; a similar one was sent on June 13, 1939, and none sent after that. The only prior message had been sent by Herbert Hoover on May 18, 1932. Harry Truman was the first president to appear at an NAACP convention on June 29, 1947, and every subsequent president has recognized the organization in some way. Hoover spoke of the "colored race," Roosevelt of the "Negro race."

21. PPA, ". . . Address at Covington, Kentucky, July 8, 1938; Felix Belair Jr., "'Not Interfering,'" *NYT,* July 9, 1938, 1.

22. Felix Belair Jr., "Roosevelt Lands; To Resume Purge," *NYT,* August 10, 1938, 1. Although Belair's story stated explicitly that if Roosevelt did what his "associates" were predicting, it would be the "first time that the quiescent 'purge' of refractory elements of the Democratic party is brought into the open," the *Times* headline writers wrote "To Resume Purge." Most historians have followed the headlines rather than the story.

23. PPA, "Address at Barnesville, Georgia, Aug. 11, 1938." Felix Belair Jr., "Roosevelt Asks Defeat of George and Talmadge as Foes of Liberalism," *NYT,* August 12, 1938, 1, indicates that George had his remarks written out. Roosevelt had endorsed Camp at a luncheon at Warm Springs the day before. "Move Is a Surprise," *NYT,* August 11, 1938, 1. William Anderson, *The Wild Man from Sugar Creek: The Political Career of Eugene Talmadge,* 172–75, cites a 1971 interview with Lawrence W. (Chip) Robert, a Roosevelt insider who was treasurer of the Democratic Party, saying that Roosevelt would have preferred an ineffective Talmadge in the Senate to an influential George.

24. PPA, "Informal, Extemporaneous Remarks at Greenville, South Carolina, Aug. 11, 1938"; "President Appeals to South Carolina," *NYT,* August 12, 1938, 4.

25. Felix Belair Jr., "Roosevelt Puts O'Connor and Tydings on Purge List," *NYT,* August 14, 1938, 1; "Roosevelt Urges Defeat of O'Connor and Tydings," *NYT,* August 17, 1938, 1.

26. PPA, "Radio Address on the Third Anniversary of the Social Security Act, Washington, D.C., Aug. 15, 1938." After each of his defeats in Senate races, Lewis received a patronage appointment: Wilson put him on the U.S. Tariff Commission in 1917, and Roosevelt named him to the National Mediation Board in 1939.

27. *Press Conf* #476 (August 16, 1938), 12:24–27; "Fay, New Deal Ally, to Fight O'Connor," *NYT,* August 12, 1938, 1; "O'Connor Sees Red Trend," *NYT,* August 12, 1938, 4; Richard Polenberg, "Franklin Roosevelt and the Purge of John O'Connor: The Impact of Urban Change on Political Parties"; James A. Hagerty, "President Wants Fay Nominated, White House Says," *NYT,* September 18, 1938, 1.

28. Anderson, *Wild Man,* 181. For an analysis of the complexities of the South Carolina primary, see David Robertson, *Sly and Able: A Political Biography of James F. Byrnes,* 271–74; and "Tydings Lead Increases," *NYT,* September 14, 1938, 18.

29. "Republicans Find Cheer in Kentucky," *NYT,* August 9, 1938, 2.

30. Polenberg, "Purge of John O'Connor," 325. Fay was aided by Mayor La Guardia's active campaigning and his arranging an American Labor Party nomination for him. Fay got more than five thousand votes on the ALP line, more than twice his margin of victory. After unseating O'Connor, he won reelection in 1940, lost in 1942, and won again in 1944. New York's governor, Thomas E. Dewey, accused him of being familiar with the notorious gangster Frank Costello. During his six years in the House, he had no visible impact on significant legislation. "Dewey Says Issue Is Tammany Rule," *NYT,* October 29, 1943, 1; "James H. Fay Dies, Ex-Representative," *NYT,* September 10, 1948, 23.

31. Burns, *Lion and the Fox,* 346; David M. Kennedy, *Freedom from Fear: The American People in Depression and War,* 349. Each is highly selective in his electoral analysis. Burns notes McAdoo's loss in California to a maverick Sheridan Downey but ignores the triumph of Culbert Olson, who became, with Roosevelt's endorsement, California's first Democratic governor in the twentieth century, while Kennedy says, "Rooseveltian liberals fell like dead timber before the rising conservative wind," noting the defeat of New Deal liberal Maury Maverick in one House race in Texas while ignoring Lyndon Johnson's victory in another (348).

32. Polenberg, *Reorganizing Roosevelt's Government,* 181; Brownlow, *A Passion for Anonymity.*

33. Bureau of Labor Statistics data describe annual average unemployment as a percentage of the labor force. The figures before 1940 are so "iffy," to use a favorite Roosevelt expression, that I am reluctant to put them in a chart. 1933, 24.9; 1934, 21.7; 1935, 20.1; 1936, 17.0; 1937, 14.3; 1938, 19.0; 1939, 17.2; 1940, 14.6; and 1941, 9.9. Robert VanGiezen and Albert E. Schwenk, "Compensation from before World War I through the Great Depression," *Compensation and Working Conditions* (Fall 2001), available on the Bureau of Labor Statistics website, March 2009.

34. *Press Conf #458* (May 13, 1938), 11:413.

35. PPA, "Radio Address on the Election of Liberals, Nov. 4, 1938."

36. PPA, "A Request for a Report by the National Economic Council on the Problems and Needs of the South, June 22, 1938" and "A Message to the Conference on Economic Conditions of the South, July 4 1938," and appended note; Louis Stark, "South Is Declared 'No. 1' by President in Economic Need," *NYT*, July 6, 1938, 1; National Emergency Council, *Report on Economic Conditions of the South*. William E. Leuchtenburg, *The White House Looks South: Franklin D. Roosevelt, Harry S. Truman, Lyndon B. Johnson*, 112–17, has a trenchant section on the conference, the report, and its short- and long-term significance, but his treatment follows an explication of the purge, when, as his narrative shows, it preceded and in a way showcased it.

37. PPA, "Address at the University of Georgia, Athens, Aug. 11, 1938."

38. PPA, "A Recommendation for Liberalizing the Old-Age Insurance System," April 28, 1938," and appended note, and "Radio Address on the Third Anniversary of the Social Security Act, White House, Washington, D. C., Aug. 15, 1938."

39. This curious linkage occurred because the nation's first health insurance program, to provide hospitals for merchant seamen in John Adams's administration, was financed by a twenty-cent monthly deduction from the wages of seamen to be paid to the collectors of customs, who were Treasury officials. It mimicked practices begun by Britain after the defeat of the Spanish Armada. In the colonial era, the wages of American seamen were levied for the support of the British hospital at Greenwich.

40. PPA, "A Call for a Coordinated National Health Program, July 15, 1938," and appended note. For Josephine Roche, see the *ANB* sketch by Peter Wallenstein; and S. Ware, *Beyond Suffrage*.

41. DALLEK, 144–68.

42. An electronic search of his *Public Papers* is the authority for that statement. The only exception was in Proclamation 2222, January 23, 1937, when he used the word in connection with the great Ohio River flood. It occurs nineteen more times between March 24, 1938, and June 12, 1944.

43. PPA, "The United States Moves to Help Refugees from Germany, State Department Release, Mar. 24, 1938," and appended note; *Press Conf #445* (March 25, 1938), 11:249; "U.S. Asks Powers to Aid Refugees Flee Nazis," *NYT*, March 25, 1938, 1; "Study of Refugees Begins Wednesday," *NYT*, April 9, 1938, 5; "President Confers on Aid to Refugees," *NYT*, April 14, 1938, 16; "M. C. Taylor Named to Help Refugees," *NYT*, May 1, 1938, 1. Barbara McDonald Stewart, *United States Government Policy on Refugees from Nazism, 1933–1940*, is an important account by McDonald's daughter. See also two volumes she edited with Richard Breitman, Barbara McDonald Stewart, and Severin Hochberg, *Advocate for the Doomed: James G. McDonald* and *Refugees and Rescue:*

The Diaries and Papers of James G. McDonald, 1935–1945; and "James McDonald, Ex-Ambassador to Israel, Dies," *NYT,* September 27, 1964, 86. Hull, *Memoirs,* 1:578–79, writes as if the invitations were the State Department's idea and makes no mention of either McDonald or the Advisory Committee. Perkins, the cabinet member most involved with the Advisory Committee, makes no mention of it in her published memoir, *The Roosevelt I Knew,* though she speaks of Roosevelt's attitudes toward refugees at 348ff. Her biographer George Martin does not discuss refugees. For a detailed account, see Bat-Ami Zucker, "Frances Perkins and the German-Jewish Refugees." For some notion of the twenty-first-century debate on this topic, see Richard Breitman and Allan J. Lichtman, *FDR and the Jews;* and my review in *American Jewish History* (January 2014): 30–31.

44. Kristallnacht is now commonly translated as "Night of Broken Glass," a reference to the untold numbers of broken windows of synagogues, Jewish-owned stores, community centers, and homes plundered and destroyed during the pogroms. Encouraged by the Nazi regime, the rioters burned or destroyed 267 synagogues, vandalized or looted seventy-five hundred Jewish businesses, and killed at least ninety-one Jews. They also damaged many Jewish cemeteries, hospitals, schools, and homes as police and fire brigades stood aside. Kristallnacht was a turning point in history. The pogroms marked an intensification of Nazi anti-Jewish policy that would culminate in the Holocaust—the systematic, state-sponsored murder of Jews. Website of the U.S. National Holocaust Memorial Museum.

45. The fullest account of Évian and its aftermath is in the three volumes on McDonald, cited above. See also Stewart, *Refugees from Nazism,* 282–493. Texts of Taylor's two major refugee speeches are in *NYT,* July 7, 1938, 9, and November 26, 1938, 2; *Press Conf* #501 (November 18, 1938), 12:238–41.

46. PPA, "Presidential Statement on Refugees in Palestine, Nov. 23, 1938" and "Indorsing University Scholarships for Refugees from Germany, Dec. 14, 1938"; Felix Belair Jr., "Roosevelt Is Gratified by Report That Palestine Will Take More Refugees," *NYT,* November 24, 1938, 1. See also Freidel, *Rendezvous with Destiny,* 295–96.

47. As cited in Stewart, *Refugees from Nazism,* 527–44.

48. PPA, note to "The United States Moves to Help Refugees from Germany, State Department Release, Mar. 24, 1938," and appended note. He would use the word *haven* in his June 1944 action in establishing a "token refuge" for almost a thousand refugees brought from Italy to Fort Oswego, New York.

49. Mondale speech text, Office of the Vice President's Press Secretary, July 1979, for release Saturday, July 21, 5:00 p.m. For a cogent statement of the problems involved in making such judgments, see the final chapter of Henry L. Feingold, *The Politics of Rescue: The Roosevelt Administration and the Holocaust, 1938–1945.* I have written about these matters at greater length in "American Refugee Policy in Historical Perspective" and *Guarding the Golden Door: American Immigration Policy and Immigrants since 1882.*

50. PPA, "Annual Message to the Congress, Jan, 3, 1938," "Address before the National Education Association, New York City, June 30, 1938," and "Address at Treasure Island, San Francisco, California, July 14, 1938"; Felix Belair Jr., "Roosevelt Offers to Join a World Disarmament Move," *NYT,* July 14, 1938, 1; PPA, "Address at Queen's University,

Kingston, Ontario, Canada, Aug. 18, 1938"; "Aims at Dictators," *NYT*, August 19, 1938, 1. For the agreements, see Stanley W. Dziuban, *Military Relations between the United States and Canada, 1939–1945.*

51. PPA, "The President's Message, Sept. 26, 1938, and Hitler's Reply, Sept. 27, 1938" and "The President Again Seeks Peace, Sept. 27, 1938."

52. PPA, "Radio Address to the Herald-Tribune Forum, Oct. 26, 1938"; "Roosevelt Warns Nation Must Arm in a World of Force," *NYT*, October 27, 1938, 1.

53. PPA, "Radio Address on Electing Liberals to Public Office, Nov. 4, 1938"; Felix Belair Jr., "Presses New Deal," *NYT*, November 5, 1938, 1.

54. For details of their increasing importance, see Richard Norton Smith, *Thomas E. Dewey and His Times;* and James T. Patterson, *Mr. Republican: A Biography of Robert A. Taft.* For Michigan and California, see Sidney Fine, *Frank Murphy: The New Deal Years;* and Burke, *Olson's New Deal.*

55. *Press Conf* #499 (November 11, 1938), 12:222–23.

56. *Press Conf* #502–5 (November 22, 25, 29, December 2, 1938), 12:247–76; PPA, "Address at Thanksgiving, Warm Springs, Nov. 24, 1938."

57. The SCHW (1938–48) "provided one of the earliest interracial public voices against segregation. It was a model of interracial cooperation at a time when Jim Crow was still deeply entrenched in southern culture" (Rebecca Woodham, "SCHW," in *Encyclopedia of Alabama*, http://www.encyclopediaofalabama.org/).

58. The best brief account is in Leuchtenburg, *White House Looks South*, 112–17. Eleanor Roosevelt's account is in her *This I Remember*, 173–74. Her memory was often inexact: in this instance, she remembered that the SCHW meeting was in "a church" rather than the municipal auditorium. See also Thomas Kruger, *And Promises to Keep: The Southern Conference of Human Welfare, 1938–1948;* Morton Sosna, *In Search of the Silent South: Southern Liberals and the Race Issue;* and John Egerton, *Speak Now against the Day: The Generation before the Civil Rights Movement in the South.*

59. The letter is not in PPA but is printed in the first of two press accounts: Winifred Mallon, "Sweeping Moves Urged to Aid South," *NYT*, November 23, 1938, 23; and "Black Hails Gain in Rights in South," *NYT*, November 24, 1938, 33.

60. For Graham, see Leuchtenburg's *ANB* sketch. Felix Belair Jr., "Roosevelt to Talk on Foreign Affairs," *NYT*, December 4, 1938, 1; "World Will Hear Roosevelt Speak Today," *NYT*, December 5, 1938, 1.

61. PPA, "Address at University of North Carolina, Chapel Hill, Dec. 5, 1938"; Felix Belair Jr., "Roosevelt Urges Nation to Continue Liberalism," *NYT*, December 6, 1938, 1.

62. The quotation is of the longtime editorialist for the *New York Herald-Tribune* Walter Millis (1899–1968), in Burns, *Lion and the Fox*, 375, with the accolade "The passage of time has not invalidated this judgment."

63. *Press Conf* #506–7 (December 6, 9, 1938), 12:277–92.

64. *Press Conf* #508 (December 10, 1938), 12:293–305. In addition to Morison and Walker, the members were, in Roosevelt's words, "Ambassador Dodd; President Graham of North Carolina University; Archie MacLeish, a writer and I think he has been connected with 'Time'; Randolph Adams, the Librarian of the University of Michigan; Edmond E. Day; Dr. [Robert D. W.] Connor [the archivist]; Dr. [Alexander C.] Flick, State Historian at Albany; Dr. Charles A. Beard; Professor Frankfurter; Stuart Chase;

Samuel I. Rosenman . . . ; Ernest Lindley . . . ; President [Frederic L.] Paxson, of the American Historical Association; Dr. [Julian P.] Boyd of the Historical Society of Pennsylvania; Mrs. Helen Taft Manning of Bryn Mawr; [and] Miss Marguerite Wells, President of the League of Women Voters."

65. For Dewson, see Susan Ware's *ANB* sketch and her *Partner and I*. Her *Beyond Suffrage* is the best account of its subject. "Miss Dewson Quits Social Security Board," *NYT,* December 21, 1938, 2; *Press Conf* #511 (December 20, 1938), 12:314–15.

66. Salmond, *Southern Rebel,* 102–4; "Hopkins Sworn in, Faces Senate Test," *NYT,* December 25, 1938, 1. There is no biography of Harrington; his *NYT* obituary is October 1, 1940, 32.

67. Dr. George Gallup, "Finds Prejudice Is Facing Hopkins," *NYT,* December 23, 1938, 2.

68. DALLEK, 176–77; Hull, *Memoirs,* 1:601–12. He calls that chapter "New World Alerted."

69. PPA, "Address on Lighting the Community Christmas Tree, Washington, Dec. 24, 1938." The text is Isaiah 2:4.

Works Consulted

Abbazia, Patrick. *Mr. Roosevelt's Navy: The Private War of the U.S. Atlantic Fleet, 1939–1942.* Annapolis, Md.: Naval Institute Press, 1975.

Adams, Henry H. *Harry Hopkins: A Biography.* New York: Putnam, 1977.

Agawa, Hiroyuki. *The Reluctant Admiral: Yamamoto and the Imperial Navy.* Translated by John Bester. New York: Kodansha International, 1979.

Albertson, Dean. *Roosevelt's Farmer: Claude R. Wickard in the New Deal.* New York: Columbia University Press, 1955.

Allen, Frederick Lewis. *Since Yesterday: The Nineteen-Thirties in America.* New York: Harper, 1939.

Allen, George E. *Presidents Who Have Known Me.* New York: Simon and Schuster, 1950.

Allen, William C. *History of the United States Capitol.* Washington, D.C.: Government Printing Office, 2001.

Alsop, Joseph W., with Adam Platt. *"I've Seen the Best of It."* New York: W. W. Norton, 1992.

American Defense League. *Gardner or Daniels?* New York: American Defense Society, [1915?].

American Legion. *Proceedings of the Sixteenth National Convention of the American Legion, Miami, Florida, October 22–25, 1934.* Washington, D.C.: Government Printing Office, 1935.

American National Biography. http://www.anb.org.

Anderson, Karen. *Wartime Women: Sex Roles, Family Relations, and the Status of Women during World War II.* Westport, Conn.: Greenwood Press, 1981.

Anderson, Margo. *The American Census: A Social History.* New Haven, Conn.: Yale University Press, 1988.

Anderson, Michael J. "The Presidential Election of 1944." Ph.D. diss., University of Cincinnati, 1990.

Anderson, Paul Y. "Armed Rebellion on the Right." *Nation,* August 7, 1937, 146–47.

Anderson, William. *The Wild Man from Sugar Creek: The Political Career of Eugene Talmadge.* Baton Rouge: Louisiana State University Press, 1975.

Annunziata, Frank. "Governor of New York." In *Franklin D. Roosevelt: His Life and Times; An Encyclopedic View,* edited by Otis L. Graham Jr. and Meghan R. Wander, 159–61. Boston: G. K. Hall, 1983.

Arnold, Henry Harley. *Global Mission.* New York: Harper, 1949.

Arsenault, Raymond. *The Sound of Freedom: Marian Anderson, the Lincoln Memorial, and the Concert That Awakened America.* New York: Bloomsbury Press, 2009.

Asbell, Bernard. *Mother and Daughter: The Letters of Eleanor and Anna Roosevelt.* New York: Coward, McCann, and Geoghegan, 1982.

Ashburn, Frank D. *Peabody of Groton: A Portrait*. New York: Coward, McCann, 1944.

Ashley, Clifford W. *Whaleships of New Bedford*. Boston: Houghton Mifflin, 1929.

Auerbach, Jerold S. *Labor and Liberty: The La Follette Committee and the New Deal*. Indianapolis: Bobbs-Merrill, 1966.

———. "New Deal, Old Deal, or Raw Deal: Some Thoughts on New Left Historiography." *Journal of Southern History* 35 (1969): 18–30.

Austin, Allan W. *From Concentration Camp to Campus: Japanese American Students and World War II*. Urbana: University of Illinois Press, 2004.

Baer, George W. *The Coming of the Italian-Ethiopian War*. Cambridge, Mass.: Harvard University Press, 1967.

Bagby, Wesley M. *The Road to Normalcy: The Presidential Campaign and Election of 1920*. Baltimore: Johns Hopkins University Press, 1962.

Bailey, Anthony. *America, Lost & Found*. New York: Random House, 1980.

Barnard, Ellsworth. *Wendell Willkie, Fighter for Freedom*. Marquette: Northern Michigan University Press, 1966.

Barnouw, Eric. *The Golden Web: A History of Broadcasting in the United States, 1933 to 1953*. New York: Oxford University Press, 1968.

Bayly, Christopher, and Tim Harper. *Forgotten Armies: The Fall of British Asia, 1941–1945*. Cambridge, Mass.: Harvard University Press, 2005.

Bazer, Gerald. "Baseball during World War II: The Reaction and Encouragement of Franklin Delano Roosevelt and Others." *Nine: A Journal of Baseball History and Culture* 10 (Fall 2001): 114–29.

Beard, Charles A. *American Foreign Policy in the Making, 1932–1940: A Study in Responsibilities*. New Haven, Conn.: Yale University Press, 1946.

———. *President Roosevelt and the Coming of War, 1941: A Study in Appearances and Realities*. New Haven, Conn.: Yale University Press, 1948.

Beasley, Maurine H. *Eleanor Roosevelt and the Media: A Public Quest for Self-fulfillment*. Urbana: University of Illinois Press, 1987.

———, ed. *The White House Press Conferences of Eleanor Roosevelt*. New York: Garland, 1983.

Belair, Felix. "F. D. Roosevelt: Assistant Secretary." *New York Times Magazine,* March 17, 1940, 8, 18.

Belknap, Michal K. "A Putrid Pedigree: The Bush Administration's Military Tribunals in Historical Perspective." *California Western Law Review* 38 (2002): 433, 471–79.

———. "The Supreme Court Goes to War: The Meaning and Implications of the Nazi Saboteurs Case." *Military Law Review* 89 (1980): 59.

Bellush, Bernard. *The Failure of the NRA*. New York: W. W. Norton, 1975.

———. *Franklin D. Roosevelt as Governor of New York*. New York: Columbia University Press, 1955.

———. *He Walked Alone: A Biography of John G. Winant*. The Hague: Mouton, 1968.

Berg, A. Scott. *Lindbergh*. New York: Putnam, 1998.

Berle, Adolf A. *Navigating the Rapids, 1918–1971: From the Papers of Adolf A. Berle*. Edited by Beatrice Bishop Berle and Travis Beal Jacobs. New York: Harcourt Brace Jovanovich, 1973.

Bernstein, Barton J. "The New Deal: The Conservative Achievements of Liberal Reform." In *Towards a New Past: Dissenting Essays in American History*, edited by Barton J. Bernstein, 263–88. New York: Pantheon, 1968.

Bernstein, Irving. *A Caring Society: The New Deal, the Worker and the Great Depression*. Boston: Houghton Mifflin, 1985.

———. *The New Deal Collective Bargaining Policy*. Berkeley: University of California Press, 1950.

———. *Turbulent Years: A History of the American Worker, 1933–1941*. Boston: Houghton Mifflin, 1969.

Beschloss, Michael R. *Kennedy and Roosevelt: The Uneasy Alliance*. New York: W. W. Norton, 1980.

Biddle, Francis. *In Brief Authority*. New York: Doubleday, 1962.

Biles, Roger. *Big City Boss in Depression and War: Mayor Edward J. Kelly of Chicago*. DeKalb: Northern Illinois University Press, 1984.

———. *Crusading Liberal: Paul H. Douglas of Illinois*. DeKalb: Northern Illinois University Press, 2002.

Biographical Directory of the United States Congress, 1774–Present. http://bioguide.congress .gov.

Birmingham, Stephen. *Our Crowd: The Great Jewish Families of New York*. New York: Harper & Row, 1967.

Bishop, Jim. *FDR's Last Year*. New York: William Morrow, 1974.

Blackorby, Edwin C. *Prairie Rebel: The Public Life of William Lemke*. Lincoln: University of Nebraska Press, 1963.

Blum, John Morton. *From the Morgenthau Diaries: Years of Crisis, 1928–1938*. Boston: Houghton Mifflin, 1959.

———. *From the Morgenthau Diaries: Years of War, 1941–1945*. Boston: Houghton Mifflin, 1967.

———. *The Price of Vision: The Diary of Henry A. Wallace, 1942–1946*. Boston: Houghton Mifflin, 1973.

———. *Roosevelt and Morgenthau*. Boston: Houghton Mifflin, 1970.

Boettiger, John R. *A Love in Shadow*. New York: W. W. Norton, 1978.

Bohlen, Charles E. *Witness to History, 1929–1969*. New York: W. W. Norton, 1973.

Borg, Dorothy. "Notes on Roosevelt's Quarantine Speech." *Political Science Quarterly* 72 (1957): 405–33.

Bower, Kevin P. "Relief, Reform, and Youth: The National Youth Administration in Ohio, 1935–1943. Ph.D. diss., University of Cincinnati, 2003.

Boyer, Paul S., ed. *The Oxford Companion to United States History*. New York: Oxford University Press, 2001.

Braeman, John, Robert H. Bremner, and Everett Walters, eds. *Change and Continuity in Twentieth Century America*. Columbus: Ohio State University Press, 1964.

Brandeis, Louis D. *Other People's Money and How the Bankers Use It*. New York: Stokes, 1914.

Brandes, Stuart D. *American Welfare Capitalism, 1880–1940*. Chicago: University of Chicago Press, 1976.

Brandt, Irving. *Adventures in Conservation with Franklin D. Roosevelt.* Flagstaff, Ariz.: Northland, 1988.

Breitman, Richard, and Allan J. Lichtman. *FDR and the Jews.* Cambridge, Mass.: Harvard University Press, 2013.

Breitman, Richard, Barbara McDonald Stewart, and Severin Hochberg, eds. *Advocate for the Doomed: James G. McDonald.* Bloomington: Indiana University Press, 2007.

———. *Refugees and Rescue: The Diaries and Papers of James G. McDonald, 1935–1945.* Bloomington: Indiana University Press, 2009.

Bremer, William W. *Depression Winters: New York Social Workers and the New Deal.* Philadelphia: Temple University Press, 1984.

Brinkley, Alan. *The End of Reform: New Deal Liberalism in Recession and War.* New York: Alfred A. Knopf, 1995.

———. "The National Resources Planning Board and the Reconstruction of Planning." In *The American Planning Tradition: Culture and Policy,* edited by Robert Fishman, 173–92. Baltimore: Johns Hopkins University Press, 2000.

———. *Voices of Protest: Huey Long, Father Coughlin, and the Great Depression.* New York: Alfred A. Knopf, 1982.

Brock, William R. *Welfare, Democracy and the New Deal.* Cambridge: Cambridge University Press, 1988.

Broesamle, John J. *William Gibbs McAdoo: A Passion for Change, 1863–1917.* Port Washington, N.Y.: Kennikat, 1973.

Browder, Robert Paul, and Thomas G. Smith. *Independent: A Biography of Lewis W. Douglas.* New York: Alfred A. Knopf, 1986.

Brown, D. Clayton. *Electricity for Rural America: The Fight for REA.* Westport, Conn.: Greenwood Press, 1980.

Brown, John Mason. *The Ordeal of a Playwright.* New York: Harper, 1970.

———. *The Worlds of Robert E. Sherwood: Mirror to His Times, 1896–1939.* New York: Harper, 1965.

Brownlow, Louis. *Administrative Management in the Government of the United States.* Washington, D.C.: Government Printing Office, 1937. [United States, President's Committee on Administrative Management].

———. *A Passion for Anonymity.* Chicago: University of Chicago Press, 1958.

Bruenn, Howard G. "Clinical Notes on the Illness and Death of President Franklin D. Roosevelt." *Annals of Internal Medicine* 72 (1970): 571–92.

Bruère, Henry. *America's Unemployment Problem.* Philadelphia: n.p., 1915.

Buell, Thomas B. *Master of Sea Power: A Biography of Fleet Admiral Ernest J. King.* Boston: Little, Brown, 1980.

Buenker, John D. *Urban Liberalism and Progressive Reform.* New York: Scribner's, 1973.

Buhite, Russell D., and David Levy, eds. *FDR's Fireside Chats.* Norman: University of Oklahoma Press, 1992.

Bunche, Ralph J. *The Political Status of the Negro in the Age of FDR.* Chicago: University of Chicago Press, 1973.

Buni, Andrew. *Robert L. Vann and the "Pittsburgh Courier": Politics and Black Journalism.* Pittsburgh: University of Pittsburgh Press, 1974.

Burke, Robert E., ed. *Diary Letters of Hiram Johnson, 1917–1945.* 7 vols. New York: Garland, 1983.

———. *Olson's New Deal for California.* Berkeley: University of California Press, 1953.

Burns, James MacGregor. *Roosevelt: The Lion and the Fox.* New York: Harcourt, Brace, 1956.

———. *Roosevelt: The Soldier of Freedom.* New York: Harcourt Brace Jovanovich, 1970.

Burns, James MacGregor, and Susan Dunn. *The Three Roosevelts: Patrician Leaders Who Transformed America.* Boston: Atlantic Monthly Press, 2001.

Butler, J. R. M. *History of the Second World War.* United Kingdom Military Series, Grand Strategy. Vol. 2, *September 1939–June 1941.* London: Her Majesty's Stationery Office, 1957.

Butler, Susan. *My Dear Mr. Stalin.* New Haven, Conn.: Yale University Press, 2005.

Butow, Robert J. C. "The FDR Tapes: Secret Recordings Made in the Oval Office of the President in the Autumn of 1940." *American Heritage* (February–March 1982): 23–24.

———. *The John Doe Associates: Backdoor Diplomacy for Peace.* Stanford, Calif.: Stanford University Press, 1974.

———. "A Notable Passage to China: Myth and Memory in FDR's Family History." *Prologue* 31 (Fall 1999): 159–77.

———. *Tojo and the Coming of War.* Stanford, Calif.: Stanford University Press, 1961.

Byrnes, James F. *All in One Lifetime.* New York: Harper, 1958.

———. *Speaking Frankly.* New York: Harper, 1947.

Cadogan, Alexander. *The Diaries of Sir Alexander Cadogan, O.M., 1938–1945.* New York: Putnam, 1972.

Calef, Wesley C. *Private Grazing and Public Lands: Studies of the Local Management of the Taylor Grazing Act.* Chicago: University of Chicago Press, 1960.

Campbell, Thomas M., and George C. Herring, eds. *The Diaries of Edward R. Stettinius, Jr., 1943–1946.* New York: New Viewpoints, 1975.

Cannadine, David. *Mellon: An American Life.* New York: Alfred A. Knopf, 2006.

Capeci, Dominic J. *Race Relations in Wartime Detroit: The Sojourner Truth Housing Controversy of 1942.* Philadelphia: Temple University Press, 1984.

Caro, Robert A. *The Power Broker: Robert Moses and the Fall of New York.* New York: Alfred A. Knopf, 1974.

Caroli, Betty Boyd. *The Roosevelt Women: A Portrait in Five Generations.* New York: Basic Books, 1998.

Carosso, Vincent P., with the assistance of Rose C. Carosso. *The Morgans: Private Investment Bankers, 1854–1913.* Cambridge, Mass.: Harvard University Press, 1987.

Carter, Dan T. *Scottsboro: A Tragedy of the American South.* New York: Oxford University Press, 1969.

Catton, Bruce. *The War Lords of Washington.* New York: Harcourt, Brace, 1948.

Cebula, James E. *James M. Cox: Journalist and Politician.* New York: Garland, 1985.

Champagne, Anthony. *Congressman Sam Rayburn.* New Brunswick, N.J.: Rutgers University Press, 1984.

Chang, Hsin-pao. *Commissioner Lin and the Opium War.* Cambridge, Mass.: Harvard University Press, 1964.

Churchill, Winston S. *The Grand Alliance.* Boston: Houghton Mifflin, 1950.

———. *The Hinge of Fate.* Boston: Houghton Mifflin, 1950.

———. *The World Crisis, 1916–1918.* New York: Scribner's, 1927.

Clawson, Marian. *New Deal Planning: The National Resources Planning Board.* Baltimore: Johns Hopkins University Press, 1981.

Clemens, Diane Shaver. *Yalta.* New York: Oxford University Press, 1975.

Cline, Ray S. *Washington Command Post: The Operations Division.* 1951. Reprint, Washington, D.C.: Center for Military History, 2003.

Coady, Joseph W. "Franklin D. Roosevelt's Early Washington Years (1913–1920)." Ph.D. diss., St. John's University, 1968.

Coben, Stanley. *A. Mitchell Palmer: Politician.* New York: Columbia University Press, 1963.

Cohodas, Nadine. *Strom Thurmond and the Politics of Southern Change.* New York: Simon and Schuster, 1993.

Cole, Hugh M. *The Ardennes: Battle of the Bulge.* Washington, D.C.: Government Printing Office, 1965.

Cole, Olen, Jr. *The African-American Experience in the Civilian Conservation Corps.* Gainesville: University Press of Florida, 1999.

Cole, Wayne S. *America First: The Battle against Intervention.* Madison: University of Wisconsin Press, 1953.

———. *Roosevelt and the Isolationists, 1932–1945.* Lincoln: University of Nebraska Press, 1983.

Coletta, Paolo E., ed. *American Secretaries of the Navy.* Annapolis, Md.: Naval Institute Press, 1980.

Commission on Wartime Relocation and Internment of Civilians. *Personal Justice Denied.* Washington, D.C.: Government Printing Office, 1982.

Conkin, Paul. *Tomorrow a New World: The New Deal Community Program.* Ithaca, N.Y.: Cornell University Press, 1958.

Conn, Stetson. "The Decision to Relocate the Japanese from the Pacific Coast." In *Command Decisions,* edited by Kent Roberts Greenfield, 125–49. New York: Harcourt, 1959.

Conn, Stetson, Rose C. Engleman, and Byron Fairchild. *Guarding the United States and Its Outposts.* Washington, D.C.: Office of the Chief of Military History, Department of the Army, 1964.

Cook, Blanche Wiesen. *Eleanor Roosevelt.* Vol. 1, *1884–1933.* Vol. 2, *1933–1938.* New York: Viking, 1992, 1999.

Coox, Alvin D. *Nomonhan: Japan against Russia, 1939.* 2 vols. Stanford, Calif.: Stanford University Press, 1985.

Cordery, Stacy A. *Alice: Alice Roosevelt Longworth, from White House Princess to Washington Power Broker.* New York: Viking, 2007.

Cox, James M. *Journey through My Years.* New York: Simon and Schuster, 1946.

Craven, Wesley F., and James L. Cate, eds. *The Army Air Forces in World War II.* 7 vols. Washington, D.C.: Government Printing Office, 1948–58.

Creel, George. *Rebel at Large: Recollections of Fifty Crowded Years.* New York: G. P. Putnam's Sons, 1947.

Cronon, E. David, ed. *The Cabinet Diaries of Josephus Daniels, 1913–1921.* Lincoln: University of Nebraska Press, 1963.

———. *Josephus Daniels in Mexico.* Madison: University of Wisconsin Press, 1960.

Crosby, Alfred W. *America's Forgotten Pandemic: The Influenza of 1918.* New York: Cambridge University Press, 1989.

Cross, Robert F. *Sailor in the White House: The Seafaring Life of FDR.* Annapolis, Md.: Naval Institute Press, 1999.

Culley, John Joel. "Enemy Alien Control in the United States during World War II." In *Alien Justice: Wartime Internment in Australia and North America,* edited by Kay Saunders and Roger Daniels, 138–51. St. Lucia: University of Queensland, 2000.

Curtis, James C. *Mind's Eye, Mind's Truth: FSA Photography Reconsidered.* Philadelphia: Temple University Press, 1989.

Cutlip, Scott M. *Fund Raising in the United States: Its Role in American Philanthropy.* 1965. Reprint, New Brunswick, N.J.: Transaction, 1990.

Dallek, Robert. *Democrat and Diplomat: The Life of William E. Dodd.* New York: Oxford University Press, 1968.

———. *Franklin D. Roosevelt and American Foreign Policy, 1932–1945.* New York: Oxford University Press, 1979.

Dangerfield, George. *Chancellor Robert R. Livingston of New York, 1746–1813.* New York: Harcourt, Brace, 1960.

Daniels, Jonathan. *The Time between the Wars: Armistice to Pearl Harbor.* New York: Doubleday, 1966.

———. *Washington Quadrille: The Dance beside the Documents.* New York: Doubleday, 1968.

———. *White House Witness, 1942–1945.* New York: Doubleday, 1975.

Daniels, Josephus. *Editor in Politics.* Chapel Hill: University of North Carolina Press, 1941.

———. *Shirt-Sleeve Diplomat.* Chapel Hill: University of North Carolina Press, 1947.

———. *The Wilson Era: Years of Peace, 1910–1917.* Chapel Hill: University of North Carolina Press, 1944.

———. *The Wilson Era: Years of War and After, 1917–1923.* Chapel Hill: University of North Carolina Press, 1946.

Daniels, Roger, ed. *American Concentration Camps: A Documentary History of the Relocation and Incarceration of Japanese Americans, 1941–1945.* 9 vols. New York: Garland, 1989.

———. "American Refugee Policy in Historical Perspective." In *The Muses Flee Hitler: Cultural Transfer and Adaptation, 1930–1945,* edited by Jarrell C. Jackman and Carla M. Borden, 61–77. Washington, D.C.: Smithsonian Institution Press, 1983.

———. *Asian America: Chinese and Japanese in the United States since 1850.* Seattle: University of Washington Press, 1988.

———. *The Bonus March: An Episode of the Great Depression.* Westport, Conn.: Greenwood Press, 1971.

———. *Concentration Camps, USA: Japanese Americans and World War II.* New York: Holt, Rinehart, and Winston, 1972.

———. *The Decision to Relocate the Japanese Americans.* Philadelphia: Lippincott, 1975.

———. *Guarding the Golden Door: American Immigration Policy and Immigrants since 1882*. New York: Hill and Wang, 2004.

———. "The Internment of Japanese Nationals in the United States during World War II." *Halcyon* (1995): 66–75.

———. *The Japanese American Cases: The Rule of Law in Time of War*. Lawrence: University Press of Kansas, 2013.

———. *The Politics of Prejudice: The Anti-Japanese Movement in California and the Struggle for Japanese Exclusion*. Berkeley: University of California Press, 1962.

———. *Prisoners without Trial: Japanese Americans in World War II*. New York: Hill and Wang, 1993.

Daniels, Roger, and Harry H. L. Kitano. *American Racism: Exploration of the Nature of Prejudice*. Englewood Cliffs, N.J.: Prentice Hall, 1970.

Davis, Kenneth S. *FDR: The Beckoning of Destiny*. New York: Putnam, 1972.

———. *FDR: The New York Years, 1928–1933*. New York: Random House, 1985.

———. *The Hero: Charles A. Lindbergh and the American Dream*. New York: Doubleday, 1959.

Davis, Polly. *Alben Barkley: Senate Majority Leader and Vice President*. New York: Garland, 1979.

Dawes, Charles G. *Journal as Ambassador to Great Britain*. New York: Macmillan, 1939.

Dawley, Alan. *Changing the World: American Progressives in War and Revolution*. Princeton, N.J.: Princeton University Press, 2003.

Daws, Gavan. *Prisoners of the Japanese: POWs of World War II in the Pacific*. New York: Morrow, 1994.

de Gaulle, Charles. *The Complete War Memoirs of Charles de Gaulle*. New York: Simon and Schuster, 1964.

Delano, Amasa. *Narrative of Voyages and Travels in the Northern and Southern Hemispheres, Comprising Three Voyages Round the World*. Boston: E. G. House, 1817.

Delano, Daniel W., Jr. *Franklin Roosevelt and the Delano Influence*. Pittsburgh: James S. Nudi, 1946.

Dewey, George. *Autobiography of George Dewey, Admiral of the Navy*. New York: Scribner's, 1913.

DeWitt, Larry. "Historical Background and Development of Social Security." http://www.ssa.gov/history/briefhistory3.html.

Dierenfield, Bruce J. *Keeper of the Rules: Howard W. Smith of Virginia*. Charlottesville: University Press of Virginia, 1987.

Divine, Robert A. *Roosevelt and World War II*. Baltimore: Johns Hopkins University Press, 1969.

Dorsett, Lyle W. *Franklin D. Roosevelt and the City Bosses*. Port Washington, N.Y.: Kennikat, 1977.

Dorwart, Jeffery M. *Conflict of Duty: The U.S. Navy's Intelligence Dilemma, 1919–1945*. Annapolis, Md.: Naval Institute Press, 1983.

Douglas, Paul H. *The Coming of a New Party*. New York: McGraw-Hill, 1931.

———. *In the Fullness of Time: The Memoirs of Paul H. Douglas*. New York: Harcourt Brace Jovanovich, 1972.

Downey, Kirstin. *The Woman behind the New Deal*. New York: Doubleday, 2009.

Downs, Jacques M. *The Golden Ghetto: The American Commercial Community at Canton and the Shaping of American China Policy, 1784–1844*. Bethlehem, Pa.: Lehigh University Press, 1997.

Doyle, William. *Inside the Oval Office: The White House Tapes from FDR to Clinton*. New York: Kodansha International, 1999.

Droze, Wilmon H. *Trees, Prairies, and People: A History of Tree Planting in the Plains States*. Denton: Texas Woman's University, 1997.

Dubofsky, Melvin, and Warren Van Tine. *John L. Lewis: A Biography*. New York: Quadrangle, 1977.

Dunne, Gerald T. *Grenville Clark: Public Citizen*. New York: Farrar, Straus, and Giroux, 1986.

Dykeman, Wilma. *Seeds of Southern Change: The Life of Will Alexander*. Chicago: University of Chicago Press, 1962.

Dziuban, Stanley W. *Military Relations between the United States and Canada, 1939–1945*. Washington, D.C.: Government Printing Office, 1959.

Eccles, Marriner S. *Beckoning Frontiers: Public and Personal Recollections*. Edited by Sidney Hymon. New York: Alfred A. Knopf, 1951.

Eddy, William A. *F.D.R. Meets Ibn Saud*. New York: American Friends of the Middle East, 1954.

Egerton, John. *Speak Now against the Day: The Generation before the Civil Rights Movement in the South*. New York: Alfred A. Knopf, 1994.

Eisel, Braxton. *The Flying Tigers: Chennault's American Volunteer Group in China*. Washington, D.C.: Air Force History and Museums Program, 2009.

Eisenhower, Dwight D. *Crusade in Europe*. New York: Doubleday, 1948.

Eliot, Thomas Hopkinson. *Recollections of the New Deal: When the People Mattered*. Boston: Northeastern University Press, 1992.

Elsey, George M. *An Unplanned Life*. Columbia: University of Missouri Press, 2005.

Emerson, William. "Franklin Roosevelt as Commander-in-Chief in World War II." *Military Affairs* 22 (Winter 1958–59): 181–207.

"F. D. Roosevelt: The World's Best Known Stamp Collector." *Stamp & Coin Collector* 3 (January 1966).

Falk, I. S. "The Committee on the Costs of Medical Care: 25 Years of Progress." *American Journal of Public Health* 48 (1958): 979–82.

Farley, James A. *Behind the Ballots: The Personal History of a Politician*. New York: Harcourt, Brace, 1938.

———. *Jim Farley's Story: The Roosevelt Years*. New York: Whittlesey House, 1948.

Feingold, Henry L. *The Politics of Rescue: The Roosevelt Administration and the Holocaust, 1938–1945*. New Brunswick, N.J.: Rutgers University Press, 1970).

Feis, Herbert. *The China Tangle: The American Effort in China from Pearl Harbor to the Marshall Mission*. Princeton, N.J.: Princeton University Press, 1953.

———. *1933: Characters in Crisis*. Boston: Little, Brown, 1966.

Ferrell, Robert H. *The Dying President: Franklin D. Roosevelt, 1944–45*. Columbia: University of Missouri Press, 1998.

Fielding, Raymond. *The American Newsreel, 1911–1967*. Norman: University of Oklahoma Press, 1972

Finan, Christopher M. *Alfred E. Smith: The Happy Warrior.* New York: Hill and Wang, 2002.

Fine, Sidney. *Frank Murphy: The Detroit Years.* Ann Arbor: University of Michigan Press, 1975.

———. *Frank Murphy: The New Deal Years.* Ann Arbor: University of Michigan Press, 1979.

Fisher, Louis. *Nazi Saboteurs on Trial: A Military Tribunal and American Law.* Lawrence: University Press of Kansas, 2003.

Fleming, Donald. "Albert Einstein: Letter to Franklin D. Roosevelt, 1939." In *An American Primer,* edited by Daniel J. Boorstin, 857–62. Chicago: University of Chicago Press, 1966.

Flynn, Edward J. *You're the Boss.* 1947. Reprint, New York: Collier Books, 1962.

Flynn, John T. *Country Squire in the White House.* New York: Doubleday, Doran, 1940.

Flynt, Wayne. *Duncan Upshaw Fletcher, Dixie's Reluctant Progressive.* Tallahassee: Florida State University Press, 1971.

Fogarty, Gerald P., S.J. *The Vatican and the American Hierarchy from 1870 to 1965.* Stuttgart: Hiersmann, 1982.

Frankfurter, Felix. *Felix Frankfurter Reminisces: Recorded in Talks with Dr. Harlan B. Phillips.* New York: Reynal, 1990.

Freedman, Max, ed. *Roosevelt and Frankfurter: Their Correspondence, 1928–1945.* Boston: Little, Brown, 1967.

Freidel, Frank. "The Dutchness of the Roosevelts." In *A Bilateral Bicentennial: A History of Dutch American Relations, 1782–1982,* edited by J. W. Schulte Nordholt and Robert P. Swierenga, 157–67. New York: Octagon Books, 1982.

———. *Franklin D. Roosevelt: The Apprenticeship.* Boston: Little, Brown, 1952.

———. *Franklin D. Roosevelt: Launching the New Deal.* Boston: Little, Brown, 1973.

———. *Franklin D. Roosevelt: The Ordeal.* Boston: Little, Brown, 1954.

———. *Franklin D. Roosevelt: A Rendezvous with Destiny.* Boston: Little, Brown, 1990.

———. *Franklin D. Roosevelt: The Triumph.* Boston: Little, Brown, 1956.

———. "Franklin D. Roosevelt in the Northwest: Informal Glimpses." *Pacific Northwest Quarterly* 76 (1985): 122–31.

———. "Herbert Hoover and Franklin Roosevelt: Reminiscent Reflections." In *Understanding Herbert Hoover: Ten Perspectives,* edited by Lee Nash, 125–40. Stanford, Calif.: Hoover Institution, 1987.

Friedman, Max Paul. *Nazis and Good Neighbors: The United States Campaign against the Germans of Latin America in World War II.* Cambridge: Cambridge University Press, 2003.

Friend, Theodore. *Between Two Empires: Philippine Ordeal and Development from the Great Depression through the Pacific War, 1929–1946.* New Haven, Conn.: Yale University Press, 1965.

Fritz, Sherilyn C. "Twentieth-Century Salinity and Water-Level Fluctuations in Devils Lake, North Dakota: Test of a Diatom-Based Transfer Function." *Limnology and Oceanography* 35 (1990): 1771–81.

Fry, Varian. *Surrender on Demand.* New York: Random House, 1945.

Galbraith, John Kenneth. *The Great Crash.* London: Hamish Hamilton, 1955.

———. "How Keynes Came to America." In *A Contemporary Guide to Economics, Peace, and Laughter,* by John Kenneth Galbraith, 43–59. Boston: Houghton Mifflin, 1971.

———. *A Life in Our Times.* Boston: Houghton Mifflin, 1981.

———. *Name Dropping: From F.D.R. On.* Boston: Houghton Mifflin, 1999.

Gallagher, Hugh G. *FDR's Splendid Deception.* New York: Dodd, Mead, 1985.

Garrison, Lloyd K. "The National Labor Boards." *Annals* 184 (1936): 138–46.

Gaydowski, J. D. "Eight Letters to the Editor: The Genesis of the Townsend Plan." *Southern California Quarterly* 52 (1970): 365–82.

Gellman, Irwin F. *Good Neighbor Diplomacy: United States Policies in Latin America, 1933–1945.* Baltimore: Johns Hopkins University Press, 1979.

———. *Secret Affairs: Franklin D. Roosevelt, Cordell Hull, and Sumner Welles.* Baltimore: Johns Hopkins University Press, 1995.

Gilbert, Martin. *Churchill: A Life.* New York: Henry Holt, 1991.

———. *Churchill and America.* New York: Free Press, 2005.

Glennon, Robert J. *The Iconoclast as Reformer.* Ithaca, N.Y.: Cornell University Press, 1985.

Glines, Carroll V. *Doolittle's Tokyo Raiders.* Princeton, N.J.: Van Nostrand, 1964.

Goldberg, Richard Thayer. *The Making of Franklin D. Roosevelt: Triumph over Disability.* Cambridge, Mass.: Abt Books, 1981.

González, Gilbert G. *Labor and Community: Mexican Citrus Worker Villages in a Southern California County, 1900–1950.* Urbana: University of Illinois Press, 1994.

Goodwin, Doris Kearns. *The Fitzgeralds and the Kennedys.* New York: Simon and Schuster, 1987.

———. *No Ordinary Time: Franklin and Eleanor Roosevelt; The Home Front in World War II.* New York: Simon and Schuster, 1994.

Gosnell, Harold F. *Boss Platt and His New York Machine: A Study of the Political Leadership of Thomas C. Platt, Theodore Roosevelt, and Others.* Chicago: University of Chicago Press, 1924.

———. *Champion Campaigner: Franklin D. Roosevelt.* New York: Macmillan, 1952.

Graebner, Norman A. *An Uncertain Tradition: American Secretaries of State in the Twentieth Century.* New York: McGraw-Hill, 1961.

Graham, Otis L. *An Encore for Reform: Old Progressives and the New Deal.* New York: Oxford University Press, 1967.

Graham, Otis L., Jr., and Meghan R. Wander, eds. *Franklin D. Roosevelt: His Life and Times; An Encyclopedic View.* Boston: G. K. Hall, 1983.

Gravlee, G. Jack. "Stephen T. Early: The 'Advance Man.'" *Speech Monographs* 30 (1963): 441–49.

Green, Marguerite. *The National Civic Federation and the American Labor Movement.* Westport, Conn.: Greenwood Press, 1956.

Greenfield, Kent Roberts. *American Strategy in World War II: A Reconsideration.* Baltimore: Johns Hopkins University Press, 1963, especially "Franklin D. Roosevelt: Commander-in-Chief," 49–84, 126–31.

Greer, Thomas H. *What Roosevelt Thought: The Social and Political Ideas of Franklin D. Roosevelt.* East Lansing: Michigan State University Press, 1958.

Gregory, Cleburne F. "Franklin D. Roosevelt Will Swim to Health." *Atlanta Journal Sunday Magazine,* October 26, 1924.

Griswold, Erwin W. "Government in Ignorance of the Law: A Plea for Better Publication of Executive Legislation." *Harvard Law Review* 48 (1934).

Gruening, Ernest. *Many Battles: The Autobiography of Ernest Gruening.* New York: Liveright, 1973.

Gunther, John. *Roosevelt in Retrospect: A Profile in History.* New York: Harper, 1950.

Haight, John M. *American Aid to France, 1938–1940.* New York: Atheneum, 1970.

Hall, Kermit L., ed. *The Oxford Guide to Supreme Court Decisions.* New York: Oxford University Press, 1999.

Halsey, William F., and J. Bryan III. *Admiral Halsey's Story.* New York: Whittlesey House, 1947.

Hand, Samuel B. *Counsel and Advise: A Political Biography of Samuel I. Rosenman.* New York: Garland, 1979.

Handlin, Oscar. *Al Smith and His America.* Boston: Little, Brown, 1958.

Harbaugh, William H. *The Life and Times of Theodore Roosevelt.* New York: Oxford University Press, 1975.

——. "Roosevelt, Theodore." In *American National Biography.* New York: Oxford University Press, 2000.

Hargrove, Erwin C. "The Task of Leadership: The Board Chairman." In *TVA: Fifty Years of Grass Roots Democracy,* edited by Erwin C. Hargrove and Paul K. Conkin. Urbana: University of Illinois Press, 1984

Harriman, W. Averell, and Elie Abel. *Special Envoy to Churchill and Stalin, 1941–1946.* New York: Random House, 1975.

Harrington, Jerry. "Senator Guy Gillette Foils the Execution Committee." *Palimpsest* 62 (1981): 170–80.

Harris, Joseph E. *African-American Reactions to War in Ethiopia, 1936–1941.* Baton Rouge: Louisiana State University Press, 1994.

Harriss, C. Lowell. *History and Policies of the Home Owners' Loan Corporation.* New York: National Bureau of Economic Research, 1951.

Harrod, Frederick S. *Manning the New Navy: Development of a Modern Naval Enlisted Force, 1899–1940.* Westport, Conn.: Greenwood Press, 1978.

Hartmann, Susan M. *The Home Front and Beyond: American Women in the 1940s.* Boston: Twayne, 1982.

Harvard Alumni Bulletin 47 (April 28, 1945).

Hassett, William D. *Off the Record with FDR, 1942–1945.* New Brunswick, N.J.: Rutgers University Press, 1958.

Hawkins, Helen S. *A New Deal for the Newcomer: The Federal Transient Service.* New York: Garland, 1991.

Hawley, Ellis W. *The New Deal and the Problem of Monopoly.* Princeton, N.J.: Princeton University Press, 1966.

Healy, David. *Gunboat Diplomacy in the Wilson Era: The U.S. Navy in Haiti, 1915–1916.* Madison: University of Wisconsin Press, 1976.

Heinemann, Ronald L. *Depression and New Deal in Virginia.* Charlottesville: University Press of Virginia, 1986.

Herman, Jan Kenneth. "The President's Cardiologist." *Navy Medicine* 81 (March–April 1990): 6–13.

Herring, E. Pendleton. "Second Session of the Seventy-Third Congress, January 3rd, 1934, to June 18th, 1934." *American Political Science Review* 28 (1934): 852–66.

Herring, George C. *Aid to Russia, 1941–46.* New York: Columbia University Press, 1973.

Hershberg, James. *James B. Conant: Harvard to Hiroshima and the Making of the Nuclear Age.* New York: Alfred A. Knopf, 1993.

Hess, Stephen. "The Roosevelt Dynasty." In *America's Political Dynasties,* by Stephen Hess, 167–217. 2nd ed. New Brunswick, N.J.: Transaction, 1997.

Higham, John. *Strangers in the Land: Patterns of American Nativism, 1860–1924.* New Brunswick, N.J.: Rutgers University Press, 1955.

Hine, Darlene Clark. "Black Professionals and Race Consciousness: Origins of the Civil Rights Movement, 1890–1950." *Journal of American History* 89 (2003): 1279–95.

Hofstadter, Richard. *The American Political Tradition and the Men Who Made It.* New York: Alfred A. Knopf, 1948.

Hofstadter, Richard, William Miller, and Daniel Aaron. *The United States: The History of a Republic.* Englewood Cliffs, N.J.: Prentice Hall, 1957.

Holley, Donald. "Trouble in Paradise: Dyess Colony and Arkansas Politics." *Arkansas Historical Quarterly* 32 (Autumn 1973): 203–16.

———. *Uncle Sam's Farmers: The New Deal Communities in the Lower Mississippi Valley.* Urbana: University of Illinois Press, 1975.

Holtzman, Abraham. *The Townsend Movement: A Study of Old Age Pressure Politics.* New York: Bookman Associates, 1963.

Hoover, Herbert C. *The Memoirs of Herbert Hoover: The Great Depression, 1929–1941.* New York: Macmillan, 1952.

———. *Public Papers of the Presidents of the United States.* 4 vols. Washington, D.C.: Government Printing Office, 1974.

Hoover, Irwin H. *Forty-Two Years in the White House.* Boston: Houghton Mifflin, 1934.

Hopkins, Harry L. *Spending to Save: The Complete Story of Relief.* New York: W. W. Norton, 1936.

Hopkins, June. *Harry Hopkins: Sudden Hero, Brash Reformer.* New York: St. Martin's, 1999.

Howard, Donald S. *The WPA and Federal Relief Policy.* New York: Russell Sage Foundation, 1943.

Howe, George F. *Northwest Africa: Seizing the Initiative in the West.* Washington, D.C.: Office of the Chief of Military History, Department of the Army, 1957.

Howe, Louis McHenry. "The President's Mailbag." *American Magazine,* June 1934, 34.

———. "The Winner." *Saturday Evening Post,* February 25, 1935.

Howlett, Charles F., ed. *History of the American Peace Movement, 1890–2000: The Emergence of a New Scholarly Tradition.* Lewiston, N.Y.: Edwin Mellen Press, 2005.

Hull, Cordell. *The Memoirs of Cordell Hull.* New York: Macmillan, 1948.

Hurd, Charles W. "Hopkins: Right-Hand Man." *New York Times Magazine,* April 11, 1940, 6, 22.

———. *When the New Deal Was Young and Gay.* New York: Hawthorn Books, 1965.

Huthmacher, J. Joseph. *Senator Robert F. Wagner and the Rise of Urban Liberalism.* Cambridge, Mass.: Harvard University Press, 1968.

Hyman, Sidney. *Marriner S. Eccles: Private Entrepreneur and Public Servant.* Stanford, Calif.: Stanford University, School of Business Administration, 1976.

Ickes, Harold L. *The Autobiography of a Curmudgeon.* New York: Reynal and Hitchcock, 1943.

———. *The Secret Diary of Harold L. Ickes.* 3 vols. New York: Simon and Schuster, 1954.

Iriye, Akira. *Across the Pacific: An Inner History of American–East Asian Relations.* New York: Harcourt, Brace & World, 1961.

Ismay, Hastings Lionel. *Memoirs.* New York: Viking, 1960.

Jackman, Jarrell C., and Carla M. Borden, eds. *The Muses Flee Hitler: Cultural Transfer and Adaptation, 1930–1945.* Washington, D.C.: Smithsonian Institution Press, 1983.

Jackson, Carlton. *Presidential Vetoes, 1792–1945.* Athens: University of Georgia Press, 1967.

Jackson, Kenneth T. "Race, Ethnicity, and Real Estate Appraisal: The Home Owners Loan Corporation and the Federal Housing Administration." *Journal of Urban History* 6 (1980): 419–62.

Jackson, Robert H. *That Man: An Insider's Portrait of Franklin D. Roosevelt.* New York: Oxford University Press, 2003.

James, D. Clayton. *The Years of MacArthur.* Vols. 1–2. Boston: Houghton Mifflin, 1970, 1975.

Janeway, Eliot. *The Struggle for Survival.* New Haven, Conn.: Yale University Press, 1951.

Jeffries, John. "A 'Third New Deal'? Liberal Policy and the American State, 1937–1945." *Journal of Policy History* 8 (1996): 387–409.

———. *Wartime America: The World War II Home Front.* Chicago: Ivan R. Dee, 1998.

Jensen, Joan M. *The Price of Vigilance.* Chicago: Rand McNally, 1968.

Johnson, Charles W., and Charles O. Jackson. *City behind a Fence: Oak Ridge, Tennessee, 1942–1946.* Knoxville: University of Tennessee Press, 1981.

Johnson, Hugh S. *The Blue Eagle from Egg to Earth.* New York: Doubleday, 1935.

Johnson, Walter. *The Battle against Isolation.* Chicago: University of Chicago Press, 1944.

———. "Edward R. Stettinius, Jr." In *An Uncertain Tradition: American Secretaries of State in the Twentieth Century,* edited by Norman A. Graebner, 2110–23. New York: McGraw-Hill, 1961.

———, ed. *Selected Letters of William Allen White.* New York: Holt, 1947.

Jones, Jesse H., with Edward Angly. *Fifty Billion Dollars: My Thirteen Years with the RFC.* New York: Macmillan, 1951.

Jong, Louis de. *The German Fifth Column in the Second World War.* Chicago: University of Chicago Press, 1956.

Kantowicz, Edward R. "Cardinal Mundelein of Chicago and the Shaping of Twentieth-Century American Catholicism." *Journal of American History* 68 (1981).

———. *Corporation Sole: Cardinal Mundelein and Chicago Catholicism.* Notre Dame: University of Notre Dame Press, 1983.

Katznelson, Ira. *Fear Itself: The New Deal and the Origin of Our Time.* New York: Liverright, 2013.

Kauffman, Reginald W. *Jesse Isidor Straus: A Biographical Portrait*. New York: n.p., 1973.

Kaye, Harvey J. *The Fight for the Four Freedoms*. New York: Simon and Schuster, 2014.

Kearney, James R. *Anna Eleanor Roosevelt: The Evolution of a Reformer*. Boston: Houghton Mifflin, 1968.

Kelly, Lawrence C. *The Assault on Assimilation: John Collier and the Origins of Indian Policy Reform*. Albuquerque: University of New Mexico Press, 1983.

Kendrick, Alexander. *Prime Time: The Life of Edward R. Murrow*. Boston: Little, Brown, 1969.

Kennan, George F. *American Diplomacy, 1900–1950*. Chicago: University of Chicago Press, 1951.

Kennedy, David M. *Freedom from Fear: The American People in Depression and War*. New York: Oxford University Press, 1999.

Kennedy, Susan E. *The Banking Crisis of 1933*. Lexington: University Press of Kentucky, 1973.

Kersten, Andrew E. *A. Philip Randolph: A Life in the Vanguard*. Lanham, Md.: Rowman & Littlefield, 2007.

———. *Clarence Darrow: American Iconoclast*. New York: Hill and Wang, 2011.

———. *Race, Jobs, and the War: The FEPC in the Midwest, 1941–46*. Urbana: University of Illinois Press, 2000.

Kessner, Thomas. *Fiorello H. La Guardia and the Making of Modern New York*. New York: McGraw-Hill, 1989.

Keynes, John Maynard. *The Economic Consequences of the Peace*. New York: Harcourt, Brace, and Howe, 1920.

———. *Essays in Persuasion*. New York: Harcourt, Brace, 1932.

Kilpatrick, Carroll, ed. *Roosevelt and Daniels: A Friendship in Politics*. Chapel Hill: University of North Carolina Press, 1952.

Kimball, Warren F., ed. *Churchill and Roosevelt: The Complete Correspondence*. 3 vols. Princeton, N.J.: Princeton University Press, 1984. The 1987 paperback edition, with errata, is definitive.

———. *Forged in War: Roosevelt, Churchill, and the Second World War*. New York: Morrow, 1997.

———. *The Juggler: Franklin Roosevelt as Wartime Statesman*. Princeton, N.J.: Princeton University Press, 1991.

———. *The Most Unsordid Act: Lend Lease, 1939–1941*. Baltimore: Johns Hopkins University Press, 1969.

Kirkendall, Richard S. "Agricultural Adjustment Act." In *Franklin D. Roosevelt: His Life and Times; An Encyclopedic View*, edited by Otis L. Graham Jr. and Meghan R. Wander. Boston: G. K. Hall, 1983.

———. "Agriculture." In *Franklin D. Roosevelt: His Life and Times; An Encyclopedic View*, edited by Otis L. Graham Jr. and Meghan R. Wander. Boston: G. K. Hall, 1983.

Klaw, Spencer. "Labor's Non-Partisan League: An Experiment in Labor Politics." Master's thesis, Harvard University, 1941.

Kleeman, Rita Halle. *Gracious Lady: The Life of Sara Delano Roosevelt*. New York: D. Appleton–Century, 1935.

Klehr, Harvey, and John Haynes. "The Comintern's Open Secrets." *American Spectator* 25 (December 1992): 34–41.

Klein, Joe. *Woody Guthrie: A Life.* New York: Dell, 1980.

Kochavi, Arieh J. *Prelude to Nuremberg: Allied War Crimes Policy and the Question of Punishment.* Chapel Hill: University of North Carolina Press, 1998.

Koop, Theodore F. *Weapon of Silence.* Chicago: University of Chicago Press, 1946.

Kruger, Thomas. *And Promises to Keep: The Southern Conference of Human Welfare, 1938–1948.* Nashville: Vanderbilt University Press, 1967.

Kutler, Stanley I. *The American Inquisition: Justice and Injustice in the Cold War.* New York: Hill and Wang, 1982.

Kyvig, David E. *Explicit and Authentic Acts: Amending the U.S. Constitution, 1776–1995.* Lawrence: University Press of Kansas, 1996.

———. *Repealing National Prohibition.* Chicago: University of Chicago Press, 1979.

Lane, Anne Wintermute, and Louise Herrick Wall, eds. *The Letters of Franklin K. Lane, Personal and Political.* Boston: Houghton Mifflin, 1922.

Larrabee, Eric. *Commander in Chief: Franklin D. Roosevelt, His Lieutenants & Their War.* New York: Harper & Row, 1987.

Lash, Joseph P. *Eleanor and Franklin: The Story of Their Relationship, Based on Eleanor Roosevelt's Private Papers.* New York: W. W. Norton, 1971.

———. *Love, Eleanor: Eleanor Roosevelt and Her Friends.* New York: Doubleday, 1982.

Lasser, William. *Benjamin V. Cohen: Architect of the New Deal.* New Haven, Conn.: Yale University Press, 2002.

Leab, Daniel J. "United We Eat: The Creation and Organization of Unemployed Councils in 1930." *Labor History* 8 (1967): 300–315.

Leahy, William D. *I Was There.* New York: Whittlesey House, 1950.

Leff, Mark H. *The Limits of Symbolic Reform: The New Deal and Taxation, 1933–1939.* New York: Cambridge University Press, 1994.

Leighton, Richard M., and Robert W. Coakey. *Global Logistics and Strategy, 1940–1943.* 1955. Reprint, Washington, D.C.: Government Printing Office, 1995.

Lekachman, Robert. *The Age of Keynes.* New York: Random House, 1966.

Leotta, Louis. "Abraham Epstein and the Movement for Old Age Security." *Labor History* 16 (Summer 1975): 359–77.

Lepawsky, Albert. "The Planning Apparatus: A Vignette of the New Deal." *American Institute of Planners Journal* 42 (January 1976): 25.

Lerner, Barron H. "Crafting Medical History: Revisiting the 'Definitive' Account of Franklin D. Roosevelt's Terminal Illness." *Bulletin of the History of Medicine* 81, no. 2 (2007): 386–406.

Leuchtenburg, William E. "Charles Evans Hughes: The Center Holds." *North Carolina Law Review* 83 (June 2005): 1187–1204.

———. *The FDR Years: On Roosevelt and His Legacy.* New York: Columbia University Press, 1995.

———. *Flood Control Politics: The Connecticut River Valley Problem, 1927–1950.* Cambridge, Mass.: Harvard University Press, 1953.

———. *Franklin D. Roosevelt and the New Deal.* New York: Harper, 1963.

———. *In the Shadow of FDR: From Harry Truman to Barack Obama.* Ithaca, N.Y.: Cornell University Press, 2009.

———. "The New Deal and the Analogue of War." In *Change and Continuity in Twentieth Century America,* edited by John Braeman, Robert H. Bremner, and Everett Walters, 81–144. Columbus: Ohio State University Press, 1964.

———. *The Supreme Court Reborn: The Constitutional Revolution in the Age of Roosevelt.* New York: Oxford University Press, 1995.

———. *The White House Looks South: Franklin D. Roosevelt, Harry S. Truman, Lyndon B. Johnson.* Baton Rouge: Louisiana State University Press, 2005.

Levin, Linda Lotridge. *The Making of FDR: The Story of Stephen T. Early, America's First Modern Press Secretary.* Amherst, N.Y.: Prometheus, 2008.

Levine, Lawrence W., and Cornelia R. Levine. *The People and the President: America's Conversation with FDR.* Boston: Beacon Press, 2002.

Lichtenstein, Nelson. *Labor's War at Home.* New York: Cambridge University Press, 1982.

Lilienthal, David E. *The Journals of David E. Lilienthal: The TVA Years, 1939–1945.* New York: Harper & Row, 1964.

———. *TVA: Democracy on the March.* New York: Harper, 1944.

Lindenmeyer, Kriste. *The Greatest Generation Grows Up: American Childhood in the 1930s.* Chicago: Ivan R. Dee, 2005.

———. *"A Right to Childhood": The U.S. Children's Bureau and Child Welfare, 1912–1946.* Urbana: University of Illinois Press, 1997.

Lindley, Ernest K. *Franklin D. Roosevelt: A Career in Progressive Democracy.* New York: Blue Ribbon Books, 1931.

Link, Arthur S. *Wilson: The Struggle for Neutrality, 1914–1915.* Princeton, N.J.: Princeton University Press, 1960.

Link, Arthur S, et al., eds. *The Papers of Woodrow Wilson.* 69 vols. Princeton, N.J.: Princeton University Press, 1966–94.

Lippman, Thomas W. *Arabian Knight: Colonel Bill Eddy USMC and the Rise of American Power in the Middle East.* Vista, Calif.: Selwa Press, 2008.

Lippmann, Walter. "First Roosevelt Policies." March 11, 1933. Reprinted in *Interpretations, 1933–1935,* edited by Allan Nevins, 27. New York: Macmillan, 1936.

———. "Governor Roosevelt's Candidacy." January 8, 1932. Reprinted in *Interpretations, 1931–1932,* edited by Allan Nevins, 261–62. New York: Macmillan, 1932.

Livermore, Seward W. *Politics Is Adjourned: Woodrow Wilson and the War Congress, 1916–1918.* Middletown, Conn.: Wesleyan University Press, 1966.

Loewenheim, Francis L., Harold D. Langley, and Manfred Jonas. *Roosevelt and Churchill, Their Secret Wartime Correspondence.* New York: Saturday Review Press, 1975.

Looker, Earle. *This Man Roosevelt.* New York: Brewer, Warren & Putnam, 1932.

Lord, Russell. *The Wallaces of Iowa.* Boston: Houghton Mifflin, 1947.

Lorentz, Pare. *FDR's Moviemaker: Memoirs and Scripts.* Reno: University of Nevada Press, 1992.

Lowenstein, Sharon R. *Token Refuge: The Story of the Jewish Refugee Shelter at Oswego, 1944–1946.* Bloomington: Indiana University Press, 1986.

Lowitt, Richard. *George W. Norris: The Persistence of a Progressive, 1913–1933.* Urbana: University of Illinois Press, 1971.

———. *George W. Norris: The Triumph of a Progressive, 1933–1944.* Urbana: University of Illinois Press, 1978.

Lowitt, Richard, and Maurine Beasley, eds. *One Third of a Nation: Lorena Hickok Reports on the Great Depression.* Urbana: University of Illinois Press, 1981.

Lubell, Samuel. *The Future of American Politics.* New York: Harper, 1952.

Madison, James H. *The Indiana Way: A State History.* Bloomington: Indiana University Press, 1986.

Malcolm, James, ed. *The New York Red Book.* Albany: J. B. Lyon, 1930.

Manning, Thomas G. *The Office of Price Administration: A World War II Agency of Control.* New York: Holy, 1960.

Marks, Edward B., Jr. *Token Refuge: The Story of America's War Refugee Shelter.* Washington, D.C.: Government Printing Office, 1946.

Marolda, Edward J., ed. *FDR and the U.S. Navy.* New York: St. Martin's, 1998.

Marquis, Albert N., ed. *Who's Who in America, 1934–35.* Chicago: A. N. Marquis, 1934.

Martin, George. *Madam Secretary: Frances Perkins.* Boston: Houghton Mifflin, 1976.

Masters, Charles J. *Governor Henry Horner, Chicago Politics and the Great Depression.* Carbondale: Southern Illinois University Press, 2007.

Matloff, Maurice. *Strategic Planning for Coalition Warfare, 1943–44.* 1959. Reprint, Washington, D.C.: Government Printing Office, 1990.

Matloff, Maurice, and Edwin M. Snell. *Strategic Planning for Coalition Warfare, 1941–42.* 1953. Reprint, Washington, D.C.: Government Printing Office, 1999.

May, Dean L. *From the New Deal to the New Economics.* New York: Garland, 1981.

May, Irvin M. *Marvin Jones: The Public Life of an Agrarian Advocate.* College Station: Texas A&M University Press, 1980.

McCoy, Donald R. "The Good Neighbor League and the Presidential Campaign of 1936." *Western Political Quarterly* 13 (1960): 1011–21.

———. *Landon of Kansas.* Lincoln: University of Nebraska Press, 1966.

McElvaine, Robert S., ed. *Encyclopedia of the Great Depression.* New York: Thompson/Gale, 2004.

McFarland, Keith. *Harry H. Woodring: A Political Biography of FDR's Controversial Secretary of War.* Lawrence: University Press of Kansas, 1975.

McGraw, Thomas K. *Morgan vs. Lilienthal: The Feud within the TVA.* Chicago: University of Chicago Press, 1970.

McIntyre, Ross T. *White House Physician.* New York: G. P. Putnam, 1946.

McJimsey, George. *Harry Hopkins: Ally of the Poor and Defender of Democracy.* Cambridge, Mass.: Harvard University Press, 1987.

McKenna, Marian. *Borah.* Ann Arbor: University of Michigan Press, 1961.

———. *Franklin Roosevelt and the Great Constitutional War: The Court-Packing Crisis of 1937.* New York. Fordham University Press, 2002.

Medoff, Rafael. *Blowing the Whistle on the Holocaust: Josiah E. Dubois, Jr. and the Struggle for a U.S. Response to the Holocaust.* West Lafayette, Ind.: Purdue University Press, 2009.

Meriam, Lewis. *Relief and Social Security.* Washington, D.C.: Brookings Institution, 1946.

Meyer, Leisa D. *Creating G.I. Jane: Sexuality and Power in the Women's Army Corps during World War II*. New York: Columbia University Press, 1996.

Meyers, Susan E. *Norman Rockwell's World War II: Impressions from the Homefront*. San Antonio: USAA Foundation, 1991.

Miller, John, Jr. *Guadalcanal: The First Offensive*. Washington, D.C.: Center for Military History, 1949.

Miller, Robert E. "The War That Never Came: Civilian Defense, Mobilization, and Morale during World War II." Ph.D. diss., University of Cincinnati, 1991.

Millis, Walter. *Arms and Men: A Study in Military History*. New York: Putnam, 1956.

———. *The Road to War: America, 1914–1917*. Boston: Houghton Mifflin, 1935.

Mitchell, Broadus. *The Campaign of the Century: Upton Sinclair's Race for Governor of California and the Birth of Media Politics*. New York: Random House, 1992.

———. *Depression Decade: From New Era through New Deal*. New York: Holt, Rinehart, and Winston, 1961.

Mitgang, Herbert. *The Man Who Rode the Tiger: The Life and Times of Judge Samuel Seabury*. Philadelphia: Lippincott, 1963.

Moeller, Beverley B. *Phil Swing and Boulder Dam*. Berkeley: University of California Press, 1971.

Moley, Raymond. *After Seven Years*. New York: Harper, 1939.

Monnet, Jean. *Memoirs*. New York: Doubleday, 1978.

Moran, Baron Charles M. Wilson. *Churchill, Taken from the Diaries of Lord Moran: The Struggle for Survival, 1940–1965*. Boston: Houghton Mifflin, 1966.

Morgan, Arthur E. *The Making of the TVA*. Buffalo, N.Y.: Prometheus Books, 1974.

Morgan, Chester M. *Redneck Liberal: Theodore Bilbo and the New Deal*. Baton Rouge: Louisiana State University Press, 1985.

Morgan, H. Wayne. *William McKinley and His America*. Syracuse, N.Y.: Syracuse University Press, 1963.

Morison, Elting E., ed. *The Letters of Theodore Roosevelt*. Vols. 2–3, 6. Cambridge, Mass.: Harvard University Press, 1951–52.

Morison, Samuel E. *History of United States Naval Operations in World War II*. 15 vols. Boston: Little, Brown, 1947–62.

———. *The Two Ocean War: A Short History of the United States Navy in World War Two*. Boston: Little, Brown, 1963.

Morris, Edmund. *The Rise of Theodore Roosevelt*. New York: Coward, McCann, Geoghegan, 1979.

Morrison, Joseph L. *Josephus Daniels: The Small-d Democrat*. Chapel Hill: University of North Carolina Press, 1966.

———. *Josephus Daniels Says . . . : An Editor's Political Odyssey from Bryan to Wilson and F.D.R., 1894–1913*. Chapel Hill: University of North Carolina Press, 1962.

Morton, Louis. *The Fall of the Philippines*. Washington, D.C.: Center for Military History, 1953.

———. "War Plan Orange: Evolution of a Strategy." *World Politics* 11 (1959): 221–50.

Moscow, Warren. *Politics in the Empire State*. New York: Alfred A. Knopf, 1948.

Mowry, George E. *Theodore Roosevelt and the Progressive Movement*. Madison: University of Wisconsin Press, 1946.

Muller, Eric L. *American Inquisition: The Hunt for Japanese American Disloyalty in World War II.* Chapel Hill: University of North Carolina Press, 2007.

Murphy, Lawrence R. *Perverts by Official Order: The Campaign against Homosexuals by the United States Navy.* New York: Haworth Press, 1988.

Murphy, Robert D. *Diplomat among Warriors.* New York: Doubleday, 1964.

Murphy, Thomas D. *Ambassadors in Arms: The Story of Hawaii's 100th Battalion.* Honolulu: University of Hawaii Press, 1946.

Murray, Robert K. *The 103rd Ballot: Democrats and the Disaster in Madison Square Garden.* New York: Harper & Row, 1976.

———. *Red Scare: A Study in National Hysteria, 1919–1920.* Minneapolis: University of Minnesota Press, 1955.

Murray, Stuart, and James McCabe. *Norman Rockwell's Four Freedoms: Images That Inspired a Nation.* Stockbridge, Mass.: Norman Rockwell Museum, 1993.

Myers, Howard B. "Corrington Calhoun Gill, 1898–1945." *Journal of the American Statistical Association* 41 (September 1948).

Myers, William S., and Walter H. Newton. *The Hoover Administration: A Documented Narrative.* New York: Scribner's, 1936.

Myrdal, Gunnar. *An American Dilemma: The Negro Problem and Modern Democracy.* New York: Harper, 1944.

National Emergency Council. *Report on the Economic Conditions of the South.* Washington, D.C.: Government Printing Office, 1938.

Neal, Steve. *Dark Horse: A Biography of Wendell Willkie.* New York: Doubleday, 1984.

Nelson, Donald M. *Arsenal of Democracy: The Story of American War Production.* New York: Harcourt, Brace, 1946.

Neumann, William L. "Franklin D. Roosevelt and Japan, 1913–1933." *Pacific Historical Review* 22 (1953): 143–53.

Nevins, Allan. *Herbert H. Lehman and His Era.* New York: Scribner's, 1963.

Newman, Roger K. *Hugo Black: A Biography.* New York: Pantheon, 1994.

Newton, Verne, ed. *FDR and the Holocaust.* New York: St. Martin's, 1996.

New York State. *Old Age Security: Report of the New York State Commission.* Albany: J. B. Lyon, 1930.

New York [State] Governor's Commission on Unemployment. *Less Unemployment through Stabilization of Operations.* Albany: J. B. Lyon, 1930.

———. *Problems: Preventing Unemployment; Preliminary Report. . . .* Albany: J. B. Lyon, 1930.

Nixon, Edgar B., ed. *Franklin D. Roosevelt and Conservation, 1911–1945.* 2 vols. Hyde Park, N.Y.: FDR Library, 1957.

———. *Franklin D. Roosevelt and Foreign Affairs.* 17 vols. Cambridge, Mass.: Harvard University Press, 1969–79.

North, Douglas. *Growth and Welfare in the American Past.* Englewood Cliffs, N.J.: Prentice Hall, 1966.

Numbers, Ronald L. *Almost Persuaded: American Physicians and Compulsory Health Insurance, 1912–1920.* Baltimore: Johns Hopkins University Press, 1978.

O'Brien, David M. *Storm Center: The Supreme Court in American Politics.* New York: W. W. Norton, 1986.

Official Report of the Proceedings of the Democratic National Convention . . . 1920. Indianapolis: Bookwalter-Ball, 1920.

Ohl, John Kennedy. *Hugh S. Johnson and the New Deal.* DeKalb: Northern Illinois University Press, 1985.

———. *Supplying the Troops: General Somervell and American Logistics in WWII.* DeKalb: Northern Illinois University Press, 1994.

Okihiro, Gary Y. *Cane Fires: The Anti-Japanese Movement in Hawaii, 1865–1945.* Philadelphia: Temple University Press, 1991.

Olson, James S. *Saving Capitalism: The Reconstruction Finance Corporation and the New Deal, 1933–1940.* Princeton, N.J.: Princeton University Press, 1988.

O'Reilly, Kenneth, ed. *The FBI File on the House Committee on Un-American Activities.* Microfilm. Wilmington, Del.: Scholarly Resources, 1986.

Osborn, Chase S. *The Iron Hunter.* Edited by Robert M. Warner. 1919. Reprint, Detroit: Wayne State University Press, 2002.

Oshinsky, David. *Polio: An American Story.* New York: Oxford University Press, 2005.

Parrish, Michael E. *Securities Regulation and the New Deal.* New Haven, Conn.: Yale University Press, 1970.

Patterson, James T. *Congressional Conservatism and the New Deal: The Growth of the Congressional Coalition in Congress, 1933–1939.* Lexington: University Press of Kentucky, 1967.

———. *Mr. Republican: A Biography of Robert A. Taft.* Boston: Houghton Mifflin, 1972.

Pecora, Ferdinand. *Wall Street under Oath: The Story of Our Modern Money Changers.* New York: Simon and Schuster, 1939.

Peek, George N., with Samuel Crowther. *Why Quit Our Own.* New York: D. Van Nostrand, 1936.

Perkins, Frances. *The Roosevelt I Knew.* New York: Viking, 1946.

Perry, Elisabeth Israels. *Belle Moskowitz: Feminine Politics and the Exercise of Power in the Age of Alfred E. Smith.* New York: Oxford University Press, 1987.

Persico, Joseph E. *Franklin and Lucy.* New York: Random House, 2008.

Pivar, David J. *Purity and Hygiene: Women, Prostitution, and the "American Plan," 1900–1930.* Westport, Conn.: Greenwood Press, 2002.

Piven, Frances Fox, and Richard Cloward. *Regulating the Poor: The Functions of Public Welfare.* New York: Pantheon, 1971.

Plokhy, S. M. *Yalta: The Price of Peace.* Cambridge, Mass.: Harvard University Press, 2010.

Pogue, Forrest C. *George C. Marshall.* 4 vols. New York: Viking, 1963–87.

Polenberg, Richard. "Franklin Roosevelt and the Purge of John O'Connor: The Impact of Urban Change on Political Parties." *New York History* 49 (1968): 306–26.

———. *Reorganizing Roosevelt's Government.* Cambridge, Mass.: Harvard University Press, 1966.

———. *War and Society.* New York: Lippincott, 1973.

Potter, E. B. *Fleet Admiral Chester W. Nimitz.* New York: St. Martin's, 1993.

Potter, E. B., and Chester W. Nimitz. *Triumph in the Pacific: The Navy's Struggle against Japan.* Englewood Cliffs, N.J.: Prentice Hall, 1963.

Prados, John. *The White House Tapes: Eavesdropping on the President.* New York: New Press, 2003.

Pritchett, C. Herman. *The Roosevelt Court: A Study in Judicial Politics and Values, 1937–1947.* New York: Macmillan, 1948.

———. *The Tennessee Valley Authority: A Study in Public Administration.* Chapel Hill: University of North Carolina Press, 1943.

Proskauer, Joseph M. *A Segment of My Times.* New York: Farrar, Straus, 1956.

Quirk, Robert E. *An Affair of Honor: Woodrow Wilson and the Occupation of Vera Cruz.* Lexington: University Press of Kentucky, 1962.

Radford, Gail. *Modern Housing for America: Policy Struggles in the New Deal Era.* Chicago: University of Chicago Press, 1996.

Radomski, Alexander L. *Work Relief in New York State, 1931–1935.* New York: Kings Crown, 1947.

Randolph, A. Philip. "Why and How the March Was Postponed." *Black Worker* 7, no. 8 (1941): 1–2.

Rauchway, Eric. *Murdering McKinley: The Making of Theodore Roosevelt's America.* New York: Hill and Wang, 2003.

Rawick, George P. "The New Deal and Youth: The Civilian Conservation Corps, the National Youth Administration, and the American Youth Congress." Ph.D. diss., University of Wisconsin, 1957.

Reilly, Michael F. *Reilly of the White House.* New York: Simon and Schuster, 1947.

Reiman, Richard A. *The New Deal and American Youth: Ideas and Ideals in a Depression Decade.* Athens: University of Georgia Press, 1992.

———. "The New Deal for Youth: A Cincinnati Connection." *Queen City Heritage* 44 (1986): 36–48.

Reingold, Nathan. "Vannevar Bush's New Deal for Research." *Historical Studies in the Physical and Biological Sciences* 17, no. 2 (1987).

Reynolds, David. *From Munich to Pearl Harbor: Roosevelt's America and the Origins of the Second World War.* Chicago: Ivan R. Dee, 2001.

Rice, Diana. "Mrs. Roosevelt Takes on Another Task." *New York Times Magazine,* December 2, 1928.

Rigdon, William M. *White House Sailor.* New York: Doubleday, 1974.

Riggs, Fred W. *Pressures on Congress: A Study of the Repeal of Chinese Exclusion.* New York: King's Crown, 1950.

Riis, Jacob A. *Theodore Roosevelt: The Citizen.* Washington, D.C.: Johnson, Wynne, 1904.

Ritchie, Donald. *James M. Landis, Dean of the Regulators.* Cambridge, Mass.: Harvard University Press, 1980.

Robertson, David. *Sly and Able: A Political Biography of James F. Byrnes.* New York: W. W. Norton, 1994.

Robinson, Edgar E. *The Presidential Vote, 1896–1932.* Stanford, Calif.: Stanford University Press, 1934.

———. *They Voted for Roosevelt.* Stanford, Calif.: Stanford University Press, 1947.

Robinson, Greg. *By Order of the President: FDR and the Internment of Japanese Americans.* Cambridge, Mass.: Harvard University Press, 2001.

Rogers, Naomi. *Dirt and Disease: Polio before FDR.* New Brunswick, N.J.: Rutgers University Press, 1992.

———. "Race and the Politics of Polio: Warm Springs, Tuskegee, and the March of Dimes." *American Journal of Public Health* 97 (2007): 784–95.

Rollins, Alfred B., Jr. *Roosevelt and Howe.* New York: Alfred A. Knopf, 1962.

Romasco, Albert U. *The Poverty of Abundance: Hoover, the Nation, the Depression.* New York: Oxford University Press, 1965.

Roose, Kenneth D. "The Depression of 1937–38." *Journal of Political Economy* 56 (1948): 239–48.

Roosevelt, Eleanor. *On My Own.* New York: Harper, 1958

———. *This I Remember.* New York: Harper, 1949.

———. *This Is My Story.* New York: Harper, 1937.

———. "Women Must Learn to Play the Game as Men Do." *Red Book,* April 1928, 78–79, 141–42.

Roosevelt, Elliott, ed. *F.D.R.: His Personal Letters.* 3 vols. New York: Duell, Sloan, and Pearce, 1950.

———. "The Most Unforgettable Character I've Met." *Reader's Digest,* February 1953, 26–30.

Roosevelt, Franklin D. *The Complete Presidential Press Conferences of Franklin D. Roosevelt.* 25 vols. New York: Da Capo Press, 1972.

———. "Shall We Trust Japan?" *Asia* 23 (1923): 475–78, 526, 528.

———. "The New Deal: An Interpretation." *Liberty,* December 10, 1932, 7–8.

———. "Our Foreign Policy: A Democratic View." *Foreign Affairs* 6 (1928): 573–86.

———. *Public Papers of Franklin D. Roosevelt, Forty-Eighth Governor of New York.* 4 vols. Albany: J. B. Lyon, 1929–33.

———. "The Real Meaning of the Power Problem." *Forum* 82 (1929): 327–32.

———. *Whither Bound?* Boston: Houghton Mifflin, 1926.

Roosevelt, James, with Bill Libby. *My Parents: A Differing View.* Chicago: Playboy Press, 1976.

Roosevelt, James, and Sidney Shalett. *Affectionately, F.D.R.: A Son's Story of a Lonely Man.* New York: Harcourt, Brace, 1959.

Roosevelt, Sara Delano. *My Boy Franklin, as Told by Mrs. James Roosevelt to Isabel Leighton and Gabrielle Forbush.* New York: R. Long & R. R. Smith, 1933.

Roosevelt, Theodore. *An Autobiography.* 1913. Reprint, New York: Scribner's, 1923.

———. *Letters from Theodore Roosevelt to Anna Roosevelt Cowles, 1870–1918.* New York: Scribner's, 1924.

Roper, Daniel C., with the collaboration of Frank H. Lovette. *Fifty Years of Public Life.* Durham, N.C.: Duke University Press, 1941.

Rose, Mark H. *Interstate: Express Highway Politics, 1941–1956.* Lawrence: University Press of Kansas, 1969.

Rosenbaum, Herbert D., and Elizabeth Bartelme, eds. *Franklin D. Roosevelt: The Man, the Myth, the Era, 1882–1945.* Westport, Conn.: Greenwood Press, 1987.

Rosenberg, Charles. "Martin Arrowsmith: The Scientist as Hero." *American Quarterly* 15 (1963): 447–58.

Rosenman, Samuel I., ed. *Public Papers and Addresses of Franklin D. Roosevelt.* 13 vols. New York: Random House, 1938–50.

———. *Working with Roosevelt.* New York: Harper, 1952.

Ross, Davis R. B. *Preparing for Ulysses: Politics and Veterans during WW II*. New York: Columbia University Press, 1969.

Rossiter, Clinton. *The American Presidency*. New York: Harcourt, Brace, 1960.

Rostow, Eugene V. "The Japanese American Cases: A Disaster." *Yale Law Journal* 54 (July 1945): 498–533.

———. "Our Worst Wartime Mistake." *Harper's Magazine*, September 1945, 193–201.

Rovere, Richard H. *The Goldwater Caper*. New York: Harcourt, Brace & World, 1965.

Salmond, John A. *The Civilian Conservation Corps, 1933–1942: A New Deal Case Study*. Durham, N.C.: Duke University Press, 1967.

———. *A Southern Rebel: The Life and Times of Aubrey Willis Williams, 1890–1965*. Chapel Hill: University of North Carolina Press, 1985.

Saloutos, Theodore. *The American Farmer and the New Deal*. Ames: Iowa State University Press, 1982.

Sandage, Scott A. "A Marble House Divided: The Lincoln Memorial, the Civil Rights Movement, and the Politics of Memory, 1939–1963." *Journal of American History* 80 (1993): 135–67.

Sandilands, Roger J. *The Life and Political Economy of Lauchlin Currie*. Durham, N.C.: Duke University Press, 1990.

Saunders, Kay, and Roger Daniels, eds. *Alien Justice: Wartime Internment in Australia and North America*. St. Lucia: University of Queensland, 2000.

Sautter, Udo. *Three Cheers for the Unemployed: Government and Unemployment before the New Deal*. New York: Cambridge University Press, 1991.

Schlabach, Theron F. *Edwin E. Witte: Cautious Reformer*. Madison: State Historical Society of Wisconsin, 1969.

Schlesinger, Arthur M., Jr. *The Coming of the New Deal*. Boston: Houghton Mifflin, 1958.

———. *The Crisis of the Old Order, 1919–1933*. Boston: Houghton Mifflin, 1957.

———. *The Politics of Upheaval*. Boston: Houghton Mifflin, 1960.

Schlesinger, Robert. *White House Ghosts: Presidents and Their Speechwriters*. New York: Simon and Schuster, 2008.

Schmidt, Hans. *The United States Occupation of Haiti, 1915–1934*. New Brunswick, N.J.: Rutgers University Press, 1971.

Schroeder, Paul W. *The Axis Alliance and Japanese-American Relations, 1941*. Ithaca, N.Y.: Cornell University Press, 1958.

Schwartz, Bonnie Fox. *The Civil Works Administration, 1933–1934: The Business of Emergency Employment in the New Deal*. Princeton, N.J.: Princeton University Press, 1984.

Schwarz, Jordan A. "Al Smith in the 1930s." *New York History* 45 (1964): 316–30.

———. "John Nance Garner and the Sales Tax Rebellion of 1932." *Journal of Southern History* 30 (1964): 162–80.

Scobie, Ingrid Winther. *Center Stage: Helen Gahagan Douglas, a Life*. New York: Oxford University Press, 1992.

Scott, William R. *The Sons of Sheba's Race: African-Americans and the Italo-Ethiopian War, 1935–1941*. Bloomington: Indiana University Press, 1993.

Seeber, Frances M. "I Want You to Write to Me: The Papers of Anna Eleanor Roosevelt." *Prologue* 19 (1987): 95–105.

Seidman, Joel. *American Labor from Defense to Reconversion.* Chicago: University of Chicago Press, 1953.

Seligman, Lester G., and Elmer G. Cornwell, eds. *New Deal Mosaic: Roosevelt Confers with His National Emergency Council.* Eugene: University of Oregon Books, 1965.

Sherwin, Martin J. *A World Destroyed: The Atomic Bomb and the Grand Alliance.* New York: Alfred A. Knopf, 1975.

Sherwood, Robert E. *Roosevelt and Hopkins: An Intimate History.* New York: Harper, 1948.

Shlaes, Amity. *The Forgotten Man: A New History of the Great Depression.* New York: Harper, 2007.

Shover, John L. *Cornbelt Rebellion: The Farmer's Holiday Association.* Urbana: University of Illinois Press, 1965.

Sills, David L. *The Volunteers, Means and Ends in a National Organization: A Report.* Glencoe, Ill.: Free Press, 1957.

Silva, Ruth C. *Rum, Religion, and Votes: 1928 Reconsidered.* University Park: Pennsylvania State University Press, 1962.

Sims, William S. *The Victory at Sea.* Garden City, N.Y.: Doubleday, 1920.

Sitkoff, Harvard. *A New Deal for Blacks.* New York: Oxford University Press, 1978.

Skidelsky, Robert. *John Maynard Keynes.* Vol. 1, *Hopes Betrayed, 1883–1920.* Vol. 2, *The Economist as Saviour, 1920–1937.* Vol. 3, *Fighting for Britain, 1937–1946.* London: Macmillan, 1983–2001.

Smiley, Gene. *Rethinking the Great Depression.* Chicago: Ivan R. Dee, 2002.

Smith, A. Merriman. *Thank You, Mr. President.* New York: Harper, 1946.

Smith, Elaine M. "Mary McLeod Bethune and the National Youth Administration." In *Clio Was a Woman: Studies in the History of American Women,* edited by Mabel E. Deutrich and Virginia C. Purdy, 149–77. Washington, D.C.: Howard University Press, 1980.

Smith, Ira Robert Taylor. *"Dear Mr. President . . .": Fifty Years in the White House Mail Room.* New York: J. Messner, 1949.

Smith, Neil. *American Empire: Roosevelt's Geographer and the Prelude to Globalization.* Berkeley: University of California Press, 2003.

Smith, Richard Norton. *Thomas E. Dewey and His Times.* New York: Simon and Schuster, 1982.

Snyder, Robert L. *Pare Lorentz and the Documentary Film.* Norman: University of Oklahoma Press, 1968.

Sosna, Morton. *In Search of the Silent South: Southern Liberals and the Race Issue.* New York: Columbia University Press, 1977.

Speakman, Joseph R. *At Work in Penn's Woods: The Civilian Conservation Corps in Pennsylvania.* University Park: Pennsylvania State University Press, 2006.

Spector, Ronald H. *Eagle against the Sun: The American War against Japan.* New York: Free Press, 1954.

———. "Josephus Daniels, Franklin Roosevelt, and the Reinvention of the Naval Enlisted Man." In *FDR and the U.S. Navy,* edited by Edward J. Marolda, 19–33. New York: St. Martin's, 1998.

Spencer, Thomas T. "Democratic Auxiliary and Non-party Groups in the Election of 1936." Ph.D. diss., University of Notre Dame, 1976.

———. "The Good Neighbor League Colored Committee and the 1936 Democratic Presidential Campaign." *Journal of Negro History* 63 (1978): 307–16.

Starling, Edmund W. *Starling of the White House.* New York: Simon and Schuster, 1946.

Steele, Richard W. *Propaganda in an Open Society: The Roosevelt Administration and the Media, 1933–1941.* Westport, Conn.: Greenwood Press, 1985.

Stein, Herbert. *Presidential Economics: The Making of Economic Policy from Roosevelt to Clinton.* Washington, D.C.: American Enterprise Institute for Public Policy Research, 1994.

Sterner, Richard. *The Negro's Share: A Study of Income, Consumption, Housing, and Public Assistance.* New York: Harper, 1943.

Sternsher, Bernard. *Rexford Tugwell and the New Deal.* New Brunswick, N.J.: Rutgers University Press, 1964.

Stettinius, Edward R. *Lend-Lease, Weapon for Victory.* New York: Macmillan, 1944.

———. *Roosevelt and the Russians.* New York: Doubleday, 1949.

Stewart, Barbara McDonald. *United States Government Policy on Refugees from Nazism, 1933–1940.* New York: Garland, 1982.

Stiles, Lela. *The Man behind Roosevelt: The Story of Louis McHenry Howe.* Cleveland, Ohio: World, 1954.

Stimson, Henry L., and McGeorge Bundy. *On Active Service in Peace and War.* New York: Harper, 1948.

Straus, Nathan. *Two-Thirds of a Nation: A Housing Program.* New York: Alfred A. Knopf, 1952.

Swain, Martha H. *Ellen S. Woodward: New Deal Advocate for Women.* Jackson: University Press of Mississippi, 1995.

———. *Pat Harrison: The New Deal Years.* Jackson: University Press of Mississippi, 1978.

Takei, Barbara. "Legalizing Detention: Segregated Japanese Americans and the Justice Department's Renunciation Program." *Journal of the Shaw Historical Library* 19 (2005): 75–105.

Talbert, Roy. *FDR's Utopian: Arthur Morgan of the TVA.* Jackson: University Press of Mississippi, 1987.

Taylor, A. J. P. *English History, 1914–1945.* Oxford: Oxford University Press, 1965.

Taylor, Graham D. *The New Deal and American Indian Tribalism: The Administration of the Indian Reorganization Act.* Baltimore: Johns Hopkins University Press, 1978.

Taylor, Paul S., and Norman Leon Gold. "San Francisco and the General Strike." *Survey Graphic* 23 (September 1934): 405–11.

Taylor, Quintard. *The Forging of a Black Community: Seattle's Central District, from 1870 through the Civil Rights Era.* Seattle: University of Washington Press, 1994.

Terkel, Studs. *"The Good War."* New York: Pantheon, 1984.

Theoharis, Athan G. *J. Edgar Hoover, Sex, and Crime: An Historical Antidote.* Chicago: Ivan R. Dee, 1995.

Tillett, Paul. *The Army Flies the Mails.* Tuscaloosa: University of Alabama Press, 1955.

Treadwell, Mattie E. *The Women's Army Corps.* Washington, D.C.: Government Printing Office, 1954.

Tregaskis, Richard. *Guadalcanal Diary*. New York: Random House, 1943.

Troy, Thomas F. *Donovan and the CIA: A History of the Establishment of the Central Intelligence Agency*. Langley, Va.: Central Intelligence Agency, 1981.

Truman, Harry S. *Memoirs*. 2 vols. New York: Doubleday, 1955–56.

Tugwell, Rexford G. *The Brains Trust*. New York: Viking, 1968.

——. *The Democratic Roosevelt*. New York: Doubleday, 1957.

——. *In Search of Roosevelt*. Cambridge, Mass.: Harvard University Press, 1972.

——. "The Two Great Roosevelts." *Western Political Quarterly* 5 (March 1952): 84–93.

Tully, Grace G. *FDR, My Boss*. New York: Scribner's, 1949.

Twomey, Jane L. "May Craig: Journalist and Liberal Feminist." *Journalism History* 27, no. 3 (2001): 129–38.

U.S. Congress. Joint Committee on the Investigation of the Pearl Harbor Attack. *Pearl Harbor Attack*. Washington, D.C.: Government Printing Office, 1946.

U.S. Department of Commerce. *Historical Statistics of the United States: Colonial Times to 1957*. Washington, D.C.: Government Printing Office, 1960.

U.S. Department of State. *Foreign Relations of the United States, 1933–1945*. Washington, D.C.: Government Printing Office, 1933–45.

U.S. House of Representatives. *A Message from the President of the United States Transmitting a Report of the National Interregional Highway Committee. . . .* House Document no. 379. Washington, D.C.: Government Printing Office, 1944.

——. Tolan Committee. 77th Cong. *House Report 2124*. Washington, D.C.: Government Printing Office, 1942.

U.S. Senate. *Presidential Vetoes, 1789–1988*. S. Pub. 102-12. Washington, D.C.: Government Printing Office, 1992.

Vadney, Thomas E. *The Wayward Liberal: A Political Biography of Donald Richberg*. Lexington: University Press of Kentucky, 1970.

Vatter, Harold G. *The U.S. Economy in World War II*. New York: Columbia University Press, 1985.

Veritas Foundation. *Keynes at Harvard: Economic Deception as a Political Credo*. New York: Veritas Foundation, 1962.

Villard, Oswald Garrison. "The Plight of the Negro Voter." *Crisis* (November 1934).

Vogel, Steve. *The Pentagon*. New York: Random House, 2007.

Voorhis, Jerry. *Confessions of a Congressman*. New York: Doubleday, 1947.

Wainwright, Jonathan M. *General Wainwright's Story*. New York: Doubleday, 1946.

Walker, Frank C. *FDR's Quiet Confidant: The Autobiography of Frank C. Walker*. Edited by Robert H. Ferrell. Niwot: University Press of Colorado, 1997.

Walker, Turnley. *Roosevelt and the Fight against Polio*. London: Rider, 1954.

——. *Roosevelt and the Warm Springs Story*. London: A. A. Wyn, 1954.

Wann, A. J. "Franklin D. Roosevelt's Administrative Contributions to the Presidency." In *Franklin D. Roosevelt: The Man, the Myth, the Era, 1882–1945*, edited by Herbert D. Rosenbaum and Elizabeth Bartelme, 239–53. Westport, Conn.: Greenwood Press, 1987.

——. *The President as Chief Administrator: A Study of Franklin D. Roosevelt*. Washington, D.C.: Public Affairs Press, 1968.

Ward, Geoffrey C. *Before the Trumpet: Young Franklin Roosevelt, 1882–1905.* New York: Harper & Row, 1985.

———. *A First Class Temperament: The Emergence of Franklin Roosevelt.* New York: Harper & Row, 1989.

Ware, Gilbert. *William Hastie: Grace under Pressure.* New York: Oxford University Press, 1984.

Ware, Susan. *Beyond Suffrage: Women in the New Deal.* Cambridge, Mass.: Harvard University Press, 1981.

———. *Partner and I: Molly Dewson, Feminism, and New Deal Politics.* New Haven, Conn.: Yale University Press, 1987.

Warn, A. W. "Senator F. D. Roosevelt, Chief Insurgent at Albany." *New York Times Sunday Magazine,* January 22, 1911, 11; January 31, 1911, 3.

Warner, Hoyt Landon. *The Life of Mr. Justice Clarke: A Testament to the Power of Liberal Dissent in America.* Cleveland, Ohio: Western Reserve University Press, 1959.

Watson, Mark S. *Chief of Staff: Prewar Plans and Preparations.* 1950. Reprint, Washington, D.C.: Center of Military History, 1991.

Weil, Arthur T. "Exploding the Myth of a 'Jewish Hierarchy.'" *American Hebrew* (1934).

Weinberg, Gerhard L. *A World at Arms: A Global History of World War II.* 2nd ed. New York: Cambridge University Press, 2005.

Weingroff, Richard. "President Roosevelt and Excess Condemnation." http://www.fhwa .dot.gov/infrastructure/excess.cfm.

Weiss, Nancy J. *Charles Francis Murphy, 1858–1924: Respectability and Responsibility in Tammany Politics.* Northampton, Mass.: Smith College, 1968.

———. *Farewell to the Party of Lincoln.* Princeton, N.J.: Princeton University Press, 1983.

Weiss, Stuart L. *The President's Man: Leo T. Crowley and Franklin D. Roosevelt in Peace and War.* Carbondale: Southern Illinois University Press, 1996.

Welles, Benjamin. *Sumner Welles: FDR's Global Strategist.* New York: St. Martin's, 1997.

Welles, Sumner. *The Time for Decision.* New York: Harper, 1944.

———. *Where Are We Heading?* New York: Harper, 1946.

Westbrook, Lawrence. "The Program of Rural Rehabilitation of the FERA." *Journal of Farm Economics* 17 (1935): 89–100.

———. "Rehabilitation of Stranded Families." *Annals* 176 (1934): 74–79.

Whalen, Richard J. *The Founding Father: The Story of Joseph P. Kennedy.* New York: New American Library, 1964.

Wheeler, Burton K., with Paul F. Healy. *Yankee from the West.* New York: Doubleday, 1962.

White, W. L. *They Were Expendable.* New York: Harcourt, Brace, 1942.

White, Walter. *A Man Called White: The Autobiography of Walter White.* New York: Viking, 1948.

White, William Smith. *Majesty & Mischief: A Mixed Tribute to F.D.R.* New York: McGraw-Hill, 1961.

Whitnah, Donald R., ed. *Government Agencies.* Westport, Conn.: Greenwood Press, 1983.

Williams, T. Harry. *Huey Long.* New York: Alfred A. Knopf, 1969.

Wilmot, Chester. *The Struggle for Europe.* New York: Harper, 1952.

Wilson, Theodore. *The First Summit: Roosevelt and Churchill at Placentia Bay, 1941.* 1969. Reprint, Lawrence: University Press of Kansas, 1991.

Wilson, William H. "The Two New Deals: A Valid Concept?" *Historian* 28 (1966).

Wiltz, John E. *In Search of Peace: The Senate Munitions Inquiry, 1934–1936.* Baton Rouge: Louisiana State University Press, 1963.

Winant, John G. *A Letter from Grosvenor Square.* Boston: Houghton Mifflin, 1947.

Winfield, Betty H. *FDR and the News Media.* New York: Columbia University Press, 1990.

Winkler, Allan M. "A Forty-Year History of Civil Defense." *Bulletin of the Atomic Scientists* 40, no. 6 (1984).

———. *Franklin D. Roosevelt and the Making of Modern America.* New York: Longman, 2005.

———. *The Politics of Propaganda: The Office of War Information, 1842–1945.* New Haven, Conn.: Yale University Press, 1978.

———. *"To Everything There Is a Season": Pete Seeger and the Power of Song.* New York: Oxford University Press, 2009.

Wirth, Conrad L. *Parks, Politics, and the People.* Norman: University of Oklahoma Press, 1940.

Wladaver-Morgan, Susan. "Young Women and the New Deal: Camps and Resident Centers, 1933–1943." Ph.D. diss., Indiana University, 1982.

Wolfskill, George. *The Revolt of the Conservatives.* Boston: Houghton Mifflin, 1962.

Woodward, C. Vann. *The Battle for Leyte Gulf.* New York: Macmillan, 1947.

———. *Origins of the New South, 1877–1913.* Baton Rouge: Louisiana State University Press, 1951.

Woolf, S. J. "The Roosevelt Who Is a Firm Democrat: Governor Smith's Nominator Explains Why He Is Not of the Republican Faith—a Long Fight Won with Honor." *New York Times Sunday Magazine,* August 5, 1928, 66.

———. "A Woman Speaks Her Mind: Mrs. Franklin D. Roosevelt Points Out That in Spite of Equal Suffrage the Men Still Run the Parties." *New York Times Sunday Magazine,* April 10, 1928, 2.

Zangrando, Robert L. *The NAACP Crusade against Lynching, 1909–1950.* Philadelphia: Temple University Press, 1980.

Zawodny, Janusz K. *Death in the Forest: The Story of the Katyn Forest Massacre.* South Bend, Ind.: University of Notre Dame Press, 1962.

Ziegler, Robert H. *John L. Lewis: Labor Leader.* Boston: Twayne, 1988.

Zimand, Gertrude F. "Will the Codes Abolish Child Labor?" *Survey* 69 (August 1933).

Zinn, Howard, ed. *New Deal Thought.* Indianapolis: Bobbs-Merrill, 1966.

Zucker, Bat-Ami. "Frances Perkins and the German-Jewish Refugees." *American Jewish History* (2001): 35–59.

Index

Committee on Economic Security (CES), 195–96, 223

Committee for Industrial Organization (CIO) (1935–38), 272, 278, 341; AFL, rift between, 342

Committee of 1,000, 104

Commons, John R., 196

Communications Act (1934): Fairness Doctrine of, 194

Conant, James Bryant, 278

Conboy, Martin, 106

Congress, 115, 136, 139, 143–44, 151, 161, 170, 180–81, 184–86, 188–89, 213, 219, 221, 225, 230–31, 237, 247, 254–55, 257–58, 262, 303, 305, 315, 319, 351, 353, 360–61, 363, 368, 374, 380; antilynching bills, failure of in, 337; banking crisis, 134; congressional leadership, 107, 114, 131, 159, 232–33, 253, 259–60, 287, 332, 335, 350; constitutional authority of, 150; Democratic gains in, 109; equal-time provision, 194; Hawaiian statehood, 204; Hot Oil Act, 222–23; lame-duck sessions of, 175, 302; and NLRB, 226; NRA bill, 155, 226–27; neutrality legislation in, 307–8, 310; New Deal programs, 336; Reorganization Bill, passage of, 321; special sessions of, 123, 131–32, 153–54, 336, 346–47, 349; Social Security bill, 223–24, 228, 239; Supreme Court, unpacking of, 324–26, 338; and TVA, 147–48. *See also* House of Representatives; Senate

Congress of Industrial Organizations (1938–55). *See* Committee for Industrial Organizations (CIO)

Connell, Richard E., 24

Connery, William P., 143–44, 413n45

Connor, Eugene (Bull), 381

Connor, Robert D. W., 467n64

Constitutional Revolution of 1937, 329

Cook, Blanche Wiesen, 17, 59

Cook, Nancy, 398n40

Cooke Committee, 275

Coolidge, Calvin, 47, 64, 67–68, 95, 123, 133, 292, 294, 296, 399n71, 436n80, 462n85

Corcoran, Tom, 262, 347, 369

Corn Belt Meat Producers Association, 122

Costello, Frank, 464n30

Costigan, Edward P., 151

Coughlin, Charles E., 193, 237–38, 269, 306, 356

Council of State Governments, 419n47

Country Life Commission, 122

Couzens, James, 274

Cowles, Anna "Bamie." *See* Roosevelt, Anna "Bamie" (sister of TR)

Cox, James M., 44–45, 76, 148

Creel, George, 200, 211

Cross, Guernsey, 77

Cross, Lillian, 117

Cuba, 3–4, 294–96

Cummings, Homer S., 46, 121, 126, 196, 202, 222, 288–89, 324–25, 339, 454n22

Curaçao, 35

Currie, Lauchlin, 347, 358

Curry, John, 106–7

Cushing, Betsey, 281

Cutting, Bronson, 118, 390n45

Czechoslovakia, 378

Czolgosz, Leon, 5–6, 117

Dallek, Robert, 376

Daniels, Addie, 293

Daniels, Jonathan, 17

Daniels, Josephus, 29–33, 35–39, 41–42, 45–47, 53–54, 67, 287, 293–94

Dare, Virginia, 340

Darrow, Clarence, 184

Davis, Chester, 184, 208, 247, 272

Davis, Elmer, 63

Davis, John W., 63, 68, 76, 209

Davis, Livingston, 39

Davis, Norman H., 115, 160

Dawes, Charles G., 95

Day, Edmond E., 467n64

Declaration of Lima, 385

House, Edward M., 101
House Committee on Un-American Activities, 332
House of Representatives, 109, 173, 213, 287, 363–64, 367, 380; antilynching bill, passage of in, 337; Democratic control of, 24, 91; soldiers' bonus, 229, 255. *See also* Congress
Housing Act (1934), 215
Housing Act (1937), 461n67
Howe, Louis McHenry, 26–27, 30, 33, 37, 45–46, 49–51, 56–57, 60–62, 66–67, 76–77, 86, 91–92, 101, 104, 114, 132, 144–45, 160–61, 202, 205, 207, 227, 246, 289, 325; death of, 258; as "dirty little man," 29; as FDR's campaign manager, 28–29
Hughes, Charles Evans, 24, 122–23, 127–28, 222–23, 230–32, 254, 256, 258–59, 299, 322, 324, 328–29, 331, 340
Hull, Cordell, 62, 118, 120–21, 174, 188, 202, 246, 295, 297–300, 306, 309, 312, 314–15, 349, 385, 447n3
Humphrey, Hubert H., 125
Humphrey, William E., 163
Hunter, Howard, 268
Hurd, Charles, 160, 268, 270, 275
Hurley, Patrick J., 89
Hutchinson, William, 272
Hyde, Arthur M., 404n8
Hyde Park Democrats, 1–2
Hyde Park Roosevelts, 6, 14–15
Hylan, John F., 60

Ickes, Harold L., 122, 146–47, 156, 162–63, 167–68, 187–88, 193, 205, 222, 226, 228, 234, 242, 245, 264, 269–70, 273, 297, 325, 335, 338, 344, 353, 364, 432n27, 436n80
I, Governor of California (Sinclair), 210
Independent Offices Act, 179
Independent Offices Appropriation Act, 412n22
Indian Reorganization Act, 187
Industrial Commission, 77

The Influence of Sea Power upon History, 1660–1783 (Thayer), 3
Inter-American Peace Conference, 288, 311
Intergovernmental Committee on Political Refugees Coming from Germany, 377
International Association of Machinists (IAM), 145
International Ladies' Garment Workers' Union, 274
Interstate Commerce Commission (ICC), 194, 319
Iowa, 276
Italo-Ethiopian War, 305
Italy, 155, 376

Jackson, Andrew, 253, 263, 278–79, 352
Jackson, Robert H., 353, 356
James, William, 278
Japan, 204, 291, 294, 301–2, 305, 315, 346, 349, 375
Jefferson, Thomas, 43, 85, 191, 253, 267–68, 276, 279, 352, 421n73; and Louisiana Purchase, 260
Jim Crow, 467n57
Job Corps, 146
Johns Hopkins University, 52
Johnson, Hiram, 122, 243, 292
Johnson, Hugh S., 124, 155–57, 162–66, 183–84, 195, 203, 211
Johnson, James Weldon, 337
Johnson, Louis, 136
Johnson, Lyndon B., 125, 146, 151, 196, 302, 338, 388n17, 424n98, 464n31
Johnson Act (1934), 292, 307
Johnstown (Pennsylvania), 275
Jones, Jesse H., 164, 226, 332, 354, 356, 358, 367
J. P. Morgan and Company, 305
Justo, Augustín, 312
Justo, Liborio, 313–14

Kalinin, Mikhail, 296
Kanee, H. M., 423n89

Lubin, Isador, 357, 358, 420n60
Ludlow, Louis L., 349–50
Ludlow Amendment, 349, 351
Lunn, George R., 69
Lyman, Catherine Robbins, 7

MacArthur, Douglas, 108, 143
MacDonald, Ramsay, 296
Machado, Gerardo, 294–95
Mackenzie King, William Lyon, 270–71, 378
MacLeish, Archibald, 467n64
Madison (Wisconsin), 83
Magill, Roswell, 367
Mahan, Alfred Thayer, 3
Maine (battleship), 3
Manchuria, 291
Mandela, Nelson, 9
Manhattan Navy Club, 51
Manitoba, 429n38
Manning, Helen Taft, 467n64
March of Dimes, 59, 66
Margold, Nathan R., 420n60
Markham, Edwin M., 271, 275
Marshall, John, 190–91
Martin, Clarence, 344
Martin, George, 465n43
Mason, George, 250
Mason, Lucy Randolph, 381
Massachusetts, 75, 103
Maverick, Maury, 337, 366, 464n31
Mayo, Charles H., 207
Mayo, William J., 207
McAdoo, William Gibbs, 29, 33, 44, 46, 62–63, 66, 68, 105, 464n31
McCarthy, Charles H., 30
McCormick, Anne O'Hare, 262–63
McCormick, Robert R., 42, 345, 346
McDonald, James G., 376
McIlhenny, John A., 394n53
McIntire, Ross T., 132–33, 242, 281, 312, 411n8
McIntyre, Marvin H., 46, 132, 147, 151, 159, 179, 211, 263, 281, 339, 357, 366, 423n89

McKinley, William, 3–6, 9, 27, 117, 388n16
McNary, Charles, 254, 274, 363
McNary-Haugen bills, 170
McNutt, Paul, 275
McReynolds, James C., 141, 223, 256, 259, 329, 331
Mead, James M., 379
Medicare, 196
Mellon, Andrew W., 288–89, 399n71
Melville, Herman, 7
Memoirs (Truman), 305
Mendieta, Carlos, 295
Mennonites, 185
Mercer, Lucy, 17, 38–39, 339, 393n37
Merchants of Death: A Study of the International Armament Industry (Engelbracht and Hanighen), 450n31
Merriam, Charles E., 225, 373, 453n9
Mexican Revolution, 311
Mexico, 34, 145, 260, 293–94, 311, 365
Meyer, Eugene I., 127
Meyers, Norman, 420n60
Michelson, Charles, 257
Milbank, Jeremiah, 256
Millis, Harry A., 426n6
Millis, Walter, 307
Mills, Ogden L., 41, 89–90, 114, 125, 127
Milwaukee (Wisconsin), 83
Minnesota, 268, 274, 276
Minnesota Democratic Farmer-Labor Party, 274
Mississippi, 224
Missouri, 276
Mitchell, Arthur W., 214, 264
Mitchell, Charles E., 126
Mitchell, Wesley C., 225
Mobilization for Human Needs, 246
modern peace movement: and American peace movement, 303–4
Moley, Raymond, 102, 114–15, 119, 127, 262, 297–98, 300, 448n19
Mondale, Walter F., 378
Monroe Doctrine, 294, 378
Montana, 46, 169, 184, 206, 268, 342

Neutrality Acts, 239, 305, 309, 337, 349
Nevins, Allan, 100
New Deal, 13, 64, 80, 87, 89, 92–93, 96,
99, 108, 124–25, 131–33, 138, 142, 147–
49, 151–55, 157, 162–63, 172, 182–83,
189, 191, 194, 197, 201, 205, 208, 216,
226, 228, 232–33, 235, 238–39, 242–44,
247, 250, 262, 271, 275, 277, 279, 284,
303, 312, 321, 327, 335–36, 343, 347–48,
350–51, 363, 380, 382, 386, 433n49;
and African Americans, 214, 264,
273, 338; Agricultural Adjustment
Administration (AAA), 355; agricultural programs of, 169–71; and Christianity, 175; coalition of, 249, 263, 338,
355; as collective effort, 175; as communistic, charges of, 280, 282; Court-
packing plan, 331–32; as expensive,
176–77; farmers, deserting of, 355;
Federal National Mortgage Association (Fannie Mae), as lasting achievement of, 354; and Great Depression,
361; Harvard opposition to, 278; and
Indian New Deal, 187; Jewish influence on, 173–74; Keynes, effect on,
186; national referendum on, 212–13;
patronage politics, 161; principles of,
190; public education, 375; staffing
of, 196; as system of experiments,
171; three kinds of security of, 219;
Twenty-First Amendment, 174–75;
veterans' health care, cutting of, 137;
women, high-level positions of in,
384. *See also individual programs*
New England, 109, 271, 283, 438n4
New Haven (Connecticut), 83
New Jersey, 83
New Mexico, 142
Newport (Rhode Island) naval training
facility: homosexuality, investigation of at, 52–55, 60; and "October
surprise," 53
New York City, 59, 79, 83, 96, 165, 184;
kosher chicken industry in, 164;
Tammany graft in, 87, 89

New York State, 274–75, 328, 379,
444n68; hydroelectric power in, 80;
TERA in, 97–99
New York State Federation of Women's
Clubs, 110
New York State Wilson Conference, 28
New York University, 95
Nicaragua, 294, 296
Nixon, Richard M., 125, 302, 395n94
Norbeck, Peter, 126, 274
Norris, George W., 115, 147–48, 217, 274,
282, 287, 326, 363, 414n68
Norris-La Guardia Act (1932), 165
North Dakota, 185, 206, 268, 429n38
North Sea Mine Barrage, 37
Norton, Mary T., 364
Norway, 37
Nye, Gerald P., 183, 303, 305, 349
Nye Committee, 303–6

Oahu, 203
O'Brien, David M., 457n14
Ochs, Adolph, 60
O'Connor, Basil, 50, 65–66, 178, 332–33,
349, 354
O'Connor, John J., 228, 360, 364, 370,
372–73
O'Day, Caroline, 88, 212, 377, 400n81
O'Gorman, James A., 26
Ohio, 275
Oklahoma, 268, 276
Olds, Leland, 81, 102
Oliphant, Herman, 222, 420n58
Olson, Culbert, 464n31
Olson, Floyd B., 109, 114, 141, 207, 274,
461n67
Olympic National Monument, 343
Olympic National Park, 343
O'Mahoney, Joseph C., 281
O'Neal, Ed, 138, 141, 170, 246
Orkney Islands, 37
Osborn, William C., 41
Osborne, Thomas Mott, 27–28
Ottinger, Albert, 70, 72, 74–75
Oulahan, Richard, 69

Owen, Ruth Bryan, 293
Oyster Bay Republicans, 1–2

Pacific dependencies, 151
Palestine, 377
Palmer, A. Mitchell, 42, 44, 53
Panama, 199, 296, 311
Panama Canal Zone, 151, 199, 311, 353
Pan-American Conference, 299
Pan-Americanism, 296
Paraguay, 311
Parrish, Elsie, 328–29
Patman, Wright, 187, 229, 425n108
Paxson, Frederic L., 467n64
Peabody, Endicott, 11–13, 127, 159, 321
Peabody, George Foster, 64–65, 272–73
Pearl Harbor, 203, 211, 292, 305, 332
Pecora, Ferdinand, 126
Pecora investigation, 125–26, 154, 181
Pedro II, 312
Peek, George N., 161, 170–71, 249, 365
Pegler, Westbrook, 388n30
Pendergast, Tom, 63
Pennsylvania, 109, 213, 275
Pepper, Claude D., 352
Perkins, Frances, 77, 83–84, 94, 123, 136,
    143, 145–46, 151–52, 156, 167, 177, 185,
    194, 196, 198, 202, 288, 298, 324, 329,
    342, 356, 376–77, 384, 402n41, 402n42,
    414n58, 424n103, 435n76, 465n43
Persons, W. Frank, 145–46, 414n58
Pertinax, André Géraud, 448n19
Petroleum Board, 233
Philadelphia (Pennsylvania), 83
Philippines, 4, 121, 151, 178–79, 250, 302
Phillips, William, 292, 307
Pickford, Mary, 354
Pinchot, Amos R. E., 356–57
Pinchot, Gifford, 96, 185
Pittman, Key, 281
Pittsburgh (Pennsylvania), 83
Piven, Frances Fox, 424n98
Platt, Thomas Collier, 4–5
Platt Amendment, 295, 311

The Plow that Broke the Stars (film),
    444n71
Poland, 377
Powell, Adam Clayton Sr., 273
Prairie States Forestry Project, 185
President's Committee on Economic
    Security, 375
President's Reemployment Agreement
    (PRA), 164–65
Pressman, Lee, 174, 420n60
Procter and Gamble, 84
Progressive Era, 32
progressivism, 45
Prohibition, 61, 74, 87–88, 104, 137, 174
Proskauer, Joseph M., 62, 69, 72
Public Health Service, 375
Public Papers (FDR and Rosenman),
    133, 152, 154, 184, 212, 295, 321, 330,
    350, 353, 376–77
Public Service Commission, 80
Public Utility Holding Company Act, 239
Public Works Administration (PWA),
    156, 167–68, 187–88, 199, 227, 243,
    246, 268, 359–60, 419n40, 432n27;
    New Deal housing under, 335; slum-
    clearance projects, 248
Puerto Rico, 151, 199
Puyi, Henry, 291

radio: in American politics, importance
    of, 66
Railroad Retirement Act, 230
Railway Labor Act (1926), 165
Rainey, Henry T., 180
Rankin, John, 204
Raskob, John J., 70, 86, 88, 99, 105
Rathom, John R., 53, 397n15
Rayburn, Sam, 105, 260–61, 319, 453n10,
    454n22
Reagan, Ronald, 224, 361
Reconstruction Finance Corporation
    (RFC), 126, 142, 151–52, 169, 178, 226,
    247, 353, 354, 356, 363
Reciprocal Tariff Act, 188

Roosevelt, Franklin Delano (*continued*): administrative style of, 297–98, 359, 431n15; and African Americans, 214, 250–51, 273, 323, 338, 463n20; airline scandal, 183; Allied war debts, 113; American imperialism, involvement of in, 34; American Indians, 187; American peace movement, 303–4; American people, connection with, 160, 175–76, 208; antilynching legislation, lack of support for, 337–38, 363; armaments, increased spending on, 353–54; "Arsenal of Democracy," 386; assassination attempt on, 116–18; atomic energy, 348; authority, casual assumption of, 9; balanced budgets, belief in, 108, 186, 318–19, 346–47, 349; banking crisis, 125, 127, 134–35; as bird-watcher, 10; birth of, 6; Birthday Balls, 59, 63, 66, 178, 217, 256, 332, 349, 354; "bombshell" message of, 298; Bonus Marches, 108, 149–50; as book collector, 10; as "the Boss," 196; braggadocio of, 42; Brains Trust of, 102–3, 406n46; Buenos Aires, trip to, 311–12; business-sector support, erosion of, 209; campaign, for vice presidency, 45–47; at Carter, Ledyard, and Milburn law firm, 22; charisma of, 214; Central Statistical Board, 418n39; Civilian Conservation Corps (CCC), 142–47, 149; Civil Works Administration (CWA), recreation of, 163, 168; childhood of, 10, 16; color line, attitude toward, 34; on collective bargaining, 194, 226, 233, 238, 248, 317; Colombia, success in, 299; Committee on Economic Security, creation of, 195–96; as communist, accusations of, 278–79, 285, 302; compromising of, 26; conciliatory skills of, 79; confrontation, avoidance of, 22; conversational style of, 134; *corrido*, written in honor of, 214; corruption charges, 89–90; as country squire, 9; court-

ship of, 17; cruises of, 18, 87, 116, 159, 242, 245, 267, 269–70, 288, 297, 309, 337, 371; Cuba, policy toward, 294–96; deficits, attitude toward, 176–77, 191, 220, 280–81; at Democratic National Convention (1912), 28; Democratic Party primaries, intervening in, 369–73; destroyer, ability to steer, 11; deviousness of, 156–57; "dictatorial powers," charges of, 326, 357; drought, response to, 184–85, 206–7, 268, 272, 275, 277; Dutch stubbornness of, 16, 57; ER, public policy disagreements with, 136; at Emmett, Marvin, and Roosevelt, 49–50; engagement of, 16; as environmentalist, 225; and Executive Council, 163, 167; executive branch, reorganizing of, 319–21, 356–57; as extrovert, 47; farm policy of, 138–39, 141–42, 169–71, 246–47, 249; federal judiciary, reorganization of, 324–32; at Fidelity and Deposit Company, 49; "floating White House," 197; flood relief, 256–57, 271, 275, 323; foreign affairs, 291–315; "forgotten man" appeal to, 103, 157; future, identification with, 189; general strikes, 200–203, 323–24; gold standard, 139–40; Good Neighbor policy, 35, 68, 294–96, 299, 303, 312, 345, 394n55; as governor, 76–90, 92–99, 100–101; at Groton prep school, 11–14, 389n41; gubernatorial campaign of, 70–71; "gunboat diplomacy," role in, 34; Haiti, 34–35, 47; halo effect of, 110; Hamlet-like, 148; as "Happy Patient," 60; at Harvard, 13–16; on health care, 74, 82, 224, 375; as homeschooled, 10; honeymoon of, 21; housing policy of, 187, 215, 284; hundred days, 131, 149–50, 154, 157, 162, 178, 188–89, 209, 216, 222, 240, 411n2; image, poking fun of, 236–37; as independent, 24; as internationalist, 52, 67–68, 291, 306–7; on isolationism, 102, 291, 302–3;

Jewish advisers of, 173–74; at Fisk University, 217; Keynes, letter from (1934), 177; Keynes, letter from (1938), 347–48; Keynes, White House visit of (1934), 185–86; labor relations, 33, 166–67, 194, 198–99, 272, 277, 341–42; Landon, face-to-face meeting with, 276; landslide victory of, 109–10, 286–87; Latin American policies, 311–12; and League of Nations, 101; Lend-Lease, 292; local prejudices, pandering to, 47; London Economic Conference, 296–99; lynching law, 174; as man in the middle, 212; at Marvin, Hooker, and Roosevelt law firm, 25; Maxwell touring car of, 24; medical problems of, 55–58, 60, 63; Lucy Mercer, affair with, 38–39; metal braces of, 58; and middle class, 157; modernity, as representative of, 68; Robert Moses, animosity between, 269; National Emergency Council (NEC), creation of, 163; and National Recovery Administration, 155–56, 162, 164; National Resource Board, establishing of by, 225–26; in Navy Department, 30–33, 37, 40–42; New Deal, accomplishments of, 277; New Deal, defense of, 189, 212, 253–54; New Deal, definition of by, 175; New Deal, principles of, 190; Newport scandal, 52–55; New York bar exam, passing of, 21; as New York Senate seat candidate, 33; pardons of, 175; physical disability, acceptance of, 245; physical helplessness of, 200; and Philippines, 302; polio virus, 55, 57–59, 110–11, 333; political debut of, 23–24l political savvy of, 98; political tactics of, 79, 83, 179–80; popularity of, 157; and poverty, 171, 216, 246; as practical, 190; presidential ambitions, 87, 91–92, 96, 99–101, 103–5; presidential cabinet of, 114–15, 118–25; presidential campaigns of, 107–8, 278–79, 280–85; presi-

dential inspection trips of, 274–75; presidential nomination of, 105; presidential library of, 2, 382–83; as progressive, 42, 87; Prohibition, position on, 61, 88, 137, 174; public appearances of, as stage managed, 58; public debt, notions of, 137; public domain, management of, 187; public housing, 335; public life of, 51; public power, focus of, 80–81; public self-criticism, aversion to, 330; PWA and WPA, on jurisdictions of, 234; race issues, 144, 146, 174, 204, 233–34, 250–51, 273–74, 363–64, 370, 374–75; on rearmament, 353; reelection campaign (1936) of, 240, 248, 251, 277; refugee question, 376–78; and "reflation," 139, 172; reform credentials of, 26, 43; religion of, 12–13; Republican and independent candidates, support for, 274; "Roosevelt Coalition," 213, 287; Roosevelt recession, 167, 174, 347, 356, 360–61, 461n71; at Roosevelt and O'Connor law firm, 50; Scottsboro case, 174; "second-class intellect" comment, 134; second hundred days, 225; as secretive, 186, 324, 370, 381; securities, regulation of, 178–81; self-promotion, instinct for, 25; Upton Sinclair, meeting with, 211; Al Smith, relationship with, 60–62, 64, 72; social pioneering of, 256; Social Security, 224, 227–28, 230, 235; soldiers' bonus, battles over, 187, 228–30, 255–56; South, economic concern of, 374, 381; South, support from, 264; South American trip, 311–15; Southern Conference of Human Welfare (SCHW), 381; Soviet Union, recognition of, 299–301; Spanish Civil War and "moral embargo," 309–10; Spanish flu, victim of, 38; on speeches and speechwriters, 280; as stamp collector, 10, 389n36; Stimson doctrine, acceptance of, 291; stimulus package of, 358–61, 364, 367, 373–74;

Roosevelt, Franklin Delano (*continued*):
stock market crash, reaction to, 82;
Supreme Court, battles with, 220–23,
230–32, 258–60, 317, 318, 321–24,
426n116; as "traitor to his class," 13,
157, 209; Tammany Hall, 26, 40–41,
43, 87–88, 90, 96, 103–4, 106; tax proposals of, 235–36, 283; as tax reformer,
myth of, 236; and Tennessee Valley
Authority (TVA), 147–49, 365–66;
third term of, 373, 380; "triumphal
procession" of, 208; on unemployment, 150–52, 168, 233, 234, 317, 355,
374; unemployment insurance, 94–95,
97, 375; vacations, importance of,
159–60, 179, 197, 227, 242, 269–70;
vetoes of, 87–88, 95, 98, 136, 149, 157,
179–80, 188, 197, 227, 229–30, 255–56,
264, 267, 306, 367, 423n87; as vice
presidential candidate, 43–45; virtual
White House, 160; Walker hearings,
106; as Wall Street lawyer, 49; war
debts, 292; at Warm Springs, 64–66,
70, 82; wealth of, 1; "wealth taxes,"
236; wedding of, 18–19; whistle-and
inspection tour stops, 276–77; White
House routine of, 132–33; Wilsonian
principles of, 40, 52, 102, 345–46;
Woodrow Wilson Foundation, 51, 60,
67; work relief, 168, 182, 189, 219–20,
227–29, 355; World Court, 306
Roosevelt, Franklin Delano—AND CON-
GRESS: authority, request of from,
135, 142; congressional critics of, 135,
183; congressional leadership, 107,
114, 131, 159, 232–33, 240, 253, 259–60,
302, 318–19, 321, 324, 350–51, 355, 358;
congressional supporters of, 140,
331; cooperation with, 129–30; first
major defeat in, 306–7; last appearance before, 58; managing of, 142, 157,
205, 226; messages to, 179, 220, 225,
235, 302, 304, 317, 319–20, 349, 355,
359; personal appearance before, 229;
power struggles with, 179; praise for,

150, 253, 317, 367; relationship with,
135, 137, 150, 236, 331, 342, 370, 382;
spending struggles with, 178; veterans pay, 178, 255–56
Roosevelt, Franklin Delano—SPEECHES:
acceptance speeches, 261–62, 264–66;
ad-lib speeches, 215; annual messages, 176, 253–54, 306, 308, 317–18,
350–51; Arkansas address, 260; on
background press conferences, 365;
Bonneville Dam speech, 343; Brains
Trust radio speech, 102–3; brief
remarks, 280; broadcast annual messages, 219; budget messages, 176–78,
220–21, 254, 256, 351; campaign
speeches, 73–74, 108, 280; campaign
speeches, as blueprint for New Deal,
108; ceremonial addresses, 280;
Chautauqua speech, 37–38, 310, 345,
378, 451n48; Christmas messages,
175, 251, 288, 385; college speeches,
236–37; communism speech, 279–80;
Cotton Bowl stadium speech,
260–61; at Democratic National
Convention, 69; extemporaneous
speeches, 251, 280; Fala speech, 73;
Farm Bureau conference speech, 170;
Fireside Chats, 85, 134, 139, 150, 162,
188–91, 195, 197, 212, 228–29, 277, 327,
346, 354, 359–60, 380; Fireside Chat
"Party Primaries," 367–70; Forbes
Field speech, 280–81; foreign policy
speeches, 379; formal addresses, 312;
formal statements 250–51; Franklin
Field (Minute Man) speech, 264–66;
Georgia speech, 374–75; Governors'
Conference speech, 96; Great Plains
drought speeches, 275–76; gubernatorial acceptance speeches, 89; gubernatorial inaugural speech, 77–78,
80; Harvard speech, 278; Hawaiian
address, 204; health care speeches,
82; Hoover Dam dedication speech,
242–43; housing policy remarks, 284;
Howard University speech, 273–74;

Supreme Court: Constitutional Revolution, 329; FDR Court-packing plan, 324–32; FDR Court-packing plan, counterattack on, 328; and New Deal measure, striking down of, 220; NIRA, Section (9)c of, 221

Sutherland, George, 223, 331, 352

Swanson, Claude, 120–21

Swing, Philip D., 243

Swope, Gerard, 246, 418n32

Taft, Charles P., 198, 427n16

Taft, Robert A., 380

Taft, William Howard, 23, 28, 320, 379, 454n31

Talmadge, Eugene, 364, 371, 372

Tammany Hall, 25–28, 33, 40–41, 43–44, 61–62, 70, 72, 75, 87–88, 90, 107, 274; Seabury investigations of, 96–97, 103–4, 106

Taussig, J. K., 315

Taylor Grazing Act, 187–88

Taylor, Myron C., 86, 376–77

Teagle, Walter C., 418n32

Teamsters Union, 272

Teapot Dome scandal, 64, 121–22

Techwood Homes (Atlanta), 248, 335

Teller, Henry M., 4

Teller Amendment, 4

Temporary Emergency Relief Administration (TERA), 97–99, 101, 142, 152, 405n33

Tennessee Valley Authority (TVA), 116, 124, 147–49, 233, 256, 356, 458n30

Tenth Amendment, 254

Terra, Gabriel, 314

Texas, 185, 260

Thirteenth Amendment, 264

Thomas, Elmer, 139–40

Thomas, Norman, 109, 143, 169, 213, 274, 287, 310

Timberline Lodge, 343

Tipaldo decision, 259, 328

Tobin, Daniel J., 123, 272, 443n64

Todhunter School for Girls, 77

Townsend, Francis E., 237

Townsend Plan, 237

Trade Agreements Act (1934), 295

Trade Union Unity League, 94–95

Trading with the Enemy Act (1917), 132

Treaty of Versailles, 40, 412n32

Triborough Bridge, 268

Triborough Bridge Authority, 269

Truman, Harry S., 125, 173, 211, 213, 216, 292, 296, 302, 305, 447n3, 463n20

Truth in Securities Act. *See* Securities Act (1933)

Tsukiyama, Wilfred C., 204

Tugwell, Rexford G., 102, 108, 124, 137, 139, 161, 170–71, 177, 186, 216, 228, 230, 268, 288, 417n12, 447n100

Tully, Grace, 132–33, 272, 442n46

Tuskegee Institute, 250

Tuttle, Charles H., 88–90

Twenty-First Amendment, 137, 174

Two-Thirds of a Nation (Straus), 216

Tydings, Millard E., 372, 373, 379

Tydings-McDuffie Act, 302

Unemployed Councils, 83

United Mine Workers (UMW), 165

United States, 4, 33, 36, 46–47, 68, 72, 101, 113, 139–40, 149, 153, 184, 210, 236, 271, 291, 294, 296, 298, 301–3, 305–8, 312–13, 315, 327, 332, 335, 368, 374, 382–83, 385–86, 409n13, 448n13, 450n38, 458n30; federal budgets, 79; 1934 election of, as transformative, 213; Jewish refugees, 378; Latin America, image of in, 299; red rallies in, 83; refugees in, 377; Spanish Civil War, 309–10; unemployment, concern over in, 83–84, 86, 93

United States Housing Authority (USHA), 335

United Steelworkers of America, 376. *See also* Steel Workers Organizing Committee

University Homes (Atlanta), 248

University of North Carolina, 381

ROGER DANIELS is the Charles Phelps Taft Professor Emeritus of History at the University of Cincinnati. His many books include *Prisoners without Trial: Japanese Americans in World War II.*